Women's Lives
Themes and Variations in Gender Learning

Women's Lives
Themes and Variations in Gender Learning

Bernice Lott
University of Rhode Island

Brooks/Cole Publishing Company
Monterey, California

Brooks/Cole Publishing Company
A Division of Wadsworth, Inc.

Printed in the United States of America

10   9   8   7   6   5   4   3   2   1

Library of Congress Cataloging-in-Publication Data

Lott, Bernice E.
    Women's lives.

    Bibliography: p.
    Includes index.
    1. Sex role—United States.   2. Women—United States—
Psychology.   3. Life cycle, Human.   I. Title.
HQ1075.5.U6L68 1987   305.4′2   86-26886
ISBN 0-534-07440-5

Sponsoring Editor: Claire Verduin
Marketing Representative: Ira Zukerman
Editorial Associate: Linda Ruth Wright
Production Editor: Penelope Sky
Production Assistant: Barbara Kimmel
Manuscript Editor: Lorraine Anderson
Permissions Editor: Carline Haga
Interior Design: Victoria A. Van Deventer
Cover Illustration: Pauline Phung
Art and Photo Coordinator: Sue C. Howard
Interior Illustration: Accurate Art, Inc., and Judy Morley
Typesetting: Boyer & Brass, Inc., San Diego, California
Printing and Binding: Malloy Lithographing, Ann Arbor, Michigan

(Credits continue on page 367.)

Dedicated, with love,
to Al, Sara, Judy, and Josh,
who continue to help me grow.

Preface

This is a book about the experiences through which gender is learned and maintained by contemporary girls and women in the United States. There is a distinction between being born female and becoming a culturally defined woman, and the complex relationship between the two is influenced by parents, schooling, the mass media, employers, religious and political institutions, and the law. The issues addressed in these pages have to do with how this process of socialization affects a woman throughout the entire span of her life, from prenatal development through old age, shaping her behavior, beliefs, and attitudes, and her relationships with children, men, and other women.

While this book is intended primarily for college students in psychology and sociology classes, any interested person with some background in these areas should find it readable, engrossing, and personally relevant. As source materials I have used surveys, laboratory research, formal investigations, newspaper reports, fiction, poetry, autobiography, and personal experience: all provide evidence of common themes and variations in women's learning of gender. In addition, because I have researched the subject widely and intensively, and have concentrated on developing material that is new and timely, the book will also be valuable to graduate students and professionals who are engaged in study, teaching, or practice in which gender and women's lives are relevant.

I bring a social psychological perspective to an analysis of the process of acquiring gender—that is, to the process of becoming a woman. What a person does in a particular situation is understood to depend both upon characteristics, habits, and expectations derived from previous experiences and upon the special characteristics of the situation itself. An appreciation of the ways situational demands can influence behavior is essential to understanding how gender is acquired, how it varies in accord with individual circumstances, how it is affected by ethnic and socioeconomic factors, and how it is variously represented by different women under differing conditions.

Gender is like a prism, and there are women throughout the spectrum of possibilities. We must understand how women in our society acquire ways of thinking and behaving that are more like each other's than like men's, but we must also attend to the fact that significant differences in personal development result in diversity among women. This variety is widely demonstrated by women in the United States today; looking at other cultures, other places, and other times reveals other versions of womanhood. But the potential for women is still greater than what has been achieved. I examine women's current multiple roles as well as the even wider range of possibilities shared with men (who are, of course, also defined by the culture).

Acknowledgments

Work on this book was greatly facilitated by my having reduced departmental responsibilities for one semester at the University of Rhode Island, followed by one year of sabbatical leave that I spent at Brown University's Pembroke Center for Teaching and Research on Women. The warm hospitality and resources at the Pembroke Center provided an enriching and enabling environment for the completion of the book.

Many individuals have contributed, some indirectly, through their stimulation of ideas, raising of questions, and active pursuit of gender equity; and others more directly through their strong support, constructive criticism, and love. Included in this book is the wisdom of students, coworkers, family, friends, and unknown women, some near to me and some far away in time and place. Many of the issues that I address were formulated and discussed in papers published in professional journals and in an earlier book, *Becoming a Woman: The Socialization of Gender*, that was recognized by the Association for Women in Psychology in 1982 as meriting its Distinguished Publication Award. This and other encouragement from colleagues in psychology and in women's studies were important factors in my undertaking the writing of this volume.

Since 1972 I have been part of a group of women who meet weekly to discuss personal issues and the relationship between our experiences and the larger political, economic, and social context in which they occur. Through the years this group has said goodbye to some and welcomed others while continuing to serve a vital energizing, validating, and supportive function that for me has been strengthening, nourishing, and enlightening. Together we have experienced unemployment, enhanced job status, achievements in education and work, births, deaths, divorces, marriages, illness, aging, the growing independence of children, and significant changes in life style. To all my "sisters" in this wonderful, continuing group of giving, caring, challenging women I offer this public expression of appreciation and acknowledgment of connection.

I would also like to express my appreciation to the reviewers who offered careful, intelligent, worthwhile reactions to the book in its earlier stages. They include James W. Bartee, Pacific University, Forest Grove, Oregon; Janis Bohan, Metropolitan State College, Denver, Colorado; Alice Brown-Collins, Brown University, Providence, Rhode Island; Leigh Minturn, University of Colorado at Boulder; Bonnie Tyler, University of Maryland at College Park; and Barbara Wallston, George Peabody College of Vanderbilt University, Nashville, Tennessee.

At Brooks/Cole, I am grateful to sponsoring editor Claire Verduin for her enthusiastic interest in the project. Very special thanks go to Penelope Sky, Lorraine Anderson, and Sue Howard, who worked with me on the nitty-gritty matters and who became long-distance friends. This book has profited not only from their fine editorial talents and professionalism but also from their "tender loving care" and personal involvement with the substance of the book as well as its style.

Other special people who helped me in this project, with correspondence, manuscript typing, and related chores, are Clarice Coleman, Anne Famiglietti, and Ruth Saunders. Their assistance was always good humored, competent, and essential to the book's completion. Essential, too, was the support and sustenance I could always count on from Al Lott, from my son Joshua, and from my daughters Judith and Sara.

Whoever you are, whatever your purpose in reading this book, I hope that you find it clear and provocative, that it will raise many questions and answer some, that it will deepen your awareness of gender and society, and that it will inspire personal insights and challenges. I have certainly been enriched by teaching feminist psychology during the past decade and a half and by writing this book; I hope my enthusiasm is communicated and that it will be shared.

Bernice Lott

Contents

C   H   A   P   T   E   R   5

Adolescence:
Mixed Messages
and Real Options   68

C   H   A   P   T   E   R   6

Menstruation:
Power, Curse, or
Natural Rhythm?   85

C   H   A   P   T   E   R   7

Sexuality   101

C   H   A   P   T   E   R   8

Relationships:
Love, Marriage,
Other Options   120

Women's Lives
Themes and Variations in Gender Learning

Introduction: "Ain't I a Woman?"

The man over there says women need to be helped into carriages and lifted over ditches, and to have the best place everywhere. Nobody ever helps me into carriages or over puddles, or gives me the best place—and ain't I a woman?... I have ploughed and planted and gathered into barns, and no man could head me—and ain't I a woman? I could work as much and eat as much as a man—when I could get it—and bear the lash as well! And ain't I a woman?

Sojourner Truth, 1851   *(Flexner, 1975, p. 91)*

C H A P T E R   1

At a meeting for women's rights almost a century and a half ago in Akron, Ohio, a freed slave known as Sojourner Truth responded with the preceding words to a white clergyman who argued that because women were weak and helpless they could not (and should not) vote. But the black slave woman had never been defined in the same way as the white woman on the Southern plantation, just as the definition of the Victorian lady had never fit the working-class woman who had labored in the factories of industrialized cities. Differing conditions of life taught each different ways of being a woman. While the pre–Civil War white woman of wealth and aristocracy learned that she was weak, fragile, modest, and delicate, black women labored in the fields, were sexually assaulted by white men, and could be stripped naked and whipped. Recognition of this contradiction moved Sarah Moore Grimké, an upper-class Southern white woman, from abolitionist to radical feminist (Nies, 1977).

WHAT WOMEN DO

Women, like men, learn continuously from birth the behavior appropriate to our status and, as we grow older and the circumstances of our lives change, earlier lessons may be negated, or reinforced and affirmed. At different times and in different cultures, women's behavior has spanned the spectrum of human potential. For example, Margaret Mead, in a classic work (1949/1968), documented important variations in women's approved behaviors among different cultures in New Guinea. At one extreme were the Mundugamor women, who did all the major work of providing food, were assertive and vigorous, detested the bearing and rearing of children, and were, according to Mead, awful mothers. Kola women were described differently, as "sharp tongued and nagging" philanderers who practiced sorcery on their

husbands, while Arapesh women were seen as nurturant, maternal, cooperative, and unaggressive, like Arapesh men.

That *woman* and *man* have a variety of meanings in different cultures is abundantly illustrated in the data of cultural anthropology. As Sherry Ortner and Harriet Whitehead (1981) have noted, "What gender is, what men and women are, what sorts of relations do or should obtain between them—all of these notions do not simply reflect or elaborate upon biological 'givens,' but are largely products of social and cultural processes" (p. 1). We know that every social behavior performed by men is also done by some or many women within the same culture or another. And with the exception of a universal responsibility for the care of infants, which not all women do well or cheerfully, women's behavior across cultures varies dramatically.

Women in all cultures engage in productive work requiring different degrees of skill and physical stamina.

> Women may herd reindeer, harpoon seals, carry fifty-pound or heavier loads for miles, labor in fields, dig ditches, haul heavy bags of groceries . . . or spend most of their productive years secluded in courtyards engaged in a routine round of domestic tasks. There is extraordinary variety throughout the world in "women's work." (Tiffany, 1982, p. 4)

The photo on page 4 shows contemporary women in an unidentified Third World country hauling huge bundles of sugarcane to be used for fuel. In most societies, the gathering of firewood or crop residues for fuel is a task usually done by women (Norman, 1984). A study of 862 societies (Aronoff & Crano, 1975) found that women everywhere contribute substantially to their economies, and in some hunter-gatherer cultures, women make the major contribution to sustenance.

What women do depends upon the historical, economic, and social conditions of their lives. For example, Harriette Arnow's 1954 novel *The Dollmak-*

er describes a proud and powerful woman from the hills of Kentucky who, in one incident, purposely runs a soldier's car off the road with her mule and then, with a knife blade, cuts a hole in the swollen neck of her desperately ill, barely breathing child, as he lies on a shelf of sandstone with a rock under his head. In a different place and time, a nineteenth-century Jewish woman in an eastern European *shtetl* attracted customers to her stall in the local market with the following litany, as described by Isaac Bashevis Singer:

> You think this is a goose? God in heaven, it's a calf! Look how the fat pours off—our enemies should only melt from envy. If this goose doesn't feed you for a week, may I get a fire in my belly, a heart attack; . . . You think I'm making money from you? For every groschen profit you give me, I should get a plague . . . it's Thursday and I don't want to be stuck with the bird over the Sabbath. I don't keep meat on ice—may our enemies lie on the ground with boils and blisters on their heads, and poison in their blood. (Baum, Hyman, & Michel, 1975, p. 69)

This remembered street voice belonged to a nurturant mother and obedient wife, who was also shrewd, assertive, and competent, and was doing what was appropriate for a Jewish peasant woman—earning the bread for her family while her husband was absorbed in biblical studies and religious rituals.

Dramatic evidence of the responsiveness of sex roles to economic pressures and opportunities comes from Jagna Sharff's 1983 study of a group of poor Puerto Rican immigrants living in New York City. Sharff found that ghetto children are reared in ways that maximize the family's adaptation to socioeconomic conditions, leading to different models within the same gender. Thus, a girl might be encouraged to develop the traditional docile qualities associated with attracting a lover and husband, and thus function as a "child reproducer," or she might be trained early in her life "for dominance and assertiveness" and be reared as the family's "scholar/advocate" to whose upward mobility the entire family will contribute.

A young woman in Judith Rossner's 1983 novel *August* had been reared by two women. One had stayed at home and been "daddy": "Aside from being a superb skier and horsewoman, she knew more about animals than most veterinarians, and she could fix, or build . . . almost anything in the house. She was an excellent cook and a nearly miraculous gardener" (p. 7). The "mommy," on the other hand, cuddled the child, was a skilled dressmaker, but didn't like to cook, and went to work. She "wore make-up, jewelry and skirts . . . [and] left each morning to work as chairman of the mathematics department in a . . . high school three towns away" (p. 5). The individual patterns of skills and interests of these two women shatter our stereotypes but do not really contradict what we know about women from our own experience.

OBJECTIVES AND ORIENTATION

The preceding illustrations of the diversity and range of women's work and competencies provide a background for the major thesis of this book—that "one is not born, but rather becomes a woman," words borrowed from Simone de Beauvoir (1949/1961). This is a book about learning how, and what it means, to be a woman. Manhood, too, is learned, but the focus of this work is women and our shared experiences in the United States (primarily). The silence of women in earlier generations and our general invisibility in public history has resulted in gaps in our knowledge; as Shirley Ardener (1977) has noted, women's voices in culture have been typically muted. But what women have written in autobiographies, in fiction and in poetry, in diaries and essays, provides significant clues to common as well as differing experiences. In addition, analyses of contemporary institutions—the schools, the family, the mass media, the economy, and so on—indicate that social practices are almost everywhere differentiated by gender, that expectations are not the same for women and men, and that serious consequences to the individual follow from both conformity and deviation. Gender influences motivation, beliefs, mental health, and social behavior. Gender, in other words, organizes social life and thus much of individual experience.

The objective of this book is to trace the continuing socialization of contemporary women in the United States from birth through old age, weaving the pattern of experiences with strands taken from diverse sources—from fiction, the realities of everyday life, and the data of social psychology. We will follow critical aspects of women's experience chronologically, highlighting those pressures and sanctions that reinforce the acquiring of gender-appropriate behavior and those that enhance within-gender differences. We will be concerned with discerning the life conditions that are systematically related by cultural prescription, regulation, or arrangement to being born female in our society. We will try to identify from the available data those conditions that contribute to our learning how to behave like a woman, and we will note variations in these conditions during different periods of women's lives, and across groups differing in ethnicity, social class, and other significant characteristics. We will follow girls through childhood into adolescence and early and later adulthood, attending to sexuality, pregnancy, single and married life-styles, parenthood, employment, and mental health; we will examine the role of hostility and violence in women's lives; and we will emphasize shared experiences that link all women, as well as variations in circumstances, interests, and concerns. We will consider information about women's lives from the psychological laboratory and clinic, from observation in natural settings, from statistical summaries of quantitative data, from newspaper accounts of current events, from biography, fiction, and poetry, in the hope that from their integration might emerge verifiable and significant themes.

This is a personal book that reflects, like all human work (in science as in other spheres), the values and assumptions of its author. I have sampled and selected from the literature, and I do not give equal time to the experiences of boys and men. Although I often compare the two genders, women's lives are my central concern. My perspective is that of a behavior-focused social psychologist and a feminist, as defined and discussed below.

Focus on Social Behavior

Socialization (or enculturation) can be defined as the process of learning those behaviors that are appropriate for members of a particular status group. Some psychologists and other social scientists mainly study childhood socialization and restrict the meaning of the term to the earliest process of acquiring culture. Thus, for example, according to Diana Baumrind (1980):

> Socialization is [a] process by which developing children, through insight, training, and imitation, acquire the habits and values congruent with adaptation to their culture. At birth, a child may be viewed as a range of possibilities whose discrete potentialities are realized in interaction with the training contexts in which the child develops. (p. 640)

In this book I use the concept of socialization more broadly, and view it as a process that continues throughout a person's life. Individuals never stop acquiring cultural meanings and directions.

The differential behaviors we learn as appropriate for girls/women and for boys/men in a given society and historical period constitute the roles identified with sex. Because these behaviors are, in very large part, unrelated to the reliable biological distinctions between the sexes, we use the word *gender* to identify the learned definitions of women and men. While *female* and *male* refer to sexual distinctions across all animal species, the terms *woman* and *man* are specific to humans and denote gender—that is, learned social behavior.

The language in this book is primarily that of behavioristic social psychology. This approach focuses on what people do in particular situations, and assumes that all human behavior (beyond molecular physiological responses and innate reflex mechanisms) is learned and can be explained by a common set of interrelated principles. Explanation involves relating social behavior to its antecedents and consequences, and behavior is broadly interpreted to include all that people do and all that people say about their goals, attitudes, beliefs, feelings, perceptions, and memories.

Within this approach, the *learning-oriented* theoretical model has guided my analyses of social behavior. This model requires, on the simplest level, that explanations of behavior take into account the setting in which the behavior occurs; the individual's needs, goals, or motives as they are inferred from what the individual does or says; the range of probable responses that the individual can make in the situation (because of prior learning and physical capacity); and the consequences (provided by self, others, or events) that may follow particular acts. Because of the wide-ranging nature of the material and issues considered within this book, I use the language of learning theory with varying degrees of specificity, rigor, and consistency, and only sometimes apply learning constructs systematically. These constructs have, nevertheless, provided a framework for my thinking and have influenced both the questions I raise and the nature of the evidence I bring to bear on them.

My approach reflects a *social psychological perspective* in that I view people and environments as mutually dependent and in an interactive relationship. While the *environment* includes the immediate physical and social situation, the *person* may be said to include motives, habits, memories, physiological/neurological conditions, and structural characteristics (a product of genetic and environmental interaction), reflecting both past and future objectives and expectations. Social psychologists, whether behaviorist or cognitive in basic orientation, are optimistic about the possibilities of personal change since we see situational variables as important determinants of behavior. Our concern is always with understanding the relationships between individual behavior and conditions of the social milieu, whether these be the measurable characteristics of small groups, the contents of a persuasive message, or the norms of a culture. We assume that what persons do is relatable to their own direct experiences, to the consequences that follow their behavior, and to observations of the behavior of others.

A Feminist Perspective

The approach of the social psychologist is complemented by feminist analysis, a perspective that combines clearly articulated values with a set of research priorities. A fundamental value of feminism is that all persons should be permitted equality of opportunity for full development to the extent that this development does not impede that of others. Since there is ample historical and contemporary evidence that women as a group have experienced significantly fewer opportunities and greater restrictions than men, feminists (who may be either women or men) pay particular attention to women's experiences, needs, and circumstances.

A major objective of feminist scholarship is to examine carefully the antecedents and conditions of gender inequality, and to specify its consequences for women, for social life and institutions, and for social products such as language, art, and science. In addition, a feminist analysis proposes remedies, and feminists actively work to effect solutions and change. These objectives unify feminist scholarship in diverse fields. In literature, economics, art, history, sociology, psychology, and the natural sciences, feminist analyses have produced radical reexaminations of assumptions, and reconstructions of previously accepted interpretations. A feminist perspective, as Evelyn Keller (1983) has noted, "leads us to inquire into the simultaneous construction of both gender and science. It also provides us with a particular method for doing so" (p. 15). That method rests upon the recognition that the *personal* and the *political* are not separable. In a very explicit way, "feminist methodology seeks to bring together subjective and objective ways of knowing the world" (Rose, 1983, p. 87).

The Association for Women in Psychology (AWP), an organization of feminist psychologists founded in 1971, cites among its objectives: (a) to end the role psychology has played in perpetuating unquestioned assumptions about the "natures" of women and men; (b) to encourage research on gender; and (c) to educate the profession and the public about issues and problems of concern to women. Following the establishment of AWP, the American Psychological Association in 1973 "accepted a petition signed by 800 members and recognized the psychology of women as a separate division of the association, ending a quarter century of struggle" (Walsh, 1985, p. 199). A major objective of this group (Division 35) has been to promote and implement feminist research in order "to clarify the psychological, biological, and social-cultural determinants of behavior; . . . [accelerate] the integration of this information about women (and men) into current psychological knowledge and theories; and . . . promote the development of a benevolent society in which individual self-actualization is possible" (Task Force on Issues in Research, 1977, p. 3).

Feminist scholarship has invigorated, expanded, and transformed traditional disciplines. In psychology, as well as in other fields, the potential for enrichment has taken two interrelated forms:

> (a) self-conscious and critical analyses of the discipline to uncover its androcentric bias in both content and method . . . and (b) the indirect influence that arises from the asking of new questions, and the presentation of new hypotheses and theoretical formulations that follow from a focus on the experiences and conditions of women's lives. (Lott, 1985, p. 156)

Feminist research in psychology is distinguishable from other research not in the rigor of its methodology nor in its adherence to the rules of science, but in its choice of problems and ultimate objectives. It satisfies the primary requirements of scientific objectivity that the relationships described among events be repeatable or verifiable, and that the data brought to bear on research questions be accurate and reliable. Like other theoretical positions, this one must be judged on logical and empirical grounds. Thus, although this book reflects a particular point of view, it does so with due respect for the methods of science and in anticipation of reasoned challenges and continued inquiry into both old and newly arising questions.

Feminist psychologists have been active in research, in theoretical analysis, and in teaching. The impact we have made in the latter area can be gauged by noting that the number of psychology departments across the country that teach at least one course on the psychology of women or the female

experience has grown from 32 in 1972 to 209 in 1984–1985. The latter figure represents 23 percent of 896 departments surveyed by Mary Walsh (1985). Two psychology journals are specifically concerned with women and gender issues (*Sex Roles* and *Psychology of Women Quarterly*), and articles by feminist psychologists appear in dozens of other professional periodicals. Assessments of the current and potential impact of feminist scholarship on psychology in general and social psychology in particular (Deaux, 1985; Henley, 1985; Lott, 1985; Wallston, in press) have reviewed the significant positive contributions such research has made. These include asking new questions; making explicit the role of personal experience and values in science; treating gender as a stimulus to which persons respond; questioning earlier research that ignored or accepted unproven assumptions about women; and studying issues of particular relevance to women. Still, Barbara Wallston (in press) has urged a realistic appraisal of the impact of feminist psychology, noting that while "social psychology is being changed by work on women and gender . . . much of the adaptation by feminist researchers has gone unnoticed by the majority of social psychologists" (p. 29).

It has been reported that the term *feminist* has negative connotations for some contemporary young women (Bolotin, 1982; Friedan, 1985) and conjures up images of tough, unattractive, bitter women. But such a negative view may not be as common as the media would have us believe. A study of a large college-student sample (Berryman-Fink & Vederber, 1985), found the term *feminist* to have largely positive connotations for persons of both genders. Thus, for example, feminists were seen as logical, knowledgeable, intelligent, caring, and flexible women who were likely to be employed, ambitious, independent, active, assertive, and energetic, and who supported equal wages, equal rights, and the ERA.

A feminist orientation serves a guiding function not only in research but also in one's perceptions and responses. What another observer might ignore or find trivial, a feminist may interpret, by putting it in the context of similar events, as having important potential consequences for the lives of women. For example, a newspaper story ("Speakers," 1982) listed speakers who were in great demand as public lecturers and who earned sizable fees. A glance at the names and accompanying faces revealed that the "hot" speakers were all men. An agent for a speakers' bureau was quoted as saying, "Most of these meetings are attended by men, and men don't want to be told the facts of anything by a woman." A report with similar significance comes from a different realm. Two women, one 59 years old and the other 78, took the controls of an airplane after the pilot collapsed with a heart attack and "managed a 'magnificent' landing; though neither had [previously] flown a plane" ("Women, Nonfliers," 1983). A Civil Air Patrol officer (a man), in praising the women for bringing the airplane home, referred to them as "those two girls." A third example is that of national and international service clubs. The Jaycees, a 295,000-member national civic organization, was finally forced to admit women in 1984 (Beck, 1984). The Supreme Court, in disagreeing that the Jaycee leadership had the right to exclude women because it was a private club, made salient the still-practiced exclusion of women from equal participation in prestigious and powerful groups. In 1986, an appellate court judge in California ordered Rotary International to reinstate a chapter it had ousted for admitting three women. "Incredibly," the judge wrote, "14 years before the start of the 21st century . . . we still find ourselves having to . . . [defend] the right of American women to equal opportunity . . . " ("Rotary Ordered," 1986, p. A-1). And several months later, delegates to the annual convention of Kiwanis International voted to continue their policy of excluding women from membership ("Kiwanis Vote," 1986).

Sexism As Status Quo

Women's exclusion from particular places and situations is a general condition. The concern of feminists is not just with middle-class women who are discriminated against by being denied membership in civic clubs or excluded from decision-making positions in business or political organizations, but with the systematic exclusion of women in general from experiences necessary for our full development as human beings. Women in the United States, like women in other parts of the world, experience culturally imposed limitations on our access to resources, our access to positions of power, and our opportunity for personal growth.

Among the most devastating contemporary consequences of gender inequality in the United States is the impoverishment of millions of women and their children. The data are unambiguous and "the feminization of poverty" has become one of the catchiest new phrases in the social science lexicon. One third of all families headed by women are poor (by the most

conservative of measures, the Social Security Poverty Index) compared with 10 percent of all families and 5 percent of families headed by men; among minority families headed by women, close to 75 percent are poor. Women's poverty, according to the National Advisory Council on Economic Opportunity, is due to two major factors: women bear the primary responsibility for rearing children; and women are limited in the job market to low-paying jobs with little or no upward mobility ("Poverty Hits," 1982).

Women's relative poverty (which will be considered in greater detail in the chapter on parenthood) is but one symptom or consequence of sexism in our society. What do we mean by sexism? This concept can be defined in social psychological terms as having three related components: (a) negative attitudes toward women—generalized hostility, dislike, misogyny, or, in the more familiar term, *prejudice*; (b) a set of beliefs about women that reinforces, complements, or justifies the prejudice, involves a basic assumption of inferiority, and constitutes the *stereotypes*—well learned, widely shared, and almost irresistible generalizations about the nature of women; and (c) acts that exclude, distance, or keep women separate—that is, *discrimination*. A man is most likely to react to a woman in this way in situations where he does not expect nurturance, sexual pleasure, or some other positive response from her, and where he does not expect his behavior to be disapproved of or censured.

Recognition of the patriarchal (man-dominated) nature of our institutions and the consequences of sexism for the lives of women and men is not new. Feminist thinkers, scholars, and activists have not suddenly emerged full blown, but there have been periods of relative quiescence when the social problems associated with gender inequality have been relatively ignored. One such recent period was the 1940s and 1950s. This was followed by a growing and gnawing discontent among women, and similar messages from different places could be clearly heard. For example, in France, Simone de Beauvoir (1949/ 1961) compellingly argued in *The Second Sex* that "neither men nor women are satisfied with each other"; Germaine Greer (1970), an Australian in Great Britain, wrote convincingly in *The Female Eunuch* that "ungenteel middle-class women are calling for revolution"; and an American, Betty Friedan (1963), carefully and critically described in *The Feminine Mystique* the suffering of women experiencing the "sickness without a name." A new generation of women began to reexamine their lives and experiences.

WOMAN AS DEFINED BY MAN

"Throughout history," asserted Sigmund Freud (1933/1964), "people have knocked their heads against the riddle of the nature of femininity" (p. 113). Considering the brilliance and revolutionary nature of Freud's contributions to the understanding of human behavior and the fact that the majority of his case studies were clinical analyses of women, his admitted failure to solve the riddle of femininity is stark testimony to his androcentric bias. In a conversation with Marie Bonaparte, a respected disciple, Freud is reported by his biographer Ernest Jones (1955) to have admitted that "the great question that has never been answered and which I have not yet been able to answer, despite my thirty years of research into feminine soul, is 'What does a woman want?'" (p. 421).

The answers given to this question by men have tended to focus on a small number of similar themes. For example, when the movement for women's suffrage in the United States was close to its highest peak, Congress voted on May 7, 1914, to give women a national holiday, Mother's Day, their interpretation of what women wanted or ought to want (Rosen, 1973). The legislators believed, perhaps, along with the philosopher Immanuel Kant, that "deep meditation and a long-sustained reflection . . . do not well befit" women, and that "laborious learning or painful pondering, even if a woman should greatly succeed in it, destroy the merits that are proper to her sex"—her "unborn feeling" for beauty, her love of pleasantry and trivialities, and her good-heartedness (Agonito, 1977, p. 131). Like Kant, Freud also saw woman's main function as "ministering . . . to the needs and comforts of men," and while he believed women to be "finer and ethically nobler than men," he posited the source of women's ethical sense to be feelings and not reason (Jones, 1955, p. 421).

When Henry Higgins in *My Fair Lady* asked "Why can't a woman be more like a man?" I suspect that he did not really want a woman to be more like himself, and that he preferred to define her as the "Other." Simone de Beauvoir (1949/1961) has argued that men have found it advantageous to identify women as different from themselves, as hard to understand, complicated, ambiguous, and not the same as Man, who is the "One." Such a view appears to have served

men well, providing them with a useful scapegoat to which they could attribute the various evils and temptations of the world, ranging from lust to the excesses of greed and materialism that men claim to pursue for the sake of women (Dinnerstein, 1977).

A broad assessment of the ways women are typically presented in literature, mythology, and folklore suggests two general conclusions: women are seen to occupy a smaller, more *constricted* space in the world than men—"So much space for Man and his ideas, such cramped quarters for Woman," in the words of Michele Murray (1973, p. 28)—and attitudes toward women are typically *ambivalent*. This ambivalence appears to be related to a division of women into two categories distinguished by our level of assertiveness or independence. *If passive, then woman is good* and described as mother, virgin, saint, noble, pure, giving, fruitful, and an inspiration to man. *If active*, however, *then woman is evil* and a temptress, witch, whore, seductress, or distracter of man from his worldly or religious pursuits.

One of the most enduring and basic Judeo-Christian myths is that of Eve. This prototype of woman, fashioned from man and for man, is said to have damned the entire human species for eternity because of her sinful independent action and pursuit of knowledge. It is no wonder, then, that an Orthodox Jewish man thanks God each day in his morning prayers that he was not born a woman. In the Judeo-Christian view, woman is second to man in creation and status, and the cause of the world's troubles. In the Book of Genesis (Holy Bible, Revised Standard Version) it is written that God said to Eve, after she had eaten of the forbidden apple, "I will greatly multiply your pain in childbearing; in pain you shall bring forth your children, yet your desire shall be for your husband, and he shall rule over you" (3:16).

Eve is said to have erred more out of gullibility than malice, but before Eve there was Lilith, presented in some legends as Adam's first wife. According to Aviva Cantor (1976), "The most ancient biblical account of the Creation relates that God created the first man and the first woman at the same time. Jewish legends tell us that this woman was Lilith" (p. 5). Adam and Lilith are said to have quarreled over Lilith's refusal to obey Adam's command that she lie below him. Insisting on her equality with Adam, since they had both come from the earth, Lilith flew off in rage. In subsequent tales, Lilith appears not as a symbol of independence or equality, but as a witch/demon who is fearsome and threatening to society, who kills pregnant or birthing women, injures newborn babies, and excites men in their sleep in order to manufacture demon children from their sperm. A "female demon" with "many evil attributes," she appears in Jewish folklore as "a vampirelike child-killer and the symbol of sensual lust" (Harris & Levey, 1975, p. 1582).

The symbols of Eve and Lilith are not unique to the Judeo-Christian tradition but appear in some similar form in the legends of earlier cultures. For example, a Sanskrit myth tells of the creation of woman by Twashtri, who then "gave her to man. But after one week, man came to him and said: Lord, this creature . . . makes my life miserable . . . and so I have come to give her back." After another week, man relented and asked for the woman's return and Twashtri gave her back, but after three days man again complained to Twashtri, "She is more of a trouble than a pleasure to me." Twashtri, angered, refused to accede to man's request. "Then man said: What is to be done? For I cannot live either with her or without her" (Queen & Adams, 1955, pp. lf.). Not too dissimilar is the familiar tale of Pandora and the box, which so strikingly resembles that of Eve and the apple. An early version of the Greek story (in which there is no box and Pandora is not named) appears in *Theogony*, a genealogy of the Greek gods assumed to have been written by the poet Hesiod in the eighth century B.C.

herself and to obey her husband." *The Hindu Code of Manu V* (circa 100 A.D.) similarly asserts that "in childhood a woman must be subject to her father; in youth to her husband; when her husband is dead, to her sons. A woman must never be free of subjugation." Was it feared that otherwise a woman would act like the disobedient Pandora and unleash all the evils of the world? Thomas Aquinas in the thirteenth century (in the *Summa Theologica*) confidently repeated what Artistotle had preached sixteen centuries earlier, that "woman is defective and misbegotten . . . by nature of lower capacity and quality than man." Three centuries later, leaders of reform Protestantism like John Knox merely varied the theme to assert that "woman in her greatest perfection was made to serve and obey man." Thus, men appear to have found women praiseworthy primarily in passivity, dependency, or nurturant service, while fearing, decrying, and discouraging women's autonomy, activity, and desire for knowledge.

ORIGINS OF GENDER INEQUALITY

A number of speculative proposals have been offered to account for the historical sources of patriarchy and beliefs that support women's lesser status. They span many possibilities, including the following: (a) ancient goddess-worshiping matriarchal societies were disrupted by male revolts and men sought re-

Now when he [the God Hephaistus] had finished the lovely thing [a woman]
>   Which was evil instead of good, he brought her
>   To where the gods and men were all assembled . . .
>   They marveled at this snare men could never escape
>   For it was she who gave birth to the race of women;
>   From her came this female sex, all manner of women
>   Who live among mortal men to bring them pain.
>   (Hays, 1964, p. 80)

In a later work, Hesiod added to the story the incident of the jar. When Pandora lifted the lid, "she let forth gloomy afflictions to give men pain; . . . ten thousand sorrows fly about," and "both the earth and the sea are filled with evil" (Hays, 1964, p. 84).

Ramona Barth (1976) collected ancient "wisdom" from many sources that illustrate considerable agreement about the nature and role of women. In *The Confucian Marriage Manual* (sixth century B.C.) one finds, for example, this description: "The five worst infirmities that afflict the female are indocility, discontent, slander, jealousy and silliness . . . Such is the stupidity of woman's character, that it is incumbent upon her, in every particular way, to distrust

venge for their earlier inferior status; (b) men were jealous and fearful of women's mysterious birthgiving ability and women's tie to nature and fertility; (c) larger size and greater physical strength may have led men in some cultures to take over the tasks of hunting big game and fighting wars, with the consequence that male children were socialized for aggression and female children for docility; and/or (d) women sought to avoid dangerous situations, not for their own sake nor because they were less competent than men to deal with them, but for the sake of their infants, to whom they were biologically tied for gestation and nursing. It is likely that no one of these or other hypotheses completely explains woman's designation as the "Other," but rather multiple interdependent factors varying in significance across cultures.

A culture's emphasis on women's reproductive capacities and role in child care is the main factor that most contemporary anthropologists relate to women's lesser public influence. Dennis Werner (1984) has differentiated among three proposed explanations for this relationship: (a) child care prevents women from acquiring the knowledge, skills, or followers necessary to exert influence; (b) child care restricts women in their opportunities to obtain economic resources; and (c) child care affects the psychological makeup of caretakers in the direction of inhibiting aggressiveness, a correlate of leadership. His own research in Central Brazil did not provide clear evidence supporting any one of these explanations above the others, but he did find a significant negative correlation between the amount of time women were observed to spend on child-rearing tasks and the amount of influence other women rated them as having. Still, not all anthropologists agree that woman's role as mother is the source of her secondary status and lesser value, with some arguing that such a view "is an unwarranted projection of Western bourgeois assumptions on the rest of humanity" (Atkinson, 1982, p. 240).

Not only have many different reasons been proposed to account for women's lesser status, but the "issue of whether or not there is and always has been universal sexual asymmetry or the subordination of women is far from resolved" (Lamphere, 1977). Karen Sacks (1970), for example, has pointed out that in some cultures, like that of the Mbuti Pygmies, power, authority, and decision making appear to have been equally shared by women and men, while in other cultures, like that of the Iroquois, women have been dominant in political and economic affairs. Such illustrations support her argument that the relations between women and men, as well as feminine and masculine characteristics, are not universal, and have taken diverse forms in response to men's and women's relationships to the means of production (Sacks, 1979). Sharon Tiffany (1982) has also emphasized how women's status has changed as a result of changes in the conditions of production. According to her:

> The transition from a food foraging to a food producing economic base . . . represents a critical juncture in human history. . . . The shift from hoe agriculture and the importance of women as primary producers to labor-intensive forms of agriculture, requiring greater labor input from men, is another critical juncture. . . . As women's work is increasingly relegated to food processing and domestic tasks— . . . separated from the labor of primary production—women's reproductive roles as bearers and nurturers of children are elaborated, even idealized. (pp. 124f.)

In earliest human groups, gender differences in work and status appear to have been minimal. One theory (Fisher, 1979) is that early evolving humanity was egalitarian, and that all members of a group gathered and hunted for food. Evidence suggests that early human mothers did not stay at home with their infants but invented carriers for their babies and for food in order to free their hands and to provide storage for what was gathered. According to Tanner and Zihlman (1976), females "became innovators in the technology of gathering. They covered a wide range, knew it well, and could protect themselves and their offspring from predators" (p. 607). Nor was it the case that among hunter-gatherers it was the men who hunted and the women who gathered, as some earlier investigators assumed. Indeed, a number of foraging societies in which women hunt have now been identified, including the Agta of the Philippines (Goodman, Griffin, Estioko-Griffin, & Grove, 1985). Agta women hunt big game to about the same extent as the men do: they "hunt successfully and effectively . . . [and] are primary hunters, not assistants in male-organized hunting activities. Agta women were observed to hunt during menstruation without reluctance and to carry and nurse babies while on hunting forays" (p. 1204). No significant differences were found between Agta women who hunt and those who do not in fertility, reproductive history, height, weight, or age of youngest child. Thus, women have not been excluded from work in the public domain in all places and all times. As noted by Marion Lowe (1978), "the actual tasks and behavior allotted [to women and men] vary markedly from society to society, with no differences in sex role or behavior common to all, other than behavior directly connected with reproduction and lactation" (p. 122).

A position that attempts to reconcile the seeming contradictions among diverse sources of anthropological data has been articulated by Michelle Rosaldo (1980). Her view begins with the premise that sexual asymmetries are fundamentally social constructions and that while the biological facts of reproduction and lactation "leave their mark on women's lives" they do not by themselves explain sexual hierarchies and inequality. The limitations and constraints placed on women's access to "prestigious male pursuits" may be *understandable* consequences of women's role as mothers, but they are *not necessary* consequences. They are imposed on women to varying degrees in different societies. For example, a strong positive correlation has been found, among a sample of non-industrial societies, between a society's use of violence and its degree of sex-role rigidity or differentiation (McConahay & McConahay, 1977).

Regardless of the antecedents of women's lesser status and the variations in its extent, Rosaldo (1980) has concluded that gender inequality is widespread across cultures:

> In all known human groups—and no matter the pre-rogatives that women may in fact enjoy—the vast majority of opportunities for public influence and pres-tige, the ability to forge relationships, determine en-mities, speak up in public, use or forswear the use of force are all recognized as men's privilege and right. (p. 394)

Almost everywhere, women have functioned pri-marily in the private, domestic sphere, freeing men to operate in the public sphere, thereby giving them "privileged access to such resources, persons, and symbols as would sustain their claim to precedence, grant them power and disproportionate rewards" (p. 398). According to Louise Lamphere (1977), even where both genders contribute to the production of needed and desired commodities, inequities typically exist in what men and women receive in exchange for their labor.

It is important at this point to note that among those anthropologists who stress the universality of men's privileged position vis-à-vis women—what-ever its source(s)—and those who stress the vari-ations, there is clear agreement that: (a) women's behaviors across cultures span the range of human possibilities; (b) cultures vary in the degree to which sex roles are rigidly distinguished and in the level of overall gender inequality; and (c) where tasks are sharply distinguished by gender, those performed by men tend to be more highly valued despite the fact that there is nothing intrinsically better about one gender's domain than the other's.

WHAT WOMEN WANT: TO CAST A LONG SHADOW

The past has laid a heavy burden upon the present, and ancient myths are alarmingly congruent with some current institutional norms. But as we investi-gate the conditions of women's lives that serve to cramp and contain us, we should also come to appreciate that without the constraints imposed by ideas of gender and their translations into norms of behavior, the possibilities for women and the varia-tions in what we want and can become are vast.

History documents women's oppression, but also verifies our varied abilities and social positions. Some scholars (such as Mary Daly, 1978a) have suggested, from study of archeological finds and ancient sagas, that religions organized around mother-goddesses flourished in early civilizations. Merlin Stone (1979) has argued that the written literature and oral tradi-tions of large numbers of cultures, spanning the con-tinents, reveal that women were once viewed as deities and heroines, "as strong, determined, wise, courageous, powerful, adventurous, and able to sur-mount difficult obstacles to achieve set goals" (p. 3). Images have been found of women as judges, war-riors, and teachers; and artifacts from the Mycenaen culture (1400 B.C.) show women driving chariots and leading hunts. While the existence of ancient ma-triarchies is not well supported, new findings in archeological sites of the Neolithic period convin-cingly support arguments for the importance and visibility of women (Atkinson, 1982). Other scholars have suggested that many of the achievements that distinguished the New from the Old Stone Age, such as pottery making, weaving, planting, and harvest-ing, should be credited to women.

Thus, what contemporary women want is what has always been possible—full human status. Wom-en want, in Michele Murray's (1973) words, "to cast a shadow fully as long and as rich as the shadow cast by Man . . . not to be the Other, arranged in her place by comparison with the One, he who makes the comparison" (p. 14). We want there to be *many ways of becoming and being a woman* and to sing in celebra-tion with Denise Levertov (1973, p. 101):

> There is no savor
> more sweet, more salt
>
> than to be glad to be
> what, woman,
>
> and who, myself,
> I am, a shadow
>
> that grows longer as the sun
> moves, drawn out
>
> on a thread of wonder.

"It's a Girl!": The Nature of the Female Infant

Girls are maggots in the rice. . . .
When fishing for treasures in the
flood, be careful not to pull in girls.

Old Chinese sayings   *(Maxine Hong Kingston,*
1977, pp. 51, 62)

To understand human development we need to know a great deal more about how the environment affects physical growth and patterns, and how individual variation . . . plays into each different life history to produce adults with different competencies and potentials.

Anne Fausto-Sterling   *(1985, pp. 88f.)*

The killing of newborn children, especially girls, was widely practiced in early societies, overtly or surreptitiously, as a means to control the growth of the population (Harris, 1977). Born into a culture that for centuries killed or sold unwanted female children, Maxine Hong Kingston (1977) was never quite certain of her worth even though the possibility of her "disposal" never even remotely existed. "I am useless, one more girl who couldn't be sold. When I visit the family now, I wrap my American successes around me like a private shawl; I am worthy of eating the food" (p. 62). She remembers the old Chinese sayings with which this chapter opened:

> That is what one says about daughters. . . . I watched such words come out of my own mother's and father's mouths; I looked at their ink drawing of poor people snagging their neighbors' flotage with long flood hooks and pushing the girl babies on down the river. (p. 62)

Press reports from modern China in the early 1980s indicated that among some peasants in rural areas there had been a resurgence of ancient prejudice against girl babies and a rise in female infanticide, believed to have been sparked by the government's one-child-per-family fertility policy.

GIRLS ARE GOOD, BUT AREN'T BOYS BETTER?

Disdain for girl babies is not unique to one culture. When a boy was born among the Zulus an ox was slaughtered in celebration and to give thanks, but not for a girl, who was considered "merely a weed" (Hays, 1964). Similarly, among Orthodox Jews in eastern Europe (Baum, Hyman, & Michel, 1975), the birth of a son was a time for rejoicing, while the birth of a daughter brought "stoic acceptance." I. J. Singer has described the snickering that accompanied the public naming of his sister by their father; "Siring a female child was a shameful act for which [Hassidic Jews] occasionally flogged a young father with their belts" (Baum, Hyman, & Michel, 1975, p. 10).

One does not have to be Chinese, Zulu, or Jewish, however, to prefer boy babies to girls. While our society does not selectively discard female infants in the interest of population control, nor are fathers of girls ridiculed or flogged, girl babies continue to be seen as second best. It should not be surprising that women's lower social value is reflected in parents' attitudes and preferences. The lesser desirability of a girl, especially for a first or only child, is documented by data from a variety of sources.

Under the catchy title "Parents Still Prefer Boys," Patrice Horn (1974) reported the results of two studies separated in time by twenty years. The first investigation (by Dinitz, Dynes, and Clarke in 1954) found that a boy was preferred by 92 percent of a sample of men and 66 percent of the women, if they could have only one child. Twenty years later the same question was asked of a group of college students (by Peterson and Peterson) with comparable results. For an only child, a boy was preferred by 84 percent of the men and 64 percent of the women. Similarly, a study by Ralph Norman (1974) found that the majority of a sample of nonparent and parent students preferred boys; if they could have only one child, 86 percent of the men and 59 percent of the women wanted it to be a boy. Charles Westoff and Ronald Rindfuss (1974) analyzed responses given by 6000 women below the age of 45 in a national fertility study and found that among women still childless, 63 percent wanted their first child to be a boy. Among all women who intended to have children in the future, the sex preference ratio in favor of boys was 124 for every 100 girls. Lois Hoffman (1977), in a study of a representative national sample of married women under 40 and their husbands, found that although "most respondents wanted children of each sex, the preference was clearly for boys," so that couples who have only girls are more likely than couples who have only boys to continue to have children in order to try for a boy. After reviewing the literature on sex preferences, Nancy Williamson (1976) concluded that "there is little sign of change in attitudes" since the early 1930s. Among nonstudent populations in this country, the ratio of those preferring boys ranges from 106 to 113 for every 100 girls, clearly indicating that American parents, like those elsewhere, continue to prefer boys to girls. "Even when parents in the United States want one child of each sex, they would like the boy first. If they want an odd number of children . . . most would rather have more boys than girls" (p. 847).

One group of investigators (Calway-Fagen, Wallston, & Gabel, 1979) studied parents' sex preferences for their children by means of a clever behavioral measure. A sample of pregnant women and their spouses awaiting their first child were given a choice of four items of infant clothing as a gift. The investigators found that more than twice as many choices were made for blue rubber pants or a blue tailored shirt as for pink ruffled pants or a flowered bib; and in response to a direct question about preference, these expectant parents chose boys over girls by an even larger margin (39 to 17). Additional evidence of preference for boys has come from medical experiments on sex selection of offspring. A Chicago hospital that made a sex-determining technique available to couples using artificial insemination reported that of the first eight births using this procedure, six were boys and two were girls ("Choosing Baby's Sex," 1979). A more recent press report of a larger number of couples who used a sex-determining procedure noted that "parents requesting the technique have shown an overwhelming preference for male babies" (Lyons, 1984). Although the techniques used are not guaranteed, the success rate is claimed to be about 75 percent in birthing a child of the desired sex.

Do we continue to prefer boys to girls because we still believe the old myths about the biological inferiority of the female sex espoused by early theologians, philosophers, and scientists? Charles Darwin wrote that women's abilities represent "a past and lower state of civilization," and that intellectual eminence could only be expected of men (Agonito, 1977). Darwin was thus repeating the ancient "wisdom" of Aristotle, who maintained that

> woman is more compassionate than man, more easily moved to tears, at the same time is more jealous, more querulous, more apt to scold and to strike . . . more

prone to despondence and less hopeful than the man, more void of shame or self respect, more false of speech, more deceptive, and of more retentive memory. . . . The male is by nature superior, and the female inferior; and the one rules, and the other is ruled. (Agonito, 1977, pp. 49, 51)

In the nineteenth century, scientists paraded a continuing array of arguments and "evidence" that females were more childlike and primitive than males, that males were the agents of evolution and the more advanced representatives of the human species. Females were said to have smaller brains than males; when this was shown not to be the case in relation to body size, then the argument shifted to particular brain lobes. Females were said to have smaller frontal lobes or smaller parietal lobes, depending upon which were being identified with intelligence (Patrick, 1895/1979; cf. Shields, 1975a). Paul Broca, an influential anthropologist, never gave up his view that females were biologically impaired. Stephen Gould (1978) tells us that when Broca was confronted with the possibility that the smaller brain weight of women was related to their size, he argued that "we must not forget that women are, on average, a little less intelligent than men . . . therefore . . . the relatively small size of the female brain depends in part upon her physical inferiority and in part upon her intellectual inferiority" (p. 365). According to Gould, Broca's disciple Gustave LeBon, an early social psychologist, went further, insisting that women "represent the most inferior forms of human evolution," manifesting "absence of thought and logic, and incapacity to reason." Distinguished women were few, he said, and were "as exceptional as the birth of any monstrosity" (p. 365).

THE BIOLOGY OF SEX

Such claims regarding the innate inferiority of females did not end in the nineteenth century. Beginning in the 1970s there has been a renewed interest in establishing that sex differences in behavior and capacities originate in biology (or in "nature"), and reports of such hypotheses and related research are widely publicized. As noted by Marion Lowe (1983), "A great deal of media attention is given to biological theories that offer naturalistic explanations for the distribution of wealth and power in this society" (p. 56). In response to the widespread attention given to such theories, a number of important critiques have been published by scientists who urge us to examine the evidence carefully and who point out the interrelationships among science, culture, politics, and social policy (for example, Bleier, 1984; Fausto-Sterling, 1985; Lewontin, Rose, & Kamin, 1984). Lewontin and his colleagues, for instance, argue convincingly and explicitly that inequalities among races, social classes, and ethnic groups, in addition to those between women and men, have been contributed to and supported by certain themes in science: "Biological determinism . . . has been a powerful mode of explaining the observed inequalities of status, wealth, and power . . . and of defining human 'universals' of behavior as natural characteristics" (p. 7).

The question we must ask is, What are the "natural" characteristics of females? The answer requires that we first understand the biology of sex. We must know what structural and functional characteristics reliably distinguish a newborn child who is female from one who is male. What, in other words, is the significance of our sexual inheritance?

Sex Differentiation in the Human Embryo

Sex is defined initially by one pair of chromosomes that distinguishes females (XX) from males (XY), out of the total human complement of 23 pairs. The genetic pattern (DNA) on these chromosomes determines whether the embryonic gonads or sex glands will differentiate into ovaries (for females) or testes (for males). Another dimension of sex is morphological, defined by the external reproductive organs (vagina and penis), the development of which are under hormonal control. These two normally concordant aspects of sex—genetic pattern and morphology—are not always in harmony. The study of such sexual anomalies has contributed considerably to our understanding of the biology of sex, to the distinction among its genetic, hormonal, and morphological components, and to clarifying the relationship between these aspects and sexual identity. We will return to these anomalies shortly.

Let us now examine closely how sex differentiation occurs early in human embryonic development. At first, the newly conceived human organism is in a stage of indifferent sexuality with a single pair of embryonic gonads that can develop in either a male or female direction. The duct system structures for both are present, as can be seen in Figure 2.1. If the embryo is XX, then (by about the twelfth week) the gonads develop into ovaries; "the male duct system degenerates while the female system [the Müllerian ducts] differentiates into the internal organs of the

A. Internal structures

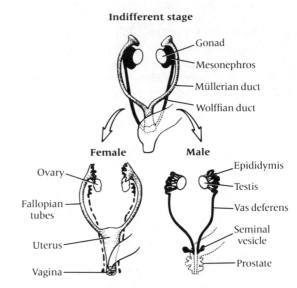

B. External structures

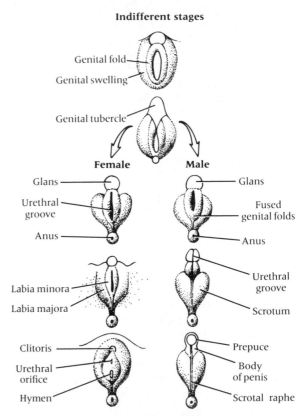

FIGURE 2.1 Embryonic development of the female and male genital structures

reproductive system [fallopian tubes and uterus]" (Fausto-Sterling, 1985, p. 81). If, however, the embryo has received an X chromosome from its mother and a Y from its father, then the genetic instructions are different; the short arm of the Y (Y_p) carries genetic chemical catalysts that direct the formation of testes (Gordon & Ruddle, 1981), followed by degeneration of the Mullerian ducts and development of the Wolffian ducts into the vas deferens and seminal vesicles. Implicated in this process is H-Y antigen, a protein synthesized by genetic information on the Y chromosome, in interaction with the X (Haseltine & Ohno, 1981). Under H-Y antigen influence, the testes are formed by about the sixth week of development. For male development to proceed, the embryonic testes must produce the Mullerian regression (or inhibiting) hormone, and testosterone. It is testosterone that is responsible for formation of the male internal genital structure, while its derivative dihydrotestosterone is necessary for development of the external genitals (Wilson, George, & Griffin, 1981). This group of interrelated hormones is called androgen.

In the first stage of human sexual development, then, the reproductive structures are identical for XX and XY embryos. Sexual differentiation proceeds gradually, with structural distinctions evident by the end of the first trimester, and the critical period extending from about the 6th to the 24th week of gestation in stages as shown in Figure 2.1. The standard description of this process assumes that sexual development proceeds in the female direction unless the embryonic testes produce androgens to direct formation of the male internal and external reproductive structures, but this interpretation has been criticized as androcentric (male centered). Anne Fausto-Sterling (1985) has questioned the assumption that females just *naturally* "develop from mammalian embryos deficient in male hormone" (p. 81), and has asked why there has been so little scientific curiosity about the precise mechanisms underlying female sexual differentiation. New work has shown that "the XX gonad begins synthesizing large quantities of estrogen at about the same time that the XY gonad begins to make testosterone" (p. 81), and some embryologists have begun to consider that the female hormones (estrogen and progesterone) produced by the placenta and present in high concentration during gestation may in fact be involved in female sexual development. Thus, both female hormones and male hormones are likely to contribute to the sexual differentiation process.

The Influence of Prenatal Hormones on Morphology

As we have seen, under normal circumstances, from initially undifferentiated gonads and ducts, an XX embryo develops ovaries and female supportive internal structures, followed by external genitalia, while an XY embryo develops testes, and then related internal and external sexual structures. But circumstances are not always normal. For example, if an enzyme necessary for androgen production is missing, or a toxic substance in utero acts as an androgen antagonist, a genetic male is born with the external genitalia of a female (labia, clitoris, and vagina). Chromosomal XY males with the syndrome of androgen insensitivity (AI) typically have a male internal structure (testes) but female external genitals because, although their testes produce androgens, their body tissues are insensitive to them. Such infants have been typically labeled as girls and reared as such. When the testes are discovered, they are surgically removed in childhood or adolescence, and estrogen therapy is provided to stimulate breast development and other female secondary sex characteristics. Research on these AI children, summarized by Anke Ehrhardt and Heino Meyer-Bahlburg (1981), indicates that the sexual identity of these genetic males is typically female, in accordance with their "postnatal rearing history."

A biological error in the opposite direction can occur among genetic females if they are exposed to excessive prenatal androgen. This can occur in children with congenital adrenal hyperplasia (CAH), in whom an excessive amount of androgen has been released in utero by the embryonic adrenal cortex (which, like the gonads, also produces sex hormones). CAH can occur in both males and females, but only the latter suffer the consequence of sexually ambiguous genitals at birth, malelike external structures with an internal reproductive system that is female. For such females to be reared as girls, early surgical correction and lifelong hormone treatment are required to ensure fertility and the capacity for normal female sexual functioning.

Some female embryos have been exposed to androgens not as a result of congenital error or malfunction, as in CAH, but as a consequence of exogenous hormones being introduced into the blood system of their pregnant mothers and passing through the placental barrier. For example, progesterone given to pregnant women to prevent spontaneous abortions (miscarriage) turned out to have an androgenic effect on the embryo. Although it is now well established that treatment with natural or synthetic progesterone (or other hormones) is largely ineffective in preventing problem pregnancies (Ehrhardt & Meyer-Bahlburg, 1981), such treatment was common in previous decades, with unanticipated serious consequences. Hermaphroditism (ambiguous genitalia) was induced in an estimated 18 percent of female offspring of progestin-treated mothers (Reinisch, 1981).

Both progestin-induced hermaphroditism (PIH) and CAH are conditions in which female sexual differentiation in the embryo has been interfered with by prenatal androgens. The primitive genital tubercle becomes an enlarged clitoris—a penis—and the labia partially fuse. Genetic females born with male genitalia who are labeled male at birth and are reared as boys require surgical removal of ovaries or hormonal treatment to prevent menstruation. Where the hermaphroditic condition is recognized at birth, surgical removal of the penis and a program of hormonal treatment make it possible for the child to be reared as a girl.

Sexual Identity

Much of the research on such "intersex" children has been done by John Money and his students and colleagues. Evidence from these studies strongly suggests that it is the sex assignment at birth and the consequent rearing and life histories of individuals, not genetic sex, that is of primary importance in sexual identity. Anke Ehrhardt and Heino Meyer-Bahlburg (1981) have concluded that in the case of genital hermaphroditism,

> gender identity agrees with the particular sex of assignment, provided that parental doubts are resolved early, and surgical corrections and postnatal hormonal therapy are in agreement with the assigned sex so that the physical appearance of such a child is unambiguously male or female. (p. 1313)

A provocative study (Imperato-McGinley, Guerrero, Gautier, & Peterson, 1974) helps to underscore and illustrate this conclusion. In the Dominican Republic, a group of interrelated families were found who suffer from an inherited deficiency of an enzyme (5α-reductase) necessary for the conversion of testosterone to dihydrotestosterone. Recall that the latter hormone is essential for the development of male external genitalia; chromosomal males with this enzyme deficiency are therefore born with ambiguous

genitals. In the investigation by Imperato-McGinley and her colleagues, 18 such children who were raised as girls were studied in adolescence. These intersex children were described as having "a blind vaginal pouch and a clitoral-like phallus" and had undergone no surgical/medical intervention at birth.

> At puberty, their voice deepens and they develop a typical male phenotype with a substantial increase in muscle mass; there is no breast enlargement. The phallus enlarges to become a functional penis . . . and the change is so striking that these individuals are referred to by the townspeople as "guevedoces"—penis at 12 (years of age) . . . the testes descend . . . and there is an ejaculate. (p. 1213)

Under such conditions—striking physical changes mediated by pubertal secretion of testosterone—it is hardly surprising that the majority of the affected individuals adopted a male sexual identity after puberty.

A lengthy critique of this investigation (Rubin, Reinisch, & Haskett, 1981) suggested that this group of children must have realized that they were different from other girls as pubertal changes gave increasing evidence of their maleness; they are reported to have experienced erections, nocturnal emissions, and to have "initiated masturbation and sexual intercourse." Only 1 of the 18 children continued to dress as a woman after puberty; another lived alone in the hills; and two were dead at the time of the investigation. While it is not clear how much confusion or concern there was about the children's abnormal genitals, it is very likely, in a society that offers little individual privacy, that the physical oddness of these children would have been noticed by their parents, siblings, and peers. One hint regarding how the children and their families interpreted their condition is provided by the seemingly good-natured acceptance of these children within the community as ones who "change at twelve," who are first woman, then man, or "machihembra" (Baker, 1980).

Some XY individuals with 5α-reductase deficiency have been studied in the United States (Rubin, Reinisch, & Haskett, 1981). They were all reared as girls, in some cases were not treated medically until puberty, and all continued to maintain their female identity. The information available on these cases suggests that as children they were "reared truly unambiguously as females," whereas the children studied in the Dominican Republic may have experienced "gender identity confusion" even before the pubertal emergence of clear signs of physical maleness. A related issue has been raised by Susan Baker (1980), who has noted that gender distinctions in Dominican culture are strong and girls marry right after puberty. In such a culture, a person without a functional vagina, who could not have intercourse or bear children, would be unlikely to remain defined as female. Thus, the findings of Imperato-McGinley and her colleagues, rather than indicating that the effect of androgen exposure in utero on the brain is so strong as to overcome the effects of nurture, as some have suggested, appear to illustrate that there is considerable plasticity in the psychological dimension, and that a change in sexual identification can occur in puberty in response to obvious sexual characteristics.

In summary, sexual identity appears to be influenced by an interaction of biological and environmental factors. As Susan Baker (1980) has suggested, "One's experience of oneself as male or female evolves over time, throughout childhood, and certainly into adolescence with its integration of a new awareness of one's self as a sexual being" (p. 95).

The Influence of Prenatal Hormones on Behavior

As previously described, genetic females who have been exposed prenatally to excessive androgen develop male external genitalia. Are there also direct consequences for behavior? This question is difficult to answer because androgen-exposed girls differ from other girls not only in prenatal exposure to male hormones but also with respect to such environmental factors as special treatment by their parents, surgery, medical attention, and hormonal therapy.

John Money and his colleagues have reported a small number of studies on CAH females who were treated early and reared as girls. Anke Ehrhardt and Heino Meyer-Bahlburg (1981) have summarized this literature as follows:

> The behavior of the prenatally androgenized girls differed significantly from that of the controls in that they typically demonstrated (i) a combination of intense active outdoor play, increased association with male peers, long-term identification as a "tomboy" by self and others . . . , and (ii) decreased parenting rehearsal such as doll play and baby care, and a low interest in the role rehearsal of wife and mother versus having a career. (p. 1314)

These conclusions have been challenged, and it would be premature to conclude that the prenatal presence of androgen has predictable "masculiniz-ing" influences on the behavior of exposed girls. A number of important questions remain unanswered: for example, Were these girls permitted greater behavioral freedom by their parents because of their unusual medical conditions? and What was the effect on these girls of their frequent medical examinations and special status? Clearly, the affected girls differed from comparison girls on variables other than just the prenatal presence or absence of excessive androgen. For example, Estelle Ramey (1976) noted that 7 of the 25 girls in one study were initially identified to their parents as boys and that this sex assignment remained unchanged for up to seven months. Others (Quadagno, Briscoe, & Quadagno, 1977) have noted that of the 17 girls in another study, 6 had received surgical correction within the first year of life, 7 between the ages of one and three, and 4 some time later, and that the affected girls had to be continually maintained on cortisone therapy. It has also been pointed out that the data obtained in these studies have come from interviews, not from observations of behavior by unbiased observers. It is likely that ambiguous genitals on a female infant influenced parental perceptions of their daughter's behavior and/or led to greater tolerance of a wider range of behavior.

Lesley Rogers and Joan Walsh (1982) have noted that CAH girls in one study were found not to differ from their mothers and siblings in choosing career over marriage; the CAH girls, in other words, had aspirations similar to others in their family. Rogers and Walsh also point out that the CAH studies typically lack clear definition of dependent measures, such as "energy expenditure"; and they ask how the rough outdoor play engaged in normally by girls can be explained in the absence of early prenatal exposure to androgen. A large majority of ordinary college women have been reported to remember themselves as tomboys in childhood (Hyde, Rosenberg, & Behrman, 1977).

No reliable differences have been reported between CAH girls and others in incidence of aggressive behaviors, fighting, or other acts of belligerence, nor have differences been found in frequency of reported daydreams about heterosexual romance and dating. Most of the androgen-exposed girls who have been studied have married in adulthood and become mothers. One seldom cited study (McGuire, Ryan, & Omenn, 1975) found no reliable differences in self-report of tomboyishness (nor on any other "femininity/masculinity" comparisons) between a group of 16 CAH young women and a control group matched in age, height, rural/urban residence, and IQ score. Thus, the small body of research considered by some to have provided the best indicators of prenatal hormone influence on behavior is not unequivocal nor free of criticism. Anke Ehrhardt and Heino Meyer-Bahlburg, who are among the most active researchers in this field, have noted that "the hormonal effects demonstrated are quite limited" (Hines, 1982, p. 72). Despite the ambiguities, contrary findings, and methodological problems, reported effects of androgen on behavior continue to be exaggerated and overgeneralized from a very small group of exposed female children who were born with genital abnormalities.

As noted earlier, exposure of female embryos to androgen has sometimes occurred not because of an adrenal gland defect (CAH) but because their mothers were treated with natural or synthetic progestins. Findings from the few studies of behavioral consequences of this exposure are difficult to interpret because there appear to be two main kinds of progestins, those chemically related most closely to progesterone, and those more related to androgenic steroids.* Among the synthetic substances there is considerable variation in chemical structure, in estrogenic or androgenic potential, and in potency. Not only do synthetic progestins come in many different combinations, but over the course of a single pregnancy a woman may have been treated with different progestins or progestin-estrogen combinations (Hines, 1982). In the majority of cases of pregnant women treated with progestins, female embryos have not developed male genitalia. Investigations of the behavior of this group of exposed children have generally used inadequate control groups and have not ruled out the influence of pregnancy conditions other than the hormones taken by the mothers (Ehrhardt & Meyer-Bahlburg, 1981). The results of these investigations have been ambiguous. Melissa Hines (1982) concluded that investigations of girls "who were exposed to unusual hormones prenatally, but who were born without abnormalities, have failed in many cases to find evidence of diminished maternal interest or masculinized play" (p. 72).

Estrogen, in the form of estradiol or diethylstilbestrol (DES), has also been used, either alone or more often in combination with progesterone, in treating problem pregnancies. Millions of pregnant women in this country took prescribed doses of such hormones in the 1940s, 1950s, and early 1960s without adequate research support for the effectiveness of this treatment in preventing miscarriage. But despite the potentially large research population, few researchers have investigated behavioral consequences of prenatal exposure to estrogen.** The available data are unclear and difficult to interpret. One study (Reinisch & Karow, 1977) examined the relationship between exposure to synthetic progestin/estrogen combinations and personality factors (as measured by a self-report test) by comparing 71 exposed offspring (of both sexes) between 5 and 17 years of age to their nonexposed siblings. There were no genital abnormalities among the exposed group and some mothers did not recall having taken any medication (although their medical records so indicated). The investigators found no significant personality differences between the exposed children and their siblings. Then the exposed offspring were subdivided into three groups: those exposed mainly to progestins, mainly to estrogens, or to a maximal level of both. When these groups were compared, the children exposed mainly to progestins were found to score higher than those exposed mainly to estrogens on 6 of 16 personality factors—independence, sensitivity, self-assurance, individualism, self-sufficiency, and pathemia (tending to feel rather than think). The investigators concluded from these data that both girls and boys with prenatal exposure to more progestin than estrogen were more inner- or self-directed. This study presents a number of problems, including the appropriateness of using a personality test developed for adults to assess children as young as five years old, and the reliability of the group divisions based on hormone ratios used in treatment of the mothers. The authors themselves noted that many of the mothers received more than one drug during a single pregnancy, and among the mothers treated mainly with progestins there were 23 different varieties. The data do not really support a conclusion that the children who were prenatally exposed mainly to progestin (assumed to be androgenic) manifested more masculine characteristics than the children who were exposed mainly to estrogen, since the obtained differences between these two groups do not reflect or correspond to our culturally stereotyped masculine

---

*It is instructive to note that the biochemical structures of female and male hormones are fundamentally similar and that each can be converted into the other. This will be discussed more fully later on.

**The consequences of DES for increased incidence of certain kinds of cancer in prenatally exposed children, especially females, have been studied and widely publicized.

and feminine patterns. Masculinity, for example, is not typically associated in our culture with sensitivity and feelings.

In a subsequent report of a study of 17 female and 8 male offspring of mothers treated during the first trimester of pregnancy with "synthetic progestins with androgenic potential," June Reinisch (1981) found that these exposed children (ranging in age from 6 to 17 years) scored significantly higher in self-reported physical aggression than their unexposed siblings on a paper-and-pencil measure of "potential for aggressive behavior." The author gives no indication of how these participants were obtained; it may be that these are the same children who were tested in the earlier study and described there as exposed mainly to progestins. If the children in the two reports are indeed the same small group (as suggested by the similarity in numbers and ages), then conclusions about the findings must certainly await replication on independent samples. Other studies have obtained negative findings. Melissa Hines (1982), for example, found no difference between 25 women prenatally exposed to DES and their sister controls on a paper-and-pencil measure of dominance, and a 1980 study by Kester, Green, Finch, and Williams (reported by Hines) found no differences on a test of personality attributes between a group of men prenatally exposed to DES and a group exposed to progesterone.

From a lengthy review of relevant research, Melissa Hines (1982) concluded that "the history of research on prenatal hormones and human behavior has been typified by reports of suggestive results, followed by realization of potential methodological problems" (p. 73). One such major problem has been in specifying what behaviors in human beings are associated with each sex. As Gina Kolata (1979) has pointed out, "It is very hard to say just what is 'masculine' or 'feminine' in human behavior" (p. 985). For example, interpreting preference for career over marriage as an indication of "masculinity" in girls is open to serious question. Hastily drawn conclusions in this area of investigation have typically been followed by negative findings from better controlled studies. One illustration is an early conclusion about intelligence and academic performance. It was first reported that prenatal exposure of females to excessive androgen resulted in higher IQ scores and school achievement, but later research that controlled for socioeconomic factors found that the hormonal exposure had no effect on these measures (Hines, 1982). Thus, the influence of prenatal hormones on human behavior has been confounded by other factors and not been satisfactorily demonstrated.

Chromosomal Anomalies

We have seen that biological sex is defined by both chromosomes and morphology, and that sometimes these do not match, because of the absence or presence of relevant hormones. Other problems of sexual definition arise from abnormal combinations of X and Y chromosomes. These have been revealed as a result of technical advances in the staining of cell nuclei (typically obtained from scraping mucosa from the inside of the cheek). Chromosomal abnormalities are believed to result from accidents occurring when ova and sperm (gametes) are formed from the division of parent germ cells. (In the case of ova, this process occurs prenatally; in the case of sperm, after puberty.) If the XX or XY chromosomes in the parent cell nucleus do not separate or if one member of the pair becomes entwined with other chromosomal material, then an ovum or sperm may be produced that either lacks a sex chromosome or has two instead of one. If such a gamete should participate in fertilization, the zygote resulting from the sperm/ovum union may have one or three sex chromosome(s) instead of the normal two.

Different categories of such abnormalities have been identified. XXY (Klinefelter's syndrome) individuals are characterized by morphological maleness but sterile testes, delayed puberty, and androgen deficiency. XO (Turner's syndrome) individuals are morphologically female with no ovaries. They are typically recognized at birth from such symptoms as webbing of the neck and kidney deformities; they tend to be deficient in gonadal hormones, short in stature, and have a number of congenital abnormalities. XXX individuals are morphologically unremarkable, and have not been much studied. In contrast, XYY individuals have received a great deal of attention, and such an abnormality has been estimated to occur in 1 out of every 1000 to 3000 live births in the United States (Probber & Ehrman, 1978). An XYY male is taller than the average XY male and is found with unusual frequency within prison populations. No causal link, however, has been reliably established between XYY chromosomal abnormality and criminal or violent behavior. Seymour Kessler and Rudolf Moos (1969) concluded, after reviewing the literature, that "no strong correlation exists between the presence of an extra Y chromosome and any specific behavioral, morphological, or physiological parameter," with possible exception of height. Herman Witkin and his colleagues (1976) found, in a large-scale and well-controlled study, that XYY men were of lower average intelligence than others but no more prone to commit violent or aggressive acts. A review of endocrine studies indicated that plasma testosterone in XYY individuals shows large variability and is "almost always comparable to that in control subjects and rarely above the normal range" (Rubin, Reinisch, & Haskett, 1981).

Sex and the Functioning of the Human Brain

Recent findings from the study of the human brain show that functions in the cortex, the brain's highest center, are specialized by hemisphere. For right-handed persons, the left hemisphere typically has primary control over verbal, linear-sequential, analytical, and mathematical processes, and the right hemisphere has primary control over spatial, holistic, intuitive, affective, and body awareness processing. That this division of function is not immutable is indicated by the fact that in children with brain injuries (and sometimes in adults) the undamaged hemisphere may take over the activities typically monitored by the injured areas. For left-handed persons, furthermore, hemispheric specialization appears to be far less developed than for right-handers.

While the scientific literature does not support any conclusions about sex differences in human brain organization at birth, nor about the effects of differential prenatal sex hormones on human brain organization, articles in popular magazines have publicized the idea that there are "male and female brains" (Bleier, 1984) and have suggested that one half of the cortex is more dominant in one sex than in the other. Whether the right or left brain has been said to be dominant in males (and vice versa for females) has, however, varied with ideas about which of the functions associated with each hemisphere are superior. Such generalizations about differential hemispheric dominance, as well as generalizations about sex differences in degree of hemispheric specialization (laterality) are not supported by the scientific literature. One of the investigators in this field, Marcel Kinsbourne (1982), a critic of "two-package brain" theories, has suggested that scholars (and nonscholars) have rushed to invoke differential hemispheric specialization "to validate their pet formulations" (p. 411) about age, sex, or culture; states Kinsbourne,

"There appear to be as many formulations of the division of function between the hemispheres as there are theorists concerned with this issue" (p. 415).

One popular attempt to divide the brain into a "his" and "hers" has given men the left hemisphere, since men are logical, sequential, and analytical (of course!); this neatly ignores the fact that verbal skills, which are also a primary function of the left brain, are said to characterize women. Instead, women have been given the right brain since they are intuitive, holistic, and sensitive (of course!); but aren't women supposed to be deficient in spatial skills, which are also a primary function of the right brain? The newest mythology appears to have reversed the earlier "his" and "hers"; the left (verbal, sequential) hemisphere has been returned to women while the right (spatial, simultaneous) hemisphere has been claimed for men. Vivian Gornick (1982) has reviewed these claims and noted that "now, suddenly, sequential reasoning is downgraded, simultaneous integration upgraded," and old assertions that men are logical while women are "hamstrung by reliance on intuitive perception" (p. 17) have been turned on their heads. As noted by Marian Lowe (1983), "Explanations that try to fit brain lateralization to sex stereotypes necessarily end up with some major contortions" (p. 52).

Michael Corballis (1980) has identified similarities between popular translations of the research findings on cortical hemisphericity and ancient myths about differences between the left and right sides of the body and their associations with gender. For example, the Taoist principles of yin and yang associate darkness, passivity, and left-sidedness with femininity, and light, activity, and right-sidedness with masculinity. Corballis also noted that hemispheric differences have not been found between persons who presumably depend more upon logical processes (such as lawyers) and those thought to be more visual/spatial (such as sculptors), and that there is evidence that both cortical hemispheres function in both simple and complex tasks, with the left hemisphere monitoring sequences and temporal judgments, and the right hemisphere better at perceptual tasks and discriminations.

Roger Sperry (1982), who received a Nobel prize for his empirical and theoretical observations of human lateralization (stimulated by discoveries he had made while working with "split-brain" patients); has proposed that "the two halves of the brain, when connected, work closely together as a functional unit with the leading control being in one or the other"

(p. 1224). In other words, under ordinary circumstances, the left and right hemispheres of the brain work together, their integration being mediated by the connecting fibers of the corpus callosum. It is not the case that one is "turned on" while the other "idles." When disconnected from the other, each hemisphere has "its own learning processes and its own separate chain of memories," but left and right processes are not antagonistic or incompatible. Instead, they manifest "a mutual and supportive complementarity." In addition, new work has emphasized the unique complexity of individual brain function and intellect, suggesting, according to Sperry, that "the individuality inherent in our brain networks makes that of fingerprints or facial features gross and simple by comparison" (p. 1225). Each human brain, in other words, is wired in a unique fashion with only rough conformity to a general plan. Recent research on brain-injured veterans of the Vietnam War also supports the general conclusion that human brains are flexible and adaptive (see Fischman, 1986).

Where reliable sex differences are found in right and left brain functioning, or in degree of hemispheric specialization for particular processes, they are small. Variation within each sex is always greater than the average difference between them, and many investigators have reported no differences. Anne Fausto-Sterling (1985) has cited an active researcher in the field, Jeanette McGlore, who in 1980 wrote that "basic patterns of male and female brain asymmetry seem to be more similar than they are different" (p. 51). Likewise, M. P. Bryden (1979) noted after reviewing the literature that inconsistencies and ambiguity in reported findings support the argument "that there are no convincing data for sex-related differences in . . . cerebral lateralization" (p. 137), and that conclusions remain speculative. This state of affairs remains unchanged in the 1980s.

There is considerable evidence that experience affects brain development. As Anne Fausto-Sterling (1985) has noted, "Extensive development of nervous connections [in the brain] occurs after birth, influenced profoundly by individual experience" (p. 77). The possibility that differential experiences have produced more communication between the two sides of the brain in women than in men was suggested by a report (DeLacoste-Utamsing & Holloway, 1982) that a portion of the corpus callosum is slightly larger in women (relative to brain weight). This serendipitous finding was obtained from a comparison between nine male and five female brains

examined in autopsies; information was not provided about their selection or other characteristics. The investigators noted that no previous data indicate "reliable sex differences in human brain morphology" (p. 1431), and replication with other samples has not yet been reported.

In general, conclusions cannot be reliably drawn from the available data about whether the brains of women differ from those of men in hemispheric specialization. As noted by Doreen Kimura (1985):

> We are finding that, depending on the particular intellectual function we're studying, women's brains may be more, less or equally diffusely organized compared with men's. No single rule holds for all aspects of thinking. . . . [Furthermore] at various periods in life, different brain structures may be undergoing more—or less—rapid growth, and patterns of brain organization will vary from time to time as a result. This may well go on throughout a person's life. (pp. 56, 58)

Brain organization patterns, according to Kimura, vary not only from person to person, but "probably even within the same person at different times" (p. 58). It seems clear, then, that conclusions about sex differences in brain function cannot be supported.

The Biological Imperatives

We have seen that biological sex refers to genetic, hormonal, and morphological distinctions between males and females that are typically (but not always) in harmony. We have also seen that (a) sexual identity is not dictated solely by genetic makeup; (b) behavior is probably not influenced by prenatal hormones; and (c) brain structure and function have not been shown to differ reliably between the sexes. This leads us to an important fundamental question: What, if any, are the inevitable consequences of one's biological sex?

According to John Money (1972), who has posed and answered this question, the biological imperatives associated with sex are only four: for females, menstruation, gestation, and lactation; and for males, impregnation. (These correlates of sex assume normal conditions and a correspondence between chromosomes and morphology.) All other sex-related characteristics are either biological options that display variations, or they represent cultural imperatives. The four biologically imperative sex differences are the only ones that are invariant for females and males (under normal conditions).

None of the secondary sex differences (such as in breast development, distribution of body hair, and voice pitch) is absolute. Within-sex variations in the quality, intensity, or frequency of these secondary characteristics "cover so wide a range that, at the extremes, individuals of one sex may be more disparate from one another than from representatives of the other sex" (Money, 1972, p. 14). Individual differences within groups of females and males are as great as the average differences between them.

Even the very limited number of sexual distinctions that constitute the biological imperatives are subject to control. Menstruation, gestation, and lactation may be capacities that are biologically limited to females, but an adult woman may choose never to experience pregnancy, in which case gestation and lactation will play no obvious part in her life despite the fact that they remain distinguishing features of her femaleness. Menstruation, too, while absolutely predictable for females, is responsive to environmental variation and can be affected by stress, exercise, and muscle/fat ratio.

OTHER SEX-LINKED PHYSICAL CHARACTERISTICS

Beyond the biological imperatives and the secondary sex characteristics, the list of reliable sex differences that can be unambiguously attributed to innate factors turns out to be very limited. This is not surprising when we consider that between genes (the starting materials for inheritance) and completed human structures and functions, a large number of processes intervene in environments that can alter, facilitate, or inhibit any aspect of human development. Victoria Freedman (1983), in a summary of recent work in genetics, has noted that

> there are . . . three fundamental, and new, concepts of the gene which are important in understanding the processes of heredity. First, in some cases, one gene does not determine one protein, but only a part of the protein. For the complete functional protein to be made, several genes must act together [especially in higher organisms]. . . . Secondly, the gene is just the beginning of a complex system of molecular activities which comprise the pathway of gene expression. In many cases, the product of that gene has to undergo many changes before it is in the operational, or active form. . . . Thirdly, the cellular environment plays a tremendous role in the final expression of gene products. (p. 30)

Whatever genetic differences there are between the sexes are carried on the X and Y chromosomes. An X chromosome accounts for 2.5 percent of the total genetic material, contains more than 100 genes, and is much more information-packed and bio-chemically active than a Y chromosome, which is smaller and controls only the differentiation of the testes (Probber & Ehrman, 1978; Lambert, 1978). Because the Y chromosome is deficient in genetic material, males are more likely than females to inherit recessive characteristics if these are carried on the male's one X chromosome, since everything on the maternal X is likely to be expressed unless modified by genes on the other chromosomes. Males are thus more likely than females to inherit the sex-linked recessive characteristics of baldness, color blindness, hemophilia, Addison's disease, and possibly muscular dystrophy.

And among newborns (neonates), infant males are more vulnerable than females and they do more poorly on a variety of psychomotor measures (Singer, Westphal, & Niswander, 1972). Natural abortion (miscarriage), stillbirth, and neonatal mortality rates are all higher for males, as well as susceptibility to infection and disease in infancy (Eme, 1979). The ratio of male to female conceptions is estimated to be 130 to 100, but at birth the ratio is down to 105 to 100 (P. S. Wood, 1980; "U.S. Study," 1985), indicating a greater risk to males even prenatally, during gestation. Although males continue to be more vulnerable during the early postnatal months of infancy, sex appears to have little relationship to health in childhood. Later on, however, differences in adolescent life-style and activities are reflected in greater male risk in athletic injuries and accidents.

Female bodies differ from male bodies in having a higher fat-to-muscle ratio; female body weight is composed, on the average, of 23 percent fat compared to 15 percent for males (Lowe, 1983). Females also exhale about 40 percent less carbon dioxide than males, differ in nitrogen metabolism, have lower metabolic rates, and a lesser vital capacity (total volume of air expelled after maximal inhalation) (Sherman, 1971). On measures of strength, women, on the average, are two thirds as strong as men, but the degree of difference varies with muscle group and is smaller when allowance is made for differences in weight and muscle fat (Lowe, 1983).

It is now well known that all of the variables relevant to physical strength can be influenced by physical regimen (activity, athletic participation, and exercise); and as Marian Lowe (1983) has noted, "There is growing evidence that differences in physical strength could come as much from differences in life experience as from innate factors" (p. 42). Males and females differ most sharply after puberty, when not only hormonal ratios but also cultural expecta-

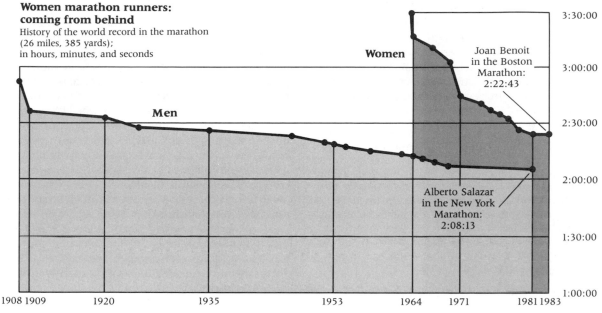

Women marathon runners: coming from behind
History of the world record in the marathon (26 miles, 385 yards); in hours, minutes, and seconds

Women

Men

Joan Benoit in the Boston Marathon: 2:22:43

Alberto Salazar in the New York Marathon: 2:08:13

3:30:00
3:00:00
2:30:00
2:00:00
1:30:00
1:00:00

1908 1909   1920   1935   1953   1964   1971   1981 1983

FIGURE 2.2   Women athletes are narrowing the gap.

tions and restrictions diverge. Thus, for example, the vital capacity of girls is only 7 percent less than that of boys, while it is 35 percent less in adult women than men. Recent studies have indicated that girls and boys in the United States are equally matched in physical ability until the ages of 10 to 13 (Streshinsky, 1975). During childhood, girls and boys are similar in all motor skills and physical activity performance, except in throwing a softball for distance.

Evidence from many sources indicates that body structure and function are responsive to variations in physical activity, training, and diet. For example, a newspaper story ("Women Changing," 1978) reported that only 14 out of 1027 female Air Force recruits failed in their performance on a mile-long obstacle course described as "the same difficult test of strength and endurance male recruits have always been subject to." Sports statistics indicate that the gap between the track and swimming records of females and males has been closing fast over the past 20 to 30 years; and it has been predicted that women will eventually do better than men in the super marathons (P. S. Wood, 1980). This is all the more extraordinary when we remember that up until the 1960s women were excluded from marathon races. In 1967 an entrant in the Boston Marathon named K. Switzer turned out to be a woman (Kathy). She ran the race "bundled in a sweatsuit because women were not allowed to compete" (Gross, 1984, p. 22E).

It was not until 1984 that the Olympics included a marathon race for women. The woman who won that event, Joan Benoit, had previously set a world record (in the 1983 Boston Marathon) of 2 hours, 22 minutes, and 43 seconds, which was faster than the record set by a man in the 1952 Olympics (Gross, 1984). The extent to which women athletes have been catching up to men in marathon running records is shown in Figure 2.2. While adult male athletes still generally outperform females, a review of relevant literature supports the conclusion that the sex gap is narrowing in many sports, and that sex comparisons are difficult to make because of differences in coaching, facilities, and training techniques (Wilmore, 1977). Marian Lowe (1983) has cited studies by Jack Wilmore that found that when nonathletic men and women were trained with weights, women's strength increased faster than men's, particularly in the arms and shoulders. This "was attributed to the fact that in daily life, American women already use their bodies in ways similar to men, but make much less use of the upper body" (p. 44). In addition, women in training lose relatively more fat than comparable men.

Physiological and body-build differences between males and females have been said to give each sex an advantage in different sports. Broader shoulders, for example, increase ability to throw and hit, while greater body fat enhances the buoyancy, endurance, and insulation needed for long-distance swimming (P. S. Wood, 1980). A wonderful example of how persons with different physiques can accomplish the same physical task in different ways has come from an informal observation by Janice Yoder (1983), who studied women in the Army Academy at West Point. All cadets of both sexes are trained on the same obstacle course.

> One obstacle is an eight-foot wall positioned between two trees. Cadets are expected to run toward the wall, plant one foot on it, push up and grasp the top, then pull themselves up and over the top. This obstacle requires upper body strength. . . . As the present author observed one day, a female cadet approached the wall, grasped the top, and rather than pull up her body weight, she began to use her legs, literally walking up the wall until both her hands and feet were on the top. She then simply pulled up her sagging bottom and disappeared over the wall. (p. 287)

While it seems likely that males will continue to be bigger and stronger, on the average, than females, we are also learning more about physical similarities between the sexes. The abdominal muscles, for example, which assist in a wide variety of sports, are as strong in females as in males.

In addition to the effects of explicit athletic training on muscles, strength, and other physical attributes, dramatic changes have been documented as a function of diet and life-style. Many years ago, anthropologist Franz Boas pointed out the striking difference in height between immigrants to the United States from eastern and southern Europe and from Asia and their significantly taller children and grandchildren. Now we have learned that since World War II changes in height and limb length have occurred in Japan for both sexes; the average height of a 20-year-old has increased three to four inches for males and two inches for females, primarily as the result of a change in leg length. The average weight for both sexes has also increased, by more than 15 pounds (Stokes, 1982). These changes are clearly attributable to modifications in life-style, posture, activity, and diet. Other factors known to affect height are incidence of disease, amount of sunshine, and physical and emotional stress (Lowe, 1983). While American women are, on the average, 40 pounds lighter than men, and have a body composition of 23 percent fat compared to 15 percent for men, "when trained men and women athletes are compared in the laboratory—muscle pound for muscle pound—there are few actual differences in their performance" (Streshinsky, 1975).

Females mature physically earlier than males as, for example, in bone development, teeth development, and in age of reaching puberty, but not in age of fertility. Females also stop growing earlier than males. By 16.5 years the average girl has attained her final height; for boys the comparable age is 17.8 years (Sherman, 1971). At maturity, the average female is five inches shorter and 30 to 40 pounds lighter than the average male (Wilmore, 1977). The shorter stature of females is thought to be related to the greater production of estrogen, which tends to inhibit the growth of long bones. Thus, age of first menses is correlated with adult height, and girls who reach puberty early tend to be shorter than girls who mature late. In addition, it has been suggested that if women were treated the same as men from birth, they might be as big and as strong since bone size is a function of calcium development, which is related to degree of muscle use. "Calcium is metabolized best when the muscles that surround the bone are being used, thus stimulating the blood flow to the area. The pull of muscles on bone may also have an effect" (Lowe, 1983, p. 45). Osteoporosis, a bone disease linked to calcium deficiencies in older people (and more common in women), is less apt to develop in individuals who exercise regularly. While large bone lengths generally differ between the sexes, it is in the shape and arrangement of the pelvic bones that female and male skeletons differ most reliably (Leibowitz, 1970).

The glands of both sexes release the same chemicals into the bloodstream. During childhood, the adrenal glands and gonads (male testes and female ovaries) produce relatively equal amounts of androgen and estrogen, but the ratios change at puberty. Although differing in relative amount, no known hormone is unique to either sex, including those specific to pregnancy, lactation, and menstrual cycle phases. The three families of steroid hormones (estrogens, progestins, and androgens) fluctuate daily in their level in any individual and under different physiological conditions, and the ranges for the two sexes overlap. There are different forms of each of these hormones, all closely related in chemical structure, and all synthesized from cholesterol, which normally metabolizes first into progesterone, which is metabolized to testosterone, which is metabolized to estradiol (Bleier, 1984).

From the preceding discussion of relatively reliable physical correlates of sex, we can see that if the parents of a newborn disregarded culture, or the consequences of socialization, the fact of their child's maleness or femaleness would permit them to make predictions about only a very small number of physical traits. The extent of within-sex variability is such that good safe bets could not even be made on some of these. Many years ago, geneticist Theodosius Dobzhansky (1967) noted that "the number of human natures is almost as great as the number of humans. Every person is unique, unprecedented, and unrepeatable" (p. 42). New investigations have revealed that even identical twins may not be absolutely identical in cytoplasm or in chromosomes.

BEHAVIORAL PLASTICITY: A KEY FEATURE OF HUMAN BIOLOGY

Each infant with a normal nervous system shares with others the specifically human characteristic of enormous *teachability and flexibility*. What is universal in the human species is a "capacity to acquire culture" (Dobzhansky, 1972) that is unmatched by other species and is indispensable to human beings; a "fundamental peculiarity of human evolution" is that we have "been selected for trainability, educability, and consequent plasticity of behavior" (p. 528).

The term *biological*, as ordinarily used and applied to descriptions of human capacities, is typically equated with genetic or innate—that is, inherited. But this is a limited and distorted meaning of the term. *It is indeed the biological nature of the human organism* that permits it to adapt to environmental conditions—*to learn*. As Helen Lambert (1978) has pointed out, "To equate biological with intrinsic, inflexible, or preprogrammed is an unfortunate misuse of the term biological. Behavior is itself a biological phenomenon, an interaction between organism and environment" (p. 104). From the very beginning of development, nature and nurture (heredity and environment) interact, and their independent contributions can rarely be clearly apportioned. The evidence from neurophysiology as well as from anthropology is compelling in support of the conclusion offered by Naomi Weisstein (1982) that "biology is a promise," that "we belong to an order stunningly flexible . . . and capable of great change within species" (p. 85). Similarly, Ruth Bleier (1984) views biology "as potential, as capacity. . . . For each person, brain-body-mind-behaviors-environment form a complex entity, the parts of which are . . . ceaselessly interacting and changing" (p. 52).

Female and male infants are similar in that each is unique and each is born with an extraordinary capacity to learn. Yet, in the eyes of their parents and the culture into which they are born, the fact of the newborn's sex is dominant; it is so important an identification that, with only rare exceptions, it is the very first thing to be publicly proclaimed at the birth of a child. In the chapters that follow, we will examine the many consequences of that excited announcement, "It's a girl!"

Infancy and Childhood: Behaving "Like a Girl"

We were required to embroider . . . I mastered the art of crocheting and tatting, and there was a lifetime's supply of dainty doilies that would never be used in sacheted dresser drawers. It went without saying that all girls could iron and wash . . .

Maya Angelou   *(1971, p. 87)*

I knew I was a girl, but that hardly seemed relevant. Girls did girls' things, but my Mum . . . trudged out and pulled the lever on the gas pumps . . . and so, later, did I, and I could wipe a fine windshield, too, shovel a walk, muck out a pigpen . . .

Marian Engel   *(1979, pp. 29f.)*

C H A P T E R 3

What does it mean to announce "It's a girl!"? Such a statement does not simply assert that this child can be expected to mature into a menstruating adult with the capacity for gestation and lactation, who will probably be sturdier in infancy, mature faster, and end up shorter than the average boy. It signifies far more. The gender designation generally carries with it the expectation of numerous traits of personality, motives, interests, capabilities, and often the general outline for an entire life script. An advertisement by IBM in popular magazines in the mid-1980s presented a pair of blue and a pair of pink booties side by side with the statement, "Guess which one will grow up to be the engineer? As things stand now, it doesn't take much of a guess" (IBM, 1985, pp. 14f.). But the behavioral predictions that knowledge of sex lets us make are the ones we have largely effected ourselves through differential socialization of our female and male children. Cultures begin at birth to shape highly flexible and teachable human infants not only into unique individuals but also into two categories of gender.

PINK BLANKETS AND PARENTAL EXPECTATIONS

In the musical *Carousel*, the hero, upon learning that his wife is pregnant, sings joyfully about what his son will be like: he'll be a heavyweight champion or president of the United States; "he'll be tall and as tough as a tree." Realization that the baby might be a girl brings an abrupt change to the lyrics. He begins to picture someone "sweet and petite . . . pink and white as peaches and cream," who will be brighter than "girls are meant to be" and, though pursued by "dozens of boys," will return each night to her dad. Such expectations mirror well the still-dominant gender ideology of our culture.

Evidence presented in the last chapter suggests that among contemporary adults, many anticipate parenthood already prejudiced to some degree against female children. Although girls may be necessary and even very nice, daughters are less expected than sons to fulfill the ambitions of their parents and to maintain continuity of the family name. In a study by Lois Hoffman (1977), the most common reasons given by women for wanting boys were to please their husbands and to carry on the family name, while the most common reasons given for desiring a girl were to have a companion and because it would be "fun to dress her and fuss with her hair." Women also said they wanted daughters because "girls are easier to raise and more obedient, . . . girls could help with and learn about housework and caring for other children, . . . girls stay closer to their parents than boys, and . . . are cuter, sweeter, or not as mean" (p. 648).

In the same study, adults who had at least one child were asked what kind of person they wanted their sons and daughters to become. For sons, parents focused on career or occupational success and said they wanted their boys to be hard-working, ambitious, intelligent, educated, honest, responsible, independent, strong-willed, and successful and respected in work. Parental hopes for daughters were different, and the themes more often centered on kindness or unselfishness, on being loving, attractive, having a good marriage, and being a good parent.

In a study of parental perceptions (Rubin, Provenzano, & Luria, 1974), parents were asked to describe their daughters and sons within the first 24 hours after birth. The infant girls were seen as softer, finer featured, smaller, more inattentive, prettier, and cuter than the infant boys; and although the fathers were more extreme in their judgments, they were largely in agreement with their wives. But objective physical measurements of these babies did not support their parents' perceptions. Ratings of the infants by the delivering doctors five to ten minutes after their birth on color, muscle tone, reflexes, heart

cathy®   by Cathy Guisewite

If it's a boy—tough and strong; if it's a girl—see her precious dimple. (CATHY. Copyright 1986, Universal Press Syndicate. Reprinted with permission. All rights reserved.)

and respiration rates, weight, and height revealed no significant sex differences. By the same token, a study of the reactions of three- and five-year-old children to a videotape of infants found remarkable similarity between their perceptions of girl and boy infants and the perceptions of adults (Haugh, Hoffman, & Cowan, 1980). After watching two infants, one labeled a boy and the other a girl (regardless of their actual gender), the observer children said, in response to questions, that the female infant was littler, more scared, slower, weaker, nicer, quieter, and softer than the boy infant. In this study, each infant observed was sometimes labeled a girl and sometimes a boy. Cathy Guisewite's cartoon suggests that stereotypical perceptions of infants, based on assumed associations with their gender, remain as common in the late 1980s as they were in earlier decades.

Research data and our own experience suggest that we typically expect and "see" in newborn girls and boys different physical and psychological characteristics and potentials. Related to this phenomenon are two important questions: (a) Do parents (and other family members) interact differently with infant girls and boys? and (b) Are there measurable and significant sex differences in behavior at birth? Few studies give reliable answers to the second question, because beyond measuring such things as reflexes, studying the behavior of neonates (infants from birth to approximately ten weeks old) is difficult. During the first two to three months of postnatal life, an infant's behavioral repertoire is limited, and responses are extremely variable. Only recently have technological advances in observation and recording equipment made the study of neonates more feasible.

Differences in Interaction with Male and Female Infants

Labeling an infant as a girl or boy, as we have already seen, gives observers what they believe to be a major clue to the child's behavior. Some researchers have gone beyond asking people to describe how they see infants labeled as girls or boys and have observed how adults actually interact with these infants. In one of the first of these studies (Seavey, Katz, & Zalk, 1975), graduate students were observed individually through a one-way mirror as they interacted for three minutes with the same three-month-old white infant dressed in a yellow jumpsuit. One third of the participants were told that the infant was a girl; another third that it was a boy; and the others were given no gender information (the "Baby X" condition). The infant was placed on a quilt in a corner of the room; near its head, on the floor, were a small rubber football, a Raggedy Ann doll, and a plastic ring. What influence, if any, did the infant's gender label have on the behavior of the adults? Both men and women used the doll most frequently in playing with the "girl," and men used the neutral plastic ring most frequently in playing with the child of unknown gender while women used either the football or the doll. Although the infant actually was a girl, 57 percent of the men and 70 percent of the women who were not told her gender guessed that she was a boy. Both boy and girl judgments were appropriately justified; those who believed that the baby was a boy "noted the strength of the grasp response or the lack of hair," while those who believed it was a girl spoke of "the baby's roundness, softness, and fragility."

In a modified replication of this study, Caroline Smith and Barbara Lloyd (1978) presented mothers of first-born infants with a previously unknown six-month-old infant dressed in "gender-appropriate" or "cross-gender" clothing and told the mothers to play with it for ten minutes. Only the infant dressed as a girl was first offered a doll by the adults, while only the infant dressed as a boy was first offered a hammer or rattle. In addition, the "boy" was verbally encouraged to physical activity more often than the "girl." A study of white middle-class expectant mothers (Bell & Carver, 1980) did not find such overall differences in interaction with six- and nine-month-old infants labeled as girls or boys. But the women who more strongly believed in sex differences offered a hammer significantly more to the boy-labeled infant than to the girl; and the total sample of expectant mothers offered toys considered "feminine" significantly more often when the infant behaved passively, and offered "masculine" toys significantly more often when the infant made noise. Another investigation using the same approach as the "Baby X" study (Sidovowicz & Lunney, 1980) found that college undergraduates of both genders who interacted with a three- to eleven-month-old dressed in diaper and shirt and believed it was a girl said she smiled a lot and was satisfied; but if they believed it was a boy, said that the infant didn't like strangers. The college students who were with a girl-labeled infant overwhelmingly chose to interact with her with a doll (as opposed to a football or a teething ring). One study examined the interactions of mother–father pairs with a six-month-old infant presented half the time as Beth (in a pink dress) and half the time as Adam (in blue overalls). The adult participants, who were parents of children of both genders, gave Beth more verbal attention and more neutral facial expressions than they gave Adam, but gave Adam more direct gazes and more smiles (Culp, Cook, & Housley, 1983).

How do parents interact with their own infants? A sample of 45 black mothers in Georgia studied by Josephine Brown and her colleagues ("The Favored Infants," 1976) responded differently to newborn girls and boys three days after giving birth, even though the behavior of the neonates did not differ significantly. "Once the feeding and caretaking chores were over, the males were rubbed, patted, rocked, touched, kissed and talked to more than the females" (p. 50). Similarly, Michael Lewis (1975) and a coworker found that on the first day of postnatal life boy babies tended to be fed by their mothers more than girl babies were.

Much cited is an early study by Howard Moss (1967), who observed interaction between 30 mothers and their first-born children for the first three months of the children's lives. The mothers of boys were observed to hold them longer at three weeks of age than were the mothers of girls (similar to the finding reported from the Georgia study). Holding time for both sexes decreased by the time the infants were three months old, but the boys were still held longer than the girls. Boys received more physical stimulation from their mothers, while girls received more reinforcement for their verbalizations—they were more frequently talked to and their babbles were more frequently imitated. A more recent study (Wasserman & Lewis, 1985) also reported, from observations of white middle-class mothers interacting with their first-born infants (11 to 14 months old) in a laboratory situation, that daughters were talked to significantly more than sons.

Not all researchers have reported differential responses to infants by their parents (it is almost always mothers who are studied) as a function of the infant's gender. For example, Kenneth Zucker and Carol Cortes (1980) found that mothers observed in a laboratory setting used gender-neutral toys in playing with their four-month-old boys and girls significantly more than they used gender-typed toys. The latter (pots and pans, dump truck), however, may have been far too advanced for four-month-old children as compared with the former (a rattle and a squeaky mouse), thus influencing the parents' choices. A more extensive and long-term study (Bee, Mitchell, Barnard, Eyves, & Hammond, 1984) of 193 mothers (primarily white) and their first-born infants, observed periodically from 1 to 48 months after delivery, reported only four significant differences (out of 42 measures) in the ways mothers interacted with girls and boys.

In sum, while some studies have reported no differences in adult or parental reactions to girl and boy neonates and infants, evidence from data collected in other well-controlled laboratory studies as well as from everyday observations, supports the conclusion that knowledge of a newborn's sex makes a difference in how the baby is handled and in the characteristics it is perceived to have. It may be that parents are more likely than other adults to respond to the individual characteristics of their own newborn infants and to be less influenced by gender expectations (at least in the early months), while other adults are more likely to be influenced in their interactions with a neonate by knowledge of its sex.

Gender Differences in the Behavior of Neonates

This brings us to our second question: Are there measurable and significant differences between girls and boys in their behavior right after birth? Among neonates, few reliable sex differences have been demonstrated, a conclusion reached by both Beverly Birns (1976) and Yvonne Brackbill and Kerri Schroder (1980) after careful analyses of the available literature. Birns reported that in 1974, Howard Moss, after summarizing ten years of his own research, noted how unstable early infant behavior is and how relatively unimportant sex differences are. He had earlier reported (1967) that the most striking characteristic of very young infants is variability, with few behaviors remaining stable from three weeks to three months after birth. Support for this conclusion with respect to even older infants has come from the work of Candice Feiring and Michael Lewis (1980), who observed the same infants at 13, 25, and 44 months and found no reliable sex differences at any of the three ages, and little individual stability over the first three years in vigor and activity levels. In 1975, an extensive review of the literature by Lyberger-Ficek revealed that most studies have "failed to show any sex differences in responses to auditory, visual, tactile, olfactory, taste or vestibular stimulation or in . . . spontaneous activities" and, thus, "labeling a newborn as male or female on the basis of its behavioral characteristics would be extremely difficult if not entirely impossible" (Birns, 1976, p. 236). Brackbill and Schroder (1980) examined the more recent literature on full-term neonates in good health (38 studies) and concluded that "insufficient grounds exist to document the existence of gender differences in neonate behavior" (p. 608). The previously mentioned study by Bee et al. (1984) found only 22 significant sex differences out of 263 variables analyzed, "only slightly above the level . . . expect[ed] by chance" (p. 790).

Some small average sex differences in spontaneous activity have been reported (Phillips, King, & DuBois, 1978) in a study of 29 neonates observed for 8 hours at 30-second intervals during nonfeeding times. On three out of six comparisons, boys were

found to be more often awake, and to make more facial grimaces and low-intensity movements. These observations, while not reported with consistency in the neonatal literature, do support a hypothesis proposed earlier by Howard Moss (1967) that males may be operating at a less well-organized level than females at birth and, hence, are more fussy or irritable and subject to more physical distress.

The most significant characteristic of the newborn of either sex is its capacity for learning. That the learning potential of human neonates is indeed enormous, and even greater than previous data had led us to believe, is shown by evidence from laboratories using refined technology and methods to gather data. Lewis Lipsitt (1977) has concluded, in an "overview of recent advances," that newborns are far more highly developed in their response capabilities and far more ready for learning than has been traditionally appreciated. Some studies have shown convincingly that learning begins even before birth, particularly through experience with sounds such as the mother's voice and heartbeat (Kolata, 1984b). Recent experiments have demonstrated conclusively that babies learn rapidly after birth, and a review of this literature led Otto Friedrich (1983) to conclude that "babies know a lot more than most people used to think. They see more, hear more, understand more" (pp. 52f.). According to Lewis Lipsitt (1977, pp. 180f.):

> The newborn comes into the world with all sensory systems functional. There is convincing evidence that the neonate responds discriminatively to exteroceptive stimulation and that sensory preferences already are present in the first few days of life. Moreover, the neonate may learn to respond differentially based upon sensory preferences and reinforcement contingencies, and in less than one hour of training may come to turn its head more in one direction than another, or more in response to one stimulus and not another. *All of this must have enormous implications for the condition of behavioral reciprocity that characterizes the early interactions of mother* [or other consistent caretaker] *and infant.* [italics added]

Research suggests that as child and parent interactions increase and as opportunities for learning expand, girls and boys begin to show those differences in behavior that the culture expects of them. In the ensuing sections of this chapter we will examine some of this evidence as we focus on the little girl's childhood, but at this point, what can we conclude about the newborn? Careful observations have indicated that the behavior of neonates is highly variable and unstable, and that there are no well-established, reliable sex differences at birth on any measure relating to behavior. One possible exception may be a greater tendency toward fussiness among newborn boys, perhaps attributable to their somewhat lesser physical maturity. Some evidence also suggests that parents (mothers have been studied more than fathers) treat infant daughters and sons differently from their earliest moments of interaction; they physically stimulate and handle their sons more during the early weeks, while they more frequently talk to and socially or vocally reinforce their daughters. The number of studies from which this conclusion stems is small because of the difficulties of this kind of research. The most certain and unambiguous conclusion we can draw is that the differential beliefs about and expectations for male and female children so common in our culture are not based on demonstrated inherent behavioral differences.

Given neonates' great capacity for learning, the caretakers of young infants can provide for them environments in which their capabilities will be developed and reinforced, and their range of behavioral and cognitive potential expanded. Unfortunately, we know only too well that adult ability to provide ideal growth-promoting environments for their children is seriously lessened by factors like poverty, ignorance, illness, and lack of access to social resources, and that these factors are related to economic class and minority status. Yet failure to provide our infants with opportunities for full development is not only a function of these social and economic factors but also of our judgments about the differential "nature" of the two sexes. Thus, we nurture our infant girls (and boys) with vision already narrowed by our preconceptions and as they so quickly learn what we teach them, our expectations are reinforced soon enough by their behavior. The female infant begins a lifelong process of becoming a culturally defined woman.

THE SEPARATE WORLDS OF GIRLS AND BOYS

Adults continue to purchase pink or blue blankets, booties, and bibs, and not frivolously. An infant's gender identity is a serious issue for the child's parents. For instance, among a sample of one- to three-month-old infants observed in suburban shopping malls (Shakin, Shakin, & Sternglanz, 1985), 75 percent of the girls wore pink (or had pink blankets or toys), but this was not true for a single boy. In contrast, 79 percent of the boys but only 8 percent of the girls were dressed in blue. Girls were also significantly

more likely to be wearing red, ruffles or lace, and puffed sleeves. The researchers noted that "the near universality of sex-typed clothing was in contrast to the low salience it displayed in parents' answers [to interview questions]. . . . Perhaps the sex-typing of clothing is such a basic given factor in clothing choice that it literally 'goes without saying'" (p. 962). But regardless of parental motives or awareness, as the researchers pointed out, "the sex labeling of infant clothing is simply one more mechanism that maintains the separate worlds of boys and girls" (p. 963).

As girls and boys leave infancy and enter childhood, adults continue to expect different things of them. This occurs despite the fact that children do not always behave in conformity to gender stereotypes. To investigate the reliability of our stereotypes, I asked adults to decide whether each of a series of jack-o'-lantern drawings had been drawn by a five-year-old girl or boy and to give their reasons (Lott, 1979). The adults said that the girls' drawings were neater, more colorful, better drawn, and had more smiling faces than the boys' drawings, and that the latter were sloppier, less careful, less symmetrical, more unconventional, and scarier, but they identified accurately the gender of the girl artists only 30 percent of the time and the gender of the boy artists 60 percent of the time. Thus, the gender beliefs of adults proved to be unreliable guides to the gender identity of these kindergarten children.

Even when there are more cues than those provided by drawings, what adults associate with gender is not necessarily true of what a stranger to the children may observe them actually doing. In a study in New Zealand (Lott, 1978b), I assessed the social behavior of four-year-old girls and boys in two schools in three different ways: direct observation in free-play situations; ratings by teachers of individual children; and ratings of "most boys/girls" by teachers and one group of parents. My direct observation yielded only 6 reliable gender differences (out of 30 social behaviors) in both schools and 8 others in one school only, compared with 18 significant gender differences that emerged from the teacher/parent ratings of "most boys/girls." But even more important was the finding that the gender differences perceived by teachers and those I observed did not always match. Present in the ideology as measured by the ratings, but missing from the observations, was the picture of four-year-old girls as dependent, helpful, and pleasant, and boys as disobedient and quarrelsome. Conversely, absent from the ideology but apparent in the observations was the picture of the girl at play alone or as onlooker, and the boy touching, chatting, and cooperating with peers.

While gender stereotypes may not accurately describe children's behavior, they are strong and widely shared beliefs that in our culture cross the lines of class, color, geographical area, and ethnicity. The dominant culture prescribes and enforces a sex-role ideology that is ubiquitous and pervasive, overt and subtle. Despite variations in, or deviations from, the cultural norms and ideals, the latter persist in specifying sex-based expectations. For example, Nancy Romer and Debra Cherry (1980) found that a sample of children aged 10 to 17 from three different ethnic and socioeconomic groups shared the perception that the "typical male" is more competent than expressive.

Some aspects of our sex-role ideology are shared with other cultures. For example, a now classic study (Barry, Bacon, & Child, 1957) found cross-cultural evidence for a common tendency to socialize girls for nurturance and responsibility, and to pressure boys for achievement and self-reliance. The researchers suggested that these differential pressures are necessary to prepare children for adult roles in which women, because they bear children, will attend to tasks near the home and minister to the needs of others, while men will do tasks away from the home that require specific skills. Each generation, in other words, is not left to its own devices but is taught sex-related behavior. Otherwise "sex differences in role would presumably be almost absent in childhood" (p. 329). A recent reanalysis of these cross-cultural data (Hendrix & Johnson, 1985) found that there tend to be more correlations than differences within each society in the socialization of girls and boys, and that "socialization varies more among societies than behavior between sexes" (p. 593). Nevertheless, the cross-cultural uniformity noted by Barry, Bacon, and Child was also supported: societies tend to emphasize "expressive traits more for girls and instrumental traits more for boys" (p. 593).

How are these cultural emphases for each gender established? They are the result of differences in (a) the situations to which girls and boys are maximally exposed; (b) the meaning and value given to these situations by adults and others; (c) the most probable responses required or demanded by these situations; (d) the opportunities girls and boys are given to practice various behaviors; and (e) the consequences (rewards and punishments) girls and boys experience or receive. Rather than just cataloging observed gender differences in children's behavior, we need to identify how the experiences of girls and boys differ along these dimensions. As an example of this approach, let us consider how the situations in which children play or behave tend to evoke those responses most appropriate to them. Children who spend their time running or playing baseball are practicing and perfecting responses and manifesting activity levels that are quite different from those of children who spend their time sitting at a table and drawing, lounging on the swings, or observing others. As a result of gender learning, which we will explore in detail in Chapter 4, girls more often play in the latter situations and boys in the former.

This raises the question of whether children who tend to behave in certain ways choose certain play situations, or whether the nature of the situation demands (and therefore precedes) certain behaviors. A study by C. Jan Carpenter and Aletha Huston-Stein (1980) addresses this question directly. Preschoolers between the ages of two-and-a-half and five were observed in five different classes. As expected, the researchers found that "girls spent more time than boys in preschool activities that were highly structured by teacher feedback or availability of adult models" (p. 870). They also found that children of both genders made more novel and creative use of materials in less-structured activities, and were more compliant in highly structured settings. Classrooms were found to differ in degree of structure, with the same behavioral consequences for children of both genders. The researchers concluded that

> the consistency between the findings for activity structure within classrooms and among classrooms adds strength to the contention that structure influences children's behavior. . . . Compliant children might select structured activities, and innovative children might select unstructured activities. [But] the classroom differences cannot be attributed to self-selection because children do not choose their classrooms. The data are therefore taken to support the proposition that boys and girls learn different skills by participating in activities differing in structure. (p. 871)

Beliefs about innate sex-related behavior differences tenaciously continue despite the existence of a large literature that documents that girls and boys are differentially exposed to different situations and that differing expectations and norms exist for their behavior. Only if environments and experiences did not vary with a child's sex could innate differences related to sex be assessed, but such conditions, necessary for testing and drawing valid conclusions about genetic determinants of sex-related behaviors, rarely exist. As Michele Wittig (1976) has noted, "Increasing the variation in child-rearing experiences to which boys are exposed and to which girls are exposed while minimizing the differences in environmental variation *between* the sexes provides one way in which to explore the answer to the question . . . of how much of a difference genes really do make in determining psychological sex differences" (p. 73). But, as we shall see, we continue to maximize between-sex differences by exposing girls and boys to differing situations and providing them with differing consequences for their behavior.

GENDER DIFFERENCES IN CHILDREN'S BEHAVIOR

In the remainder of this chapter we will consider the behavior of little girls from the end of infancy (at approximately age two) to puberty, and make comparisons with boys of the same age. We will see, as we examine first one behavior category and then another, that differences between girls and boys increase, in just about all areas, as they grow older. Jeanne Block (1976) reviewed a large body of research on gender differences previously assessed by Eleanor Maccoby and Carol Jacklin* (1974) and found more gender differences with increased age. That sex becomes increasingly predictive of behavior as children get older reflects the importance of experience, social pressures, expectations, and contingencies. *It is through socialization that sex becomes gender;* this process begins at birth and proceeds over the course of our lives.

Passivity/Dependency

Passivity denotes inaction and submissiveness, while dependency denotes subordination, control by, and reliance on others. Both are generally measured together in studies of children and are defined by such behaviors as following rather than leading, maintaining physical proximity to an adult, or low level of exploration. Despite the evidence suggesting that female neonates may be somewhat more mature and more biologically sturdy at birth than males (and certainly no less mature or sturdy), which should lead

---

*These investigations as well as others mentioned in this chapter have been primarily of white middle-class children in the United States. Exceptions will be noted where known.

to the prediction that girls are more able (and certainly not any less able) than boys to acquire independence at an early age, the cultural expectation is just the reverse. Girls are treated as though they are more fragile and are expected to be more dependent.

From an extensive survey of the relevant literature, Eleanor Maccoby and Carol Jacklin (1974) concluded that regardless of gender, dependency and attachment behavior characterize all human children during infancy and the preschool years. They further concluded that consistent differences between girls and boys have not been found in observational studies of nursery school children but that rating-scale studies, in which adults make judgments of behavior, more often report greater dependency on the part of girls. In situations in which children are confronted with something strange and unfamiliar, girls and boys have generally not been found to differ reliably on measures such as staying close to the parent (typically the mother), looking at the mother, smiling at the mother, exploration of the new environment, or degree of upset at separation from the mother. More gender differences are observed as children get older, and passive/dependent behavior in girls seems to increase with age.

Peggy Ban and Michael Lewis (1974), for example, reported finding no gender differences with respect to touching, proximity seeking, looking, or vocalizing, in a study of one-year-old infants in which the children were separately observed in interaction with mother and father. But Sharon Brehm and Marsha Weinraub (1977) reported that two-year-old girls differed from two-year-old boys in their reactions to a situational restriction. When one of two toys was placed behind a barrier, the girls more often than the boys first approached the one that was available and not barricaded. A now classic study by Jerome Kagan and Howard Moss (1962), in which the same group of persons was studied from infancy to adulthood, found that before the age of eight, girls are not significantly nor consistently more dependent than boys, but in later childhood and adolescence such a difference is more stable. Passive/dependent behavior is also more continuous among girls than among boys, as indicated by a stronger correlation for girls between measures of such behavior in childhood and adulthood. Similar evidence of increasing gender differences in passivity/dependency as children age comes from an investigation by Bonni Seegmiller (1980a) in which children aged three to five were observed under natural nursery school conditions at three-week intervals. On dependency behaviors, "three-year-old boys and girls were equal, but the four- and five-year-old boys and girls were increasingly sex-typed" (p. 32), with girls more dependent.

In the New Zealand study mentioned earlier (Lott, 1978b) in which I observed 72 four-year-old children individually during kindergarten free play, I found girls to differ reliably from boys in the following ways: more of their behaviors were adult-oriented; they more often chatted with, smiled at, and followed after adults; they more often played alone, and played quietly; they less often chatted with, cooperated with, followed the lead of, showed off with, followed after, and touched their peers; and they were less noisy and rough playing. Although there were actually more similarities than differences between girls and boys, the gender differences in behavior that I observed could be characterized by greater sociability and peer interaction on the part of the boys and by adult-centeredness and loneness on the part of the girls. Research with American children generally supports these conclusions (Maccoby & Jacklin, 1974). An analysis of the functional use of language by preschoolers, for example, found boys to differ from girls in talking more, asserting their desires, and assuming leadership; their words reflected "independence and assertiveness" more than the language used by the girls (Cook, Fritz, McCornack, & Visperas, 1985).

Why do gender differences in dependence/independence increase as children get older? To understand why this occurs, try to answer the following questions. If you were to set out to deliberately produce a dependent child (that is, to encourage a child to be clinging, submissive, non-risk taking, and to rely on others), what would you do? How would you arrange the child's environment, and what experiences and outcomes would you provide for the child? I would suggest the following: (a) restrict the child's space and the number of stimuli within it in order to deter exploration of unfamiliar territory or objects (only a limited number of responses should be required so that new behavior need not be tried out or learned); (b) provide as few opportunities as possible for the child to do anything that is self-initiated (independent) by anticipating the child's needs; (c) provide few possibilities for the child's autonomous behaviors (if they should occur) to be effective by withholding positive rewards and assuring that task success will be unlikely; (d) systematically frustrate independent responses and efforts to solve problems alone by discouraging them or making certain that

the efforts will fail to bring the desired results; and (e) positively reinforce dependent, help-seeking, and passive behaviors sufficiently often to encourage their frequent occurrence. Do we tend to arrange the environments (the learning experiences and play worlds) of our little girls so that they resemble those just described, thereby setting up conditions under which passive/dependent behaviors are likely to be acquired? Personal observation and research data suggest that we do. In Chapter 4 we will describe differences in the toys that are considered appropriate for girls and boys and note how those for girls discourage movement and initiative and encourage approval seeking and feedback from adults. Passive/dependent behavior is more likely to be manifested in some situations than in others. For example, Gail Wasserman and Michael Lewis (1985) found in a laboratory situation that when mothers were told not to interact with their 11- to 14-month-old infants, "girls showed significantly more proximal behavior (touching and staying near) than boys; . . . [but] these differences were not present when mothers were interacting with their children" (p. 672) in free play. It is interesting to note that under both conditions mothers vocalized more to their daughters than to their sons.

Activity Level

A child who plays alone, or stays close to adults and depends upon their feedback, will also most likely engage in less active play than a child who is exploring the environment, manipulating toys that move, and interacting with peers. As girls grow older, therefore, we expect to find that measures of activity level, as well as measures of independence, distinguish them from boys.

Activity level is not a stable characteristic of children younger than three and there is no single set of agreed-upon measures. Eleanor Maccoby and Carol Jacklin (1974), in summarizing the literature, have noted that "during the first year of life the evidence indicates no sex differences. From this age onward, studies vary greatly as to whether a sex difference is found, but when it is, boys are more active" (p. 177). But not all the evidence supports such a conclusion. For example, one study of 140 children, aged three to nine, who were observed playing alone in an open-field situation (that is, a room with several areas, tables, and toys) reported no significant gender differences in measures of activity level (Routh, Schroeder, & O'Tuama, 1974). When different measures are used, varied findings are sometimes reported from the same study. Thus, a well-known study (Pedersen & Bell, 1970) did not find preschool girls and boys to differ in the vigor with which they tore down a barrier to get an object, nor in running or tricycle riding, but girls did less walking than boys, and recordings of their large muscle movements yielded lower scores. These findings make sense when one learns that girls spent more time than boys with clay or play dough or on the swings, while boys spent more time with such objects as trucks and blocks.

Among girls, as among boys, play activities vary considerably. Personal observations and research data suggest that active play by girls is not always discouraged when they are young. Signe Hammer (1976) talked with a sample of mothers and daughters and found that many preadolescent girls enjoy considerable freedom from gender proscriptions and restrictions, and that they "ride bikes, climb trees, play baseball." From three independent samples—undergraduate women who wrote autobiographies, junior high school girls at a summer camp, and adult women in a shopping center who were asked to recall their childhoods—tomboyishness was found to be more typical of girls than not (Hyde, Rosenberg, & Behrman, 1977). The researchers concluded that "tomboys do not appear to be abnormal, either by definition as statistically rare or by comparison with nontomboys, from whom they do not differ on many psychological variables" (p. 75).

Where gender differences in motor behavior or physical activity are observed, they are likely to have resulted from differences in opportunities to practice as well as from differences in cultural expectations and encouragement. This conclusion is supported by a recent investigation that provides data bearing directly on this issue. Evelyn Hall and Amelia Lee (1984) studied the performance of children in grades 3, 4, and 5, during three consecutive years on five standard fitness tests including running and jumping. Among these participants in daily coed physical education classes, both genders showed continual improvement and, in the last year of the study, girls were better than boys of the same age on most of the tests. The authors concluded that "females at prepubescent ages may be expected to perform at similar levels to boys at that age . . . [if offered] equal opportunities in a coeducational situation" (p. 229).

Advertisements for children's clothes provide a dramatic illustration of cultural messages about activity levels. For example, one advertisement (Healthtex, 1982) proclaiming that "it's absolutely guaran-

teed that your boys will get dirty and messy and have a great time getting that way," presented scenes of boys camping, repairing a bicycle, preparing for a soccer game, and playing baseball. We would have a hard time finding a comparable message in an ad for girls' clothes, despite the real presence of many girls in all of these activities. Even ads for clothes for preschoolers continue, as in earlier decades, to distinguish clearly between what is appropriate for girls and for boys. In a Baby Togs, Inc. advertisement that appeared in 1981, girls are dressed in pink or red, are holding hands, and are ready to cheer for the boys, who are dressed for baseball—as a coach, a batter, and a fielder. Expectations for lesser activity by girls are found, of course, not only in the mass media and from clothing and toy manufacturers, but come also from significant adults and peers. Beverly Fagot (1984b) observed children aged 24 to 30 months in play groups and found that high activity-level play by girls "received few positive reactions from either peers or teachers," in sharp contrast to the feedback received by boys.

Play, Fantasy, and Use of Space

Children's play has been extensively investigated by Jerome Singer and Dorothy Singer (1973), who found that by three-and-one-half and four, boys and girls already differed in the themes of their make-believe play, with the latter acting out scenes relating to homemaking, school, and organized social functions while the boys played out more adventurous and fantastic themes. According to Beverly Birns (1976), other studies have shown that as early as age two or three girls move through space and explore less than boys. Dorothy and Jerome Singer (1973) found that although girls seemed more tentative in their free play in an outdoor area, both girls and boys manifested significantly more make-believe play and a greater degree of imaginativeness in free play than in structured situations. This finding supports the general proposition that what children do (in this case the degree to which they play imaginatively) is strongly influenced by the nature of their toys and the play environment to which they become accustomed.

Marsha Liss (1981) found that the type of toy children play with makes a difference in what they do. Kindergarten children were videotaped as they played with toys prejudged as masculine (for example, a truck), feminine (perhaps a doll), or neutral (like a musical instrument). The play behavior of girls and boys was found to be more alike "with male-traditional and neutral toys and less alike when playing with female-traditional toys" (p. 1148), probably reflecting the greater experience of girls with so-called boys' toys and the lesser experience of boys with toys prescribed for girls.

As with other behaviors, gender differences in play are more likely to be found as children increase in age. Thus, no gender differences were reported in a study of toy play directed toward peers or toward adults by 12- or 18-month-old infants in a playroom in which they were free to move about (Brooks-Gunn & Lewis, 1979). Studies with preschoolers sometimes report gender differences and sometimes not, depending on the measures used and other factors. Gail Melson (1977) observed four-year-olds engaged in indoor play in a nursery school over a six-month period and found no reliable gender differences in number of play areas visited, in amount or rate of indoor play use, or in frequency of contact with peers. But she did observe differences in type of activities chosen. In addition, girls played alone or with the leader more than boys, while boys played for longer periods with peers.

In the New Zealand research referred to earlier (Lott, 1978b), I found four-year-old girls and boys to differ significantly in their use of 8 out of 21 possible play areas. Girls played less often than boys in the sandpit, with the wagons, across situations in make-believe activities, and on an outdoor platform used as a staging area for dramatic play; on the other hand,

girls more often played on the swings, did painting/pasting/drawing, worked on jigsaw puzzles, or simply observed others. Girls also played more often indoors than outdoors, and differed reliably in this respect from boys. These findings are not unusual and are congruent with those reported by other researchers. For example, in every season over the course of two years, preschool girls were observed by Lawrence Harper and Karen Sanders (1975) to spend less time out-of-doors than boys. Relevant to these simple gender differences in play area is the finding in my New Zealand study that girls who did play in the areas favored by boys were less likely than other girls to conform closely to the expectations of adults with respect to such social behaviors as smiling at peers, being cooperative, not being noisy, and not playing roughly. These data suggest that the situations in which children play, or the activities they engage in, are directly related to the behavior they manifest.

The fantasies of children have also been studied (Cramer & Bryson, 1973; Cramer & Hogan, 1975). At earlier ages (nursery school through first grade) the fantasies of boys and girls are not distinguishable and, for both groups, fantasies tend to center around positive events (like eating candy) being followed by negative outcomes (like a spanking). By third through fifth grade, however, the fantasies of preadolescent girls change to reflect a pattern more characteristic of adult women—images of deprivation followed by pleasurable outcomes—while the pattern of boys' fantasies remains the same. Thus, in this behavior area, too, as in the others considered thus far, initial similarity between girls and boys gives way to differences as they grow older and their experiences diverge.

Attention, Interpersonal Sensitivity, and Prosocial Behavior

Attention to external stimuli can be measured even in neonates because it relates inversely to such relatively objective measures as heartbeat, muscular activity, and eye fixation. Such methods have not shown consistently reliable gender differences in infants in either hearing or vision. And Eleanor Maccoby and Carol Jacklin (1974) concluded from their large-scale review of the literature that girls and boys are very much alike in the amount and kind of information they are capable of extracting from their environments. Nevertheless, girls are expected to be generally more attentive than boys and more sensitive to the feelings of people, and it is likely that socialization in this direction begins very early in the girl's life. Walter Anyan and Warren W. Quillan (1971) studied the ability of a large sample of children to correctly identify the three primary colors (red, blue, yellow) at different ages. At age four the color-naming abilities of boys and girls were comparable, but by the fifth year they began to diverge, and girls were reliably superior in the sixth year. That differential learning is the major factor involved (and not differential "natures" or capabilities) is strongly suggested by the fact that among the five- and six-year-old children of both genders, those attending kindergarten outperformed those who were not in school.

Another interesting investigation of children's attention, but this time to one another, has been reported by Jerome Feldstein (1976). Girls and boys from the same day-care school were asked to identify by name photographs of their schoolmates. Despite the fact that the girls had been in the program a shorter time on the average than the boys, they made significantly fewer errors in naming their peers. Standardized measures of intelligence and memory revealed no gender differences. Had the girls already learned the importance of interpersonal sensitivity and practiced paying attention to names and faces? If, like other girls, they had spent more time indoors with a limited range of toys and more time observing "the scene," then the response of attending to persons is more likely to have been learned and less likely to have been interfered with than if they had spent a great deal of time moving about outdoors or in play in a variety of situations. In a replication of Feldstein's study by Claire Etaugh and Tommy Whittler (1982), however, preschool girls were found not to differ from boys in social memory—that is, in the accuracy of their recognition of classmates. Why the two studies obtained different findings is not clear but, as with other behaviors, gender differences in attention or sensitivity to persons are not consistently found. Kay Jennings (1977), for example, tested the widely held assumption that men (boys) are more interested in objects while women (girls) are more interested in people. She reviewed relevant studies of preschool children reported between 1955 and 1975 and concluded that the evidence does not support a conclusion of gender differences. She also tested the hypothesis by observing a sample of nursery school children, and found that "both boys and girls divided their attention evenly between people and objects" (p. 71) and that there were no gender differences in either

focus of attention or context of play, so that "boys and girls were indistinguishable" in this behavior.

So although we expect girls to be more attentive to other persons, this expectation is only sometimes supported by the evidence. We also expect girls to be more concerned about others, and to be more helpful, cooperative, sympathetic, empathic, and more considerate than boys, and thus to exhibit more of what psychologists call prosocial behavior. This set of expectations does not always turn out to be accurate either, especially among younger children. For example, in my New Zealand study (Lott, 1978b), teachers and parents of four-year-olds rated "most kindergarten girls" as being significantly more likely than "most kindergarten boys" to show affection to their peers, cooperate with them, give help to them, smile at them, and give them sympathy. But when I observed the children in free play, I saw no reliable gender differences in any of these behaviors except for cooperation—the boys were more cooperative than the girls. Eleanor Maccoby and Carol Jacklin (1974) reviewed 30 relevant studies and found no clear support for the hypothesis that girls are more empathic or sensitive to social cues than boys. On the other hand, Mark Barnett (1978) found that ten- to twelve-year-old girls tended to be less self-serving than boys in dividing up rewards in competitive situations. Boys tended to give themselves greater rewards than girls did. Perhaps girls have learned to be more concerned with other people's feelings and are thus more likely to be accommodating and generous, or perhaps girls learn that they are most likely to gain approval through positive interpersonal behavior.

Janet Lever (1978) has suggested that girls are less competitive than boys as a result of differences in the kind of games they play. She observed and interviewed a large group of fifth-grade children and studied diaries and questionnaires completed by them. Girls' games and play were found to differ from boys' in being freer of rules, providing fewer rewards based on skill, and involving less face-to-face confrontation and more turn-taking activities without explicit goals. Lever concluded that girls generally have less experience with interpersonal competition and with direct face-to-face competition. Interestingly, cross-cultural data do not support the hypothesis that boys are universally more competitive than girls. Michael Strube (1981) reviewed 95 independent tests of this hypothesis in studies of children. Only among Anglo-American and Indian cultures is the expectation supported, not among samples of Mexican-American,

Afro-American, Israeli, or Canadian children, or those from nine other cultures.

In a review of the literature on altruistic behavior (defined as behavior that benefits another but for which no external reward is expected), J. Philippe Rushton (1976) has noted that measures of altruism in children across situations do not show any discernible patterns of gender difference, and he cited a survey of gender differences (by Krebs) that gives no basis for concluding that girls are reliably more altruistic than boys. As with other behavioral dimensions we have examined, the major research objective should be to determine those conditions under which a child (of either gender) acquires the tendency to behave altruistically or sympathetically. The literature provides some hints. Rushton, for example, has noted that children who see the consequences received by altruistic models act more altruistically themselves. Are girls more likely than boys to observe altruistic models, such as their mothers? This seems likely since girls are encouraged more than boys to stay close to their mothers and to participate in mothers' activities.

A study of empathy (Barnett, Howard, King, & Dino, 1980) tells us something about this general issue of the relationship between gender differences in behavior and antecedent conditions or past experience. College students were tested for empathy; those who scored high on empathy also reported that their parents had spent more time with them, been more affectionate to them, and discussed feelings more with them than had the parents of students who scored low. This finding held for both genders, but the women students differed significantly from the men in having higher empathy scores and also in reporting having discussed feelings more with mothers and having received more affection from both parents. Thus, two of the factors found to enhance empathy are found more often in the childhood experiences of girls than of boys.

Other conditions under which children learn helpful or supportive behavior (from which we infer interpersonal sensitivity or caring about others) are suggested by cross-cultural comparisons. Beatrice Whiting and Carolyn Edwards (1973) examined data from six cultures of varied complexity and social structure. They found that where girls take care of younger children, the girls are described as helpful, supportive or nurturant, and compliant or accommodating, while the boys are more assertive, attention-getting, and engage in more rough-and-tumble play.

In cultures (such as two in East Africa) where boys care for younger siblings and do domestic chores, there are fewer gender differences; boys, too, show nurturant and helpful behavior and girls, too, are assertive and engage in rough play. Clearly, in this realm of behavior as in others, variations are best explained not by differences in biological sex but by variations in conditions and experiences.

Aggression

Eleanor Maccoby and Carol Jacklin (1974) have proposed that the evidence for greater aggressiveness (acts that are intentionally hurtful or damaging) by boys than by girls is so consistent and pervasive that it reflects a genuine sex difference, not explainable entirely by differential socialization. But this conclusion is not consistent with the available data, and has been criticized and challenged on theoretical as well as empirical grounds. For example, in the cross-cultural study by Beatrice Whiting and Carolyn Edwards (1973) previously mentioned, gender differences were found only in *provoked* aggression, and then in only two of the six cultures investigated, and only in older children (that is, in the 7-to-11 age group, but not in the 3-to-6 group). Todd Tieger (1980) analyzed the studies cited by Maccoby and Jacklin of children aged 6 or younger and found that, overall, boys were not significantly more aggressive than girls. Janet Hyde (1984) also reanalyzed the aggression studies presented by Maccoby and Jacklin and added newer investigations. She found that across a total of 108 gender comparisons in the surveyed literature, gender contributed much less than other factors to the variance in measures of aggression. According to Hyde, gender differences are greater when behavior is observed in a natural setting than in a contrived, experimental situation, are larger for physical aggression than for other kinds, and are reported less frequently in more recent investigations.

Paula Caplan (1979) concluded from an extensive review of relevant literature that in experimental studies, when girls' concerns about adult approval were reduced, the frequency of their aggressive behavior increased. This conclusion supports the view that the aggressive behavior of children (like other behavior discussed thus far) is sensitive or responsive to changes in the situation or context, and that gender differences are more likely to be found in some contexts than in others. David Barrett (1979), for example, observed five- to eight-year-old children over a six-week period in a summer day camp. Although boys were significantly more aggressive than girls overall, this was not the case when the target of aggression was considered. Boys were more aggressive than girls only to girls; to boy targets, girls and boys were equally aggressive. Barrett interpreted his data as indicating that "contextual factors . . . may affect the magnitude and even the direction of observed sex differences in children's aggression" (p. 202). Leonard Eron's (1980) research has suggested that other important variables predict aggression. In one study, aggressive behavior displayed in school by eight-year-olds of both genders was found to be related to parental nurturance and punishment: children who were aggressive were more likely to have been punished than nurtured by parents. In another study, boys and girls who were aggressive were found to share similar "interests, values, and attitudes," as illustrated by preference for violent television programs.

In their reply to Tieger's (1980) criticism of their conclusions about the innate basis of gender differences in aggression, Maccoby and Jacklin (1980) agreed with him that "human behavior is almost infinitely malleable, and the two sexes are alike in their capacity to be influenced by cultural pressures" (p. 977). They noted that there is great overlap between girls and boys in their rates of aggressiveness and that most boys are similar to most girls in this respect, but that boys are more heavily represented in the small group of extremely aggressive children. To understand why this is so, we do not need to assume innate differences, but rather to compare the typical socialization experiences of girls and boys. We know that girls are: (a) less likely than boys to have *opportunities to practice* hurting or inflicting damage; (b) less likely than boys to be assured directly (through adult and/or peer approval and encouragement) or indirectly (through observation of same-gender models) that such behavior is *appropriate and expected* (even if subject to temporary criticism); and (c) less likely than boys to *experience success* in this behavior by seeing the results of the damage or hearing the cries of the assaulted. Since we expect that "boys will be boys!" their aggressive acts typically bring a mixed message from adults; while the acts may be bad, adults recognize them as "inevitable" masculine reactions and believe that it is better to be a "real man" and to occasionally be aggressive than to be good but unmanly. (I remember my son's second grade teacher telling me with great excitement and genuine pleasure that he was beginning to act more like a "real boy"—he was getting into mischief more, working calmly and quietly less!) Girls do not face this dilemma. It is easier for them than for boys to be good, not to hurt others or inflict damage, because these acts are negatively sanctioned and are considered "unnatural" for girls. An aggressive girl thus gets a clear and unambiguous message: aggression is both wrong and decidedly unfeminine.

Probably, as the average boy begins to get taller, heavier, and stronger than the average girl, as his metabolic rate, vital capacity, and muscle-to-fat ratio increases, his ability to do damage will surpass hers. But physical capacity for inflicting hurt on others is not equivalent to the motivation for doing so, nor does it necessarily imply that aggressive behavior will be practiced. If we assume, however, that in the face of frustration (resulting from failure to attain a desired end) a person tends to persist in trying to gain gratification, then a strong response made by a strong person will likely result in damage to someone or something. Such behavior we label as aggressive. Assuming equal conditions for frustration, we can expect that what big and strong children do in natural response to it will more likely be called aggressive than what small and weak children do. If we put this possibility together with the differential consequences boys and girls are likely to experience following aggressive behavior, and the differences in opportunity to practice such behavior, then evidence of a gender difference on this dimension is not at all surprising. Consider how much greater are the opportunities to push and punch when outdoors, away from the watchful eyes of adults, and in the presence of admiring peers, than when indoors, near adults, and with no one to approve. Girls are more likely to be found in the latter than in the former scene.

Todd Tieger (1980) has offered a similar argument as follows: "Boys [may] have more weight to 'throw around' in early play interactions and thereby encounter a greater likelihood of positive reinforcement for high-amplitude behaviors" (p. 957). And Dora Ullian (1984) has proposed a complementary explanation for "why girls are good," by presenting the other side of this argument. One source of "goodness," Ullian suggests, is "the young girl's belief that she is physically vulnerable . . . fragile and defenseless" (p. 254). This contributes to her fear of aggression and her concern with potential harm. We know, of course, that young girls are not fragile and that they can be physically effective, but fewer girls than boys are expected or encouraged to see themselves as capable of self-defense or attack.

The conditions for practicing aggression are generally much less encouraging for girls than for boys. Jerome Kagan and Howard Moss (1962) found that the correlation between aggressive behavior in preschool and later childhood was lower for girls than for boys. Thus, early aggression on the part of girls tended not to be maintained, most probably because it was not reinforced. In an investigation of third- to fifth-graders of varied racial and ethnic backgrounds, Robert Deluty (1985) found that girls demonstrated less consistency in aggressive behavior than boys across situations and types of response, supporting earlier findings "that stereotypically male-appropriate behaviors tend to show greater stability for boys" (p. 1062). We know that behavior that is not reinforced by attention or other positive consequences tends not to be repeated (or, to extinguish). Thus, if aggressive acts by girls are ignored (because they do not confirm our expectations) or are otherwise devalued, such behavior will not be manifested with consistency or stability. That aggressive acts by girls and by boys are responded to differently by nursery school teachers and peers has been reported by Beverly Fagot and Richard Hagan (1985), who studied toddlers ranging in age from 18 months to three years during a ten-week period. "Girls' aggression was more likely to be ignored, with over 50 percent of their aggressive acts receiving no response. Boys, on the other hand, received a response to their initial aggression about 70 percent of the time. . . . Boys, then, are given responses which maintain aggressive interchanges, while girls' aggression is often ignored, which tends to terminate the interchanges" (p. 349).

In my study of New Zealand four-year-olds (Lott, 1978b), I found that their teachers and a group of parents believed that girls are significantly less likely than boys to disobey adults, argue with their peers, hit and fight, shout, play roughly, quarrel, and tease. But when I watched the children during free play, I saw no reliable gender differences with respect to disobeying of adults, arguing, fighting, or quarreling. The boys did do more shouting, rough playing, and teasing, and did play out-of-doors more often, and related to adults less. Since the parents and teachers expected boys to be more disobedient and quarrelsome than girls (even though they were not observed to be), and since boys' opportunities for aggression were greater (in outdoor play) than those for girls, it is likely that if I had watched older children I would have found a better match between gender ideology and the children's behavior.

While some environments discourage aggression, others appear to provide conditions that enhance it. Some girls, like boys, may learn what most girls do not, that being bad can bring more immediate rewards than being good. Agnes Smedley (1929/1973) has written of a childhood in poverty:

> I took my place as one of the leaders of the "toughest kids beyond the tracks." In school I let nothing hurt me—no reprimand of my teacher, no look or word. Swearing had always come easily and naturally with me, for my father had been a very good teacher. . . . I fought boys and girls alike in the alleys beyond the tracks, and my brothers hovered proudly under my protecting wing. (pp. 90f.)

Girls (like boys) can learn to be tough when that behavior is acceptable, brings desired ends, and is not punished. An incident at an elementary school in Rhode Island made national news when girls were separated from boys during recess "because of the girls' aggression" (Johnson, 1985). The principal of the school described the girls as "terrible"—as kicking the boys in the shins, pulling their hair, and grabbing them by their necks. The girls' objections to their punishment was widely publicized, and the schoolyard was returned to its earlier coed status. *Penthouse* later published a photograph of four of the girls with the caption "Little Amazons Attack Boys." The parents sued the magazine for libel ("Warwick Schoolgirls," 1986).

Television (particularly action shows) may teach lessons about aggression to children of both genders. In a one-year study of a sample of preschoolers, Dorothy Singer and Jerome Singer (1980) found a highly significant correlation, for both boys and girls, between observed aggression during free-play periods and both frequency of overall weekly TV viewing and the viewing of action shows in particular. Of special interest here is that the correlations between TV viewing and aggression were even larger and more dramatic for the girls than for the boys. Girls may be able to see on television what they are less likely to see in their typical interactions with peers and adults—successful, acceptable violence as a means of goal attainment or conflict resolution. Girls, under ordinary circumstances, are not taught to physically fight for what they want, but on television such images and messages abound.

Aggression is often preceded by anger in both children and adults. Do boys experience anger more often than girls? Some recent research has studied the emotional attributions made to boys and girls by adults and by children. In one study (Birnbaum, Nosanchuk, & Croll, 1980), a sample of four-year-old preschoolers and a sample of university students both associated maleness in puppies with anger, and femaleness with happiness and sadness. Leslie Brody (1984) asked children in grades 1, 3, and 5 to respond as themselves to 10 hypothetical situations, and found, similarly, that girls attributed less anger to themselves than boys did, but more sadness and more fear. In an effort to identify how the environment supports these stereotypes about children's emotions, Dana Birnbaum and William Croll (1984) examined the beliefs held by a sample of parents (primarily mothers) of preschoolers and a sample of college students, the emotional expressions of television characters, and the reactions of preschoolers to an animated video show. They found that working-class parents (but not middle-class parents) believed boys got angry more than girls and with greater intensity, and believed that girls experienced fear more often and with greater intensity than boys. In addition, anger was found to be expressed significantly more often by male than female television characters, as well as by more preschool boys than girls while watching a cartoon. The girls expressed fear and happiness significantly more often. But as with previous generalizations about the relation between gender and behavior, the situation or context appears to make a difference in expectations regarding expression of anger. Dana Birnbaum and Bruce Chemelski (1984) found that a sample of three- to five-year-olds more often attributed anger to boys than girls in a hypothetical situation in which the child's sand castle was washed away by the tide, but they saw boys and girls as equally likely to be angry in a situation in which another child grabbed the swing the first child had been playing on. Thus, stereotypes tend to lose their generality as we consider the particular characteristics of specific situations.

Performance on Cognitive Tasks

Most of the pre-1970 research on verbal, visual-spatial, and mathematical abilities shows that in childhood the performance of girls and boys in these cognitive areas overlap considerably, but that reliable gender differences appear as adolescence approaches. This was the conclusion reached by Eleanor Maccoby and Carol Jacklin (1974) after a review of this literature. Even when girls perform

cognitive tasks as well as boys do, they *expect* to do more poorly. For example, while no gender differences were found on three measures of cognitive ability among high schoolers (Gitelson, Petersen, & Tobin-Richards, 1982), the girls anticipated doing worse than the boys, saying they had less ability.

Verbal Abilities Janet Hyde (1981) has examined the studies on verbal abilities cited by Maccoby and Jacklin and found that the gender difference, overall, is very small, accounting for only 1 percent of the variation in scores on measures of such abilities. Billie Laney (1970) found that preschool girls and boys do not differ on rates of vocabulary development. But after about age 11 or 12, girls in general score higher on such verbal tasks as analogy construction, comprehension, creative writing, spelling, and fluency. By the end of high school, however, this verbal advantage on the part of girls is no longer evident on the Scholastic Aptitude Test. In 1984 the average verbal SAT score for girls was 420 compared with 433 for boys (Admissions Testing Program, 1984). The average boy's SAT score has exceeded the average girl's score every year since 1972, when reports were first issued, despite the fact that girls' grades in high school English classes are generally better than those of boys. On the separate test of Standard Written English that accompanies the SAT, girls continue to outperform boys.

Mathematical Abilities As is true for verbal ability, girls and boys in grade school are similar in acquisition of mathematical concepts and arithmetic operations. But at about the age of 12 or 13, boys first begin to show more improvement in this area than girls. This conclusion is supported by careful reviews of the literature. In one such recent review (Meece, Parsons, Kaczala, Goff, & Futterman, 1982), the authors noted that "sex differences on tests of quantitative skills do not appear with any consistency prior to the 10th grade. . . . Younger boys and girls perform equally well on tests of algebra and basic mathematical knowledge" (p. 325). They also pointed out that even at the high school level, girls sometimes are found to "outperform boys on tests of computational skills," and that differences in mathematics achievement favoring boys are not universally found among seniors and, where found, are small. Of interest in this regard is how girls and boys perform in the math classes in which they are enrolled. One study of over 2000 high school juniors by Virginia de Wolf (1981) found that the boys took more math classes than the girls but that girls significantly surpassed boys in their overall math grade point average.

Evidence for the smallness of the average difference between boys and girls in mathematical ability has come from recent research. Janet Hyde (1981) analyzed 16 studies previously cited by Maccoby and Jacklin (1974) and found considerable overlap between girls' and boys' math scores, with gender explaining only 1 percent of the variation in these scores. In a similar analysis of the test scores of mathematically precocious seventh and eighth graders reported by Camilla Benbow and Julian Stanley (1980), Joseph Rossi (1983) found that gender accounted for 4.4 percent of the variation in scores. Thus, among adolescents, the relationship between gender and mathematical test scores, while negligible, is larger than the relationship for younger children. In 1984 the average math score for boys on the SAT was 495, and the average math score for girls was 449; in each of the years since 1972 the average score for boys had exceeded that for girls by approximately 40 points (Admissions Testing Program, 1984).

Why do adolescent boys do better on these tests than girls? The findings of Benbow and Stanley (1980) with respect to gifted junior high schoolers have been interpreted by many, including the researchers themselves, as supporting the hypothesis of innate male superiority in mathematics. A story in *Science* (Kolata, 1980a) commenting on the research was headlined as follows: "Math and Sex: Are Girls Born with Less Ability? A Johns Hopkins Group Says: 'Probably.' Others Are Not So Sure" (p. 1234). The story noted that every year from 1972 to 1979, the researchers gave the SAT-M test to groups of mathematically gifted seventh and eighth graders identified through national talent searches, and every year the gifted boys scored significantly higher than the gifted girls, with the top scorer being a boy. But when we carefully examine the data presented by the researchers (Benbow & Stanley, 1980), they appear to challenge the conclusion of innate male superiority in math. In 1972, when the number of boys and girls tested was 90 and 77, respectively, the highest score for a boy was 740 and the highest score for a girl was 590 (a difference of 150 points). In 1979, when the largest number of children were tested, 2046 boys and 1628 girls, the highest score for a boy was 790 and the highest score for a girl was 760 (a difference of only 30 points!). This clear narrowing of the gap between highest scoring girls and boys during the course of seven years is surely best explained not by a change in female genes but by a documentable change in the culturally acknowledged value of mathematics for bright girls and a change in experiences, attitudes, and interests. The inferences drawn from the Benbow and Stanley data have gotten considerable criticism from many sources. The rejoinders are illustrated by an editorial in *Science* by two professors of mathematics, Alice Schafer and Mary Gray (1981), who decried the sensationalized media coverage of the Johns Hopkins study, and noted that

> environmental and cultural factors have not been ruled out. Anyone who thinks that seventh graders are free from environmental influences can hardly be living in the real world. While the formal training of all students may be essentially the same, the issues of who helps with mathematics homework, of what sort of toys and games children are exposed to, of what the expectations of parents and teachers are, and of a multitude of other factors cannot lightly be set aside. (p. 231)

Why is it that while girls do equally as well as boys in math in childhood, and as well or better in their math courses in high school, they nevertheless do not expect to do well, less often take college preparatory mathematics, and score more poorly on standardized tests of mathematical ability such as the SAT-M? Why, for example, did my middle daughter, who was an excellent and enthusiastic math student during her first two years in high school, when her math teachers were women, later lose interest in the subject and confidence in her ability? A considerable amount of current research is concerned with trying to answer such questions by searching for correlates or antecedents of mathematical skills in both genders. For example, Barbara Starr (1979) has reported that among a sample of high school seniors, girls with higher self-esteem and a sense of personal control over their environments scored higher on the SAT-M than other girls. For the boys, these personality factors had no significant relation to the measure of mathematical ability. We do not know "whether greater mathematical ability in girls gives rise to a greater sense of self-esteem and personal control, or whether girls with greater self-esteem are ones more likely to pursue the kinds of activities and goals which enhance both mathematical functioning and the setting of more diverse vocational goals in which mathematics is seen as having instrumental value" (p. 218). In any case, the lack of personality correlates for boys suggests that so many environmental factors may foster the development of mathematical ability for them that "special personality factors may not be necessary."

Other research supports the hypothesis that

mathematical ability is related to more specific variables in girls than in boys. For example, Julia Sherman (1980) reported that among a sample of high school students, while no significant gender difference in math performance was found when they were tested in eighth grade, such differences were found in grade 11. Accompanying the decline in the girls' performance were significant changes in their attitudes toward math as assessed by a variety of measures. Most important was the perception of math as a male domain; girls who saw math as a male activity were more likely to do poorly in it. Another study (Sherman, 1983) found the best predictor of continued enrollment in math courses for girls to be eighth-grade vocabulary score, followed by confidence in learning math; for boys, the latter factor was most important, followed by the former. Mary Kanarian and Kathryn Quina (1984) found no significant gender difference on 12th-grade SAT math scores among a sample of middle- to upper-class high school students, but differences favoring the boys were found on experience in math and related coursework, in perceived encouragement to study math, and in positive attitudes toward math. While 12th-grade math scores on the SAT were strongly related to an earlier measure of aptitude taken during eighth grade, these latter scores were highly related to perceived encouragement in math only for the girls, and not for the boys. The researchers concluded that "even in this well-educated, equally-able high school population, women are subjected to a support system that dictates that all men need math, but only the brightest women do" (p. 11).

A study concerned with techniques for "cultivating competence" (Bandura & Schunk, 1981) is relevant to this discussion. It reports equal gains by girls and boys, aged 7 to 10, in mastery of math after being encouraged to set attainable subgoals for themselves. Not only did these children (who had been identified by their teachers as poor in math) make substantial progress in achievement but their interest in mathematics activities also increased.

Spatial Abilities   As with mathematical ability, gender differences in visual-spatial ability are typically not found in childhood. Following a comprehensive review of the literature on human spatial abilities, Mark McGee (1979) concluded that "sex differences on tests of spatial visualization and orientation as well as on numerous tasks requiring these abilities do not reliably appear until puberty" (p. 909). A similar conclusion was reached by Herman Witkin (1979) in a review of gender differences in field dependence—independence; that is, the extent to which spatial judgments (of verticality, for example) are influenced by contextual factors. While women tend to be more field dependent than men, this difference "does not become regular or significant until around early adolescence.... [And] while this difference is a persistent one, it is small in magnitude. The range within each sex is vastly greater than the difference in means between the sexes" (p. 368). Other reviewers (Meece, Parsons, Kaczala, Goff, & Futterman, 1982) have also concluded that scores on spatial skills tests do not favor boys until about the 10th grade and, even then, not in all studies, as illustrated by a naational survey of over 3000 junior high and high school students in which girls and boys scored equally well. Thus, the data do not consistently provide evidence for gender differences in spatial skills, even at older ages. Across a range of ages the percentage of variation accounted for by gender in visual-spatial and field-articulation scores is 4.9 percent and 2.5 percent, respectively, as reported by Janet Hyde (1981).

Gender differences, although small, do appear consistently in studies of the visual-spatial abilities of adults in many cultures. But one exception to this cross-cultural generalization is among Eskimos. Two independent studies (Hier, 1979; McGee, 1979) have reported that Eskimo women and men are equal in spatial skills. In Eskimo culture both genders participate in hunting, must travel over great distances, and in order to survive must be skilled in spatial visualization and orientation. This suggests that context and experience play an important part in the development of visual-spatial skills.

A number of recent studies have demonstrated a relationship between particular experiences and visual-spatial competence. Lisa Serbin and Jane Connor (1979), for example, found that preschool children (of both genders) who preferred climbing and playing with transportation toys, blocks, and ring toss scored higher on a test of spatial ability than children who preferred to draw or to play with dolls and kitchen toys, while the latter did better on a vocabulary test. These data support Julia Sherman's (1967) suggestion that the differential practice girls and boys typically have with different kinds of play equipment is related to the later superiority of boys in visual-spatial performance. Playing with large toys, moving over large spaces, and manipulating objects are more likely to foster the development of spatial skills than sedentary play in a relatively confined area. The findings of Sharon Nash (1975) also relate to this proposition. She asked a sample of 11- and 14-year-old children to indicate whether they preferred being boys or girls, and found that within both gender groups preference for being a boy was related to better spatial performance. Whether the children in this study who said they preferred being boys did what boys typically do—engaging in activities that provide practice in visual-spatial skills—is not known, but when asked to explain their preferences, children of both genders who preferred being boys cited the greater desirability of "male activities" such as sports.

The proposed relationship between participation in certain activities and spatial ability has been studied directly. For example, in one study (Newcombe, Bandura, & Taylor, 1983) college students rated each of 231 activities as requiring or not requiring spatial abilities, and indicated whether they considered the activity "masculine" or "feminine." Activities rated as spatial were found to be considered more masculine (by both women and men), and these were ones men said they participated in more than women. The researchers also found that in another group of college students, women who reported participating in activities that require spatial skill scored higher on a standardized test of such skills than women who did not report such participation.

Training has been found to improve visual-spatial performance in children and adults of both genders. For example, the performance of first graders on an embedded figures task improved after practice (Connor, Schackman, & Serbin, 1978), although this improvement did not extend to a different spatial test (folding blocks). A study of college students in a drafting class (Johnson, Flinn, & Tyer, 1979) found that prior to training in two- and three-dimensional drawing, math or drafting majors of both genders did significantly better than liberal arts majors on an embedded figures test. Six weeks later all groups showed significant improvement on a posttest. The authors concluded that "it is not sex *per se* that matters so much as . . . interest and . . . training." A more recent study by Anne Stericker and Shirley LeVesconte (1982) found significant improvement in spatial scores after just three one-hour sessions consisting of discussions and practice among four-person groups of students. Although the men had done better as a group than the women on the pretests, both groups "benefited equally and significantly from the training." On the posttest, the trained women did as well as the group of men who had received pretest practice but no training. Three hours of training had brought the women to the men's level in tested visual-spatial ability.

These studies support the proposition that visual-spatial skill is trainable and is related to experience. Indirectly, therefore, they counter arguments that spatial ability is a fixed, inherited capacity, more likely to be found in males. One such argument is that spatial ability is carried by a recessive gene on the X chromosome and is therefore a more probable characteristic of males (who have only one X). Michele Wittig (1976, 1978) has critically examined this hypothesis and concluded that it is not well supported by the available evidence. In a direct test, Julia Sherman and Elizabeth Fennema (1978) found that the spatial test scores of a large sample of ninth-grade girls and boys did not confirm what a genetic X-linked hypothesis would predict. Thomas Bouchard and Mark McGee (1977) tested the hypothetical X-linked recessive gene effect by examining spatial ability score correlations between all possible parent-offspring combinations in 200 families. Not only did their results not conform to the expected pattern of zero father-son correlation and higher correlations between mothers and sons, but they found brother-brother correlations to be significantly greater than those between sisters, a pattern opposite to that predicted by the theory. According to the researchers, the obtained sibling correlations "are compatible with a theory which argues that boys in a family tend to be pushed into activities that foster spatial ability (sports and mechanical activities), while girls are not as consistently channeled into such activities" (p. 335). Thus, the available evidence suggests that the decreasing ability of the average girl to perform well on visual-spatial problems is a function not of some inherent weakness but of her systematic exposure to play materials and other experiences that offer little opportunity for practice in solving such problems, as well as her increasing familiarity with the cultural expectation that this is an area in which men, and not women, excel.

School Achievement

Parsons, Ruble, Hodges, and Small (1976) have suggested that as girls increase in age and experience they begin to (a) underestimate their own abilities and skills relative both to boys and to objective measures of these abilities and skills; and (b) to attribute their successes to luck or chance and their failures to stupidity or ineptitude. A dramatic illustration of girls' underestimation of themselves is provided by the work of Nicholas Pollis and Donald Doyle (1972). Each student in a first-grade class was asked to rank-order five peers on class leadership. A week later each child was asked to throw three tennis balls, one at a time, into a box concealed by a curtain so that there were no cues as to whether the throw was accurate or not, and then each child was asked to score his or her own performance (as well as that of every other child). The boys were found to outrank the girls in "class leader" nominations, and these nominations correlated significantly with attributed scores on the ball-throwing task. The boys were given higher performance scores than the girls by their classmates, despite the fact that the actual scores did not differ by gender. Only three children, all girls, achieved perfect scores on the ball-throwing task. How had they scored themselves? With scores of 0, 0, and 1 accurate throws; and this negative view had been shared by their classmates as well.

A study of children in grades four to six (Dweck, Goetz, & Strauss, 1980) found evidence that girls tend to underestimate their school achievement, regardless of the subject matter, despite the fact that their actual performance is consistently better than that of boys. The same researchers reported that while fifth-grade girls and boys reacted similarly to repeated failure (in an experimental situation involving two different tasks), by lowering their expectations, boys "bounced back" more easily. When in the presence of a new evaluator or with a new task, the expectations of the boys rose more than those of the girls.

Other research suggests that girls may feel more personal responsibility for failure than boys. For example, one study (Cooper, Burger, & Good, 1981) evaluated ten earlier investigations of elementary school children and concluded that "elementary school females took more responsibility for academic outcomes, in general, and for failure outcomes, in particular, than their male counterparts" (p. 566), but that the size of the gender difference was small. The results of their own study of over 800 children in grades three to five supported previous findings. The girls tended more often than the boys to attribute their success to an unstable characteristic like effort more than to ability. Deborah Stipek (1984) questioned a large sample of racially integrated fifth and sixth graders of varied socioeconomic status, and found that the boys perceived themselves as signifi-

cantly more competent than the girls perceived themselves in both math and spelling, despite the fact that the girls actually performed significantly better in spelling and only somewhat more poorly in math than the boys. And the girls were significantly more likely than the boys to attribute poor performance in math to low ability, while the boys were more likely than the girls to attribute good math performance to high ability.

As with the other gender differences thus far discussed, the small differences found in achievement attributions and expectancies disappear under some circumstances. Thus, for example, one study of a sample of seventh-grade girls (Van Hecke, Tracy, Cotler, & Ribordy, 1984) used a computerized task that provided its own feedback. Initial estimates of success (provided anonymously by each child) did not differ by gender, and the girls "behaved in ways that maximized achievement more often than boys did," despite the fact that to do so they had to ignore adult feedback in the form of approval for incorrect choices. Once again, this clearly shows the influence of context or situation. A similar conclusion is supported by the work of Marilyn Kourilsky and Michael Campbell (1984), who evaluated the effects of participation in a 10-week simulated economy program by over 900 eight- to twelve-year-old children. At the outset of the program both the girls and boys viewed the entrepreneurial role as more associated with men than women. But after all the children had received practice in buying and selling goods and services, teacher ratings revealed no significant gender differences in "economic success, risk taking, and entrepreneurial persistence," and the number of women perceived by the children as owners of businesses increased from the pretest.

Girls are expected to work hard in school and to get good grades, but they are not typically encouraged to believe that such achievement represents true ability or competence or is predictive of adult potential for eminence or success. Girls come to believe that when they succeed in school it is because they have put forth effort and because they want to please their parents and teachers. When boys succeed in school, our ideology tells us, it is because they are truly bright. We do not expect boys to necessarily expend their best efforts in grade school, which we regard as "feminine" places staffed by women teachers who do not really count. When boys do poorly, we tell ourselves, it is because they are not really trying. A study by Carol Dweck (cited by Parsons et al., 1976) found that teachers explicitly attributed the intellectual failure of boys to "lack of motivation" six times as often as they did for girls.

Direct support for the hypothesis that adults tend to reward girls and boys differently for achievement has come from Anthony Olejnik (1980), who had over 350 college students play the role of "teacher" and reward or punish 6- and 11-year-old hypothetical children whose performance on math problems and spelling tasks was described. Olejnik found that boys received more reinforcement than girls for their achievement in both tasks, were more likely than girls to be rewarded for high effort and positive outcome, and were more likely to be punished for low effort and negative outcome. These results suggest that adults behave as though school achievement really matters more for boys.

Recent research on computer literacy among children has found the repetition of familiar gender patterns. While women functioned in important roles and made up the majority of computer operators in the early years of the industry (Lockheed, 1985), contemporary girls appear to have less positive attitudes toward computers, less access to them, and less knowledge of them than boys do (Fetler, 1985). Among students enrolled in computer courses, however, no gender difference has been found in general ability or performance; "females are very successful and comprise a large proportion of the students who are exceptionally talented" (Linn, 1985, p. 235).

CONCLUSIONS

We can discern three general themes in the research about gender differences in the behavior of infants and children. First, gender differences are less often found in the earliest years, and more often found as children get older and as the experiences of girls vary more and more from those of boys. As socialization pressures and expectations increase, and girls and boys lead more and more different kinds of lives, they manifest more differences in behavior.

Second, regardless of gender, children's behavior is positively related to the situations in which the children are observed and in which they have had opportunities to practice appropriate and positively reinforced responses. Many of the studies discussed in this chapter illustrate this point. It must have been with this realization in mind that Marge Piercy (1976a), in her novel *Woman on the Edge of Time*, provided a picture of childhood in which sexual

identity is irrelevant to what one does, where one goes, and with what and with whom one plays. She describes a utopian society in which children live together with caregivers of both genders and are encouraged to develop individual interests and skills. A visitor to the society is told:

> Most of what children must learn they learn by doing . . . they need toys to learn coordination, dexterity; they practice tenderness on dolls. . . . We educate the senses, the imagination, the social being, the muscles, the nervous system, the intuition, the sense of beauty—as well as memory and intellect. (pp. 136, 140)

Finally, the data suggest that because of individual and group differences in children's experiences and backgrounds, our stereotyped expectations for how girls (and boys) act do not always prove to be reliable predictors of actual behavior. While children learn from their parents, teachers, and each other what is expected from persons of their gender, these lessons are not always compatible with their own experiences, observations, abilities, and interests. Rita Mae Brown (1973) has described such a contradiction in *Rubyfruit Jungle*. Molly, a poor Southern girl, is playing with her cousin Leroy and with her friend Cheryl.

> Leroy was the patient and we painted him with iodine so he'd look wounded. I wasn't gonna be no nurse. If I was gonna be something I was gonna be the doctor and give orders. I . . . told Cheryl I was the new doctor in town. Her face corroded. "You can't be a doctor. Only boys can be doctors. Leroy's got to be the doctor."
> "You're full of shit. . . . Leroy's dumber than I am . . . and being a girl don't matter."
> "You'll see [retorts Cheryl]. You think you can do what boys do but you're going to be a nurse. . . . It doesn't matter about brains, brains don't count. What counts is whether you're a boy or a girl."
> I hauled off and belted her one. . . . Course I didn't want to be a doctor. I was going to be president only I kept it a secret. (p. 31)

Some evidence suggests that girls who somehow manage to circumvent the sex-typing pressures and expectations toward passivity, dependence, and less vigorous activity are better off. For example, Joan Hemmer and Douglas Kleiber (1981) studied children in grades 3 to 6 and found that girls who were identified as tomboys by their peers and seen as somewhat "socially difficult" by their teachers in the earlier grades, were judged, by grades 5 and 6, to be "popular, cooperative, helpful, supportive of others, . . . and were regarded as leaders." Adding to our knowledge of such girls are data reported by Pat

Plumb and Gloria Cowan (1984). Self-identified tomboys in grades 4, 6, 8, and 10 were found to include more than half of the girls studied. These girls were found to differ from both boys and nontomboy girls in enjoying an expanded and varied repertoire of activities, and to be "not as gender-role bound in their preferences" (p. 711). In the earlier-mentioned New Zealand study (Lott, 1978b), I found that four-year-old girls whose observed behavior did not conform to adult expectations for girls were more creative than more conforming girls on a test of uses for everyday objects. Thus, children who do not behave in ways considered by adults to be gender-appropriate may be at an advantage relative to more narrowly conforming children, by experiencing a greater range of situations and learning a wider repertoire of responses.

Since we continue, for the most part, to provide girls and boys with differing experiences and opportunities to practice different skills and behaviors, it is not surprising that the average girl, as she grows older, becomes more and more distinguishable from the average boy in interests, goals, and responses. If we focus our attention on observing and cataloging gender differences, we shall certainly find them, although not under all circumstances and in all situations; and we will tend to forget how these differences have been created by social learning and how they continue to be maintained throughout the life span. Psychologists would do better to follow the advice of Michael Lewis (1975), who concluded from his extensive study of infant behavior that "there is no reason to study sex differences" at all. What we should be doing instead, he suggested, is studying individual differences in order to determine how behavior is modified by experience.

How Children Learn About Gender

Several families in our neighborhood gather to play touch football. Lizzy and her pal, Joey, are having fun in the melee, when another family arrives. Their daughter, demure, feminine Melissa, doesn't want to play. Suddenly Lizzy doesn't want to play either, and the adults, within earshot of Lizzy, are clucking about girls wanting to be girls.

Elizabeth Rommel   *(1984, p. 35)*

C H A P T E R   4

Our society continues to attach great importance to the careful learning of gender lessons. While exceptions exist, girls (and boys) typically acquire specific behaviors and general response tendencies and expectations that are gender-appropriate, as well as the knowledge that men and "masculine" events, objects, and actions have higher value—are more dominant and powerful—than women and that which is "feminine." In the last chapter we looked closely at the differential behaviors that boys and girls learn as they are socialized, and at some of the conditions that encourage these differential behaviors. We also noted the responsiveness of children's behavior to situational variations, and that these are related to significant differences among girls just as much as to differences between girls and boys. In this chapter we focus on children's knowledge of gender, and on the processes and agents that foster gender learning.

CHILDREN'S KNOWLEDGE OF GENDER EXPECTATIONS

In gender-sensitive societies, children learn early to associate particular behaviors, traits, activities, and occupations with women, and others with men. A variety of different studies have given clear evidence that children learn these associations as early as age two. And some have reported (for example, Leahy & Shirk, 1984) that with increasing age, children show increasing agreement with adult stereotypes regarding gender-associated personality traits and behaviors.

In a study of 2-year-olds and 3-year-olds (Kuhn, Nash, & Brucken, 1978), one of two paper dolls was selected by each child as the one who did certain things (such as play ball). All the children correctly identified the girl doll as "Lisa" and the boy doll as "Michael"; and both the girls and the boys of both ages believed that girls more than boys "like to play with dolls, like to help mother, . . . talk a lot, never hit, [and] say 'I need some help'" (p. 447). The children also believed that when boys grow up they will "be boss," while girls will "clean the house." The authors concluded that their results "clearly demonstrate that children as young as 2 years of age possess substantive knowledge of sex-role stereotypes prevailing in our culture" (p. 449). Supporting data have come from a recent investigation (Cowan & Hoffman, 1986) that found that 2½- to 3-year-olds were just as adept as 3½- to 4-year-olds in describing both infants and animals in terms of gender stereotypes. Girl babies, dogs, and horses were described as smaller, slower, weaker, quieter, and softer than boys.

By preschool age, most children are well aware of their own gender, which parent they are most like, and the gender of family members and peers. One study of a sample of children between 4 and 6 years of age found that with the exception of only one child, boys knew they would be fathers and girls that they would be mothers (Thompson & Bentler, 1973). Spencer Thompson (1975) found that 36-month-old children "consistently applied gender labels properly, were certain of their own gender, used same-sex gender labels to guide behavior and were aware of sex-role stereotyping" (p. 399).

John Masters and Alexander Wilkinson (1976) found that a sample of 4-year-olds rated 52 common toys as more likely to be used by girls or boys in a manner that was highly correlated with the ratings of adults, and that older children, 7- and 8-year-olds, rated the toys in an almost identical manner to the adults. Except at the youngest age, girls and boys exhibited "practically indistinguishable sex-stereotype norms." In a study of gender associations to adjectives describing personality, Harry Reis and Stephanie Wright (1982) found increasing stereotyping with age among children from 3 to 5 years old. The stereotypes held by girls and boys did not differ, but children with more intellectual ability also had more knowledge of gender stereotypes. According to the children, women (girls) cry a lot, are quiet and afraid, are thankful, weak, gentle, loving, and have good manners, while men (boys) are cruel, strong, get into fights, are self-reliant, and talk loudly. Using a different methodology, Wendy Matthews (1981) videotaped pairs of previously unacquainted same-gender 4-year-olds for 3 consecutive days as they engaged in an hour of free play in the absence of an adult. From an analysis of the children's imaginative role playing of mothers and fathers, she concluded that both the boys and girls saw wives as relatively helpless in comparison to husbands. Although women were seen as highly competent mothers, their competence decreased dramatically in the role of wife.

A study of older children (Connor, Serbin, & Ender, 1978) found that girls in grades 4, 6, and 8 made increasingly positive judgments of passive behavior as they got older while boys increasingly devalued such behavior. The children responded to questions about three stories in which other children were described as behaving aggressively, assertively, or passively in dealing with a problem. Children of both genders viewed passive behavior as more desirable for girls than for boys, while girls, more than boys, considered the passive approach a good and effective way to solve the problem, were willing to handle the problem in the same way as the passive character, and liked the passive character better. The same study revealed that although verbal hostility was considered a generally undesirable response, children of both genders considered it least desirable for girls.

In a different kind of study, Susanne Sandidge and Seymour Friedland (1975) asked 9- and 10-year-old boys and girls to respond to aggressive statements attributed to cartoon figures. Some children were asked to respond as a girl would and others as a boy would. The results indicated that children of both genders share "common expectations in regard to sex-appropriate behavior" and when playing the boy role, both girls and boys displayed, with equal ease, antisocial, aggressive behavior. Sheryl Olson (1984) also asked a sample of children (third graders) what girls and boys would do if attacked or if they witnessed an aggressive attack. Children of both sexes indicated that girl victims would retaliate more than boys, while boy witnesses would retaliate more than girls. Boys were thus seen as heroic, while girls were seen as reacting primarily to their own victimization.

Children show early awareness of which gender is expected to be interpersonally sensitive and helpful (in non-physically-threatening situations), and this knowledge increases with age. Beverly Fagot (1984a) observed children aged 19 to 64 months as they interacted with an adult stranger for five minutes in a playroom. Among the younger children (less than 31 months) neither the child's nor the adult's gender had any significant effect. Among the older toddlers, however, both girls and boys initiated more ball play with men, but asked for help more with women, indicating what we have seen in other studies, that children learn very early "the different roles that males and females play." In a study of older children in grades 4 to 8 (Dino, Barnett, & Howard, 1984), each was asked to indicate how their parents would respond to four interpersonal problem situations. Children of both genders expected fathers to respond to sons by suggesting choices and strategies, but expected mothers to respond to daughters in terms of feelings.

In an extensive study (Goldman & Goldman, 1983) of over 800 children aged 5 to 15 from five industrialized Western countries (including the U.S.), when children were asked in what ways mothers differed from fathers, the vast majority associated their mothers with "home duties." Also strongly associated with mothers was child care and housework, and such traditional jobs as typing and hairdressing. Mothers were seen as more loving and accommodating, fathers as more disciplining, with these attitudinal differences mentioned more frequently with increasing age. The authors' conclusion is a simple one: "Overall, children view adults in terms of traditional sex roles" (p. 811).

A great deal of research has focused on specific vocational stereotypes—whether children associate particular jobs with either men or women, how early these stereotypes emerge, whether vocational stereotyping increases or decreases with age, whether such stereotypes are currently weaker than they were in years past, and whether children's aspirations for themselves reflect the stereotypes. One of the first of such studies was reported by William Looft (1971), who asked a group of second graders to respond to the following two questions: What would you like to be when you grow up? and What do you think you *really* will do . . . ? He found that boys nominated a reliably greater variety of vocations (18 compared with 8 by girls), that boys' answers changed more than girls' from the first to the second question, and that the vocational choices were along traditional stereotyped lines. Diane Papalia and Susan Tennent (1975) repeated Looft's procedures with preschool children and also found that the children's predictions about their future vocations were highly conventional: the girls saw themselves as potential mothers, nurses, and teachers, while the boys' occupational choices "emphasized active, adventurous futures (such as policeman, fireman)." Boys were more likely than girls to change their responses to the second question in a "more realistic" and even more traditional direction.

In a more recent study, Pamela Riley (1981) asked 540 kindergarten children to "draw a picture of what you would like to be when you grow up" and then to do the same while pretending to be of the other gender. Girls chose occupations typically engaged in by women, and vice versa for boys, who selected a significantly larger variety of occupations. When taking the role of the other gender, the children's occupational aspirations again reflected traditional gender divisions. The author reported that many of the boys found the gender reversal problematic, and "moaned and groaned. Generally, a great deal of distaste seemed to be associated with the thought of being a girl" (p. 248).

One study has reported that occupational divisions by gender are found in children's aspirations even before the children recognize gender as a constant personal attribute, and that stereotyping of jobs seems unrelated to this recognition of gender stability. Eileen O'Keefe and Janet Hyde (1983) studied children from nursery school, kindergarten, third, and sixth grades and found a "tendency toward stereotyping in all groups and lack of differences between gender-stable and non-stable children" (p. 489), suggesting that children learn gender associations at a very early age.

Diana Zuckerman and Donald Sayre (1982) asked a sample of children aged four to eight about the appropriateness of various occupations for women and men, and also what the children wanted to be as adults. They found that while responses to the former question were less stereotypic than reported in earlier studies, the children's career choices for themselves were very stereotypic, with 83 percent of the boys and 68 percent of the girls choosing traditional vocations. Children of more highly educated parents expressed less stereotyped attitudes toward occupations, but parents' educational levels did not affect expectations for the children's own occupations, which were overwhelmingly traditional.

One study (Gettys & Cann, 1981) has reported

TABLE 4.1   Children's gender stereotypes of occupations

	Percentage of children assigning male doll to occupations		
Occupation	2- and 3-year-olds	4- and 5-year-olds	6- and 7-year-olds
Doctor	67	79	84
Police	67	90	92
Mayor	61	79	91
Basketball player	83	90	99
Construction worker	78	98	97
Secretary	33	34	04
Teacher	22	10	06
Dancer	39	10	09
Model	33	28	34
Librarian	56	16	03

(Adapted from Linda Gettys and Arnie Cann, *Sex Roles*, 1981, 7, 301–308, Table I)

data from children as young as 2 years old, and compared their occupational stereotypes with that of children aged four to five and six to seven. Each child was asked to assign each of ten occupations to a male or female doll. The findings are shown in Table 4.1. You can see that occupational stereotyping increased with age but was present at each level, and that girls and boys responded similarly. The authors concluded that "occupational sex stereotypes are learned very early," and suggested that their most probable sources are "television programs and children's books" (p. 306). Another investigation (Cann & Haight, 1983) found that children from kindergarten through second grade tended to select as the person who does the job "best," a male doll for jobs traditionally associated with men and a female doll for jobs traditionally ascribed to women. According to the researchers, such beliefs "that sex-appropriate individuals will be 'better' in a career role have potentially more serious implications than previous demonstrations of sex-stereotype recognition" (p. 772).

Occupational sex-typing is clearly ubiquitous. It appears in judgments about which gender does what jobs, which gender does what job best, and in children's expectations about their own future occupations. The employment status of one's mother, however, seems to make a difference. Linda Jones and Joanne McBride (1980) found that first- and second-grade children of working mothers made fewer sex-typed activity attributions than children of full-time homemakers; and Paula Selkow (1984) reported that among children aged five to seven whose mothers were working outside the home, both girls and boys chose more adult occupations for themselves than children of nonemployed mothers, and girls chose less traditionally feminine vocations if their mothers worked at less traditional jobs. Not all studies, however, report differences between children of working and nonworking mothers. For example, Bonni Seegmiller (1980b) tested 398 preschool children and found that girls' responses to occupational and toy preference questions were not influenced by the employment status of their mothers.

Another variable related to occupational stereotyping is age. Stereotyping appears to increase from preschool to about third or fourth grade (Tremaine, Schau, & Busch, 1982; Gettys & Cann, 1981), suggesting that older children have had greater exposure to cultural expectations and norms. But somewhere in mid-childhood, at about the fifth grade, children's views of occupation and gender appear to become more flexible or "liberal," with a decrease in stereotyping through adolescence. Mary Franken (1983) found that fifth graders stereotyped occupations by gender less than younger children, and Cynthia Archer (1984) found that with increasing age, children were more likely to respond with "either" when asked if various activities "should be done by a man, a woman, or either one."

We can anticipate that girls' expectations about their adult possibilities will change as they read and hear more about women astronauts like Sally Ride and Judith Resnick, see more women practicing medicine or law or doing police work, and more mothers in their neighborhoods carrying briefcases or wearing hard hats. On the other hand, stereotypes are extremely resistant to change. One group of researchers (Drabman, Robertson, Patterson, Jarvie, Hammer, & Cordura, 1981) had a sample of first, fourth, and seventh graders watch a videotape of a child visiting a doctor's office and being attended by a female physician and a male nurse. When tested immediately after the film or one week later, the first and fourth graders assigned female names to the nurse and male names to the doctor! Although the seventh graders gave name assignments in accord with the videotape when tested immediately after the film, one week later their answers were no longer correct and had reverted back to the powerful occupational stereotypes.

How do children learn such powerful associations with gender and to behave in accordance with them? The rest of this chapter is devoted to an exploration of the processes and agents of gender socialization.

PROCESSES OF GENDER LEARNING

We learn the behaviors appropriate to our gender by way of a small number of distinguishable, but related, processes that operate throughout life. While these processes are general, they are particularly relevant to the learning of gender. In this section we focus on how such learning occurs in childhood through the processes of modeling and imitation, direct positive and negative reinforcement, and labeling and cognition.

Modeling and Imitation

The proposition that children imitate those adults and peers who are, first, available, and second, likable, is supported by a good deal of evidence. Likability, in turn, derives from the association of persons with positive consequences, rewards, or satisfactions (Lott & Lott, 1968). Thus, a child will learn to like a person who is nurturant, who directly satisfies the child's needs or helps the child get her or his needs satisfied, or who is consistently associated with positive and pleasant experiences. Persons associated with punishing, frustrating, or unpleasant experiences will tend not to be liked and not to be imitated.

If this analysis is right, then one parent is as likely to be imitated as the other, and by both girls and boys. But since mothers are usually more available to their children than fathers, and since the mother's role is one of nurturing and ensuring the satisfaction of her children's needs, mother's behavior rather than father's is more probably imitated by both little boys and little girls. Imitation of mother's behavior by sons, however, presents a problem to parents in a sex-segregated and patriarchal society. For boys to be too much like their mothers for too long is not acceptable. A girl's imitation of her mother, on the other hand, is expected, approved, and encouraged.

The precise nature of the behaviors a girl acquires by imitating her mother depends on the mother's unique characteristics as well as on those she shares with other mothers. Daughters of mothers who work outside the home have been found more often, for example, to anticipate working when they grow up and to be more independent and assertive as children than the daughters of mothers who stay at home (Hoffman, 1977).

Children tend to imitate the behavior of adults who are available and rewarding, and those who have power to dispense or withhold positive outcomes (unless this power is associated primarily with painful consequences to the child, in which case the punishing person becomes one whom the child will tend to avoid rather than imitate). Diana Baumrind (1971) has reported that parents are more likely to take the role of disciplinarian with their like-gender than other-gender children, and the psychological literature supports the conclusion that the same-sex parent is typically perceived as the more powerful one (Margolin & Patterson, 1975).

In imitating the behavior of an available, likable, and powerful person, a little girl is, for all the reasons given, most likely to model her responses after those of her mother, although not consistently or entirely. In addition, a girl learns at an early age that she is in the same category as her mother and is similarly referred to as girl, sister, female, lady, woman. We will return to the significance of labeling later on, but for now it is important to understand that mother's similarity (in label, physique, dress, and so on) enhances the probability that she will be imitated by girls (and not imitated by boys). While some researchers (Kuhn, Nash, & Brucken, 1978) have suggested that gender learning is preceded by comprehension of gender constancy, or "comprehension of gender identity as a permanent, irreversible characteristic" (p. 449), others have argued that the attainment of gender constancy is not a necessary antecedent of same-gender modeling. Kay Bussey and Albert Bandura (1984) found, for example, in a study of children from 29 to 68 months of age who varied in gender constancy level, that "gender constancy reflects children's overall cognitive competencies rather than operating as a uniquely selective factor in sex role development" (p. 1296). Children with high gender constancy (who were also older) did more imitating than children with lower gender constancy (who were also younger), but did not differ in their tendency to imitate same-gender adults shown playing a game on television. Walter Emmerich and Karla Shepard (1984) have also reported from a study of over 800 black and white children between the ages of four and eight that "gender constancy . . . lagged considerably behind the development of sex-stereotyped preferences" (p. 1001).

Thus, from an early age, children imitate parents and other models who are available, likable, powerful, and similarly labeled. This occurs more frequently with increasing cognitive and discriminating skill, and covers a wide range—television characters and peers, relatives and babysitters, storybook and real-life heroes. Some research suggests that a model is more likely to be imitated if she or he is a "good

example" of her or his gender. David Perry and Kay Bussey (1979) had a sample of 9-year-olds watch groups of adult men and women make choices among tasks, and then the children themselves were given the chance to make choices. Imitation of same-gender adults was more probable when they had behaved in a sharply different manner from other-gender adults. While recall of models' behavior was not influenced by the variable of appropriateness, imitation was, with children of both genders (but boys more than girls) "matching their behavior to a model known to exemplify sex-typical behavior" (p. 1709). In a subsequent study (Bussey & Perry, 1982), the researchers found that both girls and boys from grades 3 and 4 preferred objects chosen by same-gender children, with boys being more rejecting than girls of choices made by other-gender children and of choices made by both boys and girls.

That selective preference based on same-gender modeling is not a function of selective attention or knowledge is underscored by data reported by Janice Bryan and Zella Luria (1978). Using a physiological measure of attention to stimuli with samples of children varying in age from 5 to 11, the researchers found no evidence that the children paid more attention to same-gender models, despite their stated preference for the tasks chosen by them. The authors concluded that "children look at (or have competence about) the behavior of both sexes; but their behavior (or performance) . . . is determined by other factors" (p. 21). Children learn to imitate certain models and certain behaviors, but they also learn *not* to imitate, by observing the differences between the model and themselves, by noting the divergence in behavior among models, and by observing the consequences experienced by models.

Direct Positive and Negative Reinforcement

Children also learn gender more directly. We know that behavior that is followed by positive consequences tends to be repeated while behavior followed by negative consequences tends to be avoided. Parents, other caregivers, teachers, and peers, by the way in which they react to what little girls (and boys) do, provide positive or negative sanctions or reinforcements for behavior. Consider how we let a child know that what she is doing is appropriately "feminine." We smile, applaud, provide tangible rewards, and repeat "good girl." When she imitates her sister, aunt, mother, or other appropriate female figure we reinforce the modeling. Negative consequences follow behavior considered inappropriate for girls. These need not involve physical punishment (although they sometimes do); more often in our culture we use harshly spoken "no-no's," withholding of desirable rewards, or ridicule. One form of punishment is labeling nonconforming children as deviant, along with assuming that they need help to become less deviant.

What is referred to by some psychologists as "deviant gender identity" in little boys has been identified by such behavior as rejection of toys like a football helmet, army belt with hatchet, and battery-operated electric razor (Rekers, 1975), or by behaviors such as liking to dance, or to play act, or preferring to be alone with mother rather than with father (Bates, Bentler, & Thompson, 1973). Little boys who fail to behave in an appropriately "masculine" manner are more likely to be considered deviant than "unfeminine" little girls, and during the preadolescent years being considered a sissy is likely to have more severe consequences than being considered a tomboy. Saul Feinman (1981) found that university students who were asked to indicate their degree of disapproval for "cross-sex-role" behaviors described as engaged in by 3- to 8-year-old children, indicated significantly greater disapproval of "sissy" behavior in boys. In one study (Green, Neuberg, & Finch, 1983), a small group of 4- to 10-year-old boys referred for professional assistance on the basis of "feminine" characteristics were rated by adults on the masculinity of their motor behavior as intermediate between a control group of boys and a group of girls. A similar study of little girls would be unlikely. A number of investigations have indicated that pressure for gender-appropriate behavior is applied earlier for boys than for girls (Eme, 1979) and that, among preadolescents, boys typically show greater conformity to gender expectations than girls. For example, in my previously mentioned jack-o'-lantern study (Lott, 1979), the drawings of 5-year-old boys matched more closely the stereotyped expectations of adults than did the drawings of 5-year-old girls.

Although a preadolescent girl is less likely than a boy to receive serious negative sanctions when she behaves in a gender-inappropriate manner, girls, too, may be considered "problems" and in need of help if their behavior too often resembles that of boys as defined by the adult ideology. For example, John Feinblatt and Alice Gold (1976) found that girls referred to an outpatient child-guidance clinic by their

parents or teachers were described by these adults as defiant and verbally aggressive (while boys referred to the clinic were more likely to be described as emotional or passive). These researchers also asked parents and psychology students to read hypothetical case studies in which identical behavior was attributed to a girl or to a boy. "The data from the two samples indicated that the child exhibiting the behavior inappropriate to his/her sex was seen as more severely disturbed, as more in need of treatment, and as having a less successful future than the child exhibiting sex-role appropriate behaviors" (p. 109). Similar findings were reported by Paula Caplan (1977), who had college students rate hypothetical children on the basis of the likelihood that they would be assigned to tutors for help. All the hypothetical cases were presented as children "having trouble learning grade-school subjects," but some were presented as girls or boys, and as "acting out" or "withdrawn." Both men and women raters were more likely to send girls for help if they were "acting out" and boys for help if they were "withdrawn" than vice versa, apparently believing that "deviations from the societal stereotype . . . required the most immediate attention" (p. 62).

That behavior can be modified by the way in which significant persons react to it has been demonstrated experimentally (Serbin, Connor, & Citron, 1978) with preschoolers. For a 20-minute period during each of five consecutive weeks, nursery school teachers praised one group of children for two kinds of independent behavior (playing with new toys—that is, exploration; and persisting on a task alone). At the same time, they ignored dependent behaviors (proximity-seeking and soliciting teacher attention). When this group of children was compared with children who were randomly praised (regardless of behavior), both girls and boys were found to be more independent and less dependent, indicating that the training had been effective. The researchers concluded that "the independent behaviors that were being reinforced in the training group were clearly within the repertoire of the children, but were receiving little reinforcement in the regular classroom situation" (p. 874).

Labeling and Cognition

The first step in gender learning, according to Anne Constantinople (1979), is "a labeling process." Words like *boy*, *girl*, *mommy*, and *daddy* are then joined to clothing, toys, and activities. Constantinople suggests that these "linguistic tags" serve an organizing function, while children acquire the behaviors that match one category rather than another through observation and as a result of positive and negative reinforcement. Similarly, Spencer Cahill (1983) has emphasized the importance of gender labels in guiding the child's social interactions, as well as the influence of other people's responses to the child's behavior.

Positive and negative consequences teach children to behave in ways deemed appropriate and to do the "right" thing. In addition to such positive consequences as affection, attention, or approval, and such negative consequences as punishment, disapproval, or ridicule, words or labels also have powerful reinforcing properties. Once a girl has learned that if she engages in boys' behavior she is not likely to be approved or, worse, may be derided, simply saying to her that "boys do that" serves to identify a particular activity with the possibility of negative consequences and to increase the likelihood that she will avoid it.

The effectiveness of labels has been demonstrated experimentally. In a number of studies, children were told that particular tasks or toys were preferred by their own gender, the other gender, neither, or both. Such labeling was found to reliably influence first graders' toy choices in a same-gender direction (Liebert, McCall, & Hanratty, 1971), first graders' success and liking for a task (Montemayor, 1974), their problem-solving performance (Gold & Berger, 1978), and sixth graders' expectancy for success and achievement on three different paper-and-pencil tests (Stein, Pohly, & Mueller, 1971). In another kind of investigation, fifth graders were asked to categorize 15 words as masculine or feminine and then to rate their liking for each. The girls (and boys) most preferred those items associated with their own gender (Freeman, Schockett, & Freeman, 1975). A study by Jerri Kropp and Charles Halverson (1983) found that after being read four different stories, a sample of preschool girls most preferred the one featuring a female character doing a "feminine activity" and boys preferred the story of a male character doing a "masculine activity."

Gender labels clearly serve as mediators between situations or tasks. For the average girl, whatever is associated with a same-gender label makes her anticipate positive consequences, while associations with the other-gender label are likely to elicit anticipation of either negative or neutral consequences. Gender labels probably mediate a very wide array of behavior from the time that children first begin to acquire language. Anyone who has spent time in the average preschool class has heard children being given instructions by girl/boy divisions, from lining up for milk to picking up supplies for a project. Stories the children are read tend to perpetuate gender labeling and division of activities, thus consistently and repeatedly reinforcing gender separateness. Not surprisingly, therefore, like the woman in traditional stories who is typically cooking, cleaning, or chatting indoors, the girl, too, will tend to stay inside; and like the traditional mother who stays at home alone engaged in solitary activities, and observes the behavior of husband and children, the daughter, too, will do the same. Lawrence Kohlberg (1966) has suggested that once children form their conceptions of what is appropriate for persons of their own gender, by abstracting rules from environmental cues they can direct their own behaviors accordingly. This process can be understood as related to both the mediating effect of gender labels and to learning that it is *desirable* to act "like a girl" (or "like a boy").

AGENTS OF GENDER LEARNING

The environments in which children grow and learn are filled with information about gender. Girls (and boys) observe, organize, relate themselves to their appropriate category, try out various behaviors, experience feedback from others, and acquire a gender identity that matches to some degree the ideology of their culture. This is a crucial component of one's socialization. The sheer volume of information available to a contemporary American girl about her culture and her role in it is enormous. John Condry (1984) has specified the sources of information as follows:

> In the 10 years from 4 to 14, there are 3,650 days, or 87,600 hours. If we assume that youngsters of this age range sleep about 8 hours a day, this leaves 58,400 waking or conscious hours. . . . For nine months of the year children are in school, a total of 15,200 hours; and the American child spends approximately 4 hours a day watching television, which for the 10 years in question works out to 14,600 hours. The remainder of the time (27,600 hours) is spent in the home and in the environs of the home. If we assume . . . the average child in this age range spends at least two hours a day playing . . . then the distribution of environmental sources of information is divided in about equal quarters among

the parents, the peers, the school, and the television set. (pp. 499–500)

Let us look more closely now at the most significant agents supplying children with information and lessons about gender.

Mothers and Fathers

Of all the social institutions that provide norms for behavior, the family is probably the most idiosyncratic and the most likely to provide conditions for gender learning that may be inconsistent with the dominant ideology. This is because the family serves so many and such complex social and personal needs that gender requirements may at various times be less important than others (such as economic survival, family tradition, or general nurturance and support). Some theorists like Nancy Chodorow (1978) have proposed that the family, particularly the mother, plays a crucial and primary role in teaching girls, from infancy, those attributes that our culture desires in prospective mothers, so that girls will grow up with the appropriate personality characteristics and will want to be mothers. But others see the family as only one of many socializing agents. And the family may enforce cultural stereotypes least rigidly or consistently because parents are more likely to respond to the unique characteristics of each particular child. Thus, Anne Constantinople (1979) has suggested that "siblings, peers, and outside figures of all kinds often work harder than parents to enforce sex-role stereotypes" (p. 131). This is dramatically and poignantly illustrated in Harper Lee's (1960) novel *To Kill a Mockingbird*. The eight-year-old protagonist/narrator Jean Louise (Scout) Finch had been permitted the same freedom to explore and to romp as her older brother by their decidedly nontraditional father, but when her Aunt Alexandra joined the household, a program was launched to restore Scout's "femininity." Aunt Alexandra insisted that

> I could not possibly hope to be a lady if I wore breeches; when I said I could do nothing in a dress, she said I wasn't supposed to be doing things that required pants. Aunt Alexandra's vision of my deportment involved playing with small stoves, tea sets, and wearing the Add-a-Pearl necklace she gave me when I was born. . . . I felt the starched walls of a pink cotton penitentiary closing in on me. (pp. 89, 147)

Not surprisingly, Eleanor Maccoby and Carol Jacklin's (1974) extensive review of the literature did not uncover much hard evidence in direct support of the hypothesis that parents of very young children dif-

ferentially shape the behavior of their daughters and sons. As children get older, differential parental treatment relating to gender is more frequently observed.

Some studies have provided evidence of the part parents play as agents of gender socialization. Beverly Fagot (1974), for example, found that parents of 18- to 24-month-old children may behave in ways that differ significantly from what they say they do. Those who said that most behaviors were appropriate for children of both genders showed as much sex-typing in their actual interactions with their children (when observed in their own homes) as parents who said most behaviors were more appropriate for one gender than another. Lois Hoffman (1977) has cited a number of studies that illustrate how, in important and varied ways, parents deprive daughters of the training in independence that they give sons.

> For example, Fagot (1971) . . . found that parents of toddlers were more likely to encourage daughters and discourage sons from following them around the house. . . . In another study, this time of elementary school aged children (Saegert & Hart, 1976), it was found that boys were allowed by parents to roam over a wider area of the community without special permission. (p. 649)

Research by Rosalind Barnett (1981) suggests that the beliefs and attitudes parents have about sex roles are related to the independence training they give their daughters. "For parents of girls [but not of boys], nontraditional sex-role ideology was significantly related to lower mean age of independence granting" (p. 841). Thus, while parents' traditional or nontraditional views about gender seem to make little difference when it comes to encouraging boys to be independent, such differences among parents seem to make a substantial difference in the rearing of girls. This conclusion is supported by the findings of Jeanne Brooks-Gunn (1986) that mothers of toddlers who subscribed to fewer sex-typed beliefs about children were observed to play more actively with their 2-year-olds, especially daughters.

Do mothers and fathers differ in the degree to which they enforce gender socialization or encourage sex-typing? Judith Langlois and A. Chris Downs (1980) observed 3-year-olds and 5-year-olds in a laboratory situation playing alone, with a same-gender peer, or with mother or father. When girls played with a toy preclassified as a "same-sex toy," mothers were observed to praise them and give them affection, but when they played with a "cross-sex toy," they were punished with behavioral interference or ridicule. (Peers behaved very much like mothers in this regard.) Fathers also gave "more reward for play with same-sex compared with cross-sex toys" and punished "cross-sex play" more than mothers or peers. Similar consequences to those described for girls were received by boys, with the fathers' reactions to the play behavior of boys even more pronounced than their reactions to that of girls. The researchers concluded that "socialization pressure for sex-typed behaviors may come most consistently from fathers" (p. 1245), who dispensed more vigorous differential treatment than the mothers. This conclusion of greater sex-typing by fathers has been supported by other research. For example, Beverly Fagot (1981b) has reported that parents of preschoolers who rated 30 behaviors of typical preschool children in terms of whether they were expected of girls or boys were closer to the cultural stereotypes than were child-care workers, with fathers exhibiting greater stereotyping than mothers.

Some studies have pointed to subtle and indirect gender socialization by parents. David Bellinger and Jean Gleason (1982), for example, observed a small sample of preschool children working separately with each parent on construction tasks in a laboratory setting. While there was "little evidence that parents request action differently when speaking to boys and girls," the researchers found that girls and boys tended to behave like their mothers and fathers, respectively, with fathers and sons uttering more orders and speaking more directively than mothers and daughters. In this case the evidence suggests the importance of modeling rather than the differential treatment of girls and boys by their parents.

Parental interaction with their children is likely to be strongly influenced by their immediate as well as their long-range expectations for them. Such expectations, as we have already seen, often precede a child's birth and continue, albeit with modifications, long afterward. Lois Hoffman (1977) has cited a study done in 1974 by one of her students, who interviewed a group of professional university faculty women who were also mothers. Most indicated, when asked about goals for sons and daughters, that they would be the same regardless of gender. But when asked about specific goals for only one of their children, it turned out that "despite their expressed equalitarian ideology, the mothers who discussed sons had higher academic and occupational goals in mind for them and indicated that they would be more disappointed if these goals were not achieved than did the mothers who discussed their daughters" (p. 651).

Do such differences in parental aspirations for sons and daughters, which may be unverbalized and even denied in direct questioning, emerge in subtle ways? Reporting on computer use, for example, Constance Holden (1984) noted that 93 percent of home computer users are male. Whenever there is "discretionary use" of computers, as in homes, computer camps, or arcades, boys outnumber girls among the users. This conclusion is supported by data provided by Robert Hess and Irene Miura (1985) on enrollment in computer camps and workshops across the U.S. Not as many girls as boys were enrolled at later ages and in more difficult or more expensive programs. Are parents more likely to encourage the computer interests of their sons? What parents believe and what they do in relation to their sons and daughters contribute both to the gender concepts acquired by their children and to long-term and far-reaching consequences for their children's lives.

Toys Children Play With

The toys that adults provide for children to play with are powerful agents of gender socialization. Consider, for example, the nature of the toys adults see as appropriate for girls: dolls, dress-up clothes, makeup and hairstyling kits, tea sets, kitchen utensils, paint or crayons, cuddly animals. By and large, "success" in playing with these depends upon someone else's reactions. The little girl asks: Is it pretty, nice, or good? Do you like how it looks, or what I've done with it? Such toys encourage approval-seeking and dependence on others. Toys that move or can be manipulated, on the other hand, like trucks, blocks, or tinker toys, provide their own objective test of "success" by whether or not something the child does works; such toys encourage problem solving through trial and error.

Toys associated with boys have been found in one study by E. F. Rosenfeld (Hoffman, 1977) to have more "potential for inventive use." Both girls and boys gave more varied answers when asked how such toys could be changed to make them more exciting and interesting than they gave in response to questions about "girls' toys." A Kenner toy catalog published for Christmas 1979 included photographs with a clear message. Next to the Christmas tree on the front cover was a little girl contentedly feeding her new doll while her brother was moving a robot by remote control. Inside the catalog were pictures of boys with spacecraft and science fiction characters while girls were shown talking on a telephone and mixing juices in a toy blender. The toys suggested for girls limit their imagination and reduce the need for physical movement and activity. They foster play that is passive/dependent, relatively quiet, and that does not require much peer interaction; a mother close by to smile and approve is sufficient. Much as we tend to believe that things are changing, careful observation suggests otherwise. For example, Lori Schwartz and William Markham (1985) concluded after examining retail toy catalogs and pictures of children on toy packages that "sex stereotyping in advertising is strong." In both catalogs and stores, toys for girls and boys tended to be placed in separate sections. "Girls' sections were characterized by dolls and accessories, doll houses, arts and craft kits . . . , toy beauty kits, and housekeeping and cooking toys. Building sets . . . , sports-related toys, transportation toys . . . , and workbenches and tools were featured in the boys' sections" (pp. 167f.). Thus, the toys suggested for boys are likely to evoke energetic movement, to involve objective criteria for mastery, and to encourage cooperation as well as competition and risk taking. Competence training is provided by the play equipment we purchase for little boys; approval training is what we offer girls by the toys we buy for them. And these aspects of socialization are consistent with others.

An often-heard argument is that girls like and request the toys adults buy for them, so what are adults to do? Let us consider some research that relates to this issue. In one study (Hartup, Moore, & Sager, 1963), 3- to 8-year-old children were observed in a situation in which girls could play with such toys as a football, boxing gloves, and pliers (considered "masculine" objects) or with gender-neutral toys like puzzles or a pegboard, while boys could play with the same neutral toys or with dolls, high-heeled shoes, or a purse. Avoidance of the "inappropriate sex objects" was found to increase with age, and was stronger for boys, who also showed even greater avoidance in the presence of an adult than when alone. In a similar study (Serbin, Connor, Burchardt, & Citron, 1979), 4-year-old children were observed alone, or in the presence of a same- or opposite-gender peer, in a room equipped with six toys, three considered appropriate for boys and three for girls. The researchers reported similar "effects of peer pressure" for girls and boys. Both spent significantly less time playing with opposite-sex-typed toys in the presence of an other-gender peer than when alone or with a same-gender peer. According to these researchers, "The fact that peer presence already affects the probability of

sex-typed play in the preschool age subjects suggests that children have had a learning history which has established peers, especially those of the opposite sex, as discriminative stimuli for sex role conformity" (p. 308). In another study (Downs, 1983), letters to Santa Claus written by 154 7-year-olds were analyzed. Under this private condition of letter writing, boys were found to be just as likely to request neutral (non-sex-typed) toys as "masculine" ones, but girls requested neutral toys most frequently, and more so than "feminine" toys.

Thus, children's toy choices and play behavior vary with the circumstances. For example, when nursery school teachers in one study (Kinsman & Berk, 1979) joined the traditionally separated block and housekeeping areas into one large area, they found "no indication of a sex-typed attraction to either play area." Children of both genders preferred the blocks, playing with them more than twice as often as with the housekeeping materials, and girls used the blocks in as relevant a manner as the boys. Another group of researchers (Serbin, Connor, & Iler, 1979) influenced the play behaviors of preschoolers by presenting a group of new dolls and trucks in gender neutral, nonstereotypic ways. Children who were not given gender labels for the new toys chose them for play with no relationship to gender.

While these studies tell us something about children's toy choices and play under varying conditions, we also have data on the choices adults make for children. Harriet Rheingold and Kaye Cook (1975) inventoried the contents of the rooms of four girls and four boys at each half-year of life from one month to almost 5 years old. The boys' rooms and the girls' rooms were found to be sharply and significantly different. Inside the former were more vehicles, education-art materials, sports equipment, machines, fauna, and military toys ("activities directed away from the home"), whereas the girls had more play materials in only three categories, dolls, dollhouses, and domestic toys ("activities directed toward the home—keeping house and caring for children"). Girls generally had fewer toys than boys and in fewer categories. We cannot assume that these parents (of high educational level and socioeconomic status) simply followed the wishes of their children, in light of differences that appeared even in the rooms of girls and boys as young as one month.

Parents and other adults are encouraged to make sex-typed purchases for children by other parts of the culture. Nancy Kutner and Richard Levinson (1978) had college students request help from toy salespersons in selecting birthday presents for a 5-year-old niece and nephew (twins). Almost 53 percent of the suggestions they received were for sex-stereotyped toys, and such suggestions were more likely to be made by men. The following account of a student's experience with a toy salesman illustrates the findings:

> The salesman dealt with my niece's gift first. Automatically he suggested a doll "of some kind." . . . I questioned him further by stating that my niece was rather active and had quite a number of dolls already, so could he suggest something a little more "original"? . . . He stressed that . . . my "active" niece could probably be kept occupied with dolls that talk and that must be fed, rather than ones that "just sit there." . . . I proceeded to ask for suggestions for my nephew's toy. He directed me to over six shelves full of little boys' toys—GI men, guns, trucks, boats, army men, building blocks, bat and ball sets, footballs and helmets, etc. . . . I told him that my niece and nephew were very close and that they enjoyed playing together; therefore, did he have anything that would suit *both* children? . . . His "brilliant" solution was that I should get my niece a doll family and nephew a building set so that my niece could play dolls while my nephew built the house in which the dolls would live! (p. 7)

Even more dramatic results were reported from a more recent, similar, study. Sheldon Ungar (1982) found that 67 percent of 134 toy salespersons approached for suggestions for a Christmas gift for a 5-year-old niece or nephew offered sex-stereotyped advice. Men buyers received more stereotypic advice than women, and salesmen gave such advice significantly more than saleswomen. When asked for a second suggestion, the proportion of sex-stereotyped recommendations was 69 percent, "virtually identical" to the first suggestion.

What Children Read

What children read or have read to them has been the focus of a great deal of attention in the past few years. Narrow, stereotyped images of women and girls (and less narrow but equally stereotyped images of men and boys) have been found everywhere—from nursery rhymes to coloring books, picture books, and Sunday comics, from grade school readers to high school science texts. For example, although in Mother Goose land the always late "ten-o'clock scholar" is a boy, the images of girls seem, in general, to be considerably worse, as Letty Pogrebin (1972)

has reminded us by pointing to Lazy Mary, frightened Miss Muffet, empty-headed Bo Peep, and Mary Quite Contrary. Comic strips repeat the lessons of Mother Goose. An analysis by Sarah Brabant (1976) of four popular Sunday family comics indicated that regardless of whether the major woman character was domineering or submissive in relation to her husband, she stayed at home, cooked, washed the dishes, and cleaned the house. It was the men who either worked or engaged in leisure activities such as golf, playing musical instruments, or reading. "Females might outwit males but only males read. . . . Although she may be bigger and/or smarter, the apron remains . . . the woman's trademark" (p. 337). Ten years later Sarah Brabant and Linda Mooney (1986) looked at three of these comics again (one was no longer being syndicated). While they found a narrowing of differences between the major women and men characters, the women "continued to be shown in home and child care more and in leisure activities less than [the men and] . . . were also much more likely to be portrayed as passive onlookers" (p. 147). One of the women characters was shown with reading material, but "the apron continued to be exclusively female" (p. 148). A content analysis of 100 randomly selected newspaper comics (Chavez, 1985) obtained comparable results. Men were not only far more often presented as main characters, but were also shown to be in the work force more frequently than women. While stereotypic roles predominated for both, men were presented more positively than women.

Susan Rachlin and Glenda Vogt (1974) examined 30 coloring books by five different publishers and found that boys outnumbered girls in pictures of outdoor activities, while girls starred in domestic roles (161 such pictures of girls compared to 5 of boys). Boys fished, built things, climbed trees, and rode scooters, while girls were in the sand, on the swings, or jumping rope. An analysis of prize-winning (Caldecott medal) picture books for preschoolers (Weitzman, Eifler, Hokada, & Ross, 1972) found women and girls to be underrepresented in titles, central roles, and illustrations, and depicted as passive, as followers, and as serving others. While boys were admired for achievements and for being clever, girls received praise and attention for being attractive. While men were shown in a wide variety of occupations, women were shown primarily as wives and mothers. "The world of picture books," the authors concluded, "never tells little girls that as women they might find fulfillment outside of their homes or through intellectual pursuits" (p. 1146).

A similar image of women emerged from a large-scale study of 134 grade-school readers published by 14 major publishers (Women on Words and Images, 1972). Mothers in these books were portrayed not as the nurturant, kindly, smiling bakers of yummy cookies (as we might at least have hoped) but as "limited, colorless, and mindless." According to the authors of the report, "Not only does she wash, cook, clean, and find mittens; these chores constitute her only happiness. . . . She is perpetually on call, . . . available. . . . Father is the 'good guy' in the family. He's where the fun is" (p. 40). Fathers were presented as more creative and compassionate than mothers. Boys outnumbered girls as major characters in the stories by 5 to 2, and biographies of men outnumbered those of women by a 6-to-1 ratio. Boys' themes concerned ingenuity, problem solving, heroism, apprenticeships, and adventurous/imaginative play, in sharp contrast to stories about girls, which emphasized passivity, domesticity, and incompetence, and showed girls being humiliated by boys. What a grim world is depicted for girls, portrayed as spectators of life, fearful and inadequate, who grow up to be selfless but scolding mothers. The only other popular alternative is to become a wicked witch! In 2760 stories only three mothers were shown working outside the home.

Data such as these proved sufficiently convincing that a number of book publishers agreed in the 1970s to make changes in language, stories, and pictures to provide "equal treatment" for the sexes. An example of such changes are those instituted by the McGraw-Hill Book Company (1974). A 16-page policy statement includes the following objectives:

> Men and women should be treated primarily as people, and not primarily as members of opposite sexes. Their shared humanity and common attributes should be stressed. . . . Members of both sexes should be represented as whole human beings with *human* strengths and weaknesses, not masculine or feminine ones. . . . Women and men should be treated with the same respect, dignity and seriousness. Neither should be trivialized or stereotyped. (pp. 4, 6, 7)

By 1978 almost all of the major textbook publishers had issued similar guidelines designed to discourage sexist portrayals of women (Collins, 1978). Sufficient numbers of new books are not yet available to test their impact, and determination of their effect will require that they be read by a whole new generation

of children but, as firemen give way to firefighters of either gender, the books should become both more truthful and more conducive to varied aspirations. We can hope that the books published in the next decades will not be like the 15 books that make up *The Sesame Street Library*. An analysis of these books (Charnes, Hoffman, Hoffman, & Meyers, 1980), which teach letters and numbers to preschoolers and of which an estimated 40 million copies had been sold, revealed "blatant and pervasive" sexism. Male characters are overrepresented by a 6-to-1 ratio, and the female characters are "traditional princesses and Little Miss Muffet types" who will "live happily ever after as soon as they find their prince" and who are frequently "in trouble and in need of rescuing (by a man, of course)" (p. 10).

That the books children read do have measurable effects on their behavior is supported by research. In one study (Flerx, Fidler, & Rogers, 1976), preschool children exposed to egalitarian stories for 30 minutes per day for five days gave significantly fewer stereotyped responses to questions about children's and parents' activities than children who heard traditional stories about men and women. In another investigation, Eleanor Ashton (1983) found that among a group of 5-year-olds, those who were exposed to a picture-book story in which a same-gender child played with a particular toy, later spent more time with the same toy than children who had not been exposed to the book. The effects of exposure to the picture books were greater on the girls than on the boys.

Some recent research has focused on a special group of children's books identified by publishers and feminist groups as nonsexist or nonstereotyped. Shirley St. Peter (1979) compared 43 such picture books for preschoolers with 92 conventional picture books. She found that the books identified as nonsexist far more often had women or girls as central characters, more often depicted them as engaged in instrumental activities, but infrequently showed them behaving expressively. St. Peter concluded that nonsexist books are "overcompensating" for the traditional presentation of women as expressive, dependent, and passive. A similar conclusion was reached by Albert Davis (1984), who also compared nonsexist picture books with conventional ones. He found that women and girls in the nonsexist books were presented as more independent than men and boys in both nonsexist and conventional books, thus "reversing the traditional stereotypes." But, contrary to St.

Peter's findings, Davis reported that the nonsexist female characters were shown as more emotional and less physically active than male characters in both nonsexist and conventional books, thus perpetuating traditional stereotypes. Boys in nonsexist books were presented as more nurturant, affectionate, helpful, and less hostile and destructive than in conventional books. Clearly, much can be done with the stories children read and the pictures they see to promote expectations of gender equality, and progress in this direction has begun.

Efforts to change textbooks appear to have proceeded more slowly. Florence Howe (1971) reported that early investigations of high school history and science texts revealed a generally biased presentation of women as less competent and less relevant than men. A more recent study of high school history texts (Kirby & Julian, 1981) reached much the same conclusion:

> When a textbook passage focused directly on an individual woman or topic, coverage was frequently objective and balanced. However, when a passage focused directly on another issue . . . the passage frequently omitted any mention of women or was misleading about women and their concerns. (p. 205)

The researchers concluded that women's concerns were not placed in "the mainstream of American history," and that information about women was frequently misleading or demeaning. Women's suffrage, for example, was presented "as a minor advance in the American political system" (p. 206).

What Children See on Television

Studies of television have revealed stereotyped images of women and men. For example, Sarah Sternglanz and Lisa Serbin (1974) analyzed ten television programs produced for children and found that reliably fewer women than men were shown, and that women were portrayed less often as either aggressive or constructive and more often as deferent, with negative consequences following high levels of activity. An analysis of children's television reported by Charlotte O'Kelley (1974) similarly found fewer women than men, with women in traditional roles. Pamela Reid (1978a) had observers rate videotaped episodes of ten half-hour situation comedies and found that white women were portrayed as reliably less dominant but more nurturant than white men, and black women as more nurturant but not less dominant in comparison with black men.

Probably the most extensive monitoring of the television shows typically seen by children was done by Women on Words and Images (1975). Sixteen top-rated prime-time family shows from the 1973 fall season, as well as the interspersed commercials, were observed in a systematic fashion. Here is how the authors summarized their findings:

> [Children] see, overall, more men than women on their television screens; on the exciting adventure shows, they see nearly six times as many men. The men they see work in diverse occupations, nearly twice the number of those held by women. . . . Children see that more male than female behaviors show competence, and that more female behaviors display incompetence. On the commercials, children see women taking care of their houses, their families, their shopping and their appearance, while men work and play harder and provide the voice of authority for the purchasing decisions women make.

Considering that the average American child will have spent approximately 15,000 hours watching television by the time she or he is 16 years old, which is 4,000 hours more than the number spent in classrooms (Women on Words and Images, 1975), the potential of the small screen for teaching about human relationships and behavior is awesome. Jerome Singer and Dorothy Singer (1980) have called television a "window on the world" and a "member of the family"; others have estimated that grade-school children typically spend 20 to 30 hours each week watching it. Not surprisingly, therefore, children who are frequent viewers of television have been found to hold more stereotyped beliefs about gender than less frequent viewers (Frueh & McGhee, 1975; McGhee & Frueh, 1980).

In a somewhat different approach to the same issue, Rena Repetti (1984) found that among a group of children aged 5½ to 7½, gender stereotyped responses to questions about toys and occupations were negatively correlated with the amount of educational television they regularly watched. In other words, the greater their exposure to noncommercial television, the fewer gender stereotypes they held. Michael Morgan (1982) found a significant positive correlation between frequency of commercial television viewing and sex-role stereotyping among a large sample of sixth- to tenth-grade girls and particularly among high-IQ girls, but not among boys, suggesting that the impact of television, with respect to beliefs, may be strongest on those least likely to hold traditional views. The students were tested over a 2-year period and for girls, especially those of high IQ, amount of television viewing predicted scores on a gender stereotyping measure one year later. According to Morgan:

> Television's primary function is often held to be one of ("merely") reinforcing and confirming predispositions. . . . The data support the proposition that heavy viewing works to bring into the mainstream those who would otherwise be on the periphery. . . . Television seems to have a cumulative effect on sex role stereotypes among girls. The stable assumptions and images about the norms of the adult world, as presented on television, may provide hidden yet vivid and powerful constraints on their notions about the places women should take in that world. (p. 954)

While these studies indicate a relationship between television viewing and children's beliefs about gender, most of the evidence just tells us that the two are related without telling us much about the direction of cause and effect. But evidence from experimental research suggests that children's behavior can be influenced by what they see on television. In one study (Ruble, Balaban, & Cooper, 1981), 100 preschool children were shown a one-minute toy commercial inserted in the middle of a Bugs Bunny cartoon. Among the children who understood gender constancy, those who had seen the toy played with by an other-gender child spent less time playing with it when given the opportunity later on to do so than those who had seen it played with by a same-gender child.

Some important changes have been observed in the occupations and social status of women shown on television, but children in the 1980s are still, for the most part, seeing women in dramatic shows, comedies, and commercials who do the laundry or who are secretaries to men who own companies. In addition, children are likely to see men interacting with women by avoiding or withdrawing from them. In the spring of 1986, I made an observational study of ten prime-time story-line shows that were most popular with eighth graders (Lott, 1986). I found that men characters distanced themselves from women significantly more than they did from men, and approached the latter significantly more than they did women. Women characters, on the other hand, were observed interacting no differently with women than with men, but were far more likely to be shown in scenes with men than with other women. Thus, the message emanating from commercial television continues to reflect a general devaluation of women.

Teachers and School

What parents teach their children and what children read, see, and learn from adults, one another, and the media, is also what teachers typically model in the schools and reinforce in the behavior of the children in their classes. If we look at the jobs done by women and men in the school system, we see that as in books and on television, men typically have more power and authority, and higher status. Eighty percent of elementary school principals, 93 percent of secondary school principals, and nearly 99 percent of public school superintendents are men, while 66 percent of all public school teachers and 80 percent of elementary school teachers are women (Dullea, 1975). Figures compiled in the 1980s were similar to those gathered a decade earlier (Gender Gap, 1983). Boys and girls, unaware of these figures, still know that ultimate power is found "in the principal's office," most likely occupied by a man. The cafeteria workers and teacher-aides, on the other hand, are most likely women, while the school custodian who helps to retrieve lost balls from the roof and competently opens jammed lockers is typically a man. In a recent study (Paradise & Wall, 1986), a sample of first graders in schools with women principals were found more likely to say that either women or men could be school principals than were children attending schools with a man principal.

Researchers have used several strategies to study teacher contributions to the gender learning of children: (a) relating teachers' judgments about the "masculine" and "feminine" traits of children to the degree to which these teachers like the children or rate them positively on other dimensions; (b) observing teacher-child interactions and particularly the ways in which teachers reward or punish various behaviors; and (c) measuring teachers' beliefs about gender attributes. In the first category is a study by Teresa Levitin and J. D. Chananie (1972), who asked first- and second-grade teachers to rate hypothetical children described as behaving independently, aggressively, or in an achievement-oriented manner, by indicating approval and typicalness of the behavior and how likable they found the child. These researchers found that the teachers liked an achieving girl significantly more than an achieving boy, and saw dependent girls and aggressive boys as significantly more typical than the reverse. Also, while the teachers judged dependent and aggressive boys as likable to more or less the same extent, they liked dependent girls far more than aggressive ones. We can guess pretty well how such attitudes toward children are translated into teachers' behavior in the classroom.

From studies in which teacher-child interactions have been carefully observed has come information about the different experiences girls and boys seem to have in the classroom. For example, Biber, Miller, and Dyer (1972) watched videotaped segments of ongoing classroom activity and concluded that preschool teachers had more instructional contact with girls than boys, while Heller and Parsons (1981) reported no gender difference in evaluative feedback given by teachers to seventh- and ninth-graders in math classes. But most of the research on student-teacher interaction has reported that boys receive more attention than girls. Louise Cherry (1975) listened to tape recordings of verbal interaction, and concluded that teachers' speech to boys was more directing in nature. A more comprehensive study (Serbin, O'Leary, Kent, & Tonick, 1973) involved direct observation of ongoing activities in 15 preschool classrooms. Teachers responded three times more often to aggressive behavior by boys than by girls, and gave boys loud reprimands three times as often as girls. Teachers also gave more extended directions to, and had longer conversations with, boys than girls. Girls appeared to receive teacher attention primarily when they were near the teacher, whereas proximity did not influence the amount of attention boys got. Among children who showed neither destructive nor dependent behavior, the rate of teacher response was higher for boys in all classrooms and, furthermore, teachers more often praised and hugged the boys. The researchers concluded that boys are encouraged to become involved in the classroom by being given more direction, instructions, and attention, while girls are not encouraged to become involved in problem-solving activities. If girls tend to be ignored except when within arm's reach, directly beside the teacher, it is no wonder that they are more often found there. In this same study, the researchers observed that boys were instructed on how to do things on their own, whereas girls were assisted but not sent off to work by themselves and that boys were twice as likely as girls to receive individual instructions on how to do things, either verbally or by demonstration. Girls simply received less teacher attention and consequently less actual instruction.

The conclusions that boys tend to get more atten-

tion than girls, and that specific behaviors by each gender are more likely to be reinforced than others, have been supported by other data. For example, among fifth graders observed in English, social studies, math, and science classes (Etaugh & Harlow, 1975), boys were scolded more than girls by both male and female teachers, and praised more than girls by female teachers. Beverly Fagot (1981a) observed a sample of 40 teachers in preschool play groups and found that teachers tended to interact verbally more with the girls but to join in more with the play of boys. An earlier larger-scale study of 16 junior high school classrooms (Good, Sikes, & Brophy, 1973) found evidence that teachers "provided boys with more response opportunities," asked them more different kinds of questions, and gave them more positive and negative feedback. This differential response to girls and boys was characteristic of teachers of both genders. The researchers also found that high-achievement boys received the most favorable treatment and attention of all, or "the best of everything in the classroom." A more recent study by Myra Sadker and David Sadker (1985) of over 100 fourth-, sixth-, and eighth-grade classrooms found that, in general, "boys got more than their fair share of teacher attention" (p. 56). This included being more often disciplined but also being more often instructed in how to do things. Teachers were more accepting of boys who called out answers and did not raise their hands—that is, of boys' assertive behavior. Another group of researchers (Dweck, Davidson, Nelson, & Enna, 1978) reported earlier that among a sample of fourth and fifth graders, boys received more positive teacher feedback than girls for "the intellectual quality" of their schoolwork. When making negative evaluations, teachers more often attributed girls' failures to their intellectual inadequacies but boys' failures to their lack of motivation.

The differential responses of teachers to girls and boys, documented by observational studies, would seem to reflect deeply rooted ideas about how the genders differ. Indirect evidence of such beliefs among teachers is given in data reported by Mary Gregory (1977). A large sample of elementary school teachers were asked to rate the likelihood that they would refer children with varying problems for special assistance. Boys were found to be significantly more likely to be referred for help than girls (for all problems except reading disabilities), suggesting to Gregory that teachers are "more concerned about male children." In a study aimed more directly at identifying teacher beliefs about gender, George Wise (1978) found that a large sample of public school teachers (representing kindergarten through the 12th grade) perceived girls and boys differently in a consistently stereotypic manner. According to the teachers (both women and men):

> Female students tend to be very emotional, do not hide their emotions, easily express tender feelings, are very easily hurt, cry easily, are very affectionate, very gentle, very quiet, and not at all aggressive . . . very aware of the feelings of others, very understanding of others, very helpful . . . enjoy art and literature very much, dislike math and science, are not adventurous, are not at all reckless, are very careful, are very neat . . . [and] are very interested in their appearance. (p. 609)

If adults who teach girls do so with such beliefs, and if girls play and interact with other children whose parents and teachers share these beliefs, then of course these beliefs will be perpetuated and validated through social agreement, and behavior to match them will be learned and strengthened. Such a conviction led Patrick Lee and Nancy Gropper (1974) to suggest that sexist beliefs and practices constitute a "hidden curriculum" in our schools, and spurred Congress to pass legislation in 1972 (Title IX of the Education Amendments) that prohibits sex discrimination by an educational program receiving federal financial assistance. Following approval of this law, many state education departments held conferences and workshops and issued guidelines designed to help their districts evaluate their programs, curricula, and textbooks, and to devise antisexist strategies.

The federal regulations have been noticeably effective in expanding opportunities for girls in sports and "shop" programs previously limited to boys, and in sponsoring experimental programs designed to change sexist attitudes and beliefs. Sally Koblinsky and Alan Sugawara (1984), for example, developed such a program for 3- to 5-year-olds in which some were exposed for six months to materials and activities designed as a "nonsexist curriculum" while others took part in the regular school program. The children's views about the gender appropriateness of various objects and activities were assessed before and after the program. Girls and boys were found to be equally affected by the special curriculum and manifested significantly less stereotypic views about gender after it than they did before. The importance of teacher behavior in influencing what children do has also been demonstrated in another study of preschool classes (Serbin, Connor, & Citron, 1981) in

which teachers sat in predesignated areas—ones most popular with only one gender—during free play and interacted with children. Teacher presence was very effective in helping girls overcome "sex role inhibitions against play with 'inappropriate' toys" (such as trucks and blocks). In other words, presence of a woman teacher significantly increased girls' subsequent play in a variety of play areas.

We can suppose that a little girl starts school with the very same sense of excitement as a little boy, the same sense of wonder and fear, and the expectation that something important comes from education. How unfair to shatter these anticipations by teaching girls passivity and dependency, and rewarding them for "standing by." How unfair to narrow the dreams and possibilities of children because they are poor, because they are black, native American, or Hispanic, or because they are girls. We know from our own experiences and from the results of carefully conducted research that change is possible and that stereotypes are modifiable, especially when they are first encountered, but also throughout childhood.

REDUCING THE CULTURAL EMPHASIS ON GENDER

Sandra Bem (1981, 1983) has asked *why* the category of sex has such primacy and importance in organizing ideas and behavior. Her answer is that this is neither inevitable nor necessary but simply a reflection of the culture's concern. Sex is put forth by the culture as a focus around which we process or group other material. According to Bem's gender schema theory, most children then learn to "encode and to organize information" in terms of gender; they "learn which attributes are to be linked with their own sex and, hence, with themselves," and to evaluate their "adequacy as a person according to the gender schema" (1983, p. 604). Such organization around gender divisions, however, is arbitrary.

> Given the proper social context . . . even a category like eye color could become a cognitive schema. . . . [A] category will become a schema if: (a) the social context makes it the nucleus of a large associative network . . . and (b) the social context assigns the category broad functional significance, that is, if a broad array of social institutions, norms, and taboos distinguishes between persons, behaviors, and attributes on the basis of this category. (1983, p. 608)

In our culture, gender has immense functional significance, but this is modifiable, not inevitable. As pointed out by John Condry (1984), "Gender does not have to be a central fulcrum of our identity, and it does not have to carry the baggage it does today" (p. 506). Sandra Bem (1983) has suggested that parents who wish to raise gender-aschematic children must somehow inoculate their children against seeing the world in gender terms by teaching alternative organizing principles such as individual differences. In addition, since we know that behavior often occurs in a nonverbal context and is strengthened or weakened by the overt or subtle nature of the consequences that follow, parents must come to understand the factors that influence what their children learn to do and the role played by gender-relevant variables.

Adolescence: Mixed Messages and Real Options

The passionate proclivities of the young seem especially threatening when they belong to women; so does the will to power. . . . The ends they seek—independence, control, love—characterize all adolescents—indeed all human beings.

Patricia Spacks   *(1981, pp. 119f.)*

If we were nice-looking and chaste and pleasing in manner and dress, . . . Mr. Right would come and marry us and satisfy all our desires. He would take over our father's functions in caring for us. . . .

Gail Godwin   *(1983, p. 273)*

*I*n *Woman on the Edge of Time*, Marge Piercy (1976a) wrote about a community in the year 2137 in which there is a "transit from childhood" for all girls and boys. For one month the young person stays alone in an area of wilderness and upon return home chooses an adult name and becomes a full member of the community. One young girl about to begin her rite of passage explains to a visitor from the present, "You can't expect me to go through life with an unearned name, stuck on me when I wasn't conscious yet! How can I go deep into myself and develop my own strength if I don't get to find out who I am alone as well as with others?" (p. 116). Unfortunately, rites of passage for adolescent women that encourage independence and self-knowledge remain, for the most part, securely tucked between the covers of utopian novels. In our place and time, young women are still encouraged to behave in ways our culture defines as "feminine"—to be observant and considerate of others, to attract the attentions of men, and to seek approval.

In this chapter, as we look at the experiences of girls during that period in their lives when their bodies are rapidly changing in the direction of maturity, and when they are preparing for and concerned with how they will function as adults, we will explore the messages our culture delivers to teenage girls, and their consequences. The physical changes associated with puberty, especially menstruation and hormonal fluctuations, will be discussed in the next chapter; here we will concentrate on the psychological and cultural significance of adolescence for girls. Which of the socialization pressures and conditions of childhood continue? What experiences are new? What expectations are different? What options and choices are available?

PERSONAL IDENTITY OR WAITING FOR MR. RIGHT?

Many of us have learned that the main developmental objective of the adolescent period is to establish personal identity—to identify one's adult interests and direction, to determine where one is going and why. While our culture clearly expects this of a young man, a young woman typically receives a double message. On the one hand she is encouraged to follow her interests and skills, to do well in school, and to prepare for an occupation. But at the same time, a multitude of cultural cues proclaim, with varying degrees of subtlety, that a young woman must remain flexible and adaptable because what she will become and where she will go will depend ultimately upon the man with whose life she will become identified. Consequently, the girl whose active preadolescent interest in sports was encouraged, whose high achievement in school was approved and applauded, whose aspirations for adventure, exploration, and a career were tolerated, may find adolescence to be a period of conflict and confusion.

In many ways, as we shall see, "the problems of adolescent women," as Patricia Spacks (1975) has written, "are those of all women writ large" (p. 147). In adolescence, many girls find a narrower description of how women are defined than they received in childhood, and this information comes, as before, from representatives of the significant cultural institutions—parents, friends, high school teachers, counselors, and the media. To books and television must be added pop music and films—particularly important sources of information about interpersonal relationships, love, sex, and women's value and social status. Our society's separation of girls and boys in childhood by activities, interests, and appropriate behavior continues and intensifies in adolescence. Two cultures appear, each with its own characteristics, distinctive language style, dress, informal gathering places, subjects of interest, and world view. Representatives of the two cultures meet in high school classes, at sports events, and on dates, but sexual excitement is mainly what brings the two worlds together and provides the possibility of mutual satisfaction. Fortunately, adolescent girls and boys do get to like one another as they interact, thus providing for common bonds or points of intersection between the two cultures.

Our society explicitly encourages the adolescent boy to learn to know himself, and to acquire skills sufficient to pursue his ambitions, ideals, and life goals. After he has resolved his problems of identity he is expected to search for a wife and establish a family. His heterosexuality is taken for granted. For a girl, on the other hand, the major developmental task prescribed at adolescence by our society is to enhance her attractiveness and find a boyfriend, lover, or husband. Heterosexuality is again assumed. Despite significant changes in women's roles in the family and the economy, to be discussed in detail later in this book, these generalizations appear to be as valid for contemporary teenagers as they were several generations back and are applicable across social classes and ethnic and geographic groups in the United States.

Erik Erikson (1968), an influential theorist who explored developmental issues, described adolescent objectives through a cultural lens that views boys as "the figure" and girls as "the background." Thus, for example, he wrote that "much of a young woman's identity is already defined in her kind of attractiveness and in the selective nature of her search for the man (or men) by whom she wishes to be sought" (p. 283). This message was communicated to young women in the 1950s and 1960s, regardless of whether they were pursuing higher education or career training. Jessie Bernard (1978), in commenting on her daughter's college experience in the early 1960s, noted that "if young women were going to be intellectual, they were made to understand, they better be intellectual in a charming, unchallenging, disarming, appealing—strictly feminine—way" (p. 64). Two curricula seemed offered at the women's college her daughter attended: the "official" one catering to intellectual interests, and the "hidden" one teaching "feminine style."

Can we dismiss these observations as relics of the past? Current data and the reported experiences of young women suggest not. One of my ex-students (now a colleague) shared with me a page from a 1984 gift catalogue. Featured were two books described as "perfect gifts for teenagers . . . [which] address the myths and hard realities youngsters will face when entering adulthood." Both books were journals "for self-awareness and personal planning," but the book for boys was titled *Challenges* while that for girls was called *Choices*. The cover of the former showed moving arms outstretched (on a blue background), while the cover of the latter featured lovely blossoms of pink and white. *Teen* magazine, popular with today's younger adolescent girls, still contains advertisements for "love chests" as appropriate gifts for "a contemporary young woman at graduation" (Lane, 1984).

Much has changed in the last few decades relevant to women's place and social recognition of our abilities and aspirations, but the culture still subtly, and sometimes explicitly, encourages young women to believe that their fundamental task is to find a man. Not too long ago, one of the major television networks sponsored a special program entitled "99 Ways to Attract the Right Man," a combination of comic and serious advice on "how to *recognize* him, *meet* him and *keep* him" (*TV Guide*, 1985). Messages almost everywhere encourage a young woman to believe that the activities she engages in before successfully accomplishing her fundamental task should not be taken so seriously that they interfere with it, or to see other activities as instrumental in "finding a man." Certainly, many adolescent women resist and do not accept our culture's definition of their fundamental task. These young women prepare for jobs, careers, and personal pursuits vital to their identity, integrity, and self-definition. The dominant culture, however, remains largely ambivalent about life-styles for women that do not include happiness with Mr. Right, and continues to presume that this achievement is the adolescent girl's top priority.

SOCIAL EXPECTATIONS: IT'S STILL A MAN'S WORLD

In our society men as a class are more important, more highly valued and rewarded than women, a fact that continues to be documented by informal and formal observations, personal experience, and research findings. What men do receives higher priority, more social support, higher status, and takes precedence over what women do. Margaret Mead (1949/1968) noted long ago that regardless of the nature of the activity, whether healing, weaving, doll making, fishing, or what have you, when performed by men that activity is more valued and honored than when it is merely "women's work."

Most girls begin to learn about male supremacy in childhood. They find out, by being good observers, that no matter what adults say about boys, boys really count because someday they become men. Marilyn French in *The Women's Room* (1977) described what Mira, at 15, had figured out but did not quite understand:

Everybody despised boys, everyone looked down on them, the teachers, her mother, even her father. "Boys!" they would exclaim in disgust. But everyone admired men. . . . Boys were ridiculous, troublesome, always fighting and showing off and making noise, but men strode purposefully to the center of every stage and took up the whole surface of every scene. Why was that? (p. 27)

The value of men is a lesson taught not only by parents and teachers, but also by other agents of socialization. The black heroine of Alice Walker's *Meridian* (1976) tells us about the importance of movies in her life. Not only did she learn about how white people lived and loved, but the fantasy world of films also showed young girls "the dream of happy endings: of women who had everything, of men who ran the world" (p. 75). Jessie Bernard's (1978) daughter first discovered male dominance at college:

> The young woman who in high school had written that she could "out-run, out-climb, and out-yell the boys" was writing: "It's funny but just from the few months I've been here I am convinced that at a certain age boys take over from girls intellectually because the really creative thinking seems to come from them." (p. 71)

A fascinating study of the relative size of men's and women's heads in contemporary magazine photographs, in paintings from the 17th to the 20th centuries, and in drawings made by college students, has found that men's heads are significantly more prominent—that is, larger relative to the total picture—than women's heads (Archer, Iritani, Kimes, & Barrios, 1983). Furthermore, when asked to rate photographs differing in facial prominence, a sample of students judged the more prominent faces to be more intelligent and ambitious. The researchers concluded that the greater facial prominence given to men in photographs and paintings "both reflect and contribute to thematic conceptions" about the differential intellectual qualities of men and women, and give men a clear advantage.

Steven Doloff (1983) asked his English composition students (in a business college) to write a composition "on how each would spend a day as a member of his or her respective opposite sex." His analysis of 100 in-class essays revealed that "young people even now are still burdened with sexist stereotypes and sexist self-images." In pretending to be men in their essays,

> women jauntily went places alone. . . . They threw their clothes on the floor and left dishes in the sink. More than a third of them . . . deliberately and aggressively accosted women. The male students, after their initial

paralysis wore off, did not write as much as the females. They seemed envious of very little that was female, and curious about nothing. . . . [Most] stayed home and apathetically checked off a list of domestic chores or . . . went off to work in an office. . . . [After dinner they] watched TV and went right to sleep.

Most young women across regions, ethnic groups and social classes get the message about male dominance. An important theme in Anne Campbell's (1984) book about girls in street gangs is their largely unsuccessful challenge of machismo and their emotional dependence upon men. Men's superiority is proclaimed in the intellectual sphere, in work, sports, entertainment, and political/economic influence. Jack Balswick and Bron Ingoldsby (1982) asked over 1000 high school students who their heroes and heroines were. Men were nominated overwhelmingly by a 3 to 1 ratio, by both girls and boys, black or white.

> The most outstanding finding is the extent to which sex and race do not affect the overwhelming tendency for heroes to be chosen over heroines. Black females, black males, white females, and white males chose heroes 76%, 79%, 77%, and 79% of the time, respectively. (p. 246)

Personal friends or relatives chosen as heroes or heroines were just as often women as men, but if they were public figures, men were chosen by a ratio of 7 to 1. The adolescents in this study came from Georgia. Does geography make a difference? Apparently not, since a survey among 1167 school children in Rhode Island (reported by Major, 1983) found that their ten top-ranked favorite actors or actresses were all men!

It is probably because men are so valued that adolescent women accept the necessity of finding one. High school girls have told me that having a boyfriend greatly enhances their prestige or image. A girl may be bright, friendly, competent, and attractive, but without a boyfriend she lacks social validation of these positive attributes. It is as though being selected by a boy tells others that a girl is worthwhile. Thus, a teenage girl in a story by Margaret Atwood (1984) tells us, "Once I started going out with Buddy, I found I could pass for normal. I was now included in the kinds of conversations girls held in the washroom while they were putting on their lipstick" (p. 27). When Buddy gave her his identification bracelet, "Buddy was putting his name on me, like a *Reserved* sign or an ownership label, or a tattoo on a cow's ear, or a brand. . . . It was the equivalent of a white fur sweater-collar, the kind with pom-poms. Buddy . . . was something to wear" (p. 39).

Many college or young working women also feel the need for public display of a boyfriend, despite the fact that they may be experiencing success through academic or other achievements. A cocktail napkin I picked up recently at a restaurant had the following "daffynition" on its frontside: "COED—A girl who didn't get her man in high school." (Very funny!?) A frequently repeated theme during a meeting of a group of women in science on my college campus was that it was much easier for them to pursue their scholarly ambitions if they already had the security of a personal relationship with a man. To be chosen by a man appears to confer value by showing others that a woman has been found "worthy," and frees her to focus on other interests and activities. But young women who make finding a man a top priority must accept society's prescription for their adolescent years: they must strive to be popular and feminine, flexible and nurturing.

Be Popular and Feminine

Many contemporary high school girls get up at 6 a.m. to put on their makeup before going to school. They are thus practicing pretense and, as Judith Bardwick and Elizabeth Douvan (1972) have phrased it, using a "cosmetic exterior of the self to lure men." They have learned that they are expected to be gracious, well-groomed, friendly, available, and to smile a lot. In a study of boys and girls from grades 1 through 4 and grades 9 through 12, Phyllis Berman and Vicki Smith (1984) photographed same-gender, same-grade pairs under two different sets of instructions, and found that regardless of instructions or age, girls smiled significantly more often than boys.

To be popular is a coveted achievement. In a story about an earlier generation by Alice Munro (1977), the heroine recalls how, at 13, she and her friend Lonnie used to spend their time: "We did questionnaires in magazines, to find out whether we had personality and whether we would be popular. We read articles on how to make up our faces to accentuate our good points and how to carry on a conversation" (p. 201). Contemporary magazines for young women (like *Seventeen*) have similar questionnaires and features that teach that the more "feminine" a girl looks, the more attractive she will be to boys, and that girls who act and dress appropriately will be admired, approved, and dated. A field experiment (Renne & Allen, 1976) found that college men held doors open for women four times as often as they held doors open for men, but six times as often for women who were wearing "feminine" clothes. An adolescent girl learns what kind of clothes these are from magazines, films, television, and peers. She learns to use cosmetics to highlight her "best" features and hide her "worst," and to behave in ways that will attract and keep the attention of men. When women behave in ways that men are thought to like—in "feminine" ways—they speak in soft voices, not loudly or shrilly; lower their eyes and look coy; do not talk too much when men are around; and do not sprawl or sit with feet apart (Henley & Freeman, 1976).

We might like to think that this definition of what is feminine is outmoded and old-fashioned, but when I asked a small mixed-gender high school psychology class in 1985 to list the characteristics they associated with the term *feminine*, they offered the following: intuitive, understanding, caring, graceful, soft-spoken, dainty, and curvy. The characteristics they associated with *masculine*, on the other hand, were: muscular, aggressive, brave, ambitious, rough, logical, handsome, daring, competitive, and strong. Even when contemporary advertisements for products for young women portray them as active and adventurous, the associated message is that they must retain their femininity. An ad in *Teen* magazine (Maybelline, 1984), for example, presents a girl in shorts (pink) and sneakers, who says, "I always want to look my best, even when I'm riding my bike." To "look natural, fresh and free," even when active, she advocates the use of Shine Free cosmetics!

The adolescent girl who tries to match herself to the media images of women who get men's attention may experience debilitating consequences. She may not be able to see value in her own qualities until they receive approval from a boy. For example, Judith Rossner, in her novel *August* (1983), presents us with a young woman, Sascha, who says:

> The only time I ever think I'm beautiful . . . is when some man is staring into my face in broad daylight and telling me I'm beautiful. And then as soon as he turns away for a minute I think he changed his mind. (p. 376)

Sascha's feelings may be extreme, but illustrate an adolescent girl's need to validate her attractiveness and enhance her self-esteem by the responses she elicits from young men.

Some young women who pursue men's approval with more than ordinary determination may get caught by our society's limits on how far young women can "properly" go in attracting men. The case of Vanessa Williams, chosen Miss America for 1984, is a good example. When a photographer for whom she had posed nude sold her photographs to a magazine for men, she was publicly disgraced and forced to give up her title (and the lucrative rewards attached to it). But how did she earn the title in the first place? By having more of "what it takes" than the other young women who paraded, smiling, before judges in body-accentuating gowns, in high heels and bathing suits. Vanessa Williams, however, went "too far." To exhibit one's body scantily clothed and to be seductive conforms to our society's standards for womanhood, but overtly titillating men with nude photos does not. Little sympathy was expressed for Vanessa Williams in the press, and few saw her as a victim of our culture's mixed messages. One exception to the public's general acceptance of her punishment was an editorial in *The Nation* ("There She Goes," 1984), which noted that "an honest society struggling to eradicate its sexism would excoriate the pornographer and exonerate his victim. And it would laugh the Miss America pageant right off the boardwalk" (p. 65). Andrée Nicola-McLaughlin (1985) also commented on our society's hypocrisy as revealed by the treatment of Vanessa Williams, pointing out that 80,000 young women enter state beauty contests annually, participating in the exploitation of women's sexuality, youth, and talent.

Another consequence of young women's pursuit of "femininity" is the psychological suffering this pursuit produces for many minority women. In our culture's definition of femininity, white skin is generally a requisite for attractiveness. Mary Washington (1975) has examined the writing of Afro-American women and found a preoccupation with issues of skin color, hair texture and beauty, and other evidence that the image of the white American "dream girl" has deeply affected black adolescents. She has noted that "the raving beauties every high school boy coveted were invariably light-skinned with 'good' hair" (p. xvi), and that "the idea of beauty as defined by white America has been an assault on the personhood of the black woman" (p. xvii). One story included in Washington's collection, by Gwendolyn Brooks, is entitled "If You're Light and Have Long Hair." In another story, by Paule Marshall (1975), the heroine Reena tells us that "like nearly every little black girl, I had my share of dreams of waking up to find myself with long blond curls, blue eyes, and skin like milk" (p. 122). Just such a dream is encountered in the opening pages of Maya Angelou's (1971) book about her childhood and adolescence. In the dream, she is wearing a lavender dress that makes her look like a "sweet little white girl."

> Wouldn't they be surprised when one day I woke out of my black ugly dream, and my real hair, which was long and blond, would take the place of the kinky mass that Momma wouldn't let me straighten? My light-blue eyes were going to hypnotize them. (p. 2)

In the enlightened 1980s, adolescent girls can find black models of beauty, like Vanessa Williams or Shari Belafonte-Harper, in the glamour magazines and television commercials, but these women invariably have lighter rather than darker skin. Although Afro hairstyles are sometimes in vogue for women of any skin color, the image of the long-legged, thin, magnificently hair-styled blond continues to dominate and to appear in the dreams of short-limbed, solidly built, brown-haired teenage girls.

Be Flexible and Nurturing

A persistent message to the adolescent girl is that she should be flexible and not define herself too sharply, because her ultimate identity will be defined by the man with whom she becomes associated. Erik Erikson (1968) viewed adolescence for women not as a time for active searching and exploring, but as a time of fluidity, "a psychosocial moratorium, a sanctioned period of delay of adult functioning" (p. 282). According to Erikson, the young woman's identity will come primarily from the man she marries and for whom she makes a home. While Erikson granted that a young woman also trains herself "as a worker and a citizen," the full context of his discussion makes clear that he believed her final self-definition to be powerfully shaped by the needs, ambitions, goals, and interests of her mate.

Erikson's views reflect a persistent theme in our society. Women are expected to manifest adaptability and flexibility in shaping their lives around the plans and interests of their husbands, and girls are reinforced in earlier years to consider the wishes of others and to be accommodating. A study of over 2500 students in grades 3 and 12 (Rosenberg & Simmons, 1975) found girls to be reliably more self-conscious than boys, with the gender difference increasing over time, so that by age 15, twice as many girls as boys were highly self-conscious or "other-directed." The data suggest that "girls become very worried about what other people think of them, whether they are pleasing and helpful. . . . Relative to boys, girls are much more fearful of displeasing people; they become more vulnerable than boys to criticism or disapproval" (p. 158). When asked to choose between success (being "best in things you do") and being well-liked, significantly more girls than boys chose the latter.

Studies of perceptual field dependence often find a gender difference, usually beginning at adolescence. When asked to make judgments of verticality by adjusting a movable rod within a lighted frame to an upright position, women typically show more dependence than men on features of the perceptual field. That field-dependent persons of both genders have been shown to be more sociable, more influenced by the social environment, and more concerned with making a good impression than field-independent persons, is very significant. These are motives adolescent women are encouraged to pursue. Deborah Waber (1977) has suggested that those who try to gain acceptance and prestige among their peers are more likely to rely on external social cues in monitoring their behavior.

Psychoanalytic theory regards women as more pragmatic and less principled—that is, less concerned with abstractions like justice and more with social acceptance—than men. Sigmund Freud (1933/1964) believed that a girl's superego development was inadequate because, unlike a boy, she did not experience an Oedipal conflict or castration anxiety—that is, fear of her father's reprisal for love of the mother. Without an Oedipal conflict to resolve, Freud argued, women's superego development would necessarily suffer, since it is through resolution of this conflict that social rules are internalized. Instead, wrote Freud, when the girl realizes her lack of a penis, she blames her mother, from whom she turns away with hostility, and moves toward her father with a positive attachment. The latter promises love in exchange for her renunciation of aggressive impulses. The result, according to Freud, is a wishy-washy personality without strong personal standards who is intent upon pleasing others. Was Freud describing inevitable feminine development or cultural prescription? Adolescent women, in their efforts to be pleasing, may continue behaving in many of the same ways that brought them approval when they were little girls. Generalizing from her analyses of English and American novels, Patricia Spacks (1975) concluded that young women are, in many ways, "not encouraged to grow up." Perhaps this is the reason that the

word *baby* remains so frequent in the popular music men sing to—and about—women.

That a young woman is encouraged to continue being dependent while learning that she is expected to nurture and take care of others is paradoxical. Our culture expects that she will support her family emotionally and be responsible for shaping their home into as ideal an environment as their economic circumstances permit. Beginning in childhood, girls are urged and cajoled to practice domesticity and to view themselves as sympathetic and caring persons. Both middle-class and working-class girls receive the same message, although the timing may differ. Middle-class girls who are usually encouraged to go to college, can, for a while, be autonomous and make independent choices. But they, too, have practiced and learned much the same domestic and nurturant behavior as working-class girls. Taking care of people is still a cultural imperative for young women. At 19, having never lived apart from my parents long enough to practice taking care of myself, I remember believing that I would be able to look after the older, more experienced, and troubled man I married.

TEENAGE PREGNANCIES

That an adolescent girl's sexuality is no less insistent a concern and no less a source of pleasure than it is for an adolescent boy is increasingly accepted today, but, at the same time, we still see sex as something girls "give" to boys. Such a theme appears frequently in the magazine stories and books that teenagers read. Gayle Nelson (1975) analyzed the five novels that were most commonly read by the girls in her 11th- and 12th-grade classes and found that the young women in these books were primarily concerned with clothes, dates, diets, "and whatever makes them more attractive and pleasing to the boys." In each book the heroine was depicted as coming from a nice, middle-class, conventional family and as submitting "begrudgingly to a boy's demand for sexual relations" (p. 54). Each girl was presented as having been "acted upon" and as unable to stand up for her own values. All five heroines were eventually punished; one girl died, while the other four became pregnant.

More than one million American girls between 12 and 19 have been getting pregnant each year during the past few years. Of this number, about 50 percent complete their pregnancies and have babies, and half of these mothers are not married. The pregnancy rate among girls aged 15 to 19 has increased from 99 per thousand in 1974 to 111 per thousand in 1980 ("Nation Ignoring Problem," 1986). The statistics on teenage births are complex, as has been pointed out by Diana Baumrind (1981). While teenage pregnancies have increased, the birthrate among women in general, in all age groups *including teenagers*, has been steadily decreasing. The teenage birthrate, however, has been decreasing at a slower rate than that for other age groups (and the rate for nonwhites continues to be more than twice as great as for whites). Thus, the percentage of live births to mothers under the age of 20 has increased in relation to the percentage to mothers aged 20 or older. The percentage of births to teenage mothers was 14.0 in 1960, 17.6 in 1970, and 18.9 in 1975 (Baumrind, 1981). Another complication is that while the overall birthrate among teenagers is decreasing, the percentage of out-of-wedlock births is going up, and almost quadrupled between 1960 and 1983, from 15 percent to 54 percent ("Nation Ignoring Problem," 1986). In 1983, unwed mothers of all ages accounted for 20% of all births in the United States ("Unwed Mothers," 1985).

A study by the Alan Guttmacher Institute ("U.S. Teenagers," 1985) reported that the rate of adolescent pregnancy in the United States is far higher than in any other industrialized country, despite roughly comparable levels of sexual activity. This does not seem to be due to the level of support provided by the society to pregnant mothers; indeed, in the other industrialized countries, more maternity and welfare benefits are available than under the U.S. program of Aid to Families with Dependent Children. One of the most important factors that distinguished the American teenagers in the study from the other teenagers was their far lesser use of birth control methods, and their lesser use of oral contraceptives in particular. The researchers suggested that this difference is due to the lesser availability in the United States of sex education and inexpensive contraceptive services.

> Overall, the authors of the study concluded that the lowest rates of teenage pregnancy were in countries that had liberal attitudes toward sex, had easily accessible contraceptive services for young people, with contraceptives being offered free or at low cost and without parental notification, and had comprehensive programs in sex education. (p. C-23)

This conclusion agrees with other information from studies of teenage pregnancy within the United States. Susan Phipps-Yonas (1980) concluded, from a review of the research literature, that "there is no unique psychological profile common to most, much

less all, pregnant adolescents" (p. 407); research indicates that most adolescent pregnancies result from "a quick, often unsatisfying try at sex" (DiPerna, 1984), and that teenagers know about contraceptives but are uncomfortable with them because of their potential danger to health (IUDs and the Pill) or their messiness (diaphragms, foams, and condoms). What seems implicated, then, is not any peculiarity or special attribute of individual teenagers but a social phenomenon of inadequate education about sex and birth control, and the relative difficulty of obtaining contraceptives. The teenagers who get pregnant typically have not planned to have sex. Paula DiPerna (1984) has described a group of teenage mothers in New York whom she interviewed: "For most of them, pregnancy just happened, and most of them didn't believe it when it did" (p. 61). In a 1985 episode of the soap opera "Days of Our Lives," for example, sex on the part of an unmarried teenage couple resulted in a pregnancy. Viewers might have predicted this since, as the data on real teenage pregnancies show, the sex "just happened" and no contraception was used. The adolescent girl, who had been saving money to enter hairdressing school, was presented as putting her ambitions aside and bravely facing the future as a wife and mother. True to life, her marriage ended in divorce.

Studies of pregnant teenagers have suggested that some see having a baby as a route to adulthood. Related to this is the hopelessness widespread in poor ghetto communities in which young people have little expectation of getting a good job, and feel isolated from the larger culture. Harriet Presser (1980) interviewed over 300 unmarried mothers in New York City in a 3-year study and found evidence that strongly suggested that early parenthood was often a means of achieving adult status in the absence of attainable and desirable employment. A baby can make an adolescent girl feel like an adult and a caregiver, someone of significance and importance in the life of another, and a person from whom competence is expected. One study (Falk, Gispert, & Baucom, 1981) compared a group of pregnant 15- and 16-year-old single black girls planning to have their babies with a similar group of girls planning to have abortions and a control group of girls who were not pregnant. The former group was found to differ from the others on measures that suggested that they were "attempting to fill some void and to demonstrate that they are women by assuming the role of a mother . . . [and] striving to gain status" (p. 744).

Teenage pregnancy is understandable when we realize that it is compatible with the values and beliefs acquired by young women. If an adolescent girl believes that it is a man's world and that status comes from having a boyfriend; if her sense of self or identity is waiting upon that of a future role as wife and mother; if she wants to please and be popular and to satisfy the needs of others; if her values are tentative and flexible; if she believes that having a baby and caring for it are the primary signs of womanhood; and if, at the same time, she is confused and uncertain about the various contraceptive options, does not have easy and inexpensive access to them, and is ambivalent about her sexuality, then early motherhood becomes a real possibility. Data from research supports a link between teenage pregnancy and traditional views about gender. Carol Ireson (1984) compared 43 pregnant with 118 nonpregnant but sexually active teenagers and found that the former were more traditional and sex-typed in their activities and educational expectations, as well as being lower in socioeconomic status.

Added to traditional beliefs and attitudes, which have been with us for a long time, is the increasing sexualization of teenage culture. Contemporary women expect to have heterosexual experience at an earlier age than was the case for their mothers and grandmothers. They feel the pressure for such experience from their peers and the media (especially pop music and films) and their belief that everyone else is "doing it." We will consider this issue more fully in Chapter 7, in our discussion of sexuality.

ASPIRATIONS AND ATTITUDES TOWARD WORK AND MARRIAGE

In the last chapter we noted that children generally acquire sex-typed vocational aspirations early in life. Do these limited aspirations for women continue into adolescence? For many, perhaps most, young women, they seem to. High schoolers even today seem to accept our culture's traditional gender ideology when it comes to work and marriage; and even a college education can do more to discourage than to encourage a woman's high occupational aspirations. Of course, there are wide individual variations among adolescent women in this area as in others.

Putting Marriage Before Work: Still a Prevalent Pattern

Whether or not the average high school girl is planning higher education or a career, finding a boy-friend is of highest priority to her. Despite the fact that the vast majority of women (including wives and mothers) work outside the home, the employment aspirations of adolescent girls lag behind those of boys in terms of prestige and income. Studies indicate that the majority of both genders anticipate a relatively traditional adult life of marriage in which the husband has most responsibility for providing financial resources and the wife has most responsibility for the home.

For most working-class girls, marriage is the way to adulthood. For those who are very poor and/or whose ethnicity or race is not respected, school may be a hostile place. For such girls, especially, the high school years may represent a necessary waiting period until one is old enough to attract a boy, marry him, and have children. In high school a working-class girl is likely to be directed either into a commercial or vocational course to learn typing, shorthand, and bookkeeping, or into a general course to learn homemaking, child care, and how to be a good consumer. Working-class girls who do go on to college may find that among the barriers to be overcome is that of parents, teachers, and counselors who have low expectations and assume that marriage represents the poor girl's ultimate ambition, to be realized sooner rather than later. Lillian Rubin (1976) interviewed blue-collar couples in the San Francisco area and shared this adolescent memory from one of the women with whom she spoke:

> I was a good student, and somehow I could lose myself in school. And I used to love some of my teachers. . . . So I used to dream about wanting to be a teacher. . . . I actually was in college prep in high school, even though my counselor didn't think it was such a good idea because there was nobody to help me through college . . . My counselor . . . got me a scholarship . . . to a beauty college instead of to a real college. . . . And then, not long after that—I was seventeen—I got married. (p. 44)

Rubin pointed out that despite the fact that so many married women are in the labor force, working-class girls tend to see work outside the home as temporary. Many of the jobs they see done by older working-class women in shops, offices, factories, laundries, restaurants, and other people's homes, are low in status and poorly paid, supporting the illusion that one does these things "only for a while" or "part-time" to "help out" and increase the family income. The major breadwinner is still expected to be the husband, and it is the status of his job that matters most. Not surprisingly, then, an early marriage is highly valued and sought after.

Regardless of social class, contemporary young women have lower aspirations and expectations than young men of comparable background and ability. For example, Robin Hurwitz and Mary White (1977) asked a group of high school juniors to select from a list of 40 occupations the ones that would be most appropriate for each of five students described in mock profiles; each profile was presented as that of a boy for some of the respondents and of a girl for others. The occupations selected for boys were consistently of higher status (in terms of educational level required and income to be earned) than those selected for girls. Among those students who were given prior information on new occupational opportunities for women, there was less of a difference between the occupational status scores given to boys and girls.

Not only are the occupational and educational goals of adolescent girls typically lower than those of comparable boys, but different relationships seem to exist between such aspirations and factors such as ability or social class. Thus, in a review of the literature, Margaret Marini (1978) noted that while the aspirations of teenagers are generally influenced by parental socioeconomic status, academic ability, and parental encouragement, these variables have a smaller effect on the occupational aspirations of girls than of boys. Although girls are positively influenced by their mother's employment, "girls from high socioeconomic backgrounds and with high levels of academic achievement are less likely to strive for high occupational goals than boys with similarly high levels of these resources" (p. 747). Research supporting this conclusion is illustrated by that of Elizabeth Douvan and Anne Locksley ("Teenaged Boys," 1977). Compared to boys, the girls in a midwestern high school were found to "underplan their future occupational and educational goals" in relation to their academic ability. For example, the girls who anticipated working in the lowest-status occupations had higher grade point averages than the boys who anticipated working in medium-status occupations, so academic achievement did not reliably predict girls' occupational plans. Complementing these findings, Nira Danziger (1983) has reported that among a midwestern sample of high schoolers, boys' educational aspirations were correlated with their grades, but this was not true for girls. Neither grades nor achievement test scores were significantly related

to the aspirations of girls. As Danzinger has noted, girls do not commonly see academic achievement as "the relevant message in the process of . . . aspiration formation" (p. 691). The aspirations of the girls in her study seemed to be more related to the girls' perceptions of actual opportunities.

Research designed to uncover predictors of occupational plans for girls have been uniformly unsuccessful, leading one researcher, Marilyn Ihinger-Tallman (1982), to conclude that "the variables affecting the . . . occupational-educational goals of young women continue to elude us" (p. 544). She observed parents in a laboratory situation with a son or daughter aged 12 to 15 as they played a career choice game. Although the boys and girls achieved similar "attainment value" scores in this game, encouragement from parents was relatively nonpredictive of girls', but considerably predictive of boys', job and income attainment. Similarly, Jacquelynne Eccles (1985), who followed changes in the same group of adolescents from grades 5 through 12, found that "boys and girls make different achievement decisions because they attach different values to course options [in math and English]" and that "girls seem to be ignoring information about their own talents and skills in deriving the values they attach to various achievement activities" (p. 127). An important long-term study by Martin and Cynthia Deutsch ("Girls Lose," 1981) of over 1000 children who participated in an experimental preschool program in Harlem in the 1960s found that black girls lose their earlier academic lead over boys. When examined between the ages of 18 and 22, the young men who had received the special preschool training were found to be more successful in school and in employment than those who had not received the training, but there were no differences among the young women. No more of those who had been in the preschool project were "working or going to college than those who started school at the usual age" (p. 6).

Why are the variables that predict girls' occupational goals elusive, and not the same as for boys? Is it because occupational goals for most girls are still secondary to finding a husband, and supporting *him* in his movement up the "ladder of success"? In a study of over 1000 academically exceptional high school girls who were not planning to major in a science-related field in college (McClure & Piel, 1978), the researchers found that a main reason for not choosing science was "doubts about combining family life with a science career." Traditional gender relationships, particularly in marriage and parent-hood, continue to be anticipated by most teenagers, as indicated by this and more recent studies. While many adolescents say they favor egalitarian mar-riages, their actual descriptions of expected responsi-bilities, especially for child care and home care, sug-gest that only a minority hold nontraditional views. Data from a national survey of approximately 3000 high school seniors (Herzog, Bachman, & Johnston, 1983) indicated that "many seniors still prefer a wife who works half-time or not at all." And once children arrive, "the wife is very clearly expected to drop out of the labor force or to change to part-time work" (p. 128). While the seniors said they preferred an equal division of child care, they also preferred that the woman stay at home with her young children, and that the husband work full-time. These views were found to be shared by both genders but the boys were generally more traditional than the girls. Non-traditional views were more often found among adolescent girls of high academic ability who had plans for college and liberal political beliefs, as well as among respondents of both genders with working mothers. Similar findings have been reported by Rachelle Canter and Suzanne Ageton (1984) from a 5-year study of a national sample of 1626 teenagers. Boys were found to be more traditional than girls, but there was gender agreement "on the traditional divi-sion of labor," with the majority of both genders favoring "males as breadwinner and females as care-taker of home and family" (p. 673).

In summary, then, the data indicate that (a) the occupational aspirations of the average adolescent girl are lower than those of the average adolescent boy; (b) girls' aspirations are typically not predictable from their abilities, high school grades, or other fac-tors that relate reliably to boys' aspirations; and (c) these facts make sense in light of the gender ideology prevalent among teenagers that continues to value traditional roles for women and men in marriage and family life.

Women in College

What effect does a college education have on a woman's aspirations and attitudes toward work and marriage? Some research suggests that even those young women who begin college with educational and occupational goals similar to men's in prestige show a decline in aspirations and achievement as they proceed through college. These data suggest that whether or not the women themselves value tradi-

tional roles, their experiences in college serve to ex-tinguish (through lack of reinforcement) behaviors associated with high occupational expectations. For example, Elsie Smith (1982) concluded from a re-view of relevant research that while black adolescent girls demonstrate "higher academic achievement and intellective development" than their male peers, and tend to have higher educational and career aspira-tions than comparable black male and white female high school students, these "begin to erode in college. The environmental press of the college or reassess-ment of the career opportunity structure appear to lead to traditional career goals for black college females" (p. 278).

Alexander Astin (1977) studied the effects of col-lege on beliefs, attitudes, and knowledge in a 10-year investigation of approximately 200,000 students from 300 institutions, and concluded that the under-graduate experience appears "to preserve, rather than to reduce, stereotypic differences between men and women in behavior, personality, aspirations, and achievement" (p. 216). He found that women per-sisted less in college and showed a decline in aspira-tions for advanced degrees, while men's aspirations for graduate training increased. Attending a women's college, however, may make a difference. Astin re-ported that students in women's colleges were more likely than those in coed schools to maintain, and even increase, their high aspirations and to persist to graduation. But Janet Giele (1984), in a study of over 2000 women who had graduated between 1934 and 1979 from either an elite women's college or a select coeducational college, found that the former, while more affluent, were less likely to have a career or an advanced degree, and were more likely to have mar-ried and to have children. We will return to this issue and consider the effects of attending a women's col-lege on achievement in Chapter 13.

What about coed schools that are highly selective and that admit the most competent and able women? A study of over 3000 undergraduates attending six prestigious schools in the Northeast (Brown Project, 1980) reported that, compared with men, the women students lost ambition for graduate school or a profes-sional career despite having entered college with aspirations as high as men's and despite having earned grades comparable to men's. Not only did aspirations decline relative to men, but so did self-esteem. While larger proportions of seniors than freshmen gave themselves high ratings on intellectual and social self-confidence and on academic ability, "women were markedly less likely than were men to give themselves high ratings on these three traits, and the proportion [of women] seeing themselves as highly motivated to achieve actually declined" (p. 87). With respect just to Brown University, for example, the researchers concluded that "in general, women enter Brown with a higher achievement level than men and exit with a lower achievement level. At the same time, they do not register gains in intellectual self-confidence to the same degree as do men" (p. 268).

How can we explain the differential experiences of (and outcomes for) women and men in college? In a review of research, Roberta Hall and Bernice Sandler (1982, 1984) identified factors both within and outside the classroom that do not encourage women to the same extent as men, and that tend to reduce women's aspirations and confidence.

> Despite women's gains in access to higher education . . . they frequently do not enjoy full equality of educational opportunity on campus. Students attest, and research confirms, that women students are often treated differently than men at all educational levels . . . even when they attend the same institutions, share the same classrooms, work with the same advisers, live in the same residence halls and use the same student services. (1984, p. 2)

Inequities in support services, employment, course-related experiences, and the residential, social, and cultural climate for men and women have been documented. Even college financial aid awards illustrate gender inequality. A study by the U.S. Department of Education ("Study Shows," 1984) revealed that for the year 1981–82 women were awarded "72 cents in grant money for every $1 awarded to men," despite the fact that nearly twice as many women were classified as independent of their parents. Although more women than men received Pell Grant aid, their awards averaged $880 compared to $913 for men; under the Work-Study program, the average aid given women averaged $753 compared to $830 for men. The authors of the report noted that 1981–82 was not an unusual year, and that financial aid inequity has always been the case.

Sexual harassment has also been implicated as a factor that contributes to a problematic environment for college women. Arlene McCormack (1985), for example, asked a large sample of college students who were majoring in physical or social sciences in 16 different universities about their experiences of unwelcome sexual behavior by their teachers in high school and college, and obtained reports of such behavior from 17 percent of the women and 2 percent of the men. She found that chances for victimization increased for women as they continued their education, and concluded that "sexual harassment is widespread, not discussed, and appears as an accepted part of the academic environment" (p. 29). Similar data have come from a study at the University of Rhode Island (Reilly, Lott, & Gallogly, in press). Almost one quarter of the junior, senior, and graduate women surveyed reported having personally received sexually suggestive looks or gestures from male instructors outside of the classroom; almost one fifth reported unwanted sexual teasing, jokes, comments, or questions from male teachers; and more than 8 percent reported unwanted deliberate sexual touching. Men students surveyed reported very little personal experience of sexual harassment. The women said they responded to sexual harassment by attempting to handle on their own, or avoid, situations in which it occurred. In essence, then, they were being doubly victimized.

In an introduction to an annotated bibliography on sexual harassment in education, Phyllis Crocker (1982) noted that

> sexual harassment in education is a frighteningly pervasive problem. For a woman, the injury occurs when she is confronted by an educator whose concern is not with her intellectual growth but with the satisfaction of his own sexual needs and a desire for power. (p. 91)

Billie Dzeich and Linda Weiner (1984) have estimated that overall, between 20 and 25 percent of the women attending college in the United States have been sexually harassed in some way (that is, offered unwelcome sexual attention) by their male professors. The incidence of such experiences seems to be similar for undergraduate and graduate students. In a survey of women clinical psychologists (Glaser & Thorpe, 1986), it was found that 22 percent of recent doctoral recipients had had sexual relationships with an educator, and over half of those who reported such a relationship currently saw it as coercive. In addition, sexual advances from teachers or supervisors were reported by 31 percent, most of whom judged these advances as harmful or negative in their effects. These data are similar to those reported in an earlier study (Pope & Levinson, 1979). Sexual harassment is experienced by women of all ages, not only in school, but in social and recreational situations and on the job. Because of its pervasiveness in the world of work we will discuss this issue again in Chapter 13.

Against the background of differential gender treatment and outcomes in higher education, we should note that women now outnumber men on college campuses in the United States at both the undergraduate and graduate levels. In 1980 women accounted for 50.7 percent of the 11.7 million students in postsecondary institutions ("Women Take the Lead," 1980). In 1982 this percentage had risen to 52, and women were "earning more than half of the bachelors and masters degrees and 32 percent of the doctorates" (Vetter & Babco, 1984), compared with 41.5 percent of the bachelors degrees, 39.7 percent of the masters degrees, and 13.3 percent of the doctorates in 1970, a clear indication of change in women's educational aspirations and opportunities.

Another indication of real change in young women's expectations has come from the work of Mirra Komarovsky (1982). She compared a group of college sophomore women she had studied in 1943 with a group from the same college in 1979 (one third of whom were non-Caucasian). Only 5 percent of the 1979 sample, compared to 61 percent of the earlier sample, preferred not to work after marriage; and for 42 percent of the 1979 sample, compared to 12 percent of the 1943 sample, a career was a salient, important goal with or without marriage. Thus, a college education undoubtedly has significant benefits for women with respect to occupation, income, and life-style, despite the accumulated data that indicate that college is more instrumental for men in heightening ambitions and increasing self-confidence. One documented benefit is that college-educated women and men are more likely to share roles in marriage. We will consider such issues again in later chapters.

Variations Among Adolescent Women

So far we have focused on gender differences in the aspirations and attitudes of adolescents, but it is equally important to examine within-gender variations. Some young women, as we can see from research and our own experience, do acquire motives that lead them to pursue options in employment, interests, and life-style that are enriching and wide ranging. We all remember and love spunky Dorothy from The Wizard of Oz (Baum, 1900) who successfully made it down the yellow brick road. Those who are nontraditional in their career choices, in their self-perceptions, and in their general views of what is gender-appropriate, also tend to evaluate their abilities more highly, to have higher expectations for success, and to have higher aspirations than more traditional women. These nontraditional adolescent girls appear to have been encouraged and positively reinforced for their attitudes and choices and to have been

successful in assertive and achievement-oriented behaviors. They may have had parents who provided direct reinforcement, and mothers (or other salient women) who served as models.

A study by Grace Baruch (1976) found that 10th-grade girls who perceived themselves as very competent also had mothers whose self-perceptions of competence were high and who valued ambition, independence, and being a good student. Such girls also had higher career aspirations, and wanted to have fewer children than girls with lesser feelings of competence. Such findings suggest, as the author pointed out, that "girls with higher self-perceptions of their competence have received both support for and modeling of such self-images from their mothers" (p. 46). Similarly, Sydney Altman and Frances Grossman (1977) reported that a group of college senior women who had college-educated mothers working at careers differed from a group whose mothers were homemakers, in being career-oriented and having broader conceptions of gender roles. These researchers were particularly impressed with the fact that "daughters of working mothers were unequivocal in asserting that work had provided a major source of satisfaction for their mothers" (p. 374). But some studies (such as Colangelo, Rosenthal, & Dettman, 1984) have not found significant relationships between the employment status of mothers and the aspirations of their daughters.

That models can influence women's expectations is illustrated by the results of an experiment (Geis, Brown, Jennings [Walstedt], & Porter, 1984) in which some college students were exposed to a set of four TV commercials showing women and men in traditional roles, while others viewed commercials in which traditional gender roles were reversed. Following this experience, in a seemingly unrelated task, the students wrote essays "imagining their lives and concerns 'ten years from now.'" When they analyzed these essays for themes, the researchers found that the women who had seen the reversed-role commercials showed a more even balance between achievement and homemaking interests, and their achievement scores were similar to those of men and significantly higher than those of the women who had watched the traditional commercials. A group of women who had not seen any of the commercials (the control group) wrote essays that emphasized homemaking, like the women who had been exposed to the traditional commercials. So the researchers concluded that "the traditional stimulus commercials were not creating the effect, but simply reflecting a cultural image of women's place in society as secondary in relation to men" (p. 522).

Focusing on different sets of relationships, Rebecca Wiegers and Irene Frieze (1977) reported that high school senior women who chose nontraditional careers differed from traditional girls in having higher expectancies for success, higher perceived scholastic ability, and being more confident about their skill in mathematics. Letitia Peplau (1976) also found that nontraditional college women differed from traditional women in scoring higher on career aspirations, self-ratings of intelligence, and SAT verbal scores. In another study, young women enrolled in nontraditional vocational education programs (for example, in the skilled crafts) were found to differ from comparable women studying for traditional vocations (such as secretarial) in receiving more support from friends and family, working more hours in paid employment, and in having less traditional sex-role orientations (Houser & Garvey, 1985). Similarly, Mirra Komarovsky (1982) found that among a sample of students at an elite private women's college, what distinguished career-oriented women from others was their greater endorsement of gender equality, their lesser belief in gender stereotypes, their greater support of the women's liberation movement, their greater autonomy and self-confidence, and lesser self-satisfaction. The two groups of women in this sample were found not to differ reliably on such variables as mother's or father's education or employment, nor in sexual orientation or high school dating. Thus, beliefs and attitudes seem to distinguish traditional from nontraditional adolescent girls more than background or parental characteristics.

That young women can rise above their circumstances is movingly illustrated in two fine recent novels, Alice Walker's (1982) *The Color Purple* and *Marya* by Joyce Carol Oates (1986). Both books explore a young woman's process of development and show her succeeding in her quest for independence, confidence, and competence. The heroines of both stories are born poor, and one is black, but the process through which they acquire personal strength and transcend their place and situation is applicable to girls of other backgrounds who are attempting to forge their own rites of passage and find identities that best fit their abilities and interests.

CONFLICT AND RESOLUTION

A contemporary adolescent woman inevitably has to deal with a special kind of dilemma toward which all the years of her life in our culture have propelled her.

How she solves the conflict alluded to throughout this chapter is determined by the particular ways she has been socialized, and by the behaviors that her current environment reinforces.

A conflict exists when a person must choose between two (or more) possible objectives that are incompatible and that cannot be attained at the same time. Choosing one means giving up (for the time being, at any rate) the other(s). For a young woman, such a conflict is posed by the simultaneous attractiveness of the goals of independence and public achievement, on the one hand, and attaining the cultural ideal for women, identification with a man and homemaking, on the other. Either can bring rewards, but moving in the direction of one goal may mean giving up the other. This is a classic approach-approach conflict, which can be solved only when one goal becomes more attractive and stronger, or when circumstances propel the individual toward one goal and the positive consequences that follow are sufficient to tip the balance in its favor (albeit, perhaps, only temporarily).

We can analyze the conflict a bit differently by examining the variety of consequences likely to follow from attainment of each of the opposing goals. A girl attracted by independence and personal achievement may anticipate positive consequences such as recognition, financial rewards, fulfillment, and enhanced self-esteem from their attainment, but may also have learned to expect negative social judgment from some who will regard her as less feminine and, therefore, as a less attractive (or more threatening) marriage partner. This is a powerfully punishing consequence for most young women. Rosellen Brown (1976) has shared the thoughts of a fictional young woman, Renata, who recalls her experiences in a high school botany class. "God, I remember how my teacher used to terrify me, my freshman year, by telling me I had talent" (p. 195). Renata associated talent with unattractiveness (her botany teacher was "scrawny" and had "chapped cheeks and . . . short fingernails") or with loneliness (like that of her mother who was a successful but divorced lawyer). She daydreamed about being "the first beautiful botanist" but, convinced that this was impossible, rejected the encouragement of her teacher.

When an individual expects the same objective to bring both positive and negative consequences of relatively equal strength, she confronts an approach-avoidance conflict and experiences ambivalence. In such a situation, she will tend to move back and forth, first approaching and then retreating from the objective. Picture a child at water's edge, on the beach, rushing toward the waves, and then immediately running back. Such a conflict can only be resolved when the anticipated (or actual) positive consequences become stronger than the negative ones (or vice versa). Then the ambivalence diminishes, and the person moves forward in pursuit of the positively valued goal or gives it up entirely because its consequences will be too painful.

An approach-avoidance conflict also confronts the contemporary young woman who opts for the traditional role, who finds the independence/ achievement alternative relatively unattractive and anticipates personal happiness and fulfillment from the role society considers more appropriate for her. She can anticipate approval and love, a home, husband-companion, children, financial security, possessions and perhaps luxuries, leisure (for socializing, for helping with community activities, or for doing creative, artistic work), and the vicarious pleasure to be attained through the successes of her husband and children. But today's adolescent girl can also anticipate negative consequences. She knows that as a homemaker her status, power, and influence will be low; her ability to cope with many situations will be impaired, and she may (like other women she sees around her) one day fall victim to the malaise and discontent of middle-class homemakers or be faced with severe economic hardship if she loses her husband through death or divorce.

What has been described is really a double approach-avoidance conflict, as illustrated in Figure 5.1, the most complex and difficult type of conflict to resolve. Resolution is most difficult for those young women who have become competent in nondomestic areas and who have been encouraged to be independent by their parents or other significant persons, but who have also been strongly influenced by the traditional dominant ideology through peer expectations and media models. The reality of the dilemma is illustrated by data reported by Elizabeth Douvan and Anne Locksley ("Teenaged Boys," 1977), who studied problem behavior among high school youth. They found that, contrary to popular belief, high school was not more stressful for boys than for girls, but that girls tended to express their stress in nonaggressive ways that did not challenge authority and were not "incongruent with femininity." Girls reported more frequent feelings of tension and psychosomatic symptoms than the boys, and indicated that achievement was a major source of conflict. In another study, eighth graders wrote down how they were feeling

Public Achievement versus Homemaking

Anticipated consequences of public achievement	Anticipated consequences of homemaking
Positive	*Positive*
Autonomy	Love/marriage
Excellence	Security
Self-esteem	Vicarious success
Negative	*Negative*
Less chance of marriage	Boredom/discomfort
Less chance of parenthood	Low status/power
Reduced "femininity"	Spouse-derived identity

FIGURE 5.1 The double approach-avoidance conflict faced by many adolescent women

each time a beeper they carried went off (on a preprogrammed random schedule). The researchers (Savin-Williams & Demo, 1983) found significant differences in the feelings reported by boys and girls, with the latter reporting less positive feelings than the former. The boys described themselves as powerful and in control, while the girls saw themselves as tense and unsure. These findings are congruent with others. For example, in a study (LaTorre, Yu, Fortin, & Marrache, 1983) of first-year junior-high school students, girls were found at the end of the year to have increased in measured neuroticism and alienation, while boys' scores decreased. In a more extensive study (Webb & Van Devere, 1985) that obtained self-report data from over 1000 public school students from ages 11 to 18, girls were found to express increasingly greater unhappiness than boys as they proceeded through adolescence. The researchers saw this "acquired phenomenon" as illustrating the girls' "growing awareness of an incongruency between competency and conflicting social expectations," as previously proposed by Locksley and Douvan (p. 94).

When a double approach-avoidance conflict cannot be resolved, the person may turn her back on both alternatives and withdraw, unable or unwilling to make a decision. My daughter Sara has described such a retreat in adolescence (S. Lott, 1978).

Mountain peaks—
> strong and serene,
> guide me toward mellow solitude,
> hold me in their power,

hide me in the land;
far, far, away . . .
Moods and energy
spread themselves out peacefully.
The mountain calm
heals,
    soothes,
        dissolves all worries into
tiny particles
sliding slowly away
into thin cold air.

Withdrawal, in the form of physical or psychological departure (fantasy), effectively removes the person from the conflict situation until circumstances require that it must again be confronted.

The dilemma faced by an adolescent girl may not be as exaggerated and extreme as the one illustrated in Figure 5.1, but its ingredients are real. Some adolescent girls do not experience the conflict at all and approach both objectives with equal commitment, anticipating primarily positive outcomes for both. Others experience no ambivalence during certain times in their lives, and great ambivalence earlier or later. Some young women are able to take advantage of a comfortable, socially sanctioned delay period prior to making long-range decisions—the period of college study or of job experience before marriage. During these years, successes and failures provide learning experiences that influence later choices by reinforcing particular behaviors or altering the relative strengths of the anticipated positive and negative consequences. For some young women, public achievement and the pursuit of homemaking may *not* be incompatible alternatives, and both may be approached without fear of negative consequences.

There is some reason for optimism about the possibilities for resolving the dilemma, both by older women who have reevaluated previous life-styles and acquired new skills, and by younger women now entering or leaving adolescence. For example, contemporary young people of both genders seem to see smart, accomplished, and professional women in nontraditional fields as physically attractive. Hope Lanier and Joan Byrne (1981) asked one group of high school students to select those women who were

engineers, lawyers, doctors, oceanographers, archi-
tects, and executives from a group of 20 photographs.
They asked another group of students to select from
the same photographs those women who, in high
school, had taken mechanical drawing, physics, cal-
culus, chemistry, and political science. They asked a
third group to divide the photographs into two batch-
es, of more attractive and less attractive. Judgments of
attractiveness, and judgments of having taken nontraditional courses and of working in nontraditional
fields were strongly related. These findings suggest
that high-achieving women may no longer be viewed
as unattractive oddities, and hence the choice of public achievement goals may no longer be strongly
associated with the negative consequences of decreased likelihood of marriage and family.

The less an adolescent girl accepts gender stereotypes, the less willing she will be to choose between
the alternatives of doing personally fulfilling work
and having a satisfying family life. Most young
women today say they want both. Perhaps young
women, like the one shown in the photo on page 83,
can combine love with autonomy, connectedness

with independence and adventure. Some young
women are also learning that a family is not only
defined as a heterosexual couple with children but as
any number of persons of the same or different generations who care for one another and try to meet one
another's personal needs. Attempts to raise the consciousness of girls have been successful. One project,
for example (Guttentag & Bray, 1976), consisted of a
6-week program for school children led by teachers
that was designed to explore problems of sexism and
gender stereotypes in the areas of work, family, and
personality. Ninth-grade girls were found to be most
responsive; they showed the greatest change in attitudes, the greatest increase in self-esteem, and, at the
end of the program, no longer said they believed that
personal attractiveness is the major route to success.
And some adolescent girls, like the teenage daughters
of "Kate and Allie" in the popular television series,
are helping their mothers appreciate that, while it is
not easy, a woman's life can include both rewarding
work and close interpersonal bonds with family and
friends.

Menstruation: Power, Curse, or Natural Rhythm?

What would happen . . . if suddenly . . . men could menstruate and women could not?

The answer is clear—menstruation would become an enviable, boast-worthy, masculine event:

Men would brag about how long and how much.

Boys would mark the onset of menses, that longed-for proof of manhood, with religious ritual and stag parties. . . .

Military men, right-wing politicians, and religious fundamentalists would cite menstruation (*"men-struation"*) as proof that only men could serve in the Army ("you have to give blood to take blood"), occupy political office ("can women be aggressive without that steadfast cycle governed by the planet Mars?"), be priests and ministers ("how could a woman give her blood for our sins?"), or rabbis ("without the monthly loss of impurities, women remain unclean").

Gloria Steinem   *(1978b, p. 110)*

C H A P T E R   6

*U*ntil relatively recently women did not talk much about menstruating. Except for occasional reminiscences about the "first time," how it was handled, what was said, the fear or pride it invoked, menstruation has not typically been a subject of much conversation. Yet, for all the years from puberty to menopause, normally functioning human females of all classes, cultures, and geographic areas menstruate approximately every 28 to 30 days. Contemporary women are generally healthier than those of previous generations and reach puberty considerably earlier; we normally menstruate for about four decades (from about age 12 to 52), excluding months of pregnancy. But it is the rare account of a woman's life that describes her as attending to personal needs occasioned by the menstrual flow, and until recently there was little careful scholarship on the subject.

There is now a growing interest in exploring the significance of this uniquely female experience. This new concern can be related to the influence of the feminist movement, the extraordinary publicity generated by PMS (premenstrual syndrome), and the heightened advertising campaigns of manufacturers with a wide array of new menstrual-related products. Four or five decades ago menstrual supplies consisted of a "sanitary belt" (a contraption worn around your waist with two safety pins) to hold a "sanitary napkin"; now advertisers proclaim the virtues of a variety of different tampons, maxi-pads and mini-pads (in scented and unscented varieties), pantyliners, and sea sponges. Relief from menstrual distress was once rather timidly advertised only by Midol; now the market has expanded to include at least a dozen competing brand names. Supplying women with "personal hygiene" products and medications to be used prior to and/or during menstruation is big business in the 1980s.

According to Bonnie Bullough (1974), much of the credit for taking the subject of menstruation out of the closet belongs to modern merchandisers of sanitary pads.

> The belief that menstruating women were unclean, cursed, or jinxed is as old as recorded history. Even those women in the past who were emancipated enough to ignore popular superstitions about menstruation were handicapped in their activities by the physical fact. They made various kinds of diapers and pads for themselves, but one of the reasons they wore so many petticoats was to cut down possible odors and hide the bulges; inevitably they also cut out many physical activities. . . . For this reason the development of the modern disposable, hygienic, and comparatively inexpensive sanitary napkin . . . was an important breakthrough in the emancipation of women. It first appeared on the market in 1920 as a direct result of the development of cellucotton products for surgical dressings during World War I . . . the Kimberly Clark Company hit upon the concept of selling them as sanitary pads under the name of Kotex. To be effectively merchandised the company had to bring the subject out in the open. . . . One of the first effects of the introduction of the pad was the shedding of petticoats by women, and it was no accident that the new age of the emancipated flapper coincided with the introduction of Kotex and its competitors. (p. 345)

Is menstruation no longer a taboo subject, or is it still so overlaid with anxiety and unpleasantness that we prefer not to talk much about it? Do women simply take the facts of our menstrual experience more or less for granted, adapt to its monthly occurrence, and give it little more concern than the periodic rituals of bathing or teeth brushing, or do we anticipate unpleasantness, tension, and irritability? As we shall see, menstruation denotes a set of relatively clear physiological changes, but it connotes much more and is associated with a number of acquired beliefs and attitudes.

MENARCHE

Many of us associate the first menses with the beginning of female puberty, but menarche is merely the most obvious signal and "actually occurs relatively late in a process that takes about four years if the focus is on observable changes, longer if the focus is on hormonal changes" (Petersen, 1983, p. 65). The observable changes of puberty occur between the ages of 9 and 16, and include an increase in body hair, weight gain, growth spurt, increased activity of sweat glands, growth of uterus and vagina, and changes in body proportions. Breast buds, usually the first sign of puberty, begin forming at about 11 years of age, influenced by secretion of estrogen from the ovaries and prolactin from the pituitary (Golub, 1983).

Menarche typically occurs after the first stages of pubic hair and breast development, and after the peak spurt in height. It indicates that the female's reproductive system is being readied to expel mature egg cells (ova) from the ovaries on a periodic basis. These ova have been contained within the ovaries since before birth. According to Paula Weideger (1976), the average girl at puberty has about 75,000 ova available. At puberty the ovaries begin their heightened manufacture of estrogen, thus changing the ratio of female-to-male hormones from the relative equality of childhood. For the average girl, estrogen production begins to increase at about age 11 and begins to take cyclical form about 18 months prior to menarche. Accompanying these hormonal changes are a growth spurt and the familiar secondary sex characteristics associated with femaleness, beginning with breast development.

Some new research (in Kolata, 1984a) has suggested that the onset of puberty in both sexes may be related to a decrease in nocturnal secretions of the hormone melatonin from the pineal gland, a small structure near the center of the brain. But the precise role of the gland or of melatonin has not yet been established, and the evidence relating them to puberty cannot be interpreted as showing that they cause it. No definitive answer to the question of what specifically initiates the menarche can yet be given. One hypothesis, proposed by Rose Frisch (in Weideger, 1976; and Golub, 1983) is that the triggering mechanism is a critical weight (somewhere between 94 and 103 pounds) and a critical ratio of fat-to-lean body tissue (about 22 to 24 percent fat). During puberty, up to the time of menarche, body fat increases 120 percent. By the time regular ovulation has been established, which is typically one or two years after menstruation has begun, 28 percent of the composition of a girl's body consists of fat tissue. Somehow this fat-to-lean tissue ratio signals the hypothalamus to begin, and then to maintain, the regular menstrual cycle. This hypothesis is strengthened by the fact that estrogen is synthesized from the cholesterol component of body fat.

The average age of menarche has been steadily declining for American girls; it is now 12.3 years, with a range from 9 to 17 (Bullough, 1983), and one third of all girls now reach menarche at or before age 11. Good nutrition is reliably associated with physical and sexual maturity, and improved diet, hygiene, and health are likely responsible for the steady lowering of the age at which girls reach menarche. For example, a recent study by Goodman et al., cited by Sharon Golub (1983), found no difference in age at menarche among women of Caucasian, Chinese, and Japanese ancestry living in Hawaii, supporting the role played by nutritional factors. In terms of Frisch's hypothesis, it is the age at which critical weight is reached that appears to have been changing.

THE SIGNIFICANCE OF MENSTRUATION

In most known cultures and historical periods the onset of menstruation has signified to girls, their parents, and the community that the female child is now reproductively mature. Menstruation affirms biological femaleness and the possibility of childbearing, and in all cultures menstruating persons are distinguished from others. Thus, the fact of menstruation is significant not only to the individual but also to the culture. And we know that the meaning a culture assigns to menstruation, and the attitudes engendered, are closely related to the way individual women experience it.

Cultural Meanings

Since menstruation signifies adult sexuality and reproductive capacity, we might suppose that this indication of female maturity would be culturally interpreted as a symbol of positive power. What we more typically find is the imposition of greater restrictions on girls' freedom of movement, and the belief that menstruation is unclean and women's power is evil. Even within matrilineal societies such as the Crow, where, according to Sherry Ortner (1974), women have acknowledged power and rights and function in high positions, the fact of menstruation is used to exclude them from important areas of community life. "Ultimately the line is drawn; menstruation is a threat to warfare, one of the most valued institutions of the tribe, one that is central to their self-definition" (p. 70).

M. Esther Harding (1972) has suggested that from earlier times women have been connected with the moon and its cycles. Woman's power to bear children "was thought to be the gift of the moon" and "her monthly rhythm, corresponding as it does with the moon's cycle, must have seemed the obvious result of some mysterious bond between them" (p. 25). Some cultures have identified the moon as female and in others the words for menstruation and for moon are either the same or are closely related.

Perhaps it is because of this connection that women's blood has been seen as having powerful effects, as illustrated by negative myths and taboos. For example, Lois Paul (1974) described a girl's introduction to womanhood at the age of 13 or 14 in a Guatemalan village as follows:

> When a girl suddenly finds herself bleeding and comes crying to her mother, she is given an old rag as protection and told to expect such bleeding each month. . . . No further explanation is given her . . . except for the warning never to divulge the secret of her bleeding to any male and never to let any male see her bloody rag, or catch her washing it. Because a girl's blood is "hot" when she is menstruating, she is told not to look directly at infants, turkey chicks, or sprouting beans lest these sicken and die. (p. 291)

A group of 50-year-old women in a small mining village in Australia told one researcher (Skultans, 1979) that each month during menstruation they purged themselves of "bad blood." If they had a "good clearance," this would enable them to better perform their wifely duties, and contribute to their overall good health.

Cultural prohibitions associated with menstruation have included those against cooking food for men, sexual intercourse, religious participation, contact with men preparing for battle or a hunt, or even being in the same room with a man. The early Roman writer Pliny warned his readers that menstrual blood would turn new wine sour, dry up seeds in gardens, and kill hives of bees; "to taste it drives dogs mad and infects their bites with an incurable poison" (Delaney, Lupton, & Toth, 1977, p. 7). The superstitious belief that bad luck follows from walking under a ladder might be derived, some have suggested, from the fear of ancient men that in passing under bridges

or trees the blood of a menstruating woman might fall on their heads (Harding, 1972). As Delaney, Lupton, and Toth (1977) have reported:

> In many primitive societies, the menstruating woman was excluded from the most ordinary life of her tribe for four or five days every month. Unable to plant, harvest, cook, associate with her husband, or wander freely around the village, the woman went instead to the menstrual hut, a cramped dwelling of leaves and bark, set at some distance from the village. There a menstruating woman might, depending upon her culture, be required to undergo purifying practices or simply enjoy the solitude. (pp. 7f.)

Some anthropologists have related such taboos and restrictions to men's envy and fear of women (who bring forth life), pointing out that men's sense of inferiority is evidenced in initiation rites of puberty during which men mimic or pretend to be women. While men's envy of women may be a factor in the maintenance of the menstrual taboos, women have also derived positive benefits from the prohibitions and therefore have taken part in enforcing them, as suggested by other scholars. The taboos serve to emphasize women's temporary control over men. For example, Michelle Rosaldo (1974) has noted that "many a New Guinea man will observe his wife's wishes for fear that an angry woman will serve him food while she is menstruating, or step over him, letting blood drip, while he sleeps" (p. 38). From her husband's fear a wife derives power. Menstruation has also provided women with a good reason to separate themselves from men "in societies where otherwise they may be practically slaves and are always liable to sexual demands" (Harding, 1972, p. 61).

Marla Powers (1980) has argued that Western anthropologists tend to interpret menstrual customs of other cultures in ways that reflect their own negative attitudes, and she has provided examples of native American peoples among whom the seclusion of women during menstruation should not be taken as evidence that menstruation is viewed as defilement.

> Among the Indians of California a girl at her first menstruation was thought to possess supernatural power. The onset of menstruation is regarded by the Navajo as a time for rejoicing, and the young woman becomes a tribal symbol of fecundity. . . . Among the Papago a menstruating woman is the vessel of supernatural power . . . that allows her to give birth. (pp. 56f.)

In such cultures, Powers has suggested, the separation of menstruating women from others in the community represents purification, not fear or hostility.

Powers has described the puberty rite for Oglala girls (of South Dakota) at first menses as one that initiates them into adulthood as sacred buffalo women. The shaman performs a public ceremony to "secure for the initiate the virtues most desired in an Oglala woman—chastity, fecundity, industry, and hospitality" (p. 58), and a feast is held in honor of the girl's new status. At the end of the ceremony, however, the girl's "menstrual bundle," which has been lodged in a tree, is passed from the girl's mother to the shaman to her father, "indicating that the marginal (dangerous) period has passed . . . and men need not fear contamination" (p. 61). At each menses women are secluded in special lodges and may not cook for their husbands. Among the Oglala, then, as in other cultures, menstruation may indicate a woman's power, but also her potential danger to men.

The existence of euphemisms for menstruation in our own contemporary culture attests to the ambivalence we feel about it. Virginia Ernster (1975) collected euphemisms for menstruation over a period of 10 years in the 1960s and 1970s from adolescents and adults of both genders. The terms used by women and men were found to differ in nature and also in number, with women reporting a much wider variety of expressions. Negative references (such as "the curse," "the misery," "unwell," "under the weather," "weeping womb," "bride's barf," and "tiger stepping on my toes") constituted the largest category of expressions contributed by women, followed in number by references to a visitor ("Aunt Sylvia," "Aunt Susie," "Aunt Tillie," "Granny," "Mary Lou," or simply "My Friend"). Women also reported expressions that refer to the materials used during menstruation ("riding the white horse" or "cotton pony," "mouse mattresses," "saddle blankets," or "teddy bears"). Among men the most common menstrual euphemisms were variations of "on the rag" or "flying the flag." Other researchers have listed expressions that highlight redness and blood.

> The French speak of periods as "cardinals" and "tomatoes" and of the menstruating female as . . . "the strawberry woman." Italian women may travel "the red road." . . . Polish women have "leakage" or "flow." American women may visit "my redheaded aunt from Red Bank"; may have a "red letter day," may say "I'm Bloody Mary today," or the "Red Sea's out." (Delaney, Lupton, & Toth, 1977, p. 93)

Individual Feelings and Beliefs

The importance of the menarche to women is highlighted by the finding of one study (Golub & Catalano, as reported by Golub, 1983) that a majority of a sample of women ranging in age from 13 to 45 remembered their first menstruation, and "could describe in detail where they were when it happened, what they were doing, and whom they told" (pp. 17f.). Menstruation clearly divides the sexes after childhood and leads to heightened awareness of sexual differences and identity. For contemporary women this seems no less true than it has been in the past. For example, postmenarcheal girls were found in one study (Rierdan, Koff, & Silverstone, 1978) to differ significantly from premenarcheal girls in their drawings of human figures. Comparing different girls, and the same girls at different ages, the researchers found that those who had begun to menstruate drew more sexually differentiated figures and more frequently drew a female figure before a male figure.

In our society the onset of menstruation reinforces a girl's sexual identity and also increases the socialization pressures associated with gender. It often signals to parents that the time has come to curtail and restrain their daughters and to keep a sharper eye on their activities. That menstruation is a time of greater restrictions is illustrated by the advice given in films and pamphlets written to instruct menstruating girls on how to care for themselves. A teenage girl 30 years ago might have sent a prepaid printed postcard to Personal Products Corporation (1957) that read, "Please send me, in plain wrapper, a FREE copy of 'Growing Up and Liking It.'" In this 28-page booklet she would have read that she should laugh off some "old wives' tales" like don't have a tooth filled while you're menstruating, loss of menstrual blood weakens you, spend a day or two in bed, and cold drinks give you cramps. She would also have been alerted to look for a "few little signals" just before menstruation, such as experiencing the "blues," a lack of pep, a backache, or cramps. She would have been advised to stay out of drafts, not to get a chill, and to dance with moderation. Current advice to menstruating girls in pamphlets and educational films differs from the older prescriptions and taboos in recommending lots of fresh air and exercise, but a parallel message seems to be to deodorize and sanitize (Delaney, Lupton, & Toth, 1977). This kind of contemporary advice is satirized in the Nicole Hollander cartoon on p. 90 and can be illustrated by an advertisement in *Seventeen* (FDS, 1984) that informs its teenage readers that a woman's body chemistry doesn't just change during menstruation, but every day, so that she needs a feminine deodorant spray to neutralize and absorb "embarrassing odors."

Another great idea from Sylvia   (From Mercy, It's the Revolution and I'm in My Bathrobe, *by Nicole Hollander, St. Martin's Press, Inc. Copyright © 1982 by Nicole Hollander.)*

How do today's women feel about menstruation? Pat Barker, in her recent *Union Street* (1983), has described the reaction of a fictional girl, Kelly, to the discovery of her sister's used sanitary napkins: she decided that "she certainly didn't want to drip foul-smelling, brown blood out of her fanny every month" (p. 3). The response of Kelly, while extreme, does not differ completely from those reported from a sample of seventh- and eighth-grade middle-class girls in Boston by Elissa Koff and Jill Rierdan (in Rubenstein, 1980). Postmenarcheal girls described the first menses of a hypothetical girl as a time when "she wanted to cry, die, or throw up." These girls "seemed especially self-conscious about concealing their condition, and intensely apprehensive about being discovered or being messy or unclean" (p. 38). Similarly, Jeanne Brooks-Gunn and Diane Ruble (in Golub, 1983) found mostly negative beliefs about menstruation among seventh and eighth graders of both genders: "Most believed that menstruation is accompanied by physical discomfort, increased emotionality, and a disruption of activities" (p. 27). Lenore Williams (1983) has reported that 68 percent of a sample of 9- to 12-year-old girls of varied socioeconomic status believed menstruation to be related to increased emotionality. Other researchers (Woods, Dery, & Most, 1983) asked adult women to recall how they had felt about their first menstruation. Their recollections revealed ambivalence; most had felt happy (58 percent) and proud (65 percent) but also upset (67 percent) and scared (74 percent), with the most frequently reported feeling being embarrassment (82 percent).

Beliefs about the direct effect of the menstrual cycle on moods are widespread in our society. Later in this chapter we will look at evidence that menstrual "blues" may be more influenced by their anticipation and by other social and psychological factors than by cyclical physiological changes. But regardless of the evidence, negative attitudes as well as erroneous beliefs persist. A national survey of over 1000 persons 14 years of age and older conducted by Tampax in 1981 (Milow, 1983) found that two thirds of the respondents believed menstruation was not a suitable subject for discussion socially or at work; two fifths of the women recalled having a negative reaction to their first menses; one third believed that menstruation affects a woman's ability to think; and more than one fourth thought that women cannot function normally at work while menstruating. Men's and women's beliefs were found to be generally similar.

PHYSIOLOGY OF THE MENSTRUAL CYCLE

Some of the sequence of physiological changes that occur in a periodic rhythm during a normal female's menstrual cycle have been well established; others are assumed. In general, we can trace the following chain of events. At the beginning of one cycle (and the end of the previous one) the hypothalamus (the major brain center for autonomic functions), in response to a low level of estrogen, stimulates the anterior lobe of the pituitary gland to release the follicle stimulating hormone (FSH). This hormone causes several egg-containing follicles in one of the two ovaries to ripen and develop, and also stimulates estrogen manufacture by the follicles. As the estrogen

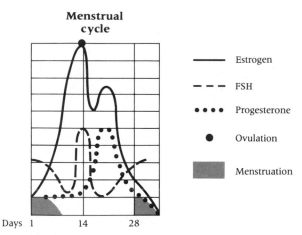

Menstrual cycle

——— Estrogen

– – – FSH

•••• Progesterone

• Ovulation

▨ Menstruation

Days 1 14 28

FIGURE 6.1 Changes in hormonal levels during the menstrual cycle

level in the bloodstream rises, this signals the anterior pituitary to decrease its production of FSH and to release luteinizing hormone (LH). During this part of the menstrual cycle, referred to as the follicular phase, important roles are played by secretions of FSH and LH in preparing an ovum, and by estrogen in thickening the uterine lining (endometrium).

During the next, ovulatory, phase, estrogen rises, and FSH first declines and then peaks along with LH. It is LH that suppresses the growth of all but one of the follicles, which then ripens and ruptures, releasing an ovum. This is known as ovulation, and occurs on the 14th day of the typical 28-day cycle. Hairlike cells of the fallopian tube sweep the egg into the oviduct, and the empty follicle is converted into the corpus luteum, secreting estrogen and progesterone, which the ripe follicle may have been secreting two to three days before ovulation. During this luteal phase, progesterone helps to prepare the uterine wall for the ovum if it becomes fertilized. When the amount of progesterone reaches a critical level, LH production is inhibited. Without implantation of a fertilized egg, the corpus luteum decays, and the manufacture of progesterone and estrogen decreases. The withdrawal of these two hormones cuts off the blood supply to the upper layer of endometrial cells; these are then shed along with blood from the broken blood vessels as the menstrual flow.

After the first one or two days of menstruation, the hypothalamus again responds to the relative absence of estrogen and the cycle begins again. Had an ovum been fertilized, the corpus luteum would have continued to function, producing progesterone and sustaining fetal development until the placenta, also a

progesterone manufacturer, was formed. Figure 6.1 shows changes in the levels of estrogen, FSH, and progesterone during various phases of the menstrual cycle and Figure 6.2 diagrams the interrelationships among the nervous, hormonal, and reproductive systems.

Accompanying the changes in hormonal levels during the menstrual cycle are other physiological changes such as in the fragility of capillaries. Progesterone, which affects the metabolism of salt and water, causes water retention and consequent temporary weight gain. Estrogen levels affect the quantity of vaginal and skin lubricants, sensitivity to odors, and have been shown to affect the sodium/potassium ratio, which is lowest during ovulation and highest during menstruation (DeMarchi, 1976). Sensitivity to pain probably peaks during ovulation (Goolkasian, 1985). Both vision and smell appear to be more acute around ovulation, and hearing seems to peak around ovulation and again at the onset of menstruation (Parlee, 1983).

Hormones other than those just discussed function in reproduction and sexuality, such as steroids from the adrenal cortex and prolactin from the pituitary. These and all of the other hormones produced by glands in female bodies are also produced in males and are qualitatively identical in both sexes. Joan Hoffman (1982) has pointed out that "the pituitary hormones involved in reproduction are exactly the same in males and females" (p. 835). That testosterone, produced in females, also fluctuates during the menstrual cycle is now recognized, but little attention has been paid, thus far, to the role played by this "male" hormone in female physiology. According to Anne Briscoe (1978):

> The hormones produced by the ovary and the testis, as well as by the adrenal cortex, belong to a class of chemical compounds called steroids [which are molecularly similar to one another] . . .
>
> The capacity of the adrenal cortex to produce hormones which are chemically similar to those of the gonads is explained by [their] common embryonic origin . . . The primitive adrenal cortex develops in the embryo adjacent to the site of development of the gonads. (p. 35f)
>
> Studies of the biosynthesis or manufacture of these sex steroids show that androgens and estrogens are interconvertible in the body and that all are present in both sexes in different amounts (p. 41).

Recent investigations have established that [progesterone] . . . is produced in the adrenal cortex and placenta as well as the corpus luteum, and possibly the testis. Males have circulating progesterone in amounts not unlike those of the preovulatory stage of the menstrual cycle in females. . . . Its presence is certain if its role is not. (p. 43)

Recall from Chapter 2 that administration of progestin (a synthetic progesterone compound) to pregnant women to prevent spontaneous abortions has sometimes produced androgenizing effects on their female embryos, clearly attesting to the chemical similarity of the sex hormones.

Not only are male and female hormones similar, but recent studies have suggested that sex hormone secretion in men is also rhythmic and cyclical as evidenced by measurable changes in testosterone concentration in the blood. The data thus far suggest a diurnal rhythm in men rather than a longer cycle but, as Joan Hoffman (1982) has pointed out, without an "external marker" in males, like the menstrual flow, "it is hard to know where to start and to stop looking for cycles" (p. 837). From a physiological perspective, according to Hoffman, the hormonal changes which characterize the menstrual cycle are modest in size and the fluctuations over 28 days are

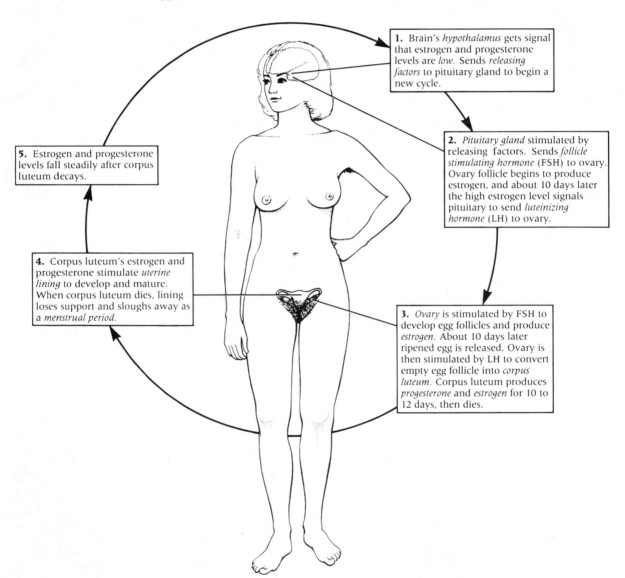

1. Brain's *hypothalamus* gets signal that estrogen and progesterone levels are *low*. Sends *releasing factors* to pituitary gland to begin a new cycle.

2. *Pituitary gland* stimulated by releasing factors. Sends *follicle stimulating hormone* (FSH) to ovary. Ovary follicle begins to produce estrogen, and about 10 days later the high estrogen level signals pituitary to send *luteinizing hormone* (LH) to ovary.

5. Estrogen and progesterone levels fall steadily after corpus luteum decays.

4. Corpus luteum's estrogen and progesterone stimulate *uterine lining* to develop and mature. When corpus luteum dies, lining loses support and sloughs away as a *menstrual period*.

3. *Ovary* is stimulated by FSH to develop egg follicles and produce *estrogen*. About 10 days later ripened egg is released. Ovary is then stimulated by LH to convert empty egg follicle into *corpus luteum*. Corpus luteum produces *progesterone* and *estrogen* for 10 to 12 days, then dies.

FIGURE 6.2   Menstrual cycle feedback system

"really not much more extreme than the diurnal [daily] changes in prolactin levels in both males and females" (p. 839).

Menstruation, like all other human physiological processes, occurs in a social, psychological, and physical context that influences it and can produce a variety of modifications. We have already noted the role of nutrition in lowering the age of menarche. Nutrition has also been implicated in delaying and in stopping menstruation (amenorrhea). Women who are undernourished as a result of famine, war, poverty, or excessive dieting often do not have menstrual periods. Menstruation is also influenced by exercise. According to Sharon Golub (1983), "Women who experience high outputs, such as ballet dancers and athletes who train intensively, have a later age at menarche and a high incidence of amenorrhea" (p. 24), and such "exercise-related alterations in reproductive function are not serious and are readily reversible" (p. 25). Anxiety or stress may also delay onset of menstruation, and women who live together tend to experience a synchronicity in their cycles.

CORRELATES OF THE MENSTRUAL CYCLE

The fact that the levels of various hormones regularly ebb and flow during the menstrual cycle is well established, but the extent to which hormonal changes are related to, and responsible for, predictable changes in mood, feelings, and behavior remains a matter of controversy. Considerable disagreement exists over whether premenstrual tension (sensitivity, anxiety, irritability, depression, and low self-esteem) is a direct consequence of physiological processes, or whether it is a learned interpretation of an altered body state and related to other conditions, beliefs, or circumstances. In this section we will examine the evidence having to do with how the menstrual cycle relates to moods and behavior. We will also consider the validity of grouping a whole range of diverse symptoms under the recently popularized name of premenstrual syndrome (PMS), and we will look at the physical complaint of dysmenorrhea.

Are Moods Related to Hormones?

Peter Farb (1978) has written with apparent confidence that for women throughout history and across cultures,

fluctuations in hormone levels during each cycle must inevitably produce emotional changes. And indeed, predictable monthly swings take place in the personality of the female that correlate closely with her menstrual cycle. The intensity of these swings . . . may be affected by cultural attitudes toward menstruation and also by the individual's own temperament and predispositions. [But, nonetheless,] . . . emotional changes during the female's monthly cycle are an objective fact related to changing hormone levels. (p. 205)

But Farb himself contradicts this generalization by pointing out elsewhere that in some cultures the emotional changes "are not very marked," and that the "majority of North American and European females, who experience premenstrual tension, apparently [do so] because it is expected of them" (p. 207), while Arapesh women of New Guinea, for example, treat menstruation as "a negligible inconvenience." If mood changes are not universally experienced then they cannot also be said to be inevitable biological facts, unless one assumes that biological femaleness in North America and Europe differs from biological femaleness in Africa, Asia, and South America.

Those who propose a hormone-mood relationship suggest that women experience tension during the premenstruum (variously defined as 2 to 7 days before menstruation) because the levels of estrogen and progesterone are rapidly declining. This period has been related not only to "feeling blue" (anxious and depressed) but also to rates of suicide, crime, psychiatric admissions to hospitals, accidents, and death. Conversely, the high estrogen period that occurs at ovulation has been associated with elevated levels of self-esteem, and feelings of well-being and competence. Psychoanalytic theory has encouraged women to believe that menstruation brings sadness because it signifies that we will not be bearing a child (through which we are said to achieve ultimate fulfillment!), and that we will remain "empty." Some of my students have reported being told as teenagers that menstruation is a "weeping of the womb" over the lost possibility of a child.

Does research support the view that women's moods fluctuate with the menstrual cycle? And what is the quality of that research? The first important, critical, and careful evaluation of the evidence relating to mood and behavior correlates of the menstrual cycle was undertaken by Mary Parlee (1973). She concluded that the available data were not rigorous or general enough to support a connection between any particular phase of the menstrual cycle and any specific way of feeling. Among the problems Parlee identified was that much of the research had used a single measure of mood, known as the Menstrual Distress Questionnaire (note its title!), which asked women to recollect how they had felt just before, during, and after their most recent menstruation. Information like this tells us only what women say in retrospect in response to questions about menstruation, which may well be influenced by shared beliefs and attitudes. Parlee also concluded that while statements implying "a direct causal relationship between physiological processes and complex psychological experiences and behaviors are abundant in the literature" (p. 461), no research has specified the mechanisms that link these processes. Others who have reviewed the literature have reinforced Parlee's conclusions. Randi Koeske (1983), for example, has questioned the concepts and methods that are taken for granted in menstrual cycle research, and has called for an approach that recognizes the complexity of interacting factors in menstruation and health. Similarly, Anne Fausto-Sterling (1985) has characterized this research as filled with inadequate sample sizes and measures, poor statistics, and badly designed studies. She asserts, "That so many scientists have been able for so long to do such poor research attests to both the unconscious social agendas of many of the researchers and to the theoretical inadequacy of the research framework used" (p. 101).

Research that has tried to overcome some of the earlier methodological problems has not found support for a direct relationship between mood and hormonal change. The new evidence suggests, instead, that anticipating menstruation causes women to respond both psychologically and physically in ways that are learned. One such study by Janet Swandby (1979) found that the same woman will give different self-reports of her daily moods in the context of a general body awareness study and in the context of a study of how she feels during different phases of her menstrual cycle. For 35 consecutive days, a small sample of women who used oral contraceptives and women who did not, as well as a sample of men, filled out a mood adjective checklist. These daily assessments showed no reliable relationship between mood and objectively determined phases of the menstrual cycle. There were large individual differences among the participants in mood patterns and, in general, the moods of the women who were not using the Pill did not differ from those of the women who were, or from those of the men. When these same persons, however, were asked to report on how they typically felt on menstrual, premenstrual, and intermenstrual days (or, if men, how their female sexual partners felt), responses conformed to stereotyped expectations, with negative feelings and physical complaints reported for the premenstrual-menstrual phases of the cycle. The men, moreover, more frequently reported negative moods for their sexual partners at the premenstrual-menstrual phases than did the women who gave self-reports.

Sharon Golub and Denise Harrington (1981) found a similar lack of agreement between responses to the standard Menstrual Distress Questionnaire and other measures of feelings administered to a sample of 10th- and 11th-grade girls during different phases of their menstrual cycles (but not in the context of menstrual-related questions). Anxiety and depression scores were not significantly higher among girls tested during premenstrual or menstrual days than among those tested during intermenstrual days (from the end of the menstrual flow to about four days prior to the next one). Nevertheless, when answering retrospective questions the same adolescent girls reported more negative feelings during premenstrual and menstrual days than intermenstrual days. Using a similar method, Mary Parlee (1982) had a small group of adult women (who were not taking oral contraceptives) report on their mood and activity levels daily for 90 days. No mention was made of menstruation except that menstrual dates were routinely reported on a biweekly health inventory. No woman was found to exhibit significant fluctuations, but as a group the women were found to show significantly greater activity levels and significantly lower tension and anxiety on weekends than on weekdays (unrelated to the menstrual cycle!) and, contrary to expectation, negative feelings were found to be less, and general activity level greater, on premenstrual and menstrual than intermenstrual days. Similarly, a 1976 study by Wilcoxon, Schrader, and Sherif (in Friedman, Hurt, Arnoff, & Clarkin, 1980) found that individual differences in negative feelings in a sample of women were due more to "the presence of stressful external events than to the specific timing of the menstrual-cycle phase" (p. 722).

Another set of studies has focused on the differences between women who often report premenstrual symptoms of negative mood and physical discomfort such as headaches or backaches and those who seldom do. Since the pattern of hormonal changes associated with the menstrual cycle is the same in all normal women who menstruate, what explains the variation in psychological and physical correlates? Do those who report going from elevated highs to bluesy lows differ on certain social or personality dimensions from women who do not report such mood swings? This question was raised by Karen Paige (1973) who, in several studies, found evidence that a woman's attitudes toward menstruation relate to other attitudes and behaviors. For example, "women who have physical discomfort and psychological stress during menstruation tend to report such symptoms in other situations as well"; they report higher psychological stress generally, greater use of medication, more aches, pains, and illnesses. Other studies have found that retrospective reports of menstrual distress are positively related to general health complaints (Carrie, 1981) as well as general anxiety (Good & Smith, 1980). Karen Matthews and Joseph Carra (1982) found that in a sample of college women, reports of menstrual distress were positively related to measures of self-consciousness and social anxiety, and that less intense menstrual distress was reported by highly achievement-oriented women.

Variations among women in their reports of negative menstrual symptoms have also been studied by Edna Menke (1983). In a sample of 30 pairs of mothers and teenage daughters, she found no significant differences between mothers and daughters in reported attitudes toward menstruation and levels of menstrual distress, suggesting that learning plays an important part in reactions to menstruation. This proposition is dramatically supported by data from a study (Ruble, 1977) in which a sample of college women were led to believe that they were closer to the beginning of menses than was actually the case. Those who had been told they were premenstrual reported significantly more pain, water retention, and change in eating habits than another group who were told they were intermenstrual, despite no differences between them in objectively measured cycle phase.

To review, then, the available evidence supports the conclusion reached by Friedman, Hurt, Arnoff, and Clarkin (1980) that mood change during the menstrual cycle "appears to be related . . . to a woman's current psychosocial experience and more enduring features of her psychological makeup such as attitudes about menstruation and personality factors" (Friedman, Hurt, Arnoff, & Clarkin, 1980, p. 726). The evidence also suggests that reported mood is unlikely to vary with menstrual phase if women are asked about their feelings in a context not related to menstruation. Additional conclusions must await research that includes studies of women in whom estrogen and progesterone vary minimally: those

with both ovaries surgically removed; pregnant women (estrogen and progesterone levels remain high until childbirth); and post-menopausal women. It would be useful to routinely include such women, as control or comparison groups, in further studies of mood correlates of the menstrual cycle.

While earlier research has focused on the roles of expectations, attitudes, and learned responses in women's experience of the menstrual cycle, newer research has focused on the role of interpretations and attributions. Simply put, the former research tested the hypothesis that a woman feels badly when she expects her period, while the latter proposes that when she feels badly, she attributes it to her period. A number of now classic studies (for example, Schachter & Singer, 1962; Storms & Nisbett, 1970) demonstrated that persons learn to attribute meaning to altered body states—such as those caused by a sharp increase or decrease in hormones—and the name we give to what we are feeling is strongly influenced by the social context or situation we are in at the time. Victor Harris and Edward Katkin (1975) concluded from a review of this literature that "cognitive evaluation of autonomic input" is of great importance in emotional experience.

Women may well learn not only to interpret hormonal fluctuations in certain ways but also to use the fact of their occurrence to explain feelings of irritability or anxiety that may stem from frustrations, disappointments, unsolved problems, or unresolved conflicts. It may be more acceptable (to oneself or to others) to attribute negative feelings to menstrual fluctuations than to admit serious problems with personal relationships or with one's work. If "the blues" are due to "that time of the month" then they will go away (until next month). This, of course, may leave long-lasting social or psychological problems unattended. Inaccurately attributing feelings of anxiety to hormonal changes may thus have serious consequences and prevent or delay the solution of significant problems. As an example of this, Judith Rodin (1976) had a sample of midcycle and a sample of premenstrual women work on a laboratory task. For some participants the task aroused little anxiety, while for others strong anxiety was aroused with threats of shock and testing. Rodin found that menstruating women who attributed their anxiety to their menstruation (and not to the task) performed the task more effectively than equally anxious nonmenstruating women and about as well as women in low-anxiety conditions. In other words, if women associate negative feelings with menstruation they may not accurately identify other sources of these feelings.

Some studies have found that other people often attribute a woman's negative/irritable mood to her being premenstrual. For example, Randi Koeske and Gary Koeske (1975) had a large sample of college students read excerpts from an interview with a woman. When she was presented as in a bad mood and also premenstrual, the students attributed her mood more often to her menstrual phase than to other possible sources such as unpleasant or dis- appointing news. In other words, these respondents discounted situational factors in favor of a biological explanation reflecting their assumptions about the link between negative moods and premenstruation. In a similar study (Ruble, Boggiano, & Brooks-Gunn, 1982), a sample of college students indicated their degree of annoyance with the various excuses a woman might use to explain her irritability. Men were found to be less annoyed when a woman gave a menstrual excuse than when she gave an ordinary pain excuse or a frustration excuse. The women re- spondents did not feel this way, and "did not feel it was justifiable to act in an antisocial way because of menstrual excuses" (p. 635). The investigators also found a significant relationship between reactions to menstrual excuses for irritability and general atti- tudes toward menstruation. Those who believed that menstruation is psychologically and physically de- bilitating were significantly less annoyed at an irri- table premenstrual or menstruating woman and were significantly less likely to blame her for being irri- table. Men were more likely than women to perceive menstruation as debilitating and to feel that "women are more tired, emotional, do not perform as well intellectually, and should have lower expectations for themselves during menstruation" (p. 633).

These data suggest, as the investigators noted, that women may respond to such beliefs on the part of men by using menstrual-related excuses to justify undesirable behavior or to get away with not doing certain things. A newspaper columnist (Patinkin, 1983) turned this around in a clever piece about men. He explained why men drop laundry on the floor, refuse to ask for directions when lost, are insensitive, and don't listen during conversations. It's all due to male hormones, he argues.

> Women's hormones make them hysterical. Ours make us stoic sorts who suppress anger, fear commitment and drink whiskey, instead of having a good cry. . . . Next time I'm told that I'm insensitive, don't listen well, drop

socks on the floor and am a lazy bum for refusing to do the dishes, I now have an answer. Don't blame me, I can't help it. It's my hormones. (p. A-3)

Behavioral Correlates

The complex relationship between hormones and mood illustrates well that we are psychosomatic or biosocial organisms with psychological and somatic processes in continuous interaction. This general proposition is further supported by critical analysis of the data bearing on a relationship between the men- strual cycle and behavior. Knowing what we do about the effects of the environment on our physio- logical functioning (for instance, as noted earlier, the menses can be delayed by weight loss or stress) may lead us to question the usual interpretation of find- ings that show a higher incidence of various antiso- cial behaviors—"crimes, accidents, suicide attempts, psychiatric crises" (Sommer, 1983, p. 531)—during the premenstruum. While such correlations with pre- menstruation have been seen as showing that hor- monal fluctuations somehow cause the behavior, it is just as "possible that the antisocial behaviors and concomitant events produce hormonal changes, rather than vice versa" (Horney, 1979, p. 31). Trauma has been found to shorten cycles, to cause dysfunctional bleeding, and to induce menstruation. Thus, that a suicide attempt or psychiatric crisis can stimulate menstruation is as likely as that onset of menstruation triggers such behavior. Horney has pointed out, for example, that women who have been in automobile accidents as passengers and are not responsible for the accident tend to menstruate shortly thereafter. Does it make sense to attribute their status as accident victims to premenstrual tension?

Regarding the generally assumed relationship be- tween menstrual cycle and women's cognitive abili- ties and task performance, studies "generally fail to demonstrate menstrual-cycle-related changes" (Friedman, Hurt, Arnoff, & Clarkin, 1980, p. 726). Employment records continue to show that men ex- ceed women in monthly absences from work due to illness, and, according to P. S. Wood (1980), "world and Olympic records have been set by women in all stages of their menstrual cycles" (p. 38). One study (Zimmerman & Parlee, 1973) found no significant relationships between menstrual cycle phases and a variety of discrete performance measures (for in- stance, reaction time, time estimation, and digit sub- stitution); only arm-hand steadiness was shown to vary, decreasing during the premenstrual days. A study of over 1000 women Air Force pilots during World War II found no relationship between menstrual phase and flying accidents or flying grades, and that women took fewer days off each month from flight training than did their male counterparts (in Keil, 1982). Sharon Golub (1976) found no difference between premenstrual and intermenstrual days in the cognitive functioning of a group of 50 adult women, even among women who complained of premenstrual symptoms. Golub concluded that "despite complaints or expectations to the contrary, a woman's ability to function intellectually is not affected by the premenstruum" (p. 103).

Although most studies have not shown fluctuations in performance related to the menstrual cycle, some have. For instance, one group of investigators (Baker, Mishara, Kostin, & Parker, 1979) found a very small average correlation between menstrual cycle and kinesthetic judgment; another study (Asso & Beech, 1975) found faster conditioning (of galvanic skin response to a light) during premenstrual than intermenstrual days among one small sample of women. Still, Barbara Sommer (1983) has examined the research and found no support, overall, for a menstrual effect on behavior. She has concluded that

> among the general population of women, menstrual cycle variables do not interfere with cognitive abilities—abilities of thinking, problem solving, learning and memory, making judgments, and other related mental activities. . . . Small changes in sensory acuity and sensitivity, and . . . motor activity . . . are neither clear nor consistent. (p. 86)

Premenstrual Syndrome (PMS): What Is It?

Much media attention has been given in recent years to claims that a new medical disorder has been discovered that afflicts millions of women, and that can be diagnosed and treated. This disorder, premenstrual syndrome (PMS), consists of a constellation of symptoms first discussed in the medical literature in the 1930s but not popularized until the mid-1970s, when the work of Katharina Dalton, a British physician, was reported widely in the press and a number of premenstrual syndrome clinics were established in the United States.

One major problem with understanding PMS is that it is said to be indicated by a large number of varied and sometimes contradictory symptoms (only some of which need be experienced by the suffering

patient), making diagnosis difficult if not impossible. Dalton has defined premenstrual syndrome as "any symptoms or complaints which regularly come just before or during menstruation but are absent at other times of the cycle" (in Sherman, 1982, p. 10). Thus, the symptoms may vary from woman to woman, making PMS, at the outset, quite different from other medical problems. Descriptions of PMS list from 20 to about 150 symptoms, including tension, depression, fatigue, irritability, backache, asthma, sinusitis, epilepsy, feelings of bloatedness, breast discomfort, headaches, acne, clumsiness, suicidal urges, herpes, hypoglycemia, sties, hoarseness, weight gain, rage, anxiety or panic attacks, food cravings, mental confusion, and seizures. Carol Turkington (1984) has pointed out that "there are no medical tests for the syndrome and no psychological evaluation which can predict its occurrence" (p. 28). Despite the lack of precise definition, however, some lawyers in Great Britain have successfully used PMS as a mitigating factor in defending women clients on assault charges (in Abplanalp, 1983), and the trustees of the American Psychiatric Association have recommended adding the category of premenstrual dysphoric disorder to its official list of psychiatric diagnoses.

We find variations not only in the suggested symptoms of PMS, but also in the estimates of its prevalence, ranging from 10 percent to 95 percent of all women. Conservative estimates like those made by Celia Helas, director of a PMS treatment program in Arizona, translate into between five and six million women who are described as "very severely affected by PMS. . . . They cannot hold jobs, they cannot maintain relationships. . . . They fear they are insane" (in Turkington, 1984, p. 28). Such assertions must be carefully scrutinized and questioned; they are not based on reliable and valid data since PMS lacks clear definition and an accepted set of symptoms.

Without precise definition and with wide variation in estimated prevalence, that PMS has no established cause and no agreed-upon treatment is not surprising. Andrea Eagan (1983) has concluded, from surveying the literature, that

> there is *nothing* in the medical literature showing clearly what causes PMS. . . . There are at least half a dozen theories as to its cause—ranging from an alteration in the way that the body uses glucose, to excessive estrogen levels—none of which have been convincingly demonstrated. (p. 28)

The most publicized hypothesis, proposed by Katharina Dalton, is that PMS results from a progesterone deficiency. Her treatment, therefore, includes administering progesterone for about 10 days before menstruation by injection or by vaginal or rectal suppositories. This treatment has been used by doctors in Britain for over 30 years, but it has not been approved by the Food and Drug Administration in the United States. All recent reviewers of the literature (for example, Abplanalp, 1983; Eagan, 1983; Fausto-Sterling, 1985; Laws, 1983) have concluded independently that medical research has thus far failed to support the hypothesis that progesterone deficiency (or any other factor) causes PMS or to support the claim that progesterone replacement therapy (or any other treatment) is helpful.

Studies have found, according to Anne Fausto-Sterling (1985), that "women under treatment for PMS respond just as well to sugar pills [placebos] as to medication containing hormones or other drugs" (p. 100). The literature, she has noted, "is filled with individual studies that permit neither replication nor comparison with one another" (p. 98). No conclusive evidence shows that PMS sufferers have lower progesterone levels or a greater estrogen-progesterone imbalance (Rubin, Reinisch, & Haskett, 1981). Another reviewer of the literature, Sophie Laws (1983), has pointed out that "the only controlled double-blind clinical trial of progesterone therapy [by Sampson in 1979] found that it performed *no better* than a placebo" (p. 25). Despite the conceptual and methodological problems and the paucity of research support, popular articles continue to exaggerate what is known about PMS. For example, a *New York Times Magazine* story asserted that "recent medical advances in the understanding and treatment of menstrual problems have been dramatic," and that PMS has been "shown to respond almost miraculously to appropriate drug therapy" (Henig, 1982, p. 65). These statements are particularly upsetting in an article entitled "Dispelling Menstrual Myths."

A dizzying array of treatments in addition to progesterone therapy have been recommended for this poorly defined syndrome, including restricting intake of diuretics; eating frequent small, high-protein meals to prevent a drop in blood sugar; reducing consumption of caffeine; increasing intake of vitamin B-6 (to prevent headache and irritability); taking oral contraceptives; exercising; taking iron and calcium supplements; reducing consumption of red meat; taking tranquilizers; and taking lithium. In a recent press report ("Premenstrual Syndrome," 1986, p. B5), the director of a PMS program in New York City

was quoted as saying, "There are now 327 different treatments for PMS."

Sophie Laws (1983) has argued that PMS is "a political construct." This should not be interpreted as denying the reality of the suffering of women who experience premenstrual discomfort. What she questions, instead, is the apparent acceptability in our patriarchal society of attributing women's "bad" behavior to "a pitiable hormonal imbalance." Laws suggests that the PMS concept "isolates the badness in women to a part of themselves which is only sometimes present and results from circumstances (hormones) beyond their control" (p. 21). To illustrate, she has described an advertisement in British medical journals for a natural progesterone product (Cyclogest) that shows the same woman before and after treatment. In the *before* photograph the woman is wearing a black T-shirt and has untidy hair and a sad expression, while in the *after* photo she has "a shining smile, shining hair" and is wearing a white blouse. A century ago, Laws has reminded us, the treatment for "female troubles" was surgical removal of the uterus and/or ovaries, and the symptoms of "female troubles" were the same as for PMS today: "'nervous prostration,' irritability, mood changes, a tendency to go mad and attack people" (p. 24).

The complaints and experiences of women with premenstrual problems must be heeded and taken seriously, but this requires better and more sophisticated research, not unskeptical acceptance of a vaguely defined disorder with no verified cause or proven treatment. The issue is complex. Some of the important questions have been raised by Anne Fausto-Sterling (1985):

> Are there women in need of proper medical treatment who do not receive it? Do some receive dangerous medication to treat nonexistent physiological problems? How often are women refused work, given lower salaries, taken less seriously because of beliefs about hormonally induced erratic behavior? In the game of PMS the stakes are high. . . . Some women probably do require medical attention for incapacitating physical changes that occur in synchrony with their menstrual cycle. Yet in the absence of any reliable medical research into the problem it is impossible to diagnose true disease or to develop rational treatment. (pp. 94f)

Dysmenorrhea

Menstrual cramps (dysmenorrhea) are sometimes grouped together with premenstrual distress, but they are a separate phenomenon. In fact, according to Joan Hoffman (1982), the literature indicates that "PMS and dysmenorrhea are seldom seen in the same individual" (p. 840).

The symptoms of dysmenorrhea are relatively clear and discrete: lower abdominal cramps (spasmodic pain) that coincide with menstruation, especially during the first day or two, and perhaps also pain in the back and upper legs, nausea, diarrhea, headache, and fatigue. Psychological factors have been implicated in this disorder; for example, a large study of adolescent and college-age women found significant correlations between reported severity of menstrual pain and not having received a clear explanation of menstruation, having been surprised by menarche, and feeling negative about menstruation (Brooks-Gunn & Ruble, 1983). Nevertheless, a widely accepted explanation for primary dysmenorrhea (where there is no known structural abnormality) is that it results from an overproduction of prostaglandins by the endometrium (lining) of the uterus. A higher prostaglandin concentration has been found in the menstrual fluid of women who suffer from menstrual cramps than from those who do not, and prostaglandins are known to trigger uterine contractions and have been used to induce labor in pregnant women (Marx, 1979a). Prostaglandins have been related to the body's calcium-magnesium balance, acting to increase the level of the former and to deplete the latter, and some have suggested that it is magnesium deficiency that causes dysmenorrhea (Friederich, 1983). Whether directly or indirectly, prostaglandins are said to produce menstrual pain through three mechanisms: "increased [muscle] contraction . . . decreased uterine blood flow . . . [and] increased sensitization of pain fibers to mechanical and chemical stimuli" (Friederich, 1983, p. 97).

Several drugs that function as prostaglandin synthesis inhibitors have been developed to treat dysmenorrhea and include ibuprofen (Motrin®), mefenamic acid (Ponstel®), and zomepirac sodium (Zomax®). (Ordinary aspirin, too, is thought to inhibit prostaglandin synthesis.) Well-controlled double-blind studies have provided evidence that these new nonnarcotic drugs are effective in reducing dysmenorrhiac symptoms and decreasing prostaglandins. Birth control pills also have been found to alleviate menstrual cramps, probably by preventing the growth and thickening of the endometrium, from which prostaglandins are released (Marx, 1979a). Penny Budoff (1982) compared Zomax® with a placebo in a six-month study and found evidence of

Zomax's® effectiveness but, interestingly, she also found the placebo to be somewhat effective; still, Zomax® was most effective. For example, before treatment 80 percent of the participants had missed at least one day of activity per month due to dysmenorrhea; this was reduced to 23 percent for those taking Zomax® and to 47 percent for those taking the placebo. W. Y. Chan (1983) studied two other prostaglandin-synthesis inhibitors, ibuprofen (Motrin®) and naproxen sodium (Anaprox®), and found them effective, but cautioned that these drugs "lack selectivity" because they suppress total-body prostaglandin synthesis, and warned that "although no serious side effects have been reported . . . , these agents are potentially toxic and should be used judiciously" (p. 249).

More research must be done to establish the long-term effects of these drugs; to contrast their efficiency with that of aspirin, which is much cheaper; to understand why placebos are sometimes able to reduce the symptoms of menstrual distress; and to identify the conditions under which excessive prostaglandins are produced. While the symptoms of physical distress that accompany menstruation seem to be directly traceable to prostaglandins, we do not know what triggers their production. Why does the uterine lining of some women but not others and, among the former, in some months but not all, release large amounts of prostaglandin? Factors other than the normal menstrual process seem to be at work, and may include exercise, stress, and diet (particularly magnesium deficiency) as well as beliefs, attitudes, and attributions. Menstrual pain can also result from such specific causes as endometriosis (abnormal growth of uterine lining cells), pelvic infection, uterine fibroids, or intrauterine birth control devices (Brody, 1981).

LIFTING THE CURSE

Menstruation is clearly something special for women to deal with—in one way or another. Sexually active women who do not want to become pregnant tend to pay close attention to signs of the imminent arrival of the menstrual flow; anxiety about pregnancy is an important phenomenon that is seldom discussed in the literature on menstrual distress. The personal hygiene aspects of menstruation are real; women need advance supplies of sanitary napkins or tampons, and it is the rare woman who has not found herself, many times, unprepared. For many women, in addition, water retention (edema) elevates weight and bloats the abdomen and breasts for some days before menstruation. When some of these relatively minor inconveniences of menstruation are combined with possible dysmenorrhea and the cultural tradition of ambivalence, expectations of distress, and avoidance, this aspect of the female experience may become problematic. Nevertheless, most women handle their monthly menstrual cycles matter-of-factly, routinely, and calmly. Even more of us would likely do so if general attitudes and expectations were unambiguously positive.

Women must understand the facts of the menstrual process and the interrelationships among its physiological, psychological, and social aspects. We must come to realize that we should not expect menstruation to be accompanied by distress or pain, and that when it is we must search for the source of the problem. If we accept uncritically the proposition that menstruation is normally associated with distress, then we may fail to identify and treat genuine problems. We must respect our bodies and maintain good health through exercise and a balanced, nutritious diet. And we must also firmly challenge the belief that women suffer from some terrible biological infirmity, some curse that can only be endured by passive resignation or taking to our beds. The fact that we must sometimes think about tampons does not mean that we cannot make decisions, do our work effectively, or lead full, productive, and healthy lives. Any suggestion to the contrary is simply not supported by historical or contemporary evidence.

Sexuality

Sex is a good gift, a delight; . . . it participates in the fullness of fruit, wine, music, amity, the vitality of the senses.

Kate Millett   *(1978, p. 80)*

Lydia had thought of the sex act . . . as something the man "took" and the woman "gave." "He took her quickly," the books would say; or, "She gave herself to him." If anything in these verbal images aroused Lydia, it was the idea of making a present of her virginity to the man to whom she could then "belong."

Gail Godwin   *(1983, p. 141)*

C   H   A   P   T   E   R   7

exual experiences might be "a good gift, a delight," but for many women they are instead something a man takes and a woman gives. Sexual interaction with a man often proves to be a disappointment to a young woman because her anticipations may differ greatly from those of her partner. For example, one woman's bitter and angry reactions to the realities of heterosexual "lovemaking" are expressed in this remarkable poem by Alta (1973):

> penus envy, they call it
> think how handy to have a thing
> that poked out; you could just shove
> it in any body, whang whang & come,
> wouldn't have to give a shit.
> you *know* you'd come!
> wouldn't have to love that person,
> trust that person,
> whang whang & come.
> if you couldn't get relief for free,
> pay a little $, whang whang & come.
> you wouldn't have to keep, or abort.
> wouldn't have to care about the kid.
> wouldn't fear sexual violation.
> penus envy, they call it.
> the man is sick in his heart,
> that's what I call it. (p. 295)

Alta's words reflect what social scientists have been validating through more systematic and objective means: the existence of two human cultures divided by gender. Women and men not only learn different role expectations and different motives and behaviors, but also divergent meanings of sexuality.

SEXUALITY AS RELATED TO GENDER

Traditional gender ideology tells us that women are less sexual than men. Further, as Patricia Miller and Martha Fowlkes (1980) have noted, "whereas males are encouraged to give full expression to their sexuality as an indication and demonstration of their masculinity, female sexual response has traditionally been thought to be appropriately derived from relationships with men and their needs" (p. 786). This traditional ideology remains dominant and generally descriptive of the behavior of contemporary adults. Thus, a recent study of sexual attitudes (Hendrick, Hendrick, Slapion-Foote, & Foote, 1985) reported substantial and significant gender differences, with college women expressing less support than college men for sexual permissiveness and more support for sexual responsibility. Philip Blumstein and Pepper Schwartz (1983) studied 12,000 American couples from varied geographical backgrounds, including heterosexual and homosexual, married and cohabiting pairs. Their conclusions support the proposition that gender plays a primary organizing role in sexuality. They found that regardless of sexual orientation, "men and women represent two very distinct modes of behavior" (p. 302). With respect to sexual motivation and attitudes, for example, "lesbians are more like heterosexual women than either is like gay or heterosexual men" (p. 303). We will explore the role played by gender in shaping sexual experience by examining contemporary and earlier views of gender differences and the responses of women to sexual imagery.

Views of Women's Sexuality, Past and Present

The belief that women are less sexual than men has not always been prevalent. The ancient Hebrews, for example, assumed that a woman's sexual desires were at least equal to those of a man's and the marriage contract, therefore, provided not only for the wife's financial security but also for her sexual satisfaction. In the *Book of Women*, compiled in the twelfth century by the physician and rabbi Maimonides (in "Holy or Wholly," 1972), the rules governing a woman's "conjugal rights" were presented in detail.

> For men who are healthy and live in comfortable and pleasurable circumstances without having to perform work that would weaken their strength, and do nought but eat and drink and sit idly in their houses, the conjugal schedule is every night. For laborers, such as tailors, weavers, masons, and the like, the conjugal schedule is twice a week if their work is in the same city, and once a week if their work is in another city. For ass drivers, the schedule is once a week; for camel drivers once in thirty days; for sailors, once in six months; for disciples of the wise, once a week, because the study of *Torah* weakens their strength. (p. 73)

Clearly, men were expected to satisfy women's sexual needs, not vice versa. The early Hebrew practice of rigidly separating men and women and imposing strict standards of modesty for women may have come about because of men's fear of women's sexuality and to help men avoid being tempted into lust.

> It was considered immoral, for example, for a [Hebrew] man to listen to a woman sing, to look at her hair, or to walk behind her in the street. Thus, the most pious men shunned all contact with women other than their wives, would not look directly at women, and avoided hearing their voices by refusing to address them by name or ask them questions ("for the voice of woman leads to lewdness"). (Baum, Hyman, & Michel, 1975, pp. 9f.)

Susan Griffin (1981) has suggested that a dominant idea in Judeo-Christian culture is that "the sight of a woman's body calls a man back to his own animal nature, and that this animal nature soon destroys him" (p. 31). It was Eve, we are told, who tempted Adam; and the belief in witchcraft was closely associated with the belief that carnal lust was insatiable in women. There is some evidence that women in pre-Christian England had considerable sexual freedom, that virginity was considered shameful, that marriage was temporary, and that women took lovers freely (Staples, 1977). According to Carolyn Heilbrun (1973), the Roman poet Ovid (who believed that women's lust was uncontrollable) recounted a story about Teiresias (the "blind prophet of Thebes"), who had been both a man and a woman and was asked to mediate a dispute between the gods Jove and Juno about which sex enjoyed lovemaking more. "He agreed with Jove that women had greater pleasure, and Juno, in a fit of temper at the decision, struck Teiresias blind" (p. 11).

Contrary to such beliefs, we have been taught that it is male sexuality that is overwhelming and powerful and more insistent than female sexuality. Women are urged to sympathize with men's sexual needs. Ross Wetzsteon (1977), in an analysis of the humor of Woody Allen, has suggested the following:

> The jokes seem to be saying that Woody Allen always wants to get laid, but that women keep rejecting him, so he feels like a schlemiel. But notice how they all assume male sexuality and female indifference—what they're actually saying then, and what men actually identify with, is that men are sex maniacs and that women don't like sex. . . . Woody Allen tells us that although we [men] have trouble with women (and we all feel we do) we don't have trouble with our sexuality . . . we're still ever-ready cocksmen. Men identify . . . not with his incompetence but with his libido. (p. 14)

Freud presented the libido as masculine, an assumption he accepted from his own time and place and then maintained and proclaimed as biological truth. Our society still views sexuality as more crucial to men's gender identity and self-worth than to women's. Ethel Person (1980) has suggested, for example, that for women "sexual expression is not critical to personality development," but for men, for whom "sexuality represents domination," it is essential. Philip Blumstein and Pepper Schwartz (1983) concluded, from their large-scale study of American couples, that it is the man who is attributed with "greater appetite" and "greater license." "Women often feel restrained and not in control of their own experience, and men feel pressed to perform" (p. 305). This same imagery, Blumstein and Schwartz assert, is shared by homosexual as well as by heterosexual couples.

There are, of course, women and men whose personal histories have reinforced sexual behavior that does not conform to the dominant gender ideology. In addition, the ideology itself does not present a simple, uncomplicated set of prescriptions. There are contradictory expectations, and we receive mixed messages. Molly Haskell (1974) has pointed out, for example, that in movies from the 1960s, a spinster like Joanne Woodward in *Rachel, Rachel* or Maggie Smith in *The Prime of Miss Jean Brodie* was depicted as suffering from "sexual malnutrition," looking "pinched and bloodless as a prune, the objective correlative of her unlubricated vagina" (p. 339). The message seemed to be that women really need sex whether they know it or not! In films of the 1980s, sexual overtures are still primarily made by men, but women are shown as acquiescing with far less hesitation than in earlier decades, and their sexual pleasure is detailed and highlighted by cameras at close range.

Contributing to the dominant gender ideology is the fact that women's experiences of sexuality were, until relatively recently, not much discussed or researched, nor described in literature by women themselves. It was primarily men who attempted descriptions of women's sexual feelings in fiction and in psychiatric and medical texts, basing their descriptions on their own assumptions. William Masters told Mary Hall (1969) in an interview that when he reviewed the literature in 1954 he found that "everything said about female orgasm was written by males." The situation is considerably changed today, and women are now describing their sexual experiences in autobiography, fiction, poetry, and in response to questions asked by researchers. Comparisons between the new information and the older assumptions reveal significant discrepancies. For those unfamiliar with the work of early sex education pioneers like Havelock Ellis and Margaret Sanger, the findings reported in the famous "Kinsey Report," *Sexual Behavior in the Human Female* (Kinsey, Pomeroy, Martin, & Gebhard, 1953), provided many surprises. The book was a landmark since the data it presented had come from women themselves. Almost 8,000 women had been interviewed and had responded to a variety of questions that had not typically been asked before. More recently, valuable information about women's sexual behavior and erotic fantasies has come from the now-classic work of William Masters and Virginia Johnson (1966) and from the inquiries of journalists like Nancy Friday (1973) and Shere Hite (1976). Women novelists have also been writing about sexuality. Erica Jong's *Fear of Flying* (1973) and *Parachutes and Kisses* (1984), Judith Rossner's *Looking for Mr. Goodbar* (1976), and Marge Piercy's *Braided Lives* (1983), to name just a few, have jolted readers into recognizing that women can be just as sexual as men and that typical differences between women and men in sexual attitudes and responses are not inevitable or innate but are consequences of cultural or social learning.

Responses to Sexual Imagery

The well-known "Kinsey Report" on the sexuality of women (Kinsey, Pomeroy, Martin, & Gebhard, 1953) suggested that women are less apt than men to be sexually stimulated by visual (or ideational) cues, and this belief has long been part of our general ideology about gender differences in sexuality. Recently, a considerable amount of interest has been

shown in this issue. Surveys have asked respondents about their exposure to, and enjoyment of, sexual material; and studies have tested reactions to such material in laboratory settings. For example, 20,000 readers of *Psychology Today* responded anonymously to a questionnaire on sexuality (Athamasion, Shaver, & Tavris, 1970). They tended to be liberal in their politics and in their sexual attitudes; the majority were young (under 30), well-educated (median level was college graduate), and of relatively high socioeconomic status. Among this highly selective sample, the voluntary exposure of men to "erotic or pornographic books, movies, magazines, etc." differed considerably from that of women. Among the women, 72 percent had viewed such materials at some time, compared to 92 percent of the men, while 8 percent of the women and 25 percent of the men viewed such materials "frequently." Also of interest is the reported response to the materials. Among the women, 51 percent said they were aroused "occasionally" or "greatly," compared to 73 percent of the men.

Experimental studies, on the other hand, have failed to validate such differences between men and women in objectively measured reactions to sexually explicit stimuli. Donn Byrne and John Lamberth (1971) tested a sample of married couples who volunteered to participate in a study described as "dealing with opinions about pornography." They were exposed to slides and literary selections depicting heterosexual, homosexual, and autosexual acts and were asked to imagine specific sexual scenes. The reactions of women and men were not reliably different, although there were wide individual differences within each group. For both women and men, instructions to imagine sexual acts produced greater arousal than exposure to either pictorial or printed presentations of the same themes. Byrne and Lamberth tried to reconcile the survey data with their findings.

> The long accepted Kinsey finding with respect to sex differences in response to erotic material has either disappeared in the years following his study or . . . the survey method simply answers a different question than does the experimental method. That is, women are relatively less likely to purchase hard core pornographic pictures or books, attend stag movies, etc., because of social pressures and custom. When asked whether they are frequently stimulated by such material, they indicate that they are not—because they are seldom exposed to these stimuli. On the other hand, when they are presented with erotic stimuli, as in an experiment, they are as sexually aroused as are males. In fact, the

females in the present experiment were significantly more aroused than were the males by the various masculine stimuli such as male nudity, male masturbation, and even homosexual fellatio. (pp. 26f.)

Support for the findings of Byrne and Lamberth has come from the work of other researchers (for example, Schmidt, Sigusch, & Schafer, 1977).

The Byrne and Lamberth findings suggest that two separate questions are at issue. The first is, To what extent do women seek erotic stimulation in pictures, books, and so on? The second question is, To what degree can women be aroused by such material? With respect to the second issue, experimental findings support the conclusion that any stimulus with sexual significance for an individual can be arousing and that this is no less true for women than for men. Julia Heiman (1975) carefully measured physiological reactions to sexual materials with a penile strain gauge and an instrument called a photoplethysmograph (which detects blood volume and pressure pulse in the penis and vagina) while college student volunteers listened to tapes of heterosexual interaction that varied in sexual context, and found that "women like erotica as much as men do, that they are as turned on by sexual descriptions, that their fantasies are as vivid and self-arousing" (p. 91). However, women in general do not seem to actively pursue sexual titillation in this way as much as men do.

In one study, William Griffitt and Donn Kaiser (1978) asked women and men to perform a discrimination task for which correct responses were followed (rewarded) by a slide of a "sexually explicit act" or by a neutral slide. Compared to same-gender persons rewarded with slides of a nonsexual nature, the performance of men was found to be "positively influenced" and that of women, "negatively influenced when correct responses [in the discrimination task] were followed by exposure to erotic stimuli" (p. 855). A peek at a "sexually explicit act" did not, apparently, function as a positive reinforcement for the women, whereas it did for the men. Perhaps these findings reflect the fact that women have learned to expect censure for the pursuit of sexual interests. Sexually explicit material, therefore, may be guilt-arousing, and the most likely response will be avoidance and not approach. Griffitt and Kaiser found that persons of both genders who scored low on a measure of "sex guilt" were more likely to repeat responses that were followed by a sexually explicit slide than were individuals who scored high on "sex guilt." On the other hand, Patricia Morokoff (1985) found that although a sample of women who scored high in sex-guilt self-reported less arousal to an erotic videotape than low sex-guilt women, the former showed significantly greater physiological arousal than the latter.

Women may not actively seek sexually explicit material because such material omits romance. Women in our culture are assumed to be more romantic than men, more concerned with relationships and less interested in sexual satisfaction that does not include love. Some evidence supports this view. One group of college women who were interviewed after seeing a series of sexually explicit films indicated that their ideal erotic film was one in which an attractive heterosexual pair is romantically and affectionately engaged in prolonged foreplay leading gradually to coitus (Steele & Walker, 1976). Another study (Kenrick, Stringfield, Wagenhals, Dahl, & Ransdell, 1980) found that a sample of college women chose to view a "loving" erotic film as opposed to a hard-core "lustful" film significantly more often than did a sample of college men. On the other hand, William Fisher and Donn Byrne (1978) found that college women and men responded very similarly to both love and lust themes in erotic films, and they concluded that affectional or romantic emphases are not preconditions for women's arousal by erotic stimuli. But they may be factors in what women seek out or prefer to view.

Erotica Distinguished from Pornography
An alternative explanation of gender differences in the pursuit of sexual imagery focuses on the nature or quality of that material. Although many writers and social science researchers fail to distinguish between erotica and pornography and use the terms interchangeably, feminists have been asserting that these terms refer to very different kinds of visual and prose materials. In erotica, sexual behavior is instrumental to mutual pleasure. Gloria Steinem (1978c) has pointed out that *erotica* comes from the root word *eros*, and that it pertains "to passionate love or sexual desire" and is defined by the depiction of sexual love. It implies positive choice, acceptance, shared pleasure, communication, and, as Maureen Howard (1983) has suggested, it may "reveal to us the wonders of our sexuality" and encourage "personal revelation." *Pornography*, on the other hand, stems from the Greek *porné*, which means prostitute, and, as Gloria Steinem (1978c) has argued, is not about sexual love or passion but about "dominance and violence against women." Pornography depicts women

being sexually dominated—coerced or conquered, degraded, humiliated, or beaten.

> It may be very blatant, with weapons of torture or bondage, wounds and bruises, some clear humiliation, or an adult's sexual power being used over a child. It may be much more subtle: a physical attitude of conqueror and victim, the use of race or class differences to imply the same thing, perhaps a very unequal nudity, with one person exposed and vulnerable while the other is clothed. In either case, there is no sense of equal choice or equal power. (Steinem, 1978, p. 54)

In pornography, men are at war against women; sexual acts are used, like weapons, to inflict pain and to defeat the enemy. In pornography, writes Maureen Howard (1983), a woman "becomes no more than a word for a part of her body, a mechanical device acted upon by a male thrust; if not willing to submit, brought to submission" (p. 326). Susan Griffin (1981) has argued that pornography is the antithesis of eroticism and, ultimately, antisexual and antinature.

> The pornographer reduces a woman to a mere thing, to an entirely material object without a soul. . . . [The woman, as object,] shows her goods. . . . Like a piece of furniture, she must be pictured from the side, and particular parts of her body, those intended for use . . . must be carefully examined. . . . There is no person there . . . this objectification of a whole being into a thing is the central metaphor. (p. 36)

Griffin has noted that while some pornography debases and humiliates men, these men are always smaller, weaker, and more "feminine" than their sexual dominators.

Pornography is not about the sexual pleasure of women. Recently, an unsolicited package of illustrated materials advertising "premiere discount erotica" (films and magazines) came by mail to my home, addressed to a young man who had been a guest some years before. The featured materials, graphically and unambiguously illustrated, were on "incest, animals, and young girls" and carried titles such as "Mammaries," "Shaved Naked Twats," "Anal Lust," and "Dominate Women." Such material is pornographic not because it is sexually explicit but because its primary message is the physical or psychological humiliation of women, which, tragically, stimulates sexual arousal in large numbers of men. Many women probably avoid pornography for these reasons. Also, for these reasons, most feminists actively discourage the distribution of such material. Research that distinguishes between erotica and pornography and that examines women's (and men's)

reactions to each should give us important information. Other questions about the effect of pornography on men's attitudes toward and interactions with women have been asked repeatedly over the past several decades and are currently being studied. We will discuss these issues in some detail in Chapter 9, where we will be concerned explicitly with violence against women.

PSYCHOPHYSIOLOGY OF SEXUAL AROUSAL AND RESPONSE

Sexuality can be considered a dimension of personality—a more or less consistent way of responding to a particular class of stimuli; and sexual arousal and response can be defined in both physiological and psychological terms. According to William Masters (in Hall, 1969), "There is no such thing as the pure physiology of sexual response. . . . From a functional point of view, the correct terminology is . . . psychophysiology" (p. 54). A comparison between women and men on this area of functioning suggests that: (a) men's and women's subjective reports of arousal and orgasm do not differ significantly; and (b) women may actually have the potential for greater sexual pleasure than men.

The clitoris is a woman's primary erogenous or sexually arousing portion of the body. For a long time this fact has been ignored or denied by a patriarchal bias in medicine. For example, Sigmund Freud (1905/1938) considered the clitoris to be an analogue of the male penis and believed that clitoral pleasure represented a childish masculinity. With mature femininity, Freud insisted, the vagina becomes the prime focus of women's sexual experience and the locus of adult orgasm. But these assumptions are contradicted by data from physiology and by reports of women's experiences. The title of a now classic paper by Anne Koedt (1973b), "The Myth of the Vaginal Orgasm," became a challenging call to debate on this issue and a feminist slogan. Little question exists that the clitoris is the major organ involved in the sexual arousal and response of women. It is, in fact, a unique human organ in that its sole function is sexual. It is thus unlike the penis in this way, although these organs originate from the same embryonic tissue and are similar in structure and function. The clitoris can become erect and enlarged (tumescent), its size changing both in diameter and in length, and its tip (glans), packed with nerve endings, is extremely sensitive to stimulation.

Physiologically, though, more is involved in sexual response than just clitoral tumescence. The muscles in the lower half of the vagina also participate by rhythmically contracting, and a thick layer of veins (venous plexus) in the vagina becomes engorged, thereby narrowing the vaginal passageway and increasing the potential for stimulation of the walls of the vagina, which contain nerve endings. The clitoris and lower third of the vagina function, to a very large extent, as an integrated unit. In addition, vaginal lubricants are released during sexual arousal. This physiological sign of a human female's sexual arousal is not hormonal but results from dilation of the venous plexus (Zuckerman, 1971).

Vaginal lubricants and clitoral erection indicate sexual arousal in women, while penile erection signifies arousal in men. How similar are the two genders in their subjective experiences and in sexual gratification or orgasm? When William Wiest (1977) asked a group of college students to choose adjectives for their experiences of orgasm, he found no significant differences between the responses of the women and those of the men. Wiest cited an earlier study by other researchers in which judges were unable to distinguish reliably between reports written by women and those written by men of "what an orgasm feels like."

Data gathered on female sexuality from observations and interviews with 387 women (Masters & Johnson, 1966) clearly indicated that sexual arousal can occur in response to anything present or imagined that has sexual meaning for a woman. Arousal can follow from particular words or images, from general body stimulation or stimulation of erogenous areas of the skin, or from direct or indirect stimulation of the clitoris. Orgasm for women was described as a complete body phenomenon involving more than just the vagina or the clitoris, and orgasmic experiences were found to vary in duration and in intensity, in extent of body involvement, and in degree of pleasure. Although simple neural reflexes for orgasmic release are involved, orgasm is not an all-or-none phenomenon. This conclusion is reinforced by the experiences reported by approximately 3000 women who responded to Shere Hite's (1976) questionnaire, and by the over 200 women studied by Michael Newcomb and P. M. Bentler (1983). Shere Hite (1976) reported that most of her informants (all women) described sexual arousal as involving sensations all over their bodies. They used such words as "tingly," "alive," "warm," "happy," "feelings of wanting to touch and be touched," while descriptions of orgasm were more confined to the genitals.

Women can experience sequential orgasm more easily than men, and retain this ability over most of their lives. This multiorgasmic potential in women has a physiological basis. The engorgement or accumulation of blood (vasocongestion) in the vaginal wall and in the clitoris is reduced with orgasm, but is promptly followed, reflexively, by reengorgement or refilling of the blood vessels. Each orgasm, therefore, produces increased vasocongestion and arousal. Sexual experience thus increases the physiological capacity of women for greater sexual pleasure. The frequency of multiple orgasms, as well as sexual gratification, has been found to increase with age and pregnancies and is potentially greatest when vaginal vasocongestion is maximal, during the postovulatory and premenstrual days of the menstrual cycle.

Mary Jane Sherfey (1970) has proposed that women "could go on having orgasms indefinitely if physical exhaustion did not intervene" and that a woman must will herself to be satisfied. Sherfey refers to this phenomenon as "the paradoxical state of sexual insatiation in the presence of the utmost sexual satiation" (p. 229). She maintains that primitive men took steps to suppress women because, unless women were confined and restricted, there could be no family life, agriculture, or civilization. (The assumption that civilization rests on the suppression of primitive urges or "instincts" is very much in the Freudian tradition. Freud, however, tended to ignore women and emphasized the destructive impulses of men.) According to Sherfey, men gradually (over thousands of years) forced women to accept monogamy, accepting it themselves only in principle in order to have knowledge of children's paternity and to ensure care of the children and stability of the family, essential for property ownership and inheritance. Regardless of the historical merits or validity of Sherfey's hypothesis, its basis in female physiology serves to counter the still prevalent view of the insistent nature of men's sexual needs and the popular denial of the importance of active sexuality to women.

THE ROLE OF LEARNING IN SEXUAL BEHAVIOR

The contradictions in historical and contemporary views of women's sexuality, and the persistence of the belief that men have the greater "need" despite contrary evidence that women are physically and psychologically able to be as sexual as men, illustrate the significance of learning (and culture) in defining sexual behavior and in affecting sexual experience. The human brain is the guardian and regulator of the body's hormones. Cognitive processes (thoughts, fantasies, expectations, and beliefs) function in sexual arousal and nonarousal, in sexual satiation and nonsatiation; and the behaviors used to achieve gratification are learned. Though all aspects of human sexuality involve the interplay of psychological and physiological factors, learning and experience are dominant. Biologist Ruth Bleier (1984) has compared sexuality with intelligence.

> Sexuality, like intelligence, is a learned relationship to the world, with an important and necessary, but not in itself determinate, biological component. For intelligence, it is not enough to have a brain and billions of neurons and synapses. Intelligence develops out of experience and learning. . . . So in sexuality, there is a real biological substrate for a range of sexual responses that involve the brain, hormones, muscles, and blood vessels. . . . But whatever or whoever arouses us . . . are . . . part of one's history of experiences and interactions with the external world. . . . There is nothing about desire, arousal, orgasms, or feelings of transcendent oneness that "comes naturally." (p. 167)

Let us examine how learning influences sexual behavior.

Human beings do not restrict their heterosexual behavior to times when females are "in heat" and when the probability of conception is maximal. The sexual behavior of lower animals generally is tied to physiological signs of readiness for mating, when a series of stereotyped, relatively inflexible, and unlearned (instinctive) responses are then triggered by appropriate stimuli. However, as noted many years ago by Frank Beach (1969), "as one moves up the evolutionary scale, there is a gradual loosening of the tie between mating [sexual behavior] and reproduction." It has long been recognized that whereas the sexual behavior of lower mammals is controlled by hormones, "in higher mammals, the balance of power shifts toward the central nervous system—and especially . . . toward the neocortex" (p. 33). The erotic responsiveness of human beings, then, depends upon the highest brain center, the cortex (the center for flexible behavior, for learning and memory), which constitutes 90 percent of the volume of brain tissue. Our closest mammalian relatives, primates such as apes and monkeys, also engage in sexual play when the female is not in estrus. In a well-known work, Harry and Margaret Harlow (1966) found that learning and experience were cru-

cial to the sexuality of the primates. Monkeys raised in social isolation or with surrogate wire mothers were not sexually competent when they became physically mature; they did not seem to know what to do and did not exhibit what is generally considered to be natural sexual behavior.

Like other mammals, humans have *biological needs* that must be satisfied if the individual is to survive. These unlearned (primary or biogenic) needs are related to human physiology and to the maintenance of a stable internal environment (homeostasis). These needs include those for oxygen, for food and water, for waste elimination, and for pain avoidance. Deprivation of nutritional satisfaction or continued exposure to an excessively aversive state (pain, for example) produces a general state of arousal characterized by intense and persistent stimulation, referred to as a *drive*, that typically activates an organism and evokes behavior. Only some of this behavior is innate (for example, reflex movements). In humans, most of the behavior exhibited in response to a state of arousal is behavior we have learned will successfully reduce the drive (the persistent and intense stimulation) because it is instrumental in obtaining what is needed (such as food to relieve hunger).

In addition to the needs originating from the nature of human physiology, a second category of needs is acquired during the course of a person's life. These needs result from experiences common to all human beings; from experiences common to a group of individuals (in particular cultures, for example); or from experiences specific to a particular person. These needs are variously described as sociogenic, psychological, secondary, or *acquired* and may be illustrated by desires for approval, for love, for affiliation or friendship, for power, for money, and so on. These needs, too, when aroused, result in a state of tension or drive and elicit behavior. Again, the behavior most successful or instrumental in reducing the person's intense state of arousal (drive) will be learned and strengthened and will tend to be elicited again. Figure 7.1 shows how these concepts are related.

Where do sexual desires stand in this dichotomy between innate/biogenic and acquired/sociogenic needs? Some human needs appear to be closely tied to physiological functions but do not require satisfaction for biological survival. Their satisfaction may simply enhance physical well-being or health, or promote more efficient or optimum functioning. One such need is for sensory and physical stimulation. We know that infants who lack such stimulation are not

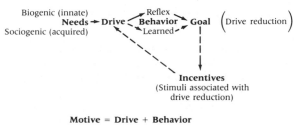

Motive = **Drive** + **Behavior**

———— Unbroken lines indicate innate connections
– – – – Broken lines indicate learned connections

FIGURE 7.1 Basic concepts in a learning model of human motivation

as healthy as those who receive it, perhaps because, as Margaret Ribble (1944) long ago suggested, blood circulation is improved with physical stimulation, exercise, and movement. Adults find sensory deprivation aversive and disorienting (which is why solitary confinement is such a severe and effective punishment). Sexual stimulation may be a variant of this more general need category and, when satisfied, may also have the effect of promoting optimum functioning without being biologically essential. As Carol Tavris told an interviewer (Hahn, 1977) after examining the responses of 100,000 women to a magazine questionnaire she had helped develop, female sexuality is "just plain fun . . . it's jolly. . . . A good, happy sex life is like having good health" (p. D-4)!

Hormonal changes at puberty appear to be associated in all cultures with increased attention to and desire for sexual experience, supporting the proposition that sexual motivation has a physiological component. On the other hand, sexual satisfaction is not necessary for the maintenance of either homeostatic equilibrium or life, and it may continue as a strong motivator in individuals with low levels of sex hormones—for example, in postmenopausal women and persons whose sex glands have been surgically removed. In normal adults, no reliable correlation exists between frequency of sexual behavior or the experience of sexual arousal (drive) and level of either androgen or estrogen. Miron Zuckerman (1971) concluded, after reviewing the literature, that "most cases of impotence in males and frigidity in women are not expressions of hormonal insufficiencies and do not respond to treatment with additional exogenous hormone" (p. 301). Only in some special instances (as for men who have underdeveloped testes) has hormone therapy been effective in increasing the frequency of sexual arousal.

As noted in a previous section of this chapter, sexual arousal is primarily a psychological phenomenon, and it can occur under a vast variety of conditions. It is affected by general physical contact or by stimulation of specific body parts, such as the clitoris, or of certain especially sensitive erogenous areas of the skin; it can also occur in response to any stimulus physically present, or to a fantasized or remembered image. Learning-oriented psychologists assume that such motivational stimuli, called *incentives* (see Figure 7.1), acquire their motivational properties through previous association with gratification or pleasure. For instance, many people of each gender attach erotic meaning to and are sexually aroused by some special song, situation, look, or memory. This approach to explaining sexual arousal, sometimes referred to as the appetitional theory of sexual motivation, contrasts sharply with Freud's libido theory, which postulates a fixed sexual drive. Ethel Person (1980) has distinguished between these two positions simply and succinctly, as follows: "In libido theory sexuality is both a motor force in culture and an innate force [in individuals] with which culture must contend. In appetitional theory the content of sexuality is formed by culture" (p. 607). In other words, as expressed by Ruth Bleier (1984), "our consciousness, our world, shapes our libido" (p. 166).

Given a state of sexual arousal, individuals behave in a variety of ways depending upon their particular past learning experiences. Among humans, all aspects of sexual *behavior* (that is, what we do to achieve satisfaction or pleasure) are acquired or learned. Just as the arousing stimuli vary, so too do the specific acts we engage in, the time and the place for the behavior, and the person(s) with whom we interact, if any. All these factors are subject to variation, depending upon one's cultural group and one's particular individual experiences as influenced by family, friends, special circumstances, and unique person/environment interactions. These variations have been well documented by social scientists and complement our personal experiences and observations.

In this view of sexuality, *homosexual* and *heterosexual* are adjectives that denote erotic attraction to same- and other-gender persons and require no major separation in a general discussion of sexual motivation or experience. We must recognize that in our society heterosexuality is typically assumed; it is only homosexuality that is questioned and examined for cause and explanation, but all expressions of sexuality have been learned. Philip Blumstein and Pepper Schwartz (1977) studied a sample of women and men who viewed themselves as bisexual and concluded that adult sexual preferences are not immutable and that either gender can be eroticized under particular circumstances. The researchers found, especially among the women, that sexual involvement followed "intense emotional attachment," which served as the "prerequisite for sexual attraction, sexual behavior, or a change in sexual identity" (p. 44). Alice Walker's novel *The Color Purple* (1982) is a compelling fictional account of such experience. The conclusion that sexual preferences can change in no way denies the validity of the experience of those persons who, from childhood or adolescence, have felt drawn to a particular sexual orientation. As noted by Carole Vance and Ann Snitow (1984):

> There are examples of both persistence and fluidity in sexual desire: for example, individuals who "knew" they were gay at an early age and remained so despite aversion therapy and incarceration, and others who "became" lesbian or gay at different stages of the life cycle in a manner suggesting internal change rather than belated expression of "repressed" desire. (p. 128)

Given the central role of learning in sexual behavior, we should not be surprised that women and men differ in the meanings they attach to sexuality. As William Simon and John Gagnon (1977) have pointed out, although adolescent boys are committed to sexuality and are encouraged to seek gratification, they receive little training in "the language and actions of romantic love," whereas adolescent girls are "committed to romantic love and relatively untrained in sexuality" (p. 126). In the process of dating, each gender must train "the other in what each wants and expects," but this exchange system does not always proceed smoothly. Researchers continue to document gender differences in the meaning and expectations of sexuality that result from social learning.

SEXUAL BEHAVIOR IN THE SERVICE OF OTHER GOALS

Sexual behavior in our culture serves a number of goals beyond the primary one of obtaining personal sexual gratification. These include serving as a symbol of autonomy or personal identity, as a status symbol, as something to be bought and sold, as a form of sport, as a way to maintain gender inequality, and as a way to communicate. In many instances, as we shall see, sex is used exploitatively in the interest of satisfying other objectives.

Sex As a Symbol of Autonomy or Personal Identity

That women are less likely than men to use sexuality to achieve identity has been argued by some writers (such as Person, 1980). Ann Snitow (1980), in reviewing how women novelists have treated sex in their works, concluded that although sex is sometimes presented as a reward for being daring and liberated, it is not presented (as in men's fiction) as a testing ground for the ego, as a way to assert oneself, or as a "symbol of triumph or defeat." Yet, such themes *have* appeared in contemporary novels by women, such as *Braided Lives* by Marge Piercy (1983), *August* by Judith Rossner (1983), and Gail Godwin's *A Mother and Two Daughters* (1983). The heroine in Marge Piercy's *Fly Away Home* (1984a), for example, recalls the beginning of her relationship with her husband as follows:

> She had slept with Ross, not out of passionate desire, not because she felt swept away, but because she was annoyed with herself for being twenty-one, graduated from college and still a virgin. . . . She was celebrating her independence of body, life, of judgment. (p. 170)

Similar reports have come from women's descriptions of their own experiences. Sarah Crichton (1983), for example, in an article about college women, began with a disclosure about herself:

> About all I can remember from spring in sophomore year is that I got myself a double bed. . . . For me, that bed was the ultimate symbol of adulthood—an advertisement that I was not only "sexually active," but that my body was my own, to do with as I pleased. (p. 68)

For this young woman, sex was a "means of defining yourself."

Maggie Scarf (1980) has presented portraits of some women for whom such an objective had serious negative consequences. During the course of her research on depression, she met women who told her that they had initiated sexual relationships "to ward off feelings of isolation" and to heighten activity or excitement. But their sexual interactions had proved to be poor substitutes for intimacy and had not increased their feelings of autonomy or control. In writing about the attitudes of black women, Toni Bambara (1974) has distinguished between control and indiscriminate sexual behavior. Among older women she remembers as having been influential in her own life, lip service was paid to virginity, but

> a greater premium was placed on sexual expertise; you were a "real woman" when you had knowledge of and

control of your sensual gifts. However, if a woman indiscriminately flaunted these gifts, she was either a loose woman or a fool. . . . So you learned growing up that . . . healthy liaisons should be based on partnership and sexual competency on both sides. (p. 41)

Sex As Status Symbol

Men boast of their sexual conquests, and women boast of the number of men who find them sexually attractive. Making such reports to friends is an attempt to gain social recognition and to enhance one's social status.

For Sylvia Plath (1972), speaking through a fictional heroine, the world in the 1950s was "divided into people who had slept with somebody and people who hadn't, and this seemed the only really significant difference between one person and another" (p. 66). Several decades later, the same issue is still salient. Since middle-class, college-educated women tend to marry later than working-class women, sexual experience outside of marriage may be a more compelling, status-relevant issue for the former. Writing from the perspective of a college woman, Sarah Crichton (1983) has described the "pressure" felt by sexually inexperienced women to whom virginity "simply means nobody wants you and you feel like shit." She quotes a 1980s junior at a midwestern university who echoes Plath's heroine of the 1950s: " 'I've got to get rid of it,' that's all you can think about" (p. 69).

Sex As a Commodity

Women have been purchased, won, conquered, taken, traded, or been part of the victor's booty in war. During the war in Bangladesh between East and West Pakistan, according to reporter Joyce Goldman (1972), "as many as 200,000 Bengali women, victims of rape by West Pakistani soldiers . . . [were] abandoned by their husbands, because no Moslem will live with a wife who has been touched by another man" (p. 84). A woman, in this view, has one owner; to be used by another man is to render her unclean and unworthy of her husband. In protest of this belief (which extends beyond the Moslem world), a group of Israeli women in a novel by E. M. Broner (1978) perform a hymenotomy on the 8-day-old daughter of one of them, saying, "May she not be delivered intact to her bridegroom or judged by her hymen but by the energies of her life" (p. 25).

Women are used to attract the attention of men and to sell products. For example, an ad for a centrifuge in a prestigious science journal reads, "The first beautiful centrifuge," and shows a beautiful blond woman in a lab coat standing next to the item. A newspaper advertisement for stereo equipment shows a cylinder surrounded by a nude woman in four different poses and asks the question, "Going 4 channel?" A magazine ad attempts to convince a prospective male buyer that "you can fit a lot of important things in Toyota's Wagon" by showing it filled with six lovely young women. A major airline attempts to lure customers by presenting a swimsuit-clad woman under a giant caption that reads, "What's your pleasure?" Women are thus used as "incentives" for men of varied backgrounds, education, and interests. A newspaper story describing how private companies "use sex to win government contracts" ("How Firms," 1980) was relegated to a midsection of the paper, presumably because this is not an unusual occurrence. The story informed its readers that sex is "routine" in the world of business and government contracting.

That sex can be exchanged for goods and services is a lesson learned across ethnic groups and is part of the experience of both black and white women. Thus, Gloria Joseph (1981b), writing about the childhood and adolescence of black women in America, has noted that in our society "sex is the dominant commodity for monetary profit, personal gains and gratifications, and human exploitation" (p. 205). Many adolescent girls are taught to "cash in" on their sex appeal, to use it to manipulate boys for material advantage. Ossie Guffy, a black woman, remembered her big sister's advice to her about sex (Guffy & Ledner, 1971):

> Boys lust even more than girls. . . . When a boy lusts after you, that's when you get him to do what you want. You've got to make them feel you're going to let them, and then when they're so horny they can't see straight, you kind of pull back and whisper you're afraid. Then . . . you start talking about how you'd love to have a charm bracelet, or a new scarf, or see a certain movie, and they'll fall all over themselves getting you what you want, 'cause they figure once you've got what *you* want, you'll give them what *they* want. (p. 63)

This advice is straight talk, direct and clear. Other girls receive similar but more subtle, ambiguous, and disguised messages from peers, parents, or the media. For example, in the real-life story of Teresa Cardenas told by Robert and Jane Coles (1978) we learn that her father, a strict, traditional patriarch, responded to knowledge of his daughter's well-paying job in a dance hall at the age of 15 by reminding her that "money is not an evil thing." When Teresa considered consulting the priest, her father said, "No—there are some things it's best not to tell priests" (p. 157).

The message that sex is exchangeable for goodies is so well accepted in our culture that we treat with good humor even the portrayal of very young girls in this role. One full-page *New York Times Magazine* ad, for example, showed a seductive little girl with a sexy look dressed as half adult, half child with an enormous fur coat under the caption, "Get what you've always wanted." Such advertisements do not produce public complaint or concern because our culture accepts and encourages women to use sexuality as a means of exchange. As noted by Andrée Nicola-McLaughlin (1985):

> Exploitation of the sexuality of women is a basic element of American enterprise—the *blood* of Big Business—by which billions of dollars in profit are amassed annually, capitalizing on women's sexuality in . . . corporate-sponsored media advertising, literature, music, movies, television, medicine, beauty pageants and pornography. (p. 33)

Sex As Sport

Sexual acts are often viewed as requiring skill, expertise, and training; persons boast of themselves or others as expert lovers or, like players of a game, they "score" or win. This attitude is reflected in the extraordinary popularity of how-to sex manuals and in the concern that some mental health practitioners have expressed about the "demands" individuals feel for sexual "performance."

The idea that sex is something a person can do well or badly seems to be an old one, and has provided both genders with a source of humor about the other's vulnerabilities. Rayna Green (1977), in an article about "bawdy lore of Southern women," shared some of the tales told by the Southern women among whom she grew up about the sexual errors of men. "Usually the subject for laughter is men's boasts, failures or inadequacies ('comeuppance for lack of uppcomance,' as one of my aunts would say)" (p. 31). Bawdy lore, according to Green, provided a safe way to laugh at men's pretensions; helped relieve women's sexual disappointments, frustrations, humiliations, and anxieties; and also provided sex education for young girls. What they did not understand in the joke (which they were supposed to hear but not supposed to hear) they later inquired about

from friends or relatives. Tony Bambara (1974) has presented a similar picture of the sex education of young black girls by older women. There is bound to be an aunt, she wrote, who will "encourage you to hang out in the beauty parlor or her living room with her and her friends and eavesdrop," where some woman will look you straight in the eye and warn, "If he don't know what he's doing, pitch him out the bed on his head," for "while the church ladies daily castigated the run-around men and adulterers, they were equally adamant about men who . . . withheld themselves or could not or would not deliver. For that was sinful, an abuse of nature" (p. 40).

When sex with others falls short of our expectations, and their or our own expertise is found wanting, we invent pleasure machines. William Masters and Virginia Johnson popularized the vibrator and, according to a recent report (Ehrenreich, Hess, & Jacobs, 1982), "a growing number of housewives can choose between a Tupperware party and a Tupper-style party where the wares are exotic sex paraphernalia instead of plastic containers" (p. 61). In his film *Sleeper*, a science fiction view of the future, Woody Allen presented the ultimate sensual device, an "orgasmatron" for one.

Recent indications that sadomasochistic sex is now popular can be viewed as another extension of sex as sport. The influence of "S & M" can be seen in women's fashions, as illustrated by an entire section in *Vogue* magazine on steel accessories worn by wide-eyed, frightened-looking models; arm shackles as bracelets, steel belts, and neck leashes were featured. The appropriate matching clothing, described in fashion jargon as "hard-edged" and "rough," was shown with jagged edges and cut-out pieces, as though ripped (Howard, 1983). The sexual innuendoes were clear from the body postures, sultry lips, and tousled hair of the models.

Sex in the Maintenance of Gender Inequality

A well-known ad for men's shoes (withdrawn after publicized protests by women's groups) showed a lovely nude woman lying contentedly next to a man's shoe, with the message "Keep her where she belongs." Although we might be inclined to laugh at this old cliché, it seems to be remarkably sturdy. In the late 1970s and early 1980s, for example, a top-selling manufacturer of women's underwear produced a series of full-page glossy ads, in color, for the

New York Times Magazine that showed women in bikini underpants and bras in outrageous places and in various roles: in telephone booths, in the subway, in an airplane cockpit, conducting an orchestra, playing basketball, as a physician talking with a patient, as a lawyer pleading a case, as a chef, as a businesswoman, as a tourist, as a musician, and so on. In every case, the only other persons in the ad were fully clothed, appropriately dressed men who functioned as obvious counterpoints to the ridiculous (but sexy) women.

This kind of sexual put-down of women, which thereby elevates men's image, is also evident in writing that emerged from the politically passionate period of the 1960s and 1970s, when sizable numbers of black and white women and men worked together to achieve common social objectives. Even within these groups, sex with men functioned to maintain women's lesser status. Stokeley Carmichael's comment about women in the civil rights movement, that their "only position" within it was "prone," has been widely quoted (see, for example, Morgan, 1970, p. 35). We have paid less attention, however, to how women saw themselves in this arena of radical political activity. Marge Piercy's (1979) Vida tells us:

> She would sometimes in the middle of a serious conversation catch herself looking at a man in a certain way she had learned over the years as apology to men for being smart, aggressive, political, for being a competitor in the real things. Putting out a certain sexual buzz was a way of apologizing for being herself. (p. 124)

Similarly, in Rosellen Brown's *Civil Wars* (1984), Jessie remembers herself as a Northern college girl working in the civil rights movement in Mississippi:

> She was Teddy's girl. . . . They made room for her, but not for herself; they respected her because they must; she walked in his aura. She was exhilarated and depressed in the same instant; then Teddy would come up behind her, turn her to him, no matter where they were, and suck a kiss so sweetly from her lips (right in the middle of conversation, as her lips formed an important word) that speech and opinion, hers at least, were put in their place. (p. 237)

Other novels about the 1960s, such as Alice Walker's *Meridian* (1976) and Sara Davidson's *Loose Change* (1978), relate how sexual relationships with men served to neutralize and diminish women's bids for leadership in radical political groups and to prevent their equal participation in decision making. Sexual involvement with a politically active man was viewed as a contribution by the woman to the "movement," just as in other times and places sexual relationships with men have been seen as contributing to their successes and progress by promoting their health and welfare.

A somewhat different motive for sexual behavior, but one that also serves to maintain gender inequality, is to obtain male protection against the demands made by other men. For example, Alice Walker (1976) has described sex for one of her heroines in high school as "not pleasure, but a sanctuary in which her mind was freed of any consideration for all the other males in the universe who might want anything of her. It was resting from pursuit" (p. 62).

Sex As a Means of Communication

Sexual play with another person involves a unique closeness achievable in no other way; it permits and provides the opportunity for the most intimate nonverbal communication. Sometimes, what a person cannot verbalize—the tenderest and most gentle of feelings—can be expressed sexually. (Or a sexual encounter can communicate the most violent and hostile of feelings, short of murder.)

Many women find it difficult to relate sexually to their husbands or lovers after an argument; their partners, on the other hand, may feel that they can "make up" by "making love." Lillian Rubin (1976) has provided examples of this kind of conflict among both working-class and middle-class married couples.

> He says, "I want to make love." She says, "It doesn't feel like love." Neither quite knows what the other is talking about; both feel vaguely guilty and uncomfortable—aware only that somehow they're passing each other, not connecting. . . . Split off, as he is, from the rest of the expressive-emotional side of himself, sex may be the one place where he can allow himself the expression of deep feelings. . . . His wife, on the other hand . . . finds it difficult to be comfortable with her feelings in the very area in which he has the greatest—sometimes the only—ease. (pp. 147f.)

With great frequency, the women who responded to Shere Hite's (1976) questionnaire told how important body contact and physical closeness were to them. Communication through touching and proximity were valued for their own sakes and not just as behavior leading to intercourse or orgasm. We can also communicate our caring and concern by providing pleasure for another person.

WOMEN'S AMBIVALENCE ABOUT SEXUALITY

Women derive pleasure from sexual arousal and orgasm. The experience of sexual gratification appears to be very comparable in women and men, both psychologically and physiologically; ample data, some of which have already been cited and discussed, support these conclusions. But the social context in which sexual behavior is learned differs in the conditions or circumstances it provides for women and men and in resultant attitudes toward sexuality. As we have seen, women's sexuality is exploited to a far greater extent than men's in our culture. Consequently, men almost always see sex as a positive goal, but women view it as having both positive and negative aspects, and women's ambivalence about sexuality often keeps us from enjoying it fully. Let us look more closely at this issue.

Woman's Role As "Gatekeeper"

Adolescent boys typically learn that sexual activity is desirable and pleasurable (and even necessary for good health). Heterosexual experience confers high status and signifies maturity and manhood. Teenage girls, however, are taught opposite or unclear values in relation to sexuality: many still learn that sexual activity is primarily a means to attract and keep a boyfriend, and that a girl should engage in sexual behavior only to the extent necessary to satisfy her boyfriend's needs, not her own. Women are still given the responsibility of restraining and tempering the sexual demands of men, whose needs, they are taught, are greater and more insistent than their own. Naomi McCormick (1979), for example, found that among a group of college students having sex was regarded "as a male goal and avoiding sex as a female goal." A subsequent study (McCormick, Brannigan, & LaPlante, 1984) supported the earlier findings and found evidence that women and men behave in accordance with these stereotypes. Thus, a sample of men college students "reported using strategies more to have sex," while "women reported using strategies more to avoid sex." Researchers continue to find that women report themselves to be less comfortable than men in initiating sex and more comfortable refusing it, thus acting as "gatekeepers." In one study (Grauerholz & Serpe, 1985), the women who did report initiating sexual intimacies were likely to have had more sexual partners and to be more aware of sexual inequalities than the other women. In general, however, these data indicated that "rising sexual intercourse rates . . . do not suggest a fundamental change in sex roles" (p. 1058).

Sexual relations with boys, though instrumental in keeping their attention, reduce an adolescent girl's status, besmirch her reputation, and mark her as a "bad girl." Lillian Rubin's (1976) study of married couples led her to conclude that although

> the media tell us that the double standard of sexual morality is dead . . . women don't believe it. They know from experience that it is alive and well, that it exists side by side with the new ideology that heralds their sexual liberation. They know all about who are the "bad girls" in school, in the neighborhood; who are the "good girls." Everybody knows! . . . The definitions of "good girl" and "bad girl" may vary somewhat according to class, but the fundamental ideas those words encompass are not yet gone either from our culture or our consciousness at any class level. (pp. 136f.)

Adolescent boys may gain respect from sexual exploits, but among girls such experiences are still considered a sign of deviance or low status. Sexual offenses are used to define delinquency for girls but not for boys, and this difference is maintained in the legal approach to prostitution. In most states, it is the seller (typically a woman) and not the buyer (typically a man) who is considered more reprehensible, threatening to society, and criminal.

Although old attitudes are resistant to change, the research literature indicates clearly that women's sexuality is now more freely and frequently expressed in behavior than during our parents' and grandparents' young adulthoods. Women's magazines have polled their readers about their sexual behavior and attitudes; for example, among *Cosmopolitan* readers, 82 percent said they had "seduced a man" at least once ("Women in Poll," 1980), and among readers of *Glamour* magazine, sex before marriage was acceptable to two thirds of the women between 18 and 24 and to one third of the women over 55 ("Poll Says," 1983). We do not know how well the respondents to these polls represent women in general, however. J. Roy Hopkins (1977) compared the results of surveys conducted before 1965 with those of surveys in the 1970s. He concluded that among young adolescents aged 13 to 15, there "is some evidence for earlier experimentation with intercourse," but that the actual number of incidences has been exaggerated and that there is more talk than action. Among college-aged women and men, the data point to a dramatic increase in sexual activity and to "intergender *convergence* in sexual behavior." Compared to earlier college surveys in which 55 percent of the men and 25 percent of the women reported premarital coitus, those conducted after 1965 found at least 60 percent of the men and at least 40 percent of the women reporting such behavior. A national survey conducted in 1983 found that among single women in their 20s, 80 percent had had sexual relations at least once, and on the average with 4.5 men, and that one third had lived with a man ("Sex Habits," 1986).

Despite the increased frequency of sexual behavior by women, researchers seem to agree that conventional attitudes and gender relationships persist. For example, comparing a sample of college women in 1973 with one in 1978, Meg Gerrard (1982) found that among the latter there was a lower correlation between sexual activity and sex guilt (defined as self-punishment for "violating standards of proper sexual conduct"). In other words, in 1978, single college women might have been sexually active even if such behavior produced feelings of guilt or psychological discomfort. There may be, in other words, a disparity between what young women do and how they feel. One group of investigators (Peplau, Rubin, & Hill, 1977), after studying a large sample of heterosexual couples who had been dating for an average of 8 months, concluded that as *individuals*, men and women had similar sexual experiences, but within *couples*, "traditional sexual role playing persists" (p. 108). This same conclusion was reached in the large-scale and more recent study of couples by Philip Blumstein and Pepper Schwartz (1983), and is complemented by other evidence. One study (Keller, Elliott, & Gunberg, 1982) of over 400 college students examined relationships between psychological characteristics and sexual behavior. Although reiterating the often-cited finding that "male and female single college students are moving toward an equal standard," the researchers found important differences between the genders. Women were more likely than men to have just one sexual partner, and men did not seem to be moving "toward sex with affection." Sexually active men self-reported more dominance in relationships, and women self-reported more affection.

In general, then, women are expressing sexuality more openly than in prior generations but in the context of intimate love relationships in which the traditional power inequalities between the genders persist. Although losing one's virginity appears to be a powerful motive among college women (and perhaps among young women in general), sexual experience does not appear to confer general likability. Luis Garcia (1982) found that women designated as being well experienced sexually were evaluated less positively by a sample of unmarried college men and women than were women with less experience; and in another study (Garcia & Derfel, 1983), women shown in slides as interacting with men in nontraditional ways (for example, staring directly at a man rather than looking down) were judged as being more sexually experienced than women whose nonverbal behavior was traditional. Heterosexual experience, therefore, may enhance a young unmarried woman's positive feelings of maturity and independence, but may also produce negative consequences—she may be evaluated less highly by her peers and be more apt to be associated with nontraditional ("unfeminine") attributes. Such a double bind is not likely to exist for a young man.

Nameless or Shameful Genitals

Other factors contribute to women's ambivalence about sex. Men experience pleasure in the use of their penises, for urination, masturbation, and copulation. Even little boys who may be told horrible tales by their parents about the evils that will befall them if they play with themselves have ample opportunities to find out differently from peers, older boys, and personal trial and error. By and large, boys acquire positive associations for that part of their body that is the focus of their sexuality. Girls, on the other hand, learn to expect largely negative consequences from their sexuality, to anticipate pain or problems during menstruation, pregnancy, childbirth, and during their first sexual intercourse.

A recent study (Gartrell & Mosbacher, 1984) has documented differences in what little girls and boys learn to call their genitals. From the retrospective responses of adults to questions about their first learning of words for genitalia, the researchers found that girls were far less likely than boys to have learned the correct anatomical names for their own genitalia as children, that both boys and girls learned *penis* significantly earlier than they learned any correct name for female genitals, and that the incorrect words taught for the latter were more euphemistic and pejorative than the nonanatomical words learned for male genitals. Thus, while *peenee* or *peter*, for example, were learned by some little boys instead of *penis*, the former terms may be considered derivatives of the latter, whereas *privates*, *shame*, *nasty*, or *down there*, words learned by the girls, have no linguistic relationship to *vagina* or *clitoris*. These data indicate that our culture regards the sexuality of boys and men not only as more important, but as nicer, cleaner, and less embarrassing than the sexuality of girls and women.

Woman As Sex Object

Sexuality to many women means being a "sex object." While this concept has been translated into humorous images for cartoons, films, and fiction, it is of utmost seriousness to women, who learn from all areas of the culture that we have "utility." One cartoon given to me by a student shows a sexily dressed woman clerk behind a drugstore counter. A sign on the counter reads, "If You Don't See It, Ask for It." The customer, a genial, well-dressed gentleman in suit, tie, and hat, smiles and asks, "Can I see your tits?" We learn that women can be bought (by favors, by being "wined and dined," or by cash), exchanged, treasured, or manhandled. I suspect that only rarely has a young woman not questioned at some point whether she was being used in a sexual relationship.

The interchangeability of women (as bodies) is the subject of a cartoon (another student donation) in which a movie "love scene" is about to be filmed. The leading man lies waiting on the bed. The male director has his arm around the voluptuous, naked woman who will also play in the scene; she is faceless, and the director shouts, "Makeup!" The strength of our culture's acceptance of (and blindness to) women's treatment as relatively interchangeable objects on display for the titillation and amusement of men can be illustrated by a report of changes being made by *Playboy* magazine to reflect gender equality. Christine Heffner, president of Playboy Enterprises, explained that "we have come through the sexual revolution and the women's movement and men and women feel more comfortable with each other now" (in Geist, 1985). In keeping with the spirit of social change, the Playboy clubs in New York hired men as "rabbits" in addition to women as "bunnies," a move that did not succeed in attracting more customers; all Playboy clubs were closed in June of 1986 for financial reasons. According to Hefner (in Geist, 1985), *Playboy* magazine now intends to emphasize relationships and to present "women as more than sex objects." Is the new emphasis illustrated by the November 1985 issue that featured a group of the smartest women in the United States (members of the high-IQ association MENSA) posing nude?

Sexual Harassment

Related to the still prevalent view of women as "curves and orifices, or tits 'n' ass with a bit of class," as Ross Wetzsteon has put it (1977), is another issue that contributes to the ambivalent nature of sexuality for women: our deeply felt fear of rape and the frequency with which we experience sexual harassment. Girls learn at an early age that we are vulnerable and largely unprotected from male predators. We try to separate the bad men (who openly leer, catcall, or follow us on the street) from the good ones (our fathers, brothers, and boyfriends), but such a classification becomes increasingly difficult as we encounter more and more men who are fathers or brothers to some other women but pinchers, leerers, or assaulters to us. Male college professors and business executives may be more subtle than the often stereotyped (and probably maligned) blue-collar construction worker, but their sexual allusions and unwanted advances are no less insistent and demeaning. As noted in a report by the Project on the Status and Education of Women ("Sexual Harassment," 1978):

> Fear of ridicule, and a sense of helplessness about the problem and a feeling that it's a personal dilemma have kept the problem concealed. Many men believe a woman's "no" is really "yes", and therefore do not accept her refusal. Additionally, when a man is in a position of power, such as employer or teacher, the woman may be coerced or feel forced to submit. Women who openly charge harassment are often not believed, may be ridiculed, may lose their job, be given a bad grade or be mistreated in some way. (p. 1)

Research has documented the widespread nature of sexual harassment. Sexual harassment has been reported by patients and clients in medical and legal settings, by students, teachers, employees, vacationers, or women just walking alone almost anywhere, and the literature on this subject continues to grow. Lin Farley (1978) found that 70 percent of the women she surveyed had personally experienced sexual harassment on the job. A study of the federal workplace, involving the largest number of randomly sampled respondents yet questioned (Tangri, Burt, & Johnson, 1982), found that 42 percent of the women reported having been sexually harassed at work within the past two years, primarily by older married men. Karen Lindsey (1977) has related the experiences of women who while working as waitresses, in assembly lines, in advertising, in hospitals, on Capitol Hill, and so on, have been approached for "sexual favors" by their male employers or coworkers. The women vary in age, position, and background, but all share the common experience of having been demeaned, frightened, and treated as a sexual commodity.

Lest we think that sexual harassment is less of a problem in the enlightened late 1980s than in previous decades, Mary Murphy (1986) has reminded us of its continued serious existence in the entertainment industry. Most people in the industry, according to Murphy, agree that harassment

> is the centerpiece of a pervasive problem in Hollywood: exploitation of women. So pervasive is it, in fact, that the Screen Actors Guild has set up a 24-hour hotline to deal with sexual harassment and other complaints. . . . The cliches . . . are all true—the casting couch, the porno-movie producers on the prowl, the agents who trade time for sexual favors. (pp. 3, 11)

A cartoon from *Playboy* tells it like it is. The leering, obviously satisfied boss is getting into his clothes while his secretary is zipping up her skimpy outfit. "By the way," says the boss, "for your raise, you have to ask Mr. Peacock"!

Women and men differ in their evaluations of the unwanted sexual initiatives received by women. For example, in a study of almost 1000 students at the University of Rhode Island (Lott, Reilly, & Howard, 1982), my colleagues and I found women and men differ significantly in their level of agreement with 11 distinct statements dealing with sexually harassing behavior (such as "An attractive woman has to expect sexual advances and should learn how to handle them"). With respect to every statement, men responded with greater tolerance for sexual harassment. In other words, the men viewed sexually related behavior on the job and at school as something to be expected and as less problematic and serious than did the women. A subsequent study has replicated these findings (Reilly, Lott, & Gallogly, in press).

When women are sexually harassed, we are often not quite certain that we have not somehow been at fault. Have we enticed the man by our manner or our dress, been too friendly or flirtatious? Women may be reluctant to discuss or report sexual harassment if they are not certain that they did not somehow provoke it. Consider how difficult it is to reconcile the humiliation experienced by receiving the unwanted attentions of a man with the feeling of flattery that

comes from being found attractive by him. Among the lessons learned by adolescent girls is that to attract a man is highest on the list of achievements, but just how to do this appropriately or respectably remains unclear. As noted by Judith Laws and Pepper Schwartz (1977):

> Those parts of the body which are sexualized in our culture—legs, face, breasts, and to a lesser extent buttocks—are subjected to special routines of display and enhancement. . . . A socialization of the young woman for the role of sex object takes place during puberty. A great deal of attention is focused on the way she looks, and she receives a lot of feedback on her "good points" and "figure faults." . . . She learns the techniques of enhancement, display and artifice. . . . The dialectic between display and concealment, or permissible flaunting and taboo, can be seen clearly in the conventions of dress. (pp. 42f.)

The results of one study (Edmonds & Cahoon, 1984) indicate that college women and men agree substantially in their ratings of women's clothing on how "sexually arousing" they appear to men. Other evidence, however, suggests that men tend to perceive the same cues as more explicitly sexual in meaning than do women. A group of researchers (Zellman, Johnson, Giarusso, & Goodchilds, 1979) studied a sizable sample of adolescents in Los Angeles and found that the young women were significantly less likely than the men to interpret behavioral cues and clothing in sexual terms. In an experimental study, Antonia Abbey (1982) had pairs of mixed-gender observers watch pairs of mixed-gender actors (all college students) carry on a five-minute discussion after which the observers rated the actors on various dimensions. The men were found to "interpret women's friendliness as an indication of sexual interest," and to see themselves and other men as well as women in a sexual context. Abbey concluded that "men are more likely to perceive the world in sexual terms and to make sexual judgments than women are" (p. 836).

Perhaps the greater primacy of sex in men's interpretations of the world contributes to the sexual harassment of women and adds to men's conviction that women who say "no" are merely being coy and hoping to be pursued further. Although our culture strongly encourages women to be attractive to men, it also promises that we will make decisions about which men to accept—that we will have choices. However, too many boys and men do not learn the necessary complementary lessons (such as taking a woman's "no" seriously) to make the cultural script of heterosexual courtship play smoothly. Part of men's reality is their higher status and power and, therefore, they can with relative impunity consider women (no matter what else they may be or what skills they may have) as fundamentally sexual objects that men have the right to use. (Some men may find it difficult to reconcile this cultural message with their own self-doubts, fears of incompetence, lack of assertiveness, and needs for acceptance.) For many men, sex and the aggressive pursuit of sex may be difficult to separate; others may not learn to distinguish well among the different forms of such pursuit, which range from visual ogling, whistling, or verbal comments about a woman's body to assault.

Performance Pressure and Fear of Pregnancy

Changing expectations for women's sexual behavior may have added to women's ambivalence about sexuality as increasingly greater demands are made of heterosexual women by husbands or boyfriends. Lillian Rubin (1976) has pointed out that

> until recently, women were expected to submit passively to sex; now they are told their passivity diminishes their husband's enjoyment. Until recently, especially among the less-educated working class, orgasm was an unexpected gift; now it is a requirement of adequate sexual performance. These new definitions of adequacy have many women feeling "under the gun"—fearful and anxious if they do not achieve orgasm; if it does not happen at the "right" moment—that is, at the instant of their husband's ejaculation; or if they are uncomfortable about engaging in behaviors that feel alien or aberrant to them. (p. 150)

One woman told Rubin that

> it's really important for him [her husband] that I reach a climax and I try to every time. He says it just doesn't make him feel good if I don't. But it's hard enough to do it once! What'll happen if he finds out about these women who have lots of climaxes? (p. 153)

A woman's orgasm signifies to a man that he has performed well and he may, therefore, require it of his partner as a validation of his sexual skill or competence.

Despite the availability of contraceptives, the fear of an unwanted pregnancy still contributes to women's ambivalence about sex. In *Meridian*, Alice Walker (1976) described a southern college for black women in which one common experience brought women from different social backgrounds together.

> Any girl who had ever prayed for her period to come was welcome to the commemoration, which was held in the guise of a slow May Day dance. . . . It was the only time in all the many social activities at Saxon that every girl was considered equal. On that day, they held each other's hands tightly. (p. 45)

It is the unusual woman who has not experienced, at some time in her life, that indescribable anxiety associated with being late, and for whom fear of pregnancy has not interfered in some way with the free expression of sexuality.

DECREASING AMBIVALENCE AND EXPLOITATION

Given the present social conditions under which young women learn sexual behavior, it seems inevitable that both lesbian and heterosexual women will feel conflict with respect to sexuality. All women in our culture experience or observe similar consequences for sexual behavior. There is the positive anticipation of pleasure from body arousal, sensual excitement, and the gratification to be derived from physical contact and affection with another person. But at the same time, there is anxiety about possible negative consequences: concern about sexual exploitation; uncertainty about one's adequacy; fear of pregnancy; social rejection for having (or for not having) a sexual relationship; and concern about the meaning of the relationship. Judith Laws and Pepper Schwartz (1977) have suggested that most young women today have been exposed to a sexual standard that emerged during the 1960s: sex is permissible if love is present. "But *when is love present*? . . . [The new standard] that both partners should love in order for sex to be acceptable . . . provides no way to tell if your partner feels the same way you do" (pp. 48f.).

Women's ambivalence about sexuality should decrease as we experience mainly positive outcomes and communicate this experience to other women. One study of two generations of college women (the classes of 1954 and 1980) from upper- and middle-class families found a largely comfortable and substantial amount of intergenerational communication reported by both daughters and mothers, with the older women "prepared to be influenced by the newer sexual mores" (Yalom, Estler, & Brewster, 1982). According to Judith Laws and Pepper Schwartz (1977), women are becoming more accepting of masturbation, "are receiving permission, instruction, and support in learning about their own bodies and the patterns of their own sexual response" (p. 62), and are more sexually assertive and less reactive or passive, are taking more responsibility for contraception, and are talking more about what maximizes their sexual pleasure.

In addition, as women grow older the pleasures derived from sexual experience and close physical contact with another person should become more potent and the negative associations of badness, of pain, and of being used should weaken. Positive outcomes may also increase as women explore more varied "sexual scripts" and experience erotic pleasure with other women. The possibility of such pleasure is increasingly discussed among women and is beginning to be explored in the media. For example, a film presented on network television in 1986 ("My Two Loves") sensitively dramatized the development of erotic attraction between two attractive upper-middle-class white women who had become close friends.

Sexual conflict for young women is unlikely to grow less intense until both genders are socialized to expect the same outcomes from their sexual experiences and to give similar meaning and value to them. This change, in turn, is not likely to occur while men and women continue to be unequal in social status. Changes in sexual standards and greater tolerance for sexuality in an otherwise unchanged world, in which women have less value and power than men, will merely compound the pressures on women, increase the chances for exploitation, and enhance the probability of conflict.

As noted by Barbara Ehrenreich, Elizabeth Hess, and Gloria Jacobs (1982), feminism is "the first political movement in history to address itself to sensual desire, . . . to personal eroticism as *political issues*" (p. 88). Intense discussion and debate is taking place today among feminists about sexual values and behavior—about dangers and pleasures in various sexual practices (for example, Ferguson, 1984; Philipson, 1984; Vance, 1984). While they have not reached consensus about what women's sexuality *should be*, most feminists would, I believe, subscribe to the values expressed by Charlotte Bunch (in Ehrenreich et al., 1982) and prefer "a sexuality that is based on exploration and freedom of choice, but that also values the human being, soul, body, and intellect . . . [and] the quality of interaction of people" (p. 87).

An important first step is understanding that women and men are fundamentally similar in sexuality in terms of psychological and physiological processes and the learning of motives and responses to sexual cues. But though necessary, this knowledge is not sufficient to eliminate either the ambivalence from women's sexual attitudes or sexual exploitation. We must also dispel other old myths about the nature of women (and men) and work toward eliminating the arbitrary differences in status, power, and role expectations that separate the genders.

Relationships: Love, Marriage, Other Options

The miracle [of love] . . . is its energy . . . the way it actually manufactures more love and further energy like a plant manufacturing chlorophyll as sustenance for the desire to manufacture more.

Robin Morgan *(1982a, p. 137)*

My wedding day came. I awoke to the sight of my bridal gown hanging on the door and my father standing by my bed smiling and mussing my hair. "I won't be waking my little girl up ever again," he said. It was a storybook day. All the details went smoothly, and when it was over, when the streamers were on the car and horns were honking and people laughing, I threw my bouquet— carefully aiming for a girlfriend. . . . We all knew what [the mandate] . . . was: each princess must find her prince. If she failed . . . she lived the reverse side of the fairy tale.

Patricia O'Brien *(1973, p. 22)*

I do not want relations which are debilitating and depressing, which sap my creative ability and capacity to love. . . . If we are not better persons for the relationship, then I can reflect, reconsider and choose to improve the situation.

Marcia Keller *(1984, p. 15)*

C H A P T E R   8

*I*n childhood and adolescence girls have entered into positive relationships with family members and peers. They have developed affection, respect, admiration, and concern for particular persons of both genders, and felt pleasure in their presence. Warm, loving relationships—with parents, siblings, children, friends, and colleagues—continue to be part of adult experience. Such relationships will be discussed in other chapters—those on parenting, adult personality, employment. In this chapter, we focus on romantic love, on the marriage of heterosexual couples, and on the nonmarried life-styles characteristic of more and more contemporary women for longer periods of our lives.

ROMANTIC LOVE

From our earliest years, women are taught to be concerned with romance. We are supposed to dream of it, long for it, weave our lives around it, and devote much energy to its pursuit and maintenance. We get this message in myriad ways from our culture's image-producers. For example, in a magazine popular with working women, *Cosmopolitan*, an advertisement for a telephone answering machine ("Record a Call," 1984), shown on page 122, tells women that we need the machine, not for messages from friends, family, or work colleagues, but so that we do not hurt our love lives by missing calls from men.

Our patriarchal, heterosexual majority culture tells women that it is through the love of a man that we will achieve completeness and mature identity. As Shulamith Firestone (1971) has put it, a woman's "whole identity hangs in the balance of her love life. She is allowed to love herself only if a man finds her worthy of love" (p. 132). Not surprisingly, then, when women have written about romantic love of men, they have typically described both passion and pain—an ambivalent experience, sought eagerly but with the anticipation of disillusionment and hurt. Our culture promises fulfillment and happiness from

love between a woman and a man, but often the promise is too great and is disconfirmed by the realities of experience. The joy to be found in love is often undermined when the partners are unequal in power and resources. Perhaps, despite films, magazines, and advertisements that continue to sell romantic love with men, many women no longer really believe in it, but pursue it, nevertheless, because it is expected and brings social rewards.

Definition

For many years Albert Lott and I have worked together in studying the antecedents and consequences of interpersonal attraction (1968, 1972, 1974). Our basic hypothesis, supported by considerable empirical data, is that people learn to like one another if, when they are together, they experience positive outcomes or pleasure. In other words, when a person is rewarded in the presence of another, she or he acquires a positive attitude toward that other, and this positive attitude defines liking or attraction. Liking depends on the frequency and quality of the reward that we experience in someone else's presence, and on the infrequency of pain or punishment. (When the same person evokes both strong positive and strong negative feelings, the result is ambivalence and a relationship characterized by conflict.) To like a particular person is to expect that we will feel good in that person's company because we will have positive or rewarding experiences. For us to like a person, that person need only be present (in the flesh or symbolically) while we are receiving rewards, whether or not the person has been responsible for providing them directly or has been instrumental in obtaining them. If a person is the direct source of gratification, or if the likelihood of pleasurable consequences is increased as a direct result of interaction with him or her, learning to like that person is even more probable.

Within this framework, love is distinguished from liking when the positive feelings for another person are especially strong, when they are derived from

Do you miss your boyfriend?

When guys call you and you're not home, who knows what you might miss?

That's why you need a telephone answering machine.

And nothing can help your love life as easily and efficiently as Record-A-Call. Thanks to the advanced micro-computer technology of our new model 580 shown.

And you can get your messages by remote control without going home when you get pleasantly delayed someplace.

So see the full line of Record-A-Calls at your dealer. And hear what you've been missing.

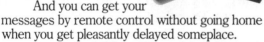

Record a Call
Because people are too good to miss.

Love lives of women are made easy and efficient with a telephone answering machine.

multiple sources or experiences with the person, and when the needs being gratified are particularly powerful and significant. It is when sexual gratification is a major source of the acquired attractiveness of a person that the term *romantic love* applies. In other words, romantic love is distinguished from liking and other forms of love by the element of sexual pleasure. Some have suggested that absorption in the relationship (Rubin, 1970) and fantasy (Berscheid & Walster, 1978) also play especially important roles in romantic love. Other descriptions of romantic love "include a sense of urgency; a high degree of possessiveness and jealousy; a diminished commitment to all outside interests; and a feverish amount of sexual passion" (Latham, 1985, p. 98).

What Love, American-Style, Promises Women

When we love another, we anticipate positive experiences in that person's presence. As a consequence, we tend to approach (to seek after) and to pay attention to those we love; to learn new behavior that the loved individual approves or supports, and to model our behavior after his or hers; to be sympathetic with a loved person's feelings; and to experience arousal (heightened motivation or drive) in that person's presence. Love, which stems fundamentally from positive experiences, endows the object of our love with "good" qualities and leads us to anticipate continued pleasure in the loved person's presence.

But instead of continued pleasure we often get pain. Our culture has made heterosexual romantic love difficult for women by encouraging us to find our worth and security in relationships instead of in the totality of our lives, and by encouraging us to confuse romance with submission, love with sacrifice, and to juxtapose man's strength against woman's weakness. Our expectations influence the kind of relationships we settle for, and too often these relationships turn out to be unsatisfactory. Let us now examine how women's experiences enhance and frustrate the development of heterosexual romantic love and what additional meanings or significance such love has for women in our culture.

Attention, Prestige, and Self-Esteem At 15, for a few brief weeks, I fabricated an imaginary boyfriend (complete with photograph) to enhance my popularity and status among my friends. "The woman in love," wrote Simone de Beauvoir (1949/1961), "feels endowed with a high and undeniable value; she is at last allowed to idolize herself through the love she inspires. She is overjoyed to find in her lover a witness . . . [that] she is a wondrous offering at the foot of the altar of her god" (pp. 607f.). In countless stories and films women are shown acquiring self-esteem by attracting the attention and receiving the approval of a man. In *An Unmarried Woman* (a 1970s film hailed by critics for its forthright depiction of the struggles of a modern woman for independence), the heroine is crushed and demoralized by the unexpected ending of her marriage. She continues her interest in her work and copes with the problems of her adolescent daughter but does not emerge from depression and self-doubt until, like the sleeping beauties in our fairy tales, she is kissed by the prince, or in this case revived by the attentions of a handsome, charming, rich, talented, and protective man. *Hannah and Her Sisters*, a 1986 film produced by Woody Allen, resolves the problems of three women by the end of the movie by settling each one into a love relationship with a man, and marriage.

A woman in a love relationship is courted, feted, admired, extolled, and flattered. Someone is paying attention and she can, by what she does and says, significantly affect another person's feelings and behavior. Data reported from a study of college students (Rubin, Peplau, & Hill, 1981) suggest that in the earliest part of a romantic relationship women may concentrate primarily on enhancing their attractiveness or desirability, while men place greater importance on the "desire to fall in love." The researchers found that men scored higher on a romanticism scale (which tapped such beliefs as in love at first sight), suggesting that "men tend to fall in love more readily than women," and in the earliest stages of a relationship men reported greater attraction and love for their girlfriends than they received in return. This state of affairs changed as the relationship continued, supporting the proposition that women may first seek to attract a man, deriving attention, prestige, and self-esteem from his expressed love for her, before her love is expressed in return.

Suffering, Sacrifice, and Service Both men and women have been led to associate a woman's love for a man with her submission to him. The macho man is expected to sweep his lady off her feet while she swoons with delight. Rhett Butler carrying the half-struggling/half-submitting Scarlett O'Hara up the staircase to bed, in the film version of *Gone With the Wind*, is still thought of by many as the prototypical romantic scene. Marilyn French (1977) has referred to the love presented in such movies as "conquest and surrender . . . a man did one and a woman did the other, and everybody knew it" (p. 31). A man "wins" a woman, if not through brutality, then through the power of his persuasiveness, charm, capacity to protect and support, or simply because he is a man and, therefore, desirable.

Women have been taught that we must be the "soft ones," the yielders, the peacemakers, that men must be "given in" to. My mother found this very difficult to do herself but encouraged this traditional role for her daughters. Folklore and media images send messages to women that we should not expect love to be associated with pleasure alone. In fiction and in popular songs we talk about loving men in whose presence (or at whose hands) we experience pain. The women who "sang the blues" in earlier decades belted out tragic stories about their no-good men who treated them rottenly, but whom they could not keep from loving. Their men shoved them around, stayed out late, came home drunk, ran around with other women, but still the refrain was, "Can't help loving that man of mine." On the cover of an album of her songs, Holly Near (1974) wrote some years ago about why she had decided to give up singing blues.

> I realized it wasn't the music that was hanging me up, it was the words . . . the words . . . are real hard to get behind. For those of you who have never heard a woman's blues, it goes something like this. "Beat me, kick me, I'll go anywhere you want me to and I won't mind."

There is some indication that the lyrics in songs sung by women are changing. Brenda Vander May and Ellen Bryant (in Stark, 1986) analyzed country music tunes from two periods, 1970 to 1972 and 1979 to 1981, and found that some women singers are standing up for themselves, renouncing their older roles, asking for equality and independence and questioning the expectations of Southern white working-class ideology that they be "nurturing, submissive and . . . forgiving of their philandering, aggressive, tough and insensitive husbands" (p. 68). While many of the old themes can still be heard, the newer music contains more contemporary images of love relationships between women and men. For example, Kitty Wells in "It Wasn't God Who Made Honky-Tonk Angels" sings: "Too many times married men think they're single . . . It's a shame that all the blame is on us women"; and Loretta Lynn sings about "The Pill" (Jean Page in Trotl, 1981).

Patricia Spacks (1975) found women's suffering and submission in love to be a major theme of nineteenth-century literature. Perhaps the most extreme literary example of the ultimate in selfless giving to the man one loves is found in a story by Nathaniel Hawthorne ("The Birthmark," 1843/1973). The male protagonist, Aylmer, is a man of science who becomes obsessed by the need to remove a small blemish from the cheek of his beautiful wife, Georgiana. He sees this mark as an intolerable defect in this otherwise perfect woman, a symbol of her liability to sin or decay, and he convinces her to permit him to perform a series of experiments. In her final moments, realizing that her husband's experiments have succeeded not only in reducing the crimson mark on her cheek but also in killing her, Georgiana speaks these words:

> "My poor Aylmer," she repeated, with a more than human tenderness, "you have aimed loftily; you have

done nobly. Do not repent that with so high and pure a feeling, you have rejected the best the earth could offer. Aylmer, dearest Aylmer, I am dying!" (p. 366)

Georgiana symbolizes the conviction that to be worthy of a man's love, a woman must serve him. In contemporary fiction, some women are shown struggling against and questioning this assumption. For example, a young college woman in Judith Rossner's *August* (1983) talks to her psychotherapist about her lover: "He was my first real love. *Is*. Tom *owns* me. Do you know what that means? If Tom throws me away . . . I'll be like a rag doll someone threw into the garbage" (p. 57). Thus, contemporary women can understand what Simone de Beauvoir (1949/1961) wrote many years ago:

> Shut up in the sphere of the relative, destined to the male from childhood, habituated to seeing in him a superb being whom she cannot possibly equal, the woman . . . will dream . . . of amalgamating herself with the sovereign. . . . She chooses to desire her enslavement so ardently that it will seem to her the expression of her liberty. . . . Love becomes for her a religion. (p. 604)

But, according to de Beauvoir, since most women do not succeed in "deifying" any of the men whom they know, love actually comes to have a "smaller place in woman's life than has often been supposed."

Our culture's insistence that women give their "love lives" a very high priority may help explain the finding (Rubin, Peplau, & Hill, 1981) that once a romantic relationship has moved past its initial stages, women tend to become more involved than their male partners. Among the college couples studied, women were considered to be the more involved partner in 45 percent of the couples, compared to 36 percent of couples in which men were considered to be the most involved. Women also were found to be more instrumental in breaking up a relationship (51 percent of the time compared to 42 percent of the time for men), citing more issues of disagreement, and indicating greater sensitivity to problems in the relationship.

Women appear to be more sensitive than men to negative messages from partners in a close heterosexual relationship, but more likely to interpret their partner's neutral communications positively. This has been reported from a study of heterosexual couples of varied socioeconomic status who had been living together for at least six months (Gaelick, Bodenhausen, & Wyer, 1985). Each couple first discussed a problem in their relationship, and then talked about the videotape of that discussion and rated their own and their partner's feelings. The obtained gender differences illustrate and confirm the general cultural expectation that it is a woman's task to nurture her male love partner and to be sensitive to his needs. While the women were accurate in perceiving their partner's hostility, the men were not accurate and tended to distort their partner's neutral communications, perceiving hostility where there was simply an absence of positive affect. Women, on the other hand, perceived the absence of hostility from their partners as indicative of positive feelings. Thus, as the investigators noted, a woman

> can elicit hostility from her partner either by a direct expression of negative affect or by simply failing to communicate positive affect because both are perceived as hostile by the man. . . . [A probable explanation for this is that] men typically expect women to be affiliative and unassertive, and consequently they interpret behavior that deviates from these expectancies as hostile. (p. 1264)

Women are not only more accurate in perceiving hostility, but their degree of satisfaction with the relationship is more strongly related to their partner's hostility than is true for men.

Gloria Steinem (1978a) has described her own feelings and those of other women who have ended relationships, as follows: "Creeping self-sacrifice (and creeping resentment of same) meant that sooner or later the only way to regain myself and my own work was to leave" (p. 87). She has argued that love is not possible when one person serves the other, but only when "I can care about the welfare of another person—not *more than* my own, as I had been trained to do, or less than my own, as men have been trained to do, but *as much* as my own" (p. 88). To give more to a love relationship than one's partner gives has the effect of lessening one's power and increasing one's uncertainty and vulnerability. One possible way to compensate is by indirectly exercising power by inducing jealousy, and Gregory White (1980) found in a study of 150 romantically involved couples that women reported using jealousy significantly more often than men. The women gave as reasons for deliberately trying to get the partners jealous, their desire to test the relationship or to increase their rewards.

Security In return for service, sacrifice, and nurturance, a woman may ask for recognition, protection, and security. To writers of 19th-century novels, as Patricia Spacks (1975) has pointed out, "the female's compulsion to find some strong male on whom she can rely appears almost as a fact of nature" (p. 58). Contemporary American women would object to such a description of themselves, and for many it would not be accurate. For example, one 26-year-old woman, a stockbroker, interviewed for an article on marriage, said, "I think women are much less frightened of going out and being alone. They get so much satisfaction from other parts of their lives that they don't rely so heavily anymore on the man in their life" (in Greer, 1986). But large numbers of today's young women are not so different from the heroines of 19th-century fiction studied by Spacks, and the desire for economic and emotional security still enters heavily into romantic relationships.

That heterosexual women tend to look for material security when searching for love is a conclusion supported by studies of personal ads placed in newspapers or magazines by single people indicating their availability and interest in a romantic relationship. Albert Harrison (1977) analyzed the content of 800 "lonely hearts" advertisements that appeared over a 6-month period in the mid-1970s in a nationally circulated weekly tabloid. In general, women were more likely than men to offer attractiveness and to seek financial security, while men offered security and sought attractive, younger women. Kay Deaux and Randel Hanna (1984) reported an analysis of 800 such ads collected from four publications equally distributed from the East and West coasts and from heterosexual and homosexual women and men. Heterosexual women were more likely than any other group to seek financial security or status and to request information about the occupations of respondents, while at the same time they were the most likely to provide information about their own physical attractiveness (as if offering to trade good looks for material goods). Men (regardless of sexual orientation) behaved in a complementary manner; they were significantly more likely than women to be seeking physical attractiveness in a partner, and to be offering financial assets, with heterosexual men the most likely to write ads with such themes.

Romantic love experienced by women who are financially independent should be less entangled with dependency and therefore ultimately more satisfying. A more independent woman should be more likely than a dependent woman to experience pleasure in the presence of her lover without the concomitant frustration or humiliation stemming from the conditions of her dependency. Women's dependence on men, however, is more than economic. After 10 years of research and more than 4000 interviews with women and men, Gerald Phillips (1983) concluded that women tend to see men as protectors who lessen their feelings of vulnerability. When the men they trust prove to be untrustworthy, women feel devastated.

Romance: Hers and His

Women often discover that our expectations of a love relationship are not the same as men's. This is not surprising in a society that separates the genders in terms of normative behavior and values. Meanings of love, as well as what each looks for in a lover, are often found to be distinguishably different for a woman and a man. In describing some of the early struggles to preserve her marriage, Robin Morgan (1978), for example, has written that "the underlying theme . . . was our love for each other, spoken in two enforcedly different languages, a woman's and a man's. There was yet no technique of translation available to us" (p. 147). And Lillian Rubin (1976) found that for many of the working-class couples she interviewed, there had been "two courtships—his and hers," so different were the two partners' memories.

That physical attractiveness is much more important to men than to women in evaluating members of the other gender is shown by considerable evidence. A review of the literature (Bar-Tal & Saxe, 1976) found agreement among studies that a woman's judged physical attractiveness, but not a man's, is positively related to her "dating popularity" and to her desirability as a mate. In *The Summer Before the Dark*, Doris Lessing's (1973) heroine Kate experiments with her meaning for men by making changes in her appearance. When her hair is styled and tinted and her dress is fashionable, she can sense men's approval and attraction; when she removes these external deceptions and is simply herself, she becomes invisible to men.

As we noted in the previously mentioned study by Kay Deaux and Randel Hanna (1984) of personal ads, men were found to seek physical attractiveness in a partner significantly more often than women. Women (regardless of sexual orientation) differed from men, in general, in seeking and offering specific personality attributes, and in seeking sincerity and a permanent relationship. Sexual orientation seemed to make the following difference in what was offered and what was sought:

> Opting for a homosexual rather than a heterosexual partner . . . appears to alter the preferences of males and females in quite different ways. For women, physical characteristics and appearance are deemphasized, and information about personal interests, hobbies, and the goals of a relationship are stressed. For men, the homosexual choice is accompanied by a greater stress on physical appearance and surface characteristics [such as racial and ethnic identification]. (p. 375)

Another study of "lonely hearts" advertisements (Lynn & Shurgot, 1984) examined the number of responses received by ads placed in a midwestern magazine for singles. Men's responses to female advertisers were found to depend more on "assurances of physical attractiveness than [did] women's responses to male advertisers" (p. 354). Jeffrey Nevid (1984) had over 500 college students rate characteristics of prospective romantic partners in the context of a sexual relationship, and separately for a meaningful long-term relationship. For both types of relationship, men placed significantly greater emphasis on physical characteristics than did women, while women rated personal qualities (such as warmth) as significantly more important than did men.

Men's concern with the physical attributes of women seems to cut across social class and ethnic background. Edith Folb (1980) analyzed the language used by black teenagers to describe the other gender and found clear indications that a primary measure of a woman's desirability is her physical attractiveness. To these young men, women appeared to be equivalent to prized possessions, and were sometimes described as different types of automobiles. Desirable parts of a woman's anatomy were called *g* or *goodies*; and sexually attractive women were referred to as *bitch*, *stallion*, and *fox*, or linked to drugs as *"stuff, main stuff, golden girl* (very fine cocaine), *silk* and *satin* (any combination of amphetamines and barbiturates). These drug-related terms suggest that desirable women get you high and make you feel good. And . . . are addictive" (p. 69). While the language used by the young women suggested that they also sought attractive physical attributes in men, they emphasized them less and were interested in a "wider range of qualities," including how the man talked and acted, sexual fidelity, intimacy, and earning power.

The primacy of a woman's physical attractiveness to men of varied backgrounds (whether urban teenagers or college-educated adults) has important im-plications. It might explain, for example, why men may fall in love more quickly, as suggested by the previously mentioned findings of Zick Rubin et al. (1981). For men, romantic feelings may be easily induced by the sight of a pretty face and sexy figure, with parts in the appreciated proportions. And since heterosexual men's preoccupation with women's physical attributes is certainly well known to women, this obviously encourages us to compete for men's attention by highlighting the attractiveness of our bodies. Makeup, perfume, and clothing manufacturers and advertisers assuredly benefit, but physical attractiveness has little relation to the probability of a mutually satisfying relationship.

As women and men differ in power generally in this society, they bring this differential status into love relationships. Thus, in trying to explain their finding that men are more romantic than women early in a relationship, the researchers in the previously cited study of heterosexual college couples (Rubin, Peplau, & Hill, 1981) pointed out that since

> the wife's status, income, and life chances are far more dependent on her husband's than vice versa [she will be] . . . more cautious, practical, and realistic. . . . Men . . . being in a position of greater power both in the larger society and in the marriage market . . . can better afford the luxury of being "romantic." (p. 831)

Studies of dating couples continue to find that most heterosexual relationships are traditional, and become even more traditional after marriage. Letitia Peplau (1979) found inconsistencies between what dating college couples say and what they actually do with respect to the division of power in their relationships. While 95 percent of the women and 87 percent of the men said they believed in equality in a relationship, less than half of each group reported equal power in their own relationship, and 45 percent of the men and 35 percent of the women said the men had a "greater say." The women expected more often than the men to use roundabout, devious means to achieve influence in decision making and activities.

Obstacles and Possibilities

Sophie Loewenstein (1977) studied passion in over 700 women by means of questionnaires and interviews, and concluded that passionate love (which she distinguishes from mature love) is a regressive experience for heterosexual women and a potential hazard to mental health, disrupting a woman's functioning, producing confusion, and interfering with reason. Are these inevitable consequences of love or are these the result of inequality in status and power?

Erich Fromm (1956) defined mature love as "union under the condition of preserving one's integrity, one's individuality"—that is, as an interdependent relationship between persons who do not lose themselves in the relationship but instead contribute their strengths to it. According to Fromm, love should permit us to overcome isolation and separateness without loss of personal integrity. If one accepts this as a statement of the ideal and then considers how young women and men in our society have learned to see themselves in relation to the other gender, then it is apparent that our culture places enormous obstacles in the path of love. When one person in a relationship perceives herself as weaker, less competent, more giving, more caring, more identified with the other, more in need of interpersonal reassurance, less powerful, less resourceful, more in need of protection, and so on, the possibility of mature love, as defined by Fromm and others, is dramatically lessened. Such partners are unequal both within their relationship and in the world outside of it. Thus, "it is not the process of love itself that is at fault," as Shulamith Firestone (1971) has put it, "but its political, i.e., unequal power, context" (p. 132). For a woman to find satisfaction in love with a man is difficult if she has been taught to lose herself in devotion to, in caring for, and in identification with him. (From the man's perspective, the complementary role that requires him to provide a woman with resources and security, to be grateful and attentive, can also be burdensome and frustrating.)

We can learn a good deal about women's beliefs and dreams about romantic love by examining the themes in the romance novels avidly read by millions of American women. A tremendous increase in the popularity of this genre has occurred since 1960, as well as some changes in their heroines and in what they seek. According to Patricia Lamb (1985), "Harlequin [the major distributor] publishes around 100,000,000 copies annually. Romance novels comprise about 40 percent of the paperback market in this country. Their devoted readers each consume anywhere from half a dozen to one hundred a month" (p. 16). In addition to the Harlequin and Silhouette lines, which are the best known, there are Rapture Romances, Loveswept, To Have and To Hold, Candlelight/Ecstasy, and Love & Life, which together "issue some 100 new romances a month" (Toth, 1984). According to Emily Toth, these books consti-

tute more than half of all book sales in the United States, are number one in popularity among books bought by noncollege women, and a close second among college-educated women, for whom historical novels are first.

What do these books say about heterosexual love, and why are they so popular among women? Janice Radway (1984) interviewed and administered questionnaires to 42 women (all homemakers in a midwestern community) who were enthusiastic readers of romance novels. She analyzed the typical plot and abstracted 13 stages in the structure of the "ideal romance." During the first stage, "the heroine's social identity is destroyed," and in the last stage, "the heroine's identity is restored." In between, the heroine meets the hero, finds him initially cold and unresponsive to her (sometimes even cruel), but toward the middle of the book she transforms him through the power of her caring and goodness into the warm, sensitive man she knew he was all along, and he confesses his love. This "magic transformation" typically occurs after a separation or misunderstanding, but is not explained. "The hero is permitted simply to graft tenderness onto his unaltered male character." According to Radway, it is woman's "sensuality and mothering capacities that will magically remake a man incapable of expressing emotions or of admitting dependency" (p. 128). From these stories the women who read them get reassurance of their worth, an emotional boost, an escape from their unexciting domestic worlds, and the hope that their man, too, like the hero, can be transformed through their efforts into the tender, gentle, loving man they still seek.

Sandra Gilbert (1984) and Patricia Lamb (1985) are highly critical of the messages conveyed by romance novels and of their pernicious influence in validating patriarchy and idealizing traditional values. Lamb has suggested that the reader of romance novels is an addict who, like other addicts,

> never learns to come to grips with her world, and . . . therefore seeks stability and reassurance through some repeated, ritualized activity. . . . [But] the problems of their daily lives, the lack of emotional sustenance, the absence of supportive, understanding, caring exchange with a partner—all these await them as they put aside the completed novel, with its happy ending of fulfillment and promise. They will be drained yet again in a day or two or three by the demands made on them and by the absence of other sources of replenishment. So they will buy another batch and read their way through those. . . . Romance novels probably perpetuate the differences and difficulties that exist in our

culture between men and women, and between men's and women's expectations of love and marriage. They inoculate, rather than vaccinate, women against the masculine ills of our world, and so the women need booster shots—lots and lots of them, and very regularly. (p. 17)

Since romance novels reiterate traditional sex roles and do not present realistic ways of improving women's relationships or status, Lamb has concluded that they are "inimical to women's real security, growth and freedom."

Janice Radway (1984) is more sympathetic both to the readers of romance novels and to the novels themselves, pointing out that the newer heroines are spirited and rebellious as well as "feminine" and that the heroes of the "ideal" (as distinct from the "failed") romances are macho only on the surface, and actually are thoughtful, giving, and warm beneath the tough exterior. Radway suggests that it is this expanded version of what men and women can offer to each other in the ideal love relationship that readers of romance novels are seeking. Similarly, Emily Toth (1984) has argued that contemporary romance novels offer readers a newer and more positive or more liberated vision of heterosexual love, and that "romances have been updated by feminism." To bolster her thesis she has noted that the heroines of the newer romances "now have well-paying jobs and independent lives, and the hero is a partner, not a reason for being." In the Harlequins published since 1982, "the major characters are equals who grow to love one another." Toth has argued that romance novels also provide women with descriptions of sex "from the woman's point of view," emphasizing not moving body parts, but emotion and sensuality.

> Successful contemporary romance writers (mostly women) make the sex a total experience: music, tastings, touchings, flowers, food, passion and words—for the ideal romantic hero is not the sullen and moody Harlequin man of the past. His appeal to the heroine is not his being handsome, but his being *verbal*, and considering her pleasure before his own. (p. 12)

Whatever we may conclude about the ultimate value and influence of romance novels, they appear to present as ideal lovers women and men who are competent, strong, and purposeful as well as expressive, nurturant, and sensitive. The separation of personal attributes into the strong, silent man and the weak, emotional woman is shown to be an obstacle to love, and the successful heroine is the one who can transform the stereotypical masculine hero into a broader human being who is caring and tender.

Evidence that adherence to gender stereotypes is a source of stress and incompatibility has come from a laboratory study (Ickes & Barnes, 1977). Pairs of pretested strangers were asked to wait together in a room for 5 minutes. Pairs of men and women who were highly sex-typed interacted less, liked each other less, and smiled and laughed less than any other pairs. That this initial discomfort might be overcome in a different setting or with continued interaction is possible, but the data suggest that, contrary to expectation, sharp gender distinctions do not provide for a smooth complementarity between women and men. Confirming evidence has come from a study by Marilyn Coleman and Lawrence Ganong (1985). Among a sample of primarily white single college students who were in heterosexual love relationships, those who self-reported both instrumental and expressive personal characteristics were found to be more loving partners than traditionally sex-typed persons of either gender. The researchers concluded that "to be a loving person it may be necessary to possess instrumental traits such as assertiveness and willingness to take risks as well as expressive traits such as sensitivity and understanding" (p. 174).

Marge Piercy (1984b) has written about romantic love in ways that emphasize the multifaceted contributions that lovers can make to each other when they get beyond gender stereotypes. Piercy's poetry articulates a feminist vision of shared struggle and attainments, for which gender is irrelevant:

> Because we work together we are obscurely
> joined deep in the soil, deep in the water
> table where the pure vulnerable stream
> flows in the dark sustaining all life. In dreams
> you walk in my head arguing, we gallop
> on thornapple quests, we lie in each other's
> arms. What a richly colored strong warm coat
> is woven when love is the warp and work is the woof.
> (p. 67)

And in another poem (Piercy, 1984c):

> I love you from my bones out, in pulses
> rising far down in the molten core
> deep as orgasm in the moist and fiery pit
> beyond ego. I love you from the center
> of my life pulsating like a storm on the sun
> shooting out arms of fire with power
> enough to run a world or scorch it.
> We are partially meshed in each other
> and partially we turn free. We are
> hooked into each other like a machine
> that could actually move forward,
> a vehicle of flesh that could bring us

and other loving travelers to a new land. (p. 31)

It is this "new land" that Simone de Beauvoir (1949/1961) was pointing toward when she wrote, "On the day when it will be possible for woman to love not in her weakness but in her strength, not to escape herself but to find herself, not to abase herself but to assert herself—on that day love will become for her, as for man, a source of life and not a mortal danger" (p. 629).

MARRIAGE

For most contemporary women, marriage continues to be, as it was for our grandmothers, a social statement that affirms the end of girlhood and assures us of a recognized place in the adult world. Lillian Rubin (1976) has pointed out that while contemporary middle-class girls can delay marriage and extend the period in which they make preparations, explore talents and aptitudes, and enjoy such privileges of adulthood as "separate domiciles and sexual relations," this luxury is less available to working-class youth, for whom adult privileges are expected to be accompanied by adult responsibilities. Both of these come with early marriage, especially for a working-class woman. For any woman to remain permanently unmarried, however, is still relatively rare, although, as we shall see, this option is being taken by more and more women in the 1980s.

In general, despite a still-increasing divorce rate, the popularity of marriage for the present generation of women remains much the same as it was for our mothers, grandmothers, and great-grandmothers. Mary Ellen Reilly (1976) analyzed the demographic data on marriage in the United States over a 100-year period and noted that 9.6 persons out of every 1000 got married in 1867, and the rate in 1976 was much the same, namely, 9.9. The marriage rate rose sharply after World War I, to close to 12 per 1000, then declined dramatically, reaching an all-time low of 7.9 in 1932 during the Great Depression. A rise in the marriage rate accompanied economic recovery in the late 1930s and early 1940s and rose to its highest peak (16.4) in 1946 following the end of World War II. The rate then fell in the 1950s (dropping to 9.9 in 1952), rose a bit in the 1960s but remained below 10 until 1968 when it reached 10.4, then declined very slowly in the 1970s. In the 1980s the marriage rate first climbed, reaching 10.6 in 1982, and then declined slowly to 10.5 in 1984 and 10.2 in 1985 ("Marriages Down," 1986). Thus, women in the 1980s are no less likely to marry than women in previous generations, with the exception of those in the late 1940s and early 1950s. Some indication that the marriage rate may be declining somewhat comes from a government report finding that in 1983, among single women aged 15 to 44, there were 99.3 marriages per 1000 women, "the first time that measure has dipped below the 100 level" ("They're Not the Marrying Kind," 1986).

While marriage remains popular for the vast majority of women and men, Census Bureau data also indicate a trend toward remaining single longer. Table 8.1 presents a comparison among the years 1970, 1980, and 1984 of the percentage of women and men in different age categories who were never married. Looking just at the figures for women, we can see that the percentage of single women in their early 30s increased by 7.1 percent between 1970 and 1984, and the percentage of single women in their late 30s increased during that same time period by 2.1 percent. Although 95 percent of all the women over 40 in 1984 were married, a figure comparable to (or somewhat higher than) that of 1970, they had married a generation or two earlier. Whether the current generation of women who are single in their 30s will eventually marry is not known. We will return later, in our discussion of single women, to a study that suggests that at least one segment of this group of women is unlikely ever to marry. But first, we will consider the experiences of women who do marry, who remain the vast majority of all women.

Related to the data just outlined and presented in Table 8.1 is the phenomenon of a significant increase in the median age of first marriage. In the first half of this century, the median age of first marriage for women declined steadily from a high of 22.0 in 1890 to a low of 20.1 in 1956. Since then, however, the median age has been rising; it was 20.3 in 1960, 20.8 in 1970, 21.1 in 1975, 22.0 in 1980, 23.0 in 1984, and 23.3 in 1985. The trend among men has been similar and complementary; the median age of first marriage was 26.1 in 1890, reached a low of 22.5 in 1956, and has been slowly increasing ever since: 23.5 in 1975, 25.4 in 1984, and 25.5 in 1985 (U.S. Bureau of the Census, "More Americans," 1985a). The median age of first marriage in 1985 was the highest it had ever been for both genders since census information was first collected in 1890.

Despite the later age of first marriage and the sharp increase in number of single adults, marriage remains the preferred way of life for most Americans. Annual studies of national samples of high school seniors begun in 1976 have found that the American

Chapter 8

TABLE 8.1 Percent of never-married persons in the United States in 1970, 1980, and 1984, by age and gender (Data taken from U.S. Bureau of the Census, 1985a, Table B, p. 2.)

	Women		Age	Men		
1970	1980	1984		1970	1980	1984
35.8	50.2	56.9	20 to 24	54.7	68.8	74.8
10.5	20.9	25.9	25 to 29	19.1	33.1	37.8
6.2	9.5	13.3	30 to 34	9.4	15.9	20.9
5.4	6.2	7.5	35 to 39	7.2	7.8	11.6
38.5	38.8	39.7	under 40	47.4	48.8	49.9
6.2	5.1	5.0	40 and over	7.4	5.7	5.8

family will "remain alive and well in the eighties" ("The Future of the Family," 1981). Four fifths of the teenagers studied said they expected to marry at some point. Daughters whose mothers are employed full-time outside the home have not been found to differ in their desire for marriage from those whose mothers are full-time homemakers. Although daughters from dual-career families have been found to prefer a less traditional, more egalitarian marriage, they choose to marry no less frequently than daughters from single-career families (Rollins & White, 1982). Many modern women still believe that marriage brings social approval and recognition. For example, in a novel by Gloria Naylor (1985), a young black woman thinks that

> marriage would set her free . . . Finally free. Freed from those endless luncheons with other lonely women . . . [for whom] something must be missing if they only had each other across the table week after week. Freed from the burden of that mental question mark on her left ring finger. What's wrong with you if no one's wanted you by now? (p. 117)

And other young women feel that, regardless of what else they do or accomplish, their parents will be disappointed in them if they never marry. Joyce Carol Oates (1986) described such a woman in her novel, *Marya*:

> One of the young women with whom she had become friendly . . . complained wistfully to Marya that, despite her numerous academic honors and prizes, despite the fact that she would be moving on, with her Ph.D., to Stanford—her family . . . seemed only to be waiting for news that she would be married. Nothing else mattered, evidently; nothing else struck them as ultimately significant. (p. 207)

What does it mean to be a bride or a wife? Let us explore this question now.

Wedding Belles

To be a bride in our society brings joy, excitement, and intensity. On the day of her wedding and during the days or months preceding it, the bride is center-stage, the object of plans, inquiries, gifts, conversation, admiration, and envy. She is the star of the show. Her hair, figure, and clothes are noticed and described. She is finally that bride doll that she has fussed over and rehearsed with during the many years of her childhood. The groom seems necessary only to validate the bride's status. Newspaper supplements that appear in local newspapers shortly before the spring wedding season still focus primarily on the bride, on how she looks, what she wears, her dreams and needs. Marriage announcements in the press are still typically accompanied by photographs of the bride alone. What has changed in the past decade in reports of engagements or weddings is that the bride's accomplishments and employment (and sometimes those of her mother and new mother-in-law) are often listed alongside those of the groom (and the father).

Women who marry in the traditional manner, in a wedding attended by family and friends, preceded by announcements, invitations, plans for flowers, for ceremony, for receptions, for food and drink and decorations, will, for a short time, have all eyes on them. Such traditional preparations are accompanied by a kind of consumer power unlikely to be enjoyed again with such freedom. While the number and nature of the purchases made varies with social class, a period of euphoric spending is experienced by both working-class and middle-class brides. That traditional marriages are once again in vogue ("Latest Rage in America," 1983) is certainly good news for business. Department stores have reported that the compiling of "bridal registries" has increased since their decline in the 1970s. These are lists of wedding gifts the young couple would like to have. For every bride registered, a store in 1983 could expect $5,000 in sales; and in the first year of marriage the newlyweds (or their parents and friends) could be expected to spend an average of $15,000 on rings, weddings, honeymoons, and household items.

Marge Piercy's book *Small Changes* (1975) opens with a description of a wedding that does not seem to be too out of date. Beth is 18 and marrying her high school boyfriend. She feels proud and grateful, and her parents have spent a great deal of money to celebrate this wedding. "This is the happiest day of your life!" her mother tells her, "The happiest day!"

"That's a thirty-five dollar headpiece, Bethie, so hold your head up proud and stop dancing like a flea on a hot griddle . . . Your family's giving you a real wedding, and don't you forget it," Mother said. "We haven't cut any corners. This is no hole in the wall at the courthouse or in the front room to save on the trimmings. You're getting married in church with flowers and bridesmaids and your father rented a hall for afterward with real caterers. And I want *you* to remember this, Nancy Rose Phail—that's how it's supposed to be. Just like we're doing for your sister Bethie, if you're a good girl and do right by your parents, your parents will do right by you." (p. 8)

Because a daughter's marriage is of major significance to working-class parents and a sign that the parental responsibility of caring for her can be relinquished and transferred to her husband, they may spend large sums of money (put aside painstakingly for this purpose) to mark the occasion. The wedding proclaims to the neighbors and to relatives that daughter and parents have "done right" by each other. The daughter has been found desirable, and all the years of parental preparation have been rewarded.

The wedding is a symbol that a young woman and a young man have done the right thing, the culturally approved thing. Society's representatives, the clergy, parents, merchants, neighbors, all smile with approval at marriage since it is through families that new members of a culture are provided for the production, distribution, and consumption of goods. Marriage, in other words, has significance for the culture for a number of reasons, including social, religious, and economic ones. Marriage remains a serious goal, extolled by all of the major institutions of our society. That wedding bells have retained their traditional meaning and desirability for most women, then, is not surprising.

Being a Wife

For the typical married woman who does not divorce or separate from her husband, the role of wife lasts longer than that of mother. This is a relatively recent historical phenomenon. Gerda Lerner (1977) has cited demographic data showing that American marriages prior to 1810 were apt to end with one spouse's death while there were still small children in the family. After 1910 a couple could anticipate less than a year of marriage without children at home. It was not until the middle of the twentieth century that wives and husbands could expect to spend a significant period of time together without children to rear, due to a steady decrease in the number of years devoted to childbearing and an increase in longevity.

Class Differences   A working-class woman whose education ends with graduation from high school will typically marry soon thereafter or after one or two years of employment. The young couple will try to settle in a neighborhood close to relatives or friends, so that the wife will have the support of continued relationships with other women as her world and that of her working husband gradually begin to separate. She and her husband will be linked together primarily by shared meals, children, a common bed, and common financial concerns. Even before there are children, and while the wife, too, may be employed outside the home, her husband's life will tend to diverge from hers. The working-class wife will spend more time with her home than with her husband. Being a wife for her literally means being a housewife. This was true of my mother, the mothers of most of my friends, and remains true today of working-class women whose self-images are enhanced by compliments about their homes and by pride in their children's accomplishments or good behavior.

Working-class wives are generally expected to submit to the authority of their husbands. They are especially dependent if they have had little work experience, have little personal knowledge of the world outside their neighborhoods, and if their education has been limited. A working-class wife may have few options and little sense of personal control over events outside the limits of her home. Lillian Rubin (1976) has reported that the most often-heard phrase among the working-class women with whom she spoke was, "He won't let me," spoken "unselfconsciously with a sense of resignation."

> On the surface, working-class women generally seem to accept and grant legitimacy to their husband's authority, largely because they understand his need for it. If not at home, where is a man who works on an assembly line, in a warehouse, or a refinery to experience himself as a person whose words have weight. . . . But just below the surface, there lies a well of ambivalence. (p. 113)

If you have few financial resources, being a housewife means doing endless, monotonous, exhausting chores. Lillian Rubin has described a composite scene of what she saw as she visited working-class neighborhoods. At ten in the morning

> mothers are catching their first free breath of the day, perhaps perched on a stool in the kitchen, coffee cup in

one hand, telephone in the other. Since five-thirty or six they have been up and about—preparing breakfast, packing lunches, feeding and changing a crying baby, scolding this child, prodding that one. (p. 15)

Being a working-class wife means experiencing financial instability that strains relationships and increases frustrations. Yet, despite hardships, disappointments, quarrels, and unrealized dreams, divorce is not more common among working-class couples than among their more affluent middle-class cohorts. Hilda Kahne (1978) has cited a study that found that for white women who separated from their husbands for the first time between 1968 and 1973 there was "no apparent relationship between family income and marital disruption" (p. 658). For black women, however, a positive relationship was found. The greater the woman's earnings, the higher were the marital "disruption probabilities." This parallels and supports a conclusion contained in a report by the U.S. Bureau of the Census (1976) that in the short run, at least, increased chances of economic independence for women "may contribute to marital dissolution." Working-class women who have little opportunity for economic independence, traditionally work very hard at making their marriages work. To be a wife and mother is what working-class girls have aspired to, expected, and been taught to value most highly.

The primary expectations that working-class wives have for their husbands are that they be steady workers, not drink to excess, and that they not be violent or abusive. Lillian Rubin (1976) noted that not one of the women in the professional middle-class families with whom she spoke mentioned any of these attributes as being ones they valued in their husbands. Instead "they tended to focus on such issues as intimacy, sharing, and communication and . . . in subtle ways, on the comforts, status, and prestige that their husband's occupation affords" (pp. 93f.). Although the working-class wives also said they valued sharing and intimacy, and quarreled with their husbands about their lack of communication, they felt guilty about doing so, as though they were asking for more than they had a right to and should be content if their husbands worked hard, brought home steady money, and were not abusive. Many of the women felt that they were much better off than their mothers had been and, thus, had no right to be dissatisfied (despite gnawing feelings of doubt).

Middle-class women expect a great deal more from marriage than a sober, paycheck-bearing hus-band, and may, in fact, expect *everything* from it. Middle-class women have articulated their disappointments, disillusionment, boredom, and frustrations, and have written and talked about the isolation, selflessness, and lack of personal fulfillment inherent in the role of wife. The growing aspirations of middle-class and college-educated women for egalitarian marriages and expressive, sensitive, caring husbands are in sharp contrast to the traditional marriage roles—the division of labor between wife and husband. These contradictions decrease the probability of satisfaction in marriage. In *A Perfect Woman* by Carolyn Slaughter (1985), Beth, a middle-class wife, reflects upon her marriage: "That trading-in of a solitary life for one which was subject to the demands and needs of one man? Of a child? Of a lifelong ritual of always being second?" (p. 14).

Traditional Values and Egalitarian Hopes

An analysis of the opinions of high school seniors, surveyed nationally each year since 1976, indicated that

both the young men and the young women want a family arrangement in which the husband consistently works full-time outside the home. . . . When small children are part of the family, the young people say they want a wife who is not spending large portions of her time working in outside employment. ("The Future of the Family," 1981, p. 8)

Similar findings were presented in the chapter on adolescence, and data from other kinds of studies reinforce the conclusion of the just-cited survey that, in general, "young people today are voicing hearty endorsement of the traditional values of marriage and family" (p. 8). John Hollender and Leslie Shafer (1981), for example, had a sample of college men view videotapes of five women who expressed different career/homemaker aspirations, after which they rated the likelihood that they could be interested in marrying someone like each of them. Most preferred was the woman who articulated the "Immediate Nurturer" role—that is, who desired marriage and a family first, and then pursuit of a job or career after her children were in school. The second-highest preference was for the "Delayed Nurturer," who would work right after marriage and then take time out for a family. Next preferred was the "Homemaker" for whom home and family are primary and continuing priorities, and then the "Integrator" (who wanted both a career and a family at the same time). Least desirable was the woman for whom "Career" was the primary focus.

Most men still expect to be the head of their family (despite the fact that the Bureau of the Census stopped using such a category in 1980). And although today's women express egalitarian attitudes more than their mothers did, much of the objective data on marriage suggests that women's aspirations are not being fulfilled. In Gail Godwin's (1983) *A Mother and Two Daughters*, one of the daughters, Cate, has just been visited by a man she loves, and she compares her behavior to that of her mother's.

> Mother, whose moods ran the gamut from wry humorist to ferocious disciplinarian when she was home alone with the girls, would turn into a smooth hostess the moment Daddy came through the door. . . . How funny that her own "hostess" voice a few moments ago had been an exact duplication of Mother's. . . . They had both been acting out the old scene of getting their man from the outside world to the kitchen, sparing him the household battleground in between. But it had confused her and Lydia, as little girls, when their mother suddenly became smaller and smoother when Daddy came home. (p. 223)

Contradictions between traditional values (or well-learned behavior) and egalitarian goals are found among both women and men. A survey conducted by a New York advertising firm (in Rice, 1980) of 452 husbands found that 65 percent believed that wives and husbands should share family responsibilities, including providing income for it, while at the same time 70 percent agreed that "a family is better off if the woman of the house does not work" and 60 percent felt that "a woman's place is in the home." Only 13 percent of the men surveyed could be classified as consistently nontraditional (egalitarian or progressive) on the basis of their responses, and the investigators concluded that most of the men were ambivalent, or more talk than action.

John Gillis and Walter Avis (1980) have investigated whether the typical difference in height between husbands and wives simply reflects average differences between men and women. They found, by checking records in one bank of the heights of couples who maintained joint checking accounts, that whereas the overall possibility of a woman being taller than a man is 2 out of 100, the actual value among the married couples was 1 out of 720, far less than might be expected by chance. In other words, there is a systematic bias in marriage that the husband should be taller than his wife. A similar systematic bias occurs with respect to age, in that husbands are typically older than their wives. This average difference in age was 2.7 years in 1983 and has changed little from previous times ("They're Not the Marrying Kind," 1986). Gloria Cowan (1984) had a large sample of college and high school students respond to scripts about heterosexual relationships in which the ages of the pairs were varied, and found evidence for a "double standard" in that respondents expressed "less optimistic views towards relationships in which the female is older than the male" (p. 22). That traditionalism is still the norm can be illustrated further by the enormous popularity of Marabel Morgan's 1973 book *The Total Woman*, which, as Ellen Ross (1980) has described it, "cheerily repudiated all the changes in marriage and women's situation since 1950" (p. 119). Morgan's book was 1975's top seller in any category, and the ninth-best-selling nonfiction book in the 1970s.

At the same time, there is evidence that women and men have different preferences with regard to decision making and performance of household chores. Marcia Kassner (1981) questioned a sample of college seniors graduating from a midwestern university and found "incongruency in attitudes between the two sexes," with men preferring traditional marriages and women preferring egalitarian ones. Similarly, when women students in a marriage course in 1978 were compared with their counterparts in 1972 and 1961, the investigators (Weeks & Gage, 1984) found a clear increase over time in egalitarian responses to a scale measuring marriage-role expectations. The greatest increase in egalitarian responses was with regard to personal characteristics and social participation. A survey of 60 thousand women conducted for *Woman's Day* magazine found that "women want more equality in marriage, with men helping out more at home and women being able to hold jobs" ("Women Want," 1986). While 70 percent of the respondents described the ideal marriage as one of shared responsibilities for earning money and caring for the children, only 53 percent felt that this characterized their own marriages.

Of particular interest, in view of the discrepancy between women's and men's attitudes, is the fact that studies of intact marriages tend to find greater harmony and satisfaction in those characterized by relative equality. A review of the literature (Gray-Little & Burks, 1983) concluded that the majority of post-1960 studies on decision making in marriage found evidence linking egalitarian patterns to high levels of marital satisfaction, although egalitarianism is not always defined in the same way. Sometimes it refers to joint decision making, and sometimes to control over separate areas or spheres. What it takes for a marriage to succeed is further suggested by the results of a study by John Antill (1983). He found that the happiness of both the husband and the wife was positively correlated with the same set of traits in their spouses, namely "sensitive, nurturant, and gentle qualities." Each member of the pair, regardless of gender, appeared to be looking for the same personal characteristics in the other. As Antill concluded, "It is the people who describe themselves as sensitive to the needs of others, compassionate, and warm that help make . . . relationships successful" (p. 153). Antill's findings are complemented by those of others. For example, one study (Neiswender-Reedy, Birren, & Schaie, 1981) of a sample of young adult, middle-aged, and older married couples (with or without children) found that the most important factors in a successful marriage were "feelings of concern, caring, trust, comfort and being able to depend on one another" (p. 62).

Housework: The Bottom Line! Research concerned with identifying the ingredients of a successful marriage may emphasize relational qualities, but the reality of women's day-to-day lives suggests that both working-class and middle-class wives are primarily associated with *things*, with duties and responsibilities, rather than with relationships per se. Remember how Golde in *The Fiddler on the Roof* answers her husband Tevye's insistent question, "Do you love me?" She reminds him that she has washed his clothes, cooked his meals, cleaned his house, given him children, and milked the cow. "If that's not love," she asks, "what is?" From Golde's old-world perspective, proof of her love is found in the meals she has cooked and the clothes she has washed. Modern Americans, especially those who are educated, professional, and middle-class, are not likely to describe love in marriage in Golde's terms, but there is evidence that the traditional view she expressed is still prevalent. For example, a marriage counselor quoted by Janet Harris (1976) reported what a couple told him about what each saw as lovable in themselves.

> The wife began by telling me that she thought she was deserving of love because she was a good housekeeper, a good cook, a good mother, that she did a lot of things for her family, that she put them first. The husband, on the other hand, thought he was lovable because he saw himself as a kindly person, with a good sense of humor, a lively imagination. . . . She perceived herself only as an object of service. (p. 109)

A woman typically expects to perform services when she marries, and her husband typically expects to receive them. Girls have practiced being housekeepers and cooks from earliest childhood play, and have been encouraged to put others first, to be good managers and tidy cleaners. If a woman can also sew or knit, manage the budget and chores economically and efficiently, so much the better. Women have been assured that if we do these things we will be appreciated and taken care of. In *A Mother and Two Daughters* (Godwin, 1983), for example, Lydia, now divorced, reflects that

> during her marriage, her compartment system had served her well. Her compartments organized *her*. If she had labeled them in her neat handwriting, they would have read something like: MOTHER. COOK. HOSTESS. INTERESTED WIFE . . . WELL-DRESSED LADY SHOPPER. AMIABLE BED PARTNER. (p. 268)

In an earlier story Gail Godwin (1977) took us through the step-by-step withdrawal from her wifely duties of a young woman whose husband and son came more and more to accept the woman's increasing isolation. Each day the woman did secret things while her husband and son were not at home. At the story's end, it is spring:

> The man and boy came home and found: five loaves of warm bread, a roast stuffed turkey, a glazed ham, three pies of different fillings, eight molds of the boy's favorite custard, two weeks' supply of fresh-laundered sheets and shirts and towels, two hand-knitted sweaters . . . , a sheath of marvelous water-color beasts accompanied by mad and fanciful stories . . . and a table full of love sonnets addressed to the man. The house smelled redolently of renewal and spring. The man ran to the little room [in which his wife had secluded herself], could not contain himself to knock, flung back the door. (p. 173)

His wife, of course, was dead, having left behind the only parts of herself he and the boy had understood and needed.

In *The Women's Room* (1977), Marilyn French offered the following description of a housewife's life:

> Years spent scraping shit out of diapers with a kitchen knife, finding places where string beans are two cents less a pound, learning to wake at the sound of a cough, spending one's intelligence in figuring the most efficient, least time-consuming way to iron men's white shirts or to wash and wax the kitchen floor or take care of the house and kids and work at the same time and save money. . . . [G]rimy details are not in the background of the lives of most women; they are the entire

surface. . . . When your body has to deal all day with shit and string beans, your mind does, too. (pp. 45f.)

Few of the married women I have known would not find these words compellingly and immediately familiar. Suppose you are more affluent, live in a suburb, and your husband is earning good money? It was such an "easier life" that French's heroine Mira, wife of a physician, finally achieved. This is her description of wifely days at home in suburbia:

More often than not, she came back from driving [her children] . . . to the bus stop to throw their breakfasts in the garbage.

After her return, after that heart-sinking moment of coming back to the greasy frying pan and the littered table, there was cleaning. The afternoons . . . were better . . . spent in an orgy of planning decor and buying furniture, rugs, draperies, lamps, pictures. Slowly the house filled up. It got to be hard to handle, so she bought herself a small file box and some packages of 2 x 3 cards. On each card she wrote one task that had to be performed, and filed them in sections. The section headed WINDOW WASHING would contain cards for each room in the house. Whenever she washed the windows in one room, she would mark the date shown on the card, and place it at the end of the section. The same was true for FURNITURE POLISHING, RUG SHAMPOOING, and CHINA. (p. 163)

Some wives, as well as their husbands, believe that it is the wife who is responsible for most of what one associates with the home. In a wonderfully funny essay called "Click! The Housewife's Moment of Truth," Jane O'Reilly (1982) wrote, "I have never met a woman who did not feel guilty . . . when a man we are attached to goes out with a button off his coat; we—not he—feel feckless" (p. 29).

Being a wife means housework for most women, excluding the "beautiful people" of great wealth and power whose housework is done by paid servants (primarily women). The family is the unit in which the housework is done and, in Marxist economic terms, "consists largely in purchasing commodities and transforming them into usable forms" (Hartmann, 1981, p. 373). Since this labor is traditionally and typically done by women, the result is exclusion from equal competition with men in the wage labor market, where husbands are supposed to provide for their families by earning a "family wage." Unlike the breadwinner, the housewife does not create surplus value (the difference between the price at which a product is sold and the cost of wages). Instead she exchanges her labor for the financial responsibility her husband assumes for her and her children. In both socialist and capitalist countries housewives constitute an unpaid labor force. According to Sylvia Porter (1985), the typical housewife (full-time homemaker) in this country spends 12 to 14 hours a day, seven days a week, attending to household activities "ranging from cooking to cleaning, from washing dishes to mending a hem." Using typical pay scales, Porter calculated what it would cost a family if it had to pay for the services provided by the housewife. In 1985 dollars, the cost came to $410 per week, or over $21,300 a year. These contributions to the nation's economy, however, are not included in our nation's GNP (gross national product) and, as Porter has noted, the housewife is thus economically "meaningless" or "nonexistent."

The modern family and the "housewife" role are relatively recent phenomena, just a little more than 100 years old. As Angela Davis (1983) has pointed out:

Housework during the colonial era was entirely different from the daily work routine of the housewife in the United States today. . . . In the agrarian economy of pre-industrial North America, a woman performing her household chores was . . . a spinner, weaver and seamstress as well as baker, butter-churner, candle-maker and soap-maker. . . . Colonial women were not "housecleaners" or "housekeepers" but rather full-fledged and accomplished workers within the home-based economy. Not only did they manufacture most of the products required by their families, they were also the guardians of their families' and their communities' health. (pp. 225f.)

According to Barbara Wertheimer (in Davis, 1983), women also ran taverns, sawmills, caned chairs, built furniture, ground eyeglasses, made rope, were housepainters and undertakers, and played a variety of other "visible roles in economic activity outside the home." Jessie Bernard (1981) has also traced changes in the family and noted that "the good provider as a specialized male role seems to have arisen in the transition from subsistence to market—especially money—economies that accelerated with the industrial revolution" (p. 2). This change, according to Bernard, kept women from direct access to money earned through their own skills and made it necessary for them to win "a good provider who would 'take care of' them."

Although it is the unusual wife today who doesn't share the "provider" role with her husband (as we shall see from data to be discussed in Chapter 12), he far less frequently shares the household chores with her. Being a wife means doing housework even when you are on vacation. The photo on page 137 presents a familiar sight, a "typical" American family enjoying summer camping in the woods. While Dad watches the children playing games, Mom is at the stove, cooking the family meal. Jane O'Reilly (1982) has reported a similar family scene illustrated by a conversation she overheard while on a boat leaving a vacation island in Maine.

> Two families were with me, and the mothers were discussing the troubles of cleaning up after a rental summer. "Bob cleaned up the bathroom for me, didn't you, honey?" she confided, gratefully patting her husband's knee. "Well, what the hell, it's vacation," he said fondly. The two women looked at each other, and the queerest change came over their faces. "I got up at six this morning to make sandwiches for the trip home from this 'vacation,'" the first one said. "So I wonder why I've thanked him at least six times for cleaning the bathroom?" (p. 23)

Being a wife means housework even when you are also employed outside the home in full-time work. There are indications of change in division of responsibilities in today's families as a result of the increased participation of wives in the paid labor force, but these changes have not yet seriously contradicted the general association between being a wife and doing most of the household chores, regardless of whatever else the wife may do. From an analysis of studies of time spent in housework, Joann Vanek (1974) concluded that married women who are not employed in jobs outside the home spend about as much time per week doing household tasks (51 to 56 hours) as women did 50 years ago, despite appliances and other modern conveniences and changes in the specific nature of the tasks done. Employed wives do less housework than full-time homemakers, but far more than their employed husbands. Vanek found that employed and nonemployed wives did not differ significantly in the extent to which their husbands helped with the housework, nor in their use of paid household help, but wives who were employed simply spent less time than other wives in doing chores at home, an average of 26 hours per week versus 51 to 56 hours. According to Heidi Hartmann (1981), regardless of whether she works outside the home "the vast majority of time spent on housework is spent by the wife, about 70 percent on the average, with both the husband and the children providing about 15 percent on average"

(p. 385). The research data show no variation in this generalization as a consequence of differences in race, ethnicity, or social class. Angela Davis (1983) has pointed out that housework has never been the central focus of black women's lives because throughout their history in the United States they have had to work outside their homes. Nevertheless, "while they have seldom been 'just housewives,' they have always done their housework . . . [and] carried the double burden of wage labor and housework" (p. 231).

Consistent with Hartmann's conclusion about the relative amount of housework done by wives and husbands are data reported by Jean Atkinson and Ted Huston (1984) from a study of 160 couples who got married in the first half of 1981 and who were interviewed periodically during the early months of their marriage. The researchers found that regardless of their employment situation, "most of the housework is done by wives," who did "from over half to more than three fourths of the household chores" (p. 341). Although differential skills predicted division of household labor better than other factors (like attitudes or personal attributes), how skillful a wife was at doing the traditional "feminine" tasks (such as cooking, shopping, laundry) did not predict how much she participated in them. In other words, wives did these chores (regardless of their level of skill) *because they were wives.* Across cultures and across classes, working outside the home has not had much of an effect on lessening a wife's home responsibilities. Lillian Rubin (1976) found that an employed working-class wife typically returns from a tedious, demeaning job to "yet another day's work before her." The employed women she interviewed were doing

> two days work in one—one on the job and the other after they get home at night. This is true . . . in working-class families [and] . . . in the professional middle-class as well. The ideology and rhetoric are different but the reality is much the same. . . . The difference is in the women's attitudes toward the situation . . . more middle-class wives are angry about the burdens they carry in the family and more able to express that anger with less fear and ambivalence than their working-class counterparts. (p. 103)

No real change seems to have occurred during the past few years in women's responsibilities for household tasks among dual-earner couples. A study of a sample of predominantly white middle-class couples (Nyquist, Slivken, Spence, & Helmreich, 1985) found

that few women received "any appreciable amount of help from their husbands on a regular basis, even when they had full-time outside employment . . . [and that] in less than 2 percent of the couples did the husband and wife share equally or the husband contribute more" (p. 31). While husbands did more of the house and yard maintenance work than their wives, such work is done less regularly and frequently than household chores, and wives contributed more to maintenance jobs than husbands contributed to household jobs. As one group of researchers concluded from a survey of husbands (in "A Man-sized Resistance," 1981), "It's easier for men to accept the possibility of women as brain surgeons than to release their own wives from the drudgery of laundry and cleaning the bathroom." Similar conclusions have come from research done in other countries. Jessie Bernard (1981) has summed up the data as follows:

> Time studies in a dozen countries—communist as well as capitalist—trace the slow and bungling process by which marriage accommodates to changing conditions. . . . For everywhere the same picture shows up in the research: an image of women sharing the provider role at the same time retaining responsibility for the household. (p. 10)

Among the 60 thousand women who responded to the previously mentioned *Women's Day* survey, 83

percent said "most men don't take on responsibilities in the home to balance those responsibilities that women have assumed in supporting the family" ("Women Want," 1986).

Women who live with men do most of the housework even if they are not legally married. Informal observations made by Vivian Estellachild (1971) in hippie communes indicated that these alternatives to conventional marriage did not free women from traditional gender-related responsibilities. Under the leadership of men, many American communal groups continued to support the older gender distinctions of our patriarchal society. Kate Wenner (1977) described what she saw on a visit to an alternative community in Tennessee: the men were doing the outside work while the women were taking care of the house and the children. "Sex roles are clearly defined: Household, health, food and child care are the exclusive domain of women; manual work, leadership and administration are jobs for the men" (p. 81). These observations are confirmed by a study that compared a sample of married couples with a sample of cohabiting couples (all white, college-educated, middle-class). The researchers (Denmark, Shaw, & Ciali, 1985) found that while the difference between women and men in the "numbers of weekly hours spent on housework was greater for married couples, unmarried females still reported spending nearly twice as many hours on housework as unmarried males" (p. 623). Unmarried couples did differ from married couples in exhibiting less consistency or greater variability in jobs done around the house, but the women did more of them, more often.

Reduced Social Status   By taking on primary responsibility for care of the home (and children), women enable their husbands to put time and energy into the pursuit of occupational success. It is the husband's work outside the home that typically has top priority in family decisions and that provides the family with its social standing in the community. Since it is the husband's occupation that matters in the community's evaluation of the family, it is not surprising to find that women make career sacrifices for the men to whom they are engaged or married. Mark Kotkin (1983) documented this process in a study of graduate student couples at the University of Pennsylvania who were interviewed and followed-up on a year later. He compared married with cohabiting engaged and nonengaged couples and found that among the married women, 70 percent had made sacrifices for their husbands' career advancement, while only 10 percent of the husbands had made sacrifices for their wives. These sacrifices included providing economic support, relocating, postponing own career, and typing papers or doing labor for the spouse. Cohabiting women had made fewer sacrifices than married women. For example, "when asked why they were currently residing in Philadelphia, most married couples (55%) specified the man's career/education, only 5% the woman's; in contrast 25% of the cohabitors listed the man's career, 15% the woman's career" (p. 978). Attitudes and plans or strategies favoring the man's career were most common among the married couples (80 percent), followed by the engaged couples (64 percent), and least common among the nonengaged couples (44 percent), reflecting least to most egalitarianism. Kotkin concluded that

> most women in the sample had already subordinated their own careers to their husbands' . . . , and most engaged women apparently were prepared to do likewise upon entrance to matrimony. Having all but guaranteed the greater earning capacity of the husbands, neither partner will be likely to risk this investment in the future. Male career precedence is thereby perpetuated. (p. 984)

It is because of a husband's position in society (and not because of his particular personal character-

istics or motives) that he has significantly more power in marriage than does his wife. A contemporary employed wife may be shocked to realize that her social status is derived from her husband's and is determined by his socioeconomic position, just as was true for her mother and grandmother. She is still formally identified as Mrs. John Doe* and, in the eyes of the community, she takes on the status of her husband and the generally lower status of married women relative to married men. This is well illustrated by findings reported by John Richardson and E. R. Mahoney (1981). A sample of college students was divided into groups, each of which read a different vignette of a family with two children in which the wife and husband were both employed full-time. What varied among the stories were the occupations of the adults. Receptionist, office manager, and English professor were used to identify women's low-, middle-, and high-status occupations, respectively, while bus driver, insurance salesman, and dentist were used for the men's jobs. When respondents were asked to rate separately the wife's and the husband's general social standing in the community on a 21-point scale, the results were clear and dramatic. The status given to the wives was not at all influenced by their own occupations, but was instead significantly influenced by that of their husbands. The social standing of the husband, on the other hand, was influenced only by his own occupation and not at all by his wife's. (There was only one exception; low-occupational-status husbands whose wives had higher-status jobs were judged to be lower in status than other husbands, presumably because their situation violated the "traditional male prerogative to confer status" rather than to derive it.) Although the wives derived their social status from their husbands' occupations (and not their own), the wives of high- and middle-status husbands were judged to be significantly lower in status than their husbands and not equal to them. The researchers concluded from these data that "being a woman has a powerful ceiling effect on attributed social status . . . [while] the general social status scores assigned to men reflect sex-role status plus or minus occupational status" (p. 1196).

Related to differences in social status are differences in role—that is, in expected ways of behaving. For example, in one study (Barnes & Buss, 1985) husbands were reported by themselves and by their

---

*In 1986, the *New York Times* finally agreed to use "Ms." as an appropriate title for women.

wives as manifesting more initiative in their marriages. Thus, within marriage as outside of it, men's greater power—their greater access to resources—is related to the fact that they are men; conversely, women are blocked from access to these resources by virtue of social position and not because of individual personal qualities.

Disappointment and Divorce

In fiction, poetry, essays, and diaries women have described disappointments in marriage that seem to reflect the differential roles our society allocates to husbands and wives. Husbands as well as wives may find their marriages disappointing and experience dissonance between their expectations and the realities. And, ironically, it is not uncommon for the most diligent and role-proper wife to be caught totally by surprise by her husband's announcement that he intends to separate from her or obtain a divorce. In *The Woman's Room* (1977), for example, Marilyn French has described what many "good wives" have experienced. The heroine (Mira) talks about all those years she spent rating herself in terms of the questionnaires one finds in women's magazines:

> Are you a good wife, are you still attractive? Are you understanding, compassionate, nutritive? Do you keep your eye shadow fresh? . . . are you OVERWEIGHT?
> Mira had pitted herself against the standard. She had dyed and dieted, spent hours trying on wigs to be sure her hairstyle suited her face, had learned the proper tone of voice in which to ask nasty questions. . . . She had been properly ginger with his male ego, his fragile pride. She needled rather than raised her voice, she never threw tantrums. . . . Her house shone. Her meals were edible. She kept her figure. She had done it all. . . . She had done everything right, she had been perfect, and he still came home saying "I want a divorce." (p. 246)

Contemporary marriages may fail for the same reason that love relationships do. Husbands and wives are not equal in status or power. In today's world this is a source of discomfort, disillusionment, distress, and real disadvantage to large numbers of women. Even when the inequality is tolerated by the wife, her husband, possessing the social advantages of worldliness and economic independence, may grow dissatisfied with his wife's contributions to his ego, physical comfort, and/or sexual pleasure, and seek to replace her with a wife who is younger, sexier, better looking, or more adoring. With more married women in the work force, an additional source of stress has been introduced; a husband's power and

authority may be threatened by his wife's economic independence and the priority she gives to her work. As a wife devotes more attention to pursuits outside the home, she has less time and energy to focus on her husband. While wives expect their spouses to be work oriented, many husbands resent the fact that their wives' employment leaves less time for attention to them and to household chores.

Surprisingly few specific answers to the question of why married couples divorce have been found, but some important information has come from a national survey of 6000 married or cohabiting couples (Blumstein & Schwartz, 1983). Conflict over the woman's job was found to be most often responsible for the breakup of heterosexual couples; and women were less likely to stay in an unhappy relationship if they were economically independent. Couples were more likely to separate if the man complained that he did more than his share of the housework, or if having a good-looking partner was very important to him. Another study (Nettles & Loevinger, 1983) focused on "problem" marriages and compared a sample of (white, middle-class) couples involved in marriage counseling with similar couples who were not in counseling. The major difference between the two groups was that in the former a greater average discrepancy existed between wives and husbands in sex-role attitudes and beliefs. The investigators concluded that "what differentiates problem marriages is not [personality] differences within the couples . . . but different expectations and attitudes about behavior and division of labor" (p. 685). What appears to introduce problems into American marriages, then, are our cultural prescriptions for gender.

Ellen Ross (1980), for example, has concluded from an analysis of advice books for married couples written during the 1970s that while a great deal of talk went on about the importance of both partners' satisfying each other's needs, "the traditional burden of female responsibility for nurturance has probably increased" (p. 112) in recent years. This conclusion is complemented by data from a study of a sample of couples (Levenson & Gottman, 1985) that found that a husband is likely to withdraw emotionally in a problematic marriage much earlier than his wife, and that his wife's initial reaction may be to increase her level of positive affect and support "to coax him back into the emotional life of the marriage" (p. 90). Thus, marital dissatisfaction was found to be related to measures of emotional response obtained three years earlier; a decline in marital satisfaction was predictable "by less positive affect on the part of the husband

and . . . by more positive affect on the part of the wife" (p. 90). Eventually, the husband's continued withdrawal is accompanied by an increase in the wife's negative emotional responses. Other data suggest that it is a woman's dissatisfaction with her marriage that leads her to search for emotional satisfaction and support in extramarital relationships. Shirley Glass and Thomas Wright (1985) found that such relationships differ significantly for women and men. Among a white middle-class highly educated sample, married women reported that their extramarital involvements were more emotional than sexual, whereas men reported the reverse, thus following "paths or codes reflect[ing] sex roles in our culture" (p. 1118).

The severity of the problems encountered in marriage is indicated by the statistics on divorce. One out of three marriages currently ends in divorce, usually within the first seven years; for first marriages, the rate is higher, almost 40 percent (Phillis & Stein, 1983). In 1984, among the population of evermarried persons, 9 percent were divorced, compared with 4 percent in 1970 and 3 percent in 1960. These figures reflect a steadily rising divorce rate. The number of divorced persons per 1000 married persons was 121 in 1984, compared with 100 in 1980, 47 in 1970, and 35 in 1960 (U.S. Bureau of the Census, 1985b). A Census Bureau study projected that nearly 60 percent of married women in their 30s in the 1980s will eventually be divorced; the projection for women in their 40s was a 45 percent divorce rate, and 50 percent for women in their 20s ("Divorce Will Touch," 1986).

Among the distresses and dislocations that accompany divorce is the tendency for a woman to blame herself for the failure of her marriage. Anecdotal reports of such feelings of guilt are common in women's conversation and women's literature. Joyce Carol Oates has captured the essence of these feelings in Monica's words in *Solstice* (1985):

> She was prevented [by losing herself in work] from lapsing into self-pity and self-recrimination and self-loathing of the kind she so abhorred in women acquaintances of hers whose marriages had "also" ended disastrously. How did I fail, these stunned women asked themselves, what did I do wrong, how could I have avoided . . . ? I, I, I . . . (p. 12)

Such feelings among divorced women may be accompanied by dislocations in social activities and friendships. Accustomed to being part of a couple, a divorced woman becomes an "extra" guest or third wheel, a source of discomfort to her acquaintances. Her phone doesn't ring as often with invitations from married friends. In *Fly Away Home* (1984a), Marge Piercy has written about a recently separated middle-class woman whose friend Annette cancels an invitation to dinner when she hears of the separation, suggesting that it would be "awkward."

> She wanted to call Annette back and berate her. What would it cost them to have one unattached woman to supper? A beggar at the banquet? Did they think she would crawl into the laps of her neighbors' husbands? They were always afraid of the damaged marriages. Avoiding the plague. (p. 192)

Beyond such problems, the most clearly established aftermath of divorce is the economic hardship suffered by women. In the chapter on parenthood we will pay particular attention to the economic circumstances of single mothers, to the conditions of poverty in which vast numbers of women and children in the United States live, but here we must attend to the fact that divorce is a major contributor to this poverty. Lenore Weitzman (1985), after a 10-year study of divorce in California, concluded that divorced women (and their children) suffer an average immediate 73 percent drop in standard of living, while that of their husbands increases in the first year after divorce by an average of 42 percent. This disparity is attributed by Weitzman to the way property settlements are mandated under new no-fault divorce laws (which now exist in all 50 states). Dividing family assets equally between husband and wife typically means that one person—the husband—gets half while the other half goes to the wife *and* her children (for whom the wife gets legal responsibility in nine out of ten divorces involving children). If a family home is sold to obtain liquid assets, the wife and children must relocate to housing of lesser value since their income has been drastically reduced. Weitzman argues that current judicial practice does not divide a couple's assets acquired during marriage equally because omitted from the legal definition of assets are those associated with the career (or job) of the husband (who is typically the major, if not the only, breadwinner). Husbands are allowed to retain their occupational assets—professional licenses, pensions, health insurance, and future earning capacities—despite the fact that their wives have invested heavily in time and human capital in their husbands' educations and occupational advancement. In recognition of the inequity produced in not considering such assets jointly owned by a wife and husband, New York state has recently legislated a new definition of community property that includes career and education investments.

Weitzman has urged that the divorce laws in all states take into account the difference between husbands and wives in current and potential social/economic position, that a woman's contributions to home life be accredited as well as her impaired earning capacity during marriage, and that women who have major responsibility for their children after divorce be provided with special economic supports. Older women, whose marriages are dissolved after decades of full-time management of a home and tending to the needs of children and husband, may be left with no job, few prospects of reasonable employment, no pension, and no health insurance. Such women, Weitzman notes, have earned alimony. It is, for them, a pension to which they are entitled for their contributions to the marriage partnership.

In the United States today, less than 15 percent of divorced women receive alimony, and the average award lasts only for 25 months. The average child support award is $200 a month for two children. Forty-four percent of divorced mothers are awarded child support, but the sum typically covers less than half the support costs and is difficult to collect. The rate of delinquent and defaulted payments is very high among fathers of all income levels. According to Census Bureau figures ("Child-support Payments Lax," 1985), of the "more than four million women who were scheduled to receive child support in 1981, only 46.7 percent received the full amount due. . . . Another 25.1 percent received partial payments . . . and 28.4 percent received nothing." A federal law passed in 1984 now mandates that defaulting fathers be found and child support payments be provided by withholding money from their paychecks, imposing liens against their property, or withholding income tax refunds. How well this new law is working has not yet been assessed nationally, but in Rhode Island, it has significantly increased the collection of court-ordered support payments for families (Chiappinelli, 1986).

Divorced women without young children and without jobs may find themselves suffering the consequences of being "displaced homemakers . . . older women who have been forcibly exiled from a role, an occupation, dependency status, and a livelihood" (Sommers & Shields, 1978, p. 34). Such women lose their sole source of income, are ineligible for unemployment insurance, do not qualify for Aid to Families with Dependent Children if their children are over 18, and find it extremely difficult to get jobs because of their age and lack of recent paid employment experience. Some states have established programs to provide free counseling, support, and job training for displaced homemakers but with funding that is generally prey to pressures for budget reductions and is consequently unstable.

Studies of divorced women have found that the majority are interested in remarriage, but the chances of such for women are 75 percent compared to 80 percent for men (Phillis & Stein, 1983). This is the case because the pool of eligible men for divorced women is restricted by age and status factors. For example, while men with higher educations have the highest rate of remarriage, "women with high incomes and/or high educations have the *lowest* remarriage rate" (Finlay, Starnes, & Alvarez, 1985, p. 641). Divorced and widowed men tend to marry women who are younger and have lesser socioeconomic status. Another factor that diminishes a divorced woman's chances for remarriage is that her attitudes regarding marriage and gender-appropriate behavior tend to be significantly more liberal and egalitarian than those of divorced men. These findings, which came from interviews with a national cross section of divorced persons, suggest that divorced women will have difficulty finding men who share their views among "their most likely source of partners," divorced men (the Virginia Slims Opinion Poll of 1979, in Finlay, Starnes, & Alvarez, 1985).

Joy and Growth

If inequality in status and power produces unhappiness in marriage, then it should follow that women have a greater chance for marital happiness the more liberated both they and their husbands are from restrictive and debilitating gender roles. Caryl Rivers' (1975) definition of a "liberated" marriage is magnificent in its simplicity. She has suggested that it is "one in which there is rough parity of both the dirtwork and the glory," and she has described her husband as "one of a growing breed of free men who have not been stamped out of a mold like a chocolate bunny, who can dry a dish or wipe a runny nose without an attack of castration anxiety" (p. 19). But good intentions are often difficult to realize in the face of both internal and external barriers of considerable strength. Robin Morgan (1978) has shared some letters she wrote to herself during the early years of her marriage. In the first, written one week prior to her wedding, she promised herself:

> I will work toward becoming a woman rather than a wife, knowing that the latter need not include the former, but rather the former can with ease and a whole graciousness bring about the latter. I will remain me. . . . I will strive to enjoy his bed truthfully, his work critically, and our life with all the endurance, passion, and honesty I, as a separate me, can bring to them. (p. 25)

Similar objectives are being sought today by many women.

In addition, some men, in response to the women's liberation movement and to economic forces that have weakened the family wage system, have begun to question their traditional role as provider and breadwinner and have come also to enjoy what used to be women's prerogatives—self-adornment, home decorating, cooking, and consumerism. Jessie Bernard (1981) has described the decline of the "good provider role" for men but cautioned that while men are finding personal benefits in sharing breadwinning responsibilities with women, they are not as eager to share women's traditional responsibilities for the household. Barbara Ehrenreich's (1983) analysis of what she has labeled "the male revolt" is even more disquieting. She has concluded that contemporary

> male culture seems to have abandoned the breadwinner role without overcoming the sexist attitudes that role has perpetrated: on the one hand, the expectation of female nurturance and submissive service as a matter of right; on the other hand, a misogynist contempt for women as "parasites" and entrappers of men. (p. 182)

Some contemporary men appear to be enjoying a new freedom to explore long-suppressed ways of behaving (previously identified with femininity), and to be reexamining and questioning traditional behaviors. They are finding out that they can do their own cooking and laundry, spend their own money, and enjoy the company of adult women and men without committing themselves to a long-term relationship. How accurate this description of the "new man" (Ehrenreich, 1983) is of men across social classes is a question for further research. For marriage to be enhancing and growth-producing, we must, as Ehrenreich suggests, "learn to be brothers and sisters," and be guided by the "feminist principle . . . that women are also persons with the same needs for respect, for satisfying work, for love and pleasure as men" (p. 182).

BEING SINGLE

While marriage remains the preferred majority lifestyle, the percentage of single adults in this country living alone or with unrelated adults of either gender has sharply risen and continues to rise. In 1985, persons over 18 years of age living alone or with nonrelatives comprised 28 percent of all U.S. households, compared with 19 percent in 1970 and 8 percent in 1940 ("Living Alone," 1984; "More People," 1985). Figure 8.1 shows the steady increase during the 40-year period between 1940 and 1980 in the percentage of "living alone" households. If the category being counted is not households but individual adults, then of all persons 18 years of age or older, 35 percent were single and living alone or with other adults in 1980 (Phillis & Stein, 1983). This includes a wide range of persons—never married, widowed, divorced, separated, single parents—but does not include college students who reside with their parents when school is not in session. Among the women who lived alone in 1980, 23 percent were never married, 5.6 percent were separated, 56.4 percent were widowed, and 15

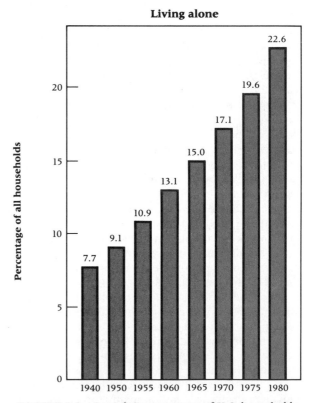

FIGURE 8.1 Growth in percentage of U.S. households containing persons living alone

percent were divorced. Comparable figures for men, in respective categories, were 45.5 percent, 13 percent, 16.1 percent, and 25.4 percent (Wolfe, 1981/1982).

Among unmarried adults two different trends in living arrangements have been noted. First, the number of unmarried-couple households has increased sharply; these include cohabiting couples as well as any other shared domestic arrangement between two adults. Since 1970, the number of such households has grown by an average of 105,000 per year, and they numbered close to 2 million in 1984 (U.S. Bureau of the Census, 1985a). Second, young adults between 18 and 34 years of age were in 1984 less likely than in 1970 "to be maintaining homes of their own and were more likely to be living in the homes of their parents" (U.S. Bureau of the Census, 1985a, p. 6); this change is more true of young men than women. Thus, among men between 25 and 34 years of age, 12.4 percent (including college students) were living with their parents in 1984 compared with 8.8 percent in 1970, while among women of the same age, 5.4 percent were living with their parents in 1984 compared to 5 percent in 1970. Contributing to this change, according to Census Bureau analysts, are such factors as "postponement of marriage, rise in divorce, emphasis on advanced education, employment problems, and high housing costs" (p. 6).

A study of census date trends has led some researchers (Bennett, Craig, & Bloom, in Greer, 1986) to conclude that

> college-educated white women who have not married by the time they are 25 years old have only a 50 percent chance of marrying. . . . Just 20 percent of the women who reach the age of 30 without marrying can be expected to marry, 5 percent of those who reached the age of 35 . . . and for those beyond 40 . . . 1 percent.

These conclusions are interpreted as suggesting that as unmarried women get older there are fewer available men to choose from. Those men who are available prefer younger women who are not as highly educated or successful; the older women have less interest in the available men and in marriage itself. Marriage is no longer viewed by some women as necessary for parenthood or for emotional or economic support and security. In some ways, however, the researchers note, today's college-educated white women may not be all that different from previous generations. For example, the average age of first marriages for such women born in the mid-1950s was 24, compared to 23 for college-educated white women born in the mid-1930s.

Stereotypes and Satisfactions

Contemporary women who lead independent lives and do not marry tend to be well educated, well employed, financially secure, and to manifest fewer signs of psychological distress than single men. Yet, old images of "the spinster" or "old maid" linger on in the pictures of never-married women we carry in our heads and see reinforced in films, television, and fiction. To the image of the sexually repressed "dried-up old prune" has been added that of the liberated "swinger" who searches actively for sexual satisfaction and the company of men. The dark side of such pursuit of sexual experience by dissatisfied, unhappy single women has been fictionalized by Judith Rossner in *Looking for Mr. Goodbar* (1976). The title suggests the theme; in this case the heroine's frantic and bewildered search ends in tragedy and violence. Other stereotypes of the unmarried woman include unusual dedication to some pursuit or career. She may be romanticized as a ballet dancer, executive, scientist, or a reclusive poet, or as someone who devotes her life to a cause or a person. She may then be viewed with some pity, since her life, though worthy, is nevertheless narrow and restricted. In fiction or films we have seen such women as teachers or daughters of demanding old parents, sometimes bitter, or, like Mary Poppins, as ever cheerful, clever, and good.

Patricia O'Brien (1973) has suggested that education and industrialization have made it possible for a single woman to live independently without the stigma of helplessness or inferior position, but the very fact that she is able to take care of herself contradicts traditional expectations about feminine behavior and is, therefore, upsetting to men and to traditional women. "Underlying all the criticisms and attacks on women alone through history has been the uneasy fear that women who seek alternatives to marriage . . . might very well find them satisfying. . . . [Thus] women who do not marry pose questions about the structure of society" (p. 74). One woman, writing to a newspaper's "share your thoughts" column, expressed her annoyance with people who (even in the enlightened eighties!) respond to her singleness "with shock, dismay, gloating or pity."

> My sister is a successful career woman [unmarried and childless]. . . . Our childhood was normal and loving, and my parents are still happily married. We both date and enjoy men's company. When I tell people about my sister's life and accomplishments, the question always comes, "Is she married?"
>
> Am I mistaken in thinking that people ask this ques-

tion as a further evaluation of worth? Is it my imagination that in this day and age there is the unfortunate concept that single men are *wisely* so by choice, and single women just "couldn't catch one"? ("She's Single," 1984)

In general, however, attitudes toward never-married persons are becoming more positive, a not-surprising correlate of the large number of single adults in this country. Within the past two decades, for example, new legislation has begun to ease the process of obtaining credit in loans and charge accounts for women who are not identified with men. Results of national opinion surveys indicate that whereas in 1957 four fifths of the respondents believed that staying unmarried was a "bad" choice and an indication of sickness, immorality, selfishness, or neuroticism, in 1976 only one fourth felt the same way ("20-year Comparison," 1979). And an investigation in 1980 found that very few adult women or their 18-year-old children unequivocally chose marriage as the better alternative to the single life; both life-styles were seen to have advantages and disadvantages ("Marriage vs. Single," 1982).

Research on unmarried adult women has found clear evidence that those who live alone or with other adults score high on physical, psychological, economic, and other criteria of well-being or life satisfaction. In some instances single women are found to do better than comparable groups of married women, and, as noted earlier, never-married women are generally better educated and employed, and more satisfied with their lives than never-married men. For example, David Bersoff and Faye Crosby (1984) analyzed data obtained from 13,500 adults in nine national opinion surveys conducted between 1972 and 1982. These adults were Caucasian, between the ages of 25 and 40, and employed at full-time jobs. Of all categories of respondents, that of single men contained the smallest percentage who indicated that they were very satisfied with their jobs (39.5 percent versus approximately 50 percent for all other groups). Single women and married women did not differ from one another on this dimension.

Single women living with young children typically face serious economic hardship in this country and differ substantially on many measures from other single adults. Thus, for example, while data from a national study revealed that adults of both genders who live alone tend to do so by choice, and are likely to be more socially integrated and to have more social contacts outside their household than adults who live with others, the women who lived alone with young

children revealed "significantly negative feelings about their life circumstances" ("Living Alone," 1984). Single parents, the vast majority of whom are women, constituted 19.5 percent of American households in 1980. In the chapter on parenthood we will discuss the special problems of single mothers related to their grossly inadequate access to economic resources. At this point it is important to recognize that single mothers are not a homogeneous group. In 1980, more than 20 percent of the over 5 million female-headed households in this country were headed by college-educated mothers (Wolfe, 1981/1982).

Single life for women without children at home is associated with high levels of personal satisfaction; this conclusion is supported by data from a variety of sources. For example, a follow-up study of children who had been identified in 1921 as highly gifted, found that those women who, in their 60s, were unmarried, childless, and employed, reported the highest level of occupational satisfaction of any group of women (Sears & Barbee, 1977). Lynn Gigy (1980) studied a sample of childless women over 30 years old who had never married and found that they differed significantly from a comparison group of married women in having had more education, in being currently employed, and in professional status of occupation. Gigy found no systematic differences between the single and married women in morale or personal adjustment, but the single women placed a higher value on personal growth and achievement and manifested a "continuing theme of self-assertiveness, determination, or independence" (p. 335). Similar findings have been reported by others. One group of researchers (Loewenstein, Bloch, Campion, Epstein, Gale, & Salvatore, 1981) interviewed 60 women between the ages of 35 and 65 who were single with no young children at home (half of whom lived alone) and found that what contributed to their feelings of satisfaction were health, living situation, friendships, and work. Family relationships were found not to be important contributors to satisfaction. Only 15 percent rated their lives as unsatisfactory and only about 30 percent of the childless women regretted not having had children. The researchers distinguished between the highly satisfied (HLS) and lesser satisfied (LLS) women as follows:

A statistical composite of a HLS single woman of this sample would be a highly educated woman in a professional, well-compensated job in which she is deeply invested. She lives with her roommate in her own house, does not feel lonely, and is in good health. She enjoys some intimate and many casual friendships. LLS women were found to suffer from ill health and loneliness. (p. 1140)

Single women between the ages of 35 and 44 are better educated and are earning substantially more money, on the average, than single men of the same age (Reilly, 1976). It is not surprising, then, that among this group of women some have begun to publicly proclaim that their single status is as significant and worthy of celebration as marriage. Beverly Stephan (1984) has written of single women who live "rich and full lives" and want others to recognize their independent life-style. Some

> celebrate this psychological turning point [when they stop waiting for Mr. Right] with an announcement or a housewarming party . . . buying a house or a set of china or getting their finances in order. The message is always the same: I am an adult. I want a whole life, not half a life. I am not willing to let life pass me by because I don't have a partner to share a mortgage or a vacation. (p. 55)

Stephan describes one such woman who at age 38 sent out announcements to 200 friends and business associates that she was "settling into Joyous Old Maidhood" and would "begin giving scintillating dinner parties and soirees" (p. 55).

Among women's reasons for choosing not to marry, the desire for personal independence has been found to rank high; so is not having found a suitable husband, incompatibility between marriage and career, and preferring to live with a woman rather than a man. Lynn Gigy (1980) found among a sample of never-married women over 30 years old that one third cited their sexual orientation as an important factor; 27 percent identified themselves as completely lesbian and 6 percent as predominantly lesbian. How representative this sample of women is of never-married women is impossible to say, but clearly, homosexual women are among those not likely to marry. This statement does not imply that lesbians never marry; a sizable number of lesbians have married and an even larger number are parents.

Letitia Peplau (1981) and her colleagues, over the course of 4 years, studied a sample of mostly white, middle-class lesbians and gay men and compared them to each other and to a sample of heterosexual women and men. She concluded that "for both homosexuals and heterosexuals, intimate relationships can—and often do—provide love and satisfaction. But neither group is immune to the perils of relationships—conflict and possible breakup" (pp.

28f.) Gender differences were found to be greater than homosexual/heterosexual differences in attitudes toward what is important in an intimate relationship, with women giving higher priority than men to emotional expressiveness. The lesbian women, however, were found to care more than any other group about shared political attitudes and about having an egalitarian relationship. What has emerged from the research on lesbian women, especially couples, is that butch-femme roles that recreate the traditional heterosexual scripts are infrequent. What is more common is "role flexibility and turn-taking" (Peplau, 1982), relationships that resemble friendships with the addition of erotic attraction, and a concern with equal power and equal involvement (Caldwell & Peplau, 1984). Jean Lynch and Mary Ellen Reilly (1985–1986) concluded from a study of 70 middle-class lesbian couples who had lived together for one or more years that, compared with heterosexual couples, "women in lesbian relationships strive to, and frequently succeed in, developing partnerships which seem to serve the needs of both individuals" (p. 15). In general, each partner in a lesbian couple was found to make relatively equal financial contributions, and to participate equally in day-to-day decision making. These findings complement those reported by Philip Blumstein and Pepper Schwartz (1983), who studied a larger sample of couples. None of the research on lesbian relationships indicates that they are free of stress, conflicts, jealousy, or frustrations, but lesbian couples are consistently found to differ from heterosexual couples and gay men in valuing and achieving egalitarianism in the relationship.

A New Definition of Family

Accompanying the steady growth in the number of single women who live alone or in households with nonrelated adults has been some change in media images of single women, particularly on television. Early pioneers like the *Mary Tyler Moore Show* and *Rhoda* have been succeeded by *Cagney and Lacey*, *Kate and Allie*, and *The Golden Girls*, which present images of strong women deriving pleasure and support from relationships with other adults to whom they are not related by birth or marriage. Jessica Fletcher in *Murder, She Wrote* is a television heroine who is a childless widow living delightfully alone in a seacoast town in Maine. She is a successful writer of mystery stories, competent, confident, assertive, busy, with many friends, places to go and things to do; she is respected, admired, liked, and sought after. There are no reasons presented to the viewer to pity her single status, and many to envy it.

The television portrayal of Fletcher's life focuses on her involvement with work and personal relationships as sources of satisfaction, thus illustrating a new conceptualization or an expanded understanding of what constitutes a family. As noted by Peter Stein (1976), single people are involved in "networks of human relationships that provide the basic satisfactions of intimacy, sharing, and continuity . . . based on a sense of choice and free exchange" (p. 109). Those persons on whom an individual can depend for emotional support, who are available in crises and emergencies, or who provide continuing affection, concern, and companionship can be said to comprise a family. Members of such a family may live together in the same household or in separate households, alone or with others; they may be related by birth or marriage, or by a choice and commitment to one another that has not been legally formalized. Thus, for example, Donald Bloch, the director of a family therapy institute, has reported that he views family therapy as appropriate for people who consider their family members to be friends, lovers, companions, and/or work colleagues (in Wolfe, 1981/ 1982). Recognition from other institutions of such an expanded meaning of family will further enhance the satisfactions unmarried women (and men) derive from their single life-style and from their varied relationships with persons of all marital categories and both genders.

Violence Against Girls and Women

every 3 minutes a woman is beaten
every five minutes a
woman is raped/every ten minutes
a lil girl is molested
yet i rode the subway today
i sat next to an old man who
may have beaten his old wife
3 minutes ago or 3 days/30 years ago
he might have sodomized his
daughter but i sat there
cuz the young men on the train
might beat some young women
later in the day or tomorrow
i might not shut my door fast
enuf/push hard enuf
every 3 minutes it happens. . . .
every three minutes
every five minutes
every ten minutes
every day

Ntozake Shange *(1978, pp. 114, 117)*

C H A P T E R   9

W omen and girls are not safe in our culture. Violence against girls and women occurs with alarming frequency. This violence is not inevitable; its roots lie in gender stereotyping and unequal power. When one gender dominates, the stage is set for the kind of violence we will explore in detail in this chapter.

SEXUAL ASSAULT

Rape is typically defined as forced sexual intercourse without the partner's consent. Such a definition is found in the legal statutes of most states, but the full meaning of rape is more complex because it is an act performed primarily by men against women. Rape, therefore, symbolizes women's *vulnerability* and in cultures where rape occurs frequently (as in our own), girls grow up fearful of the possibility that they will be overpowered and sexually violated. The possibility of rape increases a woman's need to seek out a man who will serve as her protector, and thereby increases her *dependency*. Rape connotes men taking women in the same way they take money and other goods, out of greed or temptation, thus specifying women's status as *objects* rather than persons. Rape flourishes during wars as an accompaniment of looting and other violence. Men think of rape not only as an assault of a woman but also as a crime against the man with whom she is identified—her father or her husband. The victim suffers from the brutality inflicted on her, and also from *shame* and *guilt* as though she has somehow, in some way, been an accessory.

The ancient legend of the rape of Lucretia, dating from the sixth century B.C. and later retold by Shakespeare, contains all of these major elements. Sextus Tarquinius, the son of the Etruscan king, was determined to have Lucretia, wife of a kinsman, because she was chaste, hardworking, and beautiful. He came to Lucretia one night and forced himself upon her. If she resisted, he told her, he would kill her and a male slave and then claim that he caught her in an act of adultery; by Roman law he would have the right to kill an adulterous relative. In the morning, Lucretia told her father and husband what had happened, entreated them to "avenge her dishonor," and stabbed herself to death in disgrace. The account of what took place is said to have so enraged the Romans that they overthrew the king, Tarquinius Superbus, and drove the Tarquins out of their city (V. Bullough, 1974). While the story of Lucretia enlists our sympathies for the victimized woman, it also teaches a cultural lesson. We are meant to see the rape as an act of dishonor against her father and husband that must be avenged by them; their rights and property have been trespassed against. Because Lucretia was a party to their disgrace, she is implicated and must suffer beyond the rape itself with her death. Despite her reputation for chastity and the fact that she was forced to submit to Sextus by threat of his sword, she is presented as the source of his temptation and therefore tainted by the deed. Such attitudes persist today, many centuries later.

Rape is violence in the form of forced sexual acts. Because these sexual acts may involve vaginal, oral, or anal penetration or other acts of a broadly sexual nature, and because attempted rape is sometimes successfully thwarted by the intended victim, some newly enacted state laws now refer to the behavior in question as sexual assault rather than rape and use broader definitions. Newer definitions are also gender-free in recognition of the fact that boys or men may be sexually molested, and that women are sometimes (although rarely) the perpetrators. One example of such legislation is a law passed in 1979 in Rhode Island that defines first-degree sexual assault as acts involving forced or coerced "sexual penetration with another person, not the spouse of the actor," and second-degree sexual assault as forced or coerced "sexual contact with another person." Such contact "includes the intentional touching of the victim's or actor's intimate parts, clothed or unclothed, if that intentional touching can be reasonably construed as for the purpose of sexual arousal, gratification or assault" (State of Rhode Island, 1979). In this section we will explore the problem of sexual assault in detail: its significance within society, its prevalence and the forms it takes, who perpetrates it, the phenomenon of blaming the victim, and the consequences of and possible solutions to sexual assault.

Cultural Significance of Rape

Sexual assault by men against girls and women can be related to women's status in our culture as subordinate to men, to the differential socialization of boys and girls, and to the sanctioned belief that it is a woman who attracts a man and is either his prize or prey. Sexual assault may be said to be an almost inevitable consequence of our gender stereotypes, and fear of its occurrence is part of learning what womanhood means. Women are taught to defer to men, to depend upon them for our self-definition and identity. We learn to expect that "our men" will defend and protect us against other men, and we are continually reminded and warned of the potential dangers awaiting us in unlit hallways, deserted streets, lonely roads, or the automobiles of strangers. What we are less often warned of but learn, unfortunately, from experience is that the danger is greater in our own homes, not from strangers but from men we have been urged to trust—friends and relatives. Many women would agree with Susan Griffin (1971), who wrote:

> I have never been free of the fear of rape. From a very early age I, like most women, have thought of rape as part of my natural environment—something to be feared and prayed against like fire or lightning. I never asked why men raped; I simply thought it one of the many mysteries of human nature. (p. 26)

Studies of other cultures suggest that sexual assault is not attributable to "human nature," and that cultures vary greatly in the incidence with which rape and related acts occur. Peggy Sanday (1981) examined 95 older tribal societies (from previously gathered ethnographic reports) and classified 18 percent as "rape prone" compared to 47 percent as "rape free" and 35 percent as intermediate. She concluded that "sexual assault is not a universal characteristic" (p. 9), and that rape-prone societies shared certain attributes that distinguished them from societies in which sexual assault was absent or rare. In the rape-prone societies intergroup and interpersonal violence was found to be at a high level, with frequent wars; macho ideology predominated; men had more power, authority, and public decision-making responsibility than women; women were poorly regarded; the sexes were largely segregated; and the natural environment tended to be exploited. Sanday interpreted these findings as indicating that rape is "the playing out of a socio-cultural script" by men for whom the expression of their "personhood" involves violence and toughness.

> Men are not animals whose sexual behavior is programmed by instinct. Men are human beings whose sexuality is biologically based and culturally encoded . . . Rape in tribal societies is part of a cultural configuration that includes interpersonal violence, male dominance, and sexual separation. (p. 25)

Among contemporary societies, the United States would undoubtedly be classified as rape-prone since it has the highest rate of sexual assault of any industrialized country in the world (Burt, 1980); and it can be said to share some of the just-described characteristics of other such cultures. When Susan Griffin (1971) called rape "the all-American crime," many were shocked; but her thesis is a serious one. Rape, she pointed out, "is a form of mass terrorism . . . [and] the fear of rape keeps women off the streets at night. Keeps women at home. Keeps women passive" (p. 8). Sexual assault is part of a cultural configuration that includes a view of men as predators, and of women as prey who have something men desire, need, lust after, and have a right to. When men learn that women exist for their pleasure, then women learn vulnerability, dependence, and helplessness. As Catharine MacKinnon (1983) has argued, "To be rapable, a position which is social, not biological, defines what a woman *is*" (p. 651).

In Susan Brownmiller's (1975) now-classic sociopolitical analysis of rape, the men who rape are said to perform an important function for all other men. "That some men rape provides a sufficient threat to keep all women in a constant state of intimidation" (p. 209); and the rapists, in effect, act as "front-line masculine shock troops." Although devastating and extreme, such a conclusion seems not to be greatly at variance with what we know about sexual assault: its frequency, the difficulties many people have in distinguishing between rape and seduction, the low conviction rate of accused rapists, the different attitudes toward rape expressed by men and women, and so on. For example, one consequence of women's intimidation by fear of assault, pointed out by Katha Pollitt (1985), is that in cities like New York "public space is, in fact, male turf" (p. C2). She notes that women are rarely seen alone or in small groups, unaccompanied by men, in public parks or rest areas. Women gather together outdoors primarily with their children—in playgrounds, near sandboxes and swings. While Pollitt's argument is probably exaggerated, and we can all find exceptions to her generalization, the grim picture she paints is nevertheless hauntingly familiar.

> There's the male sense of entitlement—on the street, men march boldly down the middle of the sidewalk, swinging their arms and looking ahead. . . . Women scurry along, clutching their shoulder bags, head down, weaving a zigzag path through the crowd. (p. C2)

Depictions of sexual violence against women in our mass media occur with sufficient frequency to suggest that our culture finds such images acceptable, exciting, and profitable. A review of the film *Dressed to Kill* (an example of the genre in which audiences are entertained by seeing women raped, mutilated, and killed) was headlined "De Palma Knows What Audiences Want to See" (Janusonis, 1980). The reviewer observed that the film had been "an immediate box-office hit" and received many favorable comments from the critics. "Slasher" movies are produced on small budgets, feature "bloody violence unleashed on young women," and are lucrative and well attended even if not lauded by the critics. In such "B" films, according to Barney Cohen (1984), the B refers not only to quality but also "means brutal." Neil Malamuth and Barry Spinner (1980) examined pictures published in *Playboy* and *Penthouse* and reported that between 1973 and 1977 there was a significant increase in the number depicting violent sexuality, suggesting that our tolerance for such images has increased. Explicit or suggested sexual violence against women is a common theme in cartoons, films, magazines, and television, sources of information and entertainment for a wide American audience, not just for the men who frequent peep shows in porno parlors and masturbate under their raincoats.

How Prevalent Is Rape?

Sexual assault is believed to be the least reported of all crimes, but the most frequently committed violent crime in the United States. Reported sexual assaults increased 94 percent between 1970 and 1980, when over 80,000 rapes were reported (U.S. Federal Bureau of Investigation, 1982). This is a national rate of 35.6 per 100,000 people. Statistics on rape must be approached with caution, since it is well known that sexual assaults are grossly underreported. Estimates have been made that anywhere from 3 to 10 times as many sexual assaults are committed (or attempted) as are reported. These estimates are even higher if they include assaults on young girls by their fathers, stepfathers, or other male relatives (usually categorized separately as incest), and cases of statutory rape, sexual relations with a child between the age of 12 (typically) and the age of consent (usually set at 16, but variously defined by state laws). FBI statistics on rape do not include these categories of sexual assault, nor do they include marital rape.

Judith Laws and Pepper Schwartz (1977) have noted that "according to recent statistics a forcible rape occurs every ten minutes" (p. 205); according to Ellen Weber (1977), "One girl out of every four in the United States will be sexually abused in some way before she reaches the age of 18" (p. 64); and Carole Offir (1975), basing her estimate on crime and census statistics for Los Angeles, wrote that "the chances of a Los Angeles woman meeting a rapist at some time during a 30-year period is about one in 10" (p. 73). Among the most carefully prepared estimates of the prevalence of rape in the United States is that of Allan Johnson (1980), who looked at age-specific rape rates and accumulated the risks over all ages to estimate the risk over a woman's entire life. Johnson concluded that if reported rapes are in fact the only ones that occur, and if conditions in the United States remain the same, then 12-year-old girls have an 8.5 percent chance of being subjected to a completed or attempted rape sometime during their lives. But it is well known that reported assaults represent only a small portion of the number that actually occur, and the FBI currently estimates that only 1 in 10 is reported to the police (in "Sexual Assault," 1986). In Johnson's view, a conservative assumption is that reported sexual assaults probably reflect two fifths or one third of their actual number. In that case, he has concluded, "20–30 percent of girls now under twelve years old will suffer a violent sexual attack during the remainder of their lives" (p. 145). This estimate, he reminds us, is based on data that exclude children under 12 and wives sexually assaulted by their husbands. According to Johnson:

> The average American woman is just as likely to suffer a sexual attack as she is to be diagnosed as having cancer, or to experience a divorce. . . . The numbers reiterate a

reality that American women have lived with for years: Sexual violence against women is part of the everyday fabric of American life. (p. 146)

Studies that have asked respondents about their experience of sexual assault at some time in their lives (rather than just in the preceding 12 months, as is typically asked in national crime studies) provide support for Johnson's conclusions. For example, a survey conducted by *Cosmopolitan* magazine in 1980, to which more than 106,000 women responded anonymously, revealed that 24 percent had been raped at least once; over half of the reported assaults had been perpetrated by acquaintances, relatives, or husbands, and only 38 percent by strangers (in Beneke, 1982). Diana Russell and Nancy Howell (1983) have reported results from a sample of 930 randomly selected adult women in San Francisco who were encouraged in full disclosure by well-trained interviewers matched to respondents in race/ethnicity. Within this group, 44 percent reported having experienced rape or attempted rape at some time during their lives. Based on their data, Russell and Howell calculated the probability of being the victim of attempted or completed rape during a woman's lifetime to be 46 percent; they found the most vulnerable ages to be 16 to 24, similar to other reports. Albert Gollin (1980) has concluded that "the risks of completed rape are much greater for young women (ages twelve to thirty-four), then decline sharply" (p. 347). For example, in 1985, according to the Rhode Island Rape Crisis Center, nearly 20 percent of the sexual assault victims were under the age of 13, and nearly 23 percent were between 13 and 15 (in "Sexual Assault," 1986).

In a study conducted at the University of Rhode Island (Lott, Reilly, & Howard, 1982), my colleagues and I found that among a random sample of over 500 women (students, staff, and faculty), 29.4 percent, or almost one out of every three women, reported a personal experience of sexual assault sometime during her life. Our definition of sexual assault included any sexual intrusion without consent, by force, deception, or threat of violence. A survey of 470 resident undergraduate women at the University of Massachusetts obtained comparable results, from which the researchers concluded that 25 percent had experienced at least one sexual assault sometime during her life (Everywoman's Center, 1980).

Sexual assaults can occur anywhere and at any time, but are more likely to take place on the weekend, during evening or early morning hours,

during summer months, and in urban areas. In 1985, almost one third of the assaults reported to the Rhode Island Rape Crisis Center occurred in the victims' homes, 15 percent in the assaulters' homes, and 15 percent in homes the victim and assaulter shared (in "Sexual Assault," 1986). My colleagues and I (Lott, Reilly, & Howard, 1982) also found that homes are places of risk. Among those in our university sample who had experienced sexual assault, 42 percent were assaulted in someone's residence, and 39 percent in the victim's home, as compared to 32 percent outdoors and 24 percent in a parking lot. National data support the conclusion that the single most common place of attack is in a woman's own residence—approximately 30 percent of all reported cases.

The victim and the attacker are of the same race 93 percent of the time ("The Problem of Rape," 1978), and typically also of the same social class. According to Susan Brownmiller (1975), those who run the greatest risk of being assaulted are black, teenage, urban working-class girls. But rape reports come from all segments of the population, and victims' ages range from infancy to old age. Sexual assault appears to be occurring with greater frequency on college campuses throughout the country, and women have been sexually abused by their psychiatrists and other trusted professionals. According to Robert Trotter (1982):

> Single case histories   usually a woman complaining that she was sexually abused by her therapist—have appeared from time to time in psychology journals, on television documentaries, and in movies. But the extent of the problem has been difficult to determine because of its intimate and often embarrassing nature. (p. 78)

Documentation of the seriousness of the problem of sexual assault by therapists has now been provided by a number of studies. For example, a national survey showed that 5.5 percent of male clinical psychologists had had sexual relations with their clients (Holroyd & Brodsky, 1977). In a subsequent study cited by Trotter (1982), 700 licensed clinical psychologists in California responded anonymously to a mailed questionnaire and gave details on 559 cases of sexual intimacy between patients and therapists. In the vast majority of cases some harm to the patients was reported. Almost all the offending psychotherapists were men, while almost all of the patients involved in the intimacies were women, who ranged in age from 13 to 58. Laws making it illegal for therapists or physicians to have sex with their patients have been passed by several states, including Arizona, California, New Jersey, New York, Ohio, Rhode Island, and Wisconsin. Another indication of the significance of this problem comes from a report that the American Psychiatric Association (APA) voted no longer to cover sexual misconduct in its malpractice insurance ("Therapists Lose," 1985). In explaining the change in policy, a spokesperson noted that "allegations of sexual misconduct make up about 10 percent of the complaints that come before the APA's professional liability insurance committee but account for 15 percent of the insurance losses." The financial cost of sexual license and misconduct with patients has apparently become too great to be tolerated. Paul Slawson, chairperson of the APA's insurance committee, is quoted in the press report as follows:

> Back when insurance cost a few hundred dollars, people didn't worry about it. . . . But now they cost thousands. And members felt they didn't want to pay extra thousands a year for what they felt was unethical behavior . . . [that] shouldn't in any way be sanctioned.

The prevalence of sexual assault in homes, offices, familiar and unfamiliar places can only be estimated, since most victims do not report this experience to official agencies, and many do not talk about it to anyone. A woman may not report sexual abuse because she doesn't realize that what happened to her is a legally punishable offense. She may have been assaulted on a date, by a family member, or while intoxicated. She may be embarrassed and ashamed; she may wish to avoid the unsympathetic (and sometimes callous) treatment she anticipates from the police and in the courts; she may want to avoid continued references and attention to a deeply painful experience; or she may simply feel helpless and confused. A child may not report a sexual assault for the same reasons as an adult, but, in addition, the child may fear reprisals, may not fully comprehend what has occurred until later, or may be convinced that she is now a "bad" girl and that no one can help her.

Sexual Assault by Nonstrangers

Reports of sexual assault indicate that more than half are committed by someone known to the victim. This is especially true when the victim is a child, but is also the case for older victims. Instances of assault by a stranger are known to be more likely reported than assault by a person with whom the victim has voluntarily interacted in social or other situations; thus, official reports of assault by known attackers are very likely to underestimate the actual number of such cases. Figures for 1985 reported by the Rhode Island Crisis Center (in "Sexual Assault," 1986) indicated that the assaulter was a stranger to the victim in only 18.7 percent of the cases; 31.8 percent of the time the sexual assault was committed by a relative; 26 percent of the time the victim knew the offender well; and in 23.5 percent of the cases the victim was acquainted with the attacker. These data are likely to be similar to those from other states, and complement information accumulating from many sources. Sexual assault by nonstrangers includes incest, date rape, and wife rape, and each will be discussed in more detail.

Incest David Finkelhor (1979) surveyed almost 800 New England college students and found that 19 percent of the women (and 9 percent of the men) reported having been sexually abused as children, primarily by male friends or acquaintances of the family or by family members. The probability of sexual abuse by an adult was greater in poor and rural families but was also found within suburban and urban families of all social classes. Approximately 1 percent of the women had been sexually victimized by their fathers or stepfathers.

Judith Herman and Lisa Hirschman (1977), basing their estimate on the reports of psychotherapists, have suggested that at least 2 to 3 percent of women have been the victims of father-daughter incest. They found that the age of onset of such a relationship varied from 4 to 14 and that the occupation of the father spanned socioeconomic categories. Similarly, Louise Armstrong (1978), who interviewed 183 women who had been sexually assaulted by their fathers, reported that they came "from all classes, all races, all parts of the country" (p. 232). The National Incidence Study commissioned by the Children's Bureau (*Executive Summary*, 1982) collected data on reported child abuse between May 1979 and April 1980 from a sample of 26 counties in 10 states, including urban, suburban, and rural areas. On the basis of their data they estimated that almost 6 children are abused out of every 1000 children in this country and that 1 out of every 1000 is a victim of sexual exploitation. The authors of the study, however, emphasized that their figures reflect "*a bare minimum* number" (p. 3) because of the very strict definitions used, the restriction of data collection only to public facilities, and variation in the level of cooperation among public agencies.

Among anonymous respondents to a *Cosmopolitan* survey, 10 percent indicated that they had been victims of incest (in Beneke, 1982). According to a recent summary of all available national data (*Developing a National Agenda*, 1985), "Incest is estimated to occur in 14 percent of families and is found in all family types and social classes" (p. 12); in 75 percent of the cases, fathers have abused daughters; and when boys are victimized, they are also likely to be sexually assaulted by men in their own families. Some estimates are even higher. For example, Vincent Fontana, who has chaired government commissions investigating child abuse, believes that one of every five girls and one of every nine boys is sexually abused by an adult, and in 8 of 10 cases the assaulter is known to the child and is most often a family member, typically the father or stepfather (in May, 1986). Finally, in a survey of 3000 college women in Rhode Island, Joan Crook (1986) identified 30 as father-daughter incest survivors, supporting the often-cited figure of a 1-percent incidence.

While estimates of the true prevalence of sexual exploitation of children by adults (and particularly by family members) vary, all investigators agree that the number is far greater than was suspected a decade or two ago. Slowly, reports by women of childhood sexual victimization by men in their families have been matched and corroborated by data gathered by social scientists. Maya Angelou (1971) has written of her experience as an 8-year-old when she went to live with her mother and her mother's friend, Mr. Freeman, who used to hold and fondle her, and press his "thing" against her leg. Eventually he raped her. In a novel by Marian Engel (1979), the heroine recalls her childhood experiences with Uncle Eddie, who would

> put his arm around me and tell me what a good girl I was and try to get his finger up my pants. I hated him, but I knew if I told my mother she'd think I invited it or invented it. (p. 23)

Gail Godwin (1978) has told a similar story about a young girl who would awaken in the middle of the night to find her stepfather "kneeling and panting in the dark beside her bed" (p. 311). After Senator Paula Hawkins of Florida disclosed at a national conference that she had been sexually molested as a child, she reported being "bombarded by letters" from women who had been similarly victimized ("Molestation Story," 1984).

Ellen Weber (1977) has found that the sexual abuse of a child often begins before she understands its significance and that it need not, therefore, involve the use of force; "the perpetrator uses his position of authority or trust to convince the naive child that their relationship is 'for her own good,' or a normal part of growing up" (p. 64). Accounts by women who have told their own stories, like Katherine Brady (1979) in *Father's Days*, Louise Armstrong (1978) in *Kiss Daddy Goodnight*, and four women who appear in the documentary film *Incest: The Victim Nobody Believes*, suggest that the process described by Weber is typical. When the girl begins to understand what has been happening to her

> she may feel both betrayed by the offender, and guilty and ashamed. . . . [She] will usually resist the relationship, only to be frightened with stronger and stronger threats; but her own sense of complicity may prevent her from asking anyone else for help. . . . The family may close its eyes . . . out of a sense of loyalty to the offender, the fear of public embarrassment, or perhaps the loss of a father's income. (Weber, 1977, p. 64)

While no consistent profile of the abuser appears in the literature, one general attribute is repeatedly reported: the abuser is described retrospectively by his victimized daughter as having been authoritarian, punitive, and threatening. According to Judith Herman and Lisa Hirschman (1977), the victim of incest tends to feel "overwhelmed by her father's superior power and unable to resist him; she may feel disgust, loathing, and shame. But at the same time . . . that this is the only kind of love she can get" (p. 748). In their study of 40 women in psychotherapy who were victims of father-daughter incest (defined as any physical contact that had to be kept a secret), Herman and Hirschman (1981) found that the fathers were often described as having dominated their families by physical force or intimidation. And Louise Armstrong (1978) concluded that the abusive father

> must have a sense of paternalistic prerogative in order to even begin to rationalize what he's doing. . . . Weak or authoritarian in nature, he must have a perception of his children as possessions, as *objects*. He must see his children as there to meet his needs. (pp. 234f.)

Data reported by Joan Crook (1986) also indicate significant differences between fathers of incest survivors and fathers of a comparison group, with the former reported by their daughters to have been more verbally aggressive, violent, punishing, and less supportive.

In the traditional psychiatric literature about incest, the mother has been blamed for her daughter's abuse either because she presumably shut her eyes to what was going on and refused to believe her daughter's claims or hints, or because of her overly dependent, passive personality. Thus, for example, in a report on the wife in cases of father-daughter incest, it was noted, without supporting data, that she usually "has an extremely passive personality" ("Paper Urges," 1982). A widely held view is that the mother is somehow responsible for her husband's behavior, by her passivity or her unavailability for sex or her failure to protect her child. Some researchers (such as Armstrong, 1978; Herman & Hirschman, 1981) have reported that while incest survivors are typically angry with their mothers for not having protected them, or for not having been powerful enough to punish their fathers, these daughters judge their mothers not so much as at fault or as somehow responsible, but blame them for having failed to give their daughters the support they needed to prevent the fathers from acting as they did. Herman and Hirschman maintain that

> the message that these mothers transmitted over and over to their daughters was: your father first, you second. It is dangerous to fight back, for if I lose him I lose everything. For my own survival . . . I cannot defend you, and if necessary I will sacrifice you to your father. (p. 746)

A study by Margaret Myer (in "Research Dispels," 1984), however, has concluded that mothers of incest victims cannot be grouped into any one category and that "they vary markedly not only in their initial response to the revelation of sexual abuse, but in their ability to protect their daughters and maintain the family unit" (p. 3). Fixty-six percent of the 43 mothers studied were found to have protected their daughters and rejected their husbands when the incest was discovered or disclosed, and at least 75 percent of the mothers had not known about their husband's sexual abuse of their daughters. Similar findings and conclusions have been reported by Joan Crook (1986), who compared 30 college women incest survivors on descriptions of family functioning and other variables with a matched group from a large sample. She found no evidence that the mothers of incest survivors had played any role in maintenance of the father's behavior. They did not differ from mothers of the women who had not been sexually abused by their fathers on any measure "except that they seemed to be more verbally aggressive, perhaps their way of acting out under the stressful conditions of their lives" (p. 58). The daughters reported that their mothers had been unaware of the abuse, and that most had been "helpful and supportive" when they did learn of it. Perhaps, as Crook suggests, the incest survivors who are supported by their mothers (the majority in her sample, 22 of 30)

do not consult psychotherapists, while those who have had little or no parental assistance are more likely later to be seen in therapy. She concluded that "incest happens in a large number of families whether or not the mother is a strong and protective parent figure" (p. 56).

Traditional psychiatric analyses of incest have blamed not only the mothers but the victims themselves for their "seductiveness" (in Rush, 1971). That such views are still held is illustrated by the public statements of two judges from different regions of the United States. In sentencing a man convicted of first-degree sexual assault, a judge in Wisconsin said of the 5-year-old victim, "I am satisfied we have an unusually sexually permissive young lady. And [the defendant] did not know enough to refuse. No way do I believe [he] . . . initiated sexual contact" ("Judge's Recall Sought," 1982). Similarly, a judge in Rhode Island suggested that some victims of incest "really enjoy it," don't complain "until they get hurt or something," and thus must share guilt with their abusers ("Judge Defends Comments," 1982). When Sigmund Freud proposed in an 1896 paper ("The Aetiology of Hysteria") that women's neuroses were caused by childhood experiences of sexual abuse within their own families, the response of the medical community was outrage, and Freud was ostracized. He soon abandoned this hypothesis in favor of one that was more acceptable, namely that the women were obsessed with sex and that their stories about seduction and sexual violence were not memories but rather wish-fulfilling fantasies. An analysis of the events in this process of change in Freud's position has been carefully presented in a book by Jeffrey Masson (1983).

The reality for daughters sexually victimized by family members, especially fathers, has been painfully reported to psychotherapists and survey researchers, and described in articles and books. From a number of such first-person accounts, Wini Breines and Linda Gordon (1983) concluded that

> the daughter may gain a semblance of power in the family through bargaining with the father for things she wants. But her main experience is shame and guilt, isolation, and an oppressive, disproportionate sense of responsibility for holding the family together, which she accomplishes in part by keeping her secret. (p. 526)

Joan Crook (1986) found that "most survivors did not tell anyone about the abuse at the time, and the reason given was usually fear" (p. 59). Effects of the abuse reported by her sample of college women included problems with interpersonal relationships, trusting others, and sexual difficulties. We will focus on the effects of sexual assault in general in a later section in this chapter.

Date Rape Reports of the widespread sexual exploitation of women by men we know and trust enough to go out with have come from a number of studies. For example, on one college campus (Koss, Leonard, Beezley, & Oros, 1985), almost 32 percent of approximately 2000 men surveyed admitted having used some degree of physical or emotional coercion to have sex with an unwilling woman. In all cases the nonconsensual sex reported was with an acquaintance. The men who reported having threatened or browbeaten women into sexual contact with them were undetected offenders since the assaults they committed were never reported, and the women who experienced sexual victimization without reporting it were hidden rape victims. Elsewhere, Mary Koss (1981) has reported that the women in this same study who did not label their experience of forced sexual intercourse as rape tended to be romantically involved with the offender. For approximately 40 percent of the hidden rape victims, their first sexual experience had been a sexually aggressive one!

Another group of researchers (Giarrusso, Johnson, Goodchilds, & Zellman, 1979) asked a sample of 14- to 18-year-olds in Los Angeles, "Under what circumstances is it OK for a guy to hold a girl down and force her to have sexual intercourse?" When presented with nine specific circumstances, only 44 percent of the girls and 24 percent of the boys maintained that it was *never* acceptable to use force. Both genders ranked the circumstances under which force is acceptable in very similar ways, and believed it was most acceptable "when a girl gets a guy sexually excited." The investigators concluded that

> a likely scenario involves a young man's interpreting a young woman's behavior as indicative of sexual intent or perhaps even a tacit agreement to sexual intercourse; whereas, the young woman is unaware of this ostensible contract and acts accordingly. In such a conflict, our findings suggest, there may well be a resolution through the use of force. The stage seems set for nonstranger rape. (p. 7)

In an informal interview with students at an eastern university, Karen Barrett (1982) was told by one man that he gets told "no," but keeps on going since "nobody complains afterward." Another man told her, "I guess it's hard to believe a girl could really mind that much. Because the guy's never even imagined a negative sexual experience, he can't quite

relate to the significance of coercion. After all, sex is fun, right?" (p. 50). Among the letters that followed the publication of Barrett's article on date rape in *Ms.* was one from a woman who wrote that she had been forced to engage in sex with a boy she was dating as a teenager because he had told her that she "shouldn't have started something" she "wasn't prepared to finish" ("Letters," 1982, p. 7).

Wife Rape Another group of hidden rape victims are wives forced to submit to their husband's sexual demands. Husbands have typically been excluded from state rape laws because marriage is considered a contract that gives a man the right to "carnal knowledge" of his wife. But while wife rape has not been considered a criminal offense and is, thus, rarely reported to the police or to other agencies, Diana Russell (1982) found, among a sample of respondents in San Francisco, that 14 percent had been sexually assaulted by their husbands. In *Vida*, a novel by Marge Piercy (1979), two sisters are talking about rape and one is reminded of experiences with her husband.

> She saw herself pinned on the bed under Vasos, unable to cry out because there was nothing but humiliation in screaming when your own lawfully wedded husband exercised his conjugal rights. . . .
> "But it isn't rape if you know the guy."
> "If you murder somebody you know, it's murder. If you rob somebody you know, it's robbery." (pp. 200f.)

Marital rape has been found to be embedded in violent marriages. Irene Frieze (1983) interviewed almost 300 women in Pittsburgh and found that among those who had reported being physically assaulted by their husbands, 73 percent also said they were pressured to have sex, and 34 percent said they had been raped. Among the women in a nonviolent comparison group, 37 percent reported pressure for sex and 1 percent reported rape. In a study of a random sample of adults in Texas, Charles Jeffords (1984) found that persons who have tolerant attitudes toward forced marital intercourse are also likely to be highly traditional in their sex-role attitudes. These data complement Frieze's findings that husbands who forced sex on their wives did so, according to their wives, to prove their manhood, and to obtain services they believed their wives were obligated to perform.

In December 1978, an Oregon man went on trial for raping his wife, the first such prosecution in this country. He was acquitted by a jury of four men and eight women who deliberated for three hours.

Almost 6 years later in Florida, in August 1984, a man was convicted for the first time for the rape of his wife. Between these two events the laws in several states were changed. Before 1979, husbands could be prosecuted for sexually assaulting their wives only in the states of Delaware, Iowa, Nebraska, New Jersey, and Oregon, but 18 states had been added to this list by the end of 1984 ("New Laws," 1984). These other states include California, Connecticut, Florida, Illinois, Massachusetts, Minnesota, New Hampshire, New York, Pennsylvania, Virginia, Wisconsin, and the District of Columbia. Still, many states provide no legal recourse for a woman whose husband forces her to have sex with him. And in 1980, 13 states broadened their marital rape exemptions to prevent prosecution of a man who rapes the woman with whom he is cohabiting (*Docket Report*, 1983–1984). At the same time, the New York Court of Appeals, in December 1984, voted unanimously in *People v. Liberta* to overturn New York state's marital rape exemption, ruling that such an exemption denied married women equal protection of the law. This was "the first top state court to rule that laws are unconstitutional which permit married men to legally rape their wives," and to assure married women "the same right to control over their bodies" guaranteed to unmarried women (*Docket Report*, 1985–1986, p. 25).

Who Commits Sexual Assault?

Information about the characteristics of sexual assaulters comes primarily from those who have been identified, arrested, tried, and convicted. What we know about men who sexually assault women is thus very limited, since most perpetrators are never identified by legal or social service agencies. For example, the Rhode Island Governor's Justice Commission reported that in 1981 and 1982, although arrests were made in the majority of sexual assault cases reported to the police, the number of arrests was only one third of the number of sexual assaults reported to the Rape Crisis Center (in Landis, 1983). While more reports are made to such an agency than to the police, even more assaults are suffered painfully alone, or humiliatingly shared only with a friend or relative. Even when a sexual assault has been reported, an arrest does not always follow, and prosecution does not always lead to a conviction. According to Susan Brownmiller (1975), "In reported rape cases where the police do believe the victim, only 51 percent of the offenders are actually apprehended, and of these, 76 percent are prosecuted, and of these 47 percent are

acquitted or have their case dismissed" (p. 175). Reports of conviction rates around the country have varied from 10 to 50 percent, and Karen Barrett (1982) has reported only a 16 percent national rate. Of the four major violent crimes—rape, murder, aggravated assault, and armed robbery—rape has the highest acquittal/dismissal rate and the lowest rate of conviction.

Those who collect data on sexual assaults agree that no "typical portrait" of a potential rapist exists. He may be single, married, or divorced; of any stature, physique, or degree of intelligence; drunk or sober; in any occupation; and aged 14 to over 50. A. Nicholas Groth (1979) studied over 500 convicted rapists and concluded that

> rape is a complex act that serves a number of retaliatory and compensatory aims in the psychological functioning of the offender. It is an effort to discharge his anger, contempt, and hostility toward women—to hurt, degrade, and humiliate . . . to assert his strength and power—to control and exploit. . . . Sexuality is not the only—nor the primary—motive underlying rape. It is, however, the means through which conflicts surrounding issues of anger and power become discharged. (p. 60)

Judith Becker and Gene Abel (1978), who also studied men convicted of sexual assault, concluded that rapists select their victims on the basis of availability and vulnerability, and that rape is a "crime of opportunity." Personality tests, according to Neil Malamuth (1981), have not found reliable differences between rapists and nonrapists, but the former have been found to be more likely "1) to hold callous attitudes about rape and to believe in rape myths, and 2) to show relatively high levels of sexual arousal to depictions of rape" (p. 142). But some researchers have failed to find reliable differences between convicted rapists and matched groups of men on measures of attitudes toward women (for example, Sattem, Savells, & Murray, 1984; Scully & Marolla, 1981).

The data reported by Koss and her colleagues (1985) from their previously mentioned survey of 2000 men on one college campus are particularly significant because the men who admitted using coercion to get sex were undetected offenders (the majority of rapists). The researchers were able to distinguish four groups among the college men they studied: *sexually assaultive* men (4.3 percent), who had had intercourse with a woman through threat or actual use of physical force; *sexually abusive* men (4.9 percent), who had forced sexual contact on women without intercourse; *sexually coercive* men (22.4 percent), who used extreme verbal pressure and made emotional or psychological threats; and *sexually nonaggressive* men (59 percent), who reported sexual experiences characterized only by mutual consent. A small group of men (9.4 percent) could not be classified. The researchers found within their sample

> that men who have threatened or actually used force to gain nonconsensual sexual intercourse with female acquaintances differed from sexually nonaggressive men in their degree of adherence to several rape-supportive attitudes. The more sexually aggressive a man had been, the more likely he was to attribute adversial qualities to interpersonal relationships, to accept sex-role stereotypes, to believe myths about rape, to feel that rape prevention is the woman's responsibility, and to view as normal an intermingling of aggression and sexuality. (p. 989)

While sexually coercive men differed sharply from other men in their attitudes and beliefs about gender attributes and about rape, they were not distinguishable on any measure of psychopathology.

A series of studies by Neil Malamuth and his colleagues have revealed that sexual assault is not beyond the realm of contemplation for a surprisingly large number of ordinary, middle-class, college men. While Koss and her colleagues asked college students to report on their actual behavior, in the studies described by Malamuth (1981), participants read a description of a sexual assault and were then asked to indicate, on a 5-point scale, the likelihood that they would behave like the assailant under similar circumstances if they were assured of not being caught and punished. Among various samples of college men, 35 percent have indicated some likelihood that they would engage in sexual acts with a woman forcibly and without her consent. These men, in other words, did not respond to the question by saying there was *no likelihood at all* that they would behave in this way. When compared with men who self-reported no likelihood of rape (low LR scorers), those with higher LR scores were found to have more callous attitudes toward rape, to believe more in rape myths, and to be more sexually aroused to depictions of rape. Thus, ordinary college men who admit that they might assault a woman under certain circumstances are similar both to undetected offenders and to convicted rapists. Malamuth and his colleagues have also found that

> men with a higher LR self-rating are more inclined to perceive rape as a sexual act which women desire and enjoy whereas those with lower LR reports perceive

rape more in terms of an act of violence with serious consequences to the victim. (p. 150)

In addition, men with high LR ratings were found to more often report that they had personally used force against women in sexual relations, and might do so again. In another study of college men (Check & Malamuth, 1983), those with high sex-role stereotyping scores were found to show levels of arousal to a rape depiction that were as high as those of a previously tested group of rapists. Among the men with highly stereotyped beliefs, 44 percent self-reported some likelihood that they might sexually assault a woman if they could be certain of no punishment.

Factors Influencing Judgments About Assault

What people believe about rape, about what is appropriate behavior for women and men, and about gender-differentiated responsibilities and attributes affects judgments about guilt or innocence of accused offenders and about whether a particular incident is sexual assault. Even when a described incident is one in which sexual relations were forced without consent, thus meeting the legal definition of sexual assault, persons asked to make judgments about the situation appear to be influenced by other factors—particularly their attitudes about rape, whether the victim and offender were acquainted, and characteristics of the persons involved. Often these other factors militate toward a judgment that the victim was somehow to blame for the assault. Let us look more closely at these factors.

Greater Callousness of Men Evidence from varied sources suggests that men in general do not consider sexual assault to be as serious a personal violation as do women, and that they are more likely to subscribe to myths about rape. Many men seem really to believe that a woman can "lie back and enjoy it"; that she has somehow "asked for it" by her manner of dress, walk, speech, or by the fact that she was out alone, hitchhiking, or in a bar; and that women entice and lure men and really want to be "taken" by strong and forceful ones. For example, in one study (Malamuth, Heim, & Feshbach, 1980), when the reactions of college men and women to a depiction of rape were compared, the men were found to be significantly more aroused when the victim was described as experiencing both orgasm and pain. In addition, the men, overall, self-reported significantly less frustration, anger, and negative feelings than the women after reading rape stories.

Judith Krulewitz (1978) has reported that when victims were described to a sample of men and women as having come to a rape crisis center for help, the women expressed more interest in talking with the victim, saw her as more upset and frightened, expected her to experience psychological problems as a consequence of the rape, were consistently more supportive, and perceived the situation as more serious than the men. According to Krulewitz, the men did not see rape as being as serious and traumatic an experience as the women did. Similarly, Hubert Feild (1978a) found in comparing 528 adult women with an equal number of men from the same community that the men believed more than the women that it is women's responsibility to prevent rape, that victims "precipitate rape" by how they look or behave, that rapists are not motivated by a need for power over women, that a raped woman becomes less attractive, that women should not resist during rape, and that punishment for rape should be harsh. Except for the opinion about punishment, each of the beliefs about rape held by the men was also found among a group of convicted rapists. The views of the men were closer to those of the rapists and to a sample of male police officers than they were to those of rape crisis counselors. Like the rapists, the male police officers believed that rape is motivated by a desire for sex and not by a need for power, that rapists are not mentally normal, and that after a rape a woman is a less desirable person.

In light of such beliefs, it is not surprising that many victims of sexual assault have found their treatment by the police to be less than sympathetic and to range from harsh and superficially objective to leering and voyeuristic. Complainants have been made to feel that they have committed some crime—the crime of being out alone at night, of having accepted a ride in someone's car, of having bathed away the signs of the rape, of having improperly secured their door, or simply of being a woman and an available target. Many police departments are trying to sensitize police officers to understand rape from the victim's perspective, to ask questions with sympathy, and to not assume that the complainant is lying or at fault; in addition, some departments are putting rape cases in the hands of policewomen.

In a recent study (Deitz, Littman, & Bentley, 1984), a sample of college women and men were found to differ significantly in their responses to 7 out of 12 questions about a rape, the men believing more

than the women that the victim somehow encouraged the rape, that the psychological impact of the rape was not too severe, and that rape is not a very serious crime. The men identified less with the victim and more with the defendant, had less positive feelings toward the victim, and were less certain of the defendant's guilt.

Rape Myths Among Women   Although women are generally more upset and disturbed than men by stories or reports of rape, some women believe the culturally supported myths about rape and ascribe blame to the victim. The following public letter, for example, was written by a woman in response to a trial in Massachusetts of several men accused of having raped a woman in a bar.

> There are women who ask to be raped, and they get what they deserve. There are also women who are raped and don't deserve it. The first kind are those who dress themselves indecently and flaunt themselves in front of men or throw themselves at men and go into barrooms by themselves. . . .
> I was one who didn't deserve it. . . . I was raped because the boyfriend I was seeing was trying to prove his masculinity to his mother. . . . I'll tell you what I intend to do if a women's libber ever approaches me. I'm going to shove her teeth down her throat . . . [because] it's you I blame for my getting raped. (Barb, 1984, p. A16)

Large numbers of women as well as men continue to perceive a victim as somehow being implicated in, or responsible for, her assault. Martha Burt (1980), for example, found among a random sample of almost 600 Minnesota adults that one half agreed with the statement, "In the majority of rapes, the victim was promiscuous or had a bad reputation." Such myths persist, and the victim is blamed for having somehow provoked (if not enjoyed) her assault. Burt found that acceptance of rape myths was not related to personality variables but, among both genders, was "strongly connected to other deeply held and pervasive attitudes such as sex role stereotyping, distrust of the opposite sex (adversial sexual beliefs), and acceptance of interpersonal violence" (p. 229). Acceptance of violence in personal relationships correlated most strongly with acceptance of myths about rape.

Other studies have found that women and men sometimes respond similarly to reported cases of sexual assault and are similarly influenced by the situational context of the incidents and specific characteristics of victims and offenders. Hubert Feild (1978b), for example, compared a large sample of adult white women with an equal number of men who served as mock jurors in a rape case and found no relationship between a juror's gender and sentencing of the defendant.

Victim/Offender Acquaintance　People seem less ready to call an attack rape when the victim was previously acquainted with the offender, even though, as we have noted, more than half of all sexual assaults are committed by nonstrangers. In one study, for example, Susan Klemmack and David Klemmack (1976) interviewed over 200 adult women in Alabama and asked each to evaluate the degree to which she believed a rape to have occurred in seven different situations that met the legal definition of rape. Where there was any prior relationship or acquaintance between the victim and her attacker, fewer than 50 percent of the respondents considered the described incident of forced nonconsensual sex to be a rape. The situation that was labeled as rape by the largest percentage of respondents described a woman assaulted by a stranger in a parking lot after 11 p.m. as she was walking to her car after work. But even this seemingly unambiguous rape story was judged not to be rape by 8 percent of the respondents. Another study (L'Armand & Pepitone, 1982) found that college students who read stories of rape trials were significantly more likely to recommend more lenient sentences, to perceive less damage to the victim, and to blame the victim more and the rapist less, if the victim and rapist had dated or been previously intimate than if they were strangers.

A suggestion as to why acquaintance in a sexual assault decreases the likelihood that it will be judged a criminal act is found in data reported by James Check and Neil Malamuth (1983). Their sample of college students (both men and women) perceived the victim of a depicted assault to react to it more favorably if she was assaulted by an acquaintance than by a stranger; and persons with highly stereotyped gender beliefs were even more likely to perceive favorable reactions on the part of acquaintance-rape victims, despite the complete absence of such cues in the stories read. Another study, of over 400 teenagers in Los Angeles, found evidence supporting the importance of victim-offender acquaintance in judgments about rape (Zellman, Goodchilds, Johnson, & Giarusso, 1981). This sample was evenly divided by gender and included one third Anglos, one third blacks, and one third Hispanics. The researchers found that nonconsensual sex was most likely to be labeled rape by both girls and boys in "situations in which the boy used physical force and the couple had just met" and least likely "when nonconsensual sex occurred between dating partners, and a minimum of force was used" (p. 6). The researchers concluded that "victims of nonstranger rape are likely to receive little sympathy from individuals or institutions" (p. 8), because they are likely to be seen as having provoked or enjoyed the violent encounter.

Evidence of Resistance　Another circumstance likely to influence judgments about sexual assault is evidence of resistance. To convict an accused rapist, many state laws require proof that the victim actively resisted; the greater the number of cuts, bruises, and broken bones, therefore, the more believable is her story. Thus, for example, a judge in Hawaii dismissed a rape charge in the case of a woman who maintained that while jogging on a rural road she was run down by a car, threatened with broken glass, and raped ("Rape Case Decision," 1978). The judge ruled that the woman did not show enough resistance.

Studies of judgments of rape victims and their assailants have found that degree of victim resistance is an important variable. Mary Kanarian (1980) has reported that a sample of men students attributed more responsibility for a sexual assault to the victim when she did not physically resist. And another group of investigators (Wyer, Bodenhausen, & Gorman, 1985) found that a victim who did not resist was judged by student raters to be less credible, less likely to have been harmed, and more responsible for the incident than one who resisted.

Respectability of the Victim　Sometimes, however, even corroboration of resistance is not sufficient to convince others that rape has occurred. In a much-publicized rape decision in Wisconsin ("Judge Says," 1977) that resulted in the judge's removal from the bench by an incensed community, the judge based his acquittal of an accused teenage boy on his belief that all men carry lust in their hearts that can be triggered by a woman in provocative clothing. The assaulted girl in this case had been wearing jeans and a sweater. In Los Angeles, a judge reversed the conviction of a man found guilty of raping a woman hitchhiker. In support of his decision, he wrote the following:

> The lone female hitchhiker in the absence of an emergency situation . . . advises all who pass by that she is willing to enter the vehicle with anyone who stops and in doing so advertises she has less concern for the consequences than the average female.

Under such circumstances it would not be unreasonable for a man in the position of defendant here to believe that the female would consent to sexual relations. ("Women Hitchhikers," 1977)

In a Massachusetts case, five young men were acquitted of raping and beating a woman who was left nude, battered, and abandoned on a winter night, but they were convicted of wrecking her car ("5 Acquitted," 1983). The defendants had previously pleaded guilty to the rape charges in a plea-bargaining agreement and had received $500 fines and suspended sentences. A new trial was ordered when additional new evidence was brought forward, but despite testimony against the defendants from an admitted participant, the men were judged not guilty. The victim was a former "beauty queen" whose character was questioned by the defense attorney, who claimed she had offered the defendants sex for money but that things had gotten "out of hand." In another nationally publicized Massachusetts trial, the Big Dan rape case, six men were accused of sexually assaulting a woman (in front of onlookers) on a pool table in a tavern. During the trial she was questioned by the defense attorneys about whether she had tried to keep her legs together, how much she had had to drink, whether she had ever had psychiatric treatment, and whether she had violated the welfare code by living with her boyfriend while collecting public assistance. These efforts to discredit the victim and to influence the jurors to perceive what had occurred as something other than rape proved unsuccessful and some of the defendants were convicted.

The respectability of the victim and her sexual history have been found to influence the extent to which she is blamed or held responsible for her sexual assault. In one study (Luginbuhl & Mullin, 1981) in which college students read a description of a rape, men recommended a significantly lighter sentence for the offender when the victim was described as a topless dancer who took drugs than when she was described as a married social worker. The character of the topless dancer was seen as a more important causal factor than chance. Similarly, in another study (Acock & Ireland, 1983), college students of both genders perceived a rape victim described as a service station attendant who had given a man a ride as more to blame for her assault, and saw the rapist as less to blame, than when the victim was described as a college student on her way home from the library. Other studies have shown a greater assignment of responsibility (or blame) to a forcibly assaulted victim if she failed to take precautions in avoiding a poorly lighted

street (Pallak & Davies, 1982); if she was intoxicated (Richardson & Campbell, 1982); if she was attractive (Jacobson & Popovich, 1983); and if her previous sexual history was part of the material presented to evaluators (L'Armand & Pepitone, 1982).

Some states now bar evidence about a rape victim's past sexual conduct from the trial proceedings. A survey of state laws (Borgida, Oksner, & Tomkins, 1978) found that 11 states (including the District of Columbia) admitted such evidence on a relatively unlimited basis, 21 states admitted such evidence on a limited basis subject to the discretion of the judge, and 19 states totally excluded such evidence. Since this survey was published, other states (such as Connecticut and Illinois) have joined the last category. The same researchers reported finding that significantly more guilty verdicts are reached by a simulated jury under conditions in which evidence relating to a victim's previous sexual experiences is not allowed than under conditions in which such evidence is presented. It is distressing to note that another study found that simply being a woman increases the chances of being held responsible for one's victimization. Judith Howard (1984) found that college students (especially those with traditional sex-role attitudes) blamed women victims more than men victims in a rape or a robbery, and when the victim was described as a jogger or a hitchhiker.

Attributes of the Offender   Some research has also been concerned with the influence of characteristics of offenders (or defendants) in judgments about sexual assault. Marsha Jacobson (1981) has reported that a physically attractive defendant is more likely than an unattractive defendant to be believed in his version of the assault; is less likely to be judged as guilty; and is more likely to be given a shorter sentence. Defendants in simulated rape trials were also more likely to be judged not guilty by groups of college students when they were defended by a woman than by a man attorney (Villemur & Hyde, 1983). Deborah Richardson and Jennifer Campbell (1982) found that a sample of college students judged an offender in a rape case to be less to blame when he was described as intoxicated than when he was described as sober. This was opposite to their judgment of the victim, who was considered less moral, less likable, and more responsible for the assault when she was drunk than when she was sober.

The race of a defendant accused of rape has also been found to be an important factor in influencing judgments. Hubert Feild (1979) found in a study of white students who served as jurors in a mock rape case that when the victim was white, black defendants were punished more severely than white defendants. The use of excessive penalties against black men for the sexual assault of white women is a matter of historical record. In 1972, before the Supreme Court abolished capital punishment (now again permissible under certain conditions), death was the prescribed punishment for rape in 14 states. Of 455 men executed for rape between 1930 (when national figures began to be published) and 1972, 405 were black, and overwhelmingly these were men who had been convicted of raping white women. While 38 percent of convicted black rapists in Georgia, for example, were sentenced to death before 1972, only one half of 1 percent of convicted white rapists were similarly sentenced (Lear, 1972).

Consequences of Sexual Assault

Considering the continued strength of myths about rape, it is not surprising to find that victims of sexual assault suffer not only from shock, physical bruises and lacerations, disruption of their lives, invasion of their safety and integrity, but also from confusion about responsibility for their victimization and embarrassment. Some victims blame themselves (as cultural beliefs have taught us to do) and may retreat into an isolation of shame and helplessness. C. Buf Meyer and Shelley Taylor (1986) obtained answers to questions from 58 women who had reported a sexual assault to a rape crisis center and found that nearly half "mentioned some form of self-blame" and, further, that self-blame of any form was reliably related to poor adjustment.

Some women do not forcefully fight back against an attacker. Women tend to believe that we are physically weaker than men (and in the case of the average woman vis-à-vis the average man, this is typically true); and most women have had very little practice in physical self-defense. Many rapists have weapons—knives or guns—and we fear for our lives should we resist. To not resist is what we were urged to do in the past by parents and police, so as to avoid serious injury or death at the hands of an enraged attacker. At the same time, evidence of resistance (and injury) is often required in order to convict an accused rapist. This dilemma has been described by Pauline Bart and Patricia O'Brien (1984) as follows:

> Women threatened with rape are in a double bind. On the one hand we are told, "Fighting back will only excite him. . . . " We are warned . . . that resistance will

result in serious injury, if not mutilation and death . . . On the other hand . . . in order to prove legally that what happened was rape, the woman has to prove that it was indeed against her will. . . . The best way to prove that the act is not mutually consensual is by physically resisting. (pp. 83f.)

Recent advice from feminists, rape crisis counselors, and psychologists who have worked with rapists is to scream, make a scene, attempt to break away, and fight back, if at all possible. Susan Brownmiller's (1975) analysis of available data convinced her that lack of resistance provides no guarantee of lesser injury. James Selkin (1975), basing his advice on what he has learned from clinical experience with rapists, has suggested that a woman's best strategy is to resist, and to do so immediately. He believes that most rapists first test and then threaten a prospective victim. This new message to women, that we should attempt escape by physically resisting or by creating a scene, may add to the negative consequences experienced by a rape victim; having been unable to fend off an attacker, she may feel the additional pain of failure to fight back effectively. Pauline Bart and Patricia O'Brien (1984) found in an interview study of women who had been raped that those who had used physical strategies were less likely to be depressed than those who had used verbal or no strategies, even though they had failed to stop the rape. Women who had effectively avoided rape differed from those who had not in having used some varied strategies against the attacker, and in having used some "combination of screaming/yelling and physical resistance" (p. 91). Fighting back was found to have not resulted in more injury than not fighting, and thus to have been an effective response.

Two women made headlines in the 1970s by fighting back and killing their assailants. In March 1974, Inez Garcia of Soledad, California, after having been beaten by two men and raped by one of them, pursued her attackers with a rifle and shot one to death. She was tried and found guilty of second-degree murder, but, after a national campaign that brought psychological and financial support, she was acquitted in a second trial in 1977. The photo on page 162 shows her during an interview in San Francisco. A brochure circulated by the Inez Garcia Defense Committee contains this statement:

> I am not ashamed of what I have done. I was afraid and I had to defend myself. I would like other women to know about my case; I think they can identify with me. And if they had the same thing happen to them, they will know how I felt. Maybe it will stop more rapes.

In San Francisco on February 10, 1977, Inez Garcia is being interviewed about her second trial.

Joan Little, a 20-year-old black woman, fought off with an ice pick her 62-year-old white jailer who was sexually molesting her in a cell in Beaufort County, North Carolina; she fled the jail, leaving the man dying of stab wounds. She was charged with first-degree murder and the state requested the death penalty, but she was acquitted in a widely observed trial. Both of these cases captured the public's attention at a time when the women's movement was openly discussing sexual assault and violence and their effects on women's lives.

Personal testimony and more formal research indicates that the lives of sexual assault survivors are not only temporarily disrupted but are often permanently altered. Ann Burgess and Lynda Holmstrom (1976) provided 24-hour-a-day immediate counseling for rape victims who came to the emergency room of a Boston hospital, later followed by telephone counseling or a home visit. They found serious disruptions in the performance of important life tasks and diagnosed 79 percent of the victims they saw as having suffered from "rape trauma," or acute disorganization. Among students, 41 percent either stopped attending classes or changed their schools; unemployed married women experienced disruptions in homemaking and parenting; and among the women whose main activity was employment, half changed or quit their jobs within six months after having been assaulted. The assaulted women made changes in their residences, phone numbers, and transportation habits.

The consequences for children who have been sexually abused, especially for those who have been repeatedly assaulted by family members, may be even more severe. Many adolescent runaways or drug addicts were sexually abused earlier in their lives. Ellen Weber (1977) has cited a study of adolescent prostitutes in the Minneapolis area that found that 75 percent had been victims of incest. Almost every one of a group of 15 incest victims being treated by Judith Herman and Lisa Hirschman (1977) described herself as a witch, bitch, or whore, branded or marked. Dorothy Bianco (1984) found that 53 percent of a sample of adolescent women in a residential drug treatment program "had been sexually or physically abused at some time during their childhood or early adolescence" (p. 167), and found a significant relationship between poor treatment outcome and prior abuse by a family member or family friend. And in a study of father-daughter relationships among a group of college women, Joseph LaBarbera (1984) found that those who reported sexually seductive behavior on the part of their fathers had more negative views of themselves and "attributed more danger to male sexuality" than the other women. A panel of psychologists who participated in a national symposium on the subject of childhood sexual abuse reported (in Fisher, 1985) that

> adults who were sexually abused as children are more likely to be depressed, to abuse drugs and alcohol, and have difficulty in sexual relationships than those who were not abused . . . [and psychotherapists should] be more aware of sex abuse as a possible cause of psychological problems in adult women. (p. 12)

David Finkelhor, one of the participants, suggested that the trauma of sexual abuse does not stem only from the sexual acts, but is a process that antedates the abuse and continues afterward. A review of research on the long-term effects of sexual abuse of children (including forced or coerced sexual activity imposed on a child and sexual activity between a child and a person 5 or more years older) led to the following conclusions by Angela Browne and David Finkelhor (1986):

Adult women victimized as children are more likely to manifest depression, self-destructive behavior, anxiety, feelings of isolation and stigma, poor self-esteem, a tendency toward revictimization, and substance abuse. (p. 72)

The greatest negative impact was found to be suffered by women who experienced childhood sexual abuse by their fathers or stepfathers.

Among the most significant and general social consequences of the widespread prevalence of sexual assault by men against women is that girls and women learn to be fearful; we perceive ourselves as vulnerable, and curtail our activities. Martha Burt and Rhoda Estep (1981) interviewed a sample of college seniors and found that the women differed significantly from the men in experiencing more fear in places usually associated with possible danger (vacant lots, bus stations), and in receiving more warnings from others. The findings suggested that this gender difference emerged in adolescence. The researchers concluded that

adult women report a sense of sexual vulnerability both in their own concerns and in the concerns for them expressed by their family and friends as warnings designed to increase their vigilance and safety. Adult males do not share this sense of the world as a sexually dangerous place, and . . . report less overall sense of danger. (p. 520)

Similar findings have been reported by Stephanie Riger and Margaret Gordon (1981) from an interview study of a sample of urban adults. Forty-four percent of the women, compared with 18 percent of the men, reported being very or somewhat afraid when out alone at night. Elderly black and Hispanic women, those with the least formal education and lowest incomes, carried "the heaviest burden of fear." The precautions taken by women result in a restriction of freedom. Seventy-five percent of the men but only 30 percent of the women reported that "they never let fear deter them" from doing what they want to do. Thus, as the investigators concluded, "high fear seems to shrink the scope of women's choices about their lives by restricting their movement through time and space" (p. 87).

Another consequence of the prevalence of rape is that it becomes part of the nightmares and fantasies of women who have learned to expect that they will be "taken" by, and forced to submit to, men. Those who have studied such fantasies, like E. Barbara Hariton (1973), have argued that they represent a woman's attempts to order or control a seduction. Rape fantasies do not, for the most part, involve frightening acts of violence but deal more typically with acts of passion under circumscribed (usually romantic or exotic) conditions, with men of one's own choice. Although the dreams of some women, while asleep or awake, do contain elements of brutal violation, these are not common. More typically, fantasies represent efforts to control experience. As Robin Morgan (1982a) has suggested, "If you feel you *have* control, you are free to abandon it, knowing as you do that it is yours to pick up again whenever you choose" (p. 131).

Solutions

Men have said very little about rape until quite recently. It is primarily women who have spoken out, protested, examined the problem, and suggested solutions. Women's experiences have been recounted in interviews, essays, autobiography, fiction, and poetry. Through articulate voices, like that of Marge Piercy (1976b), women are saying:

There is no difference between being raped
and being pushed down a flight of cement steps
except that the wounds also bleed inside.

There is no difference between being raped
and being run over by a truck
except that afterward men ask if you enjoyed it.

There is no difference between being raped
and being bitten on the ankle by a rattlesnake
except that people ask if your skirt was short
and why were you out alone anyhow.

There is no difference between being raped
and going head first through a windshield
except that afterward you are afraid
not of cars
but of half the human race. (p. 88)

Solutions to the problem of sexual violence against women are possible. There have already been a number of significant legal reforms. Several states now define rape in terms of the rapist's conduct (force) rather than by the victim's behavior (resistance) or state of mind (lack of consent). It has been suggested, but not yet adopted into law, that in sexual assault cases consent should have to be proved by the defense rather than disproved by the prosecution (MacKinnon, 1983). Some states have defined rape as gender-neutral, and others have replaced the term with the broader one of sexual assault. The excessive penalties for rape in some states must be reduced, because they stand in the way of obtaining convictions and because they have been used selectively against black men. Another misguided solution is the ordering by some judges of chemical castration for convicted rapists. The administration of Depo-Provera suppresses testosterone production, but its use as a punishment for convicted rapists reinforces the myth that men commit acts of sexual assault because of uncontrollable sexual urges. We know that this is not the case.

Some have proposed that psychological treatment for convicted rapists be given a greater priority. The first treatment program for imprisoned sex offenders was begun in California in 1948. Since then approximately 17 other states have provided some kind of intensive therapy opportunity in prison programs, and successful outcomes of treatment have been claimed by the providers. For example, Robert Freeman-Longo and Ronald Wall (1986), who run such a program in Oregon, have reported that

> most untreated sex offenders released from prison go on to commit more offenses—indeed as many as 80 percent do. By contrast, the recidivism rate for sex offenders who have completed state-run treatment programs is estimated by the programs at between 10 and 25 percent. Of those who have completed all three phases of our treatment program, fewer than 10 percent have reoffended sexually. (p. 64)

The Oregon program is multifocused and attempts to change attitudes and beliefs about rape, to enhance social skills, and to improve general psychological and sexual functioning. It reaches only a small number of convicted rapists, however. It is a voluntary program, from which more than 50 percent drop out. And, as we know, convicted rapists represent only a very small proportion of men who sexually assault women or other men.

Sexual assault is a cultural problem. Educating women and men about the facts of rape and how it can be prevented has become the focus of many programs instituted by local communities, crisis intervention centers, universities, and so on. One rape-prevention program in an urban area ("Community Action Strategies," 1980) found that workshop participants gained knowledge and decreased their adherence to myths about sexual assault. In addition, "participants reported increased practice of confrontation and self-defense skills, decreased fear, and increased confidence in their ability to defend themselves if attacked" (p. S241).

Rape crisis centers and telephone hot lines have been organized by concerned women around the country to help victims deal with the psychological

and physical trauma of sexual assault, to work cooperatively and innovatively with law enforcement and medical agencies, and to encourage increased rates of reporting, arrests, and convictions. Some communities also offer special programs for incest victims and their families. The most typical intervention involves immediate assistance to the victim (survivor) in dealing with the crisis, an opportunity to talk, and help in regaining control over daily tasks and more long-term pursuits. Rape victims are reassured that they were not at fault, are assisted in putting the incident into a realistic perspective, and are offered emotional as well as practical support. Elizabeth King and Carol Webb (1981) found, from a survey of rape crisis centers around the country, that 62 percent of clients receive at least one follow-up contact and that a third of the centers provide two to five contacts. The researchers noted that while these centers are recognized and lauded for contributions to their communities, their funding "remains tenuous and professional staffing is minimal" (p. 102).

Lynda Holmstrom and Ann Burgess (1978), who followed almost 150 rape victims from the time they arrived at a city hospital emergency room to the final outcome of legal proceedings, concluded that what was necessary for change was first and foremost

> to *delegitimize* rape. . . . This means changing the social definition of rape . . . seeing rape as an act of aggression and violence, motivated primarily by power and anger, rather than by sexuality. And it means seeing that rape . . . can occur in many circumstances . . . when the victim initially accompanies the offender willingly, between people who are not strangers, when the victim is not a virgin, when there are no bruises because the victim did not dare to fight, and when both offender and victim are of the same race. (p. 262)

Thus, we must continue improving the quality and extent of community services for assault victims, and at the same time continue discussing the cultural significance of rape. Women must achieve physical competence *and* maintain feminist consciousness. And most important of all, we must continue to question and evaluate what we teach our children about the differential roles of women and men. Martha Burt (1980) concluded from her study of belief in rape myths that the most fruitful long-range strategy for change was to counter gender stereotypes of children at very young ages. She argued that since "rape is the logical and psychological extension of a dominant-submissive, competitive, sex-role stereotyped culture . . . the task of preventing rape is tantamount to revamping a significant proportion of our societal values" (p. 229).

PHYSICAL ASSAULT

The physical and psychological damage done to women through acts of sexual assault represents the extreme end of a continuum of hostile responses to women by men that are observable in a variety of contexts. For example, consider how some men in movie audiences react with signs of pleasure to events on the screen that demean women; when a woman gets slapped, roughed-up, or insulted in a film, some male voices in the audience invariably cheer. And, until very recently, it has been acceptable in our culture for a man to hit a woman in a family argument. In an experiment in which college students observed staged assaults (Shotland & Straw, 1976), in some cases the student observers were told that the assaulter and victim were strangers, while in other cases they were told that the two persons were a married couple. Despite the fact that the fight was identical under both conditions, students intervened more frequently when they believed the fight to involve strangers. Under the married couple condition, the woman was less often perceived as in danger or as wanting help. When observers were given little information about the conflict, they were more likely to see the quarrel as between "dates, lovers, or married couples," and were less likely to intervene even though they were observing a man physically attacking a woman. When a husband hits his wife, it is commonly assumed that it is for a "reason," and that the woman must have been "asking for it."

That such an assumption is often made is a conclusion supported from a number of sources, including the widespread prevalence of wife beating in this country. Each year, an estimated 2 million women in the United States, or 4 to 5 percent of all wives, are injured by their husbands (Straus, 1978a). Among persons attending two conferences on battering (students, professionals, and interested members of the community), 36 percent of the women (compared to none of the men) reported having been physically abused at least once as an adult by a member of the opposite sex; for 25 percent of the women, physical abuse was an occasional or frequent experience (Stringer-Moore, Pepitone-Arreola-Rockwell, & Rozèe-Koker, 1984). A national study was reported in the press to have found that "attacks by husbands on wives result in more injuries requiring medical treatment than rapes, muggings and auto accidents combined" ("Carnage of Violence," 1984, p. A-2). Richard Gelles (1974) found that one fourth of the women who were beaten by their husbands were pregnant; and other investigators have reported that 25 percent of suicide attempts by women and 20 percent of visits by women to emergency medical services are the result of battering (in Cultural Information Service, 1984).

Abusers and Victims

Erin Pizzey's (1974) now-classic book, *Scream Quietly or the Neighbours Will Hear*, startled some of us into public recognition of what we had really known for a long time, that large numbers of women were being physically and emotionally brutalized by their husbands (or cohabiting boyfriends) and that these women had virtually no place to go for advice, support, or assistance. Since then a great deal of attention has been paid to the problem, much research has been done, and many cities and towns have established facilities to assist battered women. The information accumulated by crisis intervention workers, social service and law enforcement agencies, and regional and national surveys (for example, Martin, 1976; Straus, Gelles, and Steinmetz, 1981; Walker, 1979) contradicts prevalent myths about wife abuse.

We now know that family violence cuts across socioeconomic classes as well as racial and ethnic categories. Neither the men who batter nor the women they abuse fit into clear categories or support our stereotypes. In writing about the problem of battered women in Afro-American communities, Beth Richie (1985) has urged that the violence against women committed by black men not be excused as the result of racism and black men's frustrations. The struggle of black people for equal opportunities "must not be done at the physical and psychological expense of black women" (p. 43), which Richie maintains is too often the case. Men of all skin colors, ethnic groups, and varied socioeconomic status have physically abused their wives or lovers.

> Women have been battered by doctors, lawyers, dock workers, judges, school teachers, ministers, cab drivers, and every other variety of worker. . . . [And] a battered woman may be elderly, teen-aged, or middle-aged. . . . She may work inside or outside the home as a housewife, teacher, prostitute, student or laborer. (Massachusetts Coalition, 1981, p. 9)

A story carried by the national press dramatically illustrates the fact that wife abuse occurs at all social levels. The head of the Securities and Exchange Commission appointed by President Reagan resigned his position after his wife alleged in suing for divorce that he had repeatedly abused her during their 18-year marriage ("SEC Enforcer," 1985). Like other abused wives, this woman had tolerated the abuse because she thought she was "the only one" subjected to it, and she had blamed herself for not pleasing her husband.

In a review of Maria Roy's book *Battered Women*, I drew the following conclusions from information presented by a variety of researchers and practitioners (Lott, 1978a):

> Wife battering identifies repeated acts of violence by men distinguishable from other men by no special class or ethnic background. For such men, violence is an acceptable and effective method of wielding power over their wives because it has been amply reinforced by historical precedent; prior family experiences; cultural sanction; personal identification with stereotyped "masculinity"; toleration by neighbors, police and judges; and has evoked few, if any, aversive consequences from friends, relatives, or society (p. 668).
>
> Just as the potential victim of rape is any woman, the potential victim of wife-beating is any wife. Those who remain in marriage with a brutal spouse do so for some combination of a number of very powerful reasons: they have children to care for and no resources for outside child care; they have fulfilled the prophecies of a sexist society and have learned behaviors appropriate to low-status persons; they are discouraged by unsympathetic police officers who rarely arrest abusive husbands, and by a legal and social service system which does all that it can to preserve the family at all costs; they may fear reprisals from their husbands; and most have literally "no place to go," no psychological or physical refuge. (p. 669)

Richard Gelles and Murray Straus have proposed that family violence is related to the level of conflict and stress experienced within the family. This hypothesis was tested by Straus (1978b) in a national interview study of over 2000 adults who were living with a member of the opposite sex as a couple. He found that "the higher the stress score the higher the rate of assault between husband and wife" (p. 10), and that family violence was also related to the husband's dominance.

> Men who assault their wives believe that physical punishment of children and slapping a spouse are appropriate behavior. . . . Education does not affect the link between stress and violence. . . . Men who believe

that husbands should be the dominant person in a marriage, and especially husbands who have actually achieved such a power position, had assault rates from one and a half to three times higher than the men without such values who were also under stress. (p. 16)

Similar findings have been reported by Irene Frieze (1979), who interviewed a sample of battered women and compared them to a sample of nonbattered women. She concluded that violent marriages are characterized by "high husband dominance," and the use by husbands of coercive power.

The sequence of events that involve a husband's abuse of power and use of violence has been described by Lenore Walker (1978), who has proposed a "cycle theory of battering incidents." In phase one, tension builds and "the woman usually attempts to calm the batterer. . . . She may become nurturing, compliant and anticipate his every whim, or she may stay out of his way" (pp. 146f.). During phase two, the tension is released destructively, and the batterer's rage is out of control. It may be triggered by a specific incident (almost any excuse will do) or occur without an obvious reason. According to Walker, "It is not uncommon for the batterer to wake the woman out of a deep sleep to begin his assault" (p. 151). In the third phase, the batterer knows he has gone too far; is contrite, kind, and charming; begs forgiveness; promises that he will never again hurt the woman he loves, and that he will change. In this phase, "the woman gets a glimpse of her original dream of how wonderful love is . . . [which provides] reinforcement for staying in the relationship" (p. 152); so she will "try again."

Phase three may not be reached if the battering ends in serious injury or murder. According to Pauline Gee (1983), one fourth of all murders in the United States occur within a family, and half of these are husband-wife killings. The Kansas City Police Department found that in 85 percent of domestic homicide cases, the police had been summoned at least once to stop a beating before the murder occurred (Massachusetts Coalition, 1981). And according to Ann Jones (1980), "One of every four murder victims is a woman. Nine out of ten murdered women are murdered by men. Four out of five are murdered at home. Almost three out of four are murdered by husbands or lovers" (pp. 319f.).

The long-range consequences of continued physical abuse by one's husband or lover may be murder, scars, broken bones and other bodily damage, or psychological and emotional injury—feelings of valuelessness, extreme helplessness, and disillusionment. In describing her feelings as a battered wife, Andrea Dworkin (1978) has reflected the experiences of others. To be physically abused by one's husband is particularly shattering and life-diminishing because his violence contradicts everything that we have "been taught about life, marriage, love and the sanctity of the family" (p. 34); "The fear does not let go. The fear is the eternal legacy" (p. 35).

Women Who Fight Back

A great deal of press attention was given to a report by Suzanne Steinmetz (1977–78) that more women batter husbands than vice versa, data she obtained from the same national survey of over 2000 American families analyzed by Murray Straus (1978b). Critics responded that the statistics were taken out of context of the total investigation and were being misinterpreted. Richard Gelles (1979), for example, who along with Steinmetz and Straus had been one of the project's major investigators, pointed out that the violent acts reported by the wives tended to be "protective reactions," acts of self-defense against physical attack or its threat. In addition, Gelles noted:

> Examining the social context and social consequences of marital violence, one finds that irrespective of the kind of hitting that goes on, women are much more likely to get the worst of it. In many cases of marital violence women are physically helpless . . . and almost completely unable to adequately defend themselves. (p. 72)

Battered wives are typically trapped in violent marriages as a result of their social, legal, and economic disadvantage and, according to Gelles, defensive, protective hitting of their husbands may be their only option.

The data gathered in this national survey (Straus, Gelles, & Steinmetz, 1981) do not tell us what proportion of the violent acts committed by wives was in response to those initiated by their husbands, but it is likely to have been high. It is also important to know that the data came from self-reports; that is, each respondent was asked about acts of violence that he or she had committed. Murray Straus (1978b) has cited evidence from another study that husbands tend to *underreport* their own acts of violence. He suggested that this is "probably because the use of physical force is so much a part of the male way of life that it is not salient for men" (p. 22). Straus has also noted that husbands have higher rates than wives in the most injurious forms of violence (beating up and

using weapons), and that violent acts are repeated more by husbands than by wives.

Others have pointed out that although husbands and wives kill each other with about equal frequency, wives are seven times more likely to murder their husbands in self-defense (Jones, 1980). The nationally televised dramatization in October 1984 of Faith McNulty's (1981) book *The Burning Bed* presented the true story of such a murder to millions of viewers. Francine Hughes, an Iowa wife and mother, after years of abuse and unsuccessful efforts to dissolve her marriage, poured gasoline around the bed on which her husband was sleeping and set fire to the house, killing her husband. She was acquitted by a jury that found her not guilty by reason of temporary insanity. Expert testimony about the behavior of women who have been repeatedly abused by their spouses, and the reality of their fear of imminent danger, was not admissible as evidence to help establish her claim of self-defense at the time of Hughes' trial in 1977. Since then, however, a number of states have permitted such testimony. Nevertheless, while some women have been acquitted on the grounds of self-defense for the murder of husbands who have physically abused them for many years (for example, Dorothy Rapp of New Jersey in 1981, and Sherrie Allery of Washington in 1984), many more women have been convicted and jailed. Ann Jones (1980) has pointed out that women acquitted of murdering their husbands have made headlines "precisely because they were the exception and not the rule" (p. 292).

Community Interventions

Physically abused women who try to avoid beatings by seeking assistance from relatives, friends, the police, social service agencies, and the courts typically meet barriers in their attempts to improve their situations. Cases such as that of Francine Hughes (McNulty, 1981) provide striking documentation of the many efforts a woman may make to escape from an abusive husband. A study of 45 women who succeeded in getting out of violent relationships (and staying out for at least one year) provides information on the factors that contributed to their success (Wagner, n.d.). The women reported that they managed to get out primarily on their own or with the help of a friend or relative rather than through the assistance of a traditional community service. Among the institutional services used, the police was mentioned by 55 percent of the women, a private attorney by 53 percent, the clergy by 18 percent, and counseling by 12 percent. The most significant factor that enabled a woman to leave her husband was finding employment.

It was not until 1974 that shelters for battered women were opened in the United States, following their inauguration in England through the efforts of Erin Pizzey (1974) and her colleagues. Such shelters were a response to the impossible situation that faces most battered wives: police reluctance to intervene in "family squabbles"; the focus of social workers on "reconciliations" to save the family; lack of financial resources or a place to go; and fear of further harassment from their husbands. By 1976, a sufficient number of shelters had been established to warrant publication of the first national directory. Most shelters, staffed by volunteers, provide 24-hour telephone hot lines; emergency temporary shelter for women and their children; support groups; information about, and referral to, legal services, welfare, housing, and counseling; and educational programs for the community through speakers, slides, and so on. In 1978, one directory (reported by Dworkin, 1978) listed 2000 shelters across the country.

As a result of public concern and publicity about wife abuse, new police policies and new state laws that have been found successful in reducing the incidence of family violence have been implemented. For example, an analysis of 300 cases in Minneapolis revealed that arrest of the husband was significantly more effective in preventing future wife battering than either attempting to counsel both parties or sending the assailant away from home for a few hours ("New Police Policy," 1984). Previously, arrests could only be made if an assault was witnessed by a police officer or if the wife made a citizen's arrest, but the new policy in Minneapolis permits an arrest if probable cause exists to believe an assault has taken place within four hours before the police arrive on the scene. The police department of Oakland, California, changed their arrest policy in response to a class action suit filed against it by a group of battered women who claimed that their constitutional right to equal protection (guaranteed by the Fourteenth Amendment) had been violated by the police department's reluctance to arrest assaulting husbands.

> The defendants' nonintervention and arrest-avoidance policy was argued to be an invidious discrimination against the plaintiffs on the basis of sex, in that it encourages violence against women and is based on "biased and archaic" sexist assumptions that what a man does in his home is not the state's business and that

a man has a legal right to punish and restrain his wife physically. (Gee, 1983, p. 558)

This case was settled out of court in November 1979 with a promise from the police to treat domestic violence like any other criminal behavior and a promise from the city to provide support services for the victims of such violence.

This case and a similar one against the New York City Police Department settled in 1978 (Jones, 1980) set a precedent and have been models for change elsewhere. In Rhode Island, for example, a new law lets an abused spouse get a temporary restraining order against the alleged abuser without the aid of a lawyer. This protective order removes the abuser from the family for up to 30 days until a hearing is held before a judge. And a federal jury in Connecticut ruled that police in the town of Torrington had not adequately protected an abused wife from her husband, thus denying her equal protection under the law. The woman, Tracey Thurman, scarred and paralyzed, was awarded $1.9 million after an appeal by the Torrington Police Department. Despite numerous prior complaints, the husband had not been taken into custody until after he had stabbed her 13 times. When the police arrived 25 minutes after Tracey Thurman's call for help, she was lying wounded in her front yard and her husband was standing over her with a knife. As a direct result of this case, the state of Connecticut passed a family violence law in 1986 "that ranks among the strongest in the nation. Under the law, Connecticut becomes the seventh state to require an arrest in cases of probable domestic assault, regardless of whether the victim is willing to sign a complaint" (Johnson, 1986, p. E9). Connecticut's law requires court hearings the day following an assault, establishes court-appointed advocates for victims, and provides special training on domestic violence for law enforcement personnel. Tracey Thurman's husband has been convicted of assault and sentenced to 20 years in prison.

PORNOGRAPHY

Hostility toward women is manifested in a great many ways: in humorous put-downs, insults, harassment, and by sexual and physical violence. Some men experience pleasure when women are humiliated, attacked, or punished, and images of such treatment of women are for sale and easily obtainable in the form of photographs, stories, cartoons, films, videos, or live peep shows.

The formal, intentional pornography business is more profitable than the popular record industry; the California Department of Justice has estimated that pornography earns $4 billion a year (Lederer, 1980). According to David Friendly (1985), "Every week Americans buy an estimated 2 million tickets to X-rated films resulting in an annual box-office take of about $500 million even before they reach the burgeoning home-video market" (p. 62). Pornographic video cassettes have been said to account for 20 percent of sales by New York's Radio Shack chain ("The War," 1985). A *Newsweek* poll found that nearly 40 percent of VCR owners bought or rented an X-rated cassette during 1982; and pornography producer Chuck Vincent has said that video sales make up 70 percent of his profit.

But incidental and free pornography also appears as advertisements on billboards, in fashion magazines, and on record covers. Media images of women as dehumanized objects, with focus on our body parts, or as chained, bound, treated with contempt, or abused, are familiar to all of us, and are found in supermarkets, drugstores, films, and on the television screen. The number of pornographic magazines available at newsstands has grown from none in 1953 to 40 in 1977 (Longino, 1980), and the easy availability of VCRs has vastly increased the market for pornography. "The media have subjected women to dramatized rapings, stabbings, burnings, beatings, gaggings, bindings, dismemberments, mutilations, and deaths in the name of male sexual pleasure or sheer entertainment" (Lederer, 1980, p. 16).

Feminists who are critical of pornography do not object to its explicit sexual content but to its degrading and demeaning portrayal of women as objects to be used by men for their satisfaction. As discussed in the chapter on sexuality, the dominant view among feminists is that pornography is clearly distinguishable from erotica. While the latter portrays mutually satisfying and consensual sex, or the beauty of the human body, what appears in magazines like *Playboy* or *Hustler* is not erotica but pornography because women are presented as men's toys, things, pets, servicers, or meat.

Effects of Pornography

Research has shown that exposure to pornography has demonstrable effects on attitudes, beliefs, and aggressive behavior toward women. Edward Donnerstein (1983) has summarized the research on arousal, attitudes, and beliefs, and concluded that a positive relationship exists between men's exposure to pornography and sexual arousal, self-generated rape fantasies, lessened sensitivity to rape, increased acceptance of rape myths and interpersonal violence, and increased self-reported likelihood of sexually assaulting a woman. Illustrative of this research is an experiment in which college students were first exposed to slides (varying in content for different groups of viewers) and then asked to read the testimony of a rape victim and make judgments about the case (Wyer, Bodenhausen, & Gorman, 1985). For men participants, prior exposure to visual materials that portrayed women as sex objects significantly decreased their belief that the rape victim was telling the truth (that is, decreased her credibility) and increased their belief that she was responsible for the sexual assault.

Such findings demonstrate that beliefs about women are influenced by media images. Other data indicate that such images directly mediate aggressive acts against women. In a series of experiments, Edward Donnerstein and his colleagues showed that men in a laboratory situation in which they were given a second chance to apply electric shocks to others, gave shocks of higher intensity to women than to men if they had first been exposed to a sexually explicit film; that men who had first seen an aggressive-erotic film gave higher intensity shocks to women than to men even if they were not angry at the women they shocked; and that, when angered, men exposed to either an aggressive-erotic or an aggressive film in which a woman was physically abused, behaved more aggressively toward women targets than men not exposed to such materials. Donnerstein (1980) suggested that a woman's "association with observed violence was an important contributor to the aggressive responses toward her" (p. 286). In another study, Neil Malamuth (1983) found that after men had been angered, those who were more accepting of rape myths and who had previously been sexually aroused by a rape depiction were more likely to deliver aversive noise to a woman as punishment for incorrect responses on a laboratory task.

Thus, laboratory research has demonstrated not only that men exposed to pornographic materials are likely to experience rape fantasies, to report greater acceptance of rape myths, question the credibility of rape victims, and to be more likely to say they might sexually assault a woman (if no possibility of punishment exists), but also that such men behave more aggressively toward women, whether or not they are angry at them. Finding such a relationship between what people see and hear and what they feel, believe, and do is not surprising. To expect that pornography would not affect attitudes, beliefs, and behavior would counter much of what we know about human learning. Much in our culture teaches ordinary men that women's abuse can be a source of amusement and pleasure, or can be justified by male privilege and dominance. Until we make serious changes in these messages, too many women will continue to experience what Marge Piercy has described in "The Ordinary Gauntlet" (1984d, p. 32):

> . . . making my necessary
> way through streets I am impaled
> on shish-kabob stares,
> slobbering invitations,
> smutfires of violence.
> The man who blocks my path,
> the man who asks my price,
> the man who grabs with fat
> hands like sweating crabs. . . .
> they prance in ugly numbers.

Making Changes

How to make the necessary changes is an issue on which feminists and others are divided. Some have supported efforts to censor pornography, but only a very small minority of feminists would take this route, most agreeing with Erica Jong (in Blakely, 1985) that "censorship only springs back against the givers of culture" (p. 38). Another route, strongly supported by some, is legislation that defines pornography as sex discrimination and gives victims the right to sue for damages under civil law if they can support the claim that they were injured by it. Such an ordinance, drafted by Catharine MacKinnon and Andrea Dworkin, was twice passed by the Minneapolis city council, and twice vetoed by the mayor. In Indianapolis a similar ordinance, limited to violent pornography, was approved by the city council and signed by the mayor, but challenged by "a coalition of booksellers, distributors, and publishers" (Blakely, 1985, p. 44). A federal district judge upheld the suit;

an appeal was filed and lost by the City of Indianapolis; and in 1986, the Supreme Court affirmed the appeals court ruling "that the city law violated the constitutional guarantee of freedom of speech" ("High Court," 1986, p. A-4) under the First Amendment. The central proposition explicit in the ordinance struck down by the court is that "pornography fosters the subordination and exploitation of women and leads to rape and other violent acts against women" ("High Court," 1986, p. A-4). While the appeals court judges agreed that pornography influences how people behave and perceive women and social relationships, they argued that freedom of speech could not be regulated solely because speech contributes to people's beliefs.

Other attempts will probably be made to give victims the legal right to sue those who produce and distribute pornography, although no agreement exists on whether this is the most effective way to solve the problem. In 1986, a federal panel (The Attorney General's Commission on Pornography) concluded that "There is a connection between most pornography and violence" (Shenon, 1986), and made a large number of recommendations for community action and legislation. There is considerable disagreement, however, among social scientists and others about how direct a causal link there is between exposure to pornography and acts of sexual violence. Some critics of the Commission's report fear that its intent is to interfere with the distribution of all sexually explicit material (including erotica), to dictate traditional standards of morality, and to restrict and legislate sexual behavior. Whether the consequences of the Commission's report will be to raise the consciousness of the country about the negative impact of pornography, as some believe, or to enforce a narrow morality, as others fear, remains to be seen. In the meantime, as Mary Kay Blakely (1985) has argued, the challenge "to create a safer reality for women" in verbal and pictorial images has begun. This challenge can include educational campaigns, organized demonstrations, personal protests, continued discussion of the issues, as well as new proposals for legislation that will protect women without interfering with legitimate civil liberties.

Birth Control, Pregnancy, and Childbirth: New Choices

I have lain down.

I have lain down and sweated and shaken
and passed blood and feces and water and
slowly alone in the center of a circle I have
passed the new person out
and they have lifted the new person free of
                          that
language of blood like praise all over the
                          body.

I have done what you wanted to do, Walt
                         Whitman,

Allen Ginsberg, I have done this thing,
I and the other women this exceptional
act with the exceptional heroic body,
this giving birth, this glistening verb,
and I am putting my proud American boast
right here with the others.

                Sharon Olds   *(1980, p. 44f.)*

No woman can call herself free who does not own and
control her own body. No woman can call herself free
until she can choose conscientiously whether she will or
will not be a mother.

                Margaret Sanger   *(1920, p. 94)*

C   H   A   P   T   E   R   10

All three of the biological imperatives that distinguish females from males (as discussed in Chapter 2) are related to childbearing. *Menstruation* is a precondition for reproduction; *lactation* provides for maintaining the life of a newborn child; and *gestation* refers to the prenatal sheltering and nourishing of a developing new human organism. The female's ability to become pregnant and bear a child is what identifies her as biologically distinct from the male and provides the primary definition of our sex.

Although this has always been true, women have never before had so many choices to make about our childbearing capabilities. A woman today can truly "choose conscientiously whether she will or will not be a mother," with contraception, abortion, and role models for a child-free life available. Women who choose motherhood can choose the timing and the conditions for conception, pregnancy, and childbirth. In all of these areas, women's needs are being reflected in culturally approved options.

TO HAVE OR NOT TO HAVE; NOW OR LATER

Like marriage, pregnancy is still very much the norm for women, regardless of any other decisions pertaining to education, work, career, or life-style. Over 90 percent of married women over 25 in the United States end up having at least one child. Still, the number of childless women is increasing, and there is a growing trend toward having fewer children, later in life. Women seem to be making different choices about children than our mothers and grandmothers did; indeed, we are far more able than were our mothers and grandmothers to regulate the number and timing of children that we have and to make the more fundamental decision as to whether or not we want to experience pregnancy at all.

Smaller Families and Later Parenthood

The number of children the average American woman will have in her lifetime has been declining steadily since 1800, when the rate was seven children per woman. Among white women, the average dropped sharply from 3.6 children in 1957 to 1.7 in 1975, "where it has hovered ever since" ("Declining Birthrates," 1985, p. 3). The average number of children among black women has also dropped, but not as sharply, and stands now at 2. This decrease in birthrate is strongly associated with the reduction of unplanned pregnancies. In 1982, according to data gathered by the National Center for Health Statistics, the percentage of wanted births was 90 percent, compared with 86 percent in 1973, while unwanted births declined correspondingly from 14 to 10 percent ("Unwanted Births Decline," 1985). Unwanted births have been reduced among both white and black women but remain higher among the latter.

In addition to average family size, another measure of fertility is the number of births per 1000 women of childbearing age (between 15 and 44 years old). Among American women this rate was 68.4 in 1980 and 66 in 1984 ("Nation's Birthrate," 1985). Although there have been yearly fluctuations, the birthrate remains lower in the 1980s than it was in the 1970s, 1960s, and 1950s. In fact, according to Martin O'Connell of the Census Bureau, discussing the statistics for 1984, "the fertility rate now is about half what it was in the late 1950s and early 60s" (in "Fertility Rate's," 1985, p. E7). In 1980, Hispanic women had the highest fertility rate (95.4), white women the lowest (62.4), with Afro-American women in between (90.7) (Amaro, 1986). While the national birthrate has been declining generally, births to single women have been increasing, particularly among teenaged women and women between 35 and 39 years of age. In 1983, according to the National Center for Health Statistics, one out of every five births in the United States was to an unmarried mother (in "U.S. Study," 1985).

Fertility rates for single and married women in their 30s have been rising sharply. Between 1975 and 1978 there was a 37 percent rate of increase in the number of first-time mothers among women aged 30 to 34, and a 22 percent increase among those aged 35 to 39. Between 1970 and 1979 the number of women between 30 and 34 who gave birth to their first child doubled (Collins, 1980). This trend has continued into the 1980s, but at a slower rate. For every 1000 women between the ages of 30 and 34 in 1984, there were 72.2 births, compared to 60 in 1980 and 56.4 in 1976 ("Fertility Rate's," 1985). The contemporary trend for women to have a first child at later ages is not an entirely new phenomenon. In fact, it appears to repeat the state of affairs of the late 1920s and the 1930s. Ravenna Helson (1986) found, for example, in studying the alumni of an upper-middle-class college for women, that those who had graduated between 1921 and 1925 had married at an average age of over 28 and had their first child at around 30; those who had graduated between 1931 and 1935 had married at 27 and had their first child at age 30. From that point, a downward trend began for both age at marriage and age at first childbirth, with this trend beginning an upward reversal again with graduating classes in the 1960s.

How can we account for this new trend toward later parenthood? Kathy Weingarten and Pamela Daniels (1981) studied a sample of first-time parents from diverse backgrounds and found that the older women tended to be better educated, more affluent, more likely to hold professional jobs, and more "settled" in their lives. They had put off having children until they had the "right man" in their lives, had achieved a secure relationship, or had experienced some degree of success in their careers.

Another correlate of the increased birthrate among women over 30 may be the insistent message of the mass media that they should "hurry up" and have their babies. Some doctors and the press have been quick to suggest to women over 30 that they consider motherhood before their "biological clocks" click to midnight. For example, newspapers all over the country publicized the findings of a group of French researchers (Federation CECOS, Schwartz, & Mayaux, 1982) that among a sample of over 2000 women, the successful pregnancy rate dropped from 73.5 percent for women under 30 to 61 percent for women between 31 and 35, and to 54 percent for women over 35. What was also true, however, but infrequently included in the news reports, was that the women in the study were married to sterile men and had been artificially inseminated.

Other research, given far less publicity, has indicated that it takes older couples only slightly longer than younger ones to conceive their first child. A letter to the *New York Times* (Brickman & Beckwith, 1982) cited a study by Alan Guttmacher, for example, that found that it took couples in the 15-to-24 age group 2 months to succeed in a planned first pregnancy as compared to 3.8 months for couples in the 35-to-44 age group, a modest difference of 1.8 months. A group of researchers (Buehler et al., 1986) has reported a 50 percent drop in pregnancy-related deaths among women over 35 years of age, from a rate of 47.5 such deaths per 100,000 live births in the late 1970s to 24.2 maternal deaths per 100,000 live births in 1982. The decline, the researchers suggested, could be attributed to the higher socioeconomic status of older women having babies as well as to advances in medical care. The risk of maternal death for black women in the over-35 group was reported to be almost four times as high as that for white women. In an analysis and review of over 100 studies dealing with the pregnancies of older mothers, Phyllis Mansfield (in Woodall, 1983) concluded that maternal age by itself is irrelevant to the prediction of such negative outcomes as miscarriage, intense labor, problem pregnancies, birth defects, and so on.

The only greater risk statistically linked to maternal age is that of having a child with Down's syndrome. This condition has recently been linked to the age of the father in addition to that of the mother. Early research on Down's syndrome children obtained data only on the ages of the mothers at pregnancy, ignoring the possible role played by the sperm-contributing fathers. New studies indicate that paternal age may be as important a predictor of Down's syndrome as maternal age (Horn, 1979), and that the two are highly correlated since older women are usually impregnated by older men. Taking only maternal age into account, the risk of having a child with Down's syndrome is 1 in 40 for women over 40, compared with 1 in 300 for women between 35 and 39, and 1 in 1500 for women under 30 (Francke,

1982). The etiology of this syndrome in the fetus is not known but is thought to be due to chromosomal defects in the ovum or the sperm or to abnormal conditions present during cell division, resulting in the development of three (rather than two) chromosomes in the pair identified as number 21.

Birth Control Methods

All societies have tried to regulate their birthrates in one way or another; and women have sought to understand our role in procreation, to control our own bodies, and to limit the size of our families. Birth control has always been practiced, but with limited knowledge and with varying degrees of safety and success. While there is as yet no one method of birth control, outside of abstinence, that is both infallible and completely nonhazardous to women's health, a number of relatively safe and effective alternative methods are now available. According to a national survey (reported in "Sterilization Leads," 1984), 55 percent of all women in the United States between the ages of 15 and 44 used some form of contraception in 1982. Only about 3 million women, or 6 percent of those of childbearing age, have never used any form of birth control, as estimated by the Alan Guttmacher Institute (Kash, 1984a).

The natural, artificial, and social means of birth control used by different cultures have included abstinence; taboos on intercourse with lactating women; vaginal douches; the use by men of penis sheaths (condoms) and by women of cervical plugs or caps (pessaries); abortion; and infanticide (Newman, 1972). Before the nineteenth century, the only truly effective method of pregnancy prevention was abstinence, although various other techniques were tried, including the rhythm method, sponges, potions, and powders. The earliest contraceptive used by women was the pessary—some material placed over the cervix to prevent the sperm from reaching the uterus. According to Newman, pessaries were made of many substances "including leaves, gum arabic, grasses, camel dung [or crocodile or elephant dung], cork, honey, cotton and hemp" (p. 8). Vaginal washes (douches) of vinegar, lemon juice, gum arabic, boric acid, or other substances have also long been used, their contraceptive effectiveness dependent upon their degree of acidity to counteract the alkaline environment necessary for the survival of sperm. The diaphragm was developed in the 1880s; and, after the vulcanization of rubber was perfected, relatively safe and cheap condoms replaced the types made from such materials as fish skins, bladders, intestines, and the skins of goats and sheep. The modern condom is used to protect against venereal disease and AIDS, as well as to prevent pregnancy.

Surprisingly, voluntary sterilization is now the most widely used method of birth control in the United States. A survey of almost 7000 women ranging in age from 18 to 44 (reported by Kash, 1984a) found that almost one third had either been sterilized themselves (by means of a tubal ligation) or had husbands/partners who had had vasectomies; sterilized women made up the larger group. Sterilization is most popular with women over 35 and with married couples. A survey of almost 8000 women by the National Center for Health Statistics (in Shipp, 1985) found that 26 percent of married women and 15 percent of married men had been sterilized in 1982, compared with 7 percent of women and 5 percent of men in 1965. The greatest increase in use of sterilization was found to be among middle-class couples with at least one child in which the wife was between 35 and 44 years old. Surgical sterilization is almost always irreversible, and while it is most often a matter of informed choice, some poor women, especially minority women on welfare, have been bullied or coerced into accepting such a procedure. Sometimes doctors have agreed to perform an abortion only as a "package deal" that includes sterilization; some women have reported signing papers they didn't understand and then discovering later that they had had their tubes tied (Dreifus, 1975).

The second most widely used contraceptive method is the Pill, used primarily by younger women, and more by white women. Eighty-two percent of Pill users are under 30, with the largest group between 20 and 24 years of age (Kash, 1984a). Pill use among married women has declined from a peak of 36 percent in 1973 to 20 percent in 1982 (Shipp, 1985). The Pill is 98 percent effective; and recent research has indicated that it is far safer than previously thought and may, in fact, protect women against cancer of the ovary and uterus, pelvic inflammatory disease, toxic-shock syndrome, rheumatoid arthritis, and dysmenorrhea ("The Pill," 1982). The changed evaluation of the Pill's safety is mainly due to changes in its production. Sequential pills (a series of only estrogen, followed by a shorter series of only progestin) have been replaced by combination pills (a mixture of the two hormones); and the dosage has decreased dramatically from the 5 to 10 mg. per day in the 1960s to today's .5 to 1 mg. (Djerassi, 1981). Progestin is the active contraceptive agent that inhibits ovulation, thereby preventing pregnancy, while estrogen is added to overcome the menstrual irregularities that would otherwise occur. Since the cardiovascular risks previously found to be associated with the Pill are attributable to the intake of large dosages of estrogen, some experts advise taking an oral contraceptive with the lowest possible estrogen content. On the other hand, high-progestin pills have been found to increase the level of LDL, the dangerous form of cholesterol (reported by Emery, 1983). What is important is clearly the proper balance between progestin and estrogen. A new oral contraceptive, Triphasil, approved by the Food and Drug Administration in 1984, contains 31 percent less hormone than the lowest dose combination pill manufactured and is adjusted to administer different ratios of estrogen and progestin on different days during the menstrual cycle ("Safer Birth Control," 1984). Women over 35, however, are still advised against using the Pill in any form, especially if they smoke, since these women are at greater risk for vascular problems.

Another birth control method commonly used by women is the diaphragm, preferred by higher-income women. It has about a 13 percent failure rate, but is safe and has no identified side effects. It is often used in conjunction with a spermicidal cream. The IUD, which was widely used until the mid-1980s, had a 4 percent failure rate but adverse and serious side effects, particularly pelvic inflammatory disease and perforations of the uterus. The most serious offender, the Dalkon Shield, was removed from the market by its manufacturer in 1975 and was the target of thousands of lawsuits brought by women who had suffered serious consequences. Women who had used IUDs were found to have a drastically increased chance of infertility as a result of infection (reported by Emery, 1985). As a consequence of this research, public criticism, and lawsuits, all American manufacturers have ceased production of IUDs. How IUDs worked is not completely understood, but the IUD's presence in the uterus was thought to produce a local inflammation that destroyed sperm or inhibited the implantation of a fertilized egg.

Depo-Provera, a progestogen, is widely used for contraception around the world and has been judged safe by the World Health Organization. A single injection of it can stop ovulation for three months. However, a panel of experts convened by the Food and Drug Administration concluded, after studying relevant data for two years, that the safety of Depo-Provera was unproved and recommended that the drug not be approved for widespread use in the United States (Sun, 1984). The fear is that Depo-Provera is a potential human carcinogen.

"Natural birth control," a sophisticated form of the rhythm method, depends for its success on an accurate assessment of when a woman has ovulated (Skolnik, 1983). Monitoring of body temperature is essential since just prior to ovulation, temperature drops slightly and then rises about one degree, remaining high until about a day or so before menstruation. One technique requires monitoring the cervical mucus to check for changes in amount, translucency, and elasticity. Some newly developed methods have combined the essentials of rhythm with modern computerized technology. For example, a "bioself" invented in Switzerland registers a woman's temperature and calculates the days of the month she is fertile ("Device Flashes," 1982); and a "sexometer" developed in England transmits a woman's body temperature through an electronic sensor in her mouth to a miniature microcomputer that stores the daily information ("Fertility Signal," 1981).

A new contraceptive sponge is a variation of the diaphragm (or older pessary); the two-inch polyurethane cushion contains a spermicide that is activated by being put in water. It is low in cost and available over the counter, but too new for its side effects, long-range safety, or effectiveness to have been established (Eagan, 1984). In addition, some women use a cervical cap; 1.5 million American women use only a spermicidal foam or suppository, which can be purchased without a prescription and has an estimated failure rate of 15 percent.

The contraceptive methods currently available to American men are withdrawal (very unreliable), the condom, and vasectomy. Condoms are very popular and are relied on by 4.5 million women, generally under age 30 (Kash, 1984a). The failure rate is estimated to be about 10 percent. After a long period of contraception research concentrated mainly on methods for women, methods for men are now being seriously investigated. One procedure being studied involves a synthetic form of the hormone that turns off testicular function (LHRH); another involves gossypol, a derivative of cottonseed oil that interferes with sperm production (Brody, 1983b). Gossypol has been tested on a large scale in China and found to be safe, effective, inexpensive, and reversible; it can be taken orally and is relatively economical (Djerassi, 1981), but for unknown reasons is not yet available in the United States.

Despite the lesser attention given by drug companies and researchers to birth control methods for men, we seem to be approaching a state of affairs that Carl Djerassi (1981) has proposed for the future: a "contraceptive supermarket" that allows women and men to choose among devices on the basis of health factors as well as cultural, religious, and moral preferences. Modern women are thus close to having complete control over our procreative capacities. Under these conditions, with choice and control possible, why does a contemporary woman choose to have a child?

Motives for Childbearing

The argument that motherhood is the direct result of an instinctive biological mechanism is no longer taken seriously. There is no evidence that human females are universally driven to perform a series of complex, unlearned, species-specific acts, triggered by discrete internal and/or external stimuli, that result in impregnation. Nevertheless, a more sophisticated version of the biological argument that "anatomy is destiny" is still persuasive for many. Sigmund Freud's view was that motherhood is a woman's ultimate destiny, not only because our bodies are supremely equipped and fashioned for it, but also because it is in this way that we can resolve our early envy of the penis.

> The wish for a penis is replaced by one for a baby. . . . It has not escaped us that the girl has wishes for a baby earlier . . . that, of course, was the meaning of her playing with dolls. But that play . . . served as an identification with her mother. . . . Not until the emergence of the wish for a penis does the doll-baby become a baby from the girl's father, and thereafter the aim of the most powerful feminine wish. Her happiness is great if later on this wish for a baby finds fulfillment in reality, and quite especially so if the baby is a little boy who brings the longed-for penis with him. (Freud, 1933/1964, p. 128)

How cleverly Freud turned our anatomy against us by arguing that we must have babies not so much to realize our reproductive capacities (which is at least a positive approach) but in order to correct our anatomical deficiency. By having a baby (especially a male baby), according to Freud, a woman can overcome nature's unfairness and provide herself with a substitute for the penis she never can have.

Psychoanalytic theorists after Freud modified his thesis, but in ways that embellished and strengthened it. Helene Deutsch (1944), for example, who could not as a woman take the penis-envy proposition too seriously, suggested that women's urge for motherhood stemmed from our tender and erotic motives. Our sexuality, she said, serves reproduction; and the major goal of the truly feminine woman is motherhood, a goal toward which the development of a woman's entire personality has been directed. In this view, a woman who does not accept motherhood is deviant and suffers from a "masculinity complex." Erik Erikson (1968) suggested that the design of women's bodies with vagina and uterus served to focus our adult motives on receiving, enclosing, and protecting. Without a child, Erikson told us, a woman feels unfulfilled and empty. Even Karen Horney (1931/1967), who recognized the patriarchal bias in Freud's assumptions and the role of culture and socialization in the development of personal motives, believed, nevertheless, that a woman's desire for a child is a primary unlearned drive "instinctually anchored deeply in the biological sphere" (p. 106).

Ideas such as these have served to reinforce the belief that pregnancy, even more than marriage, certifies that one is a genuine woman. In *Small Changes*, Marge Piercy (1975) lets us listen to Miriam and Neil, a sophisticated, highly educated, and professionally employed couple, as they consider why they should have a child. Neil speaks first:

> Here we are in our own house. A big house with plenty of room. I'm thirty, you're twenty-six. We're not kids. I was so late finding my own woman, we're behind for our ages. Shouldn't we start a family? It would get Mother off our backs. I know you don't like needling. But they say it's harder to have a baby later on, harder to conceive, harder to carry and deliver. (p. 376)

Miriam considers Neil's arguments:

> A baby in her arms. That whole adventure. To feel life in her quickening, to grow large with life. She would be a real woman then, she would be what they all tried to prove she was not. . . . She would prove that Neil was right to love her and marry her, to take a chance on her. She would validate her womanhood. . . . She saw herself stepping proudly through her pregnancy, ripe as a pear and glowing, full and beautiful as a sheaf of ripe wheat. Suckling her own baby. . . . She would have Neil's child and he would love her even more, they would really be bound together securely. . . . He wanted that from her. . . . She would satisfy him. She would be a mother, a good mother, warm and nurturing and protective. Why not? (p. 377)

Between them, Neil and Miriam seem to have mentioned all the usual reasons for having a child except the economic ones (another pair of hands for the farm or another potential wage earner). Like our mothers and grandmothers, contemporary women also want to please our husbands and to prove that we are true women. We also want to experience the special sensations of pregnancy, actualize our biological potential, provide nurturance and guidance for a developing human being, and embark on an adventure unique to our sex. These were my objectives, and I was eager to partake of woman's grand experience, to know what it felt like to have another's life and body inside of me, to follow its development and marvel at its possibilities.

None of these motives, however, are simply "natural" to women. We have learned them all, and are reinforced for pursuing them. Our society, like others, provides the appropriate institutional pressures and rewards, and the necessary conditions for learning that a woman should *want* to have a child. This process has been described and analyzed by Nancy Chodorow (1978) as the "reproduction of mothering." Girls receive consistent encouragement and practice in caring for children, planning for children, and in expressing delight about motherhood. Thus, a fictional character in a novel by Carolyn Slaughter (1985), a woman leading a nontraditional, liberated life, is described as reacting to her pregnancy as follows:

> Sylvie got out of bed and lifted her arms high. She was naked, her body, so taut and well-tuned, was touching now because of the round, hard belly. She put her hands to her large breasts and felt them, womanly and large, but with reason now for being so. She was complete. (p. 162)

But this reaction is no more natural than that of the Mundugumor of New Guinea, who, as described many years ago by Margaret Mead (1949/1968), did not welcome pregnancy and punished it by social disapproval.

Among contemporary American women the desire to bear a child has remained strong at the same time that family planning and women's right to reproductive freedom are supported. Thus, in samples of college students, Stephanie Shields and Pamela Cooper (1983) found that only 4 percent were definitely planning not to have children, and Mary-Joan Gerson (1980) found that 9 percent wanted no children. In another study (Knaub, Eversoll, & Voss, 1983), 95 percent of the white college women surveyed said that they expected to be mothers at some time during their lives, while most also supported delayed parenthood and strongly rejected such traditional ideas as "children are necessary to a woman's sense of fulfillment or happiness, . . . [and] represent an expression of mature love" (p. 361). Another study of college students (Hare-Mustin, Bennett, & Broderick, 1983) found that while most respondents subscribed to the position that "motherhood is a woman's choice," the men subscribed more than the women to idealizations of motherhood (for example, that no child is unwanted by a normal woman, and that having a baby fulfills a woman totally), and the younger college women supported such beliefs significantly more than a sample of older women who were already mothers.

Women who have borne and reared children learn that the reality is far different from the idealized expectations. Thus, for example, in reviewing a series of national studies about the psychological well-being of Americans, Angus Campbell ("The Paradox of Well-being," 1981) concluded that

> children are not necessary either for a successful marriage or for a happy and satisfying life. Married men and women over 30 who do not have children are more positive than the parents of young children . . . and have about the same feelings of well-being as married people who are parents of grown children. (p. 5)

Among the happiest of all, concluded Campbell, are young married women without children!

These conclusions, though based on data gathered over many years from representative samples and reinforced by other studies, contradict our still-prevalent stereotypes. Stephanie Shields and Pamela Cooper (1983), for example, asked a sample of college students to react to a hypothetical 25-year-old happily married career woman who was described as intentionally child-free, or pregnant but unhappy, or pregnant and happy. The latter woman was "consistently evaluated most positively." The picture that emerged of the happily pregnant woman, although more idyllic for men than for women, was, for both genders, someone "who radiates happiness and competence." In sharp contrast, the unhappily pregnant woman was described by the women respondents as confused and dissatisfied, while the men were even harsher, judging her to be bitter, fearful, moody, resentful, and self-centered. Such adjectives as *mature, understanding,* or *warm* were seldom used to describe her.

The anticipation that a woman will be perceived negatively if she chooses not to bear a child must surely evoke anxiety, and avoidance of anxiety is a powerful motivator of behavior. We can reasonably hypothesize, therefore, that one reason young women continue to seek motherhood is to gain the approval of their community and to avoid being judged as self-centered, immature, and cold. Rolf Peterson (1983) found that voluntary childlessness was viewed by a sample of college students as a temporary or misguided intention that was not positively regarded. Similarly, in another study (Ross & Kahan, 1983), college students asked to respond to vignettes about a couple who had been married for five years "either refused to accept the fact that the couple could be childfree, or saw the ultimate effect as negative" (p. 75) and projected selfishness, loneliness, and regret as consequences. Children were seen as more important for a woman's life satisfaction than graduate school and job advancement.

The strength of the motivation for motherhood on the part of contemporary women can be illustrated by the extent to which infertile women, or those married to sterile men, have gone in their pursuit of the opportunity to bear a child. Such women have voluntarily endured pain and discomfort and submitted their bodies to a variety of exploratory, problematic, and unreliable techniques. As described by Christopher Norwood (1985), "For decades, infertile women were experimentally pumped with hormones, subjected to repeated surgery, endometrial biopsies, tubal insufflation, and laparoscopy" (p. 40). More than 100 test-tube baby centers around the world now provide in vitro fertilization (IVF); these, added to centers providing artificial insemination with donor sperm (AID), have increased women's childbearing possibilities.

Motives for Childlessness

That pronatalism is a dominant theme in our culture has been documented by Jean Veevers (1982) in a review of the literature. And Adrienne Rich (1977) has noted the difficulty we have in talking about women who, through choice or necessity, do not have children. "In the interstices of language lie powerful secrets of the culture" (p. 253): thus, Rich has noted, we speak of women without children as *barren* or *childless*, both terms implying some lack, failure, or emptiness; or we use the word *child-free*, suggesting a refusal to be a mother. In a poem, Lyn Lifshin (1975) has talked about the

> years apologizing for not
> having babies laughing
> when someone pulled
> a baby gerber jar out
> of a closet and held it in
> front of my eyes like
> a cross or a star. (p. 41)

But despite the strength of our traditional ideology and the fact that most women bear at least one child, millions of women choose not to have children, and perhaps even larger numbers may have them but would have preferred not to. The vitality of those who believe strongly in the soundness and acceptability of a child-free life-style is illustrated by a group called the National Alliance for Optional Parenthood (NAOP), which was organized in 1972 to gain public acceptance of couples who do not have children and to counter pronatalist bias in laws and customs (Varro, 1980). What motivates an increasing number of women to remain childless? Each woman probably has her own reasons, but studies have offered clues to general patterns of motives.

In a study of a sample of college women and men, I found that an expressed desire to have and to rear children was related to certain other variables (Lott, 1973). Those who were moderate or less positive in their attitudes and not eager to rear children differed reliably from those whose attitudes were highly positive, in viewing child rearing as a less creative activity; in believing less strongly that child rearing is of value to society; and in remembering less energy and attention being devoted to their care as children by their mothers and also by their fathers. In addition, among women (but not among men) those who were less eager to have and rear children had stronger pro—women's liberation views than those who were more eager to be mothers. In replications of this study, Mary-Joan Gerson (1980) also found that the desire for parenthood among a sample of unmarried college women was most related to a recollection of loving behavior by their own mothers; and another group of researchers (Biaggio, Mohan, & Baldwin, 1985) reported support for the earlier findings that non—child-oriented adults associate child rearing with less creativity and social value than those more eager to have them, and that proliferation women are less personally interested in child rearing than more traditional women. Among a group of unmarried college women, Mary-Joan Gerson (1984) found that those most supportive of and identified with the feminist movement believe that "motherhood offers opportunities for active mastery and assertiveness" but, at the same time, that there are costs associated with motherhood centering on "loss of freedom with regard to self and career" (p. 395).

Couples who decide to remain childless may do so because they regard parenthood as having more disadvantages than "blessings." Susan Bram (1978) compared 30 such couples on a variety of measures with a similar group of parents and a group of still-childless couples who intended to have children. She found that the first group was distinguishable from the other two by an expressed desire to balance work achievement with home life without the interference of children; a greater value placed on work by the wives; and a general desire of both wives and husbands to maximize their individual freedom, as well as freedom in the marriage. In a subsequent analysis of these interview data, Bram (1984) compared only the women. She concluded that the childless women differed from those who were already parents as well as from those who were delaying parenthood in being less traditional in behavior, attitudes, and self-image. For the childless woman

> the themes of achievement and egalitarianism emerge repeatedly. The childless woman is more committed to her work . . . views her marriage as a source of personal companionship and growth . . . adheres to principles of equal participation of the sexes in public and private life . . . [and] views herself in strongly individualistic terms. (p. 203)

Jean Veevers (1982) has reviewed the literature on voluntarily childless couples and found that, in general, they are similar to couples with only one or two children in being likely to live in a large urban area, having married later, and being above average in education and below average in religious identification or church attendance. With respect to the women, the data indicate that those who are childless are significantly more likely than other women to be employed outside the home, to be committed to a career, and to be earning higher incomes at higher-status jobs. The psychological differences center on independence as a value and as a personal characteristic.

Sharon Houseknecht (1979) interviewed 51 women who had been married for at least 5 years and who did not intend to have children. She found that only 19 had made this decision early in their lives. The remainder had come to this decision after they were married and after they had experienced the satisfaction of work and other activities. These findings are particularly important because they emphasize that different women may decide not to have children at different times during their adult lives.

Abortion

Reasoned and thoughtful decision making does not precede every pregnancy, and women throughout history have become pregnant as a result of force,

coercion, ignorance, thoughtlessness, or carelessness. A child conceived under such conditions may not be wanted; this may also be the case if the pregnancy threatens a woman's physical or mental health, her obligations to herself or to others, or if she knows in advance that the child will be born with serious mental or physical handicaps. Once begun, pregnancies can only be terminated by natural or induced abortion.

Worldwide, an estimated 30 to 55 million abortions were performed in 1980, about half of them illegally, according to a United Nations conference (reported in "A Look at Abortion Laws," 1981). Thus, for every ten live births in the world, there were 4.5 interrupted pregnancies. After the Portuguese parliament voted to legalize abortion in 1984, Ireland and Belgium remained the only Western countries in which abortion is forbidden by law under all conditions. In 12 Western countries, abortion on demand is permitted during the first three months of pregnancy (Francke, 1982).

In the United States the number of legal abortions performed varies widely among states. Data reported by the U.S. Bureau of the Census (1985b) indicate that the national rate is 426 abortions for every 1000 births (similar to the worldwide figure). New York has the highest abortion rate (731 per 1000 live births) while Utah has the lowest rate (100 per 1000 births). More than 1 million legal abortions are performed in the United States each year, making it the most common surgical procedure in the country (Hayler, 1979). The number of abortions has remained relatively stable since 1973, when abortion was legalized, and most experts agree that about 70 percent of the legal abortions now performed have merely replaced the earlier illegal abortions. Two thirds of the women who have abortions are single; and 95 percent of the abortions are performed during the first trimester, when they are safest, simplest, and least problematic.

The Legality of Abortion   "Hardly any society is known that has not at some time and for some reason practiced abortion," according to Lucile Newman (1972, p. 8). But although abortion is a universal occurrence, not every culture has recognized it as legal. In the United States, abortions were relatively common and not punished or censured until about 150 years ago. The first statutes prohibiting abortion were passed in the nineteenth century; and by 1850 to 1890 every state had enacted legislation specifying that abortions could be performed only if the pregnancy was life-threatening and then only by a doctor. But abortions did not cease; they just went underground. Leo Kanowitz (1969) has estimated that before the liberalization of abortion laws in some states in the late 1960s, a vast abortion black market was thriving in the United States, and that each year over a million abortions were performed, resulting in the deaths of between 5 and 10 thousand women.

After decades of debate and state reforms of restrictive abortion legislation, the Supreme Court ruled in 1973 (*Roe v. Wade* and *Doe v. Bolton*) that no state can pass laws prohibiting or restricting a woman's right to an abortion during the first trimester of pregnancy. The Court intended that a woman and her doctor should be free of state interference for the first three months in determining whether an abortion is in the best interests of the mother, with attention paid to her psychological, emotional, and physical circumstances. During the next six months, according to the ruling, a state can regulate abortion procedures in ways that reasonably relate to maternal health, and only in the last 10 weeks can a state ban abortions entirely, except where they are necessary to preserve the woman's life or health. The Jane Roe in the historic *Roe v. Wade* decision was Norma McCorvey, who in 1973 was a 25-year-old divorced waitress from Texas who five years earlier had been gang-raped and severely beaten. Too poor to seek a legal abortion outside of Texas, which did not permit one, she had sued the state. When the Supreme Court finally decided her case, the child that she had given up for adoption was four years old (Brasher, 1983).

As of this writing, the Court's 1973 decision that guarantees a woman the unconditional right to terminate her pregnancy during the first trimester is still the law of the land. Repeated attempts by state legislatures to impose restrictions have been declared unconstitutional by several federal district judges, and by the Supreme Court itself in 1983. The State of Rhode Island, for example, has passed at least a half-dozen laws since 1973 designed to interfere with a woman's decision to terminate her pregnancy. Each of these laws has been legally challenged, and then enacted again in some other form by the state legislature. In 1984, U.S. District Court Judge Raymond Pettine once again found three antiabortion laws to be unconstitutional. One required physicians to notify a woman's husband before performing an abortion (unless she had confirmed in writing that she had already done so, or there was a medical emergency, or her husband was not responsible for

the pregnancy). The other two laws limited women's rights to receive insurance coverage for abortions: one law prohibited municipalities from providing their employees with insurance for abortions; the other statute allowed abortion coverage to be sold to women by insurance companies as an optional rider for an additional premium and gave insurance companies (or employers paying for health insurance benefits) the right to deny the rider to single women (or to others). These laws are illustrative of others passed by other states. In declaring these unconstitutional, Judge Pettine

> noted that in the Roe vs. Wade decision of 1973, the Supreme Court recognized two compelling interests that may lead states to lawfully inhibit a woman's right to an abortion—the interest in the mother's health, which may only come into play after the first three months of pregnancy, and the interest in potential life, which is relevant once the fetus can live outside its mother. (Krupa, 1984)

Still enforced in Rhode Island (where I live) is a law prohibiting state employees and their families from medical coverage for induced abortions if their health insurance plans are state financed. Medical procedures to terminate a pregnancy are covered by health insurance only in cases of rape or incest, or if the mother's life is in danger. State employees wishing insurance for abortions for other reasons must purchase additional coverage at their own expense.

The Supreme Court itself reaffirmed its 1973 ruling 10 years later by declaring unconstitutional certain state statutes regulating abortion: requirements for informed consent procedures, fetal disposal, 24-hour waiting periods, enforced counseling, and second-trimester hospitalization. The Court did uphold the right of states to require parental (or in some cases, court) consent for minors (Wolfson, 1983). The 1983 Supreme Court decision was widely interpreted as indicating a clear, unequivocal reaffirmation of a woman's constitutional right to decide whether or not to continue her pregnancy. In 1986, the Supreme Court again acted in a 5 to 4 decision to curb the rights of states to regulate abortion. "In striking down Pennsylvania's 'informed consent' requirement and other provisions . . . , Justice Harry A. Blackmun wrote in the majority opinion that some of them were designed to 'intimidate women into continuing pregnancies'" (Taylor, 1986, p. E1).

On the other hand, the Supreme Court has permitted the federal government (and states) to deny public funds to poor women who wish to exercise

A new compromise on reproductive rights? (*From* Mercy, It's The Revolution and I'm In My Bathrobe, *by Nicole Hollander, St. Martin's Press, Inc. Copyright © 1982 by Nicole Hollander.*)

their constitutional right to an abortion but cannot afford to pay for it themselves. The Hyde Amendment, passed by Congress in 1977, prohibits the use of Medicaid funds for abortion except in cases of promptly reported rape or incest, or when the mother's life is endangered. This legislation enables states and cities to issue similar prohibitions with regard to the use of public funds. In 1980, Federal District Judge John Dooling of New York declared the Hyde Amendment to be unconstitutional on the grounds that it interfered with a woman's religious beliefs favoring abortion, that it violated her right to privacy, and represented unequal treatment for indigent women. The Supreme Court disagreed and in a 5 to 4 decision in 1980 (*Harris v. McRae*) upheld the constitutionality of the Hyde Amendment. The majority opinion was that Congress had the right to establish the favoring of childbirth as national policy and to further that objective by denying the use of federal funds for abortions. The Court argued that a woman still had the right to have an abortion, and if her poverty prevented it, that was not the fault of the government.

As a consequence of the Hyde Amendment and the McRae decision, poor women are restricted in the exercise of their constitutional right to terminate a pregnancy. While states are free to use their own welfare funds to finance an abortion for a woman who cannot pay for it herself, only 15 states do so, under conditions that vary from state to state (Bakst, 1984). The Center for Disease Control has reported ("Hyde Amendment," 1981) that the majority of poor women who have sought abortions have been

able to get them because they live in states that provide funds for them, or have been subsidized by clinics like Planned Parenthood (which offers low-cost abortions). But the report also noted that in the year after the Hyde Amendment took effect, of 300,000 Medicaid-eligible women who wanted an abortion, about 5 percent continued their pregnancies and 1 percent "resorted to illegal or self-induced abortions." If these figures can be generalized to subsequent years, then approximately 3000 women each year are forced to face the shame, terror, pain, and potential danger of back-room abortions simply because they are poor.

Opponents of free choice are continuing their efforts to abolish women's right to abortion. These efforts include lobbying for a constitutional prohibition amendment and/or legislation that would specify that human life begins at conception. The cartoon by Nicole Hollander (1982) shown on this page gives an ironic view of the continuing debate and legislative proposals.

Attitudes Toward Abortion   A summary of the results of nationwide opinion polls indicates that 80 to 90 percent of Americans support abortion when a woman's health is endangered, when there is a chance of serious fetal abnormality, or when the pregnancy has resulted from rape or incest; support for abortion for economic, social, or personal reasons is found among 40 to 50 percent of adults ("Views on Sex," 1985). One study found that among women undergoing amniocentesis to find out if there was abnormality in the embryo (a procedure that currently can be performed no earlier than the 14th week of pregnancy*), 70 percent indicated that they would definitely get an abortion if a serious genetic birth defect were detected, and only 4 to 6 percent said that they would not consider abortion under any conditions ("Tests Change Abortion Attitudes," 1984). Indications of fetal abnormalities are detected in 3 percent of all amniocentesis tests.

In 1982 the National Coalition of American Nuns issued a statement affirming its own opposition to abortion but also its conviction that women have the right to make this decision for themselves ("Nuns' Group Opposes," 1982). Two years later, "24 nuns and four priests and religious brothers were among . . . 97 signers of . . . [an] advertisement that asserted 'a diversity of opinion exists among committed Catholics on the abortion issue'" ("Vatican Seeks," 1986, p. C-22). After the Vatican demanded a retraction from the religious signers, the four men did so but some of the nuns have continued to resist. Among a representative sample of law students polled by the American Bar Association, two thirds were found to believe that a woman has an unconditional right to an abortion ("Most Law Students," 1985). On the other hand, lobbying for antichoice legislation has remained strong, and in the past few years women entering abortion clinics and clinic personnel have been harassed. Such clinics as well as family planning centers around the country have been threatened with violence or been its victims; in 1984, 24 bombings were reported.

Both Deirdre English (1981) and Kristin Luker (1984) have argued that women who are most strongly antichoice differ from those who are pro-choice not so much in ideology, religion, or the value they place on children and families, but in social circumstances. Those who adamantly oppose anyone's right to terminate a pregnancy by choice tend to be less well-educated and to be married to husbands who are skilled workers or small-business operators. They typically married young, have had relatively large families, and have devoted their adult lives to homemaking and motherhood. They perceive legalized abortion as a profound threat to their way of life.

> The women who staff the right-to-life movement . . . are . . . homemakers . . . whose lack of job training

gives them few employment options, but who expect their husbands' salaries—at whatever income—to protect them from being put at the mercy of the job market. In a twist that perhaps only someone who has been a full-time housewife can totally appreciate, the antiabortion movement accomplishes two things at once for these women: it defends their role as women in the home, and it gets them out of the house. (English, 1981, pp. 16f.)

Those who have been in the vanguard of the movement for legalized abortion, on the other hand, are more likely to be women eager to enter, or retain their competitive position in, the professional work force.

Abortion Methods   Methods used to terminate pregnancy have varied throughout history with the technology available and the legality or illegality of the procedure. Linda Francke (1982) has described some of the ancient methods as follows:

> Over 5,000 years ago in China, women drank quicksilver fired in oil or swallowed fourteen live tadpoles three days after they had missed a menstrual period in the hope of bringing it on. . . . In more modern times, Russian women attempted to abort themselves by squatting over pots of boiling onions, while members of certain Indian tribes climbed up and down coconut palms, striking their stomachs against the trunks. (p. 24)

Before 1973, when abortion was available only for narrowly defined medical reasons, millions of women in this country underwent humiliating and dangerous procedures to end their pregnancies. In *Braided Lives*, Marge Piercy (1983) has presented an unforgettable fictional account of the way it used to be for women whose only means of terminating a pregnancy was an illegal abortion in a back room or on a kitchen table. Part of becoming a woman, for me, was going very early one morning to a fashionable address in New York City with a brown paper bag containing a supply of sanitary napkins and $350 in cash. When I arrived (alone), the physician gave me an injection of penicillin and took me to a small room behind his office. There, with no nurse in attendance and no anesthetic, I was aborted (dilation and curettage) as I screamed and he angrily shouted at me to keep quiet. For an hour afterward I was able to rest on a cot but, before his office filled with his regular patients, I had to leave as surreptitiously as I had come. My experience was not unusual and, in some respects, it was much better than that of other women who have had illegal abortions. Adrienne Rich (1977) has cataloged some of the methods resorted to

---

*A new technique (chorionic villus biopsy) may replace amniocentesis and permit prenatal testing for genetic disorders much earlier during the first trimester (Kolata, 1983).

by American women unable to obtain legal, safe, and low-cost abortions:

> Wire coat-hangers, knitting needles, goose quills dipped in turpentine, celery stalks, drenching the cervix with detergent, lye, soap, Ultra-Jel (a commercial preparation of castor oil, soap, and iodine), drinking purgatives of mercury, applying hot coals to the body. The underworld . . . abortionists, often alcoholic, disenfranchised members of the medical profession, besides operating in septic surroundings . . . frequently rape or sexually molest their patients. . . . An illegal or self-induced abortion is no casual experience. It is painful, dangerous, and cloaked in the guilt of criminality. (p. 272)

In these days of legal abortions in hospitals or clinics and by professional medical personnel, the most common procedure is vacuum aspiration (suction), which can be performed during the first trimester (up to 12 weeks) under local anesthetic and takes about 10 minutes. Dilation and curettage (D & C), also a first trimester procedure, involves scraping the uterine lining and may require a night in the hospital. Second trimester abortion procedures (which represent only 5 percent of those performed) include injection of saline solution, intraamniotic prostaglandin injection, and dilation and evacuation (D & E). The latter, the least traumatic and safest of the late-pregnancy techniques, involves a combination of suction and curettage, takes less than half an hour, and requires only a local anesthetic (Francke, 1982).

First trimester abortions need not be performed in a hospital, but states may regulate the location of second-trimester abortions, most of which are done in hospitals. Most facilities in which abortions are performed provide counseling before and after the procedure and are staffed by supportive, empathetic personnel. According to Linda Francke (1982), "The legalization of abortion has brought with it the development of an abortion industry that is at the same time both profitable to its members and supportive and safe for the women seeking its services" (p. 40).

The Decision to Abort Terminating a pregnancy is a decision made by a very large number of women, but I have never spoken with, read about, or heard about a woman whose abortion decision was made quickly and effortlessly. The very personal decision to end a pregnancy is made in a social context in which abortion is negatively evaluated by many persons, hysterically condemned by a highly vocal minority, considered sinful by a significant and powerful church, not approved for support by public funds, and was illegal and punishable until the early 1970s. For most women, abortion is a last resort. Religious, moral, and medical considerations enter in; so do fear for one's health and safety and for one's future ability to have children. Issues must also be resolved relating to the relationship with the man who participated in the conception. New reproductive technology has increased the dilemma of choosing for some women, as pointed out by Barbara Rothman (1986). Through amniocentesis, diagnoses in utero can now be made of certain kidney diseases, Tay Sachs disease, anencephalus (absence of brain and spinal cord), and chromosomal abnormalities, in addition to Down's syndrome. Thus, a decision to terminate a pregnancy may be based on probable outcomes for the fetus if it is carried to term, adding new factors to be taken into account and to the stress of decision making.

Following an abortion, the emotions a woman experiences may range from renewed self-confidence to guilt and depression, or some combination of these. Linda Francke (1982) interviewed women who had had abortions and found examples of all of these emotions and reactions. Lisa Shusterman (1976) reviewed the literature on psychosocial factors in abortion and concluded that women who obtain legal abortions on request are typically young and unmarried, not in a good position to bear or care for a child, and are influenced by social and economic factors in their decisions to abort; the psychological consequences for them, according to Shusterman, have been "mostly benign." Women who experience negative effects tend to be less certain of their decision and to be involved in less stable heterosexual relationships. A similar conclusion from a review of research findings was reached by Nancy Adler (1979). She found that most women who had legal abortions experienced relief and positive emotions afterwards, although not unmixed with some negative feelings. She pointed out that much of the stress

> is associated with the discovery and acknowledgement of an unwanted pregnancy and the need for a decision about whether to continue or terminate it. . . . Women generally report that the time of greatest distress is between the discovery that they are pregnant and the abortion. Thus, the psychological aftereffects of abortion must be viewed not only as reactions to abortion, per se, but also as reactions to the experience of having had . . . an unwanted pregnancy. (p. 112)

Most researchers agree that reactions to an unwanted pregnancy and to the decision to end it are strongly influenced by a woman's social and economic circumstances, by the meaning the pregnancy has for her, by the resources and support available to her, and by her previously developed skills in coping with stressful situations.

A study that offers considerable insight into the decision-making process of women faced with an unwanted pregnancy was done by Carol Gilligan (1977). She interviewed 29 women (varying in age, race, and social class) referred to her by abortion and pregnancy counseling services. Of this group, 4 decided to complete their pregnancies, 21 decided to end them, 1 woman miscarried, and 3 remained in doubt about what to do. Gilligan reported that in confronting their dilemma the women tended to define the moral problem as "one of obligation to exercise care and avoid hurt" (p. 492). According to Gilligan, this perspective differs sharply from the way men generally view morality—in terms of rights, not responsibilities. Gilligan found that the women's discussions of abortion proceeded from an initial focus on the self to considerations of responsibility for others. At this level, what was "good" was equated with the care of others. When a woman began to ask herself "whether it is selfish or responsible, moral or immoral, to include her own needs within the compass of her care and concern" (p. 498) then it was possible for her to establish a balance between selfishness and responsibility. Once she accepted the extension of obligation to include herself, she was able to make judgments and choices. The decision to end a pregnancy is made within the same moral and psychological framework as the decision to initiate or continue it. To be concerned about persons, to be instrumental to their care, to avoid inflicting injury—these Gilligan found to be major elements in the moral judgments of the women she studied. When self was seen as equally worthy of care as others, then the ethic of responsibility became a general guiding principle. Women have not typically received encouragement or reinforcement for taking this final step. Instead, we have been taught to look to authority, to male teachings, to our husbands, or to others for approval of what we do.

In a study of a small sample of women who had had abortions, a colleague and I (Quina & Lott, 1986) found that, for most, it had been a reasoned decision, and 75 percent of the women had consulted their sex partners, all of whom had agreed with the decision to terminate the pregnancy. In retrospect, 65 percent felt that their decision had been very wise, and an additional 25 percent that it had been moderately wise. All the women said that they would support a friend in her decision to end a pregnancy, but 20 percent would probably not have an abortion again. The women in our sample varied in current age from 21 to 52 and varied in age at which they had had an abortion from 15 to 43; they also varied in the number of years ago that they had had this experience, the conditions of the abortion, its legality, and so on. The sample was heterogeneous with respect to ethnicity, religion, sexual preference, and marital status. What unified this group of women were the reasons they gave for having decided on an abortion, and the ways in which this decision had affected their lives. The abortion, in most cases, had served an enabling function by permitting the women to move ahead in their lives. The women told us that the abortion had enabled them to provide care and affection for the children they already had; to complete their education; to find better employment; to solve debilitating problems (such as drinking); to mature emotionally/psychologically before having a child; and to avoid financial hardship (welfare). Most of the women recognized both positive and negative outcomes and their reported immediate and longer-range reactions revealed complex experiences, but 75 percent believed, strongly or moderately, that their abortion had changed their lives for the better.

From the statistics on abortion cited earlier in this section, we know that members of all social classes, all regions of the country, all ethnic and religious groups (with only rare exceptions), have taken the opportunity now provided by law to exercise choice over their pregnancies. These women have exercised their right (or obligation) to make decisions about their bodies and lives. As expressed by Marge Piercy (1984e), a woman who advocates or practices choice is saying:

> I will choose what enters me, what becomes
> flesh of my flesh. Without choice, no politics,
> no ethics lives. I am not your cornfield,
> not your uranium mine, not your calf
> for fattening, nor your cow for milking.
> You may not use me as your factory.
> Priests and legislators do not hold
> shares in my womb or my mind.
> This is my body. If I give it to you
> I want it back. My life
> is a non-negotiable demand. (p. 97)

Many women have children out of the need to validate their womanliness, to do the correct thing, to please others, to fulfill the expectations of parents and culture, and because few attractive alternatives exist. If these are her motives, then the willful termination of a pregnancy may leave a woman confused, uncertain of her worth, questioning her womanly qualities and her goodness as a person. On the other hand, a woman may choose to experience pregnancy, childbirth, and motherhood because she wishes to extend her experiences and personal development through caring interaction with a growing human being; she may want to share her skills and use her adult competencies to assist a helpless infant; she may want to give and receive attention and love. If such objectives are not likely to be realized, if childbirth is likely to result in both the woman and child being diminished, exploited, and hurt, then a decision to end a pregnancy becomes one that is made out of a sense of morality in which responsibility and the avoidance of hurt are key elements.

PREGNANCY

Most women in our society continue to have babies, although we now want fewer than our mothers and grandmothers did, and we have them at later ages, spaced at more convenient and sensible intervals. Our unique female capacity to sustain developing human life within our bodies remains a source of delight, excitement, and awe; and those remarkable months of pregnancy continue to be experienced at least once by the vast majority of women.

The normal changes that occur inside a pregnant woman's body during the nine months of gestation are extraordinary and intricate, involving practically every organ and all major physiological systems. Niles Newton and Charlotte Modahl (1978) have discussed some of the profound physical changes a pregnant woman undergoes. These include rapid increase in production of progesterone, which will be maintained throughout the pregnancy; heightened and continued production of estrogen; high expenditure of energy; tiredness; possible nausea; frequent need to urinate as the growing embryo presses on the bladder; the possibility of dietary deficiencies (perhaps associated with specific food cravings), since the fetus must obtain from its mother all nutrients and vitamins and makes particularly heavy demands on calcium, iron, and protein; rapid weight gain (approximately 24 pounds); and the physical discomforts and postural adjustments that may accompany changes in body weight and distribution.

Experiences of Pregnant Women

Although all pregnant women undergo the same general physical and physiological changes, their subjective experiences of pregnancy can vary widely. For example, during her pregnancy, Miriam in *Small Changes* (Piercy, 1975) dragged her heavy body to bed, where

> she was launched on her nightly vigil. . . . The baby was a night person. Soon as she got ready for bed he—it—started to dance. . . . Even if the fetus would sleep at night . . . how could she sleep with having to pee every time he moved? . . . She counted the days until the baby was due . . . [when] she would get rid of this overstuffed disgusting body that could no longer do anything right—heartburn . . . , backaches, water on the knee and swollen ankles. Soon she would have . . . her own body back, lively and properly shaped, and then *she* would do the dancing. (pp. 381f.)

In contrast, Roslyn Willett (1971) wrote of herself:

> I had been married for ten years before I decided to have a child. . . . I . . . [worked] until the night before the baby was born, putting on a very successful client party less than two weeks before, at which I did not sit down at all. . . . My feeling about work was clued to my observation of pregnant alley cats. Belly or no, they continue to jump over fences and grub around in garbage cans. So can most women. When I was asked how I could continue to work with such a massive handicap, the answer was easy: a big belly only interferes with tying your shoelaces; it does not impair your intelligence. Ask any man with one. (pp. 374f.)

How a woman experiences her pregnancy reflects her past history and present situation. Clearly, pregnancy has differing meanings for women in different circumstances and has varied consequences for our lives. Myra Leifer (1980) has noted that few psychological studies "have dealt with women's subjective reactions to pregnancy" (p. 758). Much of what we know of these has come from feminist literature and the women's health movement. The empirical findings regarding psychological changes typically fluctuate between an emphasis on positive feelings of well-being, hope, eager anticipation, and calm, to descriptions of pregnant women as vulnerable and stressed. A pregnant woman may confront fears of death, of unattractiveness, of loss of figure and beauty, or that the child will be born defective or deformed. A pregnant woman is nurturing a developing human being (literally giving it all she has) and at the same time is typically enjoying some special care and attention from husband, lover, friends, or relatives. Thus, pregnancy involves both positive and negative experiences, which may fluctuate or occur simultaneously.

How the pregnant woman will react to the changes taking place in her body depends upon the interaction between these changes and the environment in which she experiences them, with environment broadly defined to include cultural, social, economic, and physical conditions as well as her attitudes toward herself, the pregnancy, her marriage, her job, and so on. Myra Leifer (1980) concluded from a review of the literature on pregnancy that the degree to which it "is experienced as a time of well-being or stress may be critically related to the quality and extent of social and interpersonal support received" (p. 760). For example, a study of 98 pregnant women (reported by Newton and Modahl, 1978) found that those with good marital relationships were less likely to feel depressed or anxious than those whose marriages were not happy ones. In addition, those who said they had wanted to be pregnant were less likely to have childbirth complications than women who had not wanted to become pregnant. These data and others suggest a strong relationship between a woman's general feeling of well-being or satisfaction and the extent to which she will enjoy or feel positively about her pregnancy. Cherylynn Carrie (1981) collected responses to a lengthy questionnaire from a large sample of women who were visiting an obstetrician. She found that the report of negative symptoms by pregnant women was most related to their general health and to their tendency to report symptoms in general, and she concluded that "reproductive symptom reports can . . . be seen as part of a general tendency to react to stressors with somatic and emotional symptoms" (p. 185).

What we have learned to expect, and how we define or label our experiences, greatly influence how we feel and what we do. Nausea, for example, accompanies the first trimester of pregnancy for many, but by no means all, women. It is instructive to note what Margaret Mead (1949/1968) long ago observed among women in different cultures of the South Seas regarding how variations in personal experience are correlated with cultural emphases. She wrote:

> Morning-sickness in pregnancy may be completely ignored, or it may be expected of every woman, so that the woman who displays no nausea is the exception or it may be stylized as occurring for the first child only. But in those societies which . . . ignore it . . . there are still a few women who have extreme nausea. . . . We may say of morning-sickness that where it is culturally

stylized as appropriate for any period of pregnancy or order of pregnancy . . . , a large majority of women will show this behavior; where it is not, only a very few will. Convulsive vomiting is a capacity of every human organism, which can be elaborated, neglected, or to a large degree disallowed. (p. 221)

After reviewing the relevant literature, Myra Leifer (1980) concluded that little is known about "what proportion of women actually experience these symptoms [nausea and vomiting], nor do researchers agree on the biological, psychological, or sociological factors associated with them" (p. 756).

A pregnant woman's view of herself is influenced not only by general cultural emphases but also by the way her neighbors, family, employer, and others react to her. Pregnant women often appear to make those around them (particularly men) feel uneasy. Shelley Taylor and Ellen Langer (1977) found that people in an elevator showed a strong preference for standing next to a nonpregnant as opposed to a pregnant woman. They found that the pregnant woman was avoided more by men than by women and that staring was a very common reaction. In another study, Dianne Horgan (1983) found that department stores differentially frequented by upper- and working-class pregnant women displayed maternity clothes in very different places. High-status stores displayed maternity clothes adjacent to lingerie or loungewear, whereas lower-status stores placed them near uniforms or clothes for large women. These findings suggested to Horgan that perhaps "in the high status stores, pregnancy is seen as feminine, delicate, luxurious, joyous, personal, and private. In the lower status stores, pregnancy is viewed as a job, a period when one is fat" (p. 336). Complementing Horgan's department store data are differences in attitudes assessed from responses to a brief survey filled out by women who were waiting to see their obstetricians. Upper-middle-class women were found to differ from working-class women in reporting that they felt sexier, that they were treated differently when pregnant, and were more likely to be returning to work after giving birth. We should note briefly here that pregnancy has been used as a reason to discriminate against women in employment, and many regulations, policies, and practices still treat women differently from men on the job because women are potential childbearers. Some employers discriminate against women during pregnancy, or after they return to work from maternity leave ("Pregnancy Discrimination," 1985). We will return to this issue in the chapter on employment.

Fears and Taboos

In addition to physiological and physical changes, feelings about the extent to which the pregnancy was planned or desired, and fears for her own safety and competence in a new role, yet another factor contributes to the stress of pregnancy for contemporary women. This is our feeling of responsibility for the health of the fetus and our awareness of the large number of factors that can threaten normal development. In many cultures, special regimens, rituals, or taboos are related to such fears. For example, within the Guatemalan village of San Pedro (Paul, 1974), a pregnant woman is believed to be especially vulnerable to harmful influences. It is considered dangerous for her to be outside at midday when the sun is strongest or during a thunderstorm, or for her to look at the full moon or point to a rainbow; failure to observe such precautions, it is believed, can result in a defective child. It is also believed that a pregnant woman can endanger others by gazing directly at babies, young plants, or animals, causing these to die since her blood during pregnancy (as during menstruation) is "hot" or "strong." Lucile Newman (1969) found pregnancy apprehensions and superstitions among women in our own culture, in a group of black and white obstetric patients in California. Newman suggested that one factor that

> sustains pregnancy superstitions is the irrational and ineffable definition of the pregnant woman as particularly vulnerable to magical forces. She is, for the time, in a "dangerous" situation, . . . set apart from the other members of society by her condition and by their feelings about her. Superstition and magic are brought to bear upon her to counteract her supernormal and dangerous aspects. (p. 123)

Even if we do not subscribe to superstition and magic, even if we know that it is safe during pregnancy to swim, ski, dance, work, look at the moon, and be out in thunderstorms, modern women have other things to worry about, other proscriptions and another list of don'ts. Most of us have learned how intimately fetus and mother are connected, how vital it is that our health be good, that we walk enough and rest enough, that our diet be nutritious, and that our spirits be high. Everything we do and ingest will have some consequence for the developing fetus. Despite the fact that our doctors are the ones responsible for the tragedy of deformed children born to mothers who took prescribed thalidomide, and for the tragedy of cancer in the reproductive tissues of children born to mothers who took prescribed DES, the mother is the one who feels the guilt. We are responsible for this new human being growing in our bodies. We must avoid X rays, be wary of contracting German measles and herpes, avoid drugs, alcohol, and cigarettes.

Research indicates that pregnant women should be very cautious about consuming alcoholic beverages. There is evidence of a "fetal alcohol syndrome" characterized by a set of abnormalities evident after birth: growth deficiencies, mental retardation, body organ defects, and/or psychomotor disturbances. A review of the research (Streissguth, Landesman-Dwyer, Martin, & Smith, 1980) concluded that "the lower limit of alcohol necessary to produce a harmful effect has not been determined" (p. 359), but clear indications exist that alcohol is a teratogen (that is, it freely passes across the placental barrier and affects fetal development). Although the mechanisms through which alcohol affects the fetus are still unclear, and variations among individuals in alcohol metabolism are poorly understood, adverse effects have been found in the offspring of women reporting an average consumption of two alcoholic drinks per day. Binge drinking has been found to be particularly harmful and can produce different congenital abnormalities at different times during fetal growth.

Smoking and aspirin have also been found to adversely affect prenatal development. Data from a national study of over 50,000 pregnancies implicated smoking as a factor in spontaneous abortions, stillbirths, premature births, and crib death. The danger of smoking stems from its reduction of blood flow to the placenta; aspirin is believed to interfere with the circulation of oxygen. New research has also indicated that caffeine consumption may be dangerous to the fetus, as well as sexual intercourse during the second and third trimesters of pregnancy (reported by Connelly, 1981). Heavy caffeine use (equivalent to about five cups of coffee a day) is associated with an increased likelihood of breech births, miscarriages, low birth weight, stillbirths, and premature births. The danger of sexual intercourse comes from the possibility that seminal fluid may introduce or activate bacterial infection that can spread to the amniotic fluid surrounding the fetus and cause premature labor. Such infections are the most frequent cause of premature birth in the United States.

Sherryl Connelly (1981) has listed the following other things that are "not good for the unborn": gaining too much weight or too little weight (the new medical advice is 25 pounds for a woman with a normal prepregnancy weight); eating a diet deficient in vitamins and minerals; using Bendectin as an antinausea drug (it has been implicated in birth defects and, since Connelly's article, has been removed from the market); using diazepam (marketed as Valium); and being exposed to cats or cat litter. There may be additional risks, not yet discovered, from the use of ultrasound to observe the fetus, a practice that has become almost a routine part of the examination of pregnant women. Ruth Hubbard (1982) has cautioned that there is no certainty that ultrasound is safe when used frequently.

> We know only that so far, babies show no signs of damage. But that was also true for X-rays. To know more will take time and careful studies; but in the meanwhile more and more fetuses are being exposed to numerous ultrasound examinations. (p. 32)

The net effect of these considerations is that a pregnant woman can hardly avoid feelings of apprehension and concern about whether or not she is doing all that she can to enhance the health and proper development of the fetus. If it is born defective will it have been her fault?

CHILDBIRTH

Nancy Dean and Myra Stark (1977) have suggested that childbirth is a woman's biological test of courage, a natural occasion for bravery that men have tried to match by constructing battlefields. In childbirth we risk our lives, demonstrate strength, and withstand pain. The result of such courage is the bringing forth of life (and not the destruction of lives as in the wars men fight against each other). I do not mean to imply, by presenting and extending this analogy, that women see childbirth this way, nor that they should, nor that women's strength cannot be exhibited in every sphere of human activity. It can and it is. But childbirth is in a separate and unique category, and for women who choose to experience it, the element of deeply rooted challenge and risk remains. Robin Morgan (1978), for example, described her feelings shortly before giving birth to her child as follows:

> As any woman . . . I was prey to deep, almost archetypal feelings that I must be ready for the possibility of losing the child—or of dying, myself, in childbirth. No matter how "modern" we become, it will take still more time and consciousness . . . before the imprint of a million ghosts dead in childbirth will be erased from the secret thoughts of a pregnant woman. (p. 50)

What triggers the end of gestation and the beginning of childbirth is not yet entirely clear. Believed to be involved are hormones from the pituitary—namely, oxytocin and prostaglandins—as well as progesterone. The first sign of childbirth (parturition) is expulsion of a mucous plug from the cervix, often followed closely by rupture of the amniotic sac (the "bag of waters" housing the fetus) and release of its fluid contents. This is normally followed by the first stage of labor, uterine contractions that take place at regular intervals while the cervix dilates. This first stage may last from 2 to 16 or more hours. During the second, briefer, stage, the fetus is expelled (normally head first) down the vaginal canal, accompanied by a different kind of uterine contraction. During the last stage the placenta is expelled.

The Cultural Context of Childbirth

How a woman experiences childbirth varies widely from culture to culture, and within our own culture variation exists among groups of women who have received different kinds of prenatal preparation and whose babies are born under different conditions. Niles Newton and Charlotte Modahl (1978) have pointed out that "in societies that look upon birth as a fearful and secret experience, women often have long, difficult labors. In societies that are open about childbirth and expect it to be simple, women usually have short, uncomplicated labors" (p. 47).

In some cultures, childbirth is a relatively public event at which other individuals are expected to be present and to assist; in other cultures, childbirth is private. For example, in the Guatemalan village of San Pedro (Paul, 1974), a childbirth is attended by the husband, his parents, possibly the woman's parents, and the midwife. Women are expected not to cry or scream "lest the neighbors hear them," and the husband assists by supporting his wife from behind "as she squats to deliver her child." In contrast, among the Siriono Indians of Bolivia (Newton, 1970), birth takes place in a communal hut where the mother lies in a hammock and her groans appear to disturb no one; labor tends to be short, and the woman is not usually assisted. Cultures vary in the number and kind of special taboos observed just before the birth is expected. The woman may be required to leave her village, go alone into the bush and care for her own needs entirely, or food may be brought and left for her. In still other cultures, the father may be encouraged to behave in a parallel manner to his childbearing wife (couvade), thus incorporating him more closely with the birth of his child. As Sheila Kitzinger (1979) has noted, anthropological data clearly indicate that human childbirth is a cultural act in which spontaneous physiological processes operate within a context of customs, the performance of which is considered essential or desirable for a safe outcome. . . . [Birth] is surrounded and shaped by ritual and myth, injunction, prohibitions and taboos. (p. 83)

Our society has tended to encourage fear of childbirth, the expectation of terrible pain and helplessness, and an increasing dependence upon a male-dominated medical system. In earlier times, childbirth took place in a different context: it was the domain of women. Historian Nancy Dye (1980) has noted that

> until the late eighteenth century, birth [in America] was an exclusively female affair, a social rather than a medical event, managed by midwives and attended by friends and relatives. . . . From the late eighteenth century [and] throughout the first decades of the twentieth century, [there] was a long transition between "social childbirth" and medically managed birth. Gradually, male physicians replaced midwives and transformed birth into a medical event. By the 1920's . . . the medical profession [had] consolidated its control of birth management. (p. 98)

Viewing childbirth as a medical event transfers its control from the woman to medical personnel. Childbirth is equated with illness and the baby is "delivered" in a hospital by a doctor. The entire experience encourages dependence, passivity, uninformed reliance on authority, and anxiety. The pregnant woman is virtually powerless; the doctor (usually male) is powerful and in control. The powerlessness and helplessness of the woman is even further aggravated by what happens to her in the hospital. She is undressed, her genital area is shaved ("prepped"), she is given an enema and sedated; later she is typically drugged more heavily, wheeled out, and strapped down. She is probably also patronized, poked, and prodded by nurses and interns, and told to be a "good girl."

Such experiences elicit anxiety and increase the probability of a painful and prolonged labor. Giving birth is not an easy thing to do. It is stressful; it is a physiological, psychological, and emotional challenge. But we know that a woman's discomfort in labor is greatly increased if she is fearful.

> The excessive amounts of adrenaline that fear can place in a woman's bloodstream may counteract the work of hormones like oxytocin that help labor progress. Anxiety may cause the mother's muscles to become tense, converting simple contractions into painful cramps. (Newton & Modahl, 1978, p. 47)

A study by John Kennel in a Guatemalan hospital, for example, found that women who were assisted during labor and delivery by a friendly woman companion (an untrained stranger) were in labor less than half as many hours, had simpler deliveries, and were more affectionate to their babies during the first 45 minutes after birth than a comparable group of women who received traditional childbirth care from medical personnel. The connection between fear and pain was articulated very persuasively by Grantly Dick-Read (1959), the champion of "natural" childbirth. He asserted that the "fear-tension-pain" syndrome worked to counteract the birth process by pitting two sets of muscles against one another. Fear produces tension in the muscles controlling the cervix, acting to close it, while the muscles farther up in the uterus continue to contract, producing even greater pain. To prevent this, argued Dick-Read, a woman should know in detail what takes place inside her body during the birth process, and should practice a series of exercises designed to gain control over relevant muscles; she must learn to breathe deeply and to relax completely; she must rid herself of fear. With such preparation, Dick-Read argued, a modern woman can give birth without drugs and excruciating pain if she is supported in her efforts during labor by sympathetic and calm attendants.

Our culture's dominant view of childbirth as a medical event can have negative consequences not only for the mother, but also for the child. Obstetrical procedures such as the use of forceps, overdependence on anesthetics and other medication, the use of epidural (spinal) blocks, artificial induction of labor, delaying birth until the doctor arrives, and separation of mother and infant right after birth have been found to be potentially harmful to the newborn, to prolong labor, and to increase the probability of damage to the child. For example, an epidural block (anesthetic) can lower the mother's blood pressure, decrease the oxygen supplied to the fetus, and interfere with effective pushing by the mother in the second stage of labor. Babies who have been heavily drugged during their birth (as a consequence of drugs administered to their mothers) have been found to have trouble learning to suck, to begin to gain weight later than unmedicated babies, to have slower heart and circulatory rates, and to have an impaired ability to clear mucus from air passages. Lisa Gould (1979) has summarized this research and noted that "more than 40 studies have shown that the use of perinatal obstetric medication has subsequent adverse effects on infant behavior" (p. 8), with more pronounced effects accompanying higher dosages. In a study of 3500 infants, Yvonne Brackbill and Sarah Broman (in Gould, 1979) found that medication (particularly inhalant anesthetics) had negative effects on the motor abilities of infants up to one year of age. In 1979, an advisory committee of the Food and Drug Administration unanimously agreed that obstetrical drugs produce deleterious, short-term effects on infants, but no consensus was reached on long-term effects. It is ironic that earlier in this century feminist women were leaders in the movement to make "twilight sleep" available to women during childbirth (Leavitt, 1980). They argued that the use of this scopolamine-morphine combination with narcotic and amnesiac properties would make childbirth painless (and therefore safer and easier), and that women should have this option and the right "to control the decision about what kind of labor and delivery they would have" (p. 161).

Efforts to Increase Women's Control

As early advocates for greater control by women of the childbirth process recognized, when a woman's control over her own body increases, her sense of competence and personal power is enhanced, and the pain and anxiety of childbirth are lessened. We have also learned that increasing the mother's active participation in labor and delivery promotes the health of her child. Studies of women who have given birth using more natural procedures have found that both the mothers and their infants have benefited. For example, one study (Hughey, McElin, & Young, 1978) compared 500 Lamaze-method births with an equal number of other births by mothers who were matched for age, number of previously borne children, and educational level, and significantly more positive outcomes were found for the Lamaze-prepared mothers and their babies. Among the Lamaze mothers, as compared with the controls, there were one fourth as many cesarean sections, one fifth as many cases of fetal distress, one third as many cases of postpartum infection, one third as many cases of toxemia, and half as many premature births. The Lamaze program, based on Pavlovian conditioning techniques and brought to us by way of France from Russia, involves massage, and breathing and muscle control; its success depends on blocking out sensations of pain through distraction, and making competing responses to stimuli that ordinarily evoke the perception of pain. This method involves the mother more actively than Dick-Read's relaxa-

tion approach and uses the father or other concerned adult as an assistant (Arms, 1975).

Pressure for increased control by women has led to some significant changes in the current obstetrical approach to childbirth, and to the provision of a considerable number of options, including the use of Lamaze or similar procedures and the widespread availability of childbirth-preparation classes in hospitals and clinics for expectant mothers and fathers. As a result, many women now prepare for a childbirth experience that involves them very actively in the process. One option now available to women in some hospitals is a "birthing chair," which permits a woman to give birth while reclining comfortably in a chair with a strategically located hole in the seat. In older societies, women in labor did not lie down but moved about, changed positions, and stood or squatted during the final stage. The modern birthing chair recognizes the wisdom of the older, more natural posture, which enlists gravity as an aid to both mother and child. Sheila Kitzinger (1979) has cited a study that found that "when the woman was standing, contractions were 100 percent more effective than when she lay down. Mothers in peasant cultures would probably be very surprised to learn that we have just discovered this" (p. 91).

Renewed support for midwifery and home births also aims to increase women's participation in the management of childbirth. In some modern countries, such as Holland and New Zealand, the midwife is a highly trained, specialized, and respected professional, but in the United States, according to Marion Steinmann (1975), there is wide variation in her legal status. Some states permit lay midwives to practice; others permit only nurse-midwives to practice as part of an obstetrics team; in some states all midwifery is prohibited; while in others the laws are confusing and difficult to interpret. Although most of the world's babies are still delivered by midwives, they were effectively forced out of business in the United States by restrictive laws passed in the early part of the present century. But in 1975, 16 schools were offering training programs and there were an estimated 1200 nurse-midwives in the United States.

Over 95 percent of all births in the United States take place in hospitals, but interest in home births has been increasing. Teams of doctors and midwives have provided women (and their families) with this additional option, although the dominant response by traditional medicine has been negative. Home birth advocates suggest that this response is partially motivated by fear of revenue loss. In 1981, a hospital birth

cathy® by Cathy Guisewite

CATHY, Copyright 1986, Universal Press Syndicate. Reprinted with permission. All rights reserved.

cost between $1500 and $3000, while one at home cost less than $900 (Cates, 1981). Opponents of home birth have emphasized the risks and pointed out that many hospitals now provide a more humanistic, family-centered approach to childbirth. According to a report to a congressional committee, "Fathers are now allowed to witness the births of their children at almost all American hospitals" ("Dad Gets His Turn," 1983), and are involved participants in some. Kenneth Ryan (1982), a professor of obstetrics at Harvard Medical School, has argued that hospitals have responded constructively to the criticisms leveled against them for their "dehumanization of childbirth" by making significant changes.

> The number of medicated births is decreasing; anesthesia is used less often; the father and/or a sympathetic attendant is encouraged to be present; siblings are sometimes allowed to attend; and, in general, insistence on any type of "routine" during labor has diminished . . . . The use of forceps in difficult deliveries has declined. (pp. 3f.)

Ryan has emphasized that if medical care or intervention is needed at birth, it is usually needed rapidly, and that about 20 percent of problems occur despite an initial prediction of low risk; "*When* a problem arises, a hospital is best equipped to provide complete care, and promptly" (p. 4). Home birth advocates counter that skilled midwife-physician teams will promptly move a woman to a hospital if problems arise that cannot otherwise be handled. And the personal experiences of women suggest that there is frequently a contradiction between the new rhetoric of enlightened medical practitioners about hu-

manized childbirth in hospitals and the actual procedures followed. This is well illustrated by Cathy Guisewite's cartoon, above.

The Epidemic of Cesarean Births

Just as women have achieved success in our demands to participate more actively in the birthing process and to improve the quality of prebirth education and preparation, American medicine is reasserting its dominant role in childbirth by the increased use of surgical procedures. While we have succeeded in reducing childbirth anxiety and increasing the option of drug-free and instrument-free procedures, paralleling these gains has been an alarming rise in cesarean deliveries.

In the 1970s the national rate of cesarean births tripled from 5.5 percent (up from 4 percent in the 1950s) to 18 percent by the end of the decade. This prompted an investigation by a task force of the National Institutes of Health (reported in Kolata, 1980b), which called the rapid increase in cesarean interventions "a matter of concern." No reduction in infant mortality was found to be associated with cesarean births among normal-sized infants, and the task force concluded that the number of cesareans could be reduced without added risk to babies or their mothers. But since 1980, the rate has continued to rise, and stood at 22.4 percent in 1985 (Wielawski, 1985). Thus, more than one out of every five newborns in the United States is surgically removed from its mother's uterus, a rate that is more than four times higher than it was a generation ago. In some sections of the country and in some hospitals, the rate is even higher. Joan Heilman (1980) reported, for example, that some major medical centers in New York City were performing 25 percent cesarean deliveries, and at one hospital in Rhode Island, 38.3 percent of all births were by cesarean (Wielawski, 1985). Reinforcing the recommendation of the federal task force is a study from Ireland that contradicts the claim that cesareans have helped reduce infant mortality. While the cesarean rate at Dublin's National Maternity Hospital has remained constant and unchanged for the last 15 years, the number of newborn deaths has decreased as sharply as it has in the United States ("Cesareans Don't Cut Mortality," 1983).

What is responsible for this epidemic, as it has been labeled by Gena Corea (1980) and others? From a medical perspective, cesareans are said to be indicated for the following kinds of problems: breech birth; failure to progress in labor (dystocia); baby's head too large for the mother's pelvis; or a decreased oxygen supply to the fetus (Heilman, 1980). It is widely agreed that electronic monitoring, now used routinely to check on the condition of the fetus, is partly responsible for the increase in cesareans, because the information it provides can be misinterpreted or given greater significance than it deserves. A study of nearly 35,000 pregnant women found that fetal monitors (used in about two thirds of all deliveries) were not associated with fewer birth defects or decreased infant mortality, but did motivate doctors to perform twice as many cesarean sections on low-risk mothers (in Emery, 1986). Some doctors are so enthusiastic about cesareans that they believe even more women should have babies that way because they are safe and can be scheduled at the doctor's convenience. According to Gena Corea (1980):

> Physicians refer to C-section deliveries as "from above" and vaginal deliveries as "from below." Dr. Helen Marieskind, author of a report prepared for the Department of Health, Education and Welfare (HEW), relates that while she was conducting interviews for her study on the rising Caesarean rate, obstetricians repeatedly asked her: "What's so great about delivery from below, anyway?" (p. 31)

Some critics believe that financial considerations play a major part in the increased cesarean rate. According to Joan Heilman (1980):

> Obstetricians charge more for surgery—$1,000 to $1,500—which takes much less of their time than the usual delivery, which costs $650 to $1,000; hospitals, at a time of declining births, fill their beds and nurseries for twice as many days (7–8 vs. 3–4); anesthesiologists

and other specialists get their fees if surgery is performed. (p. 88)

Thus, cesareans make more money for medical practitioners. In addition, many doctors contend that more cesareans are performed because obstetricians fear malpractice suits. Obstetricians/gynecologists (along with neurosurgeons and orthopedic surgeons) are most likely to be sued. The blame for surgical intervention is thus said by some to lie with parents who sue doctors for unfavorable outcomes of childbirth. According to one doctor, today's career-minded mothers are particularly at fault(!) because they wish to have just one or two children and therefore put "pressure . . . on the physician to assure a perfect outcome" (reported in Blakeslee, 1985, p. 24E).

Once a woman has had a cesarean, she is very likely to have one again for her next child. The number of women who deliver vaginally after having had a cesarean is very small, and at least a third of abdominal births in this country are a consequence of prior cesareans (Heilman, 1980). Perhaps this will change as a result of the public position taken by the American College of Obstetricians and Surgeons that 50 to 80 percent of women who have undergone surgical birth with a low transverse scar can deliver their next child vaginally (reported in Diamond, 1985).

Peak Experience?

If a woman is actively involved in preparing for childbirth, if she is knowledgeable about the physiological changes involved in pregnancy, and if she knows what to expect during childbirth, she is likely to be less anxious throughout the gestation period and to have less need for medication during labor, thus benefiting her child. This wisdom should be reassuring to those preparing for childbirth. Just as reassuring should be the knowledge that for some women, childbirth is a rapturous, exhilarating, exultant "peak experience" (for example, see Tanzer, 1973; Odent, 1984). But emphasis on natural, relatively painless, and joyful birth sometimes makes women even more anxious about being able to measure up to the new expectations. Will they, like the women they read and hear about, be strong, involved, calm, and capable? Will childbirth be a sensuous experience, as some have said?

Miriam in *Small Changes* (Piercy, 1975) dutifully practiced her breathing and did her exercises; she and her husband prepared for childbirth. In the hospital awaiting the birth of her child, however,

> the labor went on and on. Sometimes she felt exhausted and just wished the whole damn thing would end and forget the idiot panting and counting and carrying on. Contractions, my ass. It was pain and big pain and it hurt like hell. However, she continued. Partly she was ashamed to act as if she couldn't handle it. . . . And she wanted to be awake, she wanted that desperately. . . .
>
> Pain was pain and calling it contractions didn't make it hurt any less. . . . She panted and did her relaxations and did what she had been taught and she was angry. She did not scream, she did not cry out, she did not do any of the things she had been taught were shameful and ignorant. She panted instead of screaming. She counted instead of crying. She . . . went on. On, in the ridiculous little hospital gown designed to rob her of all her dignity. On, among the nurses and residents and doctors . . . processing her with as little nuisance to them as possible. . . . Neil was with her, she held his hand, she held tight to him, but she could feel always his fear that she would not be good enough, . . . that she would back down from the way they had chosen. (pp. 393f.)

Miriam did not want her husband to be disappointed in her; she did not want to be a "Lamaze failure." She thought that perhaps things might have been different for her if she were giving birth as she had seen her friend Sally do, surrounded by women who rubbed her stomach, kissed her, and spoke softly.

Still, despite the pain and fear they may have felt during the process, women who have observed their own children being born have described a breathlessness, an incredulity, and excitement that cannot be duplicated by any other experience. The mundane and the sublime appear in unique combination. This is Miriam's description:

> The head was blooming. . . . Huge coming through her. Ridiculous. A dark wet head emerging from the nest of towels and large sheet. . . . In the mirror a pile of laundry was giving birth. A person was emerging. Then she was laughing, because it looked ridiculous in the mirror. . . . "I did it" she cried out. . . . Gradually, gradually, the baby slipped out of her, oh, beautiful creature thrust into the world glowing and bright. (pp. 394f.)

Parenthood: The Agonies and Joys

My children cause me the most exquisite suffering of which I have any experience. It is the suffering of an ambivalence: the murderous alteration between bitter resentment and raw-edged nerves, and blissful gratitude and tenderness . . . *I love them.* But it's in the enormity and inevitability of this love that the sufferings lie.

Adrienne Rich   *(1977, p. 1f.)*

For me, the experience of motherhood has been passionate, uprooting, harsh, full of sacrifice, a sense of humility and the opportunity to experience the most powerful love I have ever known. Being a mother is one road to a deep regard for all human life.

Jane Lazarre   *(1985, p. 30)*

*L*ittle serious analysis of women's experience as mothers was done until feminist writers and scholars began in the 1960s to explore its content and significance. By and large, motherhood was simply taken for granted by social scientists, while popular images focused on aprons and home-baked cookies or on frazzled nerves and endless chores. In this chapter we will be concerned with what being a parent means for contemporary women and with the behaviors that define that role. These behaviors are related to motives, attitudes, and responses reinforced earlier in childhood and adolescence, and to the typical conditions of motherhood that serve to further socialize women into nurturant, care-giving, family-oriented persons.

In our society as in virtually all others, once a baby is born, we typically assume that its primary care giver will be a woman. First choice for the job is the baby's natural mother, but if she is not available another woman will be sought as a substitute. The fundamental relationship with which life invariably begins is between a newborn child and a woman who will mother it—that is, care for or protect it. This is, indeed, the meaning of the verb *to mother*; in contrast, *to father* is typically used to acknowledge a man's contribution to the conception of a child, not to its care.

A MOTHER'S ROLE

To be a middle-class white mother in contemporary society is typically to be the primary care giver to one's own children in a relatively isolated and relatively small family unit. This is less true for ethnic minorities such as Afro-American, Hispanic, and native American women. For example, cooperative communal exchange networks exist among women (relatives or friends) within some poor urban black communities (Stack, 1974). In many Afro-American families, roles are interchangeable and "aunts, grandmothers, older sisters, cousins and nieces . . . frequently play major roles in the care and raising of younger children" (Joseph, 1981a, p. 82). Some mothers, not part of extended families or friendship networks, form support groups to decrease their isolation, to share resources and strategies, and to provide services to themselves not otherwise available (McCoy, 1980).

Today's mothers include women of diverse lifestyles and circumstances: those who are at home with their children full-time for varying numbers of years, and those who are employed outside the home in jobs at all occupational levels and on widely varying work schedules. In 1982 almost 49 percent of married women with preschool children were employed outside the home, compared with 19 percent in 1960; and 54 percent of unmarried mothers of preschool children were working at paid jobs (Shreve, 1982). Among all women with children under the age of 18, 58.5 percent are in the labor force (Klemesrud, 1983). Women experience motherhood in varied personal, economic, and family circumstances and also at diverse ages. As noted in the previous chapter, many American women are now delaying the birth of their first child until they are in their 30s. These women are generally college-educated and in established careers. A growing number of such women are not waiting for marriage before having a child, and are choosing single parenthood as a preferred life-style or because they have not found a marriage partner. For women 30 to 34 the rate of first births nearly doubled between 1970 and 1981; but women over 30 represent only 10 percent of first-time mothers. The median age for first-time mothers has increased, but not drastically; in 1980 it was 23.1 compared to 21.8 in 1960 (Vrazo, 1984), and in the 1920s and 1930s college-educated women also tended to have their first child at later ages.

Our discussion of mothers, then, includes traditional women who begin having a family in their early 20s and stay at home for many years to care for their children; married women who combine paid employment with family responsibilities in varying ways; single mothers (divorced or never married); and mothers in complicated family situations who may share care of their children with relatives, share custody with ex-husbands, and/or who may be stepparents to the children of a new spouse. We must also recognize that not all mothers are heterosexual. The National Gay Task Force has estimated that 15 to 20 percent of all lesbians are mothers, among whom about two thirds were married when their children were born (in Beck, 1983). With the availability of artificial insemination, more lesbians are choosing to have children while remaining part of a lesbian community. A study by Sally Kweskin and Alicia Cook (1982) found no significant differences between a sample of homosexual and heterosexual single mothers in their self-descriptions, in their descriptions of preferred behaviors for children in general, and for girls and boys separately. Each mother tended to describe her ideal child as having attributes similar to her own, but these were not related to her sexual orientation.

Mothers As Nurturing Goddesses or Martyrs

The role of mother is defined by certain behaviors manifested in relationships with her children and also with others inside and outside of the family. Mothers are people who care; who provide and protect; who teach, explain, and expect; who wait and forgive. Mothers are givers, healers, and workers of miracles. Shalom Asch (in Baum, Hyman, & Michel, 1975) saw his mother's cooking pots as different from all other cooking pots. His mother

> could "milk" her pots as though they were cows. They never denied her anything. She gave them cold water—and the pots yielded yesterday's carrot soup anew; she gave them boiling water—and the pots returned a royal dish. . . . Just one formula of extortion did mother possess for use on her pots—a sigh. When the pots heard mother sigh it was as though she repeated a secret incantation over them with which she adjured them to supply the pitifully meager bit of nourishment which was all she demanded for her large brood. (p. 66)

Like the Great Mother or Great Goddess of antiquity who appears in the mythology of widely separated cultures, mothers are associated with life, peace, tenderness, concern for human welfare, and unconditional love. According to M. Esther Harding (1972), some Great Mother goddesses were moon deities (Moon Mother) and others were earth deities (Earth Mother), but there is great similarity in the ancient myths: the mother goddess represented a generative power. Harding contends that these Great Mother goddesses were always represented as virgin mothers, belonging to no man; it was their relation to their children (to humanity) that defined their primary and special quality. Adrienne Rich (1977) has described the Great Mother as giver of life and transformer of power, able to function as priestess, potter, healer, artist, wise woman, and weaver. No wonder her sighs can turn water into soup! Contemporary mothers, too, are seen as doers of magic and lesseners of hurts—the ultimate alchemists who can transform the ordinary into glitter and gold. For example, in Carolyn Slaughter's *A Perfect Woman* (1985), a daughter describes her mother as "pulling it all together somehow, making a net into which she scooped all the misery and laughter, the anguish and tears, shook it about a bit until it settled again" (p. 89). Mary McLaughlin (1974) has described changes in Western views of the "good mother." During the Middle Ages she was pious and responsible for the spiritual as well as the physical well-being of her children. Later, she came to be seen as tender, gentle, and noble, as well.

But if mothers are magical and akin to saints, they are also liable to suffer like martyrs. One study (Mamay & Simpson, 1981) found that approximately half of a sample of television commercials portrayed women in maternal role situations, and in these situations, motherhood was equated with service. The investigators concluded that

> children appear to exist primarily to be fed and doctored, get their clothes muddy, and dirty up the house. There is little indication of parent-child interaction except in mothers' services to small children. . . . Mothers do not impart moral values to their children; they give them things to consume and expect nothing in return . . . [Children's] mothers keep them healthy and supply their material wants. It is a one-way obligation. (pp. 1230, 1231)

The cartoon on page 197 illustrates this view of a mother's role.

Similar visions of martyred motherhood appear in fictionalized accounts of the lives of women. For example, in *A Perfect Woman*, Carolyn Slaughter describes a perfect mother as experiencing sadness and

> fatigue . . . when her daughters romped all over the house, spilling their enthusiasm in her lap, demanding her attention, her involvement in all of it—and yet, at the same time, making her feel curiously unnecessary,

cathy®

by Cathy Guisewite

CATHY, Copyright 1986 Universal Press Syndicate. Reprinted with permission. All rights reserved.

as if their real interests lay so far from her own, from the home, that she was just a laundry bag into which they hurled each used-up article as they tired of it. (p. 137)

And later, thinking about her children,

> you look up and see a sticky face above a bib, look up again and a schoolgirl stands awkwardly in a purple tunic; you look up yet again and a young woman is walking away—running away, desperate for a life that in no way resembles your own. (p. 165)

The exasperation experienced by a mother whose grown children continue to demand that she serve their needs graciously, has been expressed in Gail Godwin's novel *A Mother and Two Daughters* (1983) as follows:

> When the girls were growing up, Nell remembered, she had felt . . . well, loved, yes, but with the distinct air, on the girls' part, of toleration. Now both daughters were homing in on her with their frenzied passionate demands for her attention. What forms did they expect it to take? Was she to dispense wisdom? Advice? Consolation? Approval? Admiration? Was she to compensate them for not demanding these things from her sooner? (p. 346)

Mothers As Witches and Scapegoats

While our literature provides us with images of mothers who work miracles—who feed, clothe, protect, and adore their children (they are the "real" mothers)—it also shows us the witches, the mean, cruel, unfeeling, ever-demanding, and cold women (the "stepmothers" into whose evil hands children may fall). A mother's power is double-edged; she can give or withhold. We see mothers in supermarkets scowling at their children, pushing, slapping, and

shouting, and we shiver as we recall the evil witches in all the fairy tales of our childhood.

Contemporary mothers have been cartooned as controllers and dominators, as destructive wielders of power and destroyers of our children's psyches, and we respond to this stereotype more typically with guilt than with anger. Lynn Caine, in a book entitled *What Did I Do Wrong?* (1985), has argued that guilt and self-blame are occupational hazards of motherhood, that mothers tend to accept responsibility for anything that happens to their children, and that most mothers have self denouncing tapes playing continuously in their heads. In a society in which mothers are given the primary responsibility for their children's welfare, such feelings are hard to avoid; so much of what happens in the child's life is seen to be the mother's responsibility and under her control. She is accountable daily for providing good food, clean clothes, concern, love, advice, safety, permission, and answers. She is accountable for how her children turn out in the long run, but she is more likely to be blamed for failure than praised for success.

In *Cleaning House*, a novel by Nancy Hayfield (1980), the heroine, a young homemaker, is thinking about newspaper stories of child accidents, and remembers that

> they always make it a point to tell you in those stories what the mother was doing wrong—she just ran to the store for a pack of cigarettes—she just dozed off for a minute—she was talking on the phone when the kid, who was jumping on the bed, flew out of the tenth-story window. (p. 29)

The mother in Judith Rossner's *August* (1983) had received a similar message from her husband, who made it clear in a variety of ways that he considered Lulu responsible for her daughter's defection. This . . . [was the] justice under which mothers are held responsible for everything from life's random negative quality to the genesis of every neurosis developed by those passing through it. (pp. 126f.)

The pressure on women who work outside the home to put their children first is especially strong since it can be said, when things go wrong, "Aha!— look what happens when there's no mother in the home." Patricia Spacks (1975) has reported an incident that occurred when she was invited by a group of students to talk about how women might combine marriage and a family with a career.

I spoke passionately, and, I thought, eloquently about the richness of life committed to various kinds of endeavor. The students remained conspicuously unconvinced. Finally, one girl burst out, with real passion, "But do you ever send your daughter off to school with dirty underwear?" . . . I became very defensive. . . . I said my child never suffered dirty underwear. . . . My credentials as a good woman had been challenged. (p. 110)

A mother who works outside her own home, who pursues career or other interests, is liable to be accused of neglecting her children—an accusation not likely to be leveled against a working father. For example, in a story on the sexual abuse of children, Robert Lindsey (1984) quoted a psychiatrist from U.C.L.A. as follows: "There is no question . . . that the risk of exploitation for a child increases directly as the child is removed further from the care of its biological mother" (p. A21). Thus, despite the fact that no data "support the view that there is more sexual abuse of children now than in previous decades," experts are quick to point the finger of blame at working mothers. There is less disapproval of women who must work to support a family, but if we work because we want to use talents or feel the pleasure of achievement in areas outside the home, then we may be said to be selfish and more concerned with personal growth and development than with the welfare of our children.

But mothers who stay home and devote maximum time and energy to motherhood are not immune from criticism, and have been accused of smothering their children with too much attention, of crippling their initiative and prolonging their dependency. We are said to overfeed, overcontrol, overmotivate, and overwhelm. And so we mothers blame ourselves for not having done enough (or for having done too much), for not having done the right thing (or for having overdone the right thing), for having shouted too much (or too little), for having expected too much (or not enough). Our guilt is amply reinforced by the mass media, fiction, and the mental health profession. Middle-class mothers tend to blame themselves for psychological mistakes, for not having been better, calmer, or wiser, more permissive or less permissive. Working-class mothers blame themselves, in addition, because they could not do enough, provide enough in the way of resources, money, and opportunities, or because they were too tired or overburdened to pay attention to all of their children's needs. In Tillie Olsen's story "I Stand Here Ironing" (1976), a mother thinks back and remembers her relationship with her daughter. She becomes engulfed with all she "did or did not do, with what should have been and what cannot be helped" (p. 9).

Philip Wylie (1942/1955) created the classic caricature of the immature, destructive American mom in his book *A Generation of Vipers* and, later, Philip Roth (1969) gave us the unforgettable Mrs. Portnoy, whose maternal love led her son to the psychiatrist's couch. These were stay-at-home moms whose crippling effects were experienced mainly by their sons. Later, a new "blame the mom" theme appeared. Mothers pursuing careers and modeling competence and success are shown in fiction to be confusing and frightening to their daughters (for example, Brown, 1976; Rossner, 1983). Mothers have been blamed for their children's overstriving *or* underachievement, schizophrenia, school problems, suicide, drug and alcohol problems, and abuse by others. Mother, as Great Goddess, giver of life, seems thus to blend well with Pandora, on whom can be blamed all the hopes that are unfulfilled, the calamities, misfortunes, and problems of her children. Astoundingly, men, like Adam, have managed to retain their purity. Only rarely is some feeble voice heard asking, But where was the father? What was he doing? What part did he play?

The Stresses and Rewards of Motherhood

Mothers experience not only guilt and sorrow over their children's difficulties, but also pride and joy in their affection and accomplishments. A mother is rewarded by the respect of her children, friends, and neighbors. The existence of children validates a working-class woman's importance and respectability; the successful rearing of her children is dramatic testimony to the world that she has done well. She wants above all else, as my mother did, for her children to grow up to be respectable, self-supporting, and happy, and she hopes that her love will be reciprocated and that her children will value her. Middle-class mothers may expect something more, some tangible sign of achievement or success.

Much attention has been paid in the popular literature to mother-daughter conflicts or mother-son frustrations, but evidence also shows that children's empathy for, and appreciation of, their mothers increases as they get older, after they have achieved an independent identity and autonomy. For example, one study of a sample of 171 women aged 35 to 55 (Baruch & Barnett, 1983) supported the conclusion that the daughters' relationships with their mothers provided "emotional gratification" important to the "psychological well being of both" (p. 605). In *Fly Away Home* (1984a), Marge Piercy has described an adult daughter burying her mother's ashes in her garden: "Good-bye, Mama," she said to the rose bed. "In spring I will plant roses that are strong and hardy and fragrant. I remember when you were lovely. I remember when you were happy. . . . Everything I am comes from you" (p. 80).

Some ethnic groups, such as Italian-Americans and Afro-Americans, have ritualized and elaborated respect and idolization for mothers. Gloria Joseph (Joseph & Lewis, 1981) has described "Mother's Day on the Block" in black communities as "bigger than Easter, and more of a religious rite than Christmas" (p. 86), and has told how an escalating series of insults is exchanged by black urban youth when someone's mother is spoken of disparagingly. Joseph has also cautioned that although the black mother is exalted publicly, in private she may be "used, bruised, and abused"; the "ritualization of motherhood as precious . . . has its roots in African tradition and is a part of Black culture," but all is not "love, honor, respect, and appreciation" on the part of one's children (p. 92).

The role of motherhood has its stresses and strains along with its rewards. Still, it is not the fact of motherhood that is stressful, but its definition in contemporary society. A mother, by and large, is still more responsible than a father (in a two-parent family) for the day-to-day care of her children, whether or not she also has a job outside the home or receives child-care assistance from other adults. Motherhood, which most often begins with eager anticipation and determination, may become burdensome in a society that offers women educational and occupational options, and, at the same time, regards them as the primary parent responsible for the psychological and physical welfare of their children (regardless of whatever else they may do). Many full-time mothers, although eager to do the right thing and to excel in their role, may also feel that their lives are not as exciting, not as interesting, not as challenging or as pleasant as they had anticipated. They compare how they spend their days as mothers with how they used to spend them and with how their husbands (and women who are not mothers) spend theirs, and they feel dissatisfied. If they have personal objectives in addition to motherhood, the likelihood of achieving them becomes more remote, and the barriers become more formidable and impermeable, as the months at home with small children turn into years. Women who combine motherhood with a full-time job or career may also become disillusioned with their role as primary parent, and distressed by the definition of that role as one of selfless devotion and service. No wonder a number of recent studies of large national samples have reported greater well-being on the part of women whose children are grown and no longer at home than among mothers of young children (Gerson, Alpert, & Richardson, 1984).

We will further explore the role of mother as primary parent and its consequences in a later section. Now we will consider the mother's experience of the early days and months of parenthood.

EXPERIENCES OF EARLY MOTHERHOOD

In the days and months after childbirth, a woman's body adjusts to the change and, with lactation, provides for the nutritional needs of the infant. But the infant also has other needs, and filling these needs does not come naturally for any mother. She must learn to nurture her infant and to fill the role that society has prescribed for her as a mother. Some of this learning has taken place all along in her socialization, and some of it can only be done in interaction with her baby.

Postpartum Blues?

Many women learn that motherhood is likely to begin with a period of sadness, or a big letdown. Friends, neighbors, magazine articles, and doctors reinforce the expectation that after birth of a baby, the mother can expect to experience a temporary period of depression and confusion. For example, Jane Brody (1983a), in a *New York Times* story, wrote that

for up to two-thirds of new mothers, something unexpected and mystifying happens during the first week after childbirth. For no apparent reason, sadness sets in and the initial elation dissolves in teary confusion that may last for days, weeks or months.

The mother may feel irritable, hypersensitive, fatigued, restless, unable to sleep, depressed or ambivalent toward her baby. She finds herself crying at the drop of a hat. . . . This reaction . . . is so common that it is considered a normal part of the postpartum experience. (p. C6)

As is true for other aspects of women's lives, generalizations about the postpartum experience have been widely circulated and promote the expectation of dysfunction and negative mood without a firm empirical basis. We do know that childbirth is followed by a dramatic decrease in pregnancy's very high levels of estrogen and progesterone. The accompanying body changes, in tissue fluid retention, in chemical balance, metabolism, and so on, are real and, like the hormonal changes that occur during pregnancy and the menstrual cycle, these dramatic internal events must be interpreted by the person experiencing them. To be told, in advance, that many women feel blue and let down after the birth of a baby, provides us with a cognitive framework that explains, labels, and identifies our feelings, but, as with the so-called menstrual blues, no necessary connection exists between a decrease in progesterone and estrogen and feelings of depression. A review of the literature on postpartum depression (Hopkins, Marcus, & Campbell, 1984) concluded that "evidence of a direct link between hormone levels and depressed mood is lacking" (p. 506). A great deal of ambiguity exists regarding the etiology and symptoms of postpartum disturbances, as well as their frequency.

In addition to experiencing hormonal changes following childbirth (the puerperium period), many women are physically tired from the strain of labor, from inadequate hours of rest or sleep, and from focusing attention on the needs of their newborn babies. Few researchers have attended to the influence of such factors on mood. As Ann Oakley (1979) has pointed out, "What is left out of the reckoning are the social correlates of postnatal depression" (p. 616). One group of researchers (Treadway, Kane, Jarrahi-Zadeh, & Lipton, 1975) compared a sample of postpartum women (with normal deliveries) with a nonpregnant matched control group on a number of tests taken in the hospital and also six weeks earlier. Postpartum women scored higher than the control women on measures of depression and total neuroticism, and they showed an increase in time required to complete a cognitive test, but no

significant correlations were found between psychological and biochemical variables. While all postpartum women showed reductions of norepinephrine, only some were depressed while others were not. Such data are important because they indicate that factors other than normal biochemical changes following childbirth are responsible for the blues experienced by some women during this period.

As with the "menstrual blues," many women do not experience a period of sadness or general disequilibrium after childbirth. The responses mothers make to the variety of increased stresses they must cope with after the birth of a child—new stimuli (both internal and external), hormonal and metabolic changes, fatigue, new responsibilities, and changes in tasks and daily routines—vary across groups and individuals (just as is true of the responses made to pregnancy and childbirth). Women who are least anxious, who are most eager for a child, who are knowledgeable about their body changes, who are most prepared for the changes that will take place in their lives, who feel generally good about themselves and their situations, and who receive encouragement and support from family members, significant persons, and community resources are least likely to feel depressed after their child is born and most likely to continue feeling positive excitement and pleasure.

Breast-Feeding

Lactation begins during the second or third day after the birth of a child; the mammary glands swell and manufacture a milky substance filled with nutrients and antibodies. If she chooses not to breast-feed her baby, the mother must bind her breasts tightly, be given hormones to suppress the lactation, and may be uncomfortable for several days. The number of mothers who breast-feed their babies in the United States for any period of time dropped from about 90 percent early in the century to a low of 25 to 30 percent in the late 1960s, but then rose again. Among women who gave birth in 1980, for example, according to a study by the Center for Disease Control (in "Breastfeeding," 1985), 58 percent breast-fed, and this practice was twice as common among college-educated women as among women with less than nine years of schooling. Among those who breast-feed, 85 percent stop nursing by the time the baby is 10 to 12 months old (Myers & Siegel, 1985).

Women may choose to bottle-feed their babies because of the easy availability of store-bought supplies and milk products and because someone else other than the mother can then feed the child, an important consideration for working women or those with obligations to a large family. Some women associate nursing with poverty; others find it embarrassing; others want their breasts to return as soon as possible to their prepregnant size and shape. Women who decide to nurse also do so for a variety of reasons. They may be eager to provide their infants with milk that is nutritionally better, safer, and easier to digest than store-bought formulas. Nursing women find the experience pleasurable and believe it provides a unique closeness and relaxed communication with their child; some like the ease (no fuss, no bottles to sterilize); and some feel a sense of pride in the fact that their bodies can provide nourishment and natural immunities for their infant. Breast-feeding also has immediate physical benefits for the mother; it releases hormones that trigger uterine contractions that reduce the size of the uterus and speed the process of its descent from the abdomen back into the pelvic area.

Some researchers have found that mothers who breast-feed do not differ from those who bottle-feed in age, education, religion, or other social variables (Berg-Cross, Berg-Cross, & McGeehan, 1979), but are distinguishable on the basis of attitudes and beliefs. One study (Manstead, Proffitt, & Smart, 1983), for example, found that breast-feeding mothers differ significantly from bottle-feeding mothers in having stronger beliefs about the advantages of nursing; weaker beliefs that bottle-feeding allows the father greater participation and allows more careful monitoring of the baby's intake; and were less likely to feel that breast-feeding was embarrassing. Most predictive of whether a mother chose to breast-feed was whether she had done so with previous children.

Groups like La Leche League extol the pleasures and benefits of breast-feeding; and some have described nursing as a "sensuous experience" (for example, Newton, 1973). The pleasure that nursing mothers derive from the experience (whether from feelings of intimacy, power, giving, and/or sensuality) is conditioned to the infant, who is always present. As a mother continues to breast-feed, the strength of her motivation to do so increases. This conclusion has been suggested by a study reported by Harriet Myers and Paul Siegel (1985) of a sample of women who had breast-fed more than one infant. Almost all recalled positive feelings during the nursing experience and distress when their usual breast-feeding schedule was disrupted.

For some women nursing is not successful, or is painful or frustrating. A working woman who must be away from her infant for a considerable period of time each day may find it impossible to nurse comfortably, and those who can arrange to have their child brought to them may find their employers adamantly opposed. Thus, although nursing an infant can be a healthy and extraordinary experience, it is not always possible or desirable in the special circumstances of a particular woman's life. No woman who chooses to bottle-feed should feel as though she has failed some test of motherhood. As with most other behaviors, the naturalness, frequency, or duration of nursing is influenced by an array of environmental factors. In some communities choosing to breast-feed requires strong-willed commitment, and a nursing mother may meet with grudging cooperation from hospital staffs, surprise from neighbors and relatives, and frustration when trying to find a quiet spot for nursing her infant outside her home. Nutritionists and pediatricians are now recommending breast-feeding for its benefits to the infant during the first months or year of life, but few institutional supports exist for the woman who chooses it.

Learning to Nurture

The process of bonding with and nurturing one's infant begins in pregnancy but requires, more importantly, behaviors that are learned in interaction with the child. Ann Murray (1979) concluded from a review of the literature that infant cries are not "invariably effective in eliciting care-giving behavior" (p. 211) on the part of women (or men), but that care-giving responses depend upon sensitization and exposure to young children. Mothers learn to nurture. They are exposed to the stimuli of a helpless infant whose survival and development depend upon attention and care. Mothers are rewarded unambiguously, amply, and immediately by an infant when its cries cease, when it snuggles or sucks, when it smiles, coos, and babbles, when it laughs, talks, peacefully rests, and so on. A mother soon learns that these positive responses from her infant are contingent upon her behavior: on changing a diaper; providing a bottle; giving a hug, a caress, or a cookie; giving a bath; soothing, calming; and so on. Thus, a mother's nurturant behavior is powerfully reinforced, strengthened, and maintained by (a) her child's reactions of pleasure and gratitude; (b) the success of her behavior in effecting a desired change in the child's responses or circumstances; (c) the consequent feeling of competence she experiences;

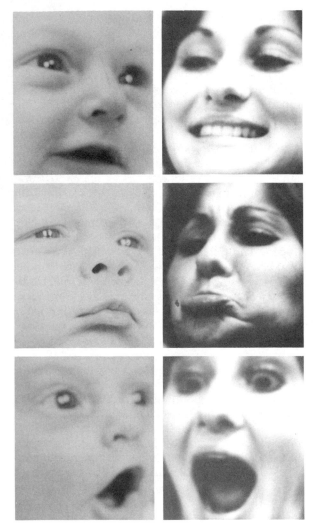

and (d) her feelings of pride and self-satisfaction for having done the right thing and having done it well.

That mother-infant attachment is not automatic but grows out of interaction has been shown by a number of studies. For example, one group of investigators (Seashore, Leifer, Barnett, & Leiderman, 1973) found that mothers who did not have early contact and care-giving experience with their firstborn premature infants had lower self-confidence and manifested less skill in handling their infants than other mothers one week after they left the hospital. Other research has shown that infants play an active role in getting their needs satisfied, by reinforcing responses that most satisfy them. Of particular significance are studies that have demonstrated the very early and

well-developed capacities of infants to identify and respond to their caretakers. For example, one study (DeCasper & Fifer, 1980) found that infants who had had no more than 12 hours of postnatal contact with their mothers were able to discriminate between the voices of their mothers and other speakers and to respond to their mothers' voices with increased sucking behavior. Another extraordinary demonstration of the capacity of neonates to discriminate and to thus provide positive reinforcement for their care givers was reported for a sample of 74 neonates whose average age was 36 hours (Field, Woodson, Greenberg, & Cohen, 1982). An adult woman modeled three facial expressions (happy, sad, and surprised) in a series of trials. Not only did the fixation responses of the neonates indicate discrimination of the different faces, but their facial movements provided evidence for imitation, such that an observer guessed at greater-than-chance accuracy what the model's expression was by observing the face of the neonate. The photographs on this page show a sample of the model's expressions and corresponding expressions of an infant.

It is likely that the relationship between nurturant behavior and certain experiences is a complex one: that women are prepared for mothering in childhood; that interaction with an infant reinforces earlier learned responses and strengthens new behavior; and that mothers develop a special perspective as a result of their experience as the nurturers of children. Sara Ruddick (1983) has elaborated the thesis that it is through maternal work—that is, caring for others—that mothers develop a distinctive perspective. This perspective is characterized by concern for others, cooperative solutions to problems, healing rather than harm-doing; it provides "a basis for pacifist commitment" (p. 6). This thesis seems to be supported by a study of over 100 women who were first surveyed as college seniors and then in their early 40s (Helson, Mitchell, & Moane, 1984). Those who had become mothers showed a significant change in certain personality attributes, including an increase in responsibility, self-control, and tolerance. Sara Ruddick, as well as other feminist writers, has noted that anyone who does maternal work can "learn its lessons," and that this work can be done by men as well as by women. On the other hand, Nancy Chodorow (1978) has suggested that caring, concern, and connectedness are attributes of women before their experience as mothers and, in fact, contribute to their desire to bear and rear children. It is because little girls learn to be affiliative and nurturant, she argues, that they are both motivated for motherhood and prepared to do its work.

We will return to Chodorow's thesis shortly. In the meantime, let us consider the following question: if nurturing behavior is learned, either earlier or later, should it be the province of only one gender, or can it be shared by both?

THE MOTHER AS PRIMARY PARENT

Although children of employed mothers are looked after for many hours each week by relatives, neighbors, fathers, and child-care workers, our society continues to regard the mother as the primary parent, and child care as her responsibility. It is she who must provide care herself or find someone else who will do it for her. Recognition of men's potential for parenting, and men's responsibilities for child care, is increasing slowly but is not yet a dominant theme in our culture. Motherhood continues to encompass the bulk of parental responsibility, especially for very young children, and fatherhood to represent general support and assistance. We see this reflected in the lives of most women, in the working class and in the middle class, among black women and white women, among women who are not employed outside the home and among those who are, among the undereducated and the highly educated, among those with unknown talents and those with known skills. Not all contemporary women who have borne children accept the role of primary child rearer, but those who do not must often apologize for their choice and experience guilt and frustration. Child care is considered a "woman's issue," a woman's problem.

Lucia Gilbert (1985), who studied dual-career families for 10 years, found that 40 percent of the fathers contribute virtually nothing to the care and maintenance of the family beyond their financial resources; the mother "does it all" and functions as a Superwoman. Another 30 percent are "participant fathers" who help with the parenting and are involved with their children but won't do any of the housework. A final 30 percent, labeled Supermen by Gilbert, are "intimately involved in parenting and share, equally with their wives, family responsibilities in and outside of the home." Such fathers, like Superwomen mothers, are, according to Gilbert, often torn between their responsibilities at home and at work, but it seems important to remember that these parent categories are far from equivalent. While the Supermom is a mother who "does it all," the Superpop is a father who *shares* parental and home chores with his wife. Is this imbalance in parenting both expected and inevitable? What are its roots and ramifications?

Child-Rearing Expectations for Women

Ann Geise (1979) examined 160 articles from the *Ladies Home Journal* and *Redbook* in two time periods, 1955–1965 and 1966–1976. She concluded that during both periods and in both magazines, the role models that were presented "quite explicitly gave family matters priority over careers. Single career girls anticipated making real sacrifices in their work upon their anticipated marriage and motherhood. Working mothers often arranged their working hours around family life" (pp. 59f.). Interviews with a group of Harvard/Radcliffe students (Klein, 1977) revealed that while both men and women talked about having careers and families, "no woman said she would put career before her family. . . . In contrast, a few men admitted that their careers would probably always come first" (p. 12). In a study of women who had graduated from a women's college in 1958 and 1960, Ravenna Helson (1986) found that during the time when they were between 27 and 37 years old, these women gave being a mother precedence over their roles as marriage partners and employed workers, as indicated by their reported percentages of high involvement in these facets of their lives. Shirley Feldman and Sharon Nash (1984) studied the impact of a firstborn child on a sample of educated, middle-class parents. They found that parenthood brought more social changes, both positive and negative, into the lives of mothers than of fathers; "women arrange their lives around the baby significantly more than they anticipated . . . while men's anticipation corresponds closely with their actual experience" (p. 72).

I first became a mother less than three decades ago. I was as highly educated as my husband, with more job experience and professional background, but it was I who went to part-time work while his career was put on a firm, full-time basis. We both believed that one of us would be much better at rearing our children and would enjoy it more than a paid baby-sitter, but we never seriously questioned that that one had to be me. When my husband stayed home one half-day each week to care for his first child all by himself, his colleagues were astounded and we considered ourselves to be radical; now our naiveté seems unbelievable. But the association between women and children is an ancient and powerful one. It persists despite our growing knowledge that men are physically, intellectually, and emotionally as capable as women of learning to care for children.

Betty Yorburg and Ibtihaj Arafat (1975) collected self-administered questionnaires from a large sample of adults in offices, campuses, and shopping centers. The surveys dealt with beliefs about men's and women's responsibilities for such tasks as housekeeping and the care of infants and children. The authors reported that 31 percent of the men and 21 percent of the women said they believed that "wife only" should take care of infants. The larger percentage who said "both" cannot be assumed to have meant both equally, however, since in response to the question, "Do you advocate the dual role of today's woman in the home and in the economy?" only 44 percent of the men and 54.8 percent of the women agreed that a woman should be both employed and a homemaker if she had children under six years of age.

More explicit information about child-rearing expectations has come from a study by Jonathan Kellerman and Ernest Katz (1978), who asked a group of parents to specify for each of 89 child-rearing tasks the percent of maternal and paternal responsibility, out of a total of 100 percent. Of 20 tasks dealing with physical caretaking, 19 were judged to be primarily the mother's responsibility, none primarily the father's responsibility, and 1 a shared responsibility. Of 31 educational guidance tasks, 11 were given to women, 3 to men, and 17 to both parents. Of 14 emotional support tasks, 9 were mother's responsibility, none were father's, and 5 were both. With respect to discipline and administrative responsibilities, of 12 tasks, 5 went to mothers, none to fathers, and 7 to both. When we look at activity and recreation we see a reversal, with primary responsibility given to fathers in 5 out of 11 areas, to mothers in 3 areas, and 3 shared. (You may recall that in children's books, too, fathers are typically shown to be "where the fun is!") In total, 53 percent of all the child-rearing responsibilities were seen as primarily the mother's, 38 percent were seen as shared with the father, and only 9 percent were seen as primarily the father's. Of special interest is the fact that when tasks were categorized into groups relating to age of the child (infant, preadolescent, and adolescent), it was found that the younger the child, the greater the attribution of primary maternal responsibility. While all of the infant tasks were seen as the primary responsibility of mothers, as were most of the 27 preadolescent tasks, none of the 5 adolescent tasks was seen as mother's responsibility alone.

The assumption that a mother's attention is vital to the health and full development of a young child is reflected in the concepts of social scientists who have labeled situations in which a maternal figure is missing from a child's environment as "maternal deprivation," but have used the term "father absence" to refer to situations in which a paternal figure is missing. The difference in meaning between these descriptive phrases is not accidental and has important implications for the behavior expected of a child's two parents.

Is Mother's Primacy Essential?

Except for breast-feeding, the care and nurturance of a human being at infancy is not dependent upon the sex of the care giver. Parenting behavior ("mothering"), bonding, or attachment depends instead upon certain features of the environment and upon previously acquired attitudes and behaviors. Important factors are (a) the physical presence of an infant; (b) the expectation that one will be caring for a child; (c) previously acquired nurturant responses; (d) opportunities for practice and reward; and (e) the quality of one's own remembered childhood—that is, the behavior of one's own parents. We have evidence of this from other cultures and other times as well as from contemporary research.

Children in different cultures and in different historical periods have been cared for in a variety of ways by a variety of different persons: looked after by siblings, grandparents, neighbors, kinfolk, nannies, or nursemaids. Extreme role specialization for mothers, with child care as a mother's major task, was the exception and not the rule in older, traditional societies (Greenfield, 1981). As Diana Baumrind (1980) has noted, "There is no evidence of a biological or psychological need for an exclusive primary bond, and certainly not a bond to a particular person" (p. 645). Children can develop important relationships with several people, and neither the gender of the person nor the biological tie with the child is an important variable. Full-time mothering by a woman who stays home just for that purpose is, in fact, a relatively recent phenomenon, which coincided with the development of a socioeconomic middle-class in nineteenth-century industrialized urban societies.

A small number of cultures are known in which

both father and mother participate in all aspects of child rearing. Among the Arapesh of New Guinea, for example, according to Margaret Mead (1935/1950), this shared responsibility began at conception and continued during pregnancy, when the father's presence and adherence to certain rituals was considered vital to the feeding and shaping of the child in its mother's womb. After the child was born, both mother and father fasted together for the first day and performed rites to "ensure the child's welfare and their ability to care for it." Despite the physical ties between the mother and child in pregnancy and breast-feeding, both mother and father were said to have borne the new child and to be equally responsible for it; thus, the care of children was said by the Arapesh to be the work of both parents. Reported Mead:

> Fathers show as little embarrassment as mothers in disposing of the very young child's excreta, and as much patience as their wives in persuading a young child to eat soup. . . . The minute day-to-day care of little children with its routine, its exasperations . . . these are as congenial to the Arapesh men as they are to the Arapesh women. (p. 38)

Some early studies of institutionalized children related their developmental deficiencies to lack of a mother's care. But we now recognize that these children had been deprived not only of a mother's attention but of good care in general, and, most importantly, of cognitive, sensory, and physical stimulation. Michael Rutter (1972) concluded, after reviewing the relevant literature, that the "deleterious influences" observed in institutionalized children were not due to their having been deprived of attachment to a mother, not due to "any form of 'loss'," but to inadequate care. The argument that a young child's bond with its mother (or mother-surrogate) is different from, and superior to, bonds that develop with other care givers has not been supported by the evidence; and researchers have begun to question the usefulness of the term "maternal deprivation."

> Most children develop bonds with several people and it appears likely that these bonds are basically similar . . . in most families the mother has most to do with the young child and as a consequence she is usually the person with whom the strongest bond is formed. But . . . the chief bond need not be with the chief caretaker and it need not be with a female. (Rutter, 1972, p. 125)

Claire Etaugh (1980) has also concluded from a review of research on the effects of nonmaternal care

that such care, if of good quality, does not adversely affect the "child's maternal attachment, intellectual development, or social-emotional behavior" (p. 309). What is important is the kind of care provided, not the care giver's gender or relationship to the child. Not all child care provided outside the home is good, but the same is true of child care within homes and by mothers. Good quality care in community centers does not harm children and, in some cases, is associated with accelerated cognitive and social development. In a study of a group of children who were cared for in day care centers for 8 hours a day, 5 days a week, from age 3 1/2 months to 30 months, Jerome Kagan and his colleagues found that "day-care children do not seem to turn out much different, emotionally or socially, from their counterparts who are raised at home" (Bush, 1976, p. 36).

Phyllis Berman (1980) reviewed research comparing the responsiveness of women and men to infants, young children, baby animals, pictures of children, and recorded baby cries. She found no consistent evidence from studies using physiological or behavioral measures to support the hypothesis that women are more responsive than men to infants or children. Only studies in which adults provided self-reports of their own responses supported a differential responsiveness hypothesis, and Berman concluded that "social factors are, to a large extent, responsible for gender inequalities in infant caretaking" (p. 692). A careful review of relevant research by Martha McClintock (1979) led her to the following conclusion:

> There is a large body of data from primates and humans which demonstrate the wide variety of environmental stimuli which can affect the development of parental behavior in females, let alone males: social contact in childhood, rehearsal during play, adolescent experiences . . . , and practice during the infant care process itself. (pp. 708f.)

Because it has been assumed for so long that women and infants will naturally display bonding or attachment toward each other, men have seldom been placed in situations where their interactions with babies could be observed over a sustained period of time. But evidence is accumulating in support of the proposition that attachment to an infant is a function of its presence and interaction with an adult, regardless of gender. For example, 3-month-old infants were conditioned to increase their vocalizations in response to a tape-recorded human voice (Banikiotes, Montgomery, & Banikiotes, 1972), and the conditioning was found to be just as rapid and effective to a man's voice as to a woman's voice. We have every reason to believe that a newborn infant would learn to respond to the voice and face of its father, as well as its mother, if the father were present and interacting with his child during the early days of its life.

In summary, then, only one of the behaviors that define the mother role or motherhood is dependent upon biological sex or femaleness. That is lactation and breast-feeding, which is, of course, optional for today's mother. All other behaviors are ones all human adults have the capacity to manifest but only some acquire because only some of us are provided with the appropriate conditions in which nurturant responses are evoked and rewarded. (In Marge Piercy's utopian novel about a nonsexist future society, *Women on the Edge of Time* [1976a], each child has three parents of mixed gender, and males can also nurse if they choose to undergo special hormonal treatment, making all aspects of child rearing available to both women and men.)

How Is Mother's Primacy Perpetuated?

If the role of mother as primary parent is not essential, how can we explain the persistence of this arrangement? In a society in which women are the primary care givers to children, girls must be socialized to want to do the work associated with motherhood and to do the job well. Thus, girls must learn attitudes and motives congenial to the role and antagonistic to other roles. Nancy Chodorow (1978) has argued that society does, in fact, reproduce motherhood by "inducing [appropriate] psychological processes" in girls. Considerable evidence supports this proposition. For example, among a group of college students who read stories about parent-child interactions, the women differed significantly from the men in reacting with greater empathy and understanding to the children's failures and problems (McBride & Black, 1984). The researchers concluded that "even before a woman has been through the biosocial experiences of pregnancy, labor, delivery, and lactation . . . socialization into gender roles by late adolescence has already paved the way for different approaches to parenting" (p. 244).

According to Chodorow (1978), maternal "capacities and needs are built into and grow out of the mother-daughter relationship itself" (p. 10), which encourages attachment and connectedness. Chodorow and Carol Gilligan (1982) have argued that the preparation of girls for maternal work is a conse-

quence of their early experience with their mothers, which they propose is very different from the experience of little boys. Chodorow has suggested that it is the tendency of mothers to connect more with daughters and separate more from sons in the early years of life that produces "a division of psychological capacities" in daughters and sons, so that girls will be "prepared psychologically for mothering"; "the relational basis for mothering is thus extended in women, and inhibited in men, who experience themselves as more separate and distinct from others" (p. 207). In this view, the familial divisions of labor are reproduced because girls, but not boys, acquire appropriate attributes for motherhood primarily as a result of the relationship their mothers have with them.

Critics of Chodorow agree that cultures prepare girls for motherhood, but argue that this training extends across the life span, is not limited to the early years, and is not primarily a function of the mother's behavior. For example, Jane Attanucci (1982) has reported that mothers experience both connectedness to and separation from both their sons and their daughters. She interviewed a heterogeneous sample of mothers of infants and found variation in the extent to which the respondents described themselves as connected or separate, and that the mothers "did not describe themselves predominantly in connected terms" (p. 31). Mothers' self-definitions were found to reflect more separation as they grew older, were married longer, and had more children. Further, the preparation of girls for motherhood varies with historical period and situation. Judith Lorber (1981), for example, has noted that social structures are the crucial explanatory variables, not personality or intrapsychic needs. Contemporary women continue to be the primary parents of their children because "intensive mothering is the choice most likely to maximize their social rewards" (p. 484).

Whether women do intensive mothering because they have been psychologically prepared since infancy or because this choice is most socially acceptable and reinforcing, maternal behaviors by girls and women become strengthened through practice, while boys and men are deprived of the opportunity to acquire them. The differential responsibilities of women and men for the care of children results in the heightening of empathy, sensitivity, and interpersonal concerns in the former, and the strengthening of assertiveness, public achievement, and risk-taking behaviors in the latter. Thus, asymmetrical parenting perpetuates differential strengths as well as "gender-related insufficiencies" (Baumrind, 1980) in both women and men.

Consequences of Asymmetrical Parenting

Some feminists believe that asymmetrical parenting is the single most important obstacle to gender equality and is closely tied to inequalities in all other spheres of social and personal life. Women and men are not likely to achieve equality of opportunity as long as the care of children is assumed to be the natural or normal responsibility primarily of mothers (or other women who substitute for them). The demands of child rearing, especially during the early years, unless they are shared, are too great to permit the primary care giver the full pursuit and development of other interests, skills, or abilities. As long as our society mandates that the person who has primary responsibility for raising the children must be a woman, the differential social status of men and women will be maintained. The primary parent (mother) will find it hard to advance in occupational status during her years of intense preoccupation with the care of her children.

Adrienne Rich (1977) has made an important theoretical distinction between motherhood as a *relationship* between a woman and a child, and motherhood as an *institution* that has been used to imprison women—to "ghettoize," degrade, and restrict. This analysis can be extended by noting that while motherhood as an institution has imprisoned women, it has also forbidden entry to men. While it has tended to incapacitate women in the pursuit of public achievement, it has incapacitated men in the expression of positive feelings and sensitivity. If a society wishes to avoid such consequences, the care and responsibility of its children must not be restricted to adults of one gender.

Child-care asymmetry also has important consequences for children's relationships with their parents. A child learns to associate its primary care giver with both gratification and pain, pleasure and frustration, and the mother thus becomes an ambivalent stimulus who can evoke both love or affection and anxiety or fear. Dorothy Dinnerstein (1977) has argued that the fact that children's earliest experiences are almost always with a woman has far-reaching and significant consequences for the personality development of both men and women, and for their relationships with one another. The earliest care giver (the mother), Dinnerstein suggests, is first experienced as an "It"—ambiguous, amor-

phous, with indistinct boundaries, and without clear identity—and will always retain some quasi-human quality. In addition, if an infant's first experience of dependence, frustration, pain, fear, and powerlessness, as well as pleasure through need satisfaction and physical and social stimulation, is in association with a woman, women become highly charged with ambivalence, evoking both positive and negative emotions. According to Dinnerstein, these conflicting attitudes toward the mother are handled or resolved differently by boys and girls as they grow up and as the father enters more and more into their lives. Sons seek to separate themselves from the hateful (yet desirable) mother and all the qualities she represents, while daughters generalize the ambivalent feelings to themselves. Dinnerstein suggests that this psychological separation of men from women—a major symptom of what she calls the human malaise—can be prevented only if parenthood is a shared enterprise from the very beginning.

> When men start participating as deeply as women in the initiation of infants into the human estate, when both male and female parents come to carry for all of us the special meanings of early childhood, the trouble we have reconciling these meanings with person-ness will finally be faced. (p. 94)

POVERTY AMONG FAMILIES HEADED BY WOMEN

One consequence of the role of mothers as primary parents that we have not mentioned yet is that when children are born to unmarried parents or when families dissolve, the mother is almost always the one who retains custody of the children. And she may do so under financial circumstances that severely hinder her ability to nurture her children. In 1984, women headed 23 percent of all families in the United States, and half of all poor families. The average income of families headed by women was $13,257, which is less than 40 percent of the $34,379 average income for two-parent families ("Families with Children," 1985). Two out of three poor adults are women, and one out of five children is poor (Stallard, Ehrenreich, & Sklar, 1983). In 1985, 15.2 percent of all four-person families (33 million people) were officially designated as below the poverty line, with median incomes less than $10,609 ("33 Million," 1985); half of these families were headed by women. Single mothers and their children are the fastest growing segment of poor in this country, and the "feminization of poverty" has become one of the catchiest new

TABLE 11.1   Median income of U.S. families (in 1984 dollars) (From K. B. Noble, "Plight of Black Family Is Studied Anew," *New York Times,* Jan 29, 1984)

	1975	1980
All families		
Black	$8,779	$12,674
White	$14,268	$21,904
Black/white ratio	62%	58%
Husband-wife families		
Black	$11,526	$18,593
White	$15,125	$23,501
Black/white ratio	76%	79%
Families headed by women		
Black	$4,898	$7,425
White	$7,651	$11,908
Black/white ratio	64%	62%

Source: Bureau of the Census

phrases in the social science lexicon.* According to Ann Withorn (1986), women's poverty has become the media's "trendy 'issue of the day'" as indicated by its featured treatment as a cover story in both *Newsweek* and *Time.*

In 1984, 59.2 percent of black families and 20.1 percent of white families with children present were single-parent families, compared with 35.7 percent and 10.1 percent, respectively, in 1970 ("Single Parents," 1985). More than 90 percent of single-parent families are maintained by women. In Table 11.1 the median earnings of these families in 1980 are compared with the earnings of husband-wife families. The shocking disparity between families headed by women and other families, and between black and white families, is clear. The median income of families headed by Hispanic women in 1980, not shown in Table 11.1, was the lowest of all, $7,031, while the median income of all families was $21,023 (Stallard, Ehrenreich, & Sklar, 1983). The National Advisory Council on Economic Opportunity (1981) reported that in 1978, while 9.1 percent of all families were poor, 31.4 percent of all families headed by women were poor, compared with only 5.3 percent of all families headed by men. Women's poverty, the Council argued, stems from two major causes: the fact that women bear the primary responsibility for rearing children; and the fact that women's occupations are limited primarily to low-paying jobs with little or no upward mobility.

*Millions of men in the United States are also poor. The intent here is not to minimize the problems of unemployed and underemployed men, but to focus on the particular impact of poverty on the lives of mothers caring for children without spouses.

In the mid-1980s, 56.2 percent of families headed by black women were designated as poor (compared to one third of all Afro-American families), and 28 percent of families headed by white women were poor (compared to 12.2 percent of all white families) (Malreaux, 1985). Most mothers living in poverty have been married, and are separated, divorced, or widowed; less than a third have never been married. Among white women, divorce and separation account for the recent increases in single-parent families; among black women, it is unwed motherhood (Cordes, 1984). In 1982, 56.7 percent of all black births and 12.1 percent of white births were to unmarried women (Pear, 1985). Approximately one half of never-married white and black mothers, and one third of never-married Hispanic mothers are in the labor force.

Reductions during the 1980s in federal spending for human services have directly affected women and worsened conditions for the poor. These reductions have been in funding for food stamps, legal aid, energy supplements, Medicaid, nutritional supplements for mothers and infants, and Aid to Families with Dependent Children (AFDC). AFDC welfare benefits vary widely from state to state, from $96 a month in Mississippi for a family of three with no other income to $614 a month in Alaska, as of March 1983 (*Beyond the Myths*, 1983). What budget cuts have meant to AFDC families was studied by Rosemary Sarri (reported in "AFDC Cuts Hurt," 1984), who interviewed more than 300 women in Michigan 12 to 18 months after their welfare benefits were completely cut off. Since AFDC automatically confers eligibility for Medicaid, these women also lost their health insurance when welfare benefits ended. Sarri found that the women who suffered the most devastating effects were "working mothers whose own earnings are too low to provide basic necessities for their children and themselves"—women working in "low-paying jobs as typists, cashiers, office and hotel cleaners, waitresses, and nurses' aides" (p. 3). After their AFDC benefits were cut off, nearly half of this sample of women had run out of food. Moreover:

89 percent said they had run out of money; 42 percent were behind in their bills by two months or more; 16 percent had experienced utilities shutoffs; 11 percent did not have telephone service.

How are they surviving? Nearly half of the families were able to obtain old produce from grocery stores and over two-thirds sought used clothing for themselves and their children. About one-third traded services or pooled resources with neighbors and one-fifth said they earned extra money by collecting bottles and cans for refunds. (p. 3)

What a middle-class mother may take for granted is a source of stress and uncertainty for a mother in poverty. For example, no more than 20 percent of pregnant women in this country get prenatal care—1 out of every 18 births ("Report Shows," 1986).

Poignant and detailed descriptions of the daily lives of poor mothers in this country have appeared in documentary and fictional accounts including Carol Stack's *All Our Kin* (1974), Susan Sheehan's *A Welfare Mother* (1975), Robert and Jane Coles' *Women of Crisis* (1978), and Carolyn Chute's *The Beans of Egypt, Maine* (1985). Such descriptions give life to the statistics supplied by economists and help us to understand what life is like for mothers living in poverty. If you are poor, you experience crowding. Whether in an urban ghetto or a rural shack, you have little chance for privacy, of maintaining a separate space. You live in substandard, deteriorating housing, surrounded by peeling paint, decay, rodents, insects, crumbling walls, the odor of garbage and urine, leaking pipes, inadequate water, inadequate heat, and poor lighting. Your home is dreary and not the sparkling clean house beautiful seen on TV. You eat a poor-quality diet of low nutritional value that affects your health and decreases your energy level. You are likely to be overweight and dressed in clothes that do not match the glowing, slender, well-groomed image of women in the media. You are constantly searching for bargains and haunting the flea markets and thrift stores, not out of chic but necessity. You have inadequate access to private and public resources—to police protection, political power, education, and to networks leading to jobs. You provide a body "on which physicians train, research and practice" in hospital clinics for the poor, in which they test out their newest chemical, procedural, and medical technologies (Hurst & Zambrana, 1980). You shop in smaller stores to which you can walk, and that give you credit, but sell you older and damaged food at higher prices. You make frequent moves due to fires, raised rent, eviction, or a constant search for something better, cheaper, cleaner, safer. Or your housing is condemned as unsafe and torn down for renewal, and profit by those who buy the land and gentrify the community.

Clearly, for women with few personal or community resources, motherhood does not provide the optimum conditions for nurturant, effective behavior. If you are poor, you are more likely to give birth to a low-weight infant who is at greater risk for infant mortality; to receive inadequate prenatal care; to experience dysfunctions during pregnancy and the birth process; and to bear and rear more children. If you are poor, you are constantly saying no to your children. You are called in by teachers who tell you that your children are slow, dirty, undisciplined, unruly, absent too often, or sick. And your children are more likely to be assaulted, victimized, murdered, arrested, unemployed, addicted, school dropouts, or social failures. That one out of five children in the U.S. in the 1980s is growing up in such circumstances is a sobering thought.

TOWARD SHARED PARENTING

Some contemporary fathers are eager to experience child rearing on an equal basis, shared cooperatively with the mothers of their children, and are learning, like the Arapesh described earlier, to find the care of little children "congenial." Letty Pogrebin (1982a) has commented on the discovery by men of the "joys of fatherhood," and suggested that "fathering is becoming a new kind of verb—an active verb—that describes a new kind of role and a new set of behaviors" (p. 43). Play groups for dads have been established (Korpivaara, 1982); workshops are being held for fathers to improve their skills as coparents or single parents; more divorced fathers are winning custody of their children either alone, or jointly with their ex-wives; and an increasing number of corporations permit paternity leaves for men. In most states, mothers no longer have an automatically greater claim than fathers to the legal custody of their children and, in cases of contested custody, fathers are now almost as likely to win as mothers, and in some circumstances more likely to win (Chesler, 1985).

A nationwide survey of employers, reported in the press ("More Fathers," 1984), found that over one third of the respondents offered men some time off for "new child-care leave," and half offered maternity leave to women. But although men are increasingly allowed to take leaves, they seldom do. This fact underscores that the redefinition of fathering as active coparenting is far from a mainstream American phenomenon. Nevertheless, fathering is now a more frequent subject of concern to young adults planning marriage and families, and an issue considered and examined in research and in the mass media. Much of this research has been encouraged and motivated by feminist concerns and analyses. Alan Booth and John Edwards (1980) studied a stratified sample of 231 Toronto families and concluded that when father's available time for child interaction is taken into account, his involvement with his children is as extensive as that between mother and child. Similarly, when Winifred Shepard (1980) asked a group of college students to report on their remembered interactions with their parents, she found more similarities than differences reported for mothers and fathers. Although mothers were seen to have had prime responsibility in areas that may be particularly important for a child's emotional life, mother-father differences in behavior and influence were small. Shepard concluded that "in general the fathers in this sample were not distant authoritarians but concerned participants in activities involving their children" (p. 425); and both parents behaved similarly toward sons and daughters, suggesting "that, in principle, parents can be interchangeable" (p. 432).

Some studies have identified variables that influence the extent and type of participation by fathers in the care of their children. Grace Baruch and Rosalind Barnett (1981) found, among a sample of fathers of preschoolers, that their independent participation in child care was positively related to their wives' labor-force status or outside employment, and to their own and their wives' nontraditional beliefs about sex roles. A subsequent study (Barnett & Baruch, 1983) in which fathers and mothers of kindergartners and fourth-graders were both interviewed found that a father tended to spend more time in interaction with his children the more hours his wife worked and the more nontraditional her attitude was toward men's roles. The researchers suggested that "the combination of the demands of a wife's employment and a non-traditional attitude both creates more demand for father's participation and may create an atmosphere that encourages fathers to be more participatory" (p. 11). Finding that fathers in dual-earner families tend to take a more active part in the care of their children than fathers who are the sole breadwinners has great social significance. Dual-earners now comprise 52 percent of all married couples, and among such couples over half have children (Presser & Cain, 1983).

Men who have assumed a sizable share of responsibility for the day-to-day rearing of their children have reported an increased respect for, and appreciation of, maternal work, and that their experiences have expanded their sensitivities and capacities. From the previously mentioned interview study of a sample of white middle-class parents of kindergartners and fourth-grade children, Grace Baruch and Rosalind Barnett (1985a) found that fathers who participated more in parenting felt more involved and competent as fathers than men who participated less, but such fathers must deal with "the problems as well as the pleasures" of daily involvement with children. Kenneth Pitchford (1978), for example, has written of his equal involvement in the raising of his son, as follows:

> In talking with men . . . if I went on to describe the amount of energy, intelligence, and sheer gray grungework my bargain has involved, I could frequently see men's reactions change before my eyes. At first they'd seemed envious: *What a rewarding experience you've had.* After hearing a few details, they radiated contempt: *You crazy masochist.* As if it were Either/Or. . . . The answer is of course to . . . admit how rewarding *and* tiring it's been to be so deeply involved in the care and feeding of another miraculous human being. (pp. 96, 98)

One of the most important consequences of his participation in child rearing, according to Pitchford, is the effect he believes it has had on his son.

> One of the most touching things about him is that he "instinctively" loves to take care of younger children. . . . It's because his earliest memories include not solely his mother but, as far back and just as often, this grumpy lovable old shoe of a person who snored sometimes when cuddling his baby asleep. It's what a Real Man does. Like his father. . . . I know . . . a child's crying will pierce his sleep as much as mine. Inherent? Instinctual? On the contrary, it's something that men can *do* in learning the work of love. (p. 99)

And Robert Miner (1980) has written very similarly about his experience as a single parent to two preschool children.

> Like most mothers I . . . think it was . . . far and away the most important experience I'd had in my life. I learned how to love, and I learned how to be emotionally available to others. I also learned that most of us men have little to congratulate ourselves for on Father's Day. (p. 6)

One interesting consequence of our contemporary "discovery" and growing acceptance of fathers as active coparents or primary care givers is their treatment by the mass media as somehow heroic or extraordinary in this role—a treatment, of course, not given to mothers. A Doonesbury cartoon (1985) (page 211) helps us laugh at this discrepancy. Well-received and well-made films like *Kramer vs. Kramer* or *Author, Author* have poignantly portrayed men as better parents (once they put their minds to it) than

Doonesbury

BY GARRY TRUDEAU

DOONESBURY, Copyright, 1985, G.B. Trudeau.
Reprinted with permission of Universal Press Syndicate.
All rights reserved.

their wives. Having discovered that a man can be a caring, sensitive parent, the media occasionally now present his role as superordinate. For example, a story headlined "'F' Is for Infants Favor Fathers' Favors" (1982) reported a pediatrician's findings that not only is "the father's role in infancy . . . more important than previously thought," but, in addition, "a father's physical play elicits more response from infants than a mother's soothing manner does"! Similarly, a news story about research indicating that babies prefer to play with their fathers because mothers are overburdened with chores was headlined "Fathers Are More Fun" ("Fathers Are," 1986) despite the fact that the major conclusion of the research was that babies are extremely perceptive "in identifying and responding to the roles parents play."

Community resources like day care centers or nurseries can encourage shared parenting but are still viewed primarily as aids for mothers. While public day care facilities for children are important, they are not the only solution. If adults worked shorter or more flexible hours, and if child care leaves were considered as necessary as sick leave and vacation time, then fathers and mothers might both be able to contribute equally to the rearing of their children, with minimum dependence upon other facilities during the first one or two years of their children's lives. The United States is the only industrial nation without a federal policy on parental leave to enable working parents to take time off from their jobs for child care without fear of being fired. As of this writing, a bill is being considered in Congress that would guarantee workers the right to a period of unpaid leave for infant or child care. We will discuss this issue more fully in the chapter on women's achievement and employment.

Modern technology has made parenting and work force participation compatible and feasible. Flexible time schedules, for example, are used widely in several European countries. A suburban community in Maryland has moved six of its schools to where parents of the children work, near major employment centers and traffic routes. These "workplace schools" are open from 7 A.M. to 6 P.M. and offer extra instruction in regular and special subjects, for a small weekly fee for each child (Wallace, 1985). Some occupations permit more personal flexibility than others. Where options in work schedules are limited, several families might work out effective cooperative child care in which all adults share equally on some rotating basis.

Cooperative child care can be encouraged by designing housing that builds in such arrangements. As noted by Dolores Hayden (1984), "To recognize the desire of women and men to be both paid workers and parents is to search for a way to overcome the physical separation of paid jobs and parenting inherent in many urban settings" (p. 69). In the 1930s, a project was designed and built in Stockholm that integrated housing, office space, food service, and child care. In the 1960s, a pioneering housing project that brought homes and jobs together for single parents was built in London. Interior corridors of the Fiona House (designed by Nina West and Sylvester Bone) "doubled as playrooms, with carpeted floors and windows from each apartment looking in, so that a parent cooking could watch a child at play. Intercoms linked apartments, enabling parents to baby-sit for each other by turning on the intercom and listening for children crying" (Hayden, 1984, p. 70). An experimental program for combining employment and housing is also in progress in the United States, by the Women's Development Corporation of Providence, Rhode Island. Other variations are possible that borrow elements from the more extensive communal arrangements represented by the kibbutz model in Israel or the commune movement in America.

If parenthood is shared and if mothers as well as fathers are encouraged to pursue personal goals, work at meaningful paid jobs, and live full busy lives, parents will be less inclined to become intensely overinvolved in the lives of their children. Children should not represent the only means of experiencing satisfaction with one's life. Still, even fulfilled and liberated parents will suffer anxieties, worries, disappointments, and frustrations, and experience elation, pride, satisfaction, and pleasure as their children grow, change, and lead autonomous lives. The many responses that make up caring are not easily extinguished. Typically, only women are expected to acquire these behaviors, but this is alterable and in the process of change. Committed parenting is maintained and strengthened in general by the rewards of society and in particular by reinforcement from one's children and one's own assessment of how well one has done as a parent. The care of children by concerned and attached adults is almost always accompanied by strongly experienced joys and agonies. These can be shared by both parents or by other adults regardless of gender or biological relationship to the child.

Work and Achievement Outside the Home

The major campaign [during World War II] conducted by OWI [Office of War Information] was the one to recruit women into the labor force. Thus . . . magazines published romances in which women who entered defense industries found fulfillment in performing important work for the nation. . . . Women [were shown obtaining] great satisfaction from employment . . . heightened . . . self-esteem . . . [and] developing into mature strong adults through meeting the challenge of long hours and hard physical labor.

Maureen Honey   *(1983, pp. 677f.)*

We've had all the career opportunities opened up to us and being a woman has even helped. . . . We're on top now. We're like men in the 50's.

Unidentified woman quoted by
Stephen Singular   *(1978, p. 18)*

C H A P T E R   12

society's views of gender can undergo remarkable changes to accommodate varied circumstances and demands, as illustrated by government propaganda produced during the Second World War to recruit women workers into defense and other essential industries. Maureen Honey (1983) has pointed out that while mass media fiction in the 1930s and early 1940s presented employed married women as "selfish and destructive to their families," wartime fiction "contained many heroines who successfully coped with both family and work responsibilities" (p. 678). Approximately 6 million new women workers entered the work force between 1941 and 1945, and Rosie the Riveter was a national symbol of the wartime American woman—strong, capable, confident, and responsible. But most women hired during the war were hired for unskilled or semiskilled jobs, and men continued to predominate in the skilled jobs within the auto, shipbuilding, steel, and other heavy industries (Gregory, 1974). After the war, when men returned to the factories, farms, and offices, the media presented Rosie as graciously relinquishing her job, taking off her work clothes, and compliantly returning to the bedroom and kitchen and to the older image of traditional femininity. Although 75 percent of the women interviewed in a 1944 Women's Bureau study said they wanted to keep their jobs after the war, when it ended 1 million were laid off and another 2.25 million quit their jobs (Gregory, 1974). During the 1950s, our society renewed its emphasis on women's home responsibilities, and forgot about the previously urged work skills and job satisfactions. Today, Rosie the Riveter's daughters and granddaughters are behaving as she did during the years of World War II.

While most contemporary American women still learn that our primary roles have to do with the care of home and family, most of us also spend many years contributing human capital to the nation's economy in the form of paid employment. Working women in this country constituted 44 percent of the total work force in 1986 ("Poll: Women," 1986) compared to 17 percent in 1930, 26 percent in 1940, 33 percent in 1960, and 38 percent in 1970 (Lindsey, 1976). Economists predict that women will comprise 45 percent of the work force by 1990. But although most women work outside the home, and although women and men work for the same reasons, the success with which we reach our objectives, or the rewards we are able to obtain, are considerably and significantly different. In this chapter we will examine the kinds of work employed women do, who constitute working women in this country, and the differences between the rewards attained by women and men for their labor.

WOMEN WHO WORK

While full-time homemakers most assuredly work, as we have seen in our discussion of wives and mothers, our attention in this chapter is focused on the experiences of employed women whose work receives compensation in the form of wages or salary. During the decades since the 1950s, participation by women in the world of paid employment has increased. In the United States, the proportion of women between 15 and 64 years of age (designated as women of working age) who were in the labor force (full- or part-time) rose from 42.6 percent in 1960 to 59.7 percent in 1980. Among Western industrialized nations, Sweden has the largest proportion of employed women, 74.1 percent in 1980 ("West's Women," 1984). Data from the U.S. Bureau of the Census (1983) indicate that between 1947 and 1980 the number of women in the work force grew by 173 percent, compared to 43 percent for men.

Of the women who work, 56 percent are married, 25 percent are single, 14 percent are divorced or separated, and 5 percent are widowed (National Commission on Working Women, 1978). Looking at these data differently, in terms of the proportion of working women within groups classified by marital status, 74 percent of divorced women hold jobs, 60.5 percent of never-married women, 22.4 percent of widows, and 47.6 percent of women with husbands present in the home ("Women Workers," 1978). In 58 percent of families with children in this country, both parents are working; and 49 percent of women with preschool-age children are employed outside the home ("18 Million Moms," 1986). The percent of employed black women has been, and continues to be, greater than that of white women. Among women 25 to 54 years of age, more than two thirds are in the work force (Serrin, 1984). Participation in the labor force is positively related to years of formal schooling.

Reflecting the role of women in today's work force are new media images. In both established women's magazines (such as *Redbook*) and newer magazines (like *New Woman*), the large majority of articles featuring a particular woman's life are about women employed full-time (Ruggiero & Weston, 1985). But the older magazines differ from the newer ones in presenting women who are "more likely to be engaged in traditional occupations . . . fairly narrow in scope," and women who are less likely to see their work as high in power and/or responsibility (p. 546).

Why Do Women Work?

Women work at jobs outside the home for the same reasons that men do. Paid employment offers the opportunity to earn needed financial resources (money and goods); become independent; have greater control of one's environment and future; contribute meaningfully to the needs of society; interact with other adults engaged in productive work; develop and use skills and talents; and experience growth, change, and personal fulfillment.

Helen Astin (1978) studied a large group of college-educated women and found that those who had been employed continuously since graduation were interested in achieving recognition, becoming authorities in their field, being financially well off, and being successful in their own business. Similarly, Linda Beckman (1978), who interviewed a sample of married women who were working full-time, reported that their most salient job rewards were social interaction; achievement, challenge, and creativity; self-definition, esteem, or independence; economic benefits; and mental stimulation. Paul Andrisani (1978) reported, from interviews with a representa-

tive national sample of approximately 5000 women (interviewed three times between 1969 and 1971), that working women in their 30s and 40s were interested in both intrinsic and extrinsic rewards. Interesting work and satisfying interpersonal relationships were the factors mentioned most frequently by both black and white women who reported themselves as being highly satisfied with their jobs.

Some studies have directly compared sources of job satisfaction among women with those reported by men. Patricia Voydanoff (1980), for example, found among a national sample of persons over age 20 who were working for pay at least 20 hours per week that for both women and men the variable that correlated most highly with job satisfaction was opportunity for self-expression. Also important for both genders were financial rewards/promotion, working conditions, minimal role strain, and quality of supervision. The author concluded that despite the significant gender difference in earnings (to be discussed later in this chapter), "men and women generally . . . require similar job characteristics to be satisfied with their jobs" (p. 185). Helen Moore (1985) tested the hypothesis that work settings are related to the satisfactions received from employment and found this to be supported by data from a national survey of employed women and men.

> Generally, both women and men in male-dominated or sex-proportionate sectors perceive their jobs as providing greater income, freedom, job involvement, job challenge, and use of their skills. These benefits are in addition to the significantly higher income for these jobs. The only benefit accruing disproportionately to the female-dominated sector is perceived support of supervisors and co-workers. (p. 676)

Linda Brown (1979) concluded from a review of research on women and men in business management that both groups "hold the same expectations of their positions. . . . The reasons women give for being satisfied with their executive jobs are similar to those given by men: they like solving problems, using their talents, and managing others" (p. 286). A study of a sample of professionals in the San Francisco Bay Area (Pines & Kafry, 1981) found that what was important for both women and men were "such positive features as success, and such negative ones as being overextended in terms of commitments and having conflicting demands" (p. 975). What differed between women and men was not what they valued in work but what they experienced.

> Men had many more positive work features than women . . . more variety, complexity, autonomy, and

influence in their work; higher demands for innovation and for proving themselves; greater opportunities for self-actualization and self-expression; a more pleasant physical environment; and more adequate tangible rewards from their work. (p. 970)

A common finding among studies of employed women, whether hard hats, white-collar workers, or professionals, is that their jobs provide needed financial resources, independence, and personal satisfaction. Thus, for example, the most common response given by a sample of women coal miners to the question of what they liked most about their work (Hammond & Mahoney, 1983) was "good money" and the satisfaction that came from providing for their children; they also said that they enjoyed the interactions with other workers and the feeling of camaraderie on the job. Of the 25 women interviewed, 22 were the primary or sole providers for their families. Responses given to Gwyned Simpson (1984) by a group of black women lawyers were not too different from those of the women who worked in the coal mines; 47 percent listed independence, mobility, or money as reasons for choosing law as a career. A group of farming women interviewed by Jessica Pearson (1980) cited the following as the satisfactions they derived from their work: being outdoors, growing crops, "battling with the elements, contact with animals, and the independence of farm work . . . identical to the satisfactions of farming articulated by the men who were interviewed" (p. 566). Thus, women look for employment that pays well, is challenging, and provides opportunities for both social and intellectual stimulation in a positive environment. The human motives for activity, exploration, and independence are reflected in women's desire to work.

What Kinds of Work Do Women Do?

In the 1980s women workers can be found in virtually every area of the economy, performing jobs at all levels of skill, from blue-collar work to public service to business/industrial management, in technical, scientific, and professional fields. Although most women continue to be employed in a narrow range of jobs (an issue we will discuss later in this chapter), breakthroughs have occurred in just about every occupation typically associated with (and reserved for) men. A 1976 issue of *Time* magazine that featured women's occupational progress included photographs of a woman garbage collector, college president, carpentry instructor, surveyor, economist,

artist, locomotive engineer, tennis professional, truck driver, author, airline flight engineer, member of Congress, surgeon, electrician, minister, naval officer, physics professor, construction worker, and chief justice of a state supreme court. Women are now a majority among "insurance adjustors, bill collectors, psychologists and assemblers" (Serrin, 1984), as well as among bank tellers and real estate agents (Noble, 1985), and among statisticians, editors, and reporters ("Women Now Hold," 1986). By February of 1986, more women than men were in the 50 occupations categorized as professional by the U.S. Labor Department. These "knowledge-based occupations" do not include executive, managerial, or administrative jobs ("Women Now Hold," 1986). Women can be found among working poets (Ostriker, 1986), orchestra conductors (Kozinn, 1985), narcotics agents (Gross, 1986), artists (Russell, 1983), scientists (Bruer, 1983), and jockeys (Duckworth, 1985); women are engaged in commercial fishing ("Life of Fishing," 1980) and in farming. According to Jessica Pearson (1980), women make up 15 percent of all persons who receive compensation for work on farms, either through wages or profits from self-employment, and 1.4 percent of all employed women are farm workers; they are "in the fields, operating farm machinery and making farm decisions" (p. 564).

More and more women are preparing for careers by attending college and earning advanced degrees from graduate and professional schools. Women now account for more than 52 percent of all college students, a phenomenon partially due to the large increase in college attendance by women aged 25 to 44 returning to school to complete their educations. In 1981, according to Lois Weis (1985), 50 percent of bachelors degrees and 51 percent of masters degrees went to women, and "women have made some progress in obtaining degrees in male-dominated areas" (p. 30). For example, it is expected that women will constitute 14 percent of all graduates from engineering colleges in 1986 (Teltsch, 1985). The percentage of doctorates granted to women has risen from 16 percent of the total in 1972 to 32 percent in 1982, when women earned 18 percent of the doctorates in business management, 29 percent in the biological sciences, 49 percent in education, 5 percent in engineering, 55 percent in foreign languages, 63 percent in library science, 14 percent in mathematics, 14 percent in the physical sciences, and 45 percent in psychology. In 1983, women earned 25 percent of all the science and engineering doctorates, compared to

13 percent in 1973 (Walsh, 1984). In 1980, women earned 23 percent of the medical degrees (compared to 8.5 percent in 1970) and 12 percent of the dentistry degrees (compared to 1 percent in 1970) (Vetter, 1981); and in 1982, women comprised 15 percent of all practicing physicians (Schreiner, 1984). Since 1981, the percentage of women in the entering classes of the 127 medical schools in the U.S. has increased from 30.7 to 33.4 percent in 1984 (Fox, 1984b). Among lawyers and judges, 15.5 percent were women in 1982 ("Change," 1985), and approximately one third of those attending law school in the 1980s are women. According to Gwyned Simpson (1984), 9 percent of women lawyers are black. Within science and engineering, the highest proportion of professional women are in the biological sciences, followed by the computer field, in which 25 percent of the software specialists are now women (Schmidt, 1985). According to Susan Merritt (1986), dean of the School of Computer Science at Pace University, women have been among the "most significant pioneers" in the field, developing electronic systems and programming languages.

There have been many occupational firsts for American women in the 1980s. In June of 1983 Sally Ride became the first of several women astronauts to work in space. After her mission, she talked about how the questions asked her by journalists had changed from the previous year ("Ride Claims," 1983).

> They started off primarily addressing questions to me about whether I would wear makeup, how my husband felt, privacy, whether I cried in the simulator. And now they seem very happy to ask me how the arm [of the space shuttle] worked. That's very gratifying.

In 1980, Evelyn Handler of the University of New Hampshire became the first woman president of a publicly supported land grant university, and in 1981 Sandra O'Connor was the first woman to be named to the Supreme Court, and Elizabeth Jones was the first woman to be appointed as chief sculptor-engraver at the U.S. Mint (Reiter, 1981). The first woman to head an elite law school in this country is Barbara Black, appointed dean of Columbia Law School in 1986 ("Woman to Head," 1986), and Eleanor Baum, dean of the Pratt Institute School of Engineering in Brooklyn, is the first and only woman in the United States to head a college of engineering (Teltsch, 1985). In December 1985, Wilma Mankiller was installed as the first woman chief of a major native American tribe, the Cherokee Nation of Oklahoma (Reinhold, 1985).

Although the Episcopal church began to ordain women ministers in 1976, and women have been ordained as rabbis within Reform and Reconstructionist Judaism since the early 1970s, it was not until 1983 that the Jewish Theological Seminary of America (the major training institution for Conservative rabbis) voted to admit women to its rabbinical studies program. In May of 1985 Amy Eilberg was ordained by the Seminary and admitted into the Rabbinical Assembly, becoming the first woman rabbi in the history of Conservative Judaism ("Conservative Jews," 1985). Another first for women occurred in 1985 when Penny Harrington became chief of the 780-member police department in Portland, Oregon.

> On her way to the top, Mrs. Harrington [had] filed a sex discrimination complaint against the department that led to changes in salaries, promotions, and other regulations, including revoking a rule that officers must stand at least 5 feet 10 inches tall. ("She's the Chief," 1985, p. 6E)

Several years earlier, in 1980, Dorothy Cousins became the first woman to command a police district in Philadelphia, one of only a handful of women in this country to hold such a job.

Jeannette Rankin from Montana was the first woman elected to the U.S. Congress, in 1916; three years later she introduced legislation for women's suffrage. But it was not until 1984 that a major political party nominated a woman, Geraldine Ferraro, for the high office of vice president of the United States. Congresswoman Ferraro did not win in 1984 but Madeleine Kunin was elected to the governorship of Vermont, the seventh woman ever to win a governor's office in the United States; and Arlene Violet of Rhode Island became the first woman ever to be elected a state attorney general. The 1984 elections also resulted in the highest number of women yet (970) winning seats in state legislatures across the country. According to one report (Tomasson, 1985), "women now constitute 14.7 percent of the lawmakers in the 50 states, or 1,097 out of the total of 7,461 legislators. Ten years ago, 604 women were legislators, about 8 percent of all state representatives and senators" (p. C14). In the spring of 1986, for the first time in American history, each of the major parties (in Nebraska) nominated a woman for governor, so that the election of a woman for this office is assured.

Women today occupy managerial/administrative posts in far greater numbers than previously (albeit at lower ranks than men). Compared with 18 percent in 1970, women now account for 31 percent of these positions (Schreiner, 1984), primarily "in the fields of

health administration; building supervision; general office management; assessors, controllers, and treasurers; and restaurant, bar, and cafeteria management" (Brown, 1979). Women managers can be found in such varied fields as the movie industry, charter jet business, banking, marketing, philanthropic foundations, and consumer products, but not yet in heavy industry or manufacturing.

The skilled trades have been as difficult for women to enter as the executive suite, but here, too, one now finds women—as bricklayers, auto mechanics, construction workers, utility service persons, maintenance workers, and electricians. By the end of 1981 there were almost 4000 women coal miners across the country (out of a total of approximately 200,000); this was eight years after women were first permitted to work in underground mines ("Superstition Crumbles," 1981). In the photo above, a woman miner at work in Ohio shovels coal onto a moving belt.

High-Achieving Women

Some research has tried to find out whether particular personality or background factors distinguish women who persist in the work force and who make progress in their jobs of careers. Women who achieve in the public sphere have been found to come from families in which independence, personal excellence,

and assertiveness were stressed and encouraged. Jeanne Lemkau (1979a) concluded from a review of the literature on women in nontraditional occupations that they tend to manifest high levels of independence, assertiveness, and adventurousness, but also to be nurturant and expressive. They are most likely to have come from homes in which they were encouraged to explore a wide range of behaviors. In her own study of a sample of employed women with masters degrees, Lemkau (1983) found that occupationally atypical women differed from a group of equally well-educated traditionally employed women in being more assertive, in having been more frequently first born, and in having had mothers who worked before they were born. Both groups of women with masters degrees, in traditional and nontraditional jobs, differed from women in general in scoring higher on measures related to competence and in manifesting less sex typing, but the occupationally atypical women were more likely

> to have been exposed to parental models and values that do not enforce a division between femininity and competence in any occupational field, to a cultural milieu more supportive of female innovation, and to early experiences contributing to . . . high confidence in being able to succeed in male domains. (p. 164)

Similarly, Gwyned Simpson (1984) reported that the black women lawyers she studied were taught by their parents that they must be autonomous and capable of taking care of themselves. "Self-reliance and economic independence were valued by both the fathers and mothers of these respondents" (p. 126).

Some researchers have reported that high-achieving women have a greater percentage of foreign-born parents and/or non-college-educated parents than would be expected by chance. Thus, for example, Dorothy Mandelbaum (1978) found that women physicians who persist in their work and do not take significant periods of time out for child rearing are likely to come from "lower social class origins," to have established their career goals early, and to have been socialized in less traditional directions. Helen Astin (1978) followed a large group of women from their entry into college until eight years after graduation and found that the married women who had worked continuously since graduating differed significantly from those who had not yet worked in having been more likely to have foreign-born or non-college-educated parents, as well as in having been more involved in extracurricular college affairs, and having majored in nontraditional fields such as natural science or business. Astin suggested that women who work continuously are likely to be motivated by a concern with social mobility—that is, to be striving to improve their social status relative to that of their parents. The college-educated women who did not work after college were more likely to have majored in fields such as the arts and the humanities, to have married men with graduate and professional degrees, to have started families early, and to have come from middle- and upper-middle-class backgrounds. An analysis of information about the lives of eminent women by Rita Mae Kelly (1983) also found that 65 percent of those who had attained political prominence had come from working-class or poor families; this was not the case for politically eminent men.

Some researchers have found that having women role models is an important correlate of work achievement by women. Thus, Mary Walshok (1981) found that most women in a sample of blue-collar workers (primarily white, and from rural backgrounds) came from families in which the mother was strong, resourceful, and employed. Similarly, among a group of black women in college, Ann Burlew (1982) found that those aiming for nontraditional professions were more likely to have had mothers who were more highly educated and had worked in nontraditional fields, than those making career choices traditional for women. A study of a group of women ministers (Steward, Steward, & Dary, 1983) reported the presence of influential mothers who

served as role models for their daughters. And Rita Mae Kelly (1983) found that very eminent women who had been political or organizational leaders were almost three times as likely to have had mothers who had worked at professional, business, or skilled jobs as women whose eminence derived from that of their husbands or who were eminent in areas other than politics or business. Similar findings were not obtained for men; thus, having a mother who served competently in an independent public role "seems to make a difference for the leadership potential of daughters, but not of sons" (p. 1077).

These studies support the conclusion that mothers serve as models for their daughters in the world of work; other women have been found to function similarly. M. Elizabeth Tidball (1980) has noted that "graduates of women's colleges are approximately twice as likely to be listed [on various registers of public achievement] as are women graduates of coeducational institutions" (pp. 506f.). One reason for the greater achievement of women's-college graduates is that they have been exposed to large numbers of women faculty. Tidball found an almost perfect positive correlation for colleges of varying sizes between the ratio of women achievers to women graduates and the ratio of women faculty to women graduates. Conversely, the correlation between the proportion of men enrolled in a college and its proportion of women achievers (cited in *Who's Who in America*) was found to be a strongly negative one. Tidball concluded that

> the larger the proportion of men students on a campus, the less likely are the women students subsequently to be cited for career achievement. . . . [But even more important is] the number of women faculty, in relation to the total faculty population and to the number of women students [which] emerges and reemerges as a major influence in the development of women students. (pp. 509, 516f.)

Other researchers who have compared graduates of women's colleges with women graduates of coeducational institutions (for example, Oates & Williamson, 1978) have found no significant differences between them in the percentage who have gone on to careers in nontraditional fields such as science, medicine, or business. But a different kind of study (Gilbert, Gallessich, & Evans, 1983) found women doctoral students who self-identified with a woman faculty member to score significantly higher in self-report measures of self-esteem, instrumentality, work commitment, and career aspirations than women students who identified with a male professor. Of

From My Weight Is Always Perfect for My Height—
Which Varies, *Nicole Hollander, St. Martin's Press, Inc.*
Copyright © 1982 by Nicole Hollander.

course, women students already high in self-esteem may tend to select women mentors or role models, but the relationship found by Gilbert et al. is nevertheless of considerable interest.

Stories about women who get ahead in the business world, like Karen Valenstein, a first vice president of E. F. Hutton & Co. (Gross, 1985), suggest that such women show extraordinary commitment to their jobs, surpassing that of men in comparable positions. Research evidence appears to confirm this view. For example, a survey conducted by *Glamour* magazine ("Career Before Fun," 1983) reported that a third more women than men executives believed their careers to be more important than their private lives, and 60 percent of the women but only 37 percent of the men said they would pass up an important family function if it conflicted with work. Similarly, a group of women senior executives were found to typically work 53 hours a week and to spend 33 days each year in out-of-town travel (Fowler, 1982). They reported spending little time on outside activities such as community service, and differed considerably in this respect from a group of male senior executives studied earlier, suggesting to the researchers that women may feel they have to work harder than men to maintain top jobs.

Rosabeth Kanter (1977) has argued that an important correlate of a woman's achievement, beyond personal characteristics, background factors, or role models, is her location or position in the work structure. According to Kanter, it is more likely that "the job shapes the person" than vice versa, and one's position within an organization has more relationship to one's productivity, self-esteem, and competence than socialization or background factors. She

studied a large corporation and found that a woman's success within it depended upon whether she was (a) a lone woman among men, and thus highly visible and vulnerable; (b) able to reward and punish subordinates; and (c) perceived as having such power.

OBSTACLES TO JOB SATISFACTION AND ACHIEVEMENT

Although women can now be found in practically every type of job performed in this country, women's numbers are small in the vast majority of cases outside of the jobs traditionally done by women. And although women work for the same reasons as men, and some women achieve as highly as some men, the average woman earns considerably less than the average man, receives fewer benefits, and works under poorer conditions. Women have been permitted entry into the world of paid employment, but with ambivalence. Women come into the work force largely through the rear door, and from the end of the line. This is even more true for women who are nonwhite and poorly educated. We will now examine in detail the obstacles women face in the paid labor market.

Job Segregation by Gender

Most employed women in this country are in narrow-option jobs in a small number of low-status fields that only meagerly provide the satisfactions and rewards generally sought for in employment. In the private sector, 34 percent of employed women are in clerical jobs and 27 percent are in service jobs (such as waitress, sales clerk, medical aide) while 57 percent

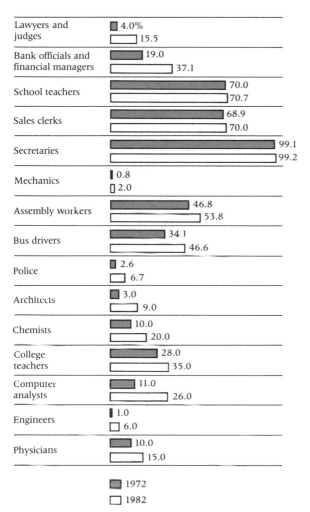

Lawyers and judges	4.0% / 15.5
Bank officials and financial managers	19.0 / 37.1
School teachers	70.0 / 70.7
Sales clerks	68.9 / 70.0
Secretaries	99.1 / 99.2
Mechanics	0.8 / 2.0
Assembly workers	46.8 / 53.8
Bus drivers	34.1 / 46.6
Police	2.6 / 6.7
Architects	3.0 / 9.0
Chemists	10.0 / 20.0
College teachers	28.0 / 35.0
Computer analysts	11.0 / 26.0
Engineers	1.0 / 6.0
Physicians	10.0 / 15.0

■ 1972
☐ 1982

FIGURE 12.1 Women as a percentage of all workers in selected occupations, 1972 and 1982

of women who work for the federal government are in clerical jobs (NOW, 1983). Overall, across the country, according to Janet Norwood, United States Commissioner of Labor Statistics, "the bulk of working women are in low-paying jobs, generally in low-paying industries or state and local government. Five of the top 10 occupations among women are sales or clerical jobs" (in Serrin, 1984).

In 1983, nearly 80 percent of women workers were in clerical, sales, service, factory, or plant jobs (National Commission on Working Women, 1983). The other occupations in which women's labor is welcome, those traditional for women, are bank teller, school teacher, nurse, and librarian. Among employed women, 40 percent are found in just ten tradi-

tional women's occupations (Pearce, 1985). In 1982, for example, women comprised 99.1 percent of all secretaries, 95.6 percent of registered nurses, and 98.5 percent of preschool and kindergarten teachers, compared to 1.4 percent of miners, 6.7 percent of police officers and detectives, 14.6 percent of doctors and dentists, and 28 percent of managers/administrators ("Poll: Women," 1986). Figure 12.1 presents comparisons between 1982 and 1972 in the percentage of women in selected occupations. Although clear gains have been made in such fields as law, medicine, bank management, computer analysis, and college teaching, relatively few women have been affected by the increased employment opportunities in these areas. The largest number of employed women are still in "pink ghetto" occupations, which pay approximately $4000 a year less than the jobs usually done by men. The well-paying unionized jobs in the skilled trades are still primarily the preserve of men. For example, women comprise 5.7 percent of construction and maintenance painters, 1.6 percent of electricians, and .4 percent of plumbers and pipefitters (Kerr, 1982).

Segregation of jobs by gender has far-reaching consequences. For example, one study investigated the general standing or prestige of a selected group of occupations among a sample of college students and found that the prestige associated with an occupation reflected the sex of the typical incumbent and thus the "sex-segregated nature of the occupational world" (Jacobs & Powell, 1985, p. 1070). A report by the Carnegie Corporation and the Departments of Education and Labor noted that "among the 503 occupations listed in the 1980 United States Census, 275 were greater than 80 percent male or female" (reported in Noble, 1985, p. A20), but "women's jobs" and "men's jobs" are not equal. "Women's jobs" are lower in status and lower in pay than "men's jobs," and are also found in fewer categories—that is, over a far narrower range. For example, the 57 jobs most frequently held by each gender account for 75 percent of all women's employment but less than half of all men's employment (Lemkau, 1979b). Women working for the federal government are segregated into the jobs with the lowest pay. Women hold 75 percent of jobs at pay grade GS-6, but only 12.4 percent of jobs at grade GS-13, for which the annual salary is two to three and a half times greater ("Women at Foot," 1984). Alice Ilchman (1986), who chaired a national committee that studied sex segregation in the workplace, has concluded that while some previously "men's jobs" have now become "women's jobs," and vice versa, "overall, the amount of sex segregation in the U.S. workplace has been virtually stable since 1900" (p. A-11).

Equal employment opportunity regulations can be circumvented by writing advertisements to appeal to women more than to men, or vice versa, and by obtaining applicants for jobs through personal contacts. For example, Daniel Socolow (in "Affirmative Action," 1978a) found that the "old boy" network still functions in the recruitment and hiring of college administrators. Although colleges advertise job openings widely to meet government requirements, administrators still phone colleagues and friends for recommended candidates. Socolow found that only 24 percent of a sample of positions advertised in the *Chronicle of Higher Education* were filled by individuals who applied directly for them "without any prior connections with the institution or the individuals doing the hiring" (p. 1).

Gender segregation in employment is reflected in the fact that the average woman's job tends to be unrelated to her level of education or background. Sandra Scarr and Gail McAvay (in Bridgwater, 1983), for example, found that among a sample of unmarried adults in their mid-20s, men with impressive family backgrounds and academic records were the most likely to have high-status jobs. Such a relationship was not found for women: "Women who did well in college were just as likely to go into relatively low-status and traditionally 'female' occupations such as public-school teaching or nursing as they were to pursue more socially prestigious professions" (p. 74).

Gender segregation exists even within the same job category. For example, women in the professional-technical category are more likely to be at the bottom of that rung; 60 percent of these women are primary or secondary school teachers or nurses, while men in the category tend to be lawyers, doctors, or college professors (National Commission on Working Women, 1978). Women scientists, according to the Scientific Manpower Commission (in Vetter, 1978), have been less likely than men to get jobs in prestigious educational institutions or in private industry and have been advanced to managerial responsibility or higher academic rank at lower rates. In an article on employment prospects for women, Peggy Schmidt (1985) noted that

> although a growing number of young women are studying the quantitatively based disciplines that prepare them for careers in science, engineering and computer science, their prospects for employment and advancement in industry and academia drag woefully behind those for men. (p. 14)

Regardless of occupation, if both women and men are represented, the latter tend to have the more powerful, prestigious, and remunerative jobs. Thus, for example, while half the musicians in regional and metropolitan orchestras in this country are women, the figure for large major orchestras is only 26 percent, and less than that in 10 of the 12 largest orchestras. The New York Philharmonic did not hire its first regular woman member until 1966, or assign a woman to a first-chair position until the early 1980s. In 1983 it had 18 women on its roster of regular members out of a total of 105 (Henahan, 1983). Matilda Butler and William Paisley (1977) studied several hundred professional couples (psychologists) and found remarkable similarity between the husbands and wives in chronological and professional age and status of university from which they graduated. Nevertheless, the husbands held more prestigious positions than their wives and were more often supervisors, administrators, or chairpersons. In medicine, too, as a study by Susan Sherman and Aaron Rosenblatt (1984) has shown, gender segregation exists in the specialties and in teaching and administration. Few women physicians are found in some areas, such as surgery, and across all specialties they tend to be overrepresented in teaching and research, and underrepresented in administration. The researchers concluded that the most powerful and financially rewarded positions are "primarily occupied by male physicians" (p. 209).

It is instructive to examine women's increased participation in the labor force by noting what kinds of jobs most women have been getting. Joan Smith (1984) concluded from such an analysis that coinciding with the massive entry of women into the work force has been the rapid expansion of the service sector of the American economy. By 1980 this sector contributed nearly 55 percent of the gross national product, and it is into this sector that women workers have been most welcomed. The service sector has the capacity to sustain high labor turnover, and derives its profits from "low-wage, intermittent, and part-time work" (p. 292). Over 75 percent of the recent growth in financial, real estate, and insurance businesses, and 60 percent of the growth of service-producing and retail food industries is attributed to the contribution of women's labor. It is in these low salary areas that most women work, as compared to men who are overrepresented in manufacturing products. According to Jennie Farley (1985), "About a third of all male workers produce goods (as opposed to services), while only 17 percent of female workers are in goods-producing industries. Fully 29 percent of women wage earners, but only 6 percent of their male counterparts, are in jobs classified as 'administrative support, including clerical' work. A fifth of the men hold jobs defined as 'precision production, craft, and repair', in contrast to the 2 percent of women workers who perform that lucrative work" (p. 585f).

Lack of Women Models in Powerful Positions

When we do not see others like ourselves occupying certain positions or visibly achieving in particular occupations or careers, we are not encouraged to feel that it is suitable or advisable to train for and aspire to them. Role models for boys and men are found in large areas of human endeavor, covering the spectrum from brawn to brains, from the active to the sedentary, the risky to the safe, and the routine to the creative. But girls who look outside the home for the presence of women find them primarily in a relatively small number of fields that do not offer much in the way of personal growth or advancement, and see only a small minority in nontraditional fields and high-status jobs. And among the latter, women are largely absent from positions of great corporate and political power. While some women have, in recent years, moved into important decision-making positions, recognition of this has been slow and hampered by continued portrayal of stereotypes in media advertisements. The photo on this page, for example, is typical of advertisements seen by readers of popular magazines in 1984 that showed women and men in their traditional roles in the office, as at home: physicians are wise men and caring parents are women.

Turn on your television set and examine the gender of the persons who are shown conferring with the President, or your governor, or the president of some major company. A woman's face is hard to find (except as an accompanying wife or staff member). In 1986 there were 2 women governors (Martha Collins in Kentucky and Madeleine Kunin in Vermont); and there was 1 woman in the President's cabinet (head of the Department of Transportation) (I cannot recall there ever having been more than 2 at the same time). There were 23 women in the House of Representatives out of 435 members, and 2 women (out of 100) in the Senate, an all-time high record, matching the one set in 1961. The situation in state legislatures is somewhat better: in 1985, 14.7 percent of all legisla-

With the ingredient doctors recommend most to reduce your child's fever fast...

Read and follow label instructions carefully

Children's Anacin-3
100% Aspirin-Free

When your child has a fever due to cold or flu, reach for the fever reducing ingredient doctors recommend most...it's in Children's Anacin-3. 100% aspirin-free.

Nothing is safer and reduces your child's fever faster than Children's Anacin-3.

tors were women, including 73 black women, 8 Hispanic women, and 2 native Americans. Of the 1096 women serving in state legislatures in 1985, 970 won their seats in 1984, when the most women were elected at one time ("Number of Women," 1985).

Both the U.S. State Department and the United Nations are overwhelmingly male in terms of senior posts with important decision-making responsibilities. A study of the State Department for the years 1970 to 1981 found that during that period the number of women Foreign Service officers remained steady at 26 percent; and in 1981 women were in only 3 percent of the senior jobs ("State Dept. Policies," 1984). Only one woman has served as an assistant secretary of state (in 1983); and there are never more than 10 percent women among the thousands of delegates chosen annually to represent the United States at international conferences. A similar situation exists within the United Nations. Of 700 professional jobs, only 22.5 percent are held by women. Among all positions at the United Nations headquarters, 44 percent are held by women, but these are "clustered in secretarial, clerical and service jobs at the bottom of the salary scale. No women are among the 27 Under Secretaries General . . . four of the 25 Assistant Secretaries General are women" (Sciolino, 1985, pp. C1, C4).

Only 8 of 75 astronauts are women ("Poll: Women," 1986); and within the military, in all branches of the armed forces except the Coast Guard, women are excluded from jobs in combat units. This has the effect of excluding women from the most important, influential posts. In the Navy, for example, women officers are primarily found in a desk-bound track as nurses or administrators in areas such as training, recruiting, and personnel records (Schwadel, 1985). Those women who are "surface warfare" officers can serve on only 33 of the Navy's 527 ships, those that are mainly repair and research vessels.

In business, women have rarely moved beyond the middle rung of responsibility, prestige, and power. Carol Bridgwater (1984) has noted that while "the number of female managers has doubled during the past 10 years, . . . the roster of the American Management Association (AMA) remains overwhelmingly male, by a margin of nine to one" (p. 17). According to Christine Doudna (1980):

> The vast majority of the new arrivals in management [with MBAs] are ranked at middle level. Women still represent a token incursion into the real power structure of most corporations. Many are vice presidents with big offices and high salaries, but they tend to be ghettoized in areas like personnel and public relations, or in corporate legal or finance departments. Rare is the woman who has her finger—or her job description—on or even near the bottom line. (p. 55)

Of two recent studies, one in 1982 found that women hold only 5 percent of executive positions in the top 50 companies in this country, while the other in 1985 reported this number to be only 2 percent (Loden, 1986). According to Marilyn Loden, "Most women in middle management today believe that their careers have reached a plateau" (p. F-2) and that they do not have the same chance for promotion as equally qualified men; because of this, a mass exodus from the corporate world of some of its best and brightest women is now taking place.

In colleges and universities, 79 percent of the key administrative jobs are held by white men, 15 percent by white women, 5 percent by minority men, and 2 percent by minority women ("Affirmative Action," 1978a). Thus, "more than 90 percent of all college students attend institutions where all three of the top administrative positions—president, chief academic officer, and dean—are held by men" ("Women Take the Lead," 1980, p. 2). In 1986, of all college or university presidents, 10 percent (300) were women; with but a few exceptions, most of these jobs were not on the most prestigious campuses. One third of women college presidents are chief administrators of small religious colleges, and 29 percent head women's colleges (Maeroff, 1986). Of the 244

women presidents identified in 1982, 20 were minority women (Touchton, 1983). Women are also seriously underrepresented among administrators at the elementary and secondary school levels. According to statistics compiled by the National Education Association (in Kleinman, 1983), although approximately 1.5 million teachers in the United States are women, compared to less than 685 thousand men teachers, women comprise only 1 percent of school superintendents and 13 percent of principals.

In colleges and universities, proportionately fewer women than men are found in higher ranks, and in the more prestigious schools and disciplines (Mason, 1980). For example:

> A 1981 survey of 1970–1974 doctoral recipients [in science] showed that 17.2 percent of the men versus 9.2 percent of the women were full professors, 50.8 percent versus 38.2 percent were associate professors, and 17.3 versus 31.7 percent were assistant professors. For this same group, 13.3 percent of the men under 35 compared to 9.4 percent of the women were tenured. For those aged 36 to 45, 80.8 percent of the men versus 62.7 percent of the women were tenured or on the tenure track. (Bruer, 1983, p. 1339)

Another study matched over 5000 triads of one woman and two men scientists by year of doctoral award, field, and race, and found differences in rank (and salary) even when they had earned their degrees and were currently employed in similarly prestigious institutions ("Misconceptions," 1982).

> Women were more likely, at each level of academic employment, to be in a non-faculty or junior faculty position than their matched male counterparts. Males were 50 percent more likely than females to have reached the status of full professor among men and women who received their doctorates between 10 and 19 years ago. . . . [And] unmarried women, or women without children fared no better with faculty promotions than women with children. (pp. 6f.)

Not until 1960 was a woman (mathematician Mina Rees) elected to the presidency of the American Association for the Advancement of Science; since that time she has been followed by only three others: anthropologist Margaret Mead in 1973, astronomer E. Margaret Burbidge in 1983; and chemist Anna Harrison in 1984 (Wrather, 1983).

Some women who have achieved important decision-making positions find that they are frequently bypassed and undervalued. Their suggestions may be ignored or recognized only later when they are repeated by a male colleague. As a college dean for six years, I often found myself in groups in which I was either the lone woman or among a very small minority of women, and my experiences matched those reported by other women in similar situations. For example, Mary Rowe (1973) has described some of "the minutiae of sexism," petty incidents that when taken together serve to impede women's job progress: a woman's name may be oddly missing from a list of announcements or invitations; her opinion may not be solicited or her work not cited; she may be loaded with extra work, or given an undesirable office.

Carol Wolman and Hal Frank (1975) found that under certain circumstances a lone woman working with a group of men can experience devastating consequences and loss of self-esteem. They studied several small ongoing groups of professional mental health workers or students, each containing only one woman. All of the women, over the course of the study, "became deviants, isolates, or low status regular members" regardless of their professional status or competence. These findings are complemented by others. Rosabeth Kanter (1977), for example, found that in a large corporation she studied where there were only a few women at the managerial level, these women were highly visible and under particular pressure to succeed; they were isolated and could share their feelings and perceptions with few others. Their chance for success was diminished by their lesser power and by the perception of others that they were less able than men to reward those whom they supervised.

Salary Discrimination

Employed women earn less than employed men, and black women earn the least of all. This reflects, first of all, the facts of job segregation we have already discussed—that women tend to be employed in occupations, in industries, and at status levels that pay less than those in which men are employed. The salary differential reflects an additional economic fact; even when men and women are in the same general occupational category or the same specific job, men receive more money than women for comparable work. Data from all areas of employment continue to show evidence of this startling phenomenon, with only rare and modest exceptions.

The wage gap has remained relatively steady, despite the ever-increasing numbers of women in the labor force. In 1982 the average woman earned 62 cents for every dollar earned by the average man. Women's earnings as a percent of men's was 64 per-

cent in 1955, 61 percent in 1960, 60 percent in 1965, 59 percent in 1970 and 1975, and 60 percent in 1980. Thus, for the past three decades, women's labor has continued to yield about 40 percent less than men's labor among *full-time* workers. The annual median income in 1982 for women was $13,014, more than $8,000 less than the annual median earnings of men, $21,077 (National Commission on Working Women, 1983). The earnings disparity between women and men in the United States is considerably greater than it is in some other comparable Western industrialized countries. For example, among industrial workers, women earn 78 percent of what men earn in Australia, 81 percent in Italy, 82 percent in Denmark, and 84 percent in Sweden (Ferber, 1982). In an analysis of incomes earned in this country by women and men between the ages of 25 and 64, Victor Fuchs (1986) found that "the average man still earns 50 percent more per hour than . . . the average woman of the same race, age, and education. This differential is also the norm within individual marriages when both spouses work for pay" (p. 232).

Black and Hispanic women in the U.S. continue to earn less than white women. The median incomes of men and women in 1982, categorized by color/ethnicity, were as follows (National Commission on Working Women, 1983):

	Men	Women
White	$21,602	$13,160
Black	15,503	12,132
Hispanic	15,382	11,112

Thus, within each group, the average man earned substantially more than the average woman, and Hispanic and black women earned 51 and 56 cents, respectively, for every dollar earned by a white man. As has already been mentioned, the difference between women and men in average income reflects not only the facts of job segregation, but also the fact that if we look at comparative earnings of women and men *within the same occupational categories* we find striking differentials in favor of men in just about every job examined. A Labor Department study in 1982 (reported by National Commission on Working Women, 1983) found that in all 100 occupations surveyed, the weekly earnings of full-time women were less than those of men. For example, for every dollar earned by men, women in the same occupation earned: 73 cents as a bookkeeper, 68 cents as a clerical worker, 80 cents as a computer programmer, 76 cents as a cook, 75 cents as a lawyer, 61 cents as an office manager, and 80 cents as a social worker. Bureau of Labor statistics have documented similar gender differentials among engineers, physicians, and accountants (Schreiner, 1984). A study of computer software specialists (in Schmidt, 1985) found that even though women in this field "earn more than do 98 percent of all working women . . . [they nevertheless] earn $9,000 a year less than men do" (p. 15).

In higher education, at all ranks from lecturer to full professor, and in public, private, and church-related colleges and universities, men earn a greater annual salary than women ("The Annual Report," 1984). The gap is greatest at the higher levels, so that the incomes of women and men full professors are further apart than the incomes of instructors. The gender gap in academic salaries has remained relatively unchanged over many years. Within the educational community, generally, women almost everywhere earn less than men. For example, women working in college development (fund raising/public relations), "regardless of their experience, educational background, and other qualifications," were found to earn 20 percent less than men in the same jobs ("Women in College," 1982); and among public school teachers, men were found to earn, on the average, $2000 more a year than women, and men superintendents almost $3000 more a year than women superintendents (Kleinman, 1983). In a study of educational researchers, being a woman was found to be "negatively related to income even when the number of articles published, number of citations received, and rated quality of one's research are statistically controlled" (Persell, 1983, p. 43).

A college education increases a person's earning power, but this is considerably more true for men than for women. A woman with a bachelors degree still typically earns less than a man who has not completed high school (NOW, 1983). Based on statistics for the years 1979 to 1981, a Census Bureau study ("Degree Can Lift," 1983) concluded that a man with a college degree can expect lifetime earnings of $1,190,000, while a comparably educated woman can expect to earn only $523,000, considerably less than half as much, over the course of her lifetime. For example, among those of the Harvard/Radcliffe class of 1961 who responded to an alumni questionnaire, the women reported earnings far below that of the men.

Half the Harvard men who replied said they earned more than $100,000 a year, with almost all the rest making more than $50,000. By contrast, a third of the Radcliffe women who responded said they earned less than $20,000 a year, and fewer than 20 percent said they earned more than $50,000. (Butterfield, 1986, p. E30)

At every educational level, white men earn the most, followed by black men, and then white women; black women earn the least.

One group of researchers (Steel, Abeles, & Card, 1982) who studied a large national sample of men and women from high school through age 29 concluded that differences between the genders in pattern of adult roles explained very little of the significant sex differences in earnings. Similar conclusions have come from another study, of a national sample of over 5000 American families studied in depth since 1968 (Corcoran, Duncan, & Hill, 1984). All the variables examined such as education, work experience, work continuity, self-imposed restrictions on work, and absenteeism "explained only about one-third of the wage gap between white men and white women and only about one-quarter of the wage gap between white men and black women" (p. 239), strongly suggesting the existence of "institutionalized discrimination against women in the working world." The researchers found that men were favored over women in finding better jobs through old-boy networks, in obtaining positions with longer training periods and advancement opportunities, and, most importantly, in obtaining jobs that gave them authority over others.

Discrimination in Benefits and Job Loss

An employed woman may find that her request for maternity leave is reacted to negatively by her employer, that she is without a pension after years in the work force, or that she is among the first to lose her job during slow periods in the economy. A law passed by Congress in 1978, the Pregnancy Discrimination Act, specifies that a pregnant woman is entitled to the same temporary disability benefits that her employer provides to all its workers. Pregnancy, childbirth, and related medical conditions must be treated as any other disability by an employer and carry entitlement to a similar period of leave. But the law does not require an employer to guarantee that the woman's job will still be available to her when she returns; and the law does not apply to companies that provide no disability benefits to men. It has been estimated, according to Tamar Lewin (1984), that more than 25 percent of working women "are employed by companies whose policies do not guarantee their return to the same or a comparable job after time off for childbirth" (p. F23). Lewin cites a study of the nation's 1000 largest industrial and 500 largest financial companies that found that

> only 38 percent of the companies guaranteed women their same jobs back after a disability leave for childbirth. Another 43 percent will provide a comparable job, and 6 percent more will give returning mothers "some job." That leaves 13 percent that make no promise of any job. (p. F23)

The millions of women who work for smaller companies, in restaurants, laundries, and the like, receive no disability leave and typically have no job waiting for them when they return to work. A survey by the New York Chamber of Commerce of 142 companies ("Taking a Break," 1981) found that 17 percent said they would hold a job open for an employee on maternity leave for 8 weeks, 17 percent would hold it for 3 months, 45 percent for 6 months or more, and 21 percent said they would not hold the job open at all. The United States is unique in this respect, and is the only industrialized country in the world that has no national policy for paid maternity leave. Many countries also permit a period of child-care leave for fathers and/or mothers. (We will return to this issue later.)

The National Federation of Business and Professional Women's Clubs ("Women's Pay," 1982) found that only 21 percent of working women are covered by pension plans. This is due to the lack of such plans by companies that employ large numbers of women, and to interrupted work patterns and changing jobs. In addition, when a woman takes time off from work to care for children at home, her Social Security contributions during that time are zero (NOW, 1983).

Some previous inequities between women and men with respect to pension benefits have been addressed and corrected by legislation and a ruling by the Supreme Court. In 1984 Congress passed legislation that requires written consent of the spouse before a retiree can waive survivor benefits, and allows former (divorced) spouses of federal workers to receive survivor benefits. A case brought to the Supreme Court by a working grandmother from Arizona has changed the prior practice of insurance companies that paid women after retirement less each month than men, regardless of whether they had made contributions to the plan equal to that of men. This practice was justified by the insurance companies on the grounds of women's greater average longevity. But in the 1983 *Norris v. Arizona* decision, the Court ruled that this practice violates Title VII of the Civil Rights Act and discriminates against women. In other words, pension or retirement benefits must be gender-neutral and calculated without regard to the sex of the beneficiary. "An individual woman," wrote Justice Thurgood Marshall for a majority of the Court, "may not be paid lower benefits simply because women as a class live longer than men" ("Supreme Court," 1983). This ruling now applies to employees of public and nonprofit institutions, but broad federal legislation prohibiting sex discrimination in all insurance plans has been proposed. Women who are retiring in the 1980s are likely to receive more retirement benefits and supplemental pensions than previous generations of women. For example, according to the Social Security Administration, about 43 percent of widowed, divorced, and single women currently retiring have pensions, compared with 25 percent in 1970 (in Collins, 1986).

The statistics on unemployment have also reflected discrimination against women, since more women than men are typically out of work and looking for jobs. According to Diana Pearce (1985), "Women's unemployment rate has historically been higher than men's, with the ratio between the two ranging from 1.09 to 1.46" (p. 445). The unemployment rate for men exceeded that for women for the first time in 1982. Highly skilled professional women in science have higher unemployment rates than men at "every degree level, in every field of science, [and] within every age group," according to Betty Vetter (1978). For example, the 1979 unemployment rates for 1977 graduates in all science fields were higher for women than for men. Among women with bachelors or masters degrees in any area of science or engineering, 4.3 percent were unemployed versus 1.7 percent of comparable men ("Unemployment," 1981). Among all workers 20 years of age or older in each of the years 1979, 1980, and 1981, the unemployment rate of women exceeded that of men ("The Employment Situation," 1981).

The differential impact that industry layoffs have on women and men can be illustrated by data from the steel industry. Among employees laid off by United States Steel Corporation in South Chicago, 63 percent of the women were reported by a union study (in Greenhouse, 1984) to be still unemployed five years after the layoff, as compared with 44 percent of the men. Women have gone from being 9 percent of the nation's steelworkers in 1980 to less than 2 percent in 1984 ("Women Face Low Pay," 1984). Similar statistics have been reported from studies of other industries. For example, within a year after a thermostat control plant shut down in Pennsylvania, 60 percent of the laid-off men had found other jobs, but only 40 percent of the women had obtained employment. A variety of inquiries indicate that

> women who have been laid off from blue-collar jobs in declining industries have the poorest prospects of ever making it back into those same jobs. The seniority rules governing layoffs and recalls are the reason . . . dislocated female workers . . . appear to have a harder time finding work and to end up earning less than their male counterparts. ("Recovery of Women Workers," 1984, p. A-15)

An analysis of unemployment benefits has led Diana Pearce (1985) to conclude that the unemployment compensation system in this country "is structurally biased against women. Consequently, women find themselves disqualified as claimants or allotted reduced benefits more often than men do" (p. 444). The bias stems from the greater probability that an unemployed woman has been in part-time employment, or earning wages so low that they do not meet the minimum earnings requirement for unemployment compensation. Thus, for example, in 1982, the highest benefits of $175 to $199 per week were received by 22 percent of all men claimants but only 3 percent of women.

Devaluation of Women's Competence

A strong conviction persists that women just cannot do certain jobs as well as men. Not too long ago a male colleague asked me in all seriousness if I really believed that a woman could handle the responsibilities of a university vice president. That he is the father of daughters who may someday be asked the same question is illustrative of the difficulty we have in overcoming the strong perceptual and cognitive habits that make up our gender stereotypes.

In every field that has been examined, evidence has been uncovered to document the devaluation of women's achievements. In art, for example, since 1970 "no fewer than five general histories of women artists have appeared, as well as a plethora of articles, exhibition catalogues, monographs, dissertations, symposia and special issues of art publications" that have been devoted to uncovering the contributions of women (Nochlin, 1979, p. 3). New scholarship on

women in music has similarly brought to public attention previously ignored gifted composers. As noted by Elizabeth Wood (1980), research has found evidence of the "historical devaluation" of women in music, identified "patterns of discrimination," and analyzed "how this has curtailed women's career opportunities. Few works by women have been performed by major orchestras; few are recorded; few women gain positions which sustain creative freedom" (p. 290). Maria Goeppert-Mayer, winner of the Nobel Prize in physics in 1963, was not offered a full-time faculty appointment in an American university until her award was widely rumored a year or two earlier (Dash, 1973). The case of biologist Rosalind Franklin is even more tragic. In an extraordinary book, Anne Sayre (1975) has documented Franklin's contributions to the discovery of the molecular structure of DNA. The scientists who received the 1962 Nobel Prize for this work (James Watson, Maurice Wilkins, and Francis Crick) were well aware of her research. In a book about the race for the Nobel Prize (The Double Helix), Watson presented a distorted characterization of Franklin, referring to her throughout as "Rosy," a name Anne Sayre maintains

> was never used by any friend of Rosalind's, and certainly by no one to her face. But beyond this, a series of minor inaccuracies of fact, each aligned in a consistent direction . . . [ensured that] the figure which emerged was . . . the perfect unadulterated stereotype of the unattractive, dowdy, rigid, aggressive, overbearing, steely, "unfeminine" bluestocking, the female grotesque we have been taught either to fear or to despise. (p. 19)

Among several factual inaccuracies is Watson's assertion that Franklin worked under the direction of Maurice Wilkins; she was, in fact, equal in status to Wilkins and was, like him, in charge of her own laboratory.

Other apparent negations of the contributions of women scientists have received public attention. The work of Jocelyn Bell (Burnell) on the discovery and understanding of pulsars was not recognized by the Nobel Prize committee in 1974 when the prize in physics for this work was awarded to two men, in the laboratory of one of whom she had worked (Wade, 1975). Similarly, in 1978, the Lasker Award for Basic Medical Research was awarded to three men for their discoveries of opiate receptors in the brain, but as noted in Science ("Lasker Award," 1979), "missing from the award citation was the name of Candace Pert," a woman who had collaborated with one of the winners "on much of the research for which he was cited." While such stories in Science have critically noted the exclusion of women from the reward system, its own editorials have reflected the same phenomenon. In a letter to the editors, Rochelle Albin (1979) charged that women were grossly underrepresented in the weekly editorial page; she presented as supporting evidence "the disturbing observation that, in the last 25 issues of 1978, a sample likely to be representative of most issues, not a single woman authored a *Science* editorial" (p. 228). A more positive illustration is that of geneticist Barbara McClintock, who received the Lasker Award in 1981 and the Nobel Prize in 1983, when she was over 80 years of age. Would recognition have come sooner if she had been a man?

A large research literature suggests that a probable answer to this question is yes. I reviewed this literature (Lott, 1985) and found support for the conclusion that a competent woman was likely to be devalued relative to an identically credentialed competent man. That gender continues to be a significant variable that affects judgments about work quality is illustrated by a recent study (Paludi & Strayer, 1985) in which college students who read articles presumably written by Joan McKay evaluated them less favorably than the same articles attributed to John McKay. This phenomenon of devaluing a woman's competence is found among different groups of people and within a variety of research settings, but is found most often in realistic contexts in which the evaluator is a real employer or personnel manager. In such studies, in which the gender of a potential employee has real significance, devaluation of women relative to men is overwhelmingly found. A more encouraging conclusion was drawn from research in which evaluations were made of women who were already known well as employees or supervisors; negative evaluations of competent women were less likely to be found in such studies. But other evidence indicates that when women are in direct competition with men for rewards, factors that are not directly work-related may influence job decisions or evaluations. For example, a field study involving interviews and analysis of job performance records of 651 employees of five different companies (Gupta, Jenkins, & Beehr, 1983), found that "while opinions (evaluations) may be positive, actions (promotions) still follow tradition" (p. 183). Women subordinates received the fewest promotions and men subordinates of men supervisors received the most frequent pay raises, regardless of the evaluations of their work.

Related research has found that the success of a woman is likely to be explained by others as due to such unstable factors as luck, effort, or easiness of the task or job. A man's success, on the other hand, is more likely to be attributed to high ability. The reverse is true for explanations of failure; men are said to fail because of bad luck, a difficult task, or low effort, whereas a woman's failure is more likely to be attributed to low ability. In addition, some research has found that competent women are more likely to be judged as having fewer stereotypically "feminine" qualities (that is, to be stronger or harder) than less competent women. A review of the literature on evaluation of women relative to men (Hansen & O'Leary, 1984) concluded that "there is a clear trend: Women are disadvantaged in the evaluation of their performance and achievement" (p. 3); in addition, effort expended on a task by a man is more likely than the same effort expended by a woman to be perceived by others as intended to produce a particular effect.

Situations in which women are likely to be evaluated negatively can be illustrated by three recent investigations. In one study (Taylor & Falcone, 1982), college students watched a videotaped interaction among three men and three women (of similar status and background) who were discussing ways to increase voter turnout. When asked to evaluate the discussants, observers rated the men as significantly more "savvy," more influential, more interesting, and more effective than the women. In another study (Gerdes & Garber, 1983), managers (mostly men) evaluated applications for both a purely technical job in chemical engineering and a technical-managerial job. The woman candidate for the latter job was rated significantly lower than the man candidate, despite identical credentials and competence. The researchers concluded that the greater ambiguity of qualifications required for a managerial position resulted in an increased chance for prejudice to operate, and that "credentials that demonstrate competence . . . are not sufficient protection from sex bias when the candidate applies for a demanding job" (p. 317). A different kind of study analyzed the actual records of 341 applicants to a medical school (Clayton, Baird, & Levinson, 1984) and found that women received lower interview ratings than men, and that the interview evaluations were more important for women than for men. Interview scores explained 42 percent of the variance in total evaluation scores for men, compared to 60 percent for women. Thus, despite no reliable gender difference in objective test scores (grade point average and MCATs), women received lower interview ratings than men and, therefore, lower overall evaluations. An earlier review by

Richard Arvey (1979) of research on employment interviews also noted that they tended to result in discrimination against women.

Clearly, women who try to achieve in areas outside the home, particularly in nontraditional fields, begin with a handicap of serious proportions, namely with negatively biased perceptions of their competence for the job. Nevertheless, the objective data that exist on the comparative quality of men's and women's work in various fields suggest that competence varies only with individual characteristics and not with gender. Women who achieve distinction in fields like engineering, science, art, business, or politics have been found to be similar to men who achieve distinction in these fields and different from persons who do not. Such a conclusion is supported by the work of Louise Bachtold (1976), who studied 863 high-achieving women in four different career categories, and by the work of Frieda Gehlen (1977), who compared the women and men who served as elected representatives to the Ninety-first and Ninety-third U.S. Congresses. Gehlen found that women and men were not distinguishable in the ratings given them by political interest groups, nor on how often they voted with or against their own party, their general effectiveness, the percentage of legislation they sponsored, and the percentage that was acted upon. I know of no evidence in any field that indicates a gender difference in competence among similarly trained and functioning persons. Thus, for example, a new Marine Corps program to teach women recruits to shoot a rifle has proven successful. While only about 40 percent of the women were expected to qualify as marksmen, 98 percent ended up qualifying, the same rate as for men recruits ("Women Marines," 1986).

Family Responsibilities and Multiple Roles

Most women, including those with careers, are also wives and mothers. Those who leave jobs or interrupt careers in order to assume primary responsibility for child care run the risk of having to start all over again when they return to the world of paid employment, since there is no legal protection against loss of job or job status. The woman who drops out of the work force for parenthood will more than likely lose her place. When she returns she may be told by prospective employers that her skills and knowledge are no longer up to date and that there are more experienced persons competing for the job, and she may have to accept the low pay and status of an entry-level position.

While professional women must be prepared for adverse career consequences after a temporary withdrawal from active participation in their fields and association with their professional colleagues, the less-educated woman who is suddenly forced into the work world by divorce or widowhood will confront an even more difficult situation. She must convince a prospective employer that she is not a "retarded housewife." A Census Bureau report (in "Women Working Less," 1984) indicated that 72 percent of employed women interrupt their jobs or careers for six months or longer, compared to 26 percent of men. While men spend an average of 2 percent of their potential work years out of the work force, the average woman spends 23 percent of these years unemployed. The major reason for this difference is that women interrupt their employment to have children and to care for them at home. A study of a group of women faculty members (Yogev & Vierra, 1983) found that 66 of the 68 who had children reported one or more interruptions in their careers, and 83 percent of these interruptions were to have or care for children.

Women who work outside the home tend also to work inside of it almost as much, in terms of chores done, as women who are full-time homemakers. An employed woman who is also a wife and mother remains primarily responsible for the good health, comfort, cleanliness, and happiness of her husband and children. Lenore Radloff (1975) found, from a survey of approximately 2500 persons, that working wives reported doing almost as much housework as did full-time homemakers. Among the employed men, 23 percent said they did some work around the house or yard each day, compared with 69 percent of the employed women and 80 percent of the full-time homemakers. Similar data were discussed earlier in the chapter on marriage. Regardless of her type of employment—blue-collar, white-collar, managerial, or professional—the average woman with children tries to find ways to accommodate her schedule to the needs of her family. For example, women who work in coal mines (Hammond & Mahoney, 1983) reported that they arrange their work shifts to be home at the same time as their school-age children. Similarly, among a group of married full-time practicing physicians whose professional productivity was unrelated to their gender, the women had primary responsibility for significantly more domestic tasks than the men and spent more than twice as much time on them (Pyke & Kahill, 1983).

Employed mothers typically devote substantially more time than employed fathers to caring for their children and their homes, accommodating the needs of family members, and tending to household responsibilities. Thus, among a sample of employees in a large corporation (Englander-Golden & Barton, 1983), although men and women without children had similar work attendance records, mothers were found to use significantly more of their sick-leave hours than fathers to attend to a child's illness or other child-related matters of importance. Professionally employed mothers seem not too different from other employed mothers in their concern for their children's well-being, and in the lack of equal time and effort forthcoming from their husbands. Donald St. John-Parsons (1978) studied ten dual-career couples (spanning 14 different professions) in which the wife had only minimally interrupted her career for childbearing. He reported that

> not one husband took sole care of the children in emergencies or illness, although four couples shared this responsibility. Where the families had hired helpers, they were invariably brought in. In the two families where the husbands were physicians, though specialists in psychiatry, the wives took sole care of sick children. (p. 35)

Inequality in household chores was also found to exist among a sample of employed psychologist couples (Bryson, Bryson, Licht, & Licht, 1976). Wives had the major responsibility for cooking, marketing, school-age child care, preschool child care, and laundry. Outside help rather than husbands assisted with house cleaning. The researchers concluded that "sharing a profession evidently does not involve sharing the housework" (p. 15), although 72 percent of the couples felt that they had worked out a satisfactory division of labor. In the chapter on parenthood, we noted that Lucia Gilbert (1985), in a study of dual-career families, found that only in 30 percent were both working parents equally involved with home and family responsibilities.

Whether we look directly at women's personal experiences or through the filtered lens of social science research we find much the same indication of the conflicting pressures married women (especially mothers) encounter in trying to fulfill the cultural expectations for being good homemakers while at the same time fulfilling work obligations or pursuing

careers. In a television interview reported in the press ("Her Uncle," 1979), Agnes de Mille, the brilliant choreographer, talked about the early years of her marriage, and her husband's expectations.

> He wanted me to do cooking [and] I'm not a cook. But he wanted me to cook and I went to cooking school secretly and I learned how. . . . One Sunday afternoon [I] made him a dinner with biscuits and all sorts of things, and you know, he wept. He'd never wept when he'd seen my dances.

A husband may expect his employed wife to behave in the traditional manner and may be disinterested in her achievements outside the home, or he may resent them and attempt to stand in her way. In Marge Piercy's (1984a) novel *Fly Away Home*, when the daughter of a successful writer of cookbooks remarks to her mother that some of her friends have seen her on television, Daria replies:

> "Well, does that bother you?" Daria felt a little pang of guilt [and] . . . quickly changed the subject. Talking too much about her work or the modest measure of celebrity it had brought felt dangerous around the house, even if Ross [her husband] wasn't in earshot. (p. 22)

Many successful women I have known have expressed the same feeling of diffidence or discomfort about discussing their public achievements in the presence of their children or husband, as though the public aspect of their lives was either not relevant or disturbing to members of their families to whom they were mother or wife.

Since employed married women with children tend to assume more household and child care responsibilities than their husbands, it is not surprising to find that more women than men in comparable careers remain unmarried, and that career women are more likely than other women to not have children. Jeanne Herman and Karen Gyllstrom (1977) have reported that among 500 employees of a midwestern university, twice as many women as men were unmarried. Others have found that women with doctorates are less likely to marry than men with doctorates. For example, one study (Glenwick, Johansson, & Bondy, 1978) found that proportionately more women assistant professors in two universities were either never married or divorced than a comparable group of men. Sara Yogev and Andrea Vierra (1983) have noted "a trend toward permanent childlessness among younger professional women" (p. 394) and found, among a sample of university faculty women, a higher rate of childlessness than in the general population for every age group sampled. In a study of a sample of alumni from a women's college who were contacted 10 years after graduation, Abigail Stewart (1980) found that "career persistence and career type were both strongly negatively predicted by marriage and children" (p. 204). And, finally, a study of 300 top women executives (in Fowler, 1982) found that only 40.7 percent were married, compared with 94 percent of a group of men executives surveyed in an earlier study. The percentage of women who had never married was 27.6 compared to 1 percent of the men.

Role overload—the necessity to fulfill many responsibilities associated with both home and personal life and employment—is clearly greater for married women than for married men. One study of married physicians (Pyke & Kahill, 1983) concluded that "practical concerns related to domestic responsibilities appear to be most problematic, and distinguish the women sharply from the men" (p. 191), while Dalia Ducker (1980), who interviewed a sample of women physicians in four different specialties, found that those with strong family commitments were likely to experience feelings of strain and conflict between the demands of home and professional work. Similarly, among a group of 232 married women doctors, lawyers, and professors, Janet Gray (1983) found that 77 percent said they often experienced strains between home and career.

Despite the reported experience of problems associated with trying to balance home and job responsibilities, and the unequal share of home responsibilities that falls to women, research on the effects of role overload does not support a conclusion of negative consequences for the married employed woman, for her job productivity, job satisfaction, or her family. Sara Yogev (1982) has reviewed relevant research on dual-career couples and concluded that for women, "the act of coping and the challenge of this lifestyle seem to outweigh the disadvantages, and there is no harm to the family unit" (p. 603). Similar conclusions with respect to family and personal functioning have been reached by others who have studied varied groups of employed women. After reviewing the sizable literature on working women and stress, James Terborg (1985) concluded that "working women as a group differ little from working men in rates of turnover, absenteeism, and illness, and both groups report similar levels of job satisfaction" (p. 254). Some research has found that employment is not only not detrimental to a woman, but, in fact, enhances her mental health; we will consider this issue in a later chapter.

Harassment on the Job

Even the most highly motivated woman who knows she has the aptitude for a particular job, who is confident that she will succeed, and who manages to receive the appropriate training, may find that she is treated differently from her male co-workers. She may be the target of hostility or suspicion. She may not be taken seriously, or she may be expected to outperform the men with whom she works. She may be the butt of tasteless jokes, pursued as easy sexual prey, or humiliated. Such reports have come from almost every occupational area, from the armed forces, coal mines, corporate offices, universities, and factories. Consider the following report by Morris Stone (1978) from the world of blue-collar labor about a woman who was hired for the bottom spot on a six-member crew that operated a heavy piece of machinery.

> Instead of offering her the customary advice and on-the-job tutoring, the men found ways to harass her, such as over-tightening bolts, forcing her to call the foreman when they had to be loosened. They looked on as she tried to move a heavy steel roller, neglecting to tell her there was special equipment for the purpose. As a result, she wrenched her back; the time she spent on sick leave . . . was proof, they claimed, that she should never have been hired. (p. F3)

Large numbers of women experience sexual harassment—unwanted, unsolicited, and nonreciprocated sexual behavior or attention. Surprisingly, however, this subject was rarely discussed openly until the mid-1970s, so well had women learned to expect such behavior by men in the workplace, as in all other settings. Catharine MacKinnon (1979) was among the first to attempt to document the frequency of sexual harassment experienced by working women and to propose definitions and remedies. In 1980, the federal Equal Employment Opportunity Commission clarified its declaration that sexual harassment is prohibited under Title VII of the Civil Rights Act of 1964 (Ferrell & Slade, 1980), and defined such behavior as "unwelcome sexual advances, requests for sexual favors, and other verbal or physical conduct of a sexual nature." It is illegal for sexual submission to be made a condition of employment or assignment, and for sexual conduct to interfere with an employee's work performance or the work environment. The Commission's guidelines hold employers liable for the behavior of their supervisors, and for sexual harassment between co-workers if the employer should have known about it.

In Chapter 7, it was argued that women's frequent experience of sexual harassment (in all areas of activity) is one of the factors contributing to our ambivalence about sex. Estimates of how widespread sexual harassment is are varied. According to the Working Women's Institute (1980), "Sexual harassment is the single most widespread occupational hazard women face in the workforce" (p. 1). They cite evidence from different sources: a study in Ithaca, New York, in which 70 percent of the women surveyed reported having experienced some unwanted sexual advances on the job; a survey by *Redbook* that found an 88 percent incidence; and an investigation in Illinois that found that 59 percent of the women questioned reported sexual harassment in their present place of employment. A study done at the United Nations (*News*, 1981) reported that one out of four women employees had been pursued for sexual favors in return for a promotion or other job benefit or experienced some other form of sexual harassment. When Kurt Waldheim, who was then Secretary General, was visited by a group of women to discuss the findings, he expressed concern, "and also questioned the group's dress (they wore black), saying he preferred the women at the United Nations to dress in pink or some other bright color"!

The most extensive and carefully executed research on this issue, involving the largest number of randomly sampled respondents (federal employees), was conducted by the United States Merit System Protection Board (Tangri, Burt, & Johnson, 1982). The investigators found that 42 percent of the women and 15 percent of the men reported having been sexually harassed at work within the past two years. Of those with this experience, 78 percent had been harassed by men. Most incidents of harassment were found to involve co-workers, but "women's harassers are most likely to be older married men . . . [and] more women than men are harassed by a superior" (p. 45). The victims of harassment seldom reported it to anyone, a finding reported by other studies as well.

During a single 12-month period the Equal Employment Opportunity Commission received 4272 discrimination cases that included charges of sexual harassment (Bartlett, 1982). It is important to understand that cases actually filed with the Commission are only a small proportion of the total number of complaints since legal redress is a course that is rarely pursued: "Women's groups counsel women to try to solve the issue at the workplace. Trials are expensive, emotionally draining and often embarrassing. And the more subtle forms of harassment are most difficult to prove" (Bartlett, 1982, p. E-3). Many large companies have programs for managers explaining what sexual harassment is and that the company can be held legally liable for such behavior. Although the subject is no longer a hidden one and some women have publicly protested their victimization, most women still "grin and bear it" or try a variety of individual solutions including leaving their jobs, suffering psychological pain and financial hardship. One example of a successful outcome from litigation is the "peephole case." Seven women coal miners from West Virginia won a lawsuit against the Pittston Company for its negligence in not having protected them from being watched by their male co-workers through peepholes as they showered and dressed in the bathhouse. Another successful outcome that took four years of hearings, negotiations, and lawsuits involved Mary Lebrato, a psychologist employed by the State of California. After she had reported being sexually harassed by one of her supervisors (an incident witnessed by many), she was passed over for a promotion promised to her. After a "long, hard road" through the courts, Lebrato's case was settled in her favor out of court. The state awarded her $150,000 and agreed "to finance for two years a project to study problems in sexual harassment in private and public employment and to pay Lebrato's salary as its manager" (Cunningham, 1984).

The United States Supreme Court made its first ruling on sexual harassment in a June 1986 decision. The majority agreed that sexual harassment violates Title VII of the Civil Rights Act of 1964 and that discrimination based on sex creates "a hostile environment" (reported in "Sexual Harassment," 1986). This ruling clearly indicates that sexually harassing behavior is against the law. How effective a deterrent it will be remains to be seen. Some indication that official agencies have already become responsive to complaints of sexual harassment has been reported by Frances Coles (1986). She examined 88 cases brought to a state agency in California and found that almost half (42) were settled in less than three months. As Coles noted, "sexual harassment has moved from back room to courtroom and from fun to fines. What used to be a joke has been discovered to be institutionalized within the workplace" (p. 81).

Other Obstacles

Some evidence shows that strategies women tend to use for obtaining employment or promotions may not be as effective as those used by men. For example, one study of a sample of PhD recipients (Leviton & Whitely, 1981) found that women tended to apply for fewer jobs than men and were more likely to depend exclusively on their professor rather than on answering ads or sending out unsolicited inquiries or resumes. Patricia Gurin (1981), in an interview study of a representative national sample of adults, found that men and women differed in the types of changes they had tried to make to improve their employment situation. Both white and black men differed significantly and sharply from white and black women in having attempted more often to change their jobs or to obtain advanced job training. The women, on the other hand, had been more likely to improve their educations: "Both groups of women, and especially Black women, more often reported efforts to improve their educational qualifications than attempts to alter their market positions through changing jobs, requesting promotions, or acquiring job training" (p. 1090).

ENDING SEXISM IN THE WORKPLACE

Women clearly face formidable obstacles to job satisfaction and achievement, growing from deeply embedded sexist notions of our capabilities, "proper" roles, and worth. To end sexism in the workplace requires an end to job segregation by gender and to salary and promotion discrimination, a recognition of the comparable worth of different jobs, and an enlightened employment policy that guarantees a leave of absence to pregnant women and to a parent of either gender for care of biological or adopted children. Let us examine some of the mechanisms that are available and that are being proposed to end sexism in the workplace.

Antidiscrimination Legislation and Lawsuits

Congress has passed a number of bills since 1963 that, if strictly enforced and interpreted, would help reduce the current differential in status between the average woman and man in the work force. The first of these was the Equal Pay Act, which prohibits wage discrimination and requires that women and men "performing work in the same establishment under similar conditions must receive the same pay if their jobs require equal skill, effort, and responsibility" (U.S. Department of Labor, 1980, p. 1). This act applies to most workers in both the public and private sectors except those in small retail and service establishments. Since 1979 it has been administered by the Equal Employment Opportunity Commission (EEOC). Title VII of the Civil Rights Act of 1964, as amended by the Equal Employment Opportunity Act of 1972, prohibits discrimination based on sex, race, color, religion, and national origin in hiring, firing, wages, fringe benefits, classification, training, apprenticeships, or any conditions of employment. It covers establishments employing 15 or more workers, and labor unions. Guidelines issued by the EEOC, which enforces Title VII, prohibit "hiring based on stereotyped characterization of the sexes, classification or labeling of 'men's jobs' and 'women's jobs', and advertising under male or female headings" (U.S. Department of Labor, 1980, p. 2). Other legislation and executive orders require that contractors doing business with the federal government not discriminate against any employee or applicant because of sex (or race, color, and so on); that qualified women have access to job training programs; and that any educational program or activity receiving federal assistance not discriminate on the basis of sex.

The U.S. Department of Labor (1980) urges women to assert their job rights by discussing them with personnel officers or supervisors, instituting grievance procedures through appropriate programs, and filing complaints with a state or federal agency. Machinery to counter sex discrimination in employment exists, but working through it is cumbersome, time-consuming, frustrating, painfully slow, and typically drains the complainant(s) of energy, money, and self-confidence. Those who make individual complaints rarely see a satisfactory solution without years of struggle. One reason is that a huge number of claims are filed with federal agencies not able to handle them quickly and efficiently. For example, by 1976, only 4 years after passage of Title IX of the Education Amendments, which prohibits sex discrimination in schools, 3000 charges of discrimination against colleges and universities had been filed with the EEOC; and in just one 12-month period from October 1, 1981, to September 30, 1982, the EEOC received 30,925 general sex-discrimination claims filed under Title VII of the Civil Rights Act (Jackman, 1983). Positive outcomes have been more likely for women acting together in class action suits.

In recent years, the charge of discrimination has been made by some men who claim that an employer's affirmative action program (designed to undo past discrimination by setting objectives for the hiring of women and minorities) has the effect of penalizing white men through "reverse discrimination." Such charges are usually well publicized, and the 1980s have witnessed a backlash against affirmative action and a presidential administration that opposes it. The cartoon on this page may help us laugh at a clearly serious situation. At the same time that affirmative action is being weakened nationally by federal disinterest and opposition, national study committees such as that chaired by Alice Ilchman (1986) for the National Research Committee are continuing to find that "the reality of sex segregation is both persistent and pervasive, and that affirmative action efforts are one of the most effective ways to weaken segregation's hold" (p. A-11).

Women have won some dramatic victories through administrative channels and in the courts. For example, the Office for Federal Contract Compliance has greatly increased the numbers of women in banking, insurance, and mining (Ilchman, 1986). And in 1980, a federal court awarded women working for Western Electric Company in New Jersey close to $9 million in back wages after finding the company guilty of sex discrimination. According to David Rosenbaum (1980), this case

> is one of hundreds in recent years in which companies and government agencies have been forced to pay back wages to women, raise their salaries and make special allowances in the future to overcome the effects of past discrimination. . . . Job discrimination suits [have been brought] on behalf of women in all walks of life . . . [and the] money involved in the settlements runs into hundreds of millions of dollars. (p. E3, Sec. 4)

Among the employers who have been forced through lawsuits to compensate women for sex discrimination are American Telephone & Telegraph; General Electric; Northwest Airlines; Uniroyal; Merrill Lynch, Pierce, Fenner & Smith; the United States Government Printing Office; United Airlines; Northwest Orient Airlines; the University of Minnesota; Brown University; and Lockheed California. At the University of Rhode Island, women classified as cleaners were paid over $150,000 in retroactive pay as a result of pressure from the U.S. Department of Labor in 1980 to equalize their wages with those paid to men doing the same work but classified as janitors. And in 1985, after years of litigation, a federal district court judge ruled that the University of Rhode Island had systematically discriminated against women faculty members by hiring them at lower ranks and

Cartoon by Bülbül © 1979.

paying them less than men with similar qualifications. The final settlement involves over $1 million.

Still, litigation in the courts requires years to be completed, and enormous amounts of money, energy, and commitment; and although many of the lawsuits brought by women have met with success, they "hardly make a ripple in the ocean of discrimination" (Rosenbaum, 1980). With respect to discrimination against women on college and university faculties, Mary Gray (1985) has noted that "in the twelve years since nondiscrimination statutes became applicable to faculty employment, . . . women have had little success in winning legal redress for employment discrimination in hiring, salary, promotion, and tenure . . . [and that] the burdens in time and money faced by those seeking remedies make litigation accessible to only a few" (p. 33). A 1985 judicial decision in favor of the Sears, Roebuck Company has been a serious setback for women's use of the law and the courts to fight job discrimination. The lawsuit against Sears was first filed in 1979 by the EEOC. While other big firms charged with sex bias, like those previously listed, settled out of court, Sears fought the charge. According to Jon Wiener (1985):

> The complaint covers the years 1973 through 1980. During that period, 60 percent of the applicants for all sales jobs at Sears and 40 percent of those qualified for commission sales posts [selling big-ticket goods, which is better paying] were women. Only 27 percent of those hired for commission jobs were women, however. Although 72 percent of Sears noncommission salespeople were women, they received only 40 percent of the promotions. (p. 174)

A federal court rejected the statistical evidence and was persuaded by the Sears lawyers that "women did not want the higher paying commission sales jobs because they had different values from men" ("Sears' Acquittal," 1986, p. A-2), were "afraid of competition with other salespeople and rejection by customers . . . [were] unfamiliar with most product lines sold on commission [which include fencing and auto parts, but also washing machines and draperies], and they didn't want additional responsibilities" (Wiener, 1985, p. 176).

Union Solidarity

Labor unions have traditionally made less effort to organize workers in industries where most women work than in those where men predominate, even though the struggles of women clothing and textile workers in the early part of this century contributed dramatically to the birth of the American labor movement. In 1975, 34.1 percent of women blue-collar workers (crafts, factories, nonfarm labor), 11.5 percent of women clerical workers, 11.1 percent of women service and private household workers, and 6.2 percent of women sales workers belonged to unions. In 1981, only 13.8 percent of full-time women workers were represented by unions or employee associations, compared to 23 percent of full-time male workers (Serrin, 1985).

Before the early 1980s, as A. H. Raskin (1977) has pointed out, "the 'Men Only' sign [was] . . . firmly in place on the staircase leading to unionism's top floor," but change has occurred, and women's potential for labor movement leadership, and the importance of organizing women, has been recognized. According to William Serrin (1985):

> Women have moved into organizing, political lobbying, research and other important staff positions in such

unions as the United Automobile Workers, the United Electrical Workers, the American Federation of State, County and Municipal Employees, the United Mine Workers of America and the Service Employees International Union. (p. A14)

Although thus far only one woman has served as president of a major union (Mary Futrell, of the National Education Association), in 1985 there were two women on the 35-member executive council of the American Federation of Labor and Congress of Industrial Organizations. The first woman ever to be elected to the executive council, in 1980, was Joyce Miller, vice president of the Amalgamated Clothing and Textile Workers Union.

In 1973, a small number of clerical workers in Boston, under the leadership of Karen Nussbaum and Ellen Cassedy, organized for "better pay, better training opportunities and greater stature in the workplace" ("Women in Clerical Jobs," 1985). From this local group grew a national organization known as 9 to 5 (the National Association of Working Women), which now has 23 chapters across the country and 14,000 members. In 1981 it joined forces with the much larger Service Employees International Union to create District 925, dedicated to organizing the "nearly 20 million female secretaries, stenographers, typists, clerks, key punch operators and other office workers in the United States" ("Working Women Join Forces," 1981). This movement among clerical workers has been successful in changing the image of the secretary, enhancing women workers' self-esteem and confidence, and improving the conditions of work. Illustrating the national recognition given to the union's strength is a front-page profile of Karen Nussbaum that appeared in the *Wall Street Journal*, in which she was referred to as "part of a small but growing nucleus of women wielding real power" (in "9 to 5 in the News," 1985, p. 4).

The Comparable Worth Movement

In an effort to reduce the differential between salaries earned by most women (in "women's jobs") and salaries earned by most men, some have proposed that jobs that involve comparable effort, training, skill, and responsibility should pay comparable wages or salaries. Carolyn Bell (1984) has pointed out that by extending the principle of equal pay for equal work to situations in which jobs are not identical but comparable, a social policy requiring equal pay for comparable jobs "would not completely wipe out wage differentials or occupational segregation by sex, but it would remove the impact of existing discriminatory practices" (p. 17). Paying workers in accordance with the value of their work to their employer would significantly enhance job equity.

Proponents of comparable worth have presented illustrations of salary inequities such as the following: in 1979 a clerk (typically a woman) employed by the state of New York earned $7195 a year, compared to a parking attendant (typically a man) employed by the state who earned $8825; in Montgomery County, Maryland, a school teacher received an average of $12,323, compared to a liquor store clerk who earned $12,479; and in Denver, Colorado, a city-employed registered nurse made $12,768 a year, while a building painter employed by the city made $14,292 (Greenhouse, 1981). A study in San Jose, California, found that city jobs generally held by women (such as librarian, nurse, recreation supervisor, stenographer) paid significantly less than comparable jobs held by men (such as electrician, plumber, carpenter, mechanic); for example, the biweekly salary of a nurse was $772, while that of a mechanic was $1152 ("Strikers Demand," 1981). In Nassau County, New York, communication technicians who send out fire trucks (mostly men) have starting salaries of $14,805 a year, while police communication and teletype operators (mostly women) start at $13,188 (Roberts & Slade, 1984). And Roslyn Feldberg (1984) has cited a study of occupational title ratings that found "child-care workers being rated lower than parking-lot attendants, . . . nursery school teachers far below marine mammal handlers, practical nurses below the offal man, and nurse-midwives below hotel clerks" (p. 324).

On the basis of such data, the principle of comparable worth has won some dramatic support. In the first of a group of recent cases, a suit brought by four Oregon prison matrons against the county that employed them (because they were paid only 70 percent as much as the male prison guards) was upheld by the Supreme Court in 1981. The Court thus acknowledged the legal validity of a comparable worth argument. Later that year, in San Jose, California, city workers won $1.5 million in equity raises in "the first successful strike over equal pay for comparable work" (Cassedy & Nussbaum, 1983, p. 45). Illustrating the facts in this strike is a comparison between the mayor's secretary and a senior air-conditioning mechanic; although they were ranked equal in skills and responsibilities, the secretary was paid 42 percent less. In 1983, a federal judge put into practice the comparable worth doctrine supported two years ear-

lier by the Supreme Court, by finding the state of Washington guilty of sex discrimination because it did not provide equal pay for jobs of comparable skill, effort, and responsibility. This decision was subsequently struck down by a U.S. court of appeals, but a promise by the union representing the state employees to take the case to the Supreme Court if necessary led to a settlement of $482 million. As noted in the press, this was the largest settlement yet and "a major victory for the comparable worth movement" ("Wash. Court," 1986, p. A-3).

Those opposed to the concept of comparable worth argue that it would radically interfere with the natural market process of supply and demand. But proponents point out that the comparable worth principle was first proposed by a federal agency, the War Labor Board, in the 1940s, when the government was eager to attract women workers to industry; and that market factors are not responsible for women's low wages as much as "a tradition that has treated women as temporary and supplementary workers, devalued women's work, and rationalized low wages as all that women *qua* women need" (Feldberg, 1984, p. 318). A case in point is that of nurses, who, while in high demand, have traditionally received lower pay than men in comparable jobs. According to economist Marianne Ferber (1982), wages are determined more by employers (and unions) than by market factors; and within a single industry "the wide range of wages paid to workers with very similar qualifications cannot be assumed to be the result of impersonal market forces" (p. 292). Widely used methods already exist for calculating the worth of jobs and for determining wages and salaries. Comparable worth advocates are suggesting that these methods be improved in the interest of gender equity. Representative Claudine Schneider (1985), for example, has pointed out that federal government workers are already classified by GS level, and that two thirds of all workers in this country work in firms where some form of job evaluation already exists. "The question," she suggests, "is not whether those classifications should exist but whether or not they are fair."

Mandating Parental Child-Care Leaves

Only the United States, among all the industrialized nations in the world, does not yet have a national policy that gives employed women a specific period of time off for childbirth with job protection and partial or full salary. The resultant "choices" faced by

cathy®   by Cathy Guisewite

an employed woman who wants to become a mother are humorously detailed in the cartoon by Cathy Guisewite. A bill before Congress at this writing (the Parental and Medical Leave Act of 1986), introduced by Representative Patricia Schroeder of Colorado, would "mandate unpaid leaves of at least 18 weeks for parents of newborn, newly adopted, or seriously ill children, as well as a 26-week unpaid leave for short-term medical disabilities of any kind" (Cordes, 1986, p. 28). This bill, which has 44 co-sponsors, does not require that parents take such leaves, but that they be granted by an employer, if requested. It would also set up a commission to recommend ways to establish a standard for providing paid leaves since many parents cannot afford to take an unpaid leave of absence for child care.

Some employers already grant child-care leaves and provide job protection to returning employees, and some unions are now making such a policy explicit in their contracts and bargaining for some form of paid leave. The city of Philadelphia is the first city in this country to have a parental leave policy that grants adoptive and biological parents of either gender unpaid leave for child care (Specter, 1986).

PROMOTING THE IDEAL THAT WOMEN NEED BOTH LOVE AND WORK

Employed women face special stresses and dilemmas not shared by working men. While the latter may also be frustrated in their search for meaningful and well-paying work that provides opportunities for advancement, their pursuit of occupational achievement is applauded and unambiguously approved by society.

This is less often the case for women. Jeanne Lemkau (1979b) has pointed out that the narrower range of job options for women decreases the likelihood that a "good fit" will be found among our skills, interests, aspirations, and employment prospects. Women are generally more educated than men in the same occupational category and are therefore more likely to experience the frustration of being underused. In jobs that are equal to women's abilities, the earnings are typically less than those of male colleagues.

The old Yiddish expression "With friends like these, who needs enemies?" may describe how some women feel after having experienced the obstacles to job satisfaction described in this chapter; some may well say, "With problems like these, who needs a job?" Thus, almost half of American married women continue to labor in their own homes and to serve their families for no wages and little social recognition, their behavior maintained by the pleasures derived from family life, the hoped-for affection of husband and children, and avoidance of the frustrations awaiting them outside.

Most American women, however, do work for money outside of our homes, expect to do so, and contradict the myth that women will be cared for by men, and that home-baked pies and a pretty face are the routes to a happy life. For example, Ravenna Helson (1986) found that among graduates of a women's college, starting in the 1960s, more women answered "always" to the question "How long did you expect that you would work?" than gave any other response. Among respondents to a nationwide Associated Press poll ("Poll: Women," 1986), 58 percent agreed that women should have an equal chance to do any job that men do; and an equal percentage of men and women said it was good that more women were now working outside the home. Younger respondents were more positive about this trend than older ones, with 60 percent of 18- to 34-year-olds agreeing that the increasing number of working women was a good phenomenon.

But, if we do not actively and explicitly promote the ideal that women should work on an equal basis with men, our culture will deny women the opportunity to acquire skills, attitudes, and objectives that maximize our potential as fully functioning members of society; prevent women from making full use of the skills and aptitudes we have learned; and increase the likelihood that women will face formidable obstacles in the work force. A study cited at the beginning of this chapter (Ruggiero & Weston, 1985) found that in a sample of women's magazines first published in the 1970s and 1980s, "working for pay is portrayed as an integral part of . . . women's self-concept" (p. 546). We can hope that such media presentations will become the norm, so that women will not have to confront the dilemma of choosing between love and work, between personal relationships and achievement, between family satisfactions and those attainable through a job or career. Women, like men, should be encouraged to strive for both.

Fulfilling and Not Fulfilling Cultural Expectations

A man of about thirty strikes us as a youthful, somewhat unformed individual, whom we expect to make powerful use of the possibilities for development opened to him by analysis. A woman of the same age, however, often frightens us by her psychical rigidity and unchangeability. . . .There are no paths open to further development . . . as though, indeed, the difficult development to femininity had exhausted the possibilities of the person concerned.

Sigmund Freud   *(1933/1964, p. 134f)*

The membership committee of a business and professional club was considering what object might make an attractive bonus for new members. I suggested a canvas bag. "Men won't carry it" was the immediate consensus. At first I pushed my point. . . . But even as I spoke, my mind's eye had trouble visualizing great numbers of men with bags in hand, while the images of women carrying all manner of totes was an easy one to conjure. . . . When men carry things, what they carry is usually associated with their work or leisure activities . . . attache case . . . tool kits and lunch pails . . . gym bags or tennis rackets. Of course, many women carry the same labor and leisure items that men do, but . . . women also carry loads of things that maintain and enhance the lives of others . . . groceries, household supplies, laundry, baby bags and packages of assorted necessities.

Letty Pogrebin   *(1983, p. C2)*

What the human nature of males and females really consists of . . . is a capacity to learn to provide and to read depictions of masculinity and femininity and a willingness to adhere to a schedule for presenting these pictures, and this capacity they have by virtue of being persons, not females or males. . . . Gender expressions are by way of being a mere show; but a considerable amount of the substance of society is enrolled in the staging of it.

Erving Goffman   *(1979, p. 8)*

C H A P T E R   13

*O*ur culture defines womanhood differently from manhood. The former is equated with "femininity," and the typical woman is expected to behave in ways defined as feminine. The extent to which women act in "feminine" ways (and men in "masculine" ways) depends upon the success with which institutionalized sanctions and differential experiences have influenced us in the direction of fulfilling our culture's expectations.

Research suggests that a female body has few predictable consequences for behavior unless paired by culture with a complex set of demands, anticipations, and circumstances. Women and men can (and do) acquire the same habits, attitudes, aspirations, and motives under the same learning conditions, but acquire different behavioral propensities if their experiences and the way their responses are reinforced systematically differ. In other words, variations in experiences result in variations in the behaviors we learn, a theme that has been presented throughout this book. Thus, predictable personality and role consequences for women growing up in our society are not inevitable, but are related to cultural emphases and training for girls directed toward assuring gender differences. In this chapter we will consider some of the consequences for women's adult behavior, in general, of earlier socialization and continued social expectations. In other chapters, we have already dealt in detail with behavior specifically relevant to love relationships, family, and employment.

WHAT IS FEMININITY?

Dictionary definitions of the word *feminine* are surprisingly vague, typically making reference to the term *womanly* and giving one or two adjectives describing feminine traits, such as *weak, gentle, modest.* Yet, this word is used frequently in ordinary conversation and in the mass media. Janet Spence (1985) has suggested that we understand the meaning of *femininity* as a basic aspect of the individual's self-concept that *identifies* one as a woman. When *feminine* (or *masculine*) is used to denote gender identity, most of us have a firm sense of this aspect of ourselves.

We also know that to be feminine requires certain behaviors of us, and that these behaviors are important if we are to fulfill cultural expectations. As argued by Susan Brownmiller (1984), "Biological femaleness is not enough. Femininity always demands more. It must constantly reassure its audience by a willing demonstration of difference" (p. 15). Brownmiller reminds us of how often women are admonished not to "lose" their femininity, or complimented if they have managed to "retain" their femininity. "To fail at the feminine difference is to appear not to care about men, and to risk the loss of their attention and approval" (p. 15), as well as that of other women, friends, colleagues, employers. Whatever else one does, women are told, we must not compromise our femininity. Even job success depends on it, we are told by the media and advertisements such as the one shown on page 242.

So what, exactly, are the personal qualities or attributes, the specific behaviors, situations, and tasks or jobs that are associated with being feminine, as distinguished from masculine? For one view, we can look at the tests or scales some psychologists have constructed that rate a respondent's degree of femininity (or masculinity) based on the average frequency with which the respondent self-reports particular activities, interests, or characteristics. Thus, for example, an early measure of femininity constructed by Harrison Gough (1952) included such items as the following, to be answered true or false:

> I think I would like the work of a building contractor.
> I like adventure stories better than romantic stories.
> I want to be an important person in the community.
> If I get too much change in a store, I always give it back.
> I become quite irritated when I see someone spit on the sidewalk.

> The thought of being in an automobile accident is
> very frightening to me.

Obviously, to be scored "feminine" one would have to answer false to the first three self-descriptive statements and true to the last three. According to the author of these items, femininity connotes "acceptingness, softness, mildness, and tolerance" while masculinity is associated with "self-centeredness, formality, hardheadedness, and coolness" (Gough, 1952, p. 438).

Such stereotypes are also reflected in the differences women and men are assumed to manifest. Thus, diverse samples of adults in this country have been found to agree on traits that differentiate the genders (for example, Rosenkrantz, Vogel, Bee, Broverman, & Broverman, 1968; Broverman, Vogel, Broverman, Clarkson, & Rosenkrantz, 1972). Women are typically assigned such traits as the following: does not use harsh language, is talkative, tactful, gentle, aware of the feelings of others, religious, interested in own appearance, neat in habits, quiet, has strong need for security, appreciates art and literature, and expresses tender feelings. Men, on the other

You've never compromised your femininity for your success.

Maybe that's why you're so successful.

hand, are said to be aggressive, independent, unemotional, objective, active, competitive, logical, worldly, and direct. The positively valued traits attributed to men are found to cluster in a factor identified as competence-assertion-rationality, while the positively valued traits ascribed to women are said to constitute a warmth-expressiveness factor.

Recent studies using a variety of different methods (but getting information primarily from college students) have found little substantial change in the content of such gender stereotypes. Thus, for example, Paul Werner and Georgina LaRussa (1985), who directly compared the results from a 1978 study with results from 1958, found that 62 percent and 77 percent of adjectives ascribed in 1958 to men and women, respectively, remained part of the stereotypes in 1978. Although some older adjective descriptions were replaced by new ones, "in no case did an adjective change sexes over the two decades" (p. 1095). Women respondents tended to view women more favorably and men less favorably in 1978 than in 1958 but, in general, the researchers concluded, "sex-role stereotypes have changed little in recent decades" (p. 1098). The same conclusion was reached by Patricia Smith and Elizabeth Midlarsky (1985), who had equal numbers of black and white women and men rate adjectives for degree of femaleness and maleness and social desirability. They found that "current conceptions of femaleness and maleness . . . [had] marked similarities to earlier conceptions" (p. 325), with men viewed as aggressive, work-minded, and capable of leadership, and women as sensitive, affectionate, and conscious of appearance. Compared with men's views of women, women saw themselves more positively, and in terms of activities rather than traits. While there were some other differences between women and men respondents and between blacks and whites in adherence to specific items, all conformed to the same general gender stereotypes.

Hope Landrine (1985) asked a sample of college students to respond to a series of adjectives by indicating how closely they matched our society's stereotypes of women who were identified as black or white, middle-class or lower-class. She found differences related to class and to race but women were generally described in terms of the traditional stereotypes identified by earlier researchers. The white middle-class woman fit the general stereotype for women most closely, with lower-class women being rated as more confused, impulsive, and irresponsible than middle-class women, and black women as more hostile and superstitious than white women. But respondents agreed that regardless of class or race, a woman had stereotypically feminine characteristics. Their own judgments tended to be similar to those they viewed as society's, suggesting to Landrine that "general endorsement of social stereotypes persists" (p. 73). In another study (Jackson & Cash, 1985), physically attractive women and men seen in photographs were judged to be more feminine and masculine, respectively, than less attractive same-gender persons.

While most studies such as the ones just cited have reported high agreement on adjective descriptions of women and men (or of femininity and masculinity), some researchers have reported variable descriptions (in Spence, 1985) or low correlations among traits attributed to persons of the same gender. For example, Kay Deaux (1984) has cited a study with a colleague that found that when respondents were asked to estimate the probability that the average man or woman was associated with particular characteristics, behaviors, or jobs, the obtained patterns were not "of the all-or-none variety" and correlations between sets of attributes were low. Table 13.1 presents the probability judgments made by the participants in this study. In each case, the judgments made about women and men differed significantly in the direction of the prevailing stereotypes, but no attribute was judged as exclusive to one gender.

The data shown in Table 13.1 reflect a newer view of femininity: that it and masculinity are not opposite ends or poles of a single dimension but are independent. In other words, regardless of gender, a person can manifest characteristics, varying in strength, that are associated with both femininity and masculinity. This view, the "androgyny perspective," will be discussed in detail later in this chapter, as well as the more radical view that femininity and masculinity have no real meaning beyond stereotypes and should be eliminated from psychological and personal vocabularies. In the meantime, let us examine the extent to which actual women fulfill or do not fulfill our culture's expectations of femininity. This is the question to which we now turn.

GENDER DIFFERENCES IN ADULT BEHAVIOR

Behavior of adult women and men can be compared along a number of dimensions, including dependency/submissiveness versus leadership/dominance; susceptibility to social influence; confidence/self-

TABLE 13.1 Probability judgments about gender attributes made by participants in one study.
(From K. Deaux, "From individual differences to social categories," *American Psychologist*, 1984, *39*, 105–116, p. 112)

Characteristic	Judgment*	
	Men	Women
Traits		
Independent	.78	.58
Competitive	.82	.64
Warm	.66	.77
Emotional	.56	.84
Role behaviors		
Financial provider	.83	.47
Takes initiative with opposite sex	.82	.54
Takes care of children	.50	.85
Cooks meals	.42	.83
Physical characteristics		
Muscular	.64	.36
Deep voice	.73	.30
Graceful	.45	.68
Small-boned	.39	.62

*Probability that the average person of either sex would possess a characteristic

esteem; cooperativeness, concern for others, and affiliation; expressiveness; narcissism; strategies for power; and aggression. We will look at gender differences in these ways of behaving, but first we should note some considerations that affect these comparisons.

Women and men tend to describe themselves (as well as others) in ways that conform to our stereotypes about femininity and masculinity. For example, Robert Baldwin (1984) used the previously mentioned Gough Femininity Scale to test students at an urban community college in the Midwest over an 11-year period (from 1970 to 1980), and he reported an average score difference between women and men that remained generally consistent and did not differ reliably from what it was in 1952. His findings do not mean that all the women responded to the questions differently from all the men; there was considerable within-gender variability, but the average "femininity" score for women was reliably higher each year than the average score for men. In a well-known earlier study (Rosenkrantz, Vogel, Bee, Broverman, & Broverman, 1968), respondents rated themselves and the average adult man and woman on 122 bipolar adjectives (such as not at all aggressive – very aggressive) using a seven-point scale. Others were asked to indicate which pole of each of the items represented the more socially desirable behavior. The results showed that women and men agreed in their descriptions of each gender; that characteristics associated with men were perceived as more socially desirable than characteristics associated with women; and that women and men described themselves in much the same way as they described the average person of their gender. These findings were replicated with samples varying in age, religion, marital status, and education (Broverman, Vogel, Broverman, Clarkson, & Rosenkrantz, 1972). What is important to note here is that while self-reports tend to confirm gender stereotypes, in terms of average responses, observations of actual behavior tend to disclose significant within-gender variations related to differences in past and present circumstances, as we shall see from the discussion of the research that follows.

A related consideration has to do with the distinction between traits and roles in descriptions of behavior. Psychologists use the term *trait* to refer to behavior that a person tends to exhibit consistently and frequently across diverse situations (reflecting internalized attributes, or personality), and the term *role* to refer to behavior that is shown consistently in specific situations by certain classes of persons. How much of a woman's observed responses reflect one or the other of these categories of behavior is a question currently being addressed by empirical studies and theoretical arguments. This question will reappear repeatedly in this section as we examine the general behavior of adult women in a variety of situations.

Dependency/Submissiveness Versus Leadership/Dominance

Some women grow up expecting and assuming that they will be taken care of; others seek independence and acquire the requisite skills for its successful achievement but may be dissuaded by arguments that this is an undesirable path for a woman. A woman may fear independence because she has had little experience in practicing it, or because she has learned that women should be protected, defended, and guided by men. Such an assumption, challenged by many contemporary women, is still part of the dominant gender ideology of our culture.

The strength of a woman's learned motivation to put herself into the hands of a man on whom she can depend economically and emotionally is the subject of a best-selling book by Colette Dowling (1981), who labeled the phenomenon "the Cinderella complex" and described her own personal struggle to overcome it. The major elements of this syndrome are humorously illustrated in the drawing above.

Copyright © 1981 by The New York Times Company. Reprinted by permission.

Dowling's thesis is that large numbers of women fear independence and seek protection through identification and association with a man because we have not been brought up to anticipate taking care of ourselves, and because we get insufficient financial and social rewards for trying to do so. Dowling and others appear to forget, or to ignore, men's needs for affection, attention, compassion, and physical and psychological nurturance, which traditional women provide for them. When men turn to women for satisfaction of these needs, this behavior is not labeled dependence. Why not? What distinguishes a man's need for someone to take good care of him from a woman's need? We seem to accept the former uncritically, but to view the latter as a weakness and to label it pejoratively. Interdependence in relationships is sought by both women and men, despite our reluctance to admit that this is true.

Gaye Tuchman (1979) reviewed the ways in which women were presented on television in the late 1970s and found little change since 1954 in the high frequency with which we were depicted as victims. But the 1980s seem to have brought a new kind of independent heroine into television. "Kate and Allie" are divorced mothers who are shown competently, realistically, and humorously coping with interpersonal and employment demands and goals. Their lives are not problem-free, but they clearly enjoy their autonomy, and make successful use of old and new skills. "Cagney and Lacey" are police officers, sensitive but tough, women of integrity and dignity who do their jobs capably and with compassion. Jessica Fletcher, in "Murder, She Wrote," is a middle-aged widow from rural Maine who writes mysteries and is also a super sleuth, smart and risk-taking. These women are white, but Clair of "The Cosby Show" has offered television viewers a model of an assertive black woman who functions successfully as a lawyer and mother and is part of an interdependent relationship as a wife.

That such television women have proven popular suggests that for women to behave in a dominant manner, even in the presence of men, is no longer unusual. Nevertheless, clear indications exist that this is not yet the norm. Evidence shows that many women do not behave assertively in the company of men and tend to follow men's leadership in group situations. For example, John Davis (1978) had pairs of students alternately disclose information about themselves on an intimacy-scaled list of topics. Regardless of which partner had the first turn, the man in mixed-gender pairs took the lead in directing the pace at which intimacy increased during the exercise. The women matched the pace set by the men and correctly reported that they had exercised less influence. According to Edwin Hollander (1985), who has reviewed the relevant literature, "Leadership traditionally has been a male domain. . . . The evidence indicates that women and men are more inclined to expect a man rather than a woman to occupy a leader role" (p. 519). While few differences are found between women and men who occupy real leadership positions, differences in relevant behaviors continue to be found in samples of the general population.

In a study of behavior under natural conditions, Virginia Brooks (1982) observed and recorded the verbal contributions of students during 16 three-hour college classes. In classes taught by women professors, male students spoke significantly more often and significantly longer than female students; and in all classes, men interrupted more than women. Similar findings have been reported by others. Nancy Henley (1977) cited a study by Zimmerman and West in which the conversations of pairs of individuals in natural settings were tape-recorded; 96 percent of the interruptions and 100 percent of the overlaps in conversation were found to be made by men. Women were more often silent than men in mixed-gender pairs, especially after men interrupted or overlapped. Another study that recorded and analyzed the language used by men and women in same-gender and mixed-gender groups (McMillan, Clifton, McGrath, & Gale, 1977) found men to interrupt women more than five times as frequently as they were interrupted by them. The same study found support for earlier reports that women voice uncertainty more than men, particularly when in the presence of men, by making more use of "extra-baggage" intensifiers (as in "so confusing"), tagging more questions onto the ends of statements (such as "didn't it?"), and making more requests in the form of questions than in the form of direct imperatives. Other studies have found that women's speech tends to be more exaggerated, polite, hedged, and indirect than men's speech (Lakoff, 1975), and that men's speech is perceived as more dynamic (Mulac, Incontro, & James, 1985). Men have reported using profanity in daily speech more often than women, and that they believe such language demonstrates the social power or dominance of the user (Selnow, 1985). After reviewing the relevant literature, Adelaide Haas (1979) concluded that women's spoken language has generally been found to be more supportive, expressive, and polite than men's.

Women's deference (particularly in the presence of men) has also been inferred from nonverbal cues such as posture and gestures. Nancy Henley (1977) concluded that men and women in our society (like other groups differing in power) tend to use distinctive body languages. For example, women tend to take up less space (and are also assigned to smaller territories, such as smaller offices or shared offices); women tend to keep our bodies more rigid than men and to keep our legs together. Like other low-power persons, we tend to lower our eyes, stop talking when others interrupt, yield space to make room for others, and smile. We also spend more of our time waiting than do men, signifying that our time is less valuable. Relative submission is revealed by ways of moving, sitting, walking, and talking. Examples of such gender differences come from observations of behavior and also from the way women and men are presented in media messages. Erving Goffman (1979), for example, has collected and analyzed pictorial advertisements, and found that women are more often pictured receiving help from men than giving it, are more likely to be shown spatially below a man than above him, and are frequently posed "in a display of the 'bashful knee bend'" (p. 169), showing fear or shyness, smiling, and/or with body or head lowered.

Goffman noted that when "the level of the head is lowered relative to that of others, including, indirectly, the viewer of the picture . . . [this] can be read as an acceptance of subordination, an expression of ingratiation, submissiveness, and appeasement" (p. 46). An analysis of 1296 posed photographs of high school and college students and faculty (Ragan, 1982) revealed that women lowered their heads (canted) significantly more often than men. From the research currently available, it appears that deference to men is a well-learned and practiced response by women. There have not, as yet, been many studies directed toward identifying the specific circumstances or factors associated with women's leadership and dominance behaviors—behaviors amply exhibited in day-to-day situations verifiable by personal observation and experience.

Susceptibility to Social Influence

Alice Eagly (1978) examined a large body of persuasion/conformity research and concluded that women are not more easily persuaded than men by arguments on an issue. Only in group situations in which other members are the source of influence has greater influencibility of women been reported, especially in studies prior to 1970. Eagly has suggested that agreement with others in group situations, particularly on relatively unfamiliar issues, may reflect women's concern with harmonious and smooth social relations, and a feeling of "responsibility for the social-emotional aspects of the group process" (p. 105). In a reexamination of this research, Alice Eagly and Linda Carli (1981) found that women were more influenced than men in situations in which their responses were under surveillance by the influencing agent. Although this gender difference was a significant one across studies, it was nevertheless very small and of little practical value in predicting behavior. Only 1 percent of the variance in conformity or persuasion could be accounted for by gender. The analysis also revealed that greater female influencibility was significantly more likely to be reported by men than women researchers.

Most of the research on gender differences in social influence has used white middle-class participants. One exception is a study by Kathryn Adams (1980), who paired a white or black college student with a confederate of the same or different gender and of the same or different race. The confederates challenged picture preferences expressed by their partners, and Adams assessed the degree to which the

naive partners resisted changing their responses in the direction of the confederates. The white women were found to be more easily influenced than the white men, but the black women were less easily influenced than the black men, white men, or the white women. These data illustrate that cultural expectations may not be the same for all women in our society, and that not all women behave as our dominant stereotypes predict.

Other research has shown that the nature of the issue, topic, or task on which influence is attempted may also affect the extent to which the influence will be successful. People conform more readily on matters in which they have little interest or expertise. For example, Judy Morelock (1980) found that when individuals were shown the unanimous opinions of a group with whom they anticipated having a discussion, and these opinions were contrary to their own, women conformed more than men on items they knew little about (such as football and the military), while men conformed to the group opinion more than women on items they knew little about (such as day care centers and social work). The investigator concluded that "as long as social issues are perceived as sex-typed, . . . each sex will continue to have its limited domain of expertise" (p. 547) and be susceptible to social influence on the issues in which they lack knowledge.

Confidence/Self-Esteem

Research on gender differences in self-reported personal worth or self-confidence suggests that women generally manifest lower self-esteem than men. Researchers have proposed that this is a predictable consequence of women's socialization, since girls learn early that they will be less important, less powerful, and less effective than men; and adult women find that they have less control over their own lives and those of others, and less access to resources. A poem by my daughter Sara (Lott, 1985) expresses these consequences for women metaphorically:

> When I got to the station
> I thought there'd be some time
> to call and make the connection
> but my plans were out of line.
>
> Now I'm standing
> by the railroad tracks,
> waiting for a train.
> I don't care where I'm going
> 'cause each place looks the same.

I doubt it's very different
where I'm going
from where I've been.
It's this ache I carry around with me
that tells me 'bout the
shape I'm in.

Ellen Lenney (1977) reviewed the literature on self-confidence and concluded that, compared to men, women generally underestimate their abilities, and set lower educational and vocational goals that are unrelated to objective measures of their abilities. Women also tend to report lower self-confidence on tasks for which feedback is minimal or ambiguous, and in situations in which their work will be compared with that of others. But on tasks considered appropriate for women, women's self-confidence ratings are higher. Lenney's (1981) own research suggests that women's self-evaluations are more influenced by situational variables than are men's.

More recent research has sought to identify those variables that influence women's self-judgments. Ellen Lenney and Joel Gold (1982) found that on a task involving academic knowledge in which no social comparison was expected, men and women college students performed equally well and did not differ in self-evaluations of their performance. Only when they expected a comparison did the women evaluate themselves more poorly than the men. Jayne Stake (1983a) reported finding no gender differences in how well persons expected to do on a subsequent task in a study of college students who worked on a gender-neutral task under the condition of clear and unambiguous feedback about initial task success.

The importance of feedback and reduced ambiguity to women's self-judgments is further illustrated by the findings of a field study reported by Meredith Kimball and Vicky Gray (1982). Students at two universities, studying the same subject, were asked to predict their test scores before each of three examinations. In both groups, women predicted significantly lower scores than did men on the first exam. But on the next two exams, following feedback on the first one, no gender differences in expectancy were found among students in the university in which the course was taught entirely by one instructor. In the second university, where the course was taught sequentially by three different instructors, the women students manifested less self-confidence than the men on all three exams and predicted significantly lower scores, despite the fact that the women's scores were actually higher than the men's. The researchers concluded

that "the results from both courses support the hypothesis that in the absence of feedback, women have lower performance expectancies than men" (p. 1004). In the university in which there was "a new instructor and a new body of material for each examination . . . [each test became] a new situation in which the feedback from the last examination was not considered relevant" (p. 1005).

In another study (Heilman & Kram, 1984), with management employees from an insurance company, a gender difference was found in perception of one's co-workers' judgments of one's performance. but not in self-ratings. Each participant worked on a task and was led to believe that a partner was working on the same task in another room. After receiving feedback of excellent or poor for the pair's performance, women anticipated less credit for success from their partners than men, and more blame for failure. But on self-ratings of relaxation and effectiveness, no significant gender differences were found. These data suggest that women's self-reports of low-performance expectancy may reflect what they believe others expect of them, and not necessarily what they themselves believe.

Some studies continue to report a general tendency for women to state lower self-expectancies than men, to underestimate their performance on a variety of tasks, and to express less self-confidence than men (for example, Lippa & Beauvais, 1983; Instone, Major, & Bunker, 1983; McMahan, 1982). In 26 of 37 tested introductory college courses in 13 disciplines, women predicted lower grades for themselves than did men; subjects included the natural sciences, the social sciences, and the humanities (Cole, King, & Newcomb, 1977). Other research, however, has found that men and women with similar personality attributes show similar levels of self-confidence. For example, Sheryle Alagna (1982) reported that among a sample of college students, those who scored high in instrumental/agentic (that is, competent, assertive, task-oriented) characteristics had higher expectancies for performance on a task, and judged themselves to be more successful, than those who scored lower on such traits. This was true for both women and men. Another study (Senneker & Hendrick, 1983) observed the responses of participants to a simulated cry for help, and found no difference between the number of men and women who helped, but the men responded significantly faster, were more likely to report that they had had prior experience helping someone in an emergency, and the women more often reported "that they were unsure of what steps to take to try to help, that they were unsure they had the capability to help, and that they expected others to join in helping" (p. 923). While these differences indicate that gender was a significant variable, women and men who scored high on a measure of assertiveness/instrumentality tended to behave similarly and were not distinguishable in their responses to the emergency.

Attributions for Success and Failure One group of studies has assessed self-esteem or self-confidence by examining the reasons given to explain one's own success or failure. A frequently reported conclusion is that women tend to attribute their successes to external, nonstable factors such as luck, but to attribute their failures to lack of ability, while men attribute success to ability, and failure to task difficulty or low effort. But a careful review and analysis of the relevant literature (Frieze, Whitley, Hanusa, & McHugh, 1982) indicated that this generalization has been overstated and that gender differences in causal attributions for success and failure are not strongly supported across situations. A similar conclusion was reached by David Sohn (1982), who analyzed the results of 20 studies of self-attributions for achievement. He noted that "the empirical evidence does not support the proposition that the sexes differ consequentially in their use of any of the four main types of achievement self-attribution [luck, ability, effort, or difficulty of task]" (p. 354).

Although many studies have reported that women attribute their own success to ability less than men do, and attribute failure to lack of ability more than men do, the size of the gender difference is extremely small, and results are inconsistent across situations. For example, in a study of the reactions of real athletes to their performances in an intrasquad basketball scrimmage, researchers found that "successful females and males did not differ significantly in their self- and team attributions . . . [and] were generally just as inclined to take responsibility for their victory" (Croxton & Klonsky, 1982, p. 406). Cheryl Travis (1982) found the same high correlation for both men and women between objective success on a series of anagrams and expected future success, and that both genders tended to attribute their own success to high ability and their failure to task difficulty. She concluded that "sex differences provide very little information about the perception of causality" (p. 379).

Allocation of Rewards Some researchers have focused on how men and women allocate re-

wards to themselves relative to others in game or simulated work situations, and have considered such behavior to be a reflection of self-worth judgments. One study (Callahan-Levy & Messé, 1979) found that, after doing a task, women college students paid themselves less than they paid other persons and less than men paid themselves, indicating, according to the authors, "a weaker sense [of their] own equity." Interestingly, however, women in this study whose occupational preferences were nontraditional differed from more traditional women in allocating more money to themselves. Other studies have found that under certain conditions women allocate the same rewards to themselves as men do. For example, in a laboratory situation in which participants were given information on how much others paid themselves, no gender differences were found; individuals of "both sexes appeared to use the average amount taken by others as their comparison standard" (Major, McFarlin, & Gagnon, 1984, p. 1404). Another group of researchers (Wittig, Marks, & Jones, 1981) had some college students work on a task requiring luck and others on a task requiring effort, and each participant was then told that they had performed better than their partners. Both men and women who attributed their superior performance to effort tended to allocate a greater proportion of the reward to themselves than did those who attributed their superior performance to luck. No reliable gender differences were found.

Women tend to distribute rewards between themselves and a co-worker equally, while men are more likely to employ the principle of equity (allocating rewards on the basis of production or performance), but as the studies just cited indicate, not under all conditions. As noted by Michele Wittig (1985), "Such studies, which illustrate the circumstances in which previously well-established gender differences are not found, support interpretations of gender differences based on situation-sensitive norms and values, rather than situation-insensitive traits and motives" (p. 10). Some situational factors have also been found to minimize gender differences in third-party allocation strategies (rewards proposed for others, not oneself). For example, Jayne Stake (1983b), in a study in which participants were instructed to behave like work managers concerned with maintaining harmonious relationships among their employees, found that women and men used similar allocation strategies. In a subsequent study, Stake (1985) again found no gender differences when college students pretending to be managers were instructed to be fair;

under this condition more rewards were given to the faster workers by both women and men. When instructed to improve relationships among the workers, both women and men moved toward an equality principle, but when instructed to increase productivity, both used an equity principle. Similarly, Brenda Major and Jeffrey Adams (1984) found that different conditions influenced women and men in the same general way. They concluded that "gender differences in reward allocations may be due less to inherent personality or social orientation differences . . . than to situational factors within reward allocation settings that provide cues as to appropriate behavior for the sexes" (p. 879). When such cues are absent or less salient, gender is not a reliable predictor of behavior.

Men may tend to allocate rewards equitably because they have experienced such treatment themselves, in contrast to women. One study (Olejnik, Tompkins, & Heinbuck, 1982) found evidence in support of such a hypothesis. A sample of college students were instructed to imagine that they were third-grade teachers and to distribute candies to pairs of same-gender children. The men allocated more equitably than the women did, by giving more candies to the more productive child, but they rewarded the productive boys more than the deserving girls. The women, on the other hand, tended to use an equality reward strategy with girls and an equity strategy with boys. Another attempt to identify antecedents of gender differences in reward allocation behavior is illustrated by the work of Jayne Stake (1985), who asked students acting as managers in a hypothetical situation to give reasons for differences in worker productivity. Women were found to have greater sympathy for, and to be more accepting of, a slow worker than men, and to perceive the slow worker as more conscientious. Stake suggested that this finding was "consistent with differences in the socialization of men and women. . . . Women, more so than men, are expected to care for and value the individual and to place an emphasis on people rather than on tasks and end results" (p. 1628). On the other hand, in a study of 229 working administrators among whom the women and men had comparable management experience, the women were found to use equity in assigning pay raises to employees in a more discriminating way than the men ("Reward for," 1986). In making salary decisions, the women managers were more objective than the men and more responsive to subtle differences in worker performance. The investigator, Vandra Huber, concluded that women "fine-tuned the appraisal-pay system." These data clearly indicate the relevance of situational factors for behavior. When functioning in situations requiring allocation of rewards on the basis of performance, women behave accordingly and effectively.

Cooperativeness, Concern for Others, and Affiliation

Jean Baker Miller (1976) has suggested that many of the behaviors acquired by women as we are socialized to be good daughters, sisters, wives, and mothers provide us with strengths in the interpersonal domain. Thus, accepting the suggestions of others or distributing rewards equally among co-workers may be interpreted as prosocial, cooperative behaviors, which tend to promote interpersonal harmony and discourage discord. Women are expected to be agreeable and to reduce conflict. We can accomplish this by smiling, acquiescing, compromising, and not arguing too much. To steadfastly and logically defend one's position in an argument or to pay insufficient attention to what others are saying, is to risk being perceived as behaving in a "masculine" manner. The traditional woman has been taught to compromise and to consider the needs and feelings of others. Rae Carlson (1972) has suggested that women's experiences promote a communal, qualitative, and person-oriented mode of living; and Carol Gilligan (1982) has further developed this general thesis, proposing that women's morality rests upon consideration for the needs of others (that is, responsibility), whereas men's morality is concerned with abstract rules and rights (that is, justice).

While many observations of women's behavior may support the conclusion that women are more cooperative, helpful, and altruistic than men, we tend to make such observations in limited situations, ones in which cultural expectations for appropriate gender behavior are strong. When we observe people under conditions in which non–gender-related demands are more salient, we find that women can and do behave competitively and egotistically, and men cooperatively and sensitively. Careful reviews of the empirical literature typically fail to support generally accepted conclusions of stable gender differences. Thus, for example, Mary Brabeck (1983) has noted that the "empirical evidence . . . does not fully support Gilligan's claim . . . that males and females differ in moral orientations" (p. 286). In a comprehensive review of studies of gender differences in moral reasoning, Lawrence Walker (1984) found no significant differences among girls and boys in childhood and adolescence, and that the large majority of adult comparisons showed no gender differences. When such differences were found, they could be accounted for by the lesser education of the women studied.

An investigation of a sample of college students by Maureen Ford and Carol Lowery (1986) failed to confirm that women and men make differential use of "care" and "justice" orientations in resolving their own conflicts. Women differed from men in rating "their self-reported conflicts as significantly more important in their lives and their decisions as more difficult to make" (p. 779), and also in being more consistent over time in ratings of the degree to which care issues had influenced their thinking about their conflicts. But, women and men did not differ in their overall use of the two orientations. The investigators found that for both genders:

> the more important and more difficult moral decisions they have made . . . are more related to issues of care than to issues of justice . . . [and both genders] considered questions of relationships, care, and responsibility, as well as questions of fairness, justice, and rights, and they considered them fairly equally. (pp. 781, 782)

Despite these findings of no difference between women and men in the use of care and justice orientations in solving their personal moral dilemmas, the respondents in this study rated the justice orientation as more masculine and the care orientations as more feminine.

Some research continues to support gender differences in compassion or interpersonal consideration, under certain conditions. For example, a survey of a sample of adults in Massachusetts found that the women were less supportive of federal defense spending and were more worried about the likelihood of another war than the men (in "Poll: Women More Sensitive," 1983), and Michael Newcomb (1986), in a study of young adults in Los Angeles, found that women indicated more concerns about nuclear technology than men—did not believe power plants were safe and were more fearful of the threat of nuclear war. The results of both of these investigations can be interpreted as showing that women are more sensitive than men to life-threatening issues. In a study by Davis Buss (1981), a sample of college students rated the social desirability of 100 examples of dominant behavior. On 19 of these items, the ratings of men and women differed significantly. Behaviors rated more socially desirable

by the men were "expressions of self-assertion and self-expansion untempered by communion or concern with the larger groups . . . [whereas] the dominant acts that female raters judged significantly more socially desirable have a distinctly constructive, group-oriented tone" (p. 149). But studies of overt behavior less often yield evidence of gender differences than studies that rely on self-reports. For example, Martha Thompson (1981b) found that among college students who were asked to play the role of a boss who took an inequitable portion of the winnings of a group, women and men behaved no differently. When role playing a subordinate group member, however, women were more supportive of one another than men, while the latter were more concerned with avoiding conflict with the boss. Thus, gender differences appear to be highly related to the conditions under which they are assessed. When three-person same-gender groups were asked to solve problems (Wood, Polek, & Aiken, 1985), men generated more solutions to production tasks while women generated higher-quality solutions to discussion tasks; but no gender differences were found when persons worked on these tasks individually.

As noted by Catherine Greeno and Eleanor Maccoby (1986), "It is clear that women have a greater *reputation* for altruism and empathy than do men, and that women accept its validity. Whether the reputation is deserved is a more complicated question" (p. 313). The research does not support such a generalization across situations. Thus, for example, Greeno and Maccoby point out that whereas "a man is more likely to offer to change a tire, a woman [is more likely] to soothe a child" (p. 314). Overall, the available data do not support the conclusion that women are dedicated to harmony and to communal, nonegotistic goals under all conditions, across situations. But in general, the average woman in our society is more likely than the average man to be expected to pursue these objectives. Our culture still associates women with compromise, cooperation, and communal values, and with smoothing out difficulties.

Empathy and Interpersonal Sensitivity
Girls and women are encouraged to look to other persons for evidence of our effectiveness. Not surprisingly, then, we learn to be sensitive to the needs of others, to interpret subtle cues, and to behave sympathetically. Interpersonal relationships thus become highly important contributors to our feelings of self-

esteem, and women devote considerable time and energy to talking about and taking part in person-oriented activities.

Some of the antecedent conditions relevant to empathy have been identified in a study of college students (Barnett, Howard, King, & Dino, 1980) in which the women were found to score reliably higher than a comparable group of men on an empathy scale. High-empathy persons of *both genders* reported that their parents had spent more time with them, been more affectionate with them, and more often discussed feelings than was the case for low-empathy persons. With respect to these variables, women reported more than men that their mothers had discussed feelings with them, and that their parents had displayed affection toward them. Thus, the same experiences enhance empathy in both genders but are found more often in the socialization of girls.

Despite gender differences in socialization, the literature on empathy does not fully or unambiguously support the conclusion that women are more empathic than men across situations and conditions. As is true for other behaviors culturally assigned by gender, women and men have been found to differ in empathy most consistently in studies using self-report measures. This conclusion is supported by a series of analyses of relevant literature by Nancy Eisenberg and Randy Lennon (1983). According to these researchers, few gender differences are found when empathy is assessed by physiological measures or nonobvious behavioral measures. They concluded that "females' reputations for and self-report of empathic responding are much stronger than are their tendencies to respond (physiologically or non-verbally) in an empathic manner" (p. 126).

Women are also expected to be more sensitive than men and more adept at interpreting subtle interpersonal cues. Nancy Henley (1977) summarized the results of a number of studies and suggested that women are better than men at identifying emotions from nonverbal and from verbal cues. An extensive series of studies (Rosenthal, Archer, DiMatteo, Koivumaki, & Rogers, 1974) using the Profile of Nonverbal Sensitivity (which measures understanding of tone of voice, and face and body movements) found that American women are indeed "the subtler sex." Women of all ages from third grade to adult were found to show a small but reliable advantage over men, outscoring them in 81 out of 98 comparisons. But men in occupations requiring nurturant, artistic, or expressive behavior, such as actors, design-ers, artists, mental health professionals, and school teachers, were not found to be less sensitive than women. Thus, men whose work requires sensitivity to interpersonal cues learn to interpret them accurately.

Judith Hall (1978) concluded from an analysis of 75 studies of accuracy in interpreting emotion from nonverbal cues that women are better decoders than men, but that women's advantage or greater sensitivity is very small since gender accounts for only about 4 to 6 percent of the variance in decoding scores. The results of a study by Sara Snodgrass (1985) provide support for the proposition that it is not a woman's gender but her subordinate position that accounts for her greater interpersonal sensitivity. Among a sample of college students who interacted in leader-subordinate pairs for an hour, subordinates were found to be significantly more sensitive to the leaders' feelings and to the impressions they were making than vice versa. Gender made no difference, except that the role effect of being subordinate was strongest for women when their partner was a man.

Intimacy and Friendship The differences between women's and men's friendships or attachments to others have been the subject of considerable research interest in recent years. As we have already noted, Nancy Chodorow (1978) and Carol Gilligan (1979, 1982) have proposed that interpersonal bonding is a central element or theme in women's lives, and Chodorow has suggested that a woman's capacity for close ties to others has its origin in her earliest relationship with her mother; that is, because a girl is similar to her mother, she experiences connectedness rather than separation. Gilligan has drawn upon Chodorow's analysis and also emphasizes the significance of affiliation and intimacy for women. She maintains that "the elusive mystery of women's development lies in its recognition of the continuing importance of attachment in the human life cycle" (1979, p. 445).

But as with other generalizations about gender, the empirical evidence is mixed, with more recent studies and reviews finding fewer important distinctions between the friendships of women and men and the value assigned them. In one study (Wheeler & Nezlek, 1977), men's and women's social interactions in their first year of college were compared by having a sample of students living in coed dorms keep daily records of social interactions that lasted 10 minutes or more, for two weeks early in the fall semester and then again early in the spring semester. The women were found to have socialized more intensely than the men at the beginning of the year (fall term), but in the second semester differences between the men and women were minimal. Once having established relationships, the women decreased the amount of time they spent in each interaction.

The results of some studies suggest that women's friendships tend to be more intimate than men's and to include the sharing of more personal information. Thus, for example, questionnaire responses by a sample of parents of college students revealed no gender difference in frequency of contact with friends, but women more frequently than men said they talked about personal problems, intimate relationships, and daily activities (Aries & Johnson, 1983). The researchers concluded that through greater in-depth "sharing about a broad range of topics, the lives of female friends are potentially more interconnected than is the case for males" (p. 1194). Similarly, Lynne Davidson and Lucille Duberman (1982) found that women reported talking to their best friend more than men did about interpersonal relationships and personal issues; and Dorie Williams (1985) found that among a sample of college students, women reported more than men that they confided in close friends, openly expressed vulnerability and affection, emphasized mutual understanding, and discussed personal issues. On the other hand, Mayta Caldwell and Letitia Peplau (1982) found no significant gender differences among college students in total number of friends, number of intimate friends, or in hours spent with friends during an average week, but more women than men reported talking about "personal topics such as feelings and problems" and talking about other people.

Most of the empirically collected information on friendship comes from college-age women and men. How representative they may be of older persons we do not really know. It is instructive, therefore, to note differences between a group of young women (18 to 30 years old) and a group of middle-aged women (40 to 55 years old) reported by Carol Ryff and Susan Migdal (1984). Intimacy was found to be more important to the younger women, and was recalled by the older women as having been more important to them when they were younger. Paul Wright (1982) has reviewed a number of studies of friendship and concluded that, in general, women's friendships tend to be more person-oriented, supportive, self-disclosing, and holistic than men's, but

these differences are not great and, in many cases, they are so obscure that they are hard to demonstrate. In any case, the differences between women's and men's friendships diminish markedly as the strength and duration of the friendships increase. (p. 19)

Gender differences in intimacy of social interaction also diminish when information is derived from observing behavior instead of from self-reports. Thus, an investigation using both methods of assessment (Reis, Senchak, & Solomon, 1985) found that women reported more intimate interactions than men, but when observed having "an intimate conversation with their best friend, the sexes did not differ, either in their self-ratings or in the opinion of external judges" (p. 1214). The researchers concluded that "when the situation makes it desirable to do so," both genders manifest similar levels of intimacy.

Expressiveness

Another characteristic that our gender ideology tells us distinguishes women from men is that the former express emotions more readily. This generalization is so well accepted that there has been little systematic investigation of its accuracy. That women smile significantly more than men has been reported most often. For example, under conditions where same-gender pairs of college students were observed interacting in a laboratory, women were found to smile significantly more than men (LaFrance & Carmen, 1980). I also found this to be the case (Lott, 1987) in same- and mixed-gender pairs of students working together on a task. In a different kind of study, Janet Ragan (1982) had two judges rate over 1000 photographs taken from yearbooks and high school and college files. Among both students and faculty, women smiled significantly more frequently and more expansively than men.

A self-report study (Lombardo, Cretser, Lombardo, & Mathis, 1983) found that women cry more often, with greater intensity, and over a greater range of situations than men. But despite these differences, women and men were very similar in their perceptions of what might evoke tears. They "saw the same types of interpersonal relationships as making crying most likely; saw the same types of stimulus situations as most conducive to crying; and chose the same adjectives as most descriptive of their post-crying affect" (p. 994). These data suggest that women and men do not differ in feelings or emotional reactions as much as in their overt expression.

As is true of the other behaviors discussed in this chapter, individual differences within each gender can be found. Thus, Paul Cherulnik and Robert Evans (1984) reported within-gender differences and between-gender similarities in facial expressiveness among a sample of college students. Each participant in the study was videotaped while being interviewed, and judges then rated an edited tape for pleasantness, excitement, and spontaneity of facial expression. Men who scored high on a scale measuring the extent to which they monitored their own behavior were judged to be more expressive (smiling, excited, and spontaneous) than men who scored low, while the reverse was true for women. Among the women, high self-monitors smiled less than low self-monitors and showed less expression and stronger control over the outward display of their feelings.

Narcissism

Sigmund Freud (1933/1964) regarded narcissism as another one of the "psychical peculiarities of mature femininity" (p. 132); and he attributed it, in part, to women's envy of the penis. Physical vanity and the high value women place on their charms, he said, are a compensation for their "original sexual inferiority" and contribute to their stronger need to be loved than to love. But there would appear to be a more direct explanation of women's concern with adornment and beauty. We are encouraged from childhood to show off our physical attributes, to relish flattery, and to attempt to attract attention by our good looks, clothes, and demeanor. Carolyn Kizer (1973) has written about the dilemma presented to women by this cultural mandate to "preen and posture."

Our masks, always in peril of smearing or cracking,
In need of continuous check in the mirror or silverware,
Keep us in thrall to ourselves, concerned with our
    surfaces. . . .
So primp, preen, prink, pluck and prize your flesh
All posturing! All ravishment! All sensibility!
Meanwhile, have you used your mind today? (p. 133)

Black women writers have written with bitterness about the pain, bewilderment, and frustration experienced by Afro-American women who have had to measure their beauty against the standard set by white models. They have "tried to discover what happened to the black woman . . . as she looked into the mirror and tried to see beauty in full features and dark skin" (Washington, 1975, p. x). A woman in a story by Paule Marshall (1975), for example, comments, "Like nearly every little black girl, I had my share of dreams of waking up to find myself with long, blond curls, blue eyes, and skin like buttermilk" (p. 122). White girls, too, have dreamed of having hair that is curlier (or straighter), breasts that are larger (or smaller), and faces and figures that are closer to their idea of perfection. But for the black woman, "the idea of beauty as defined by white America has been an assault on . . . personhood" (Washington, 1975, p. xvii). Gloria Joseph (1981b) compared a sample of magazines most popular with black women with those read most often by white women and found that the poses, clothing, styles, and makeup featured in each were similar. The major difference she noted was that

> Black women must "become white" before they can do all the things the White women do (i.e., *be* the image). By altering their physical state to appear with lightened skin and silky hair, Black women, too, can compete and thereby gain status and security by being with (having) a man. (p. 159)

Racism has had devastating consequences for Afro-Americans of both genders, but for women (and not men) it has meant assessing one's self-worth on the basis of hair texture and skin color. All women in our society learn early that external appearance and the responses we get from others are crucial elements of our personal identities.

Strategies for Power

Beauty is enormously important to women because by being physically attractive, we are told, a woman can "get what she wants," can manipulate men and situations and obtain power. Because of our relative lack of access to the resources that would directly increase our status, women's "modes of influence"—that is, the means of controlling our lives or exerting power—are expected and observed to be different from men's.

Paula Johnson (1976) has proposed that women are expected to influence others by means that are indirect and personal. Indirect influence (or "manipulation") is exerted without direct confrontation, without the other person being aware that he or she is being influenced or persuaded to act in a particular way; it involves wheedling, flattery, and cajoling. It is devious. Johnson points out that "if a woman does use direct power, she may risk becoming known as pushy, overbearing, unfeminine, and/or castrating" (p. 101). The personal mode of influence is exerted by threatening to withdraw love, concern, and/or service and attention unless something wanted is provided. It may involve trading affection or sex (personal resources) for desired outcomes. In a questionnaire study, Paula Johnson found that respondents associated the use of personal rewards and sexuality as means of gaining influence reliably more often with women than with men.

A newspaper story advising women on how to get a man to give them the gifts they want (Winakor, 1977) provides a good illustration of indirect influence. The most important thing, women were told, is to make the man "think it's his idea." If you want jewelry, make sure he notices that you are not wearing any; if you want a new home, start finding things that are wrong with the one you have. Advertisements for daytime soap operas suggest that women's use of our charms to obtain desired ends is still expected and highly credible.

As with many of the other behaviors on which women and men are assumed to differ, self-reports of influence or power strategies tend to confirm the assumptions while observation of behavior under varying conditions is less apt to do so. Thus, for example, when college students were asked to assume the role of employee or supervisor and to answer questions about their likely behavior (Offermann & Schrier, 1985), women reported more often than men that they would use personal/dependent or negotiation strategies, and less often than men that they would use reward/coercion strategies; and, in a departure from the stereotype, the men were more likely to consider using manipulation and other indirect influence techniques. But when college students were actually observed in simulated work groups, the influence techniques they used as leaders under the same set of instructions were found to be unrelated to gender (Stitt, Schmidt, Price, & Kipnis, 1983). Both women and men "were equally able and equally willing to display autocratic and democratic leadership styles if so instructed" (p. 40).

Aggression

A review of the literature on adult aggressive behavior (Frodi, Macauley, & Thorne, 1977) found that 61 percent of the laboratory studies did not show less aggressiveness by women than by men across all conditions. Once again, as with other behaviors examined in this chapter, only in self-report studies did the authors find "the kinds of differences that sex role stereotypes would seem to predict" (p. 654). When the aggressive behavior could be justified, or when persons were acting anonymously, gender differences were less likely to be found. Robin Hasenfeld (1982) concluded from a quantitative analysis of aggression studies that there are no reliable gender differences in aggression under experimental conditions in which the aggressive behavior is believed to be justified.

Differences in aggressive behavior, both among women and between women and men, have been related to individual/personal variables as well as to situational factors. In one study, for example, college women who were sex-role traditionalists were found to respond more aggressively to an opponent (by use of electric shock in a laboratory situation) than more liberal women (Richardson, Vinsel, & Taylor, 1980). In another study (Richardson, Bernstein, & Taylor, 1979), women who were alone or women who were with a supportive observer responded "in an increasingly more aggressive manner" (in shocking an opponent) than women who were in the presence of a silent observer. The researchers concluded that the aggressiveness of the women in their study

> was largely determined by the contingencies present. The only situation in which nonaggressiveness was evidenced was in the presence of a silent observer. . . . In this case, one might expect that the women were responding to the assumed expectations of the audience. (p. 204)

Shelagh Towson and Mark Zanna (1982) found that women self-reported responding as aggressively as men to a hypothetical situation involving a frustrating incident concerned with dance exercising, but less aggressively to a frustrating incident concerned with body building. The former was rated by the women as more important to them than the latter.

Women, like men, have committed all varieties of crimes and have murdered for passion or profit (Weisheit, 1984). Between 1967 and 1976, the rate of arrest of women for all crimes rose 64 percent compared with 15 percent for men (Jones, 1980). As Karen Rosenberg (1984) has pointed out in a review of books on women's role in warfare, women have contributed to intergroup and international violence as supporters, proponents, and contributors to war efforts, and as active participants in battle. Historical and contemporary data, according to Rosenberg, do not support our culture's "cherished beliefs about female innocence"; she maintains that "conceptions of woman as nurturer, peacemaker, . . . or powerless victim . . . obscure the history of women's complicity in violence" (p. 457).

So strong are these conceptions that author Joyce Carol Oates (1981) has noted that wherever she has gone, she has been asked to explain why her writing is so violent. She finds this question "always insulting . . . always ignorant . . . [and] always sexist" (p. 35). She has been told that she should focus her writing more on "domestic" and "subjective" material. While the serious male writer is allowed (and expected) to illustrate anger and rage, the woman writer is not. The last time the question, "Why is your writing so violent?" was put to Oates, she responded:

> "Would you ask that question of a male writer?" After some hesitation, the answer came: "No."
>
> "Why not?" I asked.
>
> Herewith a long pause ensued. My interrogator knew the answer to the question but declined to answer it. Or perhaps he was thinking. I hope he still is. (p. 35)

MASCULINITY/FEMININITY: AN ARTIFICIAL DUALITY?

The fact that women's behavior does not always fulfill cultural expectations of femininity points up the role of experience in gender learning, and variations among women. Behavior depends not upon sex but upon prior experience, acquired attitudes, cultural expectations, sanctions, opportunities for practice, and situational demands. In the chapter on childhood we reviewed studies indicating that girls who behave as they are expected to—who are not aggressive, for example—are better liked by their teachers than those whose behavior is viewed as not appropriate for girls. Social sanctions exist for adults as well. Women who behave as the culture expects are perceived and treated more positively than those who do not. Elsewhere, I have argued (Lott, 1985) that

> It is not sex that matters but those life conditions that are systematically related to it by cultural prescription, regulation, or arrangement. Where such experiential/ situational correlates are weak or overriden by others, sex ceases to be a discriminating variable. We need to understand that the culture-prescribed experiential/ situational correlates of sex are only partially related to early childhood socialization and to past personal history. Sex typing is maintained in a society by contemporary cues for adult behavior and appropriate rewards and punishments. (p. 162)

A major variable that distinguishes the adult lives of most women and most men is power—that is, access to, and potential control of, resources. Socialization and differences in power between groups are interrelated: socialization describes how we learn to behave as our culture expects us to, and power differences make differential socialization necessary. Such differences are then perpetuated and reinforced by the results of differential learning. The circularity can be, and is being, broken. One requisite for change is recognizing the power differences between groups and knowing how these are related to economic, political, and other conditions. We also need to understand how we learn to behave as we do. To understand the acquisition of behavior is to understand how culture constructs gender, and that similar behavior is acquired under the same set of conditions regardless of gender.

We tend to behave as others expect us to because we are rewarded for doing what is appropriate, and because we have acquired complementary attitudes and responses through consistent sets of experiences. That expectations and responses of others can effectively influence behavior in very subtle ways was explicitly demonstrated in a study (Snyder, Tanke, & Berscheid, 1977) in which undergraduate men were asked to talk on the phone with a young woman who they believed to be either physically attractive or unattractive. The woman was unaware of how she had been described. The researchers later analyzed each phone conversation, and found that the women who were thought to be attractive "came to behave in a friendly, likeable, and sociable manner" in comparison with the women who were believed to be unattractive. In an earlier study that demonstrated the same phenomenon (Zanna & Pack, 1975), undergraduate women who had an opportunity to work on a task with a "desirable" 21-year-old male Princeton senior (with a car and without a girlfriend) portrayed themselves as being either more or less conventional in sex role depending upon whether their partner's view was stereotypically traditional or nontraditional. Furthermore, women who thought their "desirable" male partner was nontraditional outperformed those who thought otherwise (in unscrambling anagrams correctly). Women who worked with "undesirable" male partners were not influenced by their partner's beliefs. In another study (Skrypnek & Snyder, 1982), men and women were paired for a task, but some men were led to believe their partner was a man while others were told their partner was a woman. In the latter case, the men selected more stereotypically masculine activities for themselves and feminine activities for their partners. Later, the women whose partners believed they were female were more likely to choose feminine tasks for themselves than the women whose partners thought they were men, although the women did not know what their partners had been told.

Gender differences thus appear to reflect the expectations and responses of those with whom we interact. Such differences are also associated with opportunities to take part in particular activities. Rachelle Canter and Beth Meyerowitz (1984), for example, asked a sample of college students to report on their own ability, enjoyment, performance frequency, and opportunity to perform 23 "feminine" sex-typed and 22 "masculine" activities, and found a positive relationship for both genders between the opportunity to engage in an activity or behavior and the frequency of its performance.

The effect of culture on behavior becomes apparent when we compare the behavior of one gender or the other across cultures. For example, when Jean Stockard and Maureen Dougherty (1983) compared the responses of a sample of Greek young people from an isolated island village with those of a similar sample of whites from a small farming community in the western United States and of a sample of blacks from a metropolitan inner city to questions about the antecedents and consequences of success, progress, happiness, and cooperation, they found gender differences in each cultural setting but within-gender differences across cultures.

> While within each society males and females may show differences, the males in one society may be just as or even more expressive than the females in another group. Similarly, while the females in one society may be less instrumental than the men in that setting, they may be just as or even more instrumental than the men in other settings. (p. 967)

Within-gender differences, or variations in the behavior of women, are also illustrated by the experiences of contemporary women in the U.S. who behave in ways quite different from the traditional model. The complexity of modern society—the existence of numerous subcultures and disparate models and pressures—contributes to varying degrees of deviance from traditional ideals. Many women are active, independent, competitive, risk-taking, task-oriented, and concerned with achievement outside the home. Afro-American women, for example, have not been expected to fit the stereotype of femininity,

and have been portrayed in literature and the media as strong, independent, striving, or assertive. The conditions of life for a large percentage of black women have not been the same as those for most white women, just as the conditions of life for the poor are different from those for the affluent. As Linda Myers (1978) has noted, everything in the American black woman's "situation and experience [beginning with slavery] has been contrived to prohibit her fulfilling this [white] model of womanhood, even if it were worthy" (p. 3). Bonnie Dill (1979) has pointed out that black women were brought as slaves to this country "to work and to produce workers," a role that contrasts sharply with the white ideal of domesticity and dependency.

Black women tend to self-report both instrumental and expressive traits and to score as androgynous (having both "masculine" and "feminine" characteristics) on sex-role measures, a phenomenon that is not surprising since black women in America have long been accustomed to being wives and mothers who also work outside the home (Myers, 1978). Joyce Ladner (1971) found that a sample of black adolescent girls expected women to take a strong family role as well as to be economically independent, educated, resourceful, self-reliant, and upwardly mobile. Albert Lott and I (1963) studied high school seniors in a southern community and found that black girls and boys were more alike in their values and goals than white girls and boys. Our measures indicated that "the usual sex-typed goal orientations found among white youth do not exist as clearly among Negro youth" (p. 161), primarily because of differences between black and white girls, who were further apart on measures of values and goals than black and white boys. Black women seniors, for example, scored higher than their white counterparts on measures of theoretical and political values and lower on esthetic and religious values as well as on the need for love and affection. Alice Brown-Collins and Deborah Sussewell (1985) have argued that the behavior of Afro-American women can only be understood in the context of their history and in terms of the interaction between their culture and sex-role socialization. Black women have functioned as community educators, building schools and maintaining kindergartens, and as community organizers, demonstrating both agentic/instrumental and communal/affiliative attributes and concerns. As noted by Brown-Collins and Sussewell, "The irony of slave women's history is that womanhood was redefined to allow for the exploitation of their labor resulting in the development of independent, self-reliant characteristics" (p. 7).

Although differences can be found between white women and black women (or women of other oppressed minorities—Hispanics and native Americans), large areas of commonality also exist. As we have seen in earlier chapters, gender expectations sometimes supersede those associated with color, socioeconomic status, or ethnicity. Pamela Reid (1978b) has noted that black girls, too, are trained for motherhood and given the same toys as white girls to learn from and practice on; traditional behavior patterns are conveyed in the same ways and by the same agents. The pages of *Ebony* magazine, for example, provide considerable evidence that today's idealized middle-class black woman is in many ways indistinguishable from the idealized white one. A review of relevant literature by Saundra Murray and Martha Mednick (1977) found that black college and middle-class women share the traditional views of women's role held by their white counterparts. And, according to Michele Wallace (1979), growing up in Harlem meant listening "no less intently than the little white girls who grew up in Park Avenue, in Scarsdale, or on Long Island" (p. 90) to the messages that came to both groups from the same magazines, movies, and television. Thus, culture can override individual circumstances and reinforce similar ways of behaving among all women, producing common themes associated with gender. At the same time, variations among women are also found on every behavioral dimension. We know from all available evidence that behavior has no gender. Instrumental, expressive, affiliative, autonomous, self-oriented, or communal-oriented responses are teachable and, under the appropriate conditions, can be learned, maintained, and manifested by girls or boys, women or men. Knowing this, what can we conclude about the concept of femininity?

The "Female Domain" Perspective

Sigmund Freud (1933/1964), although viewing femininity as a "riddle," postulated that girls turn away from their mothers because they "hold their mother responsible for their lack of penis" (p. 124), and that femininity is characterized by envy, jealousy, narrowness, a weak superego, little sense of justice, and narcissism. His disciple Helene Deutsch (1944) later emphasized a triad of feminine traits:

passivity, narcissism, and masochism. This view assumes that femininity and masculinity are at opposite ends of a single continuum or dimension, and that the more one is feminine the less she or he can be masculine, and vice versa. For many years, this assumption was implicit in the instruments psychologists devised to measure femininity (or masculinity). And feminine qualities were typically seen as not only different from masculine qualities but also as less desirable or as weaknesses. Thus, Paula Caplan (1984) has noted that the very behaviors women are expected to manifest have been given negative labels and devalued. "Being nurturant, charitable, and so on, is labeled masochistic. . . . It is forgotten that women have been frightened by the threat of being considered unfeminine, ugly, and so on if they do not behave selflessly" (p. 137).

The unidimensional position that one is either feminine *or* masculine, has been challenged but by no means completely abandoned. At the same time that one group of feminist psychologists is presenting evidence against behavior-gender links (which we will return to shortly), another group is arguing that women's life experiences and imposed separateness from men have created a women's culture that is significant and vital. The latter point of view is that women's responsibilities and roles reinforce certain ways of behaving, attitudes and objectives, that should be respected and appreciated. This approach recognizes a "female domain" and strongly urges that it be positively valued.

Kathryn Morgan and Maryann Ayim (1984), for example, accept as "traditional female qualities" those of "nurturance, supportiveness, vulnerability, and affiliativeness," and see them as opposed to "male-identified qualities such as aggressiveness, competitiveness, and domination" (p. 196). As we noted earlier, both Jean Baker Miller (1976) and Carol Gilligan (1982) have proposed that women are more expressive and sensitive than men, and more concerned with relationships, the needs of others, interpersonal responsibility, and interpersonal harmony and cooperation. Such concerns, they suggest, can be sources of strength and not weakness, and give women a special outlook or perspective that reflects the valuing of intimacy and attachment rather than separation and autonomy, traits valued by men.

These differences, according to Nancy Chodorow (1978), emerge early in life from the infant's relationship with its mother. Chodorow argues that because mothers differ in gender from their sons, they provide the conditions that promote separation from them, encouraging autonomy and differentiation, while for daughters, mothers promote identification and attachment. Because "they are parented by a person of the same gender . . . girls come to experience themselves as less differentiated than boys, as more continuous with and related to the external object-world" (Chodorow, 1978, p. 167). This approach, known as object relations theory, accepts femininity and masculinity as separate orientations and tries to account for them by postulating different patterns of mother-infant bonding. These patterns are said to promote "ego-boundary rigidity" in boys and "boundary diffuseness" in girls, so that the former come to value separation and the latter, connectedness.

Linda Kerber (1986) has pointed out that while views such as Gilligan's are "invigorating" to women, in their "insistence that behavior once denigrated as waffling, indecisive, and demeaningly 'effeminate' ought rather to be valued as complex, constructive, and humane" (p. 306), these ideas, in somewhat different language, have been heard many times before. They have been used to keep women and men apart "in separate spheres" and to justify the separation on the grounds that reason is an attribute of men, and feeling is an attribute of women.

> This bifurcated view of reality can easily be traced at least to classical Greece, where men were understood to realize themselves best in the public sector, the polis, and women in domesticity. Ancient tradition has long been reinforced by explicit socialization that arrogated public power to men and relegated women to domestic concerns, a socialization sometimes defended by argument from expediency, sometimes by argument from biology. (Kerber, 1986, p. 306)

And Mary Brabeck (1983) has pointed out, in evaluating Gilligan's position, that

> though she places a different value on the qualities, Gilligan is arguing as Freud, Erikson, Piaget, and Kohlberg have done before her: Women are the more compassionate sex. . . . There is an intuitive appeal to these claims which speaks to an essential truth in the assertions, a truth that persists even when the evidence contradicts it. (p. 286)

Although the picture of the cooperative, caring, person-oriented adult woman drawn by the newer proponents of a feminine-masculine dichotomy is very different from the earlier negative portrait, and thus very appealing to many women, both visions have in common a focus on traits, stable personality components that are presumed to predispose to par-

ticular ways of behaving across situations. Both the older psychoanalytic and the newer "female domain" positions also ascribe to infancy an all-important role in shaping personality, and both tie a particular set of characteristics to each gender. In addition, both views have been derived from a culturally limited perspective—that of middle-class white families. In studying Afro-American return migrants to the rural South in this country, for example, Carol Stack (1986) has found more gender similarities than differences in motives and concerns. Women and men conceptualize their moral dilemmas in the same terms, and "describe with force and conviction the strength of their kinship ties to their rural southern families and the nature of these ties that bind" (p. 323).

The "female domain" arguments do not fare well when tested against observations and investigations of the actual behavior of adult women and men in diverse situations. Careful reviews of the empirical literature on gender differences typically conclude that such differences are less pervasive than has been thought, and that gender has relatively weak associations with behavior. Rhoda Unger (1981) has referred to gender differences as having a "now you see them, now you don't" quality. This is probably the case because the appearance of gender differences in behavior depends upon the social context, or particular conditions of the situation. As Deaux (1984) has suggested, some tasks are more likely than others to disclose gender differences because they are "influential sources of these differences" (p. 107). In general, concluded Deaux:

> Main effects of sex are frequently qualified by situational interactions, and the selection of tasks plays a critical role in eliciting or suppressing differences. Furthermore, the amount of variance accounted for by sex, even when main effects are reliable, is typically quite small. Thus, when any particular behavior is considered, differences between males and females may be of relatively little consequence. (p. 108)

When asked to describe their behavior in real situations in terms of active and passive, a sample of young adults in a study by Lynne Davidson (1981) gave similar examples regardless of gender. Only the reasons given for behaving in these ways differentiated women and men. "Women were passive because they felt intimidated by others, men to avoid intimidating others. Women were active . . . when they perceived the situation as 'appropriate'. Male activeness stemmed from feelings of self-confidence" (p. 345). Annual surveys administered to first-year college students have found that women are increasingly more concerned, like previous generations of men, with money and influence. As noted by John Walsh (1983), "The [gender] gap has narrowed so the greed and power quotient is up" (p. 822). Women and men in similar situations, with similar past experiences, tend to behave in ways that reflect individual differences but not gender differences. Thus, Jerome Adams (1984) found among cadets in the first three coeducational classes of West Point no gender differences in educational aspirations, professional career goals, or instrumental, assertive, and agentic personal attributes.

The Androgyny Perspective

The fact of sizable individual differences within genders and wide overlap between women and men in self-reported and observed characteristics suggests that masculinity and femininity do not represent mutually exclusive poles on a single dimension. Another view that has proved to be very popular and a strong stimulus to research, is that femininity and masculinity are each represented by a set of distinctive traits that are independent of one another, so that people may vary in the extent to which they manifest each mode, and both modes, regardless of their gender. In this approach (first proposed by Carl Jung in the early part of this century [see *The Basic Writings*, 1959]), people who describe themselves as displaying some characteristics typically associated with their own gender and some characteristics associated with the other gender are labeled androgynous. Measures have been constructed that assess sex-typed and androgynous orientations by rating respondents independently on both femininity and masculinity (Bem, 1974, 1978; Spence, Helmreich, & Stapp, 1974; Berzins, Welling, & Wetter, 1978). Developers of these measures recognized that many women and men often behave similarly to one another and manifest the same characteristics. Nevertheless, they continued to label some attributes as feminine and others as masculine, thus implying the existence of separate constellations of traits differentially associated with women and men.

But we know that any behavior can be learned by any person who is capable of performing it, given appropriate conditions for its acquisition, and that the behavior will be maintained if it continues to be situationally appropriate and is approved and not punished. No evidence exists that one group of people (distinguished by sex, color, socioeconomic level, or language) is more naturally suited for some re-

sponses than are others. To label some behaviors as feminine because our culture attempts to teach them primarily to girls and women obscures their essential humanness (and contributes to our dismay if our boys show too much of them). Some of the earlier contributors to the literature on assessment of femininity, masculinity, and androgyny have now concluded that their tests do not, in fact, measure personality constellations that can be identified by gender. For example, Janet Spence and Robert Helmreich (1980) have clearly stated that their own test, the Personal Attributes Questionnaire (PAQ), does not measure masculinity or femininity but rather gender-neutral "socially desirable instrumental and expressive characteristics" (p. 157). Elsewhere, Janet Spence (1983) has noted that

> we have probably moved more slowly than we should have away from gender-related labels for the PAQ scales and toward labels, such as instrumental and expressive or self-assertiveness and nurturance/interpersonal-concern, that are more descriptive of their actual content. (p. 442)

What so-called masculinity scales actually measure are self-reported instrumental, self-assertive, agentic, and task-oriented behaviors, while so-called femininity scales measure self-reported expressive, communal, and interpersonally oriented behaviors. There are considerable individual differences among both women and men in these attributes. Some men are more nurturant than some women, and some women are more instrumental than some men. While women and men in our society may differ, on the average, in their responses to these scales, this does not mean that the scales assess womanliness or manliness. Sandra Bem, a major contributor to the earlier androgyny literature and developer of the Bem Sex Role Inventory (BSRI), has concluded that femininity and masculinity do not have "an independent and palpable reality" (1981, p. 363), that "human behaviors and personality attributes should no longer be linked with gender, and [that] society should stop projecting gender into situations irrelevant to genitalia" (1985, p. 222).

Toward a Human Perspective

I and others have urged discontinuing the use of masculine/feminine labels because, as Barbara Wallston (1981) has put it, they "imply false dichotomies." A feminist critique of the concept of androgyny led me to the following conclusion (Lott, 1981):

No teachable human behavior belongs exclusively to any one group of persons, and both women and men manifest wide individual differences along all behavioral dimensions. It is therefore both empirically and theoretically invalid to continue to genderize behavior categories. . . . Let us investigate the conditions under which individuals learn to respond instrumentally, assertively, with compassion, or expressiveness. To understand and appreciate the modifiability of behavior requires that we study its experiential antecedents *in persons of both genders.* (p. 179)

The evidence suggests that behavioral polarities are rare, and responses to complex events tend to be multidimensional. Thus, for example, in an analysis of the research on gender differences in moral judgments, Mary Brabeck (1983) has suggested that the ideal moral decision can be understood as combining a principle of justice (as claimed for men) and an ethic of care and responsibility (as claimed for women). Moral choices, in other words, can

> reflect reasoned and deliberate judgments that ensure justice be accorded each person while maintaining a passionate concern for the well-being and care of each individual. Justice and care are then joined; . . . and the need for autonomy and for interconnection are united in an enlarged and more adequate conception of morality. (p. 289)

Such an enlarged conception of morality is not one that combines so-called masculine and feminine elements, but one that dispenses with such artificial dualities. Similarly, an enlarged conception of human personality does not first divide human functioning into two pieces and then put them back together again. Gender differences may reliably be found for some behaviors, at some ages, in some situations, at some times and places. But such differences are better understood if related to their learning antecedents and situational determinants than if simply related to sex. By "virtue of being persons," as Erving Goffman (1979) has put it, women and men have learned "to provide and to read depictions of masculinity and femininity" (p. 8) as defined within their culture. But historical and current variations among women in life-styles, aspirations, attitudes, and interests, the differences between women who are affluent and those who are poor, between white women and minority women, provide impressive evidence that we must include all within-gender variations in our understanding of what it means to be a woman.

Mental Health and Well-Being

Why is it only women who go to therapists? If Jack's in a bad mood and you ask him what's wrong he'll say he wanted to play racquetball and the weather's rotten or he's worried that Reagan's going to get the Republican nomination. . . . If you ask Jessica or me, we'll say our heads are messed up, we don't know why. Men are always looking on the outside to solve problems and women are always looking into . . . our own heads.

Judith Rossner   *(1983, p. 282)*

There is little difference between the sexes in what contributes to their satisfaction with life. Because of differential definitions of appropriate behavior, however, females experience more obstacles in attaining life-satisfying goals.

Carolyn Morgan   *(1980, p. 379)*

Our culture tends to view psychological disturbance as an acceptable feminine reaction to problems. Some have suggested that illness for women is not merely acceptable but also encouraged, as preferable to more collective (and effective) forms of reaction to stress or frustration (Cloward & Piven, 1979). Phyllis Chesler (1972) has noted that portraits of madness highlighted by both psychiatrists and novelists throughout this century have been primarily of women. Our culture is more accepting of psychological dysfunction in women, and women's socialization makes certain manifestations of dysfunction more probable than others. We will explore these issues in this chapter in the broader context of the relationship between gender and mental health.

GENDER DIFFERENCES IN DYSFUNCTIONAL BEHAVIOR

Mental health and mental illness traditionally refer to two ends of a continuum describing general functioning or day-to-day coping with life's stresses and strains. Mental health is frequently measured by answers to a series of questions that assess adjustment, well-being, self-esteem, or satisfaction. Sometimes overall functioning is assessed by self-reports of symptoms such as headaches, fatigue, and so on. Mental health is also taken to mean the absence of mental illness as diagnosed on the basis of specific symptoms that occur in conjunction with *impairment* of function and the experience of *distress* (American Psychiatric Association, 1980). Impaired mental health is also sometimes inferred from the fact of inpatient or outpatient treatment. My preference is to view behavior not on a continuum of health or illness but on one of effectiveness or optimum functioning. In this view, effective (functional or adaptive) behavior (characteristic of "mental health") is behavior that achieves a person's goals; succeeds in solving problems; reduces conflict; maximizes the attainment of positive consequences in the short run without sacrificing long-term gains; does not lead to an increase in pain or frustration; and does not create new problems or unsolvable conflicts. Dysfunctional behavior is behavior that fails to meet these criteria.

How do the genders differ in self-reported frequency of symptoms of distress and in diagnosed "mental disorders"? Overall, data from a variety of sources—community surveys, outpatient clinics, private treatment facilities, general hospitals, mental hospitals, and college or university counseling centers—have generally agreed that "women are the most frequent consumers of mental health services in this country" (*Women and Psychotherapy*, 1981, p. 1). The data on adults are in sharp contrast to those on children; studies of behavior disorders in childhood reviewed by Robert Eme (1979) reveal "a greater male prevalence" in all diagnostic categories. Furthermore, analysis of the adult data shows that only *married women* have higher rates of diagnosis and treatment for "mental disorders" than *married men*. In all other categories—never-married, divorced, or widowed—women have lower rates of diagnosed mental illness than comparable men (Gove, 1979).

A joint report by the American Psychological Association and the Federation of Organizations for Professional Women (*Developing a National Agenda*, 1985) reviewed relevant data and concluded that:

> [1] Men have higher rates of admission to mental health facilities than do women for all marital status categories, with one exception—married men have lower admission rates than do married women. This reversal is especially dramatic for minority women.
> [2] A higher percentage of women than men receive services from various types of facilities. . . . The situation is reversed in state and county mental hospitals and in public mental hospitals. . . .
> [3] Women report more worries and say more often than do men that . . . bad things happen to them. . . .

[4] In 1980 for the noninstitutionalized populations . . . women showed substantially higher rates of depressive disorders and phobias by a factor of at least two to one. In contrast, men showed higher rates of antisocial personality and alcohol abuse/dependence; women were more likely to be diagnosed as having dysthymic disorders, somatization disorders, panic disorders, obsessive/compulsive disorders, and schizophrenia. . . . Compared to men, women have higher prevalence rates of affective disorders at every age. (pp. 5, 6, 7)

The findings noted in item 4 come from a major comprehensive survey directed by the National Institute of Mental Health that involved door-to-door interviews of approximately 10,000 adults (Fox, 1984a). These researchers concluded that although women and men differ in the frequency with which they receive various diagnoses (as just indicated), the rate of mental disorders is roughly equal for both genders, as well as for blacks and whites. The conclusion of equal prevalence of psychological dysfunction in women and men contrasts with earlier data supporting the view that women outnumbered men as receivers of mental health services. But, as can be seen from distribution of the "mental illness" admissions to various types of hospital facilities in 1980 by gender and race (Figure 14.1), except for Veterans Administration hospitals and state and county hospitals, psychiatric facilities admitted women and men in roughly the same numbers. Women continue to outnumber men as clients of mental health practitioners in outpatient settings—private practice and clinics.

Depression and Suicide

Among the patterns of dysfunctional behavior manifested by women, depression is the most common. The symptoms—passivity, feelings of hopelessness and helplessness, lowered self-esteem, crying, suicidal feelings, self-accusation, slowed movement, and disturbed sleep—are congruent with women's socialization. Women are taught to look inside ourselves for the cause of unresolved problems. Women typically ask what we have done wrong, feel guilt, and punish ourselves. We are likely to turn the anger of frustration experienced when we do not meet objectives, experience success, or overcome barriers, against ourselves; and we tend to view ourselves as failures and at fault if others have not been loving, attentive, approving, or rewarding to us. Depression "is the predominant cause for admission to psychiatric services in general hospitals across

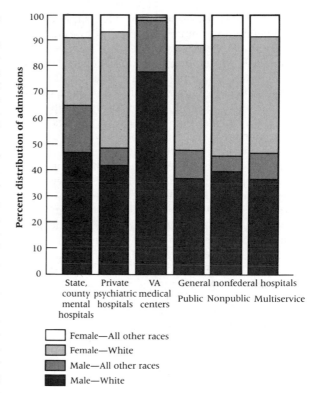

FIGURE 14.1 Distribution of admissions to inpatient psychiatric services in the United States in 1980

the nation for every female age group 18 and over" (Nickerson & Pitochelli, 1978, p. 1). Lenore Radloff (1975) measured feelings of depression in more than 1500 white adults and found married and divorced/separated women to be more depressed than comparable men, regardless of whether they stayed at home or were employed. According to Radloff, "The depressed woman is not an upper-class phenomenon . . . it is the women with low education and income who are especially depressed, compared with men" (p. 256). Most vulnerable of all are married minority women and low-income female heads of single-parent households. The latter have been found to use mental health facilities four times more frequently than married women, and to have the highest depression rate of any demographic group (*Developing a National Agenda*, 1985).

Among nonclinical samples of college students (those not undergoing treatment) who are typically single, childless, and middle-class, significant gender differences in paper-and-pencil measures of depression are not usually found (for example, Padesky &

Hammen, 1981; Elpern & Karp, 1984), or only a very small gender difference is reported (Chino & Funabiki, 1984). Paula Wise and Stephany Joy (1982), for example, found among a group of college students that self-descriptive adjectives written by the men were significantly more favorable than those written by the women, but, of the 18 most frequently used adjectives, 14 were the same for both genders. Other studies of college student samples have reported that women and men tend to manifest and to cope with depressed feelings somewhat differently. The single most discriminating behavior between women and men has been reported to be the greater tendency on the part of women to cry (Padesky & Hammen, 1981; Kleinke, Staneski, & Mason, 1982). In the latter study, women were also found to be more likely than men to eat, smoke, become short-tempered, and confront their feelings when depressed, while men were more likely to become aggressive or engage in sexual behavior. Among students who scored high in depression, men were more likely to use drugs and spend time alone, whereas women were more likely to blame themselves and seek help. College women self-report a greater readiness than college men to seek help for depression (Padesky & Hammen, 1981) and a greater tendency to eat more when depressed and to seek personal support (Chino & Funabiki, 1984).

Women attempt suicide at a rate approximately 2.3 times greater than for men, while men complete suicides more than women by the same ratio (Kushner, 1985). The rate of successful suicides is highest for white men, followed by black men, white women, and black women. Men are more likely to use guns; women are more likely to use pharmaceuticals (Heshusius, 1980). In a study of adolescents (aged 13 to 17) admitted to the emergency room of a Massachusetts hospital during the years 1979 to 1983, Eva Deykin (1984) found that the proportion of girls treated for suicidal, self-destructive emergencies was somewhat greater than for boys in four of the five year-long periods. Howard Kushner (1985) believes that the gender difference in suicidal behavior has been exaggerated, and that "if we combine completions and attempts, there is not now, nor has there ever been so far as anyone can demonstrate, any gender-specific difference in suicidal behavior" (p. 546). Kushner argues that combining the numbers of completed and attempted suicides is justified because neither reveals anything about intention. He further argues that the greater use in this country of

firearms by men in suicide simply reflects men's greater access to them. "No student of history . . . should be surprised to learn that women have had less access to lethal technology than men" (p. 551).

Alcohol and Drug Abuse

The prevalence of alcohol and drug abuse among women is difficult to assess because many women are in situations in which their chemical dependency can remain hidden. Thus "both the ability of many women to hide their excessive drinking and the great stigma attached to alcohol abuse that penalizes them for revealing their condition affects the figures on prevalence" (Marden & Kolodner, 1979, p. 13). The data sources that are available—arrest statistics, hospital admissions, physicians' reports, membership in groups like Alcoholics Anonymous, and community surveys—indicate that men outnumber women with respect to dysfunctional behavior involving chemical substance abuse but also that the number of women experiencing alcohol and drug problems has been steadily increasing. Some data have shown that the gender difference in rates of substance abuse "is smaller at younger ages, implying that the pattern of differences may change in future generations" (*Developing a National Agenda*, 1985, p. 6), approaching equal prevalence. While the general male-female ratio for alcohol problems among whites is currently 4 to 1, among blacks it is 3 to 2; and although black women are more likely to be alcohol abstainers by a 2 to 1 margin, among those who drink, black women are more likely to be heavy drinkers. One group of researchers (Gutierres, Patton, Raymond, & Rhoads, 1984) has reported that between 1969 and 1979, the ratio of male to female heroin users in New York state went from 5 to 1 to 3 to 1; and Nadine Brozan (1985) has reported that cocaine usage and addiction problems have increased among women, as indicated by the number of admissions to state-financed programs in New York City and the number of phone calls for help made to cocaine hot lines.

Although women's rate of alcohol/drug problem behavior is approaching that of men, some evidence shows gender differences in the ways substance abuse is manifested, in its associations with frustrations or life stresses, and in the reactions elicited from other people. Edith Gomberg (1979), for example, has reviewed the literature and noted that women have been found to begin heavy drinking somewhat later than men, to drink more frequently at home, alone or with their spouse, to do less binge drinking and more solitary drinking, and to be at greater risk for drug/alcohol interaction effects. In contrast, cocaine abuse appears to be more common among younger women than younger men, and women tend to use it in greater quantities. In one psychiatric facility, 53 percent of the women referred for treatment for cocaine abuse were less than 30 years old, compared with 25 percent of the men (Brozan, 1985).

Studies of nonclinical samples have found that drinking may be moderated by different variables for women than for men. For example, among a group of high school girls who reported using alcohol, drinking to be sociable was found to be negatively correlated with a measure of alienation, while drinking because of unresolved problems was positively correlated with feelings of alienation. Among the boys, neither of these relationships was significant. The researchers (Carman, Fitzgerald, & Holmgren, 1983) concluded that "drinking motivations for females are significantly more predictable from information about alienation than is the case for males" (p. 1023). A study of a college student sample (Wolfe, Lennox, & Hudiburg, 1983) found that women's reported use of alcohol was more predictable from environmental variables than men's. On the other hand, a study of over 300 patients treated for alcoholism (Cronkite & Moos, 1984) found no significant gender differences in drinking pattern, impairment, or consumption.

The consequences of alcohol dependence for married women are significantly more negative than those for married men. For example, when the patients in the Cronkite and Moos study were questioned 6 to 8 months after discharge from residential treatment facilities, the researchers found that while marriage increased the likelihood of posttreatment abstinence for men, it lowered the likelihood of abstinence for women. Other data (in *Developing a National Agenda*, 1985) indicate that women with alcohol problems frequently marry alcoholic men; that women are more likely than men to be blamed for the alcohol problems of their spouse; and that "husbands of alcoholic women are less tolerant of their spouses' drinking than are wives of alcoholic men [and] . . . are more likely to leave alcoholic spouses and fight for custody of children" (p. 23).

Our society has less tolerance and less sympathy for women with alcohol or drug problems than it has for men. A review of the literature by Jonica Homiller (1977) found that whereas 9 out of 10 women stay with an alcoholic husband, only 1 husband out of 10

stays with an alcoholic wife; and women alcoholics are generally believed to be "sicker" than their male counterparts. These findings are supported by a study in which college students read about cases of wife abuse and made judgments about responsibility (Richardson & Campbell, 1980). When the abusive husband was described as drunk, the respondents ascribed significantly more responsibility for the abuse to the situation than in the case where he was sober. On the other hand, "when the wife was drunk, she received more blame for the incident than when she was sober . . . [and] the amount of blame to the husband decreased" (p. 55).

A popular hypothesis in the substance abuse literature is that chemically dependent women have difficulties living up to their ideal standards of traditional femininity, but supporting data are sparse. Sandra Anderson (1980), for example, compared a sample of women in treatment centers for alcoholism with their nonalcoholic sisters, and found no significant differences between them on measures of conscious feminine identification, sex-role style, or unconscious masculine identification. In addition, the alcoholic women did not differ from their nonalcoholic sisters in descriptions of their parents (Anderson, 1984).

> The majority of both groups perceived their mothers as self-confident, warm and loving, and did not view her as weak or difficult to please. A slight majority of both groups viewed their father as emotionally distant, but he was not perceived as weak. (p. 284)

The alcoholic women did differ from their nonalcoholic sisters in being divorced and living alone, in recalling more parental disapproval and childhood unhappiness, and in perceiving themselves as less similar to their mothers in attitudes and interests. Another study (Rooney, Volpe, & Suziedelis, 1984) found that after 30 days in a treatment center for alcoholics, women residents experienced a substantial rise in positive self-regard and, for the younger women, this was independent of sex role and as likely to "involve a distancing from the traditional female role as its re-embracing" (p. 266). Other data suggest that family crises are an important antecedent or correlate of the abuse of chemical substances by adolescent women. Dorothy Bianco (1984) investigated the backgrounds and treatment outcomes of teenage residents of a center for alcohol and drug abuse, and found that 84 percent had an alcoholic or absent father and had experienced sexual or physical abuse, or had a mother who had been abused.

Eating Disorders

All relevant data support the conclusion that "women in general, more than men, spend a great deal of time and energy worrying about appearance and feeling too fat" (Rodin, Silberstein, & Striegel-Moore, 1985, p. 294). And more women than men manifest exaggerated patterns of eating. Rodin and her colleagues, and others (such as Brownmiller, 1984), have argued that women's preoccupation with appearance is normative in our society, that it results from social pressure, from the greater punishments experienced by obese women than men, and from the strong relationship between women's judged attractiveness and thinness. What makes attractiveness so important to women is that, historically, it "has been considered a feminine attribute, and its pursuit a feminine responsibility," and it continues to give "a woman power in terms of having more access to resources (for example, being able to attract and marry high-status men) and of being more favorably treated in social contexts" (Rodin et al., 1985, pp. 275f.). But women pursuing nontraditional roles and independent careers seem no less vulnerable than others to the exaggerated contribution of weight and appearance to feelings of self-esteem and self-worth. Career women, too, appear to use thinness as an indication of ability to control events, and as a sign of worthiness. Jane Kaplan (1980) has explored the conflict over food experienced by women in our society, a conflict visibly maintained and reinforced by the mass media. Women's magazines as well as television and newspaper ads, Kaplan argues, promote with equal intensity "delicious foods to fix, ways of taking off weight, and illustrations of lovely clothes to be worn on slim bodies. We learn how to get fat and stay slim all in the same magazine!" (p. 4).

Most women regard our weight as a crucial index of acceptability and attractiveness. A large-scale survey in 1978 found that 56 percent of all women respondents were on a diet; samples of college women consistently score higher than men on questions assessing body dissatisfaction and desire for thinness; the second most important concern expressed by a sample of elderly women, following memory loss, was increased weight, while weight concerns were not expressed by the elderly men; and among college undergraduates, weight and body shape have been found to be the central determinants of women's, but not men's, perception of their physical attractiveness (in Rodin, Silberstein, &

Striegel-Moore, 1985). A survey by *Glamour* magazine (Wooley & Wooley, 1984) found that 63 percent of the young women among their 33,000 respondents reported that weight often affected how they felt about themselves, and 42 percent said that losing weight would make them happier than would success at work, a date with an admired man, or hearing from an old friend.

Rodin et al. (1985) have noted that biological factors predispose females to accumulate more body fat than males; these include a greater production of estrogen and progesterone, and metabolic rate changes during puberty, pregnancy, and menopause. They have also reviewed the psychological and physical consequences of women's preoccupation with body weight, and have found them to include

> decreased self-esteem for failure to meet the then idealized body type, distorted body image, feelings of helplessness and frustration in response to unsuccessful dieting efforts, . . . becoming preoccupied and even victimized by consumerism [diet advertising campaigns], . . . depression . . . [and] changes in metabolic rate and in lipid and glucose metabolism. . . . Extremes in dieting behaviors, including purging, use of laxatives, and starvation, are associated with renal and liver problems, gastrointestinal disorders, and in some severe cases with death. (p. 294)

Binging and purging behavior (bulimia) is common among women on college campuses across the country, and evidence exists that women directly teach this behavior to one another. Self-induced vomiting has been found among all weight groups from the obese to the anorexic, and usually begins during adolescence. The prevalence of bulimia has been difficult to estimate because the binge eating and vomiting are typically done in secret, and because the shape and weight of bulimics are usually within normal limits, and their eating habits in social situations are appropriate (Schlesier-Stropp, 1984). Estimates of prevalence have ranged from 13 to 67 percent among normal nonclinical samples (Polivy & Herman, 1985). A survey of over 1000 high school women found that 21 percent reported binge-eating episodes at least once a week (in Rodin et al., 1985); and at one state university, 13 percent of the respondents to a survey reported experiencing all of the major symptoms of bulimia (in Schlesier-Stropp, 1984).

Robin Gibbs (1986) found among a sample of high school students that 22 percent of the girls scored sufficiently high on a measure of eating behavior to be classified as having an eating disorder. The current estimate is that 1 out of 200 American girls between 12 and 18 years of age will develop some degree of anorexia, and that 10 to 15 percent of those with this disorder will die (in "Women's Health," 1985). Susan Squire (1983) has quoted a University of California (Berkeley) sorority member as saying, "I've walked into the bathroom at the sorority house and immediately had to leave because it smelled so bad from vomit"; and David Garner, a leading researcher in this field, has calculated that about 12 percent of college-age women have serious eating behavior problems that include constant worry about food, and use of drastic weight-control techniques, laxatives, diuretics, and vomiting (in Squire, 1983).

Eating disorders can be viewed on a continuum with anorexia at the extreme end of one pole and normal eating on the other. Anorexia is diagnosed if the individual has lost at least 25 percent of body weight and feels fat even though clearly and seriously underweight. *Restrictor* anorexics maintain their emaciation by drastically restricting their intake; *bulimic* anorexics binge and then attempt to compensate by vomiting, use of laxatives, diuretics, amphetamines, and/or excessive exercise. According to Susan Squire (1983), anorexics are followed on the continuum by normal-weight bulimics, occasional purgers, occasional dieters, and finally normal eaters who are content with their bodies regardless of weight. The latter appear to be a very small minority. Janet Polivy and Peter Herman (1985) have suggested that it is dieting that precedes binging and not vice versa, and that "almost any disinhibitor may disrupt the dieter's characteristic restraint and release suppressed eating" (p. 195).

Although some consider overeating and obesity to be as serious a problem as anorexia and bulimia, far more attention has been given to the latter because it is primarily found among young women and can be life-threatening. Susie Orbach (1986) has found parallels in the hysteria associated with women in the Victorian era and today's eating disorders—in their meaning and in their treatment. She views anorexia as symbolizing *both* "stereotyped femininity and its opposite" (iron control); and suggests that, like Victorian hysteria, it expresses the "rebellion and the accommodation that women come to make in the context of a social role lived within circumscribed boundaries" (p. 24). Treatment, Orbach urges, should not center on force-feeding and forced bed rest but on the psychological antecedents and consequences of anorexic behavior.

Other Dysfunctions

Women far outnumber men among persons diagnosed as suffering from histrionic personality, the term now used in the official diagnostic manual of the American Psychiatric Association (1980) to replace hysteria (which means "wandering womb"!). According to Pauline Bart and Diana Scully (1979), a man given the diagnosis of hysteria was almost certain to be homosexual, poor, or of minority (Third World) status; and the behaviors regarded as symptomatic of hysteria represent a "stark caricature of femininity," with exaggerated dependence, exhibitionism, and manipulativeness. Others have also pointed out the correspondence between the group of symptoms labeled hysteria and the behaviors our culture teaches to women (for example, Celani, 1976). Hysteria, according to Howard Wolowitz (1972), describes the stereotyped woman whose needs for approval, dependency, and affiliation become overwhelming demands to be satisfied by the use of charm, sex, goodness, and perhaps finally illness and martyrdom. Thomas Szasz has suggested that hysteria is the vocabulary of the powerless; whereas the powerful can shout or attack to make themselves noticed, "the powerless weep or develop symptoms" (in Bart & Scully, 1979).

Another dysfunction associated primarily with women is agoraphobia, a fear of open spaces. Persons with agoraphobia experience anxiety or panic when they attempt to work, shop, visit, or do anything requiring their presence outside of their own homes; they tend to "fear any situation in which escape to safe territory or to a trusted companion might be hindered" (Chambless & Goldstein, 1980, p. 119). Some have suggested that women are vulnerable to agoraphobia because such behavior is acceptable, and the symptoms may be "reinforced by family members who feel inconvenienced but not threatened by these sex-role-appropriate behaviors" (Chambless & Goldstein, 1980, p. 131).

Richard Lewine (1981) has reviewed the literature on schizophrenia and concluded that gender differences exist in age of onset (or diagnosis) and in symptoms. Men appear to receive schizophrenia diagnoses and to be hospitalized at younger ages than women. Whether this reflects a true difference in age of onset is not known, since family members may

attend sooner to men who manifest the deviant behavior that characterizes schizophrenia (bizarre
affective and cognitive responses). Early in this century Leta Hollingworth argued that this was the case
with respect to mental retardation; men were institutionalized at earlier ages than women because young
retarded women could remain at home, serving useful functions and performing limited tasks. According
to Stephanie Shields (1975b), Hollingworth

> reasoned that since men were expected to take their
> place in society as competitive and economically-
> independent individuals, their deficiencies would be
> noted earlier. Women, on the other hand, " . . . are not
> so readily recognized as defective since they do not have
> to compete mentally to maintain themselves in the so-
> cial milieu." (p. 854)

In addition to gender differences in age of diagnosis,
Lewine also noted evidence suggesting that among
persons diagnosed as schizophrenic, women show
more unusual and affective symptoms and are less
quiet and less withdrawn than men.

As of this writing, a group of psychiatrists charged
with proposing revisions for the *Diagnostic and Statistical Manual of Mental Disorders (DSM-III)* of the
American Psychiatric Association (used by all mental
health practitioners in the United States) are planning
to designate masochism as a recognized psychiatric
disorder, to be called "self defeating personality disorder." The proposed symptoms—guilt, self-
punishment, and serving others before taking care of
oneself—have long been associated with stereotyped
femininity, and there is little doubt that this diagnosis
would be used far more often for women than for
men. According to Glenn Collins (1985):

> Richard von Krafft-Ebing, a German neurologist,
> coined the term masochism before the turn of the cen-
> tury, and Sigmund Freud theorized in 1924 that
> masochism was a feminine characteristic. His disciple
> Helene Deutsch subsequently elaborated the concept of
> women's innate masochism, while analysts like Karen
> Horney rejected the notion. (p. B12)

Paula Caplan (1984), among others, has argued that
there is no evidence to support the view that women
take pleasure in suffering (the precise meaning of
masochism), and that the new diagnostic category of
"self defeating personality" is intended to label as
"sick" women who have been victimized in abusive
relationships and women who are doing what they
are expected to do—putting the needs of others before their own.

The issue of diagnostic labels is one that we cannot
consider here without moving far from our major

focus. It is important, however, to understand that
psychiatric diagnoses are well known to be unreliable
(that is, to vary among those making the diagnosis),
and to reflect biases associated with therapists' training, and clients' social class and race. Hope Landrine
(1983) found support, in one study, for her thesis that
psychotherapists tend to describe certain diagnostic
categories with the *same terms* as they use to independently describe members of certain status groups; for
example, young white middle-class women are likely
to be described as having the same attributes as persons with histrionic personality disorders; black
lower-class men are likely to be described as having
the same attributes as persons with character disorders; and so on.

The current edition of the *DSM-III* (American
Psychiatric Association, 1980) suggests that the following disorders are more prevalent among women
than among men: agoraphobia, anxiety states, bor-
derline personality, dependent personality, depression, histrionic personality, multiple personality,
psychogenic pain disorder, sexual dysfunction, simple phobias, and somatization disorders. Men, on the
other hand, are more often diagnosed as suffering
from alcoholism, antisocial personality, compulsive
personality, drug abuse, intermittent explosive disorder, paraphilia, pathological gambling, and pyro-
mania. Carol Landau (1986) has pointed out the
remarkable fit between the categories of mental disorder said to be more prevalent among women (or
among men) and our culture's gender stereotypes
and gender socialization. This is an important issue,
to which we will now turn our attention.

GENDER STEREOTYPES AND MENTAL HEALTH

Differences in patterns of dysfunctional behavior said
to be exhibited most commonly by one gender or the
other tell us a great deal about the psychological
effects of our culture's gender stereotypes. For example, Richard Cloward and Frances Piven (1979) have
proposed that social norms govern dysfunctional as
well as functional behavior, and that women (and
men) respond to stress in "sex-appropriate" ways.
"Stresses are refracted through an ideology which
encourages women to search within their psyches
and their bodies for the sources of their problems" (p.
668). Thus, because women are encouraged to view
our problems as originating within ourselves (in our
own incompetence, inferiority, weakness, and so
on), we tend to respond either stoically, with endur-

ance, since we feel that the strength to solve problems must come from within; or self-destructively, blaming ourselves for our inability to cope.

Both the way we react to stress and the nature of the stressors we encounter are intimately related to our culture's ideas about appropriate masculine and feminine behavior. If we examine these ideas closely, we find that the traits and behaviors that our culture typically prescribes for women do not match our generally accepted criteria for mental health or maturity. On the other hand, deviation from the culturally prescribed role is typically viewed as a manifestation of maladjustment. Let us look at this double bind in more detail.

The Masculinity Stereotype As Model of Mental Health

Our culture uses as its standard of mental health the traits and behaviors of the stereotypical white male. Thus, when a woman behaves in the culturally prescribed feminine manner—that is, when she conforms to the female stereotype of dependence, expressiveness, and nonassertiveness—she may be judged by professional mental health workers and laypersons alike as behaving normally for a woman but not as one expects of a mature and healthy adult. In a now-classic study (Broverman, Broverman, Clarkson, Rosenkrantz, & Vogel, 1970), 79 psychologists, psychiatrists, and social workers (46 men and 33 women) were asked to respond to 122 bipolar adjectives by choosing the pole that best described a "mature, healthy, socially competent" adult man, adult woman, or adult person. The researchers found that the descriptions given by the men and women were similar, and that both perceived healthy persons and healthy men in the same way, but as different from women. If we use as the general standard of mental health what professionals say about adults of unspecified gender, then according to these findings, women are less likely than men to be seen as mentally healthy. Women are thus in a double bind. If we behave in ways considered desirable for mature adults we risk censure for failing to be appropriately feminine; but behaving in ways designated as feminine means being "necessarily deficient with respect to the general standards for adult behavior" (Broverman, Vogel, Broverman, Clarkson, & Rosenkrantz, 1972, p. 75).

Jeanne Brooks-Gunn and Melanie Fisch (1980) repeated the 1970 study of Broverman et al. with a large sample of college students and a different measuring instrument. They found that the men students, just like the mental health workers in the earlier study, characterized a socially competent man as having the same traits as a socially competent adult, but saw a mature, healthy woman as being significantly different from a healthy man and from a healthy adult. Women students, on the other hand, did not see socially competent men and women as differing either from each other or from a gender-neutral adult. In another replication of the 1970 Broverman et al. study, Erica Wise and Janet Rafferty (1982) found that a sample of college students (of both genders) described a normal healthy man similarly to a normal healthy adult, and a normal healthy boy similarly to a normal healthy child, but described a woman and a girl in significantly different terms from an adult and child, respectively. In addition, when asked what they had imagined when responding to the terms *adult* and *child*, the students indicated that they had more often thought of a male than a female. Roger Philips and Faith Gilroy (1985) have reported finding some support for the original Broverman findings but also some changes in a study of a sample of mental health workers (most of whom had only bachelors or masters degrees). While overall responses to healthy women and healthy adults differed (but not overall responses to healthy men and adults), examination of individual items revealed differences in degree and not in quality.

Behavior stereotypically attributed to women (considered "feminine") is more often associated with maladjustment, whether exhibited by women or by men. Thus, for example, Linda Teri (1982) found that a large sample of clinical psychologists of both genders rated hypothetical clients who were described as feeling worthless and depressed ("stereotypically feminine behavior") as more maladjusted and as functioning less adequately both socially and on the job than clients described as hostile and aggressive ("stereotypically masculine"). Similarly, members of subordinate social groups (persons with little power as a function of their age, race or ethnicity, socioeconomic status, or gender) who fulfill their roles to the maximum—that is, who conform very closely to the stereotypes subscribed to by the majority culture—are likely to be labeled mad or mentally ill, as illustrated in our earlier discussion of hysteria. To test this hypothesis, Hope Landrine (1983) asked a sample of practicing psychotherapists to make psychiatric evaluations of individuals described in varying ways. (This work was referred to earlier in the discussion of diagnostic labels.) Among her findings was that a person (gender unspecified) described as behaving like the stereotype of a young middle-class woman ("primarily concerned with cultivating an alluring, attractive physical appearance . . . has a romantic view of life, and of relationships . . . sense of self is not clearly defined") was diagnosed as having a histrionic personality disorder by 80 percent of the respondents. A person described like the stereotype of an older middle-class woman was judged to be a dependent personality 78 percent of the time and depressive 44 percent of the time. In contrast, a person described in the stereotypic terms assigned upper-class white men, the dominant social group in our culture, was judged to be normal 92 percent of the time. Landrine's research illustrates and supports her thesis that the diagnostic categories used to label mental illness reflect the existing ways in which the dominant social group describes, and tries to socialize, subordinate groups.

The Hazards of Conformity to the Femininity Stereotype

If the ways women in our culture are expected to behave deviate from our criteria for mental health, it is not surprising to find that women are less satisfied with life than men. Indeed, when Carolyn Morgan (1980) analyzed data from a national survey of over 2000 adults, she found that the three best predictors of satisfaction with life were gender (men were more satisfied than women); work satisfaction; and personal competence. And, women in general reported themselves to be significantly lower than men in personal competence, work satisfaction, and marital adjustment. In the previously mentioned survey of Harvard/Radcliffe alumni (the class of 1961), according to Fox Butterfield (1986) "the most striking theme to emerge . . . is the sharp contrast between the largely contented tone of the men's essays and the sense of frustration expressed by many of the women" (p. 30E). When women behave "appropriately," we are also more prone to depression; the symptoms of which are congruent with women's socialization. Earlier we noted that depression is the primary behavioral dysfunction for which women are admitted to treatment facilities. Hypotheses about what causes the high rate of depression for women center around its relationship to how women are expected to behave.

A number of studies have found that scores on a measure of depression are positively related to self-reported communal, expressive, and nurturant personal attributes (stereotypically labeled feminine) and negatively related to self-reported assertive, instrumental, and agentic personal attributes (stereotypically labeled masculine). A study of a graduate student sample (Elpern & Karp, 1984), for example, found that for both men and women, greater depression was associated with lower "masculinity" scores, and that among women "those that fall into the traditionally feminine category . . . are more depressed . . . than any of the other sex-role types" (p. 991). A group of middle-aged white women diagnosed as depressive were found to differ from a comparable nonclinical group (Tinsley, Sullivan-Guest, & McGuire, 1984) in being more likely to describe themselves in nurturant, expressive, and communal terms. A significant part of the variance in depression scores (37 percent) could be accounted for by variance in sex role, supporting the researchers' hypothesis that "depression in the middle-aged female is related to her degree of acceptance of the traditional feminine sex role" (p. 30).

A related hypothesis (Gove & Tudor, 1973) is that the role of full-time homemaker provides fewer satisfactions and is more ambiguous than the role of employed husband. A woman who stays at home for many years with children and housework is expected to derive satisfaction from interaction with family members, the gleam of a polished floor, the report of "no cavities" from her children's dentist, or the whiteness of her husband's laundered shirt. Unless she is also involved in activities outside the home on a paid or volunteer basis, a woman's sources of satisfaction are more limited than those of her husband. It is women's gender-restricted social role, this view argues, that increases the likelihood of greater negative than positive experiences since, while a man has two major sources of gratification, his family and his work, a full-time homemaker has only her family. Raising children and keeping house are low-prestige, frustrating, relatively unstructured, and largely invisible jobs.

Women who have learned too well the behaviors descriptive of the "feminine" mode, who have been most unambiguously socialized along normative lines, who have been most accepting of the cultural definition of women as nurturing, self-sacrificing, home-oriented adjuncts of their men, may be most vulnerable to stress. When conditions no longer make it easy to find gratification in doing the womanly, wifely, or motherly things women are expected to do, then a woman's value is called into question. Such changed conditions may result from age; illness; loss of one's husband through disinterest, death, or divorce; departure of one's children; poverty; excessive fatigue from being overburdened; or unreachable standards of "feminine accomplishment" that are imposed by oneself or others. As noted by Jeanne Lemkau and Carol Landau (in press):

> Women who adopt a posture of selflessness, in relationships with husbands, children, bosses, and friends, are typically not seen in psychotherapy until they encounter a . . . crisis which precipitates symptoms of anxiety and/or depression. (p. 5)

When the perception of being no longer useful is added to that of a woman's generally low status, she may blame herself for being unloved. Despondency can thus be understood, in some cases, as a reaction to having been discarded by others as no longer useful. The consequences may be tragic for a woman for whom traditional motives and behaviors are most important and who is not encouraged to develop new competencies.

Pauline Bart (1971) studied depression among a group of middle-aged women and found that those most likely to experience psychological distress were women whose attitudes were most traditional, who had been "supermothers" and superhousewives, who had invariably done "the right thing" and made sacrifices. With their children gone and forgetful about letters, phone calls, and other forms of recognition, traditional mothers felt let down, deserted, abandoned, and useless. Especially if their husbands were no longer alive, there were few familiar guidelines for their behavior and no one left to serve (except themselves). These women felt disappointed and helpless, and wanted desperately to regain their children's attention. Bart found that depressed reactions were more likely to occur among housewives than among employed wives, and were more likely among middle-class homemakers than among poorer working-class women.

Related to women's stereotypical role is the probability that women obtain considerably less sympathy than men when we attempt to enlist family members in helping us with our problems. A woman's traditional role may be considered easier than a man's and less stressful; the complaints of a homemaker, therefore, may be taken less seriously and considered less valid than those of her husband. In addition, it is women who are expected to be nurturers, and to know how to tend and heal and

protect. This is reflected in the following passage from Margaret Atwood's (1984) novel *Bluebeard's Egg*:

> There are some stories which my mother does not tell when there are men present. . . . She tells them to women only, [because they are too upsetting for men]. . . . Men are not to be told anything they might find too painful; the secret depths of human nature, the sordid physicalities, might overwhelm or damage them. . . . Men . . . find life more difficult than women do.

We somehow expect that women will know how to take care of the problems of their children or spouses, how to tend the sick or the troubled, to nurture and soothe, and to handle financial, emotional, and physical stress without falling apart.

Consequently, a man with problems is likely to find that his wife will want to help him, be willing to listen, and will try to be supportive. This is what wives are supposed to do. Husbands, however, are far less likely to do the same. A study by R. B. Warren found that women relied on emotional support and help with personal problems from a spouse less than did men; this discrepancy was particularly true among blue-collar couples (in Barnett & Baruch, 1978). Thus, while marriage is associated with a drastic reduction in psychological dysfunction among men, this is not the case for women. Using an index based on proportional differences between the married and the never-married, researchers have found that "marriage is associated with a 71 percent reduction in illness rates for minority men, 63 percent for white men, 28 percent for white women, and 8 percent for minority women" (*Developing a National Agenda*, 1985, p. 8).

When a woman turns to her husband for sympathy or reassurance she may be disappointed because such responses are difficult for him to make. Men have had less practice in nurturance and may experience discomfort and anxiety when asked to give emotional support. Or a man may be "too busy" with more salient concerns and responsibilities centering around his job and the financial needs of his family. In the television film *The Cracker Factory*, for example, a depressed homemaker who thinks she has achieved some insight into the cause of her problem awakens her husband late one night to share it with him, but he shrugs her off, grunting that he has to go to work early the next morning. When she persists, he tells her angrily that he does not want to hear what she has to say. "Go tell it to your shrink; that's what I pay him for, isn't it?" Men may be uncertain about their effectiveness in the area of emotional support since they have had so little practice. A fine film, *Woman Under the Influence*, about a working-class woman who "goes mad," explores her husband's struggle to be caring and sympathetic. These responses are not easily elicited from men who have seldom been called upon to make them and who have not been rewarded for their sensitivity.

The Hazards of Deviation from the Femininity Stereotype

Conforming to our culture's stereotype of femininity has negative consequences for women's mental health but, on the other hand, deviation from cultural expectations is often seen as a sign of maladjustment. Since we judge or interpret the behavior of an individual in the context of our expectations and assumptions about his or her life patterns, goals, and general nature, sometimes the same behaviors exhibited by a woman and a man are evaluated quite differently. For example, in one study (Borys & Perlman, 1985), college students who read a brief description of a lonely freshman rated this student significantly more positively on a number of dimensions if a woman than a man, suggesting that loneliness is a more acceptable attribute for the former. The general stereotype for women includes shyness, reserve, and modesty, and is therefore compatible with loneliness. One group of researchers (Israel, Raskin, Libow, & Pravder, 1978) found that a sample of college undergraduates judged female clients described as suffering from mild and common types of disturbance as being less responsible people than comparable male clients, and judged depressed female clients as more disturbed than comparable men. Differential judgments of women and men described as doing the same things have been reported by others. For example, Penelope Tilby and Rudolf Kalin (1980) had college students read descriptions of persons and then rate them on adjustment relative to work, family, sexuality, and so on. Persons whose described behavior deviated from traditional sex-role patterns were rated as "significantly more maladjusted" than traditional persons on all measures, and "the former group was described as more likely to require psychiatric help in the future" (p. 586).

Phyllis Chesler (1972) has argued that women who behave in nontraditional ways run the risk of censure and may be perceived by others as behaving oddly. Our society discourages deviance, and behaving in gender-inappropriate ways may meet with disapproval and evoke conflict. Charlotte Perkins Gilman (1891/1973), in a classic story of an upper-middle-class woman who aspires to be a writer, described the experience of a breakdown and the reactions to it by others. The woman's husband, a doctor, solicitous and sympathetic to her illness, takes her to the country to rest, and authoritatively frustrates her every attempt to write. Her brother, also a doctor, agrees that she is suffering only from "a slight hysterical tendency." She is ordered to take tonics, air, and exercise, but is "absolutely forbidden to 'work' " and is forced to write secretively. Her enforced inactivity succeeds in constricting her world more and more until she becomes the woman she has seen imprisoned in the patterned yellow wallpaper of her room. Esther Greenwood, in Sylvia Plath's *The Bell Jar* (1972), is also a deviant who fails. The reader feels Esther's pain as she realizes that she wants more for her life than the objectives generally regarded as suitable for a woman, but Esther is unable to move beyond them. She cannot act on the truths she sees so clearly. Esther sees her life branching out before her like a fig tree. On each branch is a "fat purple fig"; one is a happy home and children; others are roles as a poet, a professor, an editor. "I saw myself sitting in the crotch of this fig tree, starving to death, just because I couldn't make up my mind" (p. 63). As she sits, the figs begin "to wrinkle and go black" and to fall at her feet. She believes that to be a woman is to serve men, which she will not do. She is immobilized and finally imprisoned in her bell jar in which she sits "stewing" in her "own sour air." The tragedy of Esther Greenwood's life is her inability to make a choice, a consequence of her lack of support from others and her lack of resources and reinforcement. Her defiance does not succeed because she is alone, untutored in its expression, and uncertain of her objectives.

Data from various sources lend support to the proposition that because a woman's value to her family (and especially to her husband) is related to how well she performs her homemaking chores, a marked lapse in performance is suspect and may be interpreted as a sign of psychological disturbance, with the suggestion (or demand) that the woman seek treatment. Women who cease being considered useful may quite literally be discarded, replaced, urged to seek help, or even committed to institutions by husbands (or other family members) who find them embarrassing or burdensome. In *The Women's Room* (1977), Marilyn French introduces us to Lily, whose husband finds her increasingly unsatisfactory and demanding. As she becomes uncertain, confused, and frightened, her husband becomes more and more resentful, and finally sends her to a mental hospital for "treatment." When Lily's friend Mira visits, she finds Lily wearing "a lot of makeup," with her hair "freshly dyed."

> Other young women were introduced. They too were well-dressed and heavily made up, with brilliant eye shadow, false eyelashes, orange pancake makeup, heavy rouge, deep red lipstick. . . .
> "Those women," Mira nodded to the departing figures. "Are they guests?"
> "Oh, no. They're like me." Lily laughed. "What this place really is is a country club for women whose husbands don't want them anymore." (p. 236)

Later, after returning home from the hospital, Lily tells Mira, "Carl says I can't do anything. I don't know, Mira, I try. I clean and clean and clean. If I don't, they'll send me back" (p. 261).

In *The Stepford Wives* (1972), a macabre novel by Ira Levin, wives whose husbands find them wanting in devotion to their homemaking duties are replaced by robots, fashioned perfectly in their physical image. The robots make marvelous wives, beautiful and loving, excellent housekeepers with no outside interests; nothing diverts them from their primary role of service to their husbands. This literary theme reflects reality. Walter Reich, a psychiatrist, told a lecture audience (in Emery, 1984) about a faculty member at a prestigious medical school who brought his wife to the hospital for psychiatric help.

> The husband said his wife . . . was acting strangely. The main symptom was that she said she wanted to have a career and, as a result, the house was beginning to get messy. . . . The hospital's chief psychiatrist . . . became convinced that the woman suffered from a form of epilepsy . . . [but] Reich, who was given the job of proving it, could find nothing wrong with the woman despite repeated tests.

Phyllis Chesler reported similar cases in her important book *Women and Madness* (1972). One hospitalized woman told her, "I was so sad [after my daughter's birth] and so tired. I couldn't take care of the house right any more. My husband told me a maid would be better than me, that I was crazy" (p. 165). Chesler also cited a study by Shirley Angrist and her colleagues, who found that women who were rehospitalized as mental patients differed from those who were not rehospitalized in that they were more likely to be married, and were more likely to have refused to perform their domestic duties of "cleaning, cooking, child care, and shopping." They did not differ from women who were not rehospitalized in terms of other behaviors.

Such examples suggest that a diagnosis of mental illness may be a punishment for deviance, and that treatment may be geared toward reestablishing conformity to a socially approved role. Jane Prather and Linda Fidell (1975) examined a sample of drug advertisements that appeared in four American medical journals and found that women were portrayed more often than men as irritating others by their mental illness and as reassuming their traditional roles after they recovered. Similarly, David Stockburger and James Davis (1978), who analyzed a 10-year sample of advertisements for psychoactive drugs, noted that the content of the ads strongly suggested a treatment objective for women illustrated by an ad that "indicated that remission of a patient's symptoms would let her get the laundry done" (p. 133). Nearly a decade later, an ad for a tranquilizer (Tranxene, 1986) in *The American Journal of Psychiatry* repeats the same theme. A woman stands by her washing machine and laundry basket, holding her husband's shirt and surrounded by her three children: the caption reads, "Effective, not overpowering."

THERAPY: SEXIST OR SEX-FAIR?

As we shall see, not only mental health criteria, but also treatment objectives for "problem" behavior, are related to socially approved roles. Helplessness and despair, the most common correlates of dysfunctional behavior, can be prevented and overcome by learning how to control the events in our lives, by developing skills that will give us access to rewards and punishments, and by acquiring responses that will permit effective problem solution and the attainment of desired results. But when we look at the kind of treatment women are likely to receive from mental health professionals, such objectives are not always apparent.

Phyllis Chesler, in *Women and Madness* (1972), was among the first to examine how women are treated by a mental health profession dominated by men and by patriarchal attitudes. She pointed out that psychotherapy as traditionally practiced with women emphasizes individual solutions to problems that have societal components, and reinforces helplessness and dependence on an authority figure. But since the early 1970s, as Christine Abramowitz and Paul Dokecki (1977) have suggested, there has been an "outpouring of feminist concerns in the professional literature"; and while this outpouring has perhaps fallen short of its "goal of eliminating sex bias from clinical practice," it may have made therapists more sensitive about what they say they believe and more alert to the significance of their attitudes. Still, women need to exercise caution when seeking help with problems, to be alert for a possible sexist bias in psychotherapy, and to be aware of the existence of sex-fair and feminist therapies.

Bias in Traditional Psychotherapy

Psychotherapy is not a value-free process; it reflects our society's dominant views and expectations. Therapists who hold traditional beliefs about the differential nature and roles of women and men, regardless of their own gender, are likely to reflect these beliefs in their work with clients. An example can be drawn from one of Sigmund Freud's most celebrated cases, that of Dora. Freud's treatment of Dora, an intelligent 18-year-old woman diagnosed as a "hysteric," has been critically reviewed by Salvatore Maddi (1974), who has suggested that what Dora needed was support from Freud in her justified criticism of the adults in her life for their hypocrisy and abandonment. What she received instead was a sexual interpretation of her problems, which promoted guilt and left her feeling "depressed and suicidal." Dora, wrote Maddi, was

> a beleaguered, overwhelmed youngster caught in a fantastic web of corruption constructed by all of the important adults in her life. There is a conspiracy of silence that the girl cannot break through. . . . In various ways, these adults blame Dora for creating her own problems. . . . Dora cries out for help, and Freud wastes time trying to have her remember where she first heard about sexual intercourse and if she wet her bed as a child. (p. 99)

Roy Schaefer (1984), a renowned trainer of clinical psychologists, has described the different "story lines" he has traced in his work with men and women in therapy: "The theme of pursuing failure is relatively more conspicuous in analytic work with men, while the idealization of unhappiness is relatively more conspicuous in analytic work with women" (p. 404). These differential themes, Schaefer admits, are ones created, or sought, by the therapist. Differential treatment of men and women in therapy has also been documented by the personal testimony of John Thompson, a therapist at a coed college. Thompson "compared the kinds of services given to males and given to females," and reported his conclusions in a

paper entitled *One Male Psychotherapist's Pilgrimage into His Sexism* (1978).

> These data clearly indicated that I and my colleagues (all male) treated women significantly differently than we treated men. Women were more likely to be medicated, to be seen for counseling instead of intensive psychotherapy, and to be seen for fewer sessions . . . [supporting the view of] women as weak, dependent creatures, who needed to be reassured, supported, "patted-on-the-head," medicated and sent on their way. Men, on the other hand, had to face their problems, be aggressive and competent . . . and overcome their limitations. (p. 2)

Thus, women are encouraged to interpret personal problems in ways that underestimate their cultural meaning and overemphasize their internal and emotional components; and, at the same time, women's complaints tend to be trivialized and interpreted as transitory. Such interpretations prevent us from working out effective strategies for efficient and competent problem solving and encourage us to think that we are just "crazy."

Studies of therapists' attitudes toward women, their adherence to gender stereotypes, and the relationship between evaluation and treatment and the gender of client and/or therapist have produced ambiguous findings. In one study (Gomes & Abramowitz, 1976), for example, questionnaires returned by 30 percent of the clinical division of the American Psychological Association did not reveal any reliable prejudice against women, but whether this is also true of the 70 percent who did not respond is not, of course, known. In another study (Sherman, Koufacos, & Kenworthy, 1978), 25 percent of the therapists in one state replied to a survey of attitudes toward, and information about, women. The respondents were found to hold generally liberal attitudes, but the female therapists were better informed and held even less stereotyped beliefs than their male colleagues. A review of the literature (Abramowitz & Dokecki, 1977) did not support the conclusion that client gender is a consistent influence on therapists' judgments in simulated situations. And other reviewers (Stricker, 1977; Brodsky, 1980; Davidson & Abramowitz, 1980) have concluded that therapist bias and adherence to stereotypes are not reliably related to therapist gender.

On the other hand, in one study (Wright, Meadow, Abramowitz, & Davidson, 1980), women therapists in a community mental health center were found to be significantly more likely than men to assign benign (nonpsychotic) diagnostic labels to adult outpatients. According to John Delk (1977), of the six major studies designed to test for sex-role stereotyping by psychotherapists, five reported confirming results. Bernard Whitley (1979) concluded, from his survey of the literature, that clinicians appear to "share the sex role stereotypes of their lay contemporaries" (p. 1318); and Mary Lee Smith's (1980) analysis of relevant studies also led her to conclude that "clinicians hold negative stereotypes about women" (p. 405).

But how these views affect client treatment and outcomes has thus far not been clearly or reliably demonstrated. For example, in one study (Stearns, Penner, & Kimmel, 1980) in which a sample of psychotherapists was given information about clients who varied in gender, case history, occupation, and symptoms, the men clients were judged to have significantly more serious problems than the women, while the women were perceived as being significantly more motivated for therapy. For other judgments, however, client gender seemed less important than other information. Constance Thomas (1985) received survey responses from a small sample of psychologists and psychiatrists of both genders who practice in the Los Angeles area and concluded that the standard of mental health subscribed to by psychotherapists was the same for women as for men. She also found that "the therapist most likely to be nonsexist is a psychologist, either male or female, who has a large number of women in his or her practice. The therapist most likely to be sexist is a psychiatrist who sees relatively few women" (p. 391). We do not know the relationship between the self-reported attitudes of psychotherapists and their behavior.

What actually occurs during interaction between client and therapist over the course of many meetings is, understandably, difficult to study. While the goal of psychotherapy, to increase an individual's effective social behaviors and the probability of satisfying relationships and successful outcomes, may be the same for women and men, how these goals are interpreted may differ. Violet Franks (1979) has suggested that regardless of therapists' verbal responses to questionnaires, they likely provide subtle reinforcements for the sex-typed behaviors of their clients.

Some psychologists and other providers of mental health services are convinced that a special effort must be made to assure *sex-fair* treatment of women in psychotherapy. A consumer handbook prepared by committees from the Association for Women in Psychology and the American Psychological Association (*Women and Psychotherapy*, 1981) notes that "therapists are products of our society and as such may be influenced by societal values . . . [that] may reinforce a standard of 'normalcy' that encourages women and/or minorities to adjust to traditional, sometimes sexist/racist roles" (pp. 3f.). The handbook provides advice on selecting and evaluating a psychotherapist, on alternatives to psychotherapy, and on "how to tell whether sexism is interfering with therapy." One state psychological association officially adopted a set of guidelines to help raise the consciousness of therapists and to promote sex-fair practices. The first guideline stresses that "the options explored between client and practitioner should not be constrained by sex-role stereotypes" (Worell & Remer, 1982).

Overprescription of Mood-Altering Drugs

Seeing women's problems as trivial, transitory, and located in the individual has led to a tendency by doctors who treat women to over-prescribe mood-altering drugs. It is not unusual for a doctor to advise a troubled woman to go back home, smile at her husband or lover more often, and when things get tough, to "take a pill." Barbara Gordon's (1979) story of her addiction to prescribed Valium and its tragic consequences, told in "I'm Dancing as Fast as I Can," and a song of the 1970s by Mick Jagger and Keith Richard about "mother's little helper," the little yellow pill, reflect a reality of contemporary life. A study by the National Institute of Drug Abuse (in Scanlan, 1978) found that 80 percent of the mood-altering drugs taken by women were prescribed for them by internists, general practitioners, and obstetricians-gynecologists. The tendency of doctors to help women by prescribing tranquilizers or sedatives has been found nationwide.

Studies indicate that although women account for only 58 percent of all visits to doctors' offices, they receive 73 percent of all prescriptions written for mood-altering, psychotropic drugs (*Developing a National Agenda*, 1985). An earlier review of the literature by Linda Fidell (1973) revealed that between 45 and 50 percent of all women over 30 were estimated to use some mood-modifying medication, and that women, unlike men, tended to get drugs by prescription from a doctor and, therefore, to use them longer and more consistently. Fidell cited one study that found that women who were hospitalized for heroin detoxification were given more drugs and a greater variety of drugs while in the hospital than a comparable group of men, and another study in which Librium was judged by 87 percent of a group of doctors as legitimate for daily use by housewives while only 53 percent could justify its daily use by students.

A content analysis by Jane Prather and Linda Fidell (1975) of drug advertisements that appeared over a 5-year period in four leading medical journals found that the ads tended to associate psychoactive drugs with women patients and nonpsychoactive drugs with men, implying that women's illnesses reflect mental problems more than men's. There was also a significant difference in the symptoms men and women users of psychoactive drugs were said to manifest, men being more likely to be presented in association with specific and work-related symptoms and women with diffuse anxiety, tension, or depression. These findings have been reinforced and extended by David Stockburger and James Davis (1978). They examined human images found in ads for psychoactive drugs in the *American Journal of Psychiatry* from 1963 to 1974 and found that mentally ill persons were significantly more often shown as women (58 percent of the time) while doctors were more often shown as men (98 percent of the time). Women were disproportionately represented in three symptom categories: insomnia, depression, and anxiety. Illustrative of the use of women as models for ads for mood-altering drugs is an advertisement in *JAMA (Journal of the American Medical Association)* for a pharmaceutical (Oral Hydergine) recommended for elderly patients. The illustration accompanying the text is of a white-haired woman with varying facial expressions labeled depression, lack of self-care, dizziness, confusion, and unsociability ("A Positive Approach Helps," 1979).

Feminist Psychotherapy: A New Alternative

A radical new therapy guided by feminist principles has been proposed and is now being practiced by psychotherapists who share common values and strategies. The major therapeutic goal in feminist therapy is the discovery and pursuit of personal strengths and the achievement of independence. Such therapy encourages women to nurture themselves, to "allow themselves to do things that make them feel good" (Lerman, 1976, p. 382), and to assert their rights and needs. Anne Fishel (1979) has suggested that the major thrust and challenge of feminist therapy has been its emphasis on power; it attempts "to change the power dynamics in the therapy process itself, to help the client reclaim power in the workplace and the bedroom" (p. 79).

Feminist therapy can be said to differ in theory and objectives from traditional therapy in the following ways:

1. Feminist therapists have an obligation to make their values explicit to their clients (Rawlings & Carter, 1977).

2. The central element of feminist therapy, according to Jeanne Marecek and Diane Kravetz (1977), is a focus on society and social institutions. Feminist therapy is in this way distinguishable from sex-fair therapy. Its emphasis is on the link between personal change and sociopolitical change. Such a sociological perspective discourages the use of individual psychopathology labels (Rador, Masnick, & Hauser, 1977), and focuses instead on the sources of stress within the culture. This position is vital to feminist therapy and puts into practice the core belief of feminism that "the personal is political." As Hannah Lerman (1976) has pointed out, "Separating the internal and the external [or seeing their interrelationship] . . . serves to help a woman learn that she is not crazy" (p. 380).

3. Feminist therapists recognize women's inferior social status as an important component of psychological distress, and attribute it not to biology but to the lack of political and economic power (Rawlings & Carter, 1977).

4. In feminist therapy, therapist/client differences in status are deemphasized and "equal sharing of resources, power and responsibility" are promoted (Marecek & Kravetz, 1977); the therapy process is "democratized." The therapist does not function as an expert; rather, the client is assumed to be competent and knowledgeable about her own feelings and needs and decides what behaviors she wants to change. "Feminist values and techniques promote equalitarian rather than hierarchical relationships [and] respect for the client's expertise about herself" (Lerman, 1985, pp. 6f.).

5. Feminist therapists see themselves as participants in the women's movement, as supporters of equality between women and men, and as questioners of traditional roles. They often take social action and are advocates on behalf of their clients (Rawlings & Carter, 1977).

6. Feminist therapists assume that all social roles (and behaviors) are open to women; they encourage clients to evaluate and define their choices and to differentiate between what they have learned is

gender appropriate and what is appropriate to them as individuals. "Feminist therapists strive to restore a balance in the emphasis on work and relationships" (Rador, Masnick, & Hauser, 1977, p. 509).

7. Feminist therapists encourage women to deal with anger, to assume responsibility for their actions and feelings, and to learn how to assert power openly. They urge the client to take responsibility for doing what is needed to get what she wants for herself, and to communicate her needs to others in a straightforward manner.

8. An important goal of feminist therapy is achievement of respect and trust for other women. Feminist therapists understand that while a relationship with a man can be enriching, it is not necessary or central to a woman's mental health (Rawlings & Carter, 1977) and encourage women to view other women not as competitors for men but as sources of emotional support.

9. Feminist therapists do not view men as the enemy (Rawlings & Carter, 1977), and a relationship with a man in or outside of marriage is considered to be a "partnership of equals."

10. In feminist therapy, issues and experiences unique to women, such as menstruation, childbirth, and rape, are raised and discussed.

As Albert Bandura (1982) has suggested, people can experience two forms of futility: one deriving from self-doubt—doubt about one's competence or capacities to do what is required—and the other deriving from doubt about outcomes—fear that one's efforts will not produce the desired results because of "the unresponsiveness, negative bias, or punitiveness of the environment" (p. 140). To decrease doubts about one's competence requires expansion of one's behavioral repertoire with opportunities for practice, reinforcement, and correction; while a decrease in outcome-based futility requires a social environment that provides equitable rewards based on performance, and that does not discriminate against persons on the basis of status characteristics (such as gender, ethnicity, and occupation). Accordingly, feminist therapy acknowledges the importance of change in both the personal and the social realms.

POWER AND CONTROL: KEYS TO WELL-BEING

The fact that feminist therapy aims at helping women reclaim their power points up the central importance of a feeling of power and control to mental health and well-being. The personal traits that have clearly been shown to relate positively to measures of self-esteem or subjective well-being are the same for women as for men; and include assertiveness, independence, self-responsibility, and efficacy, characteristics typically included in the stereotype of masculinity. Of course, this is hardly surprising since measures of psychological well-being tap the same attributes; that is, a score indicating good functioning is earned *if* the respondent self-reports behaving in an assertive, independent, and effective manner. These are the characteristics our society values and the attributes that mediate the successful attainment of personal goals. Marylee Taylor and Judith Hall (1982) statistically analyzed and reviewed studies of nonclinical adult samples that compared indices of mental health with self-reported behavior. For both women and men, the major contributor to well-being scores was found to be high scores on instrumentality, which, as the researchers concluded, "pays off for individuals of both sexes . . . [and] yields positive outcomes for individuals in American society" (p. 362). Bernard Whitley has reached conclusions similar to that of Taylor and Hall. In a review of research on self-esteem (Whitley, 1983), he found that self-esteem is more related to assertive, agentic attributes than to expressive, communal ones, among both women and men. In a subsequent statistical review of studies of depression and general adjustment, Whitley (1985) again found evidence that self-reported assertiveness, independence, and instrumentality by women or men is significantly related to psychological well-being. Supporting research has involved mainly samples of college students (for example, Adams & Sherer, 1985; Frank, McLaughlin, & Crusco, 1984; Lubinski, Tellegen, & Butcher, 1981) but other populations, such as white suburban mothers, have also been sampled (Frank, Towell, & Huyck, 1985; Rendely, Holmstrom, & Karp, 1984).

Good mental health or life satisfaction is considerably diminished by circumstances in which individuals lack power or control. Jeanne Marecek (1977) has argued that powerlessness (having little or no access to the resources that enable one to influence the behavior of others or the outcomes accruing to oneself) "engenders a high risk of psychological disorder" (p. 2), and has noted that such disorders are prevalent in our society among persons who are poor and undereducated—that is, those who are chronically powerless because of social inequities. Dysfunctional behavior has also been found to accompany the temporary powerlessness that is a consequence of "abrupt economic reversals, the death of a spouse or lover, or serious illness" (p. 2), life stresses that magnify the lack of control persons have over their environment. As a status group, women have less power than men; and on an individual level, a woman's ability to control her own life varies negatively with the extent to which she conforms to traditional role expectations, and the extent to which she is discriminated against by economic, political, legal, and educational institutions.

Women are also often used as scapegoats for the frustrations of men. In an earlier chapter we discussed the hostility men direct against women in sexual and physical assault. To grow up knowing that you are an object against which someone's rage may be directed, not because of what you did or did not do but because as a woman you are weaker, have less status, and are thus a safer target than a man, is one more reason to "go mad" or become depressed. If you have personally experienced brutal forms of hostility, then your ability to function freely, easily, and confidently will likely be impaired. If you are also a member of a low-status minority group and poor, and have been exploited and terrorized, psychological dysfunction is even more understandable. One study found that among persons hospitalized for mental illness, 53 percent of the women and 23 percent of the men had histories of abuse; of those who had been sexually abused, 89 percent were women (*Developing a National Agenda*, 1985).

In a now-classic study, Barbara Dohrenwend (1973) interviewed a sample of heads of families in a New York City community and found that

> women's symptom levels were more affected by events they did not control than by all events [during the previous year], suggesting that their psychological distress tended to be associated with the lack of power to control their lives. In contrast, men's symptom levels were more closely related to life change scores based on all events. (p. 232)

Abigail Stewart and Patricia Salt (1981) had a group of 33-year-old white women (graduates of an elite women's college) respond to a questionnaire that determined the amount of life stress they had experienced over a two-year period. Life stress was found to be a reliable predictor of reported illness for single career women, and of depression for full-time homemakers. Some research has suggested that it is not the sheer number of life changes (or stressors) that is importantly linked to well-being but certain factors that mediate between the life events and their consequences, such as the degree to which the events were controllable (or controlled), access to commun-

ity or other resources, and the existence of emotional or social supports. Thus, for example, Ronald Ganellen and Paul Blaney (1984) found that among college students, those with social supports were more "hardy"—that is, more resistant to the ill effects of life stress. Similarly, data on suicide attempts suggest that women may resort to this behavior because they have few other options for solving problems or changing conditions. Lous Heshusius (1980) has summarized this proposition as follows:

> A "woman's place" does not [ordinarily] offer her the resources needed to deal effectively and adaptively with the environment. Where males most often have political power, financial power, power derived from their career status and possibilities, and sheer physical power to bring about changes in their environment, females typically lack such resources. (p. 852)

For parents, children at home are a significant source of stress and uncontrollable life changes. Not surprisingly, therefore, recent studies have found that among married persons of both genders, the "empty nest" is associated with heightened well-being and satisfaction. Thus, for example, Lenore Radloff (1980) found among a large representative sample of married white adults that those with no children living at home were significantly less depressed than those with children at home or those who had never had them. This was true for full-time homemakers as well as for employed women, and for women and men regardless of income or age. Similarly, Rosalind Barnett and Grace Baruch (1985) found, among a sample of white women between the ages of 35 and 55, that the role of parent rather than that of paid worker was their major source of stress. "Regardless of employment status, mothers experienced higher levels of role overload and anxiety than did childless women" (p. 144).

When paid employment provides control over one's life and access to resources (that is, power) it enhances well-being for both women and men. The picture beginning to emerge from a variety of studies is that, in general, for women (as for men), being involved in activities that use "one's skills and education, that offer social contacts and intimacy, and that provide income" help maintain or to foster good psychological and physical health. This conclusion was reached by Lois Verbrugge and Jennifer Madans from the results of a national health interview study (in "Busy Women," 1985). Employment was found to have the strongest and most consistent positive association with women's good health, followed by marriage, with parenthood "a weak third." Working women reported less illness, and that they felt better than women not engaged in paid employment. Another study, by Lerita Coleman and Toni Antonucci (in "Women's Well-Being," 1982), reached similar conclusions by comparing a group of working married women between 40 and 59 years of age with a group of full-time homemakers. Of all the variables tested in this study, employment was "the only significant predictor of levels of self-esteem in midlife women . . . [and] one of the most important predictors of physical health and lack of psychological anxiety" (p. 5). Grace Baruch and Rosalind Barnett (1985b) reached the same conclusion from a study of a sample of white women, aged 35 to 55. Only one social role was found to be related to an index of well-being: self-esteem was positively related to being a paid worker.

Earlier studies found full-time homemakers to be generally less happy, more discouraged, and more self-doubting than single and/or married working women (Nickerson & Pitochelli, 1978); and more recent studies (for example, Erdwins & Mellinger, 1984) continue to find that the average homemaker describes herself as feeling more fatalistic and less in control of her environment than comparable married career women. In general, the data indicate that the satisfactions women derive from employment contribute significantly to our general well-being and happiness. This relationship has been documented among women in a variety of different subgroups or populations (for example, Welch & Booth, 1977; Horwitz, 1982; Baruch, Barnett, & Rivers, 1983). Coleman and Antonucci (in "Women's Well-Being," 1982) have suggested that paid employment may not only provide direct benefits to women but may also help ameliorate the stresses associated with launching children into adulthood, with marital problems, divorce, or widowhood. In other words, paid employment can provide additional sources of potential pleasure or satisfaction (beyond family life and friends) just as it does for men.

Employment may be more associated with positive consequences under some circumstances than others. Peter Warr and Glenys Parry (1982), for example, concluded from a review of research that employment status and psychological well-being were more positively associated among working-class than middle-class women, supporting the view that a job will be "psychologically beneficial primarily for those women whose nonoccupational environment is adverse" (p. 512). Another study found that the risk of heart disease is twice as great among women

clerical workers who are married and parents than among other working women or homemakers, especially if the clerical workers were married to men with blue-collar jobs ("Women's Hearts," 1980). Constance Shehan (1984) studied married mothers of preschool children and compared full-time homemakers with clerical workers. Among this group, she found no significant differences in self-reported physical health, depression, or life satisfaction. On the other hand, Allan Horwitz (1982) found that, in general, employed married adults reported significantly fewer symptoms of psychological distress than married women and men who were unemployed, and concluded that "the resources gained through employment lead to psychological benefits for both sexes" (p. 614). But the more dominant or powerful one's position, the fewer symptoms of distress were reported, suggesting a strong positive relationship between well-being and control or dominance. According to Horwitz, "Every group in the sample with significantly fewer symptoms than average—married men and women who are chief breadwinners, married employed men, and married employed women without children—occupy roles high in resources and low in subordination" (p. 619).

Contrary to popular assumptions, multiple roles have been found to be good for women, and to be accompanied by health and positive spirits, provided that the positions occupied are ones that increase the likelihood of success and effectiveness. The same is true for men. Estelle Ramey, who has studied the effects of stress, noted in an interview that "contrary to what everyone believes . . . top-level, high-paid, successful women and men live longer than anyone else. . . . People at the top are in control of their lives, and people in control live longer" ("Success, Health Linked," 1984). Thus, one study of a sample of women between 35 and 55 years of age (Baruch, Barnett, & Rivers, 1983) found that not only did employed women report greater self-esteem and less anxiety and depression than those who were not, but also that the women with the highest degree of life satisfaction had both families and high-prestige jobs. We do not, of course, know from correlational data whether high self-esteem is an antecedent or consequence of having satisfactory personal and work situations. Among a sample of well-educated, affluent women studied by Abigail Stewart and Patricia Salt (1981), those who were married with children and careers reported the least illness of any group. The researchers noted, with regard to this finding, that "it is difficult to know whether their

Prescription for women's mental health *(From* I'm in Training to Be Tall and Blonde, *Nicole Hollander, St. Martin's Press, Inc. © 1979 by Nicole Hollander.)*

'invulnerability' lies in the variety of the stressful stimuli experienced or in the variety of the behavioral responses required of or made by the individual" (p. 1060).

The more varied one's behavioral repertoire is, the more sources of satisfaction one will likely experience. Joann Rodgers (1985) has cited a number of studies to support her thesis that what may be best for a woman's health is "juggling roles, making change, [and] taking charge" (p. 57). Among the studies cited by Rodgers is one by Suzanne Kobasa that found that men and women who stayed healthy under stress

were characterized by "the three C's": they were "committed (to self, work, family, religion, or other values); in control (over one's life); and challenged (by life's ups and downs and by change)" (p. 58). That both women and men have been expanding their behavioral repertoires and thus their potential sources of satisfaction is shown by data obtained in two large national interview studies of representative samples of American adults, in 1957 and 1976, and analyzed by Fred Bryant and Joseph Veroff (1982). These researchers concluded that women and men were more alike in their sources of well-being in 1976 than they were 19 years earlier: in 1976, as compared with 1957, women were more involved in future-oriented and work-related issues, and men were more likely to base their self-evaluations on family-life issues.

Involvement and activity contribute to health. Jobs or life situations that provide the opportunity for responsibility, control, variety, and supportive relationships enhance or help maintain psychological and physical health. Love and work, as Sigmund Freud suggested, are the twin poles around which human adult lives rotate; it is through our active engagement with their challenges, and our experience with the satisfactions that they mediate, that we derive self-esteem and well-being. Nicole Hollander's marvelous cartoon tells it like it is.

Growing Older: Special Issues for the Middle and Later Years

The midlife woman of current social science literature is . . . a far cry from the traditional psychoanalyst's woman mourning the loss of her reproductive powers. One hears less today about women's "mid-life crisis" and more about "post-menopausal zest."

Beth Hess *(1983, p. 7)*

C H A P T E R   15

ontemporary older women are not easily stereotyped as worn-out, unattractive, sickly, sexless, boring, or foolish crones. Many are experiencing the rewards of confidence and economic and emotional independence that accompany paid employment; many have returned to school and completed training for a previous or new career; many are vigorously involved in social interaction and a variety of community interests. For these women, life continues to be vital and engaging after 40, 50, 60, 70; and for some, it only begins to be so in the years following full-time child rearing or devotion to family. At the same time, women confront a number of special and potentially problematic issues or challenges as we grow older. We turn our attention to these issues now.

OLDER WOMEN'S NEGATIVE IMAGE

Older women now constitute the fastest-growing portion of the American population. Eleven percent of the American population was over 65 years old in 1980, compared to only 4 percent in 1900; and this figure is estimated to reach 12 percent by the year 2000 (Green, Parham, Kleff, & Pilisuk, 1980). Two hundred years ago the life expectancy for women was 35 (and 33 for men); by 1900 it had climbed to 48 and 46, for women and men, respectively. In this century, the longevity for both sexes has steadily increased, as well as the difference between the two, and in 1984, the average woman could expect to live to age 78 and the average man to 71 ("Men's Life," 1985). Because of the increased difference in longevity between women and men, the ratio between their numbers has gotten larger at older ages. Among persons over 65, the ratio of the number of women to men was 98 to 100 in 1900, 138 to 100 in 1970, 144 to 100 in 1980, and is estimated to reach 154 to 100 by the year 2000; in 1980 women outnumbered men in the over-75 age group by 171 to 100 (Markson & Hess, 1980; Abu-Laban, 1981). These ratios include all persons, but longevity for blacks of both sexes has continued to lag dramatically behind that of whites. In 1982, for example, white persons could expect to live to age 74.6, but black persons only to 69.3 years, a figure reached by whites 30 years earlier ("Improving Longevity," 1985).

Although the population of older women is expanding and diverse, and older women continue to grow and lead interesting lives, negative stereotypes persist. The White House Conference on Older Women held in 1981 (cited in *Developing a National Agenda*, 1985) concluded that "popular images that portray older women as inactive, unhealthy, asexual, unattractive, and ineffectual are prevalent" (p. 24). As Ethel Kahn (1984) has noted:

> Today's older woman is [typically] seen by society as a "wrinkled, greying old bag," no longer. . . sexually attractive. She finds herself in sharp contrast to the "distinguished, grey-haired, eligible bachelor" whose loss of spouse increases his attractiveness and whose work history still conveys status. She is undervalued by employers, frequently rejected in social situations, and psychologically misdiagnosed and treated. (p. 2)

Our society reacts differently to aging in women and men, and the threat to self-esteem, identity, and perceived attractiveness and desirability is far greater for older women. We are more likely than men to be ashamed of aging bodies and far more likely, as Susan Sontag (1979) has noted, to try "to cover up aging as an obscenity." An extreme example is provided by actress Brigitte Bardot, who adopted a hermitlike existence while only in her late 40s, explaining her decision as follows ("Has French Film Star," 1983):

> I have to accept old age, right? It is horrible; you rot; you fall to pieces; you stink. It scares me more than anything else. There's a beach not far away, but I never go during the day. I'm 48 and not so pretty. I wouldn't inflict this sight on anyone anymore.

It is hard to imagine a 48-year-old man responding with similar self-loathing to his graying temples or other signs of aging.

While youth is clearly highly valued by both genders in our current society, and men as well as women work to retain youthful figures and zest by watching their diets, exercising, keeping up with the fashions in dress and recreation, and resisting being categorized as old, women put more of our energies from adolescence (or earlier) into our external personas. Women learn that it is crucial for us to be slim and attractive to find love and personal happiness. As Alice Rossi (1980) has pointed out, for women

> indicators of age are important to the social self presented to others: gray hair, wrinkles, dentures, drowsiness, age spots, thickening of the waistline, sagging of abdomen and breasts, and bifocal glasses may touch aspects of aging that matter in social and, particularly, intimate interactions. (p. 21)

In Margaret Drabble's novel *The Ice Age* (1977), the heroine, a beautiful, intelligent, and very modern upper-middle-class woman, says of herself, "I am a vain, a wicked woman. . . . I cannot face old age, I cannot face ugliness and decay." She shuts the curtains and observes herself in her wardrobe mirror.

> The harsh unshaded light fell without mercy. Yes, there were wrinkles . . . there would be more. . . . The neck was slightly ringed. Rings, dark and grave, lay also beneath her eyes: dark red, weary. . . . Her face felt stiff. . . . Her hair was touched with gray. . . . When will I cease to be able to look at myself naked in the mirror? . . . Beauty had for years been [her] identity. She had no other. How could she ever make another, for the second half of her necessary life?

Gender stereotypes can be particularly crippling for older women. In Doris Lessing's *The Summer Before the Dark* (1978), the middle-aged heroine looks at herself and finds a void. She has been a devoted mother and a good wife to a successful husband. At age 45 she realizes that she is uncertain of herself and frightened, and that "a lot of time, a lot of pain, went into learning very little." Her journey into identity, stripped of illusions and gender expectations, takes her through a job, a lover, illness, disorientation, and finally self-definition and self-respect. She defiantly lets her hair go gray and returns home; and the reader is left to wonder how her renascence will be greeted. In a subsequent book, *The Diaries of Jane Somers*, Lessing (1984) has written about old women whose proud determination to live independent and meaningful lives despite their age is misunderstood, not respected, and frustrated by circumstances and social institutions. The tragic disparity between how an old woman may feel about herself and how she appears to others is described in a story by Pat Barker (1983). Alice Bell is 76 years old.

> She had hid herself from the mirror. For years she had avoided looking into it: the hag it showed bore no relation to the person she was. Inside herself, she was still sixteen. She had all the passion, all the silliness. . . . Now the dislocation between what the mirror showed and what she knew herself to be was absolute. She would have to break the glass. (p. 255)

On television, older women continue to be shown staving off obsolescence with Geritol or aspirin, baking cookies for their grandchildren, or retreating into the world of soap operas and reminiscences about unfulfilled expectations and lost dreams. The Gray Panthers monitored the image of old people on television and described what they saw as "so negatively stereotyped that it has become something to dread and feel threatened by."

> Old people are shown as ugly, toothless, sexless, and helpless. Our faces are blank and expressionless, our bodies are bent over and the "senior shuffle" is just a step away from the embalming room. We are shown as stubborn, rigid, unflexible, forgetful and confused . . . as dependent, powerless, wrinkled babies, unable to contribute to society. (Roberts, 1977, p. 4E)

According to Jeanne Schallon (cited in O'Halloren, 1977), old people on television (especially women) are either portrayed negatively or, more often, are simply ignored. "In commercials, we're buffoons. In programming, we don't exist." Women over 40 get less than 1 percent of all the continuing drama and comedy roles on television, and even game shows steer clear of older people, who are usually kept away from front-row audience seats and are rarely selected as contestants. One television comedy series about older women, "The Golden Girls," has been extremely popular and features three bright, attractive, and articulate women over 50 who share a house in Florida. But one reason for the popularity of this show may be its racy and brash language and its emphasis on the women's preoccupation with finding men and maintaining relationships with them. The elderly mother of one of the protagonists, while a very funny character, is portrayed as forgetful, scattered, and overly blunt (as a function of age). A television series that treated older women and men in a more dignified and sensitive manner and focused on a variety of themes in the lives of a group living cooperatively in a large house, "Morningstar and Eveningstar," was canceled after just one season. The other media are even less interested in older women than television. To counter the treatment of older women by the American theater as "not sexy, not intcresting, not exciting, not worth writing a play about" (cited in Robertson, 1985), a theater festival for older women was organized, featuring new plays written with women characters "well into middle age."

Besides being viewed as unattractive, older women are generally perceived as having lost their social utility, and as requiring costly institutionalized care. This latter assumption is erroneous. Although three fourths of nursing home residents are women (because of their greater longevity), 95 percent of the elderly, who are mostly women, live in the community by themselves or with others. Among this overwhelming majority of older people residing in the community, one third of the women live by themselves, while among elderly men, 17 percent live with relatives or alone, and three quarters live with their wives. Other aspects of the negative stereotype of older women are also erroneous, as will become apparent in the rest of this chapter.

PHYSICAL CHANGES OF AGING

The climacteric is a gradual aging process in both sexes that includes changes in hormonal output, in metabolism, and in the efficiency of physiological functioning—changes that affect the entire body. It is often confused with and not clearly differentiated from menopause, but the two are different, and the climacteric is experienced by men as well as women. While the process is the same for women and men, it appears to be affected by different factors, as is the case for the factors that increase the risk of death. A study of 7000 persons in California, carefully monitored since 1965, found that the most significant factors associated with increased chance of death for men were smoking, heavy alcohol usage, and not having a spouse, whereas for women they were physical inactivity, few social contacts, dissatisfaction with life, and self-perceived poor health (cited in Fisher, 1984).

Much myth and misinformation exist on the topic of menopause, and "cures" of questionable worth have been proposed. Erroneous beliefs have also developed about sexuality later in life. Let us now examine carefully these and other aspects of the physical changes associated with aging.

Menopause

Menopause refers to the cessation of ovulation and menstruation, and the gradual reduction in progesterone and estrogen production. Contemporary

women can expect to reach menopause sometime in their late 40s or early 50s. In the early years of this century, according to Paula Weideger (1976), menopause came earlier, at about the age of 40.

The primary physiological changes of menopause begin when the ovarian follicles start to decay. Recall from the discussion in Chapter 6 that during the menstrual cycle an ovum is released monthly from one of the follicles when stimulated by hormones from the pituitary. At menopause the ova begin to degenerate. No certain explanation has been found for this regression of the ovaries. The anterior pituitary continues to function and to release the hormones that have played their part in the menstrual cycle, but the ovaries lose their responsiveness to stimulation. As the ovaries cease functioning, the production of estrogen gradually diminishes. Some estrogen continues to be produced by the follicles, but not enough to trigger the next phase of the menstrual cycle and the manufacture of progesterone. Menopause thus marks the end of menstruation and the end of fertility and is considered to have occurred when a woman has not menstruated for 12 consecutive months.

Women who require surgical removal of both ovaries (for treatment of cancer, for example) experience early and sudden menopause. But for most others, the reduction of estrogen and progesterone is gradual. Estrogen continues being manufactured in the ovaries, but at a decreasing rate; and it is also produced in fat cells and by cholesterol. Progesterone also continues to be present in the bloodstream of postmenopausal women. Part of the myth and misinformation about menopause would have us believe that it results in the absence of estrogen and progesterone. This is not the case. Of the three main types of estrogen synthesized in the body, only estradiol (synthesized in the ovaries) is dramatically decreased. As noted by Anne Fausto-Sterling (1985):

> The other estrogenic hormones [estrone and estroil], as well as progesterone and testosterone, drop off to some extent but continue to be synthesized at a level comparable to that observed during the early phases of the menstrual cycle. Instead of concentrating on the notion of estrogen deficiency . . . , it is more important to point out that: (1) postmenopausally the body makes different kinds of estrogen; (2) the ovaries synthesize less and the adrenals more of these hormones; and (3) the monthly ups and downs of these hormones even out following menopause. (p. 115)

At the same time that the total level of estrogen is decreasing, FSH (follicle-stimulating hormone) and

LH (luteinizing hormone) levels increase so that the postmenopausal woman eventually has "one-and-one-half times more LH and seven times more FSH circulating in her blood than when she menstruated regularly" (Fausto-Sterling, 1985, p. 115). The consequences of this increase in the hormones are not yet understood, but one view is that they are somehow implicated in the production of hot flashes (or flushes).

The hot flash, "a sudden expansion of the blood flow into the skin" (Fausto-Sterling, 1985, p. 117), is the symptom most often linked to menopause and, for many women, serves as its symbol. It is reportedly experienced to some extent by close to 90 percent of menopausal women (Brozan, 1983), but nevertheless remains a medical mystery. While treatment with estrogen can suppress hot flashes, the normal thermal mechanism in the hypothalamus is believed to be triggered at the same time as the pituitary releases bursts of LH (Brozan, 1983), the hormone that spurs the ovaries into action. After menopause, ova are no longer released, but parts of the cycle may continue on a random basis with action by the pituitary. The hypothalamic neurons controlling the release of LH by the pituitary are very near the temperature-regulating center, suggesting that the LH surge and hot flashes may result from alterations in hypothalamic functions (Marx, 1979b). Hot flashes vary widely in frequency and duration, in the number of months or years during which they occur, and in women's reactions to them. Some women come to recognize precipitating factors such as hot drinks, alcohol, emotional upset, hot weather, or a warm bed. And in all women the flashes eventually disappear as the body naturally adjusts to the changed relative levels of LH, estrogen, and other hormones.

While the scientific literature on menopause was, until recently, both "sparse and inconclusive" (Posner, 1979, p. 189), the popular view that menopause is a difficult, troublesome, confusing, and depressing period continues. According to Sadja Greenwood (1985), "The popular image of the middle-aged woman as an emotional wreck, drenched in sweat and unable to cope, has been played up by pharmaceutical companies to persuade doctors and their patients to use drugs for this condition" (p. 79). But recent studies by psychologists and sociologists have found little evidence to support these beliefs. Alice Rossi (1980), for example, has concluded from the research literature that

> contrary to assumptions . . . menopause is rarely a crisis to women. There is more dread in the anticipation than

difficulty in the experience; and, far from being upset at the loss of an important biological function, most women feel relief to have it behind them. (p. 20)

Women in the 45-to-55 age group are not only generally happy to be done with menstruation, but are also relieved to be past the period in their lives when so much of their energies were devoted to the mothering of children. One study (Black & Hill, 1984) of over 200 women between the ages of 46 and 61 in intact marriages found that among the 71 percent who reported any symptoms of menopause, only 24 percent experienced them as negative. With respect to general happiness and marital and work satisfaction, 90 percent of this sample of well-educated and fairly affluent women rated themselves as positive. Similar data have been reported by Karen Frey (1981) from a study of 78 40- to 60-year-old women of varied background, race, and socioeconomic level, among whom 88 percent were employed. Among this sample, those going through menopause showed "no greater frequency of physical symptoms than pre- or post-menopausal women" (p. 34), and the women generally did not indicate an illness orientation toward menopause or view it as a "central distressing event" (p. 31). In an earlier study (Goodman, Stewart, & Gilbert), cited by Anne Fausto-Sterling (1985), among a large sample of women living in Hawaii, 75 percent of those who had not menstruated for at least one year were found to have reported no menopausal symptoms at all to their doctors.

The data accumulating on women's experiences during and after menopause are in sharp contrast to the traditional medical view. According to Ann Voda and Mona Eliasson (1985), current medical literature describes menopausal women as "hypogonadal, castrates, or as estrogen deficient" (p. 138) and treats menopause as a disease.

> Clinical journals in their advertising continue to project an image of the typical menopausal woman as worried, with wrinkled forehead, looking sad, and despairing over ugly aging liver spots. Menopause is seen as a time of confusion and frustration, a time in which counseling can help but can't stop vasomotor or vaginal symptoms, or retard bone loss. (p. 140)

Robert Wilson, whose 1966 book *Feminine Forever* "influenced thousands of physicians to prescribe estrogen to millions of women" (Fausto-Sterling, 1985, p. 112) and encouraged regarding all post-menopausal women as castrates, considered menopause to be an estrogen-deficiency disease, and estrogen replacement therapy (ERT) to be the only "cure." Other popular medical writers like David

Reuben (1969) have presented similarly horrifying images of postmenopausal women as sexless and shriveled: "Not really a man but no longer a functional woman, these individuals live in the world of intersex" (p. 292). Such views, as might be imagined, have helped pharmaceutical companies sell huge quantities of estrogen products to cure the "disease of menopause" despite lack of supporting data or careful investigations of the physiological and social correlates of aging.

If there are psychological and emotional correlates of menopause, these may be a function of a woman's interpretation of bodily changes, her evaluation of their significance, and the further changes she anticipates in her life. No reliable evidence links menopause to any psychopathological condition. The vaginal dryness or irritation experienced by some postmenopausal women that can make sexual intercourse painful can be safely treated with nonestrogen creams and jellies, cocoa butter, or unsaturated oils, and as Anne Fausto-Sterling (1985) has noted, "Continued sexual activity also helps—yet another example of the interaction between behavior and physiology" (p. 118). Another common complaint of postmenopausal women, difficulty in retaining urine when coughing, sneezing, or running, can be safely and simply treated by exercise—periodic tensing and relaxation of the bladder-controlling muscles, which can be done covertly at any time and place.

Osteoporosis

Osteoporosis refers to a condition of bone loss that accompanies the aging process in both sexes. As a result of a drop in the blood calcium level, bones become thin and porous, with a consequent reduction in bone mass. Sufficient calcium is required to maintain an equilibrium between the rate of normal bone breakdown and the rate of new bone formation. The blood calcium level is sensitive to, or influenced by, multiple factors, such as "chronic illness, immobilization, alcohol abuse, heavy smoking, stress, certain drugs, sedentary lifestyle, and poor nutrition" (MacPherson, 1984, p. 8). Because osteoporosis is most common among postmenopausal women, estrogen has been implicated, but the precise relationship between estrogen and the use of calcium for new bone formation is not known. According to Joan Beck (1983), about 25 to 40 percent of women, primarily Caucasian, develop osteoporosis. It appears to be more prevalent in "fair-skinned, small-boned, thin

Caucasian women" (Voda & Eliasson, 1985, p. 147). Black women, who produce more of the hormone calcitonin, are relatively immune (Greenwood, 1985). The so-called "dowager's hump" results from collapse of fractured spinal vertebra, with subsequent loss of height and a humped upper back.

Natural and safe ways to prevent osteoporosis involve making sure that one's body is getting enough calcium and using it most efficiently. This can be done by eating high-calcium foods (like dairy products, tofu, green leafy vegetables, canned salmon, and sardines), taking calcium supplements, and avoiding cigarettes, alcohol, salt, protein, and caffeine (which interfere with calcium use). Vitamin D is also necessary for new bone formation, and is obtainable from the sun or foods rich in this vitamin. Since phosphorous contributes to bone loss, avoiding excessive use of red meat, cola drinks, and processed food with phosphorous additives is important. We now know that "bones do better if you are not too thin" (Greenwood, 1985, p. 82) since fatty tissue is a source of estrogen. A reliable link has also been found between strong bones and regular exercise, especially weight-bearing exercises and those that involve movement, pull, and stress on the long bones such as walking, jogging, bicycling, and jumping rope (MacPherson, 1984; Greenwood, 1985).

Estrogen Replacement Therapy

ERT, first promoted by the pharmaceutical industry as a way to stay "forever feminine" and to prevent the "living decay" of menopause, reducing or curing so-called menopausal symptoms, was subsequently associated most specifically with osteoporosis as a method of prevention. According to Anne Fausto-Sterling (1985), "By 1975 some six million women had started long-term treatment with Premarin (Ayerst Lab's brand name for estrogen), making it the fourth or fifth most popular drug in the United States" (p. 112). It has been reported (Dejanikus, 1985) that Ayerst Labs hired a public relations firm to run a campaign about osteoporosis that succeeded in getting congressional and media attention, and financed a tour of medical experts to large cities to publicize the possible link between osteoporosis and estrogen decline.

While ERT does increase a woman's supply of estrogen, and does appear to arrest bone loss, it never replaces lost bone, and has not been conclusively related to a decreased incidence of osteoporotic bone fractures (Seidler, 1984; Voda & Eliasson, 1985). On the other hand, a sizable number of studies have shown a causal connection between estrogen intake and both endometrial and breast cancer (Seidler, 1984), and a National Institutes of Health conference in 1979 "concluded that ERT is risky" (Voda & Eliasson, 1985, p. 138). As a result of publication of the research linking estrogen treatment to uterine and breast cancer, "many women stopped taking estrogen and many physicians became more cautious about prescribing it, [but] the idea of hormone replacement therapy remains with us" (Fausto-Sterling, 1985, p. 112), and approximately 2 million postmenopausal women in this country are being treated with Premarin.

Some doctors (for example, Budoff, 1983) have suggested that the danger of estrogen replacement therapy can be offset by combining estrogen with progesterone (or progestin), but according to Sadja Greenwood (1985), progestin "raises the blood level of a type of fat that may predispose to heart disease" and the long-term consequences of exogenous estrogen and progestins "are still questioned by responsible investigators" (p. 82). Critics of pharmaceutical interventions emphasize the uncertain effects of ERT and the fact that increased calcium intake and regular exercise are cheaper and safer ways to prevent osteoporosis. While estrogen does alleviate hot flashes, these return when the estrogen is stopped, so that it appears as though ERT "merely postpones passage through the transitional period" (Voda & Eliasson, 1985, p. 148). This transitional period is one in which internally produced estrogen, progesterone, FHS, and LH reach new levels of balance. As noted earlier in our description of normal menopausal changes, menopause does not result in the absence of any hormone, but in the relative decline of some and an increase in others.

Hysterectomies

Hysterectomy is the surgical removal of the uterus (and may also include the ovaries and fallopian tubes). Various estimates have been proposed for the number of such operations performed in this country. A National Institutes of Health conference reported in 1979 that "by the time American women reach 60, upwards of one-half have had a hysterectomy" (Voda & Eliasson, 1985, p. 138). Edith Bjornson (1984) has cited estimates that one out of four American women reach menopause through surgery before the age

of 45, and that 62 percent can expect to have a hysterectomy by the time they are 70. As noted by Joanne West (1984):

> Many women as they near or pass menopause are told that they no longer need a uterus because its only function is to carry a baby, that the ovaries are not needed because they "shrivel up and die" after menopause, that the hormones that ovaries produced can be replaced with drugs . . . and that this surgery will leave their sexual lives unchanged or improved. The inference that "at this age" the uterus, cervix, and ovaries might become cancerous and that it is safer and healthier to take it all out leads many women into the operating room. (p. 4)

Hysterectomies and oopherectomies (surgical removal of the ovaries) are often performed as elective surgery—for example, to prevent cancer—and not as a procedure essential for the patient's immediate health and well-being. Edith Bjornson (1984) has reported that

> many doctors and hospitals now have a policy of removing healthy ovaries at the time of hysterectomy in all women over 40 or 45, as a "prophylactic" against possible future cancer. . . . However, studies show that this is only a 1 in 1000 chance. (pp. 5, 15)

The frequency with which American surgeons perform these operations relative to doctors in other countries has been widely criticized and has aroused suspicions that greed may be an underlying motive. Critics have argued that such surgery should be performed only when the organs are diseased and constitute a danger to continued health. Hysterectomies and oopherectomies are not reversible procedures, have potential life-altering consequences, and the missing organs may disrupt the body's biochemical balance and decrease sexual motivation and responsiveness (Morgan, 1982).

SEXUALITY

Recent studies have shown that both men and women who are in generally good health and who are motivated can continue to respond sexually and obtain gratification in their 60s, 70s, 80s, and probably indefinitely throughout their lives. A study conducted at Duke University (cited in Lobsenz, 1974) found that one in three women reported sexual interest in their 60s, but only one in five were having heterosexual relationships. The difference between interest and heterosexual activity was attributed to such factors as the lack of available men, anxiety over physical appearance, and a willingness to believe that sex should end after menopause. A more recent study of women and men between the ages of 60 and 82 (cited in "Studying Love," 1985) reported that all but a few of the persons interviewed were sexually active and experimented more with sex than they did when they were younger. The respondents described creative activities on dates: going camping, walking, going to the theater, taking weekend trips, and so on. The researchers concluded that with respect to intimacy, dating behavior, and sexuality, "old people are just younger people who have gotten older."

Zella Luria and Robert Meade (1984) have noted that the extent of sexual functioning in middle age is related to early experience and enjoyment of sex, and that in both the middle and later years, sexuality also depends upon good health and the availability of partners. An expanded sense of sexuality for older women may include masturbation and lesbian relationships. A number of researchers have reported a greater enjoyment of sex among older women than in earlier years. Lillian Rubin (1981), for example, conducted long interviews with 160 heterosexual women between 35 and 54 years of age and found that most told her that their sexual pleasure had increased with age; sex for them had "gotten better and better" (p. 74). A national survey (cited in Luria & Meade, 1984) of almost 200 middle- and upper-class women over age 50 found that 91 percent expressed interest in sex and 84 percent reported themselves to be coitally active. There has been little specific focus on Afro-American middle-aged women, but one study (Alston & Rose, 1981) found from responses to a questionnaire that a sample of black women between the ages of 40 and 65 said they found sex less enjoyable than they used to and implicated menopause as a causal factor.

Putting the information obtained from currently middle-aged and older women in a historical perspective is important. These are women born before World War II; before television; before the "sexual revolution" of liberated attitudes, sexual knowledge, and practice; and before the easy availability of reliable contraception. As Zella Luria and Robert Meade (1984) have pointed out, "Middle-aged women differ from young women not only in biology but also in the different scripts they learned for sexual experience and initiation" (p. 385). Young women of the current generation come into marriage, for example, with far greater sexual experience than was the case for their mothers or grandmothers. As newer generations of women age, then, their sexuality will likely continue to be robust and an even more important part of their lives than is true for the present cohort of older women. The lesser availability of a sexual partner may continue to be a problem for older heterosexual women, however, unless the gender difference in longevity decreases.

THE STRESSES OF WIDOWHOOD AND DIVORCE

Widows comprise almost 5 percent of the American population, and outnumber widowers by a ratio of 245 to 100, reflecting both the greater longevity of women and the custom of women marrying men older than themselves (Luria & Meade, 1984). By age 65, 20 percent of women are widowed, and by age 74, 67 percent (*Developing a National Agenda*, 1985), with very little chance of remarrying.

Widowhood brings loneliness, "the most consistent problem widows endure" (Barrett, 1981, p. 476). Karen Rook (1984), who interviewed over 100 widows between the ages of 60 and 89, found that loneliness was significantly related to having few social supports, and that negative social interactions had a potent influence on depressing general satisfaction with life. For some women, widowhood brings enforced independence and the necessity to solve problems alone. Lynn Caine (1974), whose husband died when she was still a young mother of small children, has written movingly of how widowhood forced her to regain a lost identity. While the loss of a spouse is problematic for both women and men, some women may be more vulnerable to temporary despair and panic because of their relative lack of worldliness, knowledge of mortgages, insurance, and loans, and so on. Caine, who was an educated, middle-class, and employed wife, was forced by widowhood and the necessity of caring for herself and her children to develop new skills, to acquire new behaviors, and to rediscover old strengths. For widows who are older or poorly educated this may be more difficult, but widows invariably talk about experiencing the change from dependence to autonomy and often marvel at their unanticipated competence at handling aspects of living previously attended to by their husbands. In a novel by Elizabeth Hailey (1979), for example, the heroine writes to a friend after her husband's death, "I am just beginning to learn how to live alone as an adult" (p. 123).

Despite the loneliness experienced by widows and the necessity of dealing with aspects of the world previously handled by their husbands, current research is finding that women tend to cope with the death of a spouse more successfully than do men. Margaret and Wolfgang Stroebe (1983) reviewed the relevant literature and concluded that regardless of the index used to assess well-being, men suffered more negative consequences after a spouse's death than women did.

> Whether we look at psychological distress and depression, psychiatric disorders, physical illness, mortality, or suicide, the same pattern appears to emerge: if there is a sex difference in bereavement reactions on loss of a spouse, it is always the men who appear to suffer more. (p. 294)

These conclusions are based on comparisons of widowers to married men and comparisons of widows to married women. The former differences are invariably greater than the latter, indicating a greater psychological and physical effect of bereavement on men than on women. A 12-year survey of over 4000 widowed people (Helsing, Szklo, & Comstock, 1981) found that the negative effects of widowhood for men disappeared if they remarried. Among widowed men who remarried the mortality rate was as low as or lower than among nonwidowed men, whereas those who did not remarry had a 60 percent higher chance of dying sooner than nonwidowed men in the same age group. Too few widows had remarried for a reliable assessment to be made of the effect of remarriage on their mortality, but there was a suggestion of the same phenomenon.

Even without marriage, which is unlikely for widows, women do better than men in adjusting to their spouse's death and in caring for their social, emotional, health, and practical needs. This is all the more remarkable in view of the significant negative impact widowhood has on the average woman's economic resources. Compared to a widowed man, a widowed woman is far more likely to be poor. According to Carol Barrett (1977):

> Virtually every study . . . has commented on the reduced financial resources characteristically resulting from the husband's death. Aside from the loss of income from the husband's employment and the possible freeze on bank accounts in some states, there are apt to be large bills from prolonged illness and funeral arrangements. (p. 858)

Similar financial hardships are experienced by women after a divorce, and the rate of divorce among older couples has been steadily accelerating. An estimated 100,000 people over the age of 55 get divorced in this country each year (Cain, 1982). These marriage dissolutions are said to be "overwhelmingly initiated by men," and to produce greater psychological upheaval for older than for younger women. For a woman over 60, a divorce typically comes after 30 to 40 years of marriage. Self-blame is common, and the divorce exacerbates the stress of aging. One woman interviewed by Barbara Cain (1982) noted that "divorce after 60 is a double whammy" (p. 10).

> Unlike the elderly widow, the elderly divorcee must live with the realization that her loss was deliberate, volitional, intended. . . . Moreover, the divorcee, unlike the widow, must disengage from a partner who continues to walk the face of the earth often in the same town, even the same neighborhood. (p. 92)

In *August* (1983), a novel by Judith Rossner, the protagonist, a middle-aged woman psychotherapist, is thinking the following thoughts at a party as she notes the presence of newly divorced male friends and colleagues and their much younger new wives or companions:

> These men were leaving women who were often, by the men's own admission, more than satisfactory wives. For women, this epidemic lent to the aging process a sense of doom beyond its normal difficulties and humiliations. Women looked at a gray-haired man and saw father; men looked at a gray-haired woman and ran from death. (p. 36)

Few states recognize the role of homemaker, wife, and mother in their divorce laws and most judges are not directed by law to take into account the contributions made by a woman in these roles when redistributing a divorcing couple's assets. One exception is the state of New York, which in 1980 passed an "equitable distribution" law to protect the financial security of women after divorce. A report prepared for Congress (cited in "More and More Women," 1985) conservatively estimated that the number of displaced homemakers (women between the ages of 35 and 64) had risen 28 percent since 1975 to 2.2 million. About half of this group had been plunged into sudden independence because of divorce, separation, or an absent spouse; the others were widows or women married to unemployed men not eligible for public assistance.

The rate of poverty for older women is 60 percent higher than it is for older men (Collins, 1986); and in 1985, one out of every six elderly women lived in poverty with an annual income of less than $5600

(Jaycox, 1985). Other data indicate that 50 percent of women over the age of 65 who are living alone because of widowhood or divorce have savings of less than $1000 (Greenhaus, 1983). Statistics on the poverty of older women come from many sources, use various indices, and paint a consistently depressing picture. On every measure, black, Hispanic, and native American older women are worse off than white women.

The Gray Panthers, a national advocacy organization for older Americans, maintains that health care for the elderly costs four times as much as it does for others, and that old people pay an average of 34 percent of their income for housing that is often well below standards for decency, maintenance, safety, and hygiene. Women, who have lesser financial resources than men of the same age, are more affected by the high cost of medical care and housing. Robert Butler, a geriatrics specialist (cited in Johnson, 1984), has estimated that

> women today have a 60 percent chance of being destitute in old age because of low earnings, inequalities in pensions and the tendency of couples to exhaust their assets during the last illness of the mate who dies first, usually the husband. (p. C10)

In reviewing the literature on elderly Americans who live in metropolitan areas, Elizabeth Markson and Beth Hess (1980) concluded that

> elderly widows are among the most poverty stricken of all people, with the smallest budget for housing and other services. . . . At special risk are Hispanic old women. In New York City, they live in the worst housing conditions, have the smallest incomes, the least education, and the most health problems. (p. S136)

While over three fourths of men over the age of 65 are living with a spouse, this is true of only 37.6 percent of comparable women. On the other hand, one in ten elderly men lives with one of his children, compared to two of every ten elderly women (who are likely to live in the home of a daughter).

Social Security benefits are the sole source of income for 60 percent of women aged 65 and older, but the current Social Security system shortchanges women, especially those who worked outside the home but earned less than their husbands. "A wife who worked often does not get any more in her Social Security check than she would have gotten if she had not worked even though she paid Social Security taxes" (Peterson, 1983). Proposals to reform the Social Security system by permitting each spouse to

qualify independently for a benefit based on half the couple's total earnings have been presented but not yet approved by Congress. According to statistics from the Social Security Administration, retired women receive average Social Security benefits of $380 per month compared with $495 for retired men ("Most Depend," 1986). In addition, more than 4 million women between the ages of 40 and 65 have no health coverage of any kind (Jaycox, 1985, p. 1). Among women receiving private pensions (only one in five retired women do so), the median monthly payment was $243 in 1983 compared with $473 for men, 43 percent of whom receive pensions ("Most Depend," 1986). While "retired women have significantly lower benefits, asset income, and pension protection than men do," according to Glenn Collins (1986, p. C1), the situation is improving and women who are currently retiring will be in better health and have more financial resources than previous generations of working women. One reason for the improved situation is the Retirement Equity Act passed by Congress in 1984 that expands the possibilities of private pension coverage for working women.

VITALITY IN MID-LIFE AND BEYOND

Despite the stresses and strains of aging experienced by older women, the middle and later years can be even more satisfying, rewarding, exciting, and productive than the years of early adulthood. Some women discover strengths and skills they had never previously tested, and redefine their personal identities. Other women pick up social or occupational interests and objectives where they had left them for marriage and a family. Researchers have concluded that older women often experience a heightened sense of self-esteem, a phenomenon believed to be related to the current social climate and the enhanced expectations and choices for women of all ages (Baruch, Barnett, & Rivers, 1983). Middle-aged and older women consistently report that they look forward to pleasures attainable from work, study, travel, and sociability, provided that they are in good health and not living in poverty.

Contemporary research indicates that the "empty nest" is not a source of depression for women but, on the contrary, that "the end of the active mothering function is greeted with relief" (Rubin, 1981, pp. 28f.). Among the 160 women between 35 and 54 years of age interviewed at length by Lillian Rubin, "not one . . . yearned for another chance [at motherhood]. For good or ill, they were glad the job was done, ready to move on to the next stage of life" (p. 38). Linda Beckman (1981) interviewed over 700 white women between the ages of 60 and 75 who were living in their own households. Contrary to what one might expect, the amount of contact these women had with their children had an insignificant effect on their well-being, while contact with other persons was positively and reliably related to feeling good. More important than quantity of contact was its quality. In another analysis of these data (Houser, Berkman, & Beckman, 1984), childless women were compared with those who were mothers. While each group valued the advantages of their own life-style and perceived disadvantages in that of the other, only 34 percent of mothers (and 7 percent of nonmothers) believed that not having children meant missing an important part of life.

Many older women have grown beyond a need to conform to gender stereotypes. Thus, researchers have suggested that as women and men in our culture get older, they converge more and more in self-described personal attributes. One study (Fischer & Narus, 1981) found that persons who gave non-sex-typed self-descriptions were significantly older than those giving sex-typed self-descriptions. Older women saw themselves as more autonomous and competent than younger women, and older men saw themselves as more communal and expressive than younger men. Jan Sinnott (1984) interviewed a large sample of people over 60 years of age, in good health, living in their communities, and found that the women and men described themselves in very similar ways that included attributes both stereotypically masculine and feminine. These older persons of both genders tended to see themselves as "balanced," or not sex-typed, and indicated that this was the way they believed others expected them to be.

Many new role models exist for older women. Writer May Sarton, for example, has lived alone most of her life and was long ignored by the critics, but now in her 70s is still beautiful, energetic, and at the height of her fame and popularity. Maggie Kuhn founded the Gray Panthers in 1970, with some friends, after she was forced to retire from her job at the age of 65. And there are others. Older women are "coming out" and publicly proclaiming that they are vital and interesting, with special strengths and attributes. As put in a poem by Natasha Josefowitz (1984):

> Your skins are taut
> Your faces smooth
> like fresh plums
> My skin is wrinkled
> My brow furrowed
> like a prune
> Prunes are sweeter. (p. 12)

The photograph of my mother, below, was taken when she was 77, a year before she died. Although she was physically ill toward the end of her life, she maintained her sense of personal integrity, dignity, charm, and involvement.

Contemporary older women are likely to have experienced and observed radical social changes between their earlier and later years. As Pamela Perun (1981) has noted, for many older women, investment in family did not bring the promised security and support. The vastly different social climate today from the one experienced by women when they were younger has influenced older women to change their lives and circumstances, and many are entering or reentering the work force and/or colleges and universities.

Women over 25 entering or reentering college after a significant period of time following high school graduation, whose educations were likely in-

A woman in her later years still sparkling and smiling in the sun

Older women actively participating in efforts for social change

terrupted by marriage, child rearing, employment, or a geographic move because of husband's job, now constitute a sizable proportion of the undergraduate population. This phenomenon, which began in the 1960s, appears to be continuing unabated and "has led women to outnumber men students at the undergraduate level for the first time since World War II" ("Re-entry Women," 1981a, p. 1). The number of women 35 and older enrolled in college has doubled since 1972; and in the 25-and-over age group, the ratio of women to men undergraduates is approximately 2 to 1 ("Re-entry Women," 1981b).

Older women in college, known as reentry women, face a variety of special problems ranging from the acceptance of transfer credits for courses taken many years earlier to feeling uneasy in classrooms with 20-year-olds whose lives and interests are vastly different from their own. Many reentry women have reported feeling stupid, confused, and anxious about their ability to cope with requirements and assignments. One middle-aged reentry woman interviewed by Lillian Rubin (1981) described herself as follows: "In school, I'm an absolute infant and I feel dumb, dumb, dumb—like an intellectual basket case. I don't know how to do a term paper; I didn't even know what a term paper was" (p. 155). Rubin herself returned to school after age 40, going all the way to a doctorate in sociology. Such stories are no longer uncommon. Despite the problems of initial adjustment and minority status, reentry women invariably do extraordinarily well in college. They are active participants in their education, hard workers, and responsible students. One study (Badenhoop & Johansen, 1980) compared a sample of reentry

undergraduate women with younger women students and found that the former had significantly higher grade point averages and were more likely to achieve an average of 3.5 to 4.0 on a four-point scale.

Although remarkable for their motivation, persistence, and achievements, reentry women do not seem to differ in some other important ways from other women of their generation. For example, when a sample of 30- to 50-year-old women enrolled in a BA program were compared with a sample of same-aged homemakers without college educations who were not in school (Amstey & Whitbourne, 1981), the two groups were found to be similar in measures of identity, sex-role orientation, and political views. Similarly, in another study (Ballmer & Cozby, 1981), the marital adjustment of reentry women and a comparable group of homemakers was reported not to differ, although among the former, both spouses perceived their families as having more conflict and more independence, and a greater intellectual/cultural and active recreational orientation than among the latter. Judith Gerson (1985) also compared a sample of 30- to 50-year-old married or divorced women college students with a sample of full-time homemakers and found that while the former reported more role strain, they also reported more personal benefits and general gratification.

Besides pursuing college degrees, older women in the 1980s can be found leading vigorous lives and participating fully in the workplace, in politics, and in organized efforts for social change. The goals of the Gray Panthers, an articulate and militant organization in which women hold important positions of leadership, include abolition of poverty, reform of pension plans, better health care and housing for the elderly, better monitoring of nursing care facilities, and better police protection. They have been effective in raising public consciousness about older people's skills and needs, and in influencing Congress to investigate and legislate. As illustrated by the anti-nuclear demonstrators shown in the photo on this page, older women have been working with people of all ages on programs to expand human rights and to improve the human environment, and have maintained and enhanced their effectiveness and dignity.

As women who were born in the 1950s, 1960s, and 1970s mature and grow older, their expectations and assumptions will very likely differ from those of women born in earlier decades. Alice Rossi (1980) has pointed out that the women currently studied for information about the middle years represent the cohort that pioneered the settlement of suburbia in the post—World War II period—attracted to domesticity that far exceeded in affluent possibilities what their mothers experienced in the lean years of the 1930s but more isolated from kin and friends. (p. 15)

And Beth Hess (1985) has noted that

the world of the 1970s and 80s in America is not that of the 50s and 60s. Women's life course is being transformed by delayed first marriage, lowered fertility, continuing high rates of divorce and remarriage, and ever-increasing rates of labor force participation—all in a complex cause-and-effect relationship with the feminist movement. Women today make choices and go through life stages in a radically different way from their mothers and grandmothers. (p. 6)

The daughters of today's women are more likely than their mothers to be well educated, to have explored several personal options, and to have had long years of employment experiences. They are even more likely therefore, when gray hair and wrinkles appear, to effectively resist being pushed aside.

Getting Wiser:
New Directions and Strategies

black sturdy shoulders
we are monuments that refuse to crumble
deep-rooted oaks from which the generations
like thick-leaved branches grow and thrive
we are the strong ones
having balanced the weight of the tribe
having made our planting as deep as anyman's

and yet
as women
we have known only meager harvests
we sing strong songs
and the world hums a sweet lullaby
we write rich poems
and the world offers muted applause
for a jingling rhyme

sometimes
as women only
do we weep
we are brought to whisper
when we wish to scream
assent
when we wish to defy
dance pretty
  (on tiptoe)
when we would raise circles of dust
before the charge

Gloria Gayles   *(1979, pp. 363f.)*

C H A P T E R   16

*E*verywhere we see clear indications that women's lives will not return to the status quo of earlier generations. Today's older woman is wiser, more articulate, and more skilled; and today's younger woman expects that her options will not be restricted because of her gender. If women are now less constrained by gender ideology and freer to choose who we will become, it is largely due to the efforts of the women's movement. Though the movement has changed with the times as different issues have become salient for women, it has never swerved from its insistence that women must be respected and allowed to develop as full human beings with unbound bodies and minds. In this final chapter we will look at the difference the movement has made in women's lives and at its current manifestations and challenges; and we will once again answer the question, What do women want?

THE WOMEN'S MOVEMENT: GAINS AND CHALLENGES

American women have come a long way since Lucretia Mott and Elizabeth Cady Stanton organized the first women's rights convention in 1848 at Seneca Falls, New York. One small indication of the speed with which women's issues and concerns became salient for women in the "second wave" of the post-franchise feminist movement is the growth in membership of the National Organization for Women (NOW) from 300 in 1966 to 80,000 in 1978 (Kearney, 1979). And for every woman affiliated with NOW or some other organized group, many more are sympathetic to feminist goals and act on them in diverse ways.

Affirmative action programs in business, industry, government, and education have made women visible in the public sphere, and enabled us to demonstrate our competence and our ability to solve problems and behave creatively and effectively in all areas—from accounting to zoology, in religion, science, management, the professions, skilled labor, and the arts. Title IX of the Education Amendments of 1972 (now threatened by the Supreme Court's restrictive interpretation of the *Grove City* decision in 1984*) mandated equal treatment in education for women and men by institutions receiving federal assistance. This legislation has sharply increased the number of women in fields previously dominated by men, and it has had a dramatic impact on athletics and competitive sports. Thus, for example,

> in 1970, only 300,000 high school girls participated on athletic teams sponsored by their schools. By 1979, two million girls were taking part. At the college level, there were no athletic scholarships given to women before Title IX; today there are more than 10,000 . . . [and] the National Collegiate Athletic Association sponsored 30 national championships for women. (Packwood, 1984, p. A16)

As women's presence in sports, the mass media, the world of commerce and national affairs, education, law enforcement, production, and service is observed and reflected upon, it has the further consequence of changing attitudes, beliefs, values, and expectations. A study of 1200 white women interviewed in 1962, 1963, 1966, and 1977 indicated that there had been "a dramatic increase in . . . liberal attitudes about appropriate roles for men and women in the home and at work" (cited in "Fifteen-Year Study," 1980, p. 3). For example, in response to a statement that most of the important family decisions should be made by the "man of the house," just under one third of the women respondents disagreed with this in 1962, compared with over two thirds in 1977. Egalitarian attitudes were most likely to have been adopted by younger, more educated women in the work force, but the researchers concluded that all

*The court ruled 6 to 3 that only the specific program receiving aid is subject to the antidiscrimination provisions of Title IX, not the entire institution and all of its programs, as previously understood.

groups of women had been affected by the social changes of the 1960s and 1970s having to do with women's lives. Other studies support this conclusion.

Along with more egalitarian attitudes have come changes in gender stereotypes. Women's skilled performance in the labor force and assertion of equality in personal relationships, as well as men's rediscovery of their sensitivity and ability to be nurturant lovers and fathers, have seriously challenged our cultural stereotypes about the attributes of women and men. As women (and men) are observed functioning in ways that belie the stereotypes, our beliefs begin to change, and we begin to develop new ideals for human behavior, apparent in our self-reported views of "ideal persons." Thus, for example, several researchers (Gilbert, Deutsch, & Strahan, 1978; Freeman, 1979) have reported that college student samples who have been asked to describe ideal women and men have tended to present them as more similar to one another than respondents who have been asked to describe average or typical persons. Louise Silvern and Victor Ryan (1983) found that when college students described an ideal person of unspecified gender, both women and men characterized this person as having significantly more nurturant, expressive, and people-oriented qualities than instrumental, assertive, and self-oriented ones. Women more than men described the ideal woman and the ideal person similarly and saw the ideal woman as competent and responsible. Other researchers (for example, Major, Carnevale, & Deaux, 1981) have reported that persons described as being both instrumental *and* expressive, independent as well as concerned about others, are liked best and are rated as most adjusted.

Whether or not women identify with the women's movement, our beliefs and attitudes are likely to reflect its influence. Thus, for example, one study (Bers & Mezey, 1981) found women in community leadership positions to favor specific efforts to strengthen women's status through programs for rape victims, battered wives, and displaced homemakers; equal educational opportunities for girls and boys; and sexual equality in employment. The researchers concluded that while these women did not label themselves as feminists, and did not necessarily want to change their own lives, they supported feminist goals. Similarly, another study (Smith & Self, 1981) compared a group of self-reported feminist college women with a group of traditionalists and found that both groups supported "egalitarianism in

the labor market and political arena" (p. 187). What separated the two groups was that only the feminists were willing to alter their personal relationships to achieve social equality with men. A survey of a sample of working-class (mainly white) women by Myra Ferree (1983) also found largely positive attitudes toward the goals of the women's liberation movement and toward the movement itself. Approximately 25 percent of the women studied were strong and consistent supporters; another 57 percent were sympathizers who felt that the movement had come too late to effect any meaningful changes in their own lives, but supported such efforts by others and looked "to the next generation for change" (p. 498). Generational differences in support for feminist goals have been reported (Dambrot, Papp, & Whitmore, 1984), with college women indicating more egalitarian sex-role attitudes than their mothers and grandmothers, and the latter expressing the most traditional views. And a large-scale national study of women and men who were interviewed every year from 1967 to 1978 (Doherty & Baldwin, 1985) found that women, but not men, became increasingly more likely to believe that their lives were controlled by external factors, a change the researchers attributed to women's "increased awareness of . . . structural inequalities" (p. 1051). This assumption has been supported by other data. For example, Patricia Gurin (cited in "Group Consciousness," 1982) examined the responses of a national sample of women who were interviewed three different times in the 1970s and reported that they increasingly attributed their lesser economic and social status to discrimination rather than to individual deficiencies, from 33 percent in 1972 to 55 percent in 1979.

These changes in women's sociopolitical consciousness, beliefs, and attitudes are reflected in all aspects of American life. As noted by Linda Gordon and Marla Erlien (1981), many of the gains made by women are "unmeasurable by statistics and unreachable by the law. . . . [They include raised] intellectual, economic and political expectations, an increased intolerance of wife beating, rape and other violence against women, and a redefinition of women's sexuality" (p. 578). Women country and western performers are now writing and singing songs about no longer accepting the role of honky-tonk hussy or long-suffering wife, and about the liberating consequences of the Pill (cited in Trott, 1981). Women have reappeared in major roles in television and in films as intelligent, problem-solving, effective persons; can be seen daily on the television screen as news reporters, interviewers, and anchor persons; and have even entered the world of stand-up comedy and demonstrated that they can make people laugh by using material from women's lives (Berger, 1984). For example, one Elayne Boosler line (cited in Berger) goes like this: "Hookers! How do they do it? How could any woman sleep with a man without having a dinner and a movie first?" (p. 38).

Some women are moving into high places and are realizing their own potential for public effectiveness and power. Whether defined in terms of one's ability to get others to do what you want, or one's influence over others, or one's access to resources and sanctions, power is now a word used by more and more women with less and less self-consciousness and apology. While debate continues among feminists about the dangers of behaving "like a man" (for example, Fleming, 1981), numerous workshops and books for women "on the way up" teach the old strategies as well as new ones, and *Ms* magazine has featured a test on power to enable readers to assess their P.Q. (power quotient). Carol Tavris (1982), who devised the quiz, explained that "power is not a fixed attribute . . . ; it's a shifty commodity, elusive in some situations and intrusive in others. It can be abused, misused, manipulated—or used for good" (p. 49). It is clearly something more women want more of! We know that in interactions among people of equal status, gender is less likely to be a salient variable. This has been argued by Rosabeth Kanter (1977) in the business world, and by Alice Eagly (1983) for social behavior in general.

Feminists insist that men, too, will gain from greater gender flexibility and equality and that, although men as a group (especially white middle-class men) have profited from their position of power, individual men are not "the enemy." All of us—men as well as women, our sons as well as our daughters—are denied aspects of our common humanity by sex typing. When Gloria Steinem turned 50, she was asked by an interviewer whether she had ever met a man with whom she felt she could negotiate a good life. She responded that men are *not* the problem.

> I have no complaints about individual men I've known *and* been in love with. . . . They've been generous and supportive. . . . The problem was the way society treated you, the expectation that his work would be more important, that you should take his name. It was

like racism. It's not that you can't find white people who are not racist, you can; but it's still true that when a white person and a black person enter a room together, they are regarded differently. (cited in Sinclair, 1984, p. A-6)

Men have begun to realize the price gender expectations exact from them. In this country there is now an articulate movement for men's liberation and for a nonpatriarchal society by men who have accepted the feminist agenda and share its aspirations (for example, Doyle, 1983; Lewis, 1981; Franklin, 1984). Many men and women now agree with what suffragette Crystal Eastman told an audience in 1920: "We must bring up feminist sons" (cited in Kerber, 1977, p. 48). Brothers must come to share their sisters' commitment to equality if that objective is to be realized, and to agree, as Eastman put it, that it is "womanly as well as manly to earn your own living, to stand on your own feet. And it must be manly to know how to cook and sew and clean."

But that feminist objectives are likely to continue being opposed by the majority of men is a conclusion supported by history and attention to current events. The humor in some men's reactions to women's aspirations is good for a chuckle (see the Nicole Hollander cartoons on pages 298 and 300); but a more serious analysis, presented by Arnold Kahn (1984), emphasizes the extent and ubiquitous nature of men's responses. Kahn argues that men's power (relative to women) is a key component of the masculine stereotype and self-image, and thus not easily given up or modified: "With power they are men; without it they are no better than women" (p. 238). Power enhances self-esteem, and its use is addictive, so that even men with egalitarian beliefs often fail to act accordingly. As noted by Kahn, "Men tend to be so used to exerting their power [over women] . . . that they simply do not know how to act otherwise" (p. 242). Men often interpret women's insistence on sharing power and responsibilities with them as threatening and debilitating. One particularly outrageous example of this phenomenon appeared in a press report of the reactions of people in the United States to terrorism. David Reisman, a well-known social scientist, was quoted as saying that our reactions reflect our need to feel superior, which has been heightened in recent years by our "loss of face in Vietnam, loss of economic status to Japan, and loss of identity of many men who feel threatened by the women's movement" (Trausch, 1986, p. 76). Major feminist objectives are to teach men and women to

Sylvia comes through with another great idea. *(From
Mercy, It's the Revolution and I'm in My Bathrobe, by
Nicole Hollander, St. Martin's Press, Inc. Copyright © 1982
by Nicole Hollander.)*

share power equally; to change institutions so that
this is possible and probable; and to sever the connection between power and gender (or other arbitrary
categories like race or ethnicity). The goal has never
been to punish men or to assert women's superiority.

Of course, stating principles or objectives is not
enough. In addition, for individual women to acquire
personal power within the existing system may not
be enough if that system continues to oppress most
women while permitting success for a few. The New
Woman is presented to us by the media as well-groomed, in business suit, cool, efficient, with perfect
makeup, and ready for the day's challenges. We must
ask how the fact of her new status will change the life
of the divorced mother who washes the dishes at
home before beginning a day in the typing pool or the
restaurant, who carries her lunch in a paper sack or
tote bag, not papers in an attache case. Enhanced
personal lives for some women must be accompanied
by changes in the social, economic, and political institutions that affect all of us. Many women are now
realizing their personal dreams and ambitions, are
doing responsible and worthwhile work, and are in
satisfying personal relationships, but do not connect
their present possibilities and satisfactions with the
earlier struggles of women before them or with the
continued oppression of most other women. The
media image of feminists as bitter, lonely women,
tortured, "icy monsters . . . who . . . let themselves
go physically . . . [and have] no sense of style" (Bolo-tin, 1982, p. 31) has discouraged many women from
identifying with the women's movement. While enjoying lives that promise personal rewards, young
middle-class women must also participate with other
women in a movement to abolish gender inequities
for all.

IDENTIFICATION WITH ALL WOMEN

Among the most far-reaching and significant objectives of the new women's movement is its insistence
on respect for, and empathy with, all women—regardless of marital status, color, sexual orientation,
occupation, or age. As women have begun talking to
each other openly, we have discovered common
fears, problems, and aspirations. We have found each
other likable and interesting, and capable of strong
and loving friendship. Daughters have rediscovered
their mothers, and mothers, their daughters. As Mary
Daly (1978b) has written:

> A feminist thinks of her close friends as sisters, but she
> knows that she has many sisters . . . whom she has
> never met. Sometimes she meets such women and
> some conversation unmasks the similarities between
> them. . . . The proximity that she feels is not merely
> geographic/spatial. . . . She senses gynesthetically that
> there is a convergence of personal histories, of
> wavelengths. (p. 29)

Consciousness of common experience has been
directed toward militant change and political organization, as well as toward personal change and goal
achievement. Sisterhood is thus a means both to
group and to self-understanding, a dual objective
articulated by many of the chroniclers and theorists of
the women's movement.

Raising Consciousness

Modern life in a patriarchal society tends to keep
women isolated, in the nuclear family home or alone
in a city apartment, and to convince women they are
in competition with one another for men. The
women's movement has given women a way to
break out of isolation and empower each other to see

through the patriarchal myths. In Mary Daly's (1978b) words, "Whenever two or three Self-affirming women are gathered together in our own names we are lighting our Fire" (p. 33).

Women gathering for enlightenment and support is not an altogether new phenomenon. One of the charges the churchmen of the early Massachusetts Bay Colony made against Anne Hutchinson was that women gathered regularly in her home to discuss the Scriptures and other matters of mutual interest and to comment on the weekly sermons without benefit of male leadership or guidance. For this, Hutchinson, who was a midwife, herbal healer, and mother of 15 children, was banished from Massachusetts in 1638, excommunicated from the Church, and forced to flee with her family to Rhode Island. The male clergy were threatened by Anne Hutchinson because "she dared to assert the right of women to instruct others" (Lerner, 1977, p. 465). In Nathaniel Hawthorne's (1850/1948) classic story of Puritan life, *The Scarlet Letter*, we read that Hester Prinn, who was publicly shamed for participating in adultery, was sought after toward the end of her life by women who came to her isolated cottage to share their problems, disappointments, and pain.

> Women . . . came to Hester's cottage, demanding why they were so wretched, and what the remedy! Hester comforted and counselled them, as best she might. She assured them, too, of her firm belief that, at some brighter period, when the world should have grown ripe for it . . . a new truth would be revealed, in order to establish the whole relation between man and woman on a surer ground of mutual happiness. (pp. 271f.)

Among contemporary women, what started a decade or two ago simply as informal and spontaneous "rap sessions," the discussion of mutual concerns in more-or-less regularly scheduled leaderless

Daughter and mother in sisterhood

group meetings, soon became a powerful tool for social change. The New York group Redstockings is credited with having introduced consciousness raising (CR) in the late 1960s as an American feminist version of the Chinese revolutionary practice of "speaking bitterness." It has brought women together and encouraged analyses of the interdependent relationship between self and society, the personal and the political. As noted by Catharine MacKinnon (1982):

> Through consciousness raising, women grasp the collective reality of women's condition from within the perspective of that experience, not from outside it. . . . [And] women learn they have *learned* that men are everything, women their negation, but that the sexes are equal. (pp. 536, 542)

Almost from the very beginning, the women's liberation movement has had a dual purpose: to effect massive social change *and* changes in individual lives; and the "organizational bridge between the two foci," as Naomi Rosenthal (1984) has pointed out, has been consciousness raising. "The Laingian notion that politics and experience are intertwined (i.e., the personal is political) was combined with the Marxian dictum that the development of class consciousness inevitably results in action of and for the class" (p. 313). Among the personal consequences of CR groups is that one's perception of oneself and the social environment is never the same again. Collective action directed toward change has often, but not always, followed.

Formal studies of the outcomes of CR groups, reviewed by Alberta Nassi and Stephen Abramowitz (1978), have found that participants see themselves as more competent, acquire more positive attitudes toward other women, and develop "a sociopolitical perspective that recognizes the influence of sex role conditioning and sex role expectations" (p. 150). One study (Lieberman & Bond, 1976), in which questionnaires were returned by women in 41 states, found that the most important experiences CR group members reported were sharing thoughts and feelings about being a woman and learning that their problems, feelings, and fears were not unique. Members reported positive changes in self-esteem; confidence in their own judgments; attempts to deal with problems; and feeling supported, approved of, and valued. A later analysis of data from this study (Kravetz, Marecek, & Finn, 1983) found the most important reason for joining a group to be the desire to explore women's experiences. Rose Weitz (1982) questioned a large group of women three months

© 1986, Los Angeles Times Syndicate. Reprinted with permission.

after they joined CR groups and found "a number of beneficial changes—decreased feelings of depression, isolation, helplessness, worthlessness, and self-reproach—as well as . . . increased positive attitudes towards women and feminism" (p. 237). Although largely a white middle-class phenomenon, consciousness raising has also been a goal in working-class groups (Jacoby, 1973; Van Gelder, 1979), in which the focus is more often on community problems, the need for jobs, and the desire for more education.

Women who explore common issues and their position in society invariably change in the way they relate to other women, in the ease and confidence with which they share ideas, and the respectful attention they give to one another. For example, in Carolyn Slaughter's novel *A Perfect Woman* (1985), a group of women friends is described through the eyes of a man who has come unexpectedly to visit one of the women:

> They had all welcomed him. . . . They moved back to include him, but they went on talking, in a way he wasn't familiar with. They probed and pried at one another, protected, teased, laughed. But no one was in charge. No loud male voice guided the proceedings. Everyone had a turn to talk, no one dominated. (p. 102)

And women who subscribe to feminist ideals change in other ways, also. For example, such women have been found to be more inner-directed, more self-accepting, and to value self-actualization more than conservative women (Hjelle & Butterfield, 1974); and Edwin McClain (1978) concluded that a high motivation for independence and a low motivation for affiliation reliably differentiated feminist from nonfeminist women. Feminist (or nontraditional) women have also been found to differ from other women in judging fewer personal attributes as characteristic only of men (Rapin & Cooper, 1980), and in being less likely to behave aggressively against an opponent in a laboratory situation in which pairs of persons could deliver electric shocks to one another (Richardson, Vinsel, & Taylor, 1980).

Consciousness raising has been criticized by some for emphasizing changes in personal lives, thus diverting attention and energy away from actively working for institutional changes that would benefit all women. But changes in personal attitudes and behavior are correlates of changes in culture, and pressures for the latter come from women (and men) who insist on leading fuller lives than those prescribed by the dominant gender ideology. An inventory of significant changes in the lives of members of my CR group would include decisions to work for higher degrees; the launching of a nationally known and respected women's cooperative art gallery; improved paid employment—jobs with greater responsibility and status; and participation within the larger community in political action and service to women. We have all taken greater risks and moved more assertively into the world outside of our homes. We are more confident, more responsible for our own behavior, and perceive more options. We have experienced disappointments and frustrations, job losses, divorces, problems with children, but also marriages, births, and more satisfying personal and work relationships and responsibilities.

Learning from Lesbians

Charlotte Bunch, an important feminist theorist, is reported to have said, "No woman is truly free to be anything unless she is also free to be a lesbian." Because lesbians are women who do not orient their lives around men, they represent, as Radicalesbians (1976) believe, an affront and a challenge to men and the most serious threat to patriarchal institutions. Lesbianism is thus said by some to represent the essence of women's struggle against sexism. Certainly, many active feminists report having been accused by someone at some time of being a lesbian and have had that label hurled at them angrily or seen the suspicion in bitter eyes. "Cagney and Lacey," a widely acclaimed and popular television show about two women detectives, was altered in its early years to "soften" the main characters. According to CBS, they were too tough, hard, unfeminine, and aggressive; they "were too harshly women's lib . . . more intent on fighting the system than doing police work. We perceived them as dykes" (cited in Swertlow, 1982, p. A-1). In the minds of many nonfeminists, in other words, women's liberation is equated with lesbianism. And some radical lesbian feminists argue, as has Ti Grace Atkinson, that "feminism is the theory; lesbianism is the practice" (cited in Koedt, 1973a, p. 246).

Some feminists disagree with this analysis, and the ensuing arguments have sparked emotion-laden and potentially divisive debates. But in 1977, when the representatives to the National Women's Conference in Houston voted overwhelmingly in favor of a sexual preference resolution, the event was described by Anne Fleming (1977) as follows:

> The proposition passed easily and the aisles were suddenly full of women kissing each other, on the cheek, on the mouth. . . . One had to remind oneself that at least 75 percent of the women celebrating were heterosexual. They were celebrating because for that one moment, with that one vote, they knew they were better than men. (p. 33)

Approval of the lesbian rights resolution at the Houston conference was more than an affirmation of civil rights; it represented recognition by heterosexual feminists of the special place occupied by lesbians in the women's liberation movement, of the important lessons to be learned from lesbian lives and struggles, and of the absolute necessity for unity and understanding among women.

In learning from the lesbian experience, feminists have turned the spotlight on heterosexuality, questioning both the reasons for its dominance, and its centrality to a patriarchal, sexist society in which men wield power over women. Adrienne Rich (1980), for example, has argued that women experience heterosexuality as *compulsory* and, therefore, that it "needs to be recognized and studied as a *political institution*" (p. 637). She has suggested that lesbianism be viewed as a continuum or range of woman-identified behaviors and attitudes that enhance power and include sharing, supporting, and bonding among women and resistance to marriage. Other feminists have responded that compulsory heterosexuality is only one of the mechanisms of patriarchy (Thompson, 1981a); and that to target it as the key factor in male domination is historically inaccurate and also "romanticizes lesbianism and ignores the actual quality of individual lesbian or heterosexual women's lives" (Ferguson, 1981, p. 170). Still other feminists agree with Rich that lesbianism represents resistance to patriarchy but urge that its sexual core not be understated, and that explicit attention must be given to the "deeply felt eroticism of female love and friendship that has persisted for centuries" (Zita, 1981, p. 186).

In an attempt to provide mutual support and empowerment, lesbian communities or networks have been formed in which women maintain a high level of political consciousness, shared values, and intimacy. From the energy generated in such communities has come a great deal of contemporary "women's culture"—music, art, literature (Zimmerman, 1984). According to Susan Krieger (1982), lesbian communities enhance

> sense of self . . . [and] provide a haven or home in a hostile or distrusting outside world. They lend support for what is frequently a stigmatized life-style choice. They command recognition of a distinctively lesbian sensibility—a sensibility that is unusual because of the value it places on intimacy between women. (p. 91)

But lesbian communities are not immune from externally or internally generated problems, and Krieger has noted some of these: intolerance of individual differences, exclusion, exploitation, and demands for commitment and intimacy, all of which *"may threaten as well as support* the development of individual identity" (p. 105). As with other communities, there are variations among lesbian communities as well as among the individuals who comprise them.

The earlier medical view of lesbians as sick and perverted has finally been discredited. The search for antecedents or determinants has not uncovered a link between homosexuality and pathological parent-child relationships or evidence of any one "critical period." In fact, Evelyn Hooker (1972), who chaired the National Institute of Mental Health's Task Force on Homosexuality, concluded that "adult homosexual roles may be formed by a continuous process of social-sexual learning, from early childhood to adolescent and early adult life" (p. 13). The contemporary view, based on psychological, sociological, and medical evidence, as noted by Susan Krieger (1982), is that lesbianism is

> neither a sexual nor a social disease but, rather, a lifestyle choice closely linked with a sense of personal identity . . . [and] a product of multiple influencers rather than . . . traceable to a single cause. Indeed, they [social scientists] look less at causes than at behaviors and perceptions of experience. . . . They consider lesbianism to be a matter of total personality identity . . . changeable in definition rather than as something that is a given. (pp. 93, 95)

In 1974, the American Psychiatric Association officially removed homosexuality from its classifications of mental illness, ending a long and bitter dispute. Five years later the United States Surgeon General declared that homosexuality was no longer considered a mental disease or defect, and the Immigration and Naturalization Service ordered its agents to stop preventing foreign homosexuals from coming into the country ("Ban on Homosexuals," 1979).

Homosexuals typically grow up in straight, not gay, families and social environments. And children raised by transsexual or homosexual parents have been found not to differ from children raised in more conventional family settings with respect to sexual identity, behavior, or preferences (Green, 1978). Lesbians and heterosexual women have been socialized in a common culture, and have acquired similar gender-related beliefs and ways of behaving that are reinforced and maintained by social institutions and other agents of socialization. Not surprisingly, then, research has shown few reliable differences between heterosexual women and lesbians outside the area of sexual preference. Andrea Oberstone and Harriet Sukoneck (1976) found no differences between a group of lesbians and a comparable group of single heterosexual women on a standard measure of "total psychological adjustment," nor in their responses to interview questions dealing with such items as living situation, relationships, friendship patterns, and use of drugs and alcohol. Differences were found only on items directly related to sexual orientation. This study is especially important because it did not focus on women in psychotherapy but on women recruited through referral by friends. All the women were white, single, between 20 and 45 years old, and equivalent in education and occupation. Expert judges were not able to find any distinctively lesbian characteristics that would differentiate the personality profiles of homosexual women from others, but the lesbians reported greater satisfaction in their relationships and vocations than the heterosexual women. Both groups had had very similar heterosexual experiences, but at some point the lesbians appeared to have made a choice that was not related to seduction or any other distinctive single event. A study that compared lesbian and heterosexual women on perception of their parents (Johnson, Stockard, Rothbart, & Friedman, 1981) found the women to be "remarkably similar." Most of the women, regardless of sexual preference, reported that their mother was the more supportive parent—more protective, affectionate, and tolerant of expressions of anger. But lesbians did differ from heterosexual women in reporting less affection, respect, and encouragement from their fathers.

A number of researchers have concluded that while there are more similarities than differences between lesbians and heterosexual women, in couple relationships the former tend to behave with more flexibility, cooperation, and equal sharing of responsibility and power (for example, Peplau, 1982; Lynch & Reilly, 1985–1986). On the other hand, Mayta

Caldwell and Letitia Peplau (1984) found among a group of white middle-class lesbian couples that while equal power was the ideal, a sizable minority did not achieve it, and inequality was associated with less satisfaction in the relationship (as is true among heterosexual couples). In studies comparing lesbian, gay male, and heterosexual couples, one group of researchers (Cardell, Finn, & Marecek, 1981) found the least sex typing (adherence to stereotypes) in self-reported personality traits among the lesbians. Others (Schullo & Alperson, 1984) have found "no evidence that the underlying dynamics of heterosexual and homosexual relationships are different" (p. 1000).

If lesbians are generally similar to heterosexual women, they are also, like heterosexual women, a very diverse group. Sophie Loewenstein's (1978) clinical observations and research led her to conclude that lesbians, like heterosexual women,

> are extremely diverse in personality, family constellation and developmental experiences and categorizing them as a group becomes as meaningless as categorizing all heterosexual women would be. Stereotypes of lesbians as man-haters, as obsessed with sex, as immature, as masculine or aggressive apply to some lesbians (as well as to some heterosexual women) while they are false for others. (pp. 8f.)

Brenda Vance and Vicki Green (1984) interviewed 43 predominantly white well-educated self-defined lesbians and concluded that the participants were "a very heterogeneous group, with divergent backgrounds, divergent sexual and social experiences, and divergent avenues of identifying and defining themselves as 'lesbian'" (p. 306). According to Judy Klemesrud (1971), the membership of the New York City chapter of the Daughters of Bilitis*, a lesbian organization, includes "college professors, scientists, unemployed women on welfare, editors, singers, actresses, secretaries, students, doctors, nurses, certified public accountants, housewives, and city employees."

Although homosexual women (and men) are found in every segment of society, they continue to be discriminated against in employment and housing, and to experience serious negative personal and social consequences. Only a few cities and states have recently provided formal guarantees of equal protection and nondiscrimination. The expectation that les-

bians must lose custody of their children following divorce is being challenged, as are the assumptions that they are uninterested in their children, poor mothers, or that their children will suffer ill effects. Still, in custody cases in which one parent's sexual preference is raised as an issue, 98 percent of the time the homosexual parent loses (Barclay, 1978). Sometimes the loss of custody is accompanied by reduction of visiting rights, or the stipulation that a third party of the other gender must always be present during visits. In a recent case, a Pennsylvania appeals court ruled against a lesbian mother and upheld the principle that homosexuality can be used against a parent in determining the custody of children ("Homosexuality Held a Bar," 1985). To help lesbian mothers assert their legal rights in custody cases, a group called CALM (Custody Action for Lesbian Mothers) currently offers free legal counseling and psychological support.

Many social scientists have concluded that it is homophobia and not homosexuality that is dangerous to society and dysfunctional for the individual. Homophobia results in discrimination against lesbians in the legal system, the work place, and the community. Martin Levine and Robin Leonard (1984) have reported from a review of the literature that the vast majority of lesbians hide their sexual preference from employers, and that 10 to 12 percent have been asked to resign or have been fired after disclosure. From their own research in New York City, Levine and Leonard concluded that "employment discrimination is a serious problem" (p. 705). One fourth of the lesbians studied reported discrimination in salary, promotions, and/or verbal harassment; 29 percent had not been hired, or had been fired because they were known to be lesbians. Seventy-seven percent were "closeted" on the job; and 27 percent were closeted to everyone. The extent to which heterosexual American adults still fear and misunderstand homosexuality can be illustrated by the results of a Gallup poll in 1982 (cited in Levine and Leonard) that found that only 59 percent of the respondents believed homosexuals should have equal rights with respect to employment. One group of researchers (Gross, Green, Storck, & Vanyur, 1980) found that college students made more stereotyped and negative judgments of a videotaped target person who was identified as a homosexual than if there was no such identification; and in another study (Cuenot & Fujita, 1982), college students exhibited evidence of anxiety when being interviewed by a homosexual; men exhibited greater

---

*Bilitis was a disciple of Sappho, a lyric poet of ancient Greece who was born on the island of Lesbos, from which the word *lesbian* has been derived.

avoidance of a gay male while women showed greater avoidance of a lesbian. Homophobia is also reflected in a 1986 decision by the Supreme Court that upheld the right of states to legislate against sodomy—a decision widely interpreted as a judgment about the "immorality" of homosexuality.

To counter homophobic attitudes and behaviors, lesbians and gay men have joined forces for active community organizing, demonstrations, and lobbying to demand equal rights in housing, employment, and all areas of social, political, and economic life. In addition, some national organizations have begun to educate their members. For example, the Boston chapter of NOW has published a handbook designed to combat prejudice against lesbians and to help members understand the significance of "heterosexual privilege" (*Lesbians: A Consciousness Raising Kit*, 1980). The American Psychological Association has formed a new division (Division 44) devoted to the psychological study of lesbian and gay issues, and at the 1980 national meetings of the American Association for the Advancement of Science, the National Organization of Lesbian and Gay Scientists was formed to communicate "with . . . heterosexual colleagues, and with society-at-large, about the effects of homophobia on their well-being" (Escoffier, Malyon, Morin, & Raphael, 1980, p. 340).

Sisterhood with Prostitutes and Imprisoned Women

Women have learned to identify with one another regardless of sexual preference, and also that being treated as a sexual object by men, and exchanging sex for favors of various kinds, is not unique to one class of women. The motivations and behavior of prostitutes are understandable, and we can empathize with women for whom sex provides employment. Judith Walkowitz (1980) has noted that nineteenth-century feminists saw prostitution "as the end result of the . . . constraints placed on women's social and economic activity . . . [and of the] contempt and distrust for women . . . as sexual objects to be bought and sold by men" (p. 125). Like contemporary feminists, Victorian feminists understood that the bond linking prostitutes with all other women was men's attitudes.

For an ordinary woman to be treated in ways similar to a prostitute is not unusual. For example, in 1979 a woman wrote to Ann Landers for advice, complaining that her husband "B" got furious if he woke up in the morning and found that his wife was out of bed and "not available for instant sex." Landers

responded as follows: "You don't say what is required of you in terms of time and energy. If it's only a few minutes you should agree to accommodate 'B' in exchange for his promise to leave you alone before the alarm clock goes off" (1979). I do not think that Ann Landers would give the same advice today. Ellen Strong (1970), an ex-prostitute, has argued persuasively that most girls learn "the basic principle of hustling"—that one can exchange what men want (sex) for what women want (attention, gifts, security). Most women experience some pressure at some time to take part in such an exchange. Sex, we are told, is something we can "give" to lovers or husbands in order to make them happy and satisfied; in return we will be rewarded by harmony, good treatment, or other special expressions of gratitude. In a work by Kate Millett (1971), "J" tells the following story:

> [Miles] Davis was playing in a club, and someone outside wanted to take me . . . asked me if I wanted to go in. And I knew that if I went in with him I'd have to sleep with him. But I figured it was worth it; I wanted to see Miles Davis. I had no feeling for this guy; I just wanted the ticket to get in there. I realized I'd whored—there was no way of denying the truth to myself. So when the time came a few years later and I was absolutely broke, I was ready. (p. 24)

The geisha of Japan, like the hetairai of ancient Athens, were women who were set apart from others in order to provide special attention and entertainment for men of wealth and high position. These women, versed in the arts of love and conversation, were also talented and specially educated musicians, poets, or dancers, regarded not with disrespect but with some awe. Geisha lived in separate communities and typically taught their daughters the elegant and artful behaviors they had learned. There are stories of geisha who were brilliant confidantes of, and advisors to, powerful and influential men of state and industry. Some contemporary women begin a life of prostitution with the illusion that, like the courtesans of old, such a life brings glamour and independence from a husband. But invariably and inevitably, the realities of prostitution override the illusion and promise of good times and easy money. Most women who have talked about their experiences tell much the same story of alienation, self-hatred, and increased hostility toward men. Prostitutes are abused and exploited by pimps, roughed up and victimized by the police and their clients, and taken advantage of by hotel operators, lawyers, pornographers, and organized crime. It is the rare prostitute who can live like the romanticized courtesans of old, who can survive and flourish and sometimes even work herself out of business.

Gail Sheehy (1974) spent two years exploring the world of prostitution in New York and concluded that a streetwalker rarely sees more than 5 percent of her earnings; the rest goes primarily to a pimp, for police or gangster protection, and to pay court fines. A study of street prostitutes in San Francisco cited by Kathleen Barry (1979) found that they had begun the life at an average age of 17, and that 63 percent had been runaways. Prior to prostitution, 80 percent had been victims of physical or sexual abuse; 37 percent had been victims of incest. The vast majority were working for pimps and had no savings. Another study cited by Barry found that 67 percent of a group of interviewed prostitutes had been seriously injured by customers. She concluded that "life in the brothel is not plush, erotic excitement" (p. 116). Another study of 100 San Francisco prostitutes (cited in "'Not Victimless,'" 1980) reported that nearly half were under 16 years old; most were from middle-class backgrounds; more than half had been victims of incest or sexual abuse; and 70 percent had been raped in an incident unrelated to their work. We know less about the men who buy sex than about the women who sell it. But according to Margo St. James, founder of COYOTE (Cast Off Your Old Tired Ethics), an advocacy group for prostitutes, "Studies identify the typical customer as white, about 40 years old, married and a businessman or professional" (cited in Hiltzik, 1979).

When feminists express empathy for, or solidarity with, prostitutes, the intent is not to romanticize this so-called oldest profession, but to emphasize women's common experiences. Both the paid whore and the average woman are sexually exploited in a patriarchal society that promotes the image of women as servicers of men. The prostitute magnifies one facet of our culture's picture of women, and is an object of hostility. It is she, and rarely her customers, who is derided, arrested, and liable to a fine, a jail sentence, and a police record. The infamous Jack the Ripper murdered prostitutes in London's streets a century ago, and more recently, Son of Sam aimed his gun at women who were out with men late at night in New York City. Pat Barker's novel *Blow Your House Down* (1985) describes the fears of a group of contemporary street prostitutes in England. Male police officers have long considered prostitutes fair game for mauling and sexual abuse. Society's harassment of prostitutes and benign neglect of their customers and pimps is the focus of a report by Arlene Carmen and Howard Moody (1985), who spent eight years talking to street prostitutes in Manhattan.

Judge Margaret Taylor of Manhattan made headlines when she refused to find a 14-year-old girl guilty of prostitution because of the differential treatment of prostitutes and customers ("Woman Judge Refuses," 1978). The police, she said, "harbor the attitude that women who supply sex are immoral, whereas the men who demand their services are considered blameless." A major objective of COYOTE has been to challenge local laws and police and court practices that enforce antiprostitution statutes unequally against women. The American Psychological Association's division on the Psychology of Women has approved a resolution calling for the decriminalization and destigmatization of prostitution ("Resolution For," 1984). The resolution argues that women and people of color are discriminated against in enforcement of antiprostitution laws, and that stigmatization of prostitution jeopardizes the prostitute's physical and mental well-being. By decriminalizing and destigmatizing prostitution, the intent is to reduce the victimization of women who are currently doubly oppressed and humiliated, by their customers and by the justice system.

Discrimination against women by the justice system is illustrated by its treatment of juveniles, among whom far more girls than boys get in trouble with the law for sex offenses, usually the basis of a formal charge of being a "runaway" or "intractable." Rosemary Sarri (cited in "Girls Are Different," 1977) found that girls are frequently (but boys are never) charged with promiscuity. Furthermore, once arrested, girls receive tougher penalties. According to Kenneth Wooden (1976), a study of 722 juvenile institutions found that two thirds of the girls compared with one third of the boys were imprisoned for "status offenses." These are offenses that are not considered crimes when committed by adults, such as promiscuity and running away. Many of the girls became runaways because they were escaping from the sexual advances of male relatives. Wooden concluded that while boys often received harsh and brutal treatment, the girls suffered greater psychological abuse, received less food, poorer education, and were subjected to vaginal examinations for venereal disease "with outrageous frequency."

An estimated 20,000 (5 percent) of the 400,000 inmates of state and federal prisons are women, an increase of 150 percent from 1970 to 1981 (Barclay, 1984). Among these women, 70 percent are mothers and primarily single parents. A study of Michigan prisons (cited in "Society's Losers," 1981) found that the women inmates typically came from poor families, were unskilled with little education, and often had a history of mental problems or drug addiction. Over half were minority women; and the major offenses for which the women were sent to jail were larceny, forgery, drug offenses, or prostitution. Rosemary Sarri, who has studied the sentences given to female offenders, is cited by Dolores Barclay (1984) as having concluded that "women who commit serious crimes usually are given the same penalties as men . . . [but those] convicted of less severe crimes, such as shoplifting, drug use . . . and fraud, sometimes are given stiffer sentences" (p. A-6).

Inside prison, women and men are treated differently, to the disadvantage of the former. Suzanne Sobel (1982) has noted that while women's prisons are generally more physically attractive, in rural areas, and without concrete walls and gun towers, they are also more punitive. In many state prisons, more petty restrictions are imposed on women, and they can earn fewer privileges than men. In addition to being punishment-oriented, women's prisons provide inadequate medical and psychological/counseling services and, in general, "lack the opportunities for vocational, educational, social, and personal development that are present in many prisons for male offenders" (Sobel, 1982, p. 108). One study cited by Sobel reported that the average women's prison offers 2.7 vocational programs compared to 10 offered for men. The programs for women are typically limited to cosmetology, clerical training, food services, or nurse's aide, while male inmates are often able to obtain training in "more lucrative trades, such as plumbing, auto repair and electrical work" (Barclay, 1984, p. A-6).

Because of the gender inequities in our prison system, some groups of incarcerated women have filed sex discrimination suits in federal courts. Pending as of this writing are suits against the states of Idaho, Connecticut, and Pennsylvania. A federal court ruled in favor of women prisoners in Michigan who charged that the penal system offered them educational and rehabilitation opportunities that were inferior to those provided for men ("Society's Losers," 1981). And in another case ("Women Inmates," 1982), a federal district court judge ruled that women prisoners in Kentucky would have to be given the same privileges as men, the same opportunities for vocational education and on-the-job training, and access to legal information and advice. As a result of

this decision, a unique program was instituted by Kentucky's state prison for women, which now provides eligible women an opportunity to learn to be truck drivers (Kash, 1984b). The success of this program in training and job placement illustrates the many possibilities for improving the lives of imprisoned women and increasing the probability of a dignified and responsible return to their communities. This new approach to the treatment of imprisoned women is a direct consequence of the insistence of the women's movement that women identify with one another and appreciate the special problems of particular groups.

Learning from Minority Women

For women differing in special circumstances, sexual orientation, social class, or ethnic and racial background to understand one another and to see ourselves in the same relationship to men has not been easy. Although articulate black women like Shirley Chisholm (the first black woman to serve in Congress, elected in 1968), Flo Kennedy, and Eleanor Holmes Norton have been in the forefront of the women's liberation movement, some critics have noted important differences between the immediate concerns of the average black woman and her white counterpart. According to Toni Morrison (1971), for example, "The problems of most black women . . . [are] not in getting into medical school but in getting adult education" (p. 15). And more recently, Julianne Malveaux (1985) has pointed out that "since black women head 42% of black households, the distribution of income, not the distribution of housework, is a more critical issue for black women" (p. 27). Regardless of color, working-class women have some concerns that differ sharply from those of more affluent women.

Distrust of middle-class white women can be found especially among poor women of color who have cooked the meals and cleaned the toilets in white homes. "It is a source of amusement . . . to black women to listen to [white] feminists talk of liberation while somebody's nice black grandmother shoulders daily responsibility of child rearing and floor mopping" (Morrison, 1971, p. 64). Just as heterosexuality is associated with greater privileges in our society, so too is white skin and middle-class status. Such privileges, Phyllis Palmer (1983) has pointed out, give many white women access to better incomes and social positions than they would have on their own. It is only when such previously priv-ileged women lose their spouses through divorce or death that they can appreciate the position of the many black women who do not have access to an income other than their own. In 1982, only 53.7 percent of black families lived in households with adult male earners, compared to 85.1 percent of white families (Palmer, 1983).

Gail Godwin has written in her novel *A Mother and Two Daughters* (1983) about the relationship be-tween Theodora, an elderly white woman, and Azalea, her long-time black housekeeper. When Azalea leaves her own home to come to live with Theodora, since they are both alone and aging, Theodora remarks:

> "The old order changes, Azalea. Why look at us. Who would ever have thought you and I'd be coughing each other to sleep on the opposite sides of our wall?"
>
> Azalea gave Theodora a level look . . . "You know and I know there's still that wall." (p. 580)

Thus, some feminists have challenged the meaning of the word *women*, arguing, like Chela Sandoval (1984)

> that it is impossible to utter the word . . . as if it holds some common, unified meaning. Every woman is sub-ject to . . . desires, values, and meanings that have been shaped—not only by her experiences of sexuality and gender—but by her particular experience of the in-tersections of race, culture, and class. (p. 728)

Nevertheless, unity among women is considered essential if patriarchy is to be effectively challenged, and even among those who are most passionate in raising the issues of class and ethnic differences, unity is regarded as attainable—particularly if it is based on a recognition of, and respect for, diversity.

Most black women want the same privileges and responsibilities desired by black men and do not be-lieve that it is necessary to stand several steps behind black men in order to advance the movement for civil rights and the elimination of racial discrimination. Michele Wallace (1979), for example, has written of the need for Afro-American women to enumerate their own priorities and shape their own current his-tory. Barbara Smith (1985) has eloquently articu-lated the position of contemporary black feminists as follows:

> Denying that sexual oppression exists or requiring that we wait to bring it up until racism, or in some cases capitalism, is toppled, is a bankrupt position. A Black feminist perspective has no use for ranking oppres-sions. . . . The feminist movement and the anti-racist

movement have in common trying to insure decent human life. . . . Until Black feminism, very few people besides Black women actually cared about or took seriously the demoralization of being female *and* col-ored *and* poor *and* hated. (pp. 6, 9)

The heterogeneity among Afro-American women (as among other women) in life-style and circum-stances tends not to be appreciated but is presented, instead, by the media as an apparent contradiction. Thus, as noted by Julianne Malveaux (1985):

> We black women are considered "twofers." . . . On one hand, we are superwomen who manage both child and career. On the other hand, we represent a good number of the pregnant teens who "cause" long-term social problems. On one hand, we are castrating "bitches" who emasculate our men, oppress them with our strength. On the other hand, we are lonely ladies, facing ten-to-one odds in finding a man. (p. 27)

But while Afro-American women lead many kinds of lives, the results of national polls indicate that black women, in general, support feminist goals. Pamela Reid (1984) has argued that black women, who have long functioned competently both within their fami-lies and in the work force, are good role models for young women of all races or ethnic backgrounds. In this regard, it is instructive to note that more than twice as many black women as white women hold elective office in this country today (Boyd, 1984).

While recognizing the need for cross-ethnic alliances among women, black feminists (such as Ross, 1981; Smith, 1985) are demanding their fair share of power within the women's liberation move-ment, and are resisting having their priorities set by others. Angela Davis (1982), pictured on page 308, has called for a

> multiracial women's movement, a multiracial approach to women's studies. . . . There must be a consciousness regarding the degree to which women's issues . . . must revolve, first of all, around the majority of women and those women who have the most to gain: working-class women and women of color. . . . There cannot be a white, middle-class women's movement that is going to accomplish anything of lasting value. (pp. 6, 7, 8)

Other minority women have also been demand-ing recognition, respect, appreciation, and special attention to their particular problems. Maxine Zinn (1982) has pointed out that Mexican-American women have been misrepresented as long-suffering, simple women, dependent upon insecure macho men. But careful study suggests that, like other women, "Chicanas can be active, adaptive human

Angela Davis speaking at a meeting of the American Federation of Teacher's Black Caucus in Los Angeles in July, 1983

beings despite their subordination" (p. 260), and that their oppression is a function not only of cultural tradition but of contemporary institutional discrimination that excludes them from public life. Similarly, Rayna Green (1980) has argued that our picture of the lives of native American women is unrealistic and unclear. Indian women must be seen within the context of native American life, in which they are largely responsible for maintaining "the resilient intratribal and pan-Indian networks . . . on and off reservation, networks which keep migratory and urban Indians working, educated and in touch with their Indian identities" (p. 266). Native American women have begun to describe and write eloquently about their lives, as illustrated by Louise Erdrich's novel, *Love Medicine* (1984). Correcting misrepresentations about Asian-American women has also been the objective of feminists (such as Cheng, 1984; Kingston, 1977;

Kumagai, 1978), and we are learning that traditions of women warriors exist side by side with expectations of docility and deference to men.

Jewish feminists (for example, Pogrebin, 1982b; Scheinmann, 1981) have been calling attention to the existence of deeply rooted anti-Jewish attitudes and stereotyped beliefs among women. Special issues and problems salient for Jewish feminists are discussed in a magazine called *Lilith*, "named for the legendary predecessor of Eve who insisted on equality with Adam." According to Susan Schneider (1984), editor of *Lilith*, the women's movement has been powerfully served by the energy of Jewish women who tend to identify strongly with feminist goals.

Thus, the message emanating from all the separately identifiable groups within the women's movement is largely the same. Each seems to be saying, "Respect where we have come from; recognize our special needs; guard against the negative stereotypes you have learned; and welcome our contributions." Diversity presents challenges that enhance strength as women move toward solving shared and specific problems.

ONCE AGAIN: WHAT WOMEN WANT

The answer to Freud's famous question (still asked by many men with annoyance) "What does a woman want?" is that we want a fair share of everything in an equitable, humane world in which access to resources does not depend on gender, ethnic background, or social position. As Michele Murray (1973) wrote, women want "to cast a shadow . . . [that is] long and . . . rich" (p. 14), and we want men to have an opportunity to do the same. Belva Lockwood, the first woman attorney to plead before the United States Supreme Court and who campaigned for the presidency as nominee of the National Equal Rights party (1884 and 1888), gave this answer in 1897: "I do not believe in sex distinction in literature, law, politics, or trade; or that modesty and virtue are more becoming to women than to men; but wish we had more of it everywhere" (cited in Lerner, 1977, p. 419). Ellen Willis (1981) has articulated the primary feminist objective elegantly and simply: to extend "to women—and to the entire realm of familial and sexual life—the democratic principles of self-determination, equality and the right to the pursuit of happiness" (p. 494). To this end, she argues, we must reject assumptions about "opposing masculine and feminine natures," and that men and women have monopolies on different behaviors or human capacities.

Equality Under the Law

Women want equal opportunities and treatment in employment, education, and all aspects of social and political life; and we support the need for affirmative action to help redress the negative consequences of past discrimination. Women's efforts to achieve equality in the public sphere are symbolized by our work on behalf of the Equal Rights Amendment. This amendment, proposed as the 27th to the United States Constitution, was written by Alice Paul for the National Woman's party, and was first introduced in the Congress in 1923. When it was reintroduced after World War II, it was twice passed by the Senate but the House Judiciary Committee refused to hold hearings on it. In 1967, "a stubborn Paul, then 82, persuaded the National Organization for Women to endorse the amendment" (Toufexis, 1982, p. 32) and the modern campaign began. In 1971, the ERA was finally passed by the House of Representatives, and in 1972, once again by the Senate. Section 1 of the amendment states that "equality of rights under the law shall not be denied or abridged by the United States or by any state on account of sex." Section 2 gives Congress the power to enforce the provisions, and Section 3 specifies that they will take effect two years after ratification.

The effort to ratify the ERA failed despite its approval by more than two thirds of Americans as indicated by national polls, and despite endorsements by Presidents Eisenhower, Kennedy, Johnson, Nixon, Ford, and Carter, and by 450 national, religious, labor, civic, and educational groups "from the AFL-CIO to the Y.M.C.A." (Toufexis, 1982, p. 32). The ERA gained approval from only 35 of the required number of 38 state legislatures, even after the deadline for ratification was extended an additional three years by Congress until June 30, 1982. This failure in the United States contrasts sharply with success in Canada, where in 1981 a new constitution was approved that includes an explicit guarantee of gender equality under the law.

Failure to win approval of the ERA has been a stunning disappointment to the American women's movement and has stimulated reanalysis and reassessment of strategies. Some believe that one lesson to be learned is the importance of direct dialogue with legislators and the necessity of more active participation in the electoral process. Little question exists that

the educational campaign for the Equal Rights Amendment was effective: "Public opinion polls since 1972 consistently favored the amendment, often by wide margins" (Katzenstein, 1984, p. 4), indicating that the majority of Americans of both genders favored its objectives. But one significant problem was that many people did not understand just what the ERA was. Some people who said they disapproved of the ERA indicated by their responses to other questions that they actually supported its aims. Marsha Jacobson (1983), for example, found that college students presented with the actual text of the amendment indicated significantly greater approval of it and fewer negative misconceptions about its meaning and probable consequences than students presented just with the title. Another striking example is provided by a study (Bers & Mezey, 1981) of over 200 women leaders of community organizations in a suburban area outside of Chicago. The researchers found that "although *98 percent* [italics are mine] agree that 'the U.S. and individual states should not deny any person his or her rights on account of the person's sex,' only 50.9 percent agree that the ERA should be ratified" (p. 740). Thus, people may endorse the same words as those in the amendment and not realize that this is in fact the way the ERA is written. Research suggests that women agree significantly in what we want.

Access to Political Leadership

For generations, women have run duplicating machines, stuffed envelopes, made telephone calls, and brewed coffee for male colleagues who ran for political office. Women in the 1980s are emerging more and more from behind the scenes and putting energy and knowledge to use for our own political advantage. Although few women candidates get the financial backing a successful campaign requires, some women have managed to move up front, a phenomenon most dramatically illustrated by the 1984 candidacy of Geraldine Ferraro for Vice President of the United States. This was the first time a woman had been nominated for such high office by a major political party and the first time there was ever a real chance that she could win. (Among Ferraro's predecessors have been Victoria Woodhull and Belva Lockwood of the Equal Rights party, who ran for President in 1872, and 1884, 1888, respectively; Angela Davis and Sonia Johnson, who ran for Vice President on the Communist party and Citizen's party tickets, respectively, in 1984; and Congresswoman

Shirley Chisholm, who was a candidate in 1978 for the Democratic party's presidential nomination.)

A research group at Rutgers University reported that in 1984 20 political action committees whose primary goal was the election of women to political office existed in this country. But such committees are too few to effectively counter the typical denial of funds to women by established sources. As simply put by the political director of the Democratic National Committee, "the three biggest obstacles for women candidates . . . [are] money, money and money" (in "PACs Give Women," 1984, p. A14).

In 1984, although a woman was not elected to the vice presidency, women did win significant political victories. Madeleine Kunin was elected governor of Vermont, joining the only other woman governor, Martha Collins of Kentucky. Arlene Violet of Rhode Island became the first-ever woman state attorney general, and women in Congress did not lose numbers (2 women in the Senate and 23 in the House of Representatives). As of 1985, five lieutenant governors were women, a second woman attorney general had been elected—Mary Sue Terry, in Virginia—and almost 15 percent of all state legislators were women (Gailey, 1985). And in November 1986, the people of Nebraska chose between two women for governor of their state!

Innumerable analyses of the defeat of the Mondale-Ferraro ticket in 1984 have been published. My assessment is in agreement with the conclusions of Maureen Dowd (1984); Ferraro's candidacy was not decisive in determining the outcome of the election, but it "did evoke a backlash of sexist sentiment and crude jokes," while at the same time it resoundingly "shattered stereotypes" and had an enormous influence on "the way women think about themselves and leadership" (p. 44).

A primary current objective of women legislators in Washington (working through the bipartisan Congressional Caucus for Women's Issues that was organized in 1977) is to win passage of the Economic Equity Act (Gamarekian, 1985). This legislation consists of 22 bills on such issues as pay equity, nondiscrimination in insurance, and child care in public housing. Another objective is passage of a bill (mentioned in the chapter on women and work) introduced by Congresswoman Patricia Schroeder of Colorado that mandates parental leave for care of biological or adopted children, thus establishing a national policy on employment guarantees for parents.

An End to Our Exploitation As Sex Objects

The idea that women exist "for the use and appreciation of" men (Greer, 1970) has a strong hold on the consciousness of both genders. It would be a conclusion quickly reached by visitors from another world who examined our advertisements, watched our television, and listened to our popular music. Women are everywhere on display.

To dramatize feminist opposition to the expectation that women's bodies must be enhanced to lure men, women were invited to gather in Atlantic City almost 20 years ago, on September 7, 1968, for a "day-long boardwalk-theatre event" to protest the image of Miss America ("No More Miss America," 1970). The conveners urged those who came to bring with them, for disposal into "a huge Freedom Trash Can," such items as "bras, girdles, curlers, false eyelashes, wigs" and other "such woman-garbage you have around the house" (p. 521). No bras were burned (despite the media headlines), just thrown away as symbols of women's enslavement to standards of sexual attractiveness imposed by men.

Feminists continue to work for changes in media representations of women, and have raised public awareness about pornography and its consequences. Some have used dramatic means to emphasize their message. For example, a group of women and men in Santa Cruz, California, that has grown in number from 4 in 1980 to about 1000 in 1984 has been staging a counter-pageant to that of Miss California (Elizabeth Howard, 1984). Contestants have appeared as "'Miss Used,' 'Miss Informed,' and 'Miss Directed.' One protester, 'Miss Steak,' modeled a 35-pound gown of scalloped bologna and olive loaf with a hot-dog neckline garnished with parsley. 'Judge Meat, not Women,' demonstrators chanted" (p. 24). In 1984, positive images of women were emphasized in a three-day pageant, and the pageant parade was led by a giant sculpture of an Egyptian moon goddess.

Affirmation of Joy and Adventure

Contemporary women are asking for fun, ripping off our ladylike white gloves (if we ever had them) and kicking up our heels. Erica Jong in *Fear of Flying* (1973), for example, wrote lustily about a woman's sexual and spiritual odyssey; and WITCH (1970) called on women to be "groovy, courageous, aggressive, intelligent, nonconformist, explorative, curious, independent, sexually liberated, revolutionary . . . untamed, angry, [and] joyous" (pp. 539f.).

We now read about women like Janet Guthrie who drive race cars, long-distance swimmers like Diana Nyad, marathon winners like Joan Benoit, and sailors like Naomi Jones, who in 1978 broke the previous record set by a man by sailing alone around the world, 30,000 miles, in 272 days. In 1985, and again in 1986, a woman won the Iditarod Trail sled-dog race in Alaska; and two women led a nine-member American expedition up a 26,000-foot mountain in western Nepal. Following Sally Ride, America's first woman in space, in 1983 (20 years after Valentina Tereshkova, the Russian's woman cosmonaut), other women have worked in teams in outer space, and now constitute about ten percent of the American astronaut corps. And the number of examples of women's insistence on being recognized as persons who are challenged by nature, by adventure, and by both intellectual and physical goals continues to increase.

Humane Use of Skills and Power

In a world in which oppression and suffering are realities for a majority of people, women want humane use of skills and power to be valued and cultivated by men as well as by women. A major obstacle to this has been the perception that women have a monopoly on humane behavior. Robin Morgan has noted (1982b) that women have been assigned "the positive values of 'humanism,' pacifism, nurturance, ecoconsciousness, and reverence for life. While these values have been (1) regarded by Man as amusingly irrelevant, and (2) understood by women not to be inherently 'womanly,' they are objectively positive values" (p. 101). These objectively positive values are ones we must teach to our sons as well as to our daughters; they are gender-neutral, and available to any human being.

In the chapter about the behavior of adult women in relation to cultural expectations, we mentioned the position taken by some that women's domain is separate from men's. Recall that Carol Gilligan (1982) has proposed that women are especially concerned with the welfare of others, with connectedness and other interpersonal issues, and are more likely to be guided in our behavior by an assessment of consequences and responsibilities than by abstract principles. It is true that a woman who has acquired humane values and attitudes regarding the social and political significance of her experiences as a woman is likely to reflect these in her work and in her approach to human problems. For example, two women private detectives in San Francisco, who called their agency The People's Eye, were reported to specialize in working for "underdog" clients—poor people, lesbians, and radicals ("Two Women Survive," 1978). Similarly, Eleanor Helin, who discovered a new asteroid that circles the sun once every nine months, named it Ra-Shalom, combining the name of the ancient Egyptian sun god Ra, symbol of enlightenment, with the Hebrew greeting of peace, Shalom ("New Asteroid," 1978). In one study (Merritt, 1982), 51 women municipal legislators from suburban areas and a matched group of comparable men were interviewed. Although no relationship was found between political ambition and gender, the women gave some indications of focusing more on the public interest and less on private advancement than the men, and could be characterized more by a "public serving instrumentality" (p. 1035). Another study compared a group of women managers from 50 organizations with men in similar positions (Josefowitz, 1980) and found the women to be more tolerant and encouraging of interruptions by their staff members. Each of the managers studied was observed carefully on the job, and the women were found to be more likely to have their doors open (literally and figuratively) and to walk out of their offices to talk to their subordinates.

On the other hand, as Carol Gilligan (1982) noted, the "different voice" she was describing "is characterized not by gender but by theme" and is a difference that arises "in a social context." Women are individuals, and as the contingencies influencing our behavior vary, so too do our perspectives, points of view, and subsequent actions and reactions. Linda Kerber (1986) has noted an important lesson we must bear in mind from our recent history when many suffragist feminists argued that once women were given the vote,

> the streets would be clean, child labor would be eliminated, war would be at an end. . . . [While] suffragists were right in expecting that support for peace movements and progressive legislation would come from newly enfranchised women, . . . they were wrong to predict that most women would support a political agenda drawn up from the concerns central to women's sphere. Newly enfranchised women voted as the interests of their race and class dictated. (pp. 308f.)

Thus, Sandra Day O'Connor, our first woman justice of the Supreme Court, shared the conclusions of conservative Justice William Rehnquist in 123 of the 137 cases she participated in during her first year on the bench, and

> of the 29 cases that sharply divided the Court—those 5-4 opinions that are taken by the press as ideological barometers with Rehnquist as a benchmark conservative and William Brennan as a benchmark liberal—she voted with Rehnquist in 26, with Brennan in three. (Kerr, 1982, p. 52)

I have noted elsewhere (Lott, 1985) that

> to know, for example, that Phyllis Schlafly, Margaret Thatcher, Shirley Chisholm, and Kate Millett are all women will permit reliable prediction of only some behavior. . . . Can we predict that each of these women is similar in her concern for relationships, caring, harmony, and responsibility? My guess is that we could more easily match Thatcher and Chisholm, for example, to two different men than to each other on values, interests, beliefs, and moral position. (pp. 161f.)

And while Betty Friedan (1985) has urged feminists to "affirm the differences between men and women" and to make salient in every discipline and profession the "values based on female sensitivities to life" (p. 106), she has also noted that more and more men are admitting vulnerabilities, sharing in the care of their children, and "learning to express their tenderness" (p. 106), and that women are probably not more peace-loving than men.

What is called "women's culture" or women's "different voice" is associated with particular kinds of experiences, situations, and demands, as well as with inequality in women's and men's access to social resources. If we want a more humane world, we need to provide the appropriate conditions for both genders to learn empathy, cooperation, and caring.

The Promise Fulfilled

These are not easy times for women. Many aspire to meet impossible goals without societal supports: to be perfect mothers, wives, and responsible, successful workers, while also keeping slim, attractive, exercised, healthy, and calm. Crescent Dragonwagon (1985) has satirized these expectations in describing "Today's Woman" as

> a nurturing mother who works by day, goes to law school by night, lifts weights, works hard at your marriage, and makes tortellini with fresh basil. You're equally at home in pinstripes, decolletage, and sweats, and you weigh less than you did at 12. (p. 158)

This image is a tragicomic distortion of a postfeminist future. Only a robot can blithely and confidently vacuum the rugs, go hiking with her children or friends, visit museums, pick wildflowers, work for political candidates, listen to music, repair automobiles, do the food shopping, and hold down a full-time job without assistance.

I prefer a different image of a feminist utopia, one outlined by Jane Flax (1981) that is characterized by (a) equal sharing and valuing by women and men of all socially useful work ("caring for people and interpersonal relationships, beautifying personal environments, raising children and maintaining daily life" [p. 131]); (b) redistribution of all socially necessary work (such as science, engineering, medicine, and trade) among all groups; (c) dissolution of the division between private and public work; and (d) equitable rewards for all those who participate in doing work of benefit to the human society. Such objectives are reachable and worth working for. It is in such a society that women can realize the full promise of our humanity.

Thus, this book ends with the same promise with which it began. Sojourner Truth knew that having plowed and planted, having worked in the fields and borne the lash, made her no less a woman than one whose hands bore rings, whose face was powdered, or who sewed, cooked, and tended only her own children. This book has traced the general life experiences of contemporary women as we continue to learn how to behave in accordance with our culture's definition of our character and role. We have seen that the traditional definition does an injustice to our possibilities. Let us move toward a new definition and assert that to be a woman is to be a biological complement to man, and to share with him equally a repertoire of behavior and motives bounded only by time, circumstance, and physical limitation, but not by imagination, self-esteem, or power.

References

A look at abortion laws around the world. (1981, May 20). *Providence Evening Bulletin.*

A man-sized resistance to housework. (1981, February 5). *Providence Evening Bulletin.*

A positive approach helps. (1979, April 27). *Journal of the American Medical Association, 241,* 1763.

Abbey, Antonia. (1982). Sex differences in attributions for friendly behavior: Do males misperceive females' friendliness? *Journal of Personality and Social Psychology, 42,* 830–838.

Abplanalp, Judith M. (1983). Premenstrual syndrome: A selective review. In S. Golub (Ed.), *Lifting the curse of menstruation* (pp. 107–123). New York: Haworth.

Abramowitz, Christine V., & Dokecki, Paul R. (1977). The politics of clinical judgment. *Psychological Bulletin, 84,* 460–476.

Abu-Laban, Sharon M. (1981). Women and aging: A futurist perspective. *Psychology of Women Quarterly, 6,* 85–98.

Acock, Alan C., & Ireland, Nancy K. (1983). Attribution of blame in rape cases: The impact of norm violation, gender, and sex-role attitude. *Sex Roles, 9,* 179–193.

Adams, Carol H., & Sherer, Mark. (1985). Sex-role orientation and psychological adjustment: Implications for the masculinity model. *Sex Roles, 12,* 1211–1218.

Adams, Jerome. (1984). Women at West Point: A three-year perspective. *Sex Roles, 11,* 525–541.

Adams, Kathrynn A. (1980). Who has the final word? Sex, race, and dominance behavior. *Journal of Personality and Social Psychology, 38,* 1–8.

Adler, Nancy E. (1979). Abortion: A social-psychological perspective. *Journal of Social Issues, 35*(1), 100–119.

Admissions Testing Program. (1984). *National college-bound seniors, 1984.* Princeton, NJ: College Entrance Examination Board.

AFDC cuts hurt. (1984, Spring/Summer). *ISR Newsletter,* p. 3. (Institute for Social Research, University of Michigan, Ann Arbor)

Affirmative action and employment. Top college officials are still predominantly white males. (1978a, March). *Project on the Status and Education of Women, 19.* (Association of American Colleges, Washington, DC)

Agonito, Rosemary. (1977). *History of ideas on women.* New York: Capricorn.

Alagna, Sheryle W. (1982). Sex role identity, peer evaluation of competition, and the responses of women and men in a competitive situation. *Journal of Personality and Social Psychology, 43,* 546–554.

Albin, Rochelle S. (1979). Women and *Science* editorials. *Science, 203,* 227–228.

Alston, Doris N., & Rose, Natalie. (1981). Perceptions of middle-aged black women. *Journal of General Psychology, 104,* 167–171.

Alta. (1973). penus envy, they call it. In F. Howe & E. Bass (Eds.), *No more masks! An anthology of poems by women* (p. 295). New York: Anchor.

Altman, Sydney I., & Grossman, Frances K. (1977). Women's career plans and maternal employment. *Psychology of Women Quarterly, 1,* 365–376.

Amaro, Hortensia. (1986, April 14). *A profile of Hispanic women in the United States: Health and mental health needs.* Paper read at University of Rhode Island, Kingston.

American Psychiatric Association. (1980). *Diagnostic and statistical manual of mental disorders* (3rd ed.). Washington, DC: Author.

Amstey, Frederica H., & Whitbourne, Susan K. (1981). Continuing education, identity, sex role, and psychosocial development in adult women. *Sex Roles, 7,* 49–58.

Anderson, Sandra C. (1980). Patterns of sex-role identification in alcoholic women. *Sex Roles, 6,* 231–243.

Anderson, Sandra C. (1984). Alcoholic women: Sex-role identification and perceptions of parental personality characteristics. *Sex Roles, 11,* 277–287.

Andrisani, Paul J. (1978). Job satisfaction among working women. *Signs, 3,* 588–607.

Angelou, Maya. (1971). *I know why the caged bird sings.* New York: Bantam.

Antill, John K. (1983). Sex role complementarity versus similarity in married couples. *Journal of Personality and Social Psychology, 45,* 145–155.

Anyan, Walter J. Jr., & Quillan, Warren W. II. (1971). The naming of primary colors by children. *Child Development, 42,* 1629–1632.

Archer, Cynthia J. (1984). Children's attitudes toward sex-role division in adult occupational roles. *Sex Roles, 10,* 1−10.

Archer, Dane, Iritani, Bonita, Kimes, Debra D., & Barrios, Michael. (1983). Face-ism: Five studies of sex differences in facial prominence. *Journal of Personality and Social Psychology, 45,* 725−735.

Ardener, Shirley. (1977). *Perceiving women.* New York: Halsted.

Aries, Elizabeth J., & Johnson, Fern L. (1983). Close friendship in adulthood: Conversational content between same-sex friends. *Sex Roles, 9,* 1183−1196.

Arms, Suzanne. (1977). *Immaculate deception.* New York: Bantam.

Armstrong, Louise. (1978). *Kiss daddy goodnight: A speak-out on incest.* New York: Hawthorn.

Arnow, Harriette. (1954). *The dollmaker.* New York: Avon.

Aronoff, Joel, & Crano, William D. (1975). A re-examination of the cross-cultural principles of task segregation and sex role differentiation in the family. *American Sociological Review, 40,* 12−20.

Arvey, Richard D. (1979). Unfair discrimination in the employment interview: Legal and psychological aspects. *Psychological Bulletin, 86,* 736−765.

Ashton, Eleanor. (1983). Measures of play behavior: The influence of sex-role stereotyped children's books. *Sex Roles, 9,* 43−47.

Asso, Doreen, & Beech, H. R. (1975). Susceptibility to the acquisition of a conditioned response in relation to the menstrual cycle. *Journal of Psychosomatic Research, 19,* 337−344.

Astin, Alexander W. (1977). *Four critical years.* San Francisco: Jossey-Bass.

Astin, Helen S. (1978, March). *Women and achievement: Occupational entry and persistence.* Paper presented at the meeting of the Eastern Psychological Association, Washington, DC.

Athamasion, Robert, Shaver, Phillip, & Tavris, Carol. (1970, July). Sex. *Psychology Today,* pp. 39−52.

Atkinson, Jean M. (1982). Anthropology. *Signs, 8,* 236−258.

Atkinson, Jean, & Huston, Ted L. (1984). Sex role orientation and division of labor early in marriage. *Journal of Personality and Social Psychology, 46,* 330−345.

Attanucci, Jane S. (1982, March). *"How would you describe yourself to yourself?" Mothers of infants reply.* Unpublished paper, Harvard Graduate School of Education, Cambridge, MA.

Atwood, Margaret. (1984). *Bluebeard's egg.* Toronto: Seal.

Bachtold, Louise M. (1976). Personality characteristics of women of distinction. *Psychology of Women Quarterly, 1,* 70−78.

Badenhoop, M. Suzanne, & Johansen, M. Kelly. (1980). Do reentry women have special needs? *Psychology of Women Quarterly, 4,* 591−595.

Baker, A. Harvey, Mishara, Brian L., Kostin, Irene W., & Parker, Laurence. (1979). Menstrual cycle affects kinaesthetic aftereffect, an index of personality and perceptual style. *Journal of Personality and Social Psychology, 37,* 234−246.

Baker, Susan W. (1980). Biological influences on human sex and gender. *Signs, 6,* 80−96.

Bakst, M. Charles. (1984, June 7). Walsh pledges to ease restrictions on abortion. *Providence Evening Bulletin.*

Baldwin, Robert O. (1984). Stability of masculinity-femininity scores over an eleven-year period. *Sex Roles, 10,* 251−260.

Ballmer, Helene, & Cozby, Paul C. (1981). Family environments of women who return to college. *Sex Roles, 7,* 1019−1026.

Balswick, Jack, & Ingoldsby, Bron. (1982). Heroes and heroines among American adolescents. *Sex Roles, 8,* 243−249.

Bambara, Toni C. (1974). Commentary: Sexuality of black women. In L. Gross (Ed.), *Sexual behavior: Current issues* (pp. 39−42). Flushing, NY: Spectrum.

Ban on homosexuals eased. (1979, August 19). *New York Times.*

Ban, Peggy L., & Lewis, Michael. (1974). Mothers and fathers, girls and boys; attachment behavior in the one-year-old. *Merrill-Palmer Quarterly, 20,* 195−204.

Bandura, Albert. (1982). Self-efficacy mechanism in human agency. *American Psychologist, 37,* 122−147.

Bandura, Albert, & Schunk, Dale H. (1981). Cultivating competence, self-efficacy, and intrinsic interest through proximal self-motivation. *Journal of Personality and Social Psychology, 41,* 586−598.

Banikiotes, F. G., Montgomery, A. A., & Banikiotes, P. G. (1972). Male and female auditory reinforcement of infant vocalizations. *Developmental Psychology, 6,* 476−481.

Barb. (1984, May 28). Victim blames libbers [Letter to Good Neighbors column]. *Providence Evening Bulletin,* p. A-16.

Barclay, Dolores. (1978, August 3). Gay parents struggle for child custody. *Providence Evening Bulletin.*

Barclay, Dolores. (1984, April 2). Women in prison—The numbers are increasing. *Providence Evening Bulletin,* pp. A-1, A-6.

Bardwick, Judith M., & Douvan, Elizabeth. (1972). Ambivalence: The socialization of women. In J. M. Bardwick (Ed.), *Readings on the psychology of women* (pp. 52−58). New York: Harper & Row.

Barker, Pat. (1983). *Union street.* New York: Putnam.

Barker, Pat. (1985). *Blow your house down.* New York: Putnam.

Barnes, Michael L., & Buss, David M. (1985). Sex differences in the interpersonal behavior of married couples. *Journal of Personality and Social Psychology, 48,* 654−661.

Barnett, Mark A. (1978, September). *Situational influences and sex differences in children's reward allocation behavior.* Paper presented at the meeting of the American Psychological Association, Toronto.

Barnett, Mark A., Howard, Jeffrey A., King, Laura M., & Dino, Geri A. (1980). Antecedents of empathy: Retrospective accounts of early socialization. *Personality and Social Psychology Bulletin, 6,* 361−365.

Barnett, Rosalind C. (1981). Parental sex-role attitudes and child-rearing values. *Sex Roles, 7,* 837−846.

Barnett, Rosalind C., & Baruch, Grace K. (1978). Women in the middle years: A critique of research and theory. *Psychology of Women Quarterly, 3,* 187–197.

Barnett, Rosalind C., & Baruch, Grace K. (1983, August). *Determinants of fathers' participation in family work.* Paper presented at the meeting of the American Psychological Association, Anaheim, CA.

Barnett, Rosalind C., & Baruch, Grace K. (1985). Women's involvement in multiple roles and psychological distress. *Journal of Personality and Social Psychology, 49,* 135–145.

Barrett, Carol J. (1977). Women in widowhood. *Signs, 2,* 856–868.

Barrett, Carol J. (1981). Intimacy in widowhood. *Psychology of Women Quarterly, 5,* 473–487.

Barrett, David E. (1979). A naturalistic study of sex differences in children's aggression. *Merrill-Palmer Quarterly, 25,* 193–204.

Barrett, Karen. (1982, September). Date rape: A campus epidemic? *Ms,* pp. 48–51, 130.

Barry, Herbert III, Bacon, Margaret K., & Child, Irvin L. (1957). A cross-cultural survey of some sex differences in socialization. *Journal of Abnormal and Social Psychology, 55,* 327–332.

Barry, Kathleen. (1979). *Female sexual slavery.* Englewood Cliffs, NJ: Prentice-Hall.

Bart, Pauline B. (1971). Depression in middle-aged women. In V. Gornick & B. K. Moran (Eds.), *Woman in sexist society* (pp. 99–117). New York: Basic Books.

Bart, Pauline B., & O'Brien, Patricia H. (1984). Stopping rape: Effective avoidance strategies. *Signs, 10,* 83–101.

Bart, Pauline B., & Scully, Diana H. (1979). The politics of hysteria: The case of the wandering womb. In E. S. Gomberg & V. Franks (Eds.), *Gender and disordered behavior* (pp. 354–380). New York: Brunner/Mazel.

Bar-Tal, Daniel, & Saxe, Leonard. (1976). Physical attractiveness and its relationship to sex-role stereotyping. *Sex Roles, 2,* 123–133.

Barth, Ramona. (1976). *Why we burn: A feminist exercise in exorcism.* Pittsburgh, PA: KNOW, Inc.

Bartlett, Kay. (1981, April 4). Out of the eye of the beholder and into the courtroom. *Providence Journal,* p. E-3.

Bartlett, Kay. (1982, April 4). Sexual harassment may be the 'cause' of the 1980s. *Providence Sunday Journal,* p. E-3.

Baruch, Grace K. (1976). Girls who perceive themselves as competent: Some antecedents and correlates. *Psychology of Women Quarterly, 1,* 38–49.

Baruch, Grace K., & Barnett, Rosalind C. (1981). Fathers' participation in the care of their preschool children. *Sex Roles, 7,* 1043–1055.

Baruch, Grace K., & Barnett, Rosalind C. (1983). Adult daughters' relationships with their mothers. *Journal of Marriage and the Family, 45,* 601–606.

Baruch, Grace K., & Barnett, Rosalind C. (1985a). *Consequences of fathers' participation in family work: Parents' role-strain and well-being.* Unpublished paper, Wellesley College, Center for Research on Women, Wellesley, MA.

Baruch, Grace K., & Barnett, Rosalind C. (1985b). *Role quality, multiple role involvement and psychological well-being in midlife women.* Unpublished paper, Wellesley College, Center for Research on Women, Wellesley, MA.

Baruch, Grace K., Barnett, Rosalind C., & Rivers, Caryl. (1983). *Life prints: New patterns of love and work for today's women.* New York: McGraw-Hill.

Bates, John E., Bentler, P. M., & Thompson, Spencer K. (1973). Measurement of deviant gender development in boys. *Child Development, 44,* 591–598.

Baum, Charlotte, Hyman, Paula, & Michel, Sonya. (1975). *The Jewish woman in America.* New York: New American Library.

Baum, L. Frank. (1956). *The wizard of Oz.* New York: Grosset & Dunlap.

Baumrind, Diana. (1971). Current patterns of parental authority. *Developmental Psychology Monograph, 4*(2).

Baumrind, Diana. (1980). New directions in socialization research. *American Psychologist, 35,* 639–652.

Baumrind, Diana. (1981). Clarification concerning birthrate among teenagers. *American Psychologist, 36,* 528–530.

Beach, Frank. (1969, July). It's all in your mind. *Psychology Today,* pp. 33–35, 60.

Beck, Evelyn T. (1983). The motherhood that dare not speak its name. *Women's Studies Quarterly, 11*(4), 8–11.

Beck, Joan. (1983, October 8). When greater risk is no risk at all. *Providence Evening Bulletin.*

Beck, Joan. (1984, July 17). Message to all-male civic groups. *Providence Evening Bulletin.*

Becker, Judith V., & Abel, Gene G. (1978). Men and the victimization of women. In J. R. Chapman & M. Gates (Eds.), *The victimization of women* (pp. 29–52). Beverly Hills, CA: Sage.

Beckman, Linda J. (1978). The relative rewards and costs of parenthood and employment for employed women. *Psychology of Women Quarterly, 2,* 215–234.

Beckman, Linda J. (1981). Effects of social interaction and children's relative inputs on older women's psychological well-being. *Journal of Personality and Social Psychology, 41,* 1075–1086.

Bee, Helen L., Mitchell, Sandra K., Barnard, Kathryn E., Eyves, Sandra J., & Hammond, Mary A. (1984). Predicting intellectual outcomes: Sex differences in response to early environmental stimulation. *Sex Roles, 10,* 783–803.

Bell, Carolyn S. (1984, September). After equal pay, equal worth. *The Women's Review of Books,* pp. 17–18.

Bell, Nancy J., & Carver, William. (1980). A reevaluation of gender label effects: Expectant mothers' responses to infants. *Child Development, 51,* 925–927.

Bellinger, David C., & Gleason, Jean B. (1982). Sex differences in parental directives to young children. *Sex Roles, 8,* 1123–1139.

Bem, Sandra L. (1974). The measurement of psychological androgyny. *Journal of Consulting and Clinical Psychology, 42,* 155–162.

Bem, Sandra L. (1978). *The short Bem Sex Role Inventory.* Palo Alto, CA: Consulting Psychologists Press.

Bem, Sandra L. (1981). Gender schema theory: A cognitive account of sex typing. *Psychological Review, 88,* 354–364.

Bem, Sandra L. (1983). Gender schema theory and its implications for child development: Raising gender-aschematic children in a gender-schematic society. *Signs, 8,* 598–616.

Bem, Sandra L. (1985). Androgyny and gender schema theory: A conceptual and empirical integration. In T. B. Sonderegger (Ed.), *Nebraska symposium on motivation 1984: Psychology and gender* (Vol. 32) (pp. 179–226). Lincoln: University of Nebraska Press.

Benbow, Camilla P., & Stanley, Julian. (1980). Sex differences in mathematical ability: Fact or artifact? *Science, 210,* 1261–1264.

Beneke, Timothy. (1982, July). Men talk about rape. *Mother Jones,* pp. 13–16, 20–23.

Berg-Cross, Linda, Berg-Cross, Gary, & McGeehan, Deborah. (1979). Experience and personality differences among breast- and bottle-feeding mothers. *Psychology of Women Quarterly, 3,* 344–356.

Berger, Phil. (1984, July 19). The new comediennes. *New York Times Magazine,* pp. 26–29, 32, 38, 51.

Berman, Phyllis W. (1980). Are women more responsive than men to the young? A review of developmental and situational variables. *Psychological Bulletin, 88,* 668–695.

Berman, Phyllis W., & Smith, Vicki L. (1984). Gender and situational differences in children's smiles, touch, and proxemics. *Sex Roles, 10,* 347–355.

Bernard, Jessie (with Dorothy Lee, Claude, & David). (1978). *Self-portrait of a family.* Boston: Beacon.

Bernard, Jessie (with Dorothy Lee, Claude, & David). (1978). *Self-portrait of a family.* Boston, MA: Beacon.

Berryman-Fink, Cynthia, & Verderber, Kathleen S. (1985). Attributions of the term *feminist:* A factor analytic development of a measuring instrument. *Psychology of Women Quarterly, 9,* 51–64.

Bers, Trudy H., & Mezey, Susan G. (1981). Support for feminist goals among leaders of women's community groups. *Signs, 6,* 737–748.

Berscheid, Ellen, & Walster, Elaine H. (1978). *Interpersonal attraction.* Reading, MA: Addison-Wesley.

Bersoff, David, & Crosby, Faye. (1984). Job satisfaction and family status. *Personality and Social Psychology Bulletin, 10,* 79–83.

Berzins, Juris I., Welling, M. A., & Wetter, Robert E. (1978). A new measure of psychological androgyny based on the Personality Research Form. *Journal of Consulting and Clinical Psychology, 46,* 126–138.

Beyond the myths. (1983). New York: Center on Social Welfare Policy and Law.

Biaggio, Mary Kay, Mohan, Philip J., & Baldwin, Cynthia. (1985). Relationships among attitudes toward children, women's liberation, and personality characteristics. *Sex Roles, 12,* 47–62.

Bianco, Dorothy. (1984). Adolescent female drug abusers and their families: Some variables associated with successful treatment outcome. *Dissertation Abstracts International, 45B,* 1005. (University Microfilms No. 03)

Biber, Henry, Miller, Louise B., & Dyer, J. L. (1972). Feminization in preschool. *Developmental Psychology, 7,* 86.

Birnbaum, Dana W., & Chemelski, Bruce E. (1984). Preschoolers' inferences about gender and emotion: The mediation of emotionality stereotypes. *Sex Roles, 10,* 505–511.

Birnbaum, Dana W., & Croll, William L. (1984). The etiology of children's stereotypes about sex differences in emotionality. *Sex Roles, 10,* 677–691.

Birnbaum, Dana W., Nosanchuk, T. A., & Croll, W. L. (1980). Children's stereotypes about sex differences in emotionality. *Sex Roles, 6,* 435–443.

Birns, Beverly. (1976). The emergence and socialization of sex differences in the earliest years. *Merrill-Palmer Quarterly, 22,* 229–254.

Bjornson, Edith. (1984, March/April). Sex after hysterectomy-oopherectomy: An old wives' tale revisited. *Network News,* pp. 5, 15.

Black, Sionag M., & Hill, Clara E. (1984). The psychological well-being of women in their middle years. *Psychology of Women Quarterly, 8,* 282–292.

Blakely, Mary Kay. (1985, April). Is one woman's sexuality another's pornography? *Ms,* pp. 37–47, 120–123.

Blakeslee, Sandra. (1985, March 24). Doctors debate surgery's place in the maternity ward. *New York Times,* p. E-24.

Bleier, Ruth. (1984). *Science and gender: A critique of biology and its theories on women.* New York: Pergamon.

Block, Jeanne H. (1976). Debatable conclusions about sex differences. *Contemporary Psychology, 21,* 517–522.

Blumstein, Philip, & Schwartz, Pepper. (1977). Bisexuality: Some psychological issues. *Journal of Social Issues, 33*(2), 30–45.

Blumstein, Philip, & Schwartz, Pepper. (1983). *American couples: Money, work, sex.* New York: Morrow.

Bolotin, Susan. (1982, October 17). Voices from the post-feminist generation. *New York Times Magazine,* pp. 28–31, 103–107, 114–117.

Booth, Alan, & Edwards, John N. (1980). Fathers: The invisible parent. *Sex Roles, 6,* 445–456.

Borgida, Eugene, Oksner, Phyllis, & Tomkins, Alan. (1978, August). *Perception of rape victims: The impact of evidentiary reform.* Paper presented at the meeting of the American Psychological Association, Toronto.

Borys, Shelley, & Perlman, Daniel. (1985). Gender differences in loneliness. *Personality and Social Psychology Bulletin, 11,* 63–74.

Bouchard, Thomas J. Jr., & McGee, Mark G. (1977). Sex differences in human spatial ability: Not an X-linked recessive gene effect. *Social Biology, 24,* 332–335.

Boyd, Gerald M. (1984, January 17). Black women's gains present political puzzle. *New York Times.*

Brabant, Sarah. (1976). Sex role stereotyping in the Sunday comics. *Sex Roles, 2,* 331–337.

Brabant, Sarah, & Mooney, Linda. (1986). Sex role stereotyping in the Sunday comics: Ten years later. *Sex Roles, 14,* 141–148.

Brabeck, Mary. (1983). Moral judgment: Theory and research on differences between males and females. *Developmental Review, 3,* 274–291.

Brackbill, Yvonne, & Schroder, Kerri. (1980). Circumcision, gender differences, and neonatal behavior: An update. *Developmental Psychology, 13*, 607–614.

Brady, Katherine. (1979). *Father's days.* New York: Dell.

Bram, Susan. (1978). Through the looking glass: Voluntary childlessness as a mirror of contemporary changes in the meaning of parenthood. In W. B. Miller & L. F. Newman (Eds.), *The first child and family formation* (pp. 368–391). Chapel Hill: Carolina Population Center, University of North Carolina at Chapel Hill.

Bram, Susan. (1984). Voluntarily childless women: Traditional or nontraditional? *Sex Roles, 10*, 195–206.

Brasher, Philip. (1983, January 21). Jane Roe: Battle was still worth it. *Providence Evening Bulletin.*

Breastfeeding back in style. (1985, December 26). *Providence Evening Bulletin*, p. B-4.

Brehm, Sharon S., & Weinraub, Marsha. (1977). Physical barriers and psychological reactance: Two-year-olds' responses to threats to freedom. *Journal of Personality and Social Psychology, 35*, 830–836.

Breines, Wini, & Gordon, Linda. (1983). The new scholarship on family violence. *Signs, 8*, 490–531.

Brickman, Edith, & Beckwith, Jonathan. (1982, March 14). Letters. *New York Times.*

Bridgwater, Carol A. (1983, November). Sex and the prestigious job. *Psychology Today*, p. 74.

Bridgwater, Carol A. (1984, February). Dedicated female managers. *Psychology Today*, p. 17.

Briscoe, Anne M. (1978). Hormones and gender. In E. Tobach & B. Rosoff (Eds.), *Genes and gender. I* (pp. 31–50). New York: Gordian Press.

Brodsky, Annette M. (1980). A decade of feminist influence on psychotherapy. *Psychology of Women Quarterly, 4*, 331–344.

Brody, Jane E. (1981, January 21). Personal health. *New York Times.*

Brody, Jane E. (1983a, May 11). Personal health. *New York Times*, p. C-6.

Brody, Jane E. (1983b, October 17). Research on easy-to-use male contraceptive lags. *Providence Evening Bulletin.*

Brody, Leslie R. (1984). Sex and age variations in the quality and intensity of children's emotional attributions to hypothetical situations. *Sex Roles, 11*, 51–59.

Broner, E. M. (1978). *A weave of women.* New York: Holt, Rinehart & Winston.

Brooks, Virginia R. (1982). Sex differences in student dominance behavior in female and male professors' classrooms. *Sex Roles, 8*, 683–690.

Brooks-Gunn, Jeanne. (1986). The relationship of maternal beliefs about sex typing to maternal and young children's behavior. *Sex Roles, 14*, 21–35.

Brooks-Gunn, Jeanne, & Fisch, Melanie. (1980). Psychological androgyny and college students' judgments of mental health. *Sex Roles, 6*, 575–580.

Brooks-Gunn, Jeanne, & Lewis, Michael. (1979). Effects of age and sex on infants' playroom behavior. *Journal of Genetic Psychology, 134*, 99–105.

Brooks-Gunn, Jeanne, & Ruble, Diane N. (1983). Dys-

menorrhea in adolescence. In S. Golub (Ed.), *Menarche* (pp. 251–261). Boston, MA: Lexington Books.

Broverman, Inge K., Broverman, Donald M., Clarkson, Frank E., Rosenkrantz, Paul S., & Vogel, Susan R. (1970). Sex-role stereotypes and clinical judgments of mental health. *Journal of Consulting Psychology, 34*, 1–7.

Broverman, Inge K., Vogel, Susan R., Broverman, Donald M., Clarkson, Frank E., & Rosenkrantz, Paul S. (1972). Sex-role stereotypes: A current appraisal. *Journal of Social Issues, 28*(2), 59–78.

Brown, Linda K. (1979). Women and business management. *Signs, 5*, 266–288.

Brown Project. (1980, April). *Men and women learning together: A study of college students in the late 70's.* Providence, RI: Office of the Provost, Brown University.

Brown, Rita Mae. (1973). *Rubyfruit jungle.* New York: Bantam.

Brown, Rosellen. (1976). *The autobiography of my mother.* Garden City, NJ: Doubleday.

Brown, Rosellen. (1984). *Civil wars.* New York: Knopf.

Brown-Collins, Alice R., & Sussewell, Deborah R. (1985). *Afro-American woman's emerging selves: A historical and theoretical model of self-concept.* Unpublished paper, Brown University, Providence, RI.

Browne, Angela, & Finkelhor, David. (1986). Impact of child sexual abuse: A review of the research. *Psychological Bulletin, 99*, 66–77.

Brownmiller, Susan. (1975). *Against our will: Men, women and rape.* New York: Simon & Schuster.

Brownmiller, Susan. (1984). *Femininity.* New York: Linden Press.

Brozan, Nadine. (1983, January 12). Hot flashes are topic for research and group therapy. *New York Times*, pp. C1, C14.

Brozan, Nadine. (1985, February 18). Women and cocaine: A growing problem. *New York Times*, p. C18.

Bruer, John T. (1983). Women in science: Lack of full participation. *Science, 221*, 1339.

Bryan, Janice W., & Luria, Zella. (1978). Sex-role learning: A test of the selective attention hypothesis. *Child Development, 49*, 13–23.

Bryant, Fred B., & Veroff, Joseph. (1982). The structure of psychological well-being: A sociohistorical analysis. *Journal of Personality and Social Psychology, 43*, 653–673.

Bryden, M. P. (1979). Evidence for sex-related differences in cerebral organization. In M. A. Wittig & A. C. Petersen (Eds.), *Sex-related differences in cognitive functioning* (pp. 121–143). New York: Academic Press.

Bryson, Rebecca B., Bryson, Jeff B., Licht, Mark H., & Licht, Barbara G. (1976). The professional pair: Husband and wife psychologists. *American Psychologist, 31*, 10–16.

Budoff, Penny W. (1982). Zomepirac sodium in the treatment of primary dysmenorrhea syndrome. *New England Journal of Medicine, 307*, 714–719.

Budoff, Penny W. (1983). *No more hot flashes and other good news.* New York: Putnam.

Buehler, James W., Kaunitz, A. M., Hogue, C. J. R., Hughes, J. M., Smith, J. C., & Rochat, R. W. (1986,

January). Maternal mortality in women aged 35 years or older. *Journal of the American Medical Association, 255,* 53–57.

Bullough, Bonnie. (1974). Some questions about the past and the future. In V. Bullough, *The subordinate sex: A history of attitudes toward women* (pp. 335–354). New York: Penguin.

Bullough, Vern L. (1974). *The subordinate sex: A history of attitudes toward women.* New York: Penguin.

Bullough, Vern L. (1983). Menarche and teenage pregnancy: A misuse of historical data. In S. Golub (Ed.), *Menarche* (pp. 187–193). Boston: Lexington Books.

Burgess, Ann W., & Holmstrom, Lynda L. (1976). Rape: Its effect on task performance at varying stages in the life cycle. In M. J. Walker & S. L. Brodsky (Eds.), *Sexual assault* (pp. 23–33). Lexington, MA: Heath.

Burlew, Ann K. (1982). The experiences of black females in traditional and nontraditional professions. *Psychology of Women Quarterly, 6,* 312–326.

Burt, Martha R. (1980). Cultural myths and supports for rape. *Journal of Personality and Social Psychology, 38,* 217–230.

Burt, Martha R., & Estep, Rhoda E. (1981). Apprehension and fear: Learning a sense of sexual vulnerability. *Sex Roles, 7,* 511–522.

Bush, Sherida. (1976, May). Day care is as good as home care. *Psychology Today,* pp. 36–37.

Buss, David M. (1981). Sex differences in the evaluation and performance of dominant acts. *Journal of Personality and Social Psychology, 40,* 147–154.

Bussey, Kay, & Bandura, Albert. (1984). Influence of gender constancy and social power on sex-linked modeling. *Journal of Personality and Social Psychology, 47,* 1292–1302.

Bussey, Kay, & Perry, David G. (1982). Same-sex imitation: The avoidance of cross-sex models or the acceptance of same-sex models? *Sex Roles, 8,* 773–784.

Busy women are healthier. (1985, February 20). *Providence Evening Bulletin,* pp. A-1f.

Butler, Matilda, & Paisley, William. (1977). Status of professional couples in psychology. *Psychology of Women Quarterly, 1,* 307–318.

Butterfield, Fox. (1986, July 13). The class of '61 offers some dissertations on itself. *New York Times,* p. E30.

Byrne, Donn, & Lamberth, John. (1971). The effect of erotic stimuli on sex arousal, evaluative responses, and subsequent behavior. In *Technical report of the Commission on Obscenity and Pornography* (Vol. 8). Washington, DC: U.S. Government Printing Office.

Cahill, Spencer E. (1983). Reexamining the acquisition of sex roles: A social interactionist approach. *Sex Roles, 9,* 1–15.

Cain, Barbara S. (1982, December 19). Plight of the gray divorcee. *New York Times Magazine,* pp. 89–95.

Caine, Lynn. (1974). *Widow.* New York: Morrow.

Caine, Lynn. (1985). *What did I do wrong? Mothers, children, guilt.* New York: Arbor House.

Caldwell, Mayta A., & Peplau, Letitia A. (1982). Sex differences in same-sex friendship. *Sex Roles, 8,* 721–732.

Caldwell, Mayta A., & Peplau, Letitia A. (1984). The bal-ance of power in lesbian relationships. *Sex Roles, 10,* 587–599.

Callahan-Levy, Charlene M., & Messé, Lawrence A. (1979). Sex differences in the allocation of pay. *Journal of Personality and Social Psychology, 37,* 433–446.

Calway-Fagen, Norma, Wallston, Barbara S., & Gabel, Harris. (1979). The relationship between attitudinal and behavioral measures of sex preferences. *Psychology of Women Quarterly, 4,* 274–280.

Campbell, Anne. (1984). *Girls in the gang.* New York: Basil Blackwell.

Cann, Arnie, & Haight, Jeanne M. (1983). Children's perceptions of relative competence in sex-typed occupations. *Sex Roles, 9,* 767–773.

Canter, Rachelle J., & Ageton, Suzanne S. (1984). The epidemiology of adolescent sex-role attitudes. *Sex Roles, 11,* 657–676.

Canter, Rachelle J., & Meyerowitz, Beth E. (1984). Sex-role stereotypes: Self-reports of behavior. *Sex Roles, 10,* 293–306.

Cantor, Aviva. (1976, Fall). The Lilith question. *Lilith,* pp. 5–10, 38.

Caplan, Paula J. (1977). Sex, age, behavior, and school subject as determinants of report of learning problems. *Journal of Learning Disabilities, 10,* 60–62.

Caplan, Paula J. (1979). Beyond the box score: A boundary condition for sex differences in aggression and achievement striving. In Maher, B. A. (Ed.), *Progress in experimental personality research* (Vol. 9) (pp. 42–87). New York: Academic Press.

Caplan, Paula J. (1984). The myth of women's masochism. *American Psychologist, 39,* 130–139.

Cardell, Mona, Finn, Stephen, & Marecek, Jeanne. (1981). Sex-role identity, sex-role behavior, and satisfaction in heterosexual, lesbian, and gay male couples. *Psychology of Women Quarterly, 5,* 488–494.

Career before fun for women execs? (1983, February 15). *Providence Evening Bulletin.*

Carlson, Rae. (1972). Understanding women: Implications for personality theory and research. *Journal of Social Issues, 28,* 17–32.

Carman, Roderick S., Fitzgerald, B. J., & Holmgren, Charles. (1983). Alienation and drinking motivations among adolescent females. *Journal of Personality and Social Psychology, 44,* 1021–1024.

Carmen, Arlene, & Moody, Howard. (1985). *Working women: The subterranean world of street prostitution.* New York: Harper & Row.

Carnage of violence challenges diseases as top health threat. (1984, November 27). *Providence Evening Bulletin.*

Carpenter, C. Jan, & Huston-Stein, Aletha. (1980). Activity structure and sex-typed behavior in preschool children. *Child Development, 51,* 862–872.

Carrie, Cherylynn M. (1981). Reproductive symptoms: Interrelations and determinants. *Psychology of Women Quarterly, 6,* 174–186.

Cassedy, Ellen, & Nussbaum, Karen. (1983). *9 to 5: The working woman's guide to office survival.* New York: Penguin.

Cates, Ellan. (1981, September 29). Rebellion threatens big birth business. *Providence Evening Bulletin*, p. D-1.

Celani, David. (1976). Interpersonal approach to hysteria. *American Journal of Psychiatry, 113,* 1414–1418.

Cesarians don't cut mortality—Study. (1983, January 6). *Providence Evening Bulletin*.

Chambless, Dianne L., & Goldstein, Alan J. (1980). In A. M. Brodsky & R. T. Hare-Mustin (Eds.), *Women and psychotherapy* (pp. 113–134). New York: Guilford Press.

Chan, W. Y. (1983). Prostaglandins in primary dysmenorrhea: Basis for the new therapy. In S. Golub (Ed.), *Menarche* (pp. 243–249). Boston: Lexington Books.

Change over a decade. (1985, March 10). *New York Times*, p. E24.

Charnes, Ruth, Hoffman, Kay E., Hoffman, Lyla, & Meyers, Ruth S. (1980). The Sesame Street library—Bad books bring big bucks. *Young Children, 35*(2), 10–12.

Chavez, Deborah. (1985). Perpetuation of gender inequality: A content analysis of comic strips. *Sex Roles, 13,* 93–102.

Check, James V. P., & Malamuth, Neil M. (1983). Sex role stereotyping and reactions to depictions of stranger versus acquaintance rape. *Journal of Personality and Social Psychology, 45,* 344–356.

Cheng, Lucie. (1984, February). Asian American women and feminism. *Sojourner, 10*(2), 11–12.

Cherry, Louise. (1975). The pre-school teacher-child dyad: Sex differences in verbal interaction. *Child Development, 46,* 532–535.

Cherulnik, Paul D., & Evans, Robert M. (1984). Facial expressive behaviors of high self-monitors are less sex-typed. *Sex Roles, 11,* 435–449.

Chesler, Phyllis. (1972). *Women and madness.* New York: Doubleday.

Chesler, Phyllis. (1985). *Mothers on trial: The battle for children and custody.* New York: McGraw-Hill.

Chiappinelli, S. Robert. (1986, March 14). Family-support payments up, thanks to new laws. *Providence Evening Bulletin*.

Child-support payments lax. (1985, March 14). *Providence Journal-Bulletin*.

Chino, Allan F., & Funabiki, Dean. (1984). A cross-validation of sex differences in the expression of depression. *Sex Roles, 11,* 175–187.

Chodorow, Nancy. (1978). *The reproduction of mothering: Psychoanalysis and sociology of gender.* Berkeley: University of California Press.

Choosing baby's sex is closer to reality. (1979, February 15). *Providence Evening Bulletin*.

Chute, Carolyn. (1985). *The Beans of Egypt, Maine.* New York: Ticknor & Fields.

Clayton, Obie Jr., Baird, Anne C., & Levinson, Richard M. (1984). Subjective decision making in medical school admissions: Potentials for discrimination. *Sex Roles, 10,* 527–532.

Cloward, Richard A., & Piven, Frances F. (1979). Hidden protest: The channeling of female innovation and resistance. *Signs, 4,* 651–669.

Cohen, Barney. (1984, September 9). Where B means brutal. *New York Times Magazine*, pp. 150–151, 154–155, 165.

Colangelo, Nicholas, Rosenthal, David M., & Dettman, David F. (1984). Maternal employment and job satisfaction and their relationship to children's perceptions and behaviors. *Sex Roles, 10,* 693–702.

Cole, David, King, Kraig, & Newcomb, Andrew. (1977). Grade expectations as a function of sex, academic discipline and sex of instructor. *Psychology of Women Quarterly, 1,* 380–385.

Coleman, Marilyn, & Ganong, Lawrence H. (1985). Love and sex role stereotypes: Do macho men and feminine women make better lovers? *Journal of Personality and Social Psychology, 49,* 170–176.

Coles, Frances S. (1986). Forced to quit: Sexual harassment complaints and agency response. *Sex Roles, 14,* 81–95.

Coles, Robert, & Coles, Jane H. (1978). *Women of crisis: I.* New York: Delacorte.

Collins, Glenn. (1980, September 29). More older women are becoming mothers, study shows. *New York Times*.

Collins, Glenn. (1985, December 2). Women and masochism: Debate continues. *New York Times*, p. B12.

Collins, Glenn. (1986, March 20). More women are retiring, and doing better. *New York Times*, pp. C1, C8.

Collins, Glenn. (1986, March 28). New generation of working women learn what it is to retire. *Providence Journal-Bulletin*, p. B-11.

Collins, Jean E. (1978, April 30). Publishers depict women in new ways. *New York Times*, sec. 12, p. 19.

Community Action Strategies to Stop Rape. (1980). A rape prevention program in an urban area. *Signs, 5* (Suppl.), 238–241.

Condry, John C. (1984). Gender identity and social competence. *Sex Roles, 11,* 485–511.

Connelly, Sherryl. (1981, March 5). What's not good for the unborn. *Providence Evening Bulletin*.

Connor, Jane M., Schackman, Maxine, & Serbin, Lisa A. (1978). Sex-related differences in response to practice on a visual-spatial test and generalization to a related test. *Child Development, 49,* 24–29.

Connor, Jane M., Serbin, Lisa A., & Ender, Regina A. (1978). Responses of boys and girls to aggressive, assertive, and passive behaviors of male and female characters. *Journal of Genetic Psychology, 133,* 59–69.

Conservative Jews vote to admit women rabbis. (1985, February 14). *Providence Evening Bulletin*.

Constantinople, Anne. (1979). Sex-role acquisition: In search of the elephant. *Sex Roles, 5,* 121–133.

Cook, Alice S., Fritz, Janet J., McCornack, Barbara L., & Visperas, Cris. (1985). Early gender differences in the functional usage of language. *Sex Roles, 12,* 909–915.

Cooper, Harris M., Burger, Jerry M., & Good, Thomas L. (1981). Gender differences in the academic locus of control beliefs of young children. *Journal of Personality and Social Psychology, 40,* 562–572.

Corballis, Michael C. (1980). Laterality and myth. *American Psychologist, 35,* 284–295.

Corcoran, Mary, Duncan, Greg J., & Hill, Martha S. (1984). The economic fortunes of women and children: Lessons from the panel study of income dynamics. *Signs,* *10,* 232–248.

Cordes, Colleen. (1984, August). The rise of one-parent black families. *APA Monitor,* pp. 16–18.

Cordes, Colleen. (1986, March). Parental leave: Bill, report seek time off for care. *APA Monitor,* p. 28.

Corea, Gena. (1980, July). The caesarean epidemic. *Mother Jones,* pp. 28–42.

Cowan, Gloria. (1984). The double standard in age-discrepant relationships. *Sex Roles, 11,* 17–23.

Cowan, Gloria, & Hoffman, Charles D. (1986). Gender stereotyping in young children: Evidence to support a concept-learning approach. *Sex Roles, 14,* 211–224.

Cramer, Phebe, & Bryson, Jane. (1973). The development of sex-related fantasy patterns. *Developmental Psychology, 8,* 131–134.

Cramer, Phebe, & Hogan, Katherine A. (1975). Sex differences in verbal and play fantasy. *Developmental Psychology, 11,* 145–154.

Crichton, Sarah. (1983, October). Sex and self-discovery. *Ms,* pp. 68–69.

Crocker, Phyllis L. (1982). Annotated bibliography on sexual harassment in education. *Women's Rights Law Reporter, 7,* 91–106.

Cronkite, Ruth C., & Moos, Rudolf H. (1984). Sex and marital status in relation to the treatment and outcome of alcoholic patients. *Sex Roles, 11,* 93–112.

Crook, Joan. (1986). *Family functioning in families of origin of survivors of father-daughter incest.* Unpublished master's thesis, University of Rhode Island, Kingston.

Croxton, Jack S., & Klonsky, Bruce G. (1982). Sex differences in causal attributions for success and failure in real and hypothetical sport settings. *Sex Roles, 8,* 399–409.

Cuenot, Randall G., & Fujita, Stephen S. (1982). Perceived homosexuality: Measuring heterosexual attitudinal and nonverbal reactions. *Personality and Social Psychology Bulletin, 8,* 100–106.

Culp, Rex E., Cook, Alicia S., & Housley, Patricia C. (1983). A comparison of observed and reported adult-infant interactions: Effects of perceived sex. *Sex Roles, 9,* 475–479.

Cultural Information Service. (1984). *The burning bed: October 8, 1984, 9–11 pm ET, on the NBC television network.* (PO Box 786, Madison Square Station, New York, NY 10159.)

Cunningham, Susan. (1984, January). Suit leads to study of sexual harassment on job. *APA Monitor,* p. 29.

Dad gets his turn in delivery room. (1983, November 11). *Providence Evening Bulletin.*

Daly, Mary. (1978a). *Gyn/Ecology.* Boston: Beacon.

Daly, Mary. (1978b). Sparking: The fire of female friendship. *Chrysalis, 6,* 27–35.

Dambrot, Faye H., Papp, Mary E., & Whitmore, Cheryl. (1984). The sex-role attitudes of three generations of women. *Personality and Social Psychology Bulletin, 10,* 469–473.

Danziger, Nira. (1983). Sex-related differences in the aspirations of high school students. *Sex Roles, 9,* 683–695.

Dash, Joan. (1973). *A life of one's own.* New York: Harper & Row.

Davidson, Christine V., & Abramowitz, Stephen I. (1980). Sex bias in clinical judgment: Later empirical returns. *Psychology of Women Quarterly, 4,* 377–395.

Davidson, Lynne R. (1981). Pressures and pretense: Living with gender stereotypes. *Sex Roles, 7,* 331–347.

Davidson, Lynne R., & Duberman, Lucille. (1982). Friendship: Communication and interactional patterns in same-sex dyads. *Sex Roles, 8,* 809–822.

Davidson, Sara. (1978). *Loose change.* New York: Pocket Books.

Davis, Albert J. (1984). Sex-differentiated behaviors in nonsexist picture books. *Sex Roles, 11,* 1–16.

Davis, Angela. (1982). Women, race and class: An activist perspective. *Women's Studies Quarterly, 10*(4), 5–9.

Davis, Angela Y. (1983). *Women, race, and class.* New York: Vintage.

Davis, John D. (1978). When boy meets girl: Sex roles and the negotiation of intimacy in an acquaintance exercise. *Journal of Personality and Social Psychology, 36,* 684–692.

Dean, Nancy, & Stark, Myra (Eds.). (1977). Introduction. *In the looking glass* (pp. xiii–xxii). New York: Putnam.

Deaux, Kay. (1984). From individual differences to social categories: Analysis of a decade's research on gender. *American Psychologist, 39,* 105–116.

Deaux, Kay. (1985). Sex and gender. *Annual Review of Psychology, 36,* 49–81.

Deaux, Kay, & Hanna, Randel. (1984). Courtship in the personals column: The influence of gender and sexual orientation. *Sex Roles, 11,* 363–375.

de Beauvoir, Simone. (1961). *The second sex.* New York: Bantam. (Original work published in 1949.)

DeCasper, Anthony J., & Fifer, William P. (1980). Of human bonding: Newborns prefer their mothers' voices. *Science, 208,* 1174–1176.

Declining birthrates. (1985, Spring/Summer). *ISR Newsletter,* pp. 3, 6. (Institute for Social Research, University of Michigan, Ann Arbor)

Degree can lift earnings by $300,000. (1983, March 14). *Providence Evening Bulletin.*

Deitz, Sheila R., Littman, Madeleine, & Bentley, Brenda J. (1984). Attribution of responsibility for rape: The influence of observer empathy, victim resistance, and victim attractiveness. *Sex Roles, 10,* 261–280.

Dejanikus, Tacie. (1985, May/June). Major drug manufacturer funds osteoporosis public education campaign. *Network News,* p. 1.

DeLacoste-Utamsing, Christine, & Holloway, Ralph L. (1982). Sexual dimorphism in the human corpus callosum. *Science, 216,* 1431–1432.

Delaney, Janice, Lupton, Mary J., & Toth, Emily. (1977). *The curse.* New York: New American Library.

Delk, John L. (1977). Differentiating sexist from nonsexist therapists, or my analogue can beat your analogue. *American Psychologist, 32,* 890–893.

Deluty, Robert H. (1985). Consistency of assertive, aggressive, and submissive behavior for children. *Journal of Personality and Social Psychology, 49,* 1054–1065.

DeMarchi, W. G. (1976). Psychophysiological aspects of the menstrual cycle. *Journal of Psychosomatic Research, 20,* 279–287.

Denmark, Florence L., Shaw, Jeffrey S., & Ciali, Samuel D. (1985). The relationship among sex roles, living arrangements, and the division of household responsibilities. *Sex Roles, 12,* 617–625.

Deutsch, Helene. (1944). *The psychology of women: A psychoanalytic interpretation* (Vol. 1). New York: Grune & Stratton.

Developing a national agenda to address women's mental health needs. (1985). Washington, DC: American Psychological Association.

Device flashes when woman is fertile. (1982, October 12). *Providence Evening Bulletin,* p. A-12.

de Wolf, Virginia A. (1981). High school mathematics preparation and sex differences in quantitative abilities. *Psychology of Women Quarterly, 5,* 555–567.

Deykin, Eva. (1984, February 6). *Suicidal behavior of adolescents.* Paper read at meeting of Stress Seminar, Wellesley College Center for Research on Women, Wellesley, MA.

Diamond, Pam. (1985, May). Medical news. *Ms,* p. 64.

Dick-Read, Grantly. (1959). *Childbirth without fear* (2nd ed.). New York: Harper & Row.

Dill, Bonnie T. (1979). The dialectics of black womanhood. *Signs, 4,* 543–555.

Dinnerstein, Dorothy. (1977). *The mermaid and the minotaur.* New York: Harper & Row.

Dino, Geri A., Barnett, Mark A., & Howard, Jeffrey A. (1984). Children's expectations of sex differences in parents' responses to sons and daughters encountering interpersonal problems. *Sex Roles, 11,* 709–717.

DiPerna, Paula. (1984, January). Balancing high school and motherhood. *Ms,* pp. 57–62.

Divorce will touch 60% of wives now in their 30s, study predicts. (1986, April 5). *Providence Evening Bulletin,* p. A-1.

Djerassi, Carl. (1981). *The politics of contraception.* San Francisco: Freeman.

Dobzhansky, Theodosius. (1967). Of flies and men. *American Psychologist, 22,* 41–48.

Dobzhansky, Theodosius. (1972). Genetics and the diversity of behavior. *American Psychologist, 27,* 523–530.

Docket Report. (1983–1984). New York: Center for Constitutional Rights.

Docket Report. (1985–1986). New York: Center for Constitutional Rights.

Doherty, William J., & Baldwin, Cynthia. (1985). Shifts and stability in locus of control during the 1970s: Divergence of the sexes. *Journal of Personality and Social Psychology, 48,* 1048–1053.

Dohrenwend, Barbara S. (1973). Social status and stressful life events. *Journal of Personality and Social Psychology, 28,* 225–235.

Doloff, Steven. (1983, February 19). Class struggle: Changing sex roles. *Providence Journal-Bulletin.*

Donnerstein, Edward. (1980). Pornography and violence against women: Experimental studies. *Annals of the New York Academy of Sciences, 347,* 277–288.

Donnerstein, Edward. (1983). Aggressive pornography: Can it influence aggression toward women? In G. W. Albee, S. Gordon, & H. Leitenberg (Eds.), *Promoting sexual responsibility and preventing sexual problems* (pp. 220–237). Hanover, NH: University Press of New England.

Doudna, Christine. (1980, November 30). Women at the top. *New York Times Magazine,* pp. 54–55, 115–120.

Dowd, Maureen. (1984, December 30). Reassessing women's political role. *New York Times Magazine,* pp. 18–19, 32, 42–44.

Dowling, Colette. (1981). *The Cinderella complex: Women's hidden fear of independence.* New York: Summit.

Downs, A. C. (1983). Letters to Santa Claus: Elementary school-age children's sex-typed toy preferences in a natural setting. *Sex Roles, 9,* 159–163.

Doyle, James A. (1983). *The male experience.* Dubuque, IA: William C. Brown.

Drabble, Margaret. (1977). *The ice age.* New York: Knopf.

Drabman, Ronald S., Robertson, Stephen J., Patterson, Jana N., Jarvie, Gregory J., Hammer, David, & Cordua, Glenn. (1981). Children's perception of media-portrayed sex roles. *Sex Roles, 7,* 379–389.

Dragonwagon, Crescent. (1985, May). The last word on sleepless, foodless . . . and endless good health. *Ms,* p. 158.

Dreifus, Claudia. (1975, December). Sterilizing the poor. *Progressive,* pp. 13–19.

Ducker, Dalia G. (1980). The effect of two sources of role strain on women physicians. *Sex Roles, 6,* 549–559.

Duckworth, Ed. (1985, April 9). Woman jockey succeeds—her way. *Providence Evening Bulletin.*

Dullea, Georgia. (1975, July 13). Women in classrooms not the principal's office. *New York Times,* sec. 4, p. 7.

Dweck, Carol S., Davidson, William, Nelson, Sharon, & Enna, Bradley. (1978). Sex differences in learned helplessness: II. The contingencies of evaluative feedback in the classroom, and III. An experimental analysis. *Developmental Psychology, 14,* 268–276.

Dweck, Carol S., Goetz, Therese E., & Strauss, Nan L. (1980). Sex differences in learned helplessness: IV. An experimental and naturalistic study of failure generalization and its mediators. *Journal of Personal and Social Psychology, 38,* 441–452.

Dworkin, Andrea. (1978, July). The bruise that doesn't heal. *Mother Jones,* pp. 31–36.

Dye, Nancy S. (1980). History of childbirth in America. *Signs, 6,* 97–108.

Dzeich, Billie W., & Weiner, Linda. (1984). *The lecherous professor: Sexual harassment on campus.* Boston: Beacon.

Eagan, Andrea B. (1983, October). The selling of premenstrual syndrome. *Ms,* pp. 26–31.

Eagan, Andrea B. (1984, January). The contraceptive sponge: Easy—but is it safe? *Ms,* pp. 94–95.

Eagly, Alice H. (1978). Differences in influencibility. *Psychological Bulletin, 85,* 86–116.

Eagly, Alice H. (1983). Gender and social influence: A social psychological analysis. *American Psychologist, 38,* 971–981.

Eagly, Alice H., & Carli, Linda L. (1981). Sex of researchers and sex-typed communications as determinants of sex differences in influencibility: A meta-analysis of social influence studies. *Psychological Bulletin, 90,* 1–20.

Eccles, Jacquelynne. (1985). Sex differences in achievement patterns. In T. B. Sonderegger (Ed.), *Nebraska symposium on motivation 1984: Psychology and gender* (Vol. 32) (pp. 97–132). Lincoln: University of Nebraska Press.

Edmonds, Ed M., & Cahoon, Delwin D. (1984). Female clothes preference related to male sexual interest. *Bulletin of the Psychonomic Society, 22,* 171–173.

Effective, not overpowering. (1986, September). Tranxene advertisement. *American Journal of Psychiatry, 143,* back cover.

Ehrenreich, Barbara. (1983). *The hearts of men.* Garden City, NY: Anchor/Doubleday.

Ehrenreich, Barbara, Hess, Elizabeth, & Jacobs, Gloria. (1982, March). A report on the sex crisis. *Ms,* pp. 61–64, 87–88.

Ehrhardt, Anke A., & Meyer-Bahlburg, Heino F. L. (1981). Effects of prenatal sex hormones on gender-related behavior. *Science, 211,* 1312–1318.

18 million moms doing double-duty. (1986, February 11). *Providence Evening Bulletin.*

Eisenberg, Nancy, & Lennon, Randy. (1983). Sex differences in empathy and related capacities. *Psychological Bulletin, 94,* 100–131.

Elpern, Sarah, & Karp, Stephen A. (1984). Sex-role orientation and depressive symptomatology. *Sex Roles, 10,* 987–992.

Eme, Robert F. (1979). Sex differences in childhood psychopathology: A review. *Psychological Bulletin, 86,* 574–595.

Emery, C. Eugene Jr. (1983, April 14). Balance of hormones critical to "pill" safety. *Providence Journal-Bulletin.*

Emery, C. Eugene Jr. (1984, March 22). Dissent is strange to Soviets. *Providence Evening Bulletin.*

Emery, C. Eugene Jr. (1985, April 11). 2 studies find IUDs raise infertility risk in childless women. *Providence Journal-Bulletin.*

Emery, C. Eugene Jr. (1986, September 4). Fetal monitors not really needed during low-risk births, study says. *Providence Journal–Bulletin,* p. B-8.

Emmerich, Walter, & Shepard, Karla. (1984). Cognitive factors in the development of sex-typed preferences. *Sex Roles, 11,* 997–1007.

Engel, Marian. (1979). *The glassy sea.* New York: St. Martin's Press.

Englander-Golden, Paula, & Barton, Glenn. (1983). Sex differences in absence from work: A reinterpretation. *Psychology of Women Quarterly, 8,* 185–188.

English, Deirdre. (1981, February/March). The war against choice. *Mother Jones,* pp. 16–21, 26, 28, 31–32.

Erdrich, Louise. (1984). *Love medicine.* New York: Holt, Rinehart & Winston.

Erdwins, Carol J., & Mellinger, Jeanne C. (1984). Mid-life women: Relation of age and role to personality. *Journal of Personality and Social Psychology, 47,* 390–395.

Erikson, Erik H. (1968). *Identity: Youth and crisis.* New York: Norton.

Ernster, Virginia L. (1975). American menstrual expressions. *Sex Roles, 1,* 3–13.

Eron, Leonard D. (1980). Prescription for reduction of aggression. *American Psychologist, 35,* 244–252.

Escoffier, Jeffrey, Malyon, Alan, Morin, Stephen, & Raphael, Sharon. (1980). Homophobia: Effects on scientists. *Science, 209,* 340.

Estellachild, Vivian. (1971, Winter). Hippie communes. *Women: A Journal of Liberation, 2,* 40–43.

Etaugh, Claire. (1980). Effects of nonmaternal care on children: Research evidence and popular views. *American Psychologist, 35,* 309–319.

Etaugh, Claire, & Harlow, Heidi. (1975). Behaviors of male and female teachers as related to behaviors and attitudes of elementary school children. *Journal of Genetic Psychology, 127,* 163–170.

Etaugh, Claire, & Whittler, Tommy E. (1982). Social memory of preschool girls and boys. *Psychology of Women Quarterly, 7,* 170–174.

Everywoman's Center. (1980). *Results of sexual violence survey.* Amherst: University of Massachusetts.

Executive summary: National study of the incidence and severity of child abuse and neglect. (1982). Washington, DC: Children's Bureau.

'F' is for infants favor fathers' favors. (1982, October 26). *Providence Evening Bulletin.*

Fagot, Beverly I. (1974). Sex differences in toddlers' behavior and parental reaction. *Developmental Psychology, 10,* 554–558.

Fagot, Beverly I. (1981a). Male and female teachers: Do they treat boys and girls differently? *Sex Roles, 7,* 263–271.

Fagot, Beverly I. (1981b). Stereotypes versus behavioral judgments of sex differences in young children. *Sex Roles, 7,* 1093–1096.

Fagot, Beverly I. (1984a). The child's expectations of differences in adult male and female interactions. *Sex Roles, 11,* 593–600.

Fagot, Beverly I. (1984b). Teacher and peer reactions to boys' and girls' play styles. *Sex Roles, 11,* 691–702.

Fagot, Beverly I., & Hagan, Richard. (1985). Aggression in toddlers: Responses to the assertive acts of boys and girls. *Sex Roles, 12,* 341–351.

Falk, Ruth, Gispert, Maria, & Baucom, Donald H. (1981). Personality factors related to black teenage pregnancies and abortions. *Psychology of Women Quarterly, 5,* 737–746.

Families with children falling further behind. (1985, December 26). *Providence Evening Bulletin,* p. A-1.

Farb, Peter. (1978). *Humankind.* Boston: Houghton Mifflin.

Farley, Jennie. (1985). Book reviews. *Signs, 10,* 585–588.

Farley, Lin. (1978). *Sexual shakedown.* New York: McGraw-Hill.

Fathers are more fun. (1986, May 20). *Providence Evening Bulletin,* p. A-1.

Fausto-Sterling, Anne. (1985). *Myths of gender: Biological theories about women and men.* New York: Basic Books.

FDS advertisement. (1984, April). *Seventeen* magazine.

Federation CECOS, Schwartz, D., & Mayaux, M. J. (1982). Female fecundity as a function of age. *New England Journal of Medicine, 306*, 404–406.

Feild, Hubert S. (1978a). Attitudes toward rape: A comparative analysis of police, rapists, crisis counselors, and citizens. *Journal of Personality and Social Psychology, 36*, 156–179.

Feild, Hubert S. (1978b). Juror background characteristics and attitudes toward rape. *Law and Human Behavior, 2*, 73–93.

Feild, Hubert S. (1979). Rape trials and jurors' decisions. *Law and Human Behavior, 3*, 261–284.

Feinblatt, John A., & Gold, Alice R. (1976). Sex roles and the psychiatric referral process. *Sex Roles, 2*, 109–122.

Feinman, Saul. (1981). Why is cross-sex-role behavior more approved for girls than for boys? A status characteristic approach. *Sex Roles, 7*, 289–300.

Feiring, Candice, & Lewis, Michael. (1980). Temperament: Sex differences and stability in vigor, activity and persistence in the first three years of life. *Journal of Genetic Psychology, 136*, 65–75.

Feldberg, Roslyn. (1984). Comparable worth: Toward theory and practice in the United States. *Signs, 10*, 311–328.

Feldman, S. Shirley, & Nash, Sharon C. (1984). The transition from expectancy to parenthood: Impact of the firstborn child on men and women. *Sex Roles, 11*, 61–78.

Feldstein, Jerome H. (1976). Sex differences in social memory among preschool children. *Sex Roles, 2*, 75–79.

Ferber, Marianne A. (1982). Women and work: Issues of the 1980s. *Signs, 8*, 273–295.

Ferguson, Ann. (1981). Patriarchy, sexual identity, and the sexual revolution. *Signs, 7*, 158–172.

Ferguson, Ann. (1984). Sex war: The debate between radical and libertarian feminists. *Signs, 10*, 106–112.

Ferree, Myra M. (1983). The women's movement in the working class. *Sex Roles, 9*, 493–505.

Ferrell, Tom, & Slade, Margot. (1980, April 13). Office mashers must now beware. *New York Times.*

Fertility rate's ups and downs. (1985, December 12). *New York Times*, p. E7.

Fertility signal made for women. (1981, January 21). *Providence Evening Bulletin.*

Fetler, Mark. (1985). Sex differences on the California statewide assessment of computer literacy. *Sex Roles, 13*, 181–191.

Fidell, Linda S. (1973, April). *Put her down on drugs: Prescribed drug usage in women.* Paper read at the meeting of the Western Psychological Association, Anaheim, CA.

Field, Tiffany M., Woodson, Robert, Greenberg, Reena, & Cohen, Debra. (1982). Discrimination and imitation of facial expressions by neonates. *Science, 218*, 179–181.

Fifteen-year study documents tremendous change in women's sex-role attitudes. (1980, Winter). *ISR Newsletter*, p. 3. (Institute for Social Research, University of Michigan, Ann Arbor.)

Finkelhor, David. (1979). *Sexually victimized children.* New York: Free Press.

Finlay, Barbara, Starnes, Charles E., & Alvarez, Fausto B. (1985). Recent changes in sex-role ideology among divorced men and women: Some possible causes and implications. *Sex Roles, 12*, 637–653.

Firestone, Shulamith. (1971). *The dialectic of sex.* New York: Bantam.

Fischer, Judith L., & Narus, Leonard R. (1981). Sex-role development in late adolescence and adulthood. *Sex Roles, 7*, 97–106.

Fischman, Joshua. (1986, June). The wounds of war. *Psychology Today*, pp. 8–9.

Fishel, Anne. (1979, June). What is a feminist therapist? and How to find one. *Ms*, pp. 79–81.

Fisher, Elizabeth. (1979). *Women's creation: Sexual evolution and the shaping of society.* New York: McGraw-Hill.

Fisher, Kathleen. (1984, August). Role choice linked to health. *APA Monitor*, p. 39.

Fisher, Kathleen. (1985, November). Parental support vital in coping with abuse. *APA Monitor*, p. 12.

Fisher, William A., & Byrne, Donn. (1978). Sex differences in response to erotica? Love versus lust. *Journal of Personality and Social Psychology, 36*, 117–125.

5 acquitted of 1980 Mass. rape-beating. (1983, June 18). *Providence Journal*, p. A-2.

Flax, Jane. (1981). A materialist theory of women's status. *Psychology of Women Quarterly, 6*, 123–136.

Fleming, Anne T. (1977, December 25). That week in Houston. *New York Times Magazine*, pp. 10–13, 33.

Fleming, Anne T. (1981, August 2). Women and the spoils of success. *New York Times Magazine*, pp. 30–36.

Flerx, Vicki C., Fidler, Dorothy S., & Rogers, Ronald W. (1976). Sex role stereotypes: Developmental aspects and early intervention. *Child Development, 47*, 998–1007.

Flexner, Eleanor. (1975). *Century of struggle* (Revised edition). Cambridge, MA: Belknap.

Folb, Edith A. (1980, November/December). Runnin' down some lines. *Society*, pp. 63–71.

Ford, Maureen R., & Lowery, Carol R. (1986). Gender differences in moral reasoning: A comparison of the use of justice and care orientations. *Journal of Personality and Social Psychology, 50*, 777–783.

Fowler, Elizabeth M. (1982, November 10). Women as senior executives. *New York Times.*

Fox, Jeffrey L. (1984a). NIMH study finds one in five have disorders. *Science, 226*, 324.

Fox, Jeffrey L. (1984b). Medical school enrollment still edging downward. *Science, 226*, 815.

Francke, Linda B. (1982). *The ambivalence of abortion.* New York: Laurel/Dell.

Frank, Susan J., McLaughlin, Ann M., & Crusco, April. (1984). Sex role attributes, symptom distress, and defensive style among college men and women. *Journal of Personality and Social Psychology, 47*, 182–192.

Frank, Susan J., Towell, Patricia A., & Huyck, Margaret. (1985). The effects of sex-role traits on three aspects of psychological well-being in a sample of middle-aged women. *Sex Roles, 12*, 1073–1087.

Franken, Mary W. (1983). Sex role expectations in children's vocational aspirations and perceptions of occupations. *Psychology of Women Quarterly, 8,* 59–68.

Franklin, Clyde W. II. (1984). *The changing definition of masculinity.* New York: Plenum.

Franks, Violet. (1979). Gender and psychotherapy. In E. S. Gomberg & V. Franks (Eds.), *Gender and disordered behavior* (pp. 453–485). New York: Brunner/Mazel.

Freedman, Victoria H. (1983). Update on genetics. In M. Fooden, S. Gordon, & B. Hughley (Eds.), *Genes and gender IV: The second X and women's health* (pp. 29–37). New York: Gordian Press.

Freeman, Harvey R. (1979). Sex-role stereotypes, self-concepts, and measured personality characteristics in college women and men. *Sex Roles, 5,* 99–103.

Freeman, Harvey R., Schockett, Melanie R., & Freeman, Evelyn B. (1975). Effects of gender and race on sex role preferences of fifth-grade children. *Journal of Social Psychology, 95,* 105–108.

Freeman-Longo, Robert E., & Wall, Ronald V. (1986, March). Changing a lifetime of sexual crime. *Psychology Today,* pp. 58–64.

French, Marilyn. (1977). *The women's room.* New York: Summit.

Freud, Sigmund. (1938). Three contributions to the theory of sex. In A. A. Brill (Ed.), *The basic writings of Sigmund Freud* (pp. 553–629). New York: Modern Library. (Original work published in 1905.)

Freud, Sigmund. (1964). Femininity. In *New introductory lectures on psychoanalysis* (pp. 112–135). New York: Norton. (Original work published in 1933.)

Frey, Karen A. (1981). Middle-aged women's experience and perceptions of menopause. *Women and Health, 6,* 25–36.

Friday, Nancy. (1973). *My secret garden.* New York: Pocket Books.

Friedan, Betty. (1963). *The feminine mystique.* New York: Norton.

Friedan, Betty. (1985, November 3). How to get the women's movement moving again. *New York Times Magazine,* pp. 26–28, 66–67, 84–85, 89, 98, 106–108.

Friederich, Mary A. (1983). Dysmenorrhea. In S. Golub (Ed.), *Lifting the curse of menstruation* (pp. 91–106). New York: Haworth.

Friedman, Richard C., Hurt, Stephen W., Arnoff, Michael S., & Clarkin, John. (1980). Behavior and the menstrual cycle. *Signs, 5,* 719–738.

Friedrich, Otto. (1983, August 15). What do babies know? *Time,* pp. 52–59.

Friendly, David T. (1985, March 18). This isn't Shakespeare. *Newsweek,* p. 62.

Frieze, Irene H. (1979, April). *Power and influence in violent and nonviolent marriages.* Paper read at the meeting of the Eastern Psychological Association, Philadelphia, PA.

Frieze, Irene H. (1983). Investigating the causes and consequences of marital rape. *Signs, 8,* 532–553.

Frieze, Irene H., Whitley, Bernard E. Jr., Hanusa, Barbara H., & McHugh, Maureen C. (1982). Assessing the theoretical models for sex differences in causal attributions for success and failure. *Sex Roles, 8,* 333–343.

Frodi, Ann, Macauley, Jacqueline, & Thorne, Pauline R. (1977). Are women always less aggressive than men? A review of the experimental literature. *Psychological Bulletin, 84,* 634–660.

Fromm, Erich. (1956). *The art of loving.* New York: Harper & Row.

Frueh, T., & McGhee, P. G. (1975). Traditional sex role development and amount of time spent watching television. *Developmental Psychology, 11,* 109.

Fuchs, Victor R. (1986). Sex differences in economic well-being. *Science, 232,* 459–464.

Gaelick, Lisa, Bodenhausen, Galen V., & Wyer, Robert S. Jr. (1985). Emotional communication in close relationships. *Journal of Personality and Social Psychology, 49,* 1246–1265.

Gailey, Phil. (1985, December 13). Whither the women's movement? *New York Times,* p. B10.

Gamarekian, Barbara. (1985, May 27). Women's caucus: Eight years of progress. *New York Times.*

Ganellen, Ronald J., & Blaney, Paul H. (1984). Hardiness and social supports as moderators of the effects of life stress. *Journal of Personality and Social Psychology, 47,* 156–163.

Garcia, Luis T. (1982). Sex-role orientation and stereotypes about male-female sexuality. *Sex Roles, 8,* 863–876.

Garcia, Luis T., & Derfel, Barbara. (1983). Perception of sexual experience: The impact of nonverbal behavior. *Sex Roles, 9,* 871–878.

Gartrell, Nanette, & Mosbacher, Diane. (1984). Sex differences in the naming of children's genitalia. *Sex Roles, 10,* 867–876.

Gayles, Gloria. (1979). Sometimes as women only. In R. P. Bell, B. J. Parker, & B. Guy-Sheftall (Eds.), *Sturdy black bridges* (pp. 363–364). Garden City, NY: Anchor.

Gee, Pauline W. (1983). Ensuring police protection for battered women: The *Scott v. Hart* suit. *Signs, 8,* 554–567.

Gehlen, Frieda L. (1977). Legislative role performance of female legislators. *Sex Roles, 3,* 1–18.

Geis, F. L., Brown, Virginia, Jennings (Walstedt), Joyce, & Porter, Natalie. (1984). TV commercials as achievement scripts for women. *Sex Roles, 10,* 513–525.

Geise, L. Ann. (1979). The female role in middle class women's magazines from 1955 to 1976: A content analysis of nonfiction selections. *Sex Roles, 5,* 51–62.

Geist, William E. (1985, October 2). About New York: Equality of the sexes, Playboy style. *New York Times,* p. B3.

Gelles, Richard J. (1974). *The violent home.* Beverly Hills, CA: Sage.

Gelles, Richard J. (1979, October). The myth of battered husbands. *Ms,* pp. 65–66, 71–73.

Gerdes, Eugenia P., & Garber, Douglas M. (1983). Sex bias in hiring: Effects of job demands and applicant competence. *Sex Roles, 9,* 307–315.

Gerrard, Meg. (1982). Sex, sex guilt, and contraceptive use. *Journal of Personality and Social Psychology, 42,* 153–158.

Gerson, Judith. (1985). Women returning to school: The consequences of multiple roles. *Sex Roles, 13,* 77–92.

Gerson, Mary-Joan. (1980). The lure of motherhood. *Psychology of Women Quarterly, 5,* 207–218.

Gerson, Mary-Joan. (1984). Feminism and the wish for a child. *Sex Roles, 11,* 389–398.

Gerson, Mary-Joan, Alpert, Judith L., & Richardson, Mary Sue. (1984). Mothering: The view from psychological research. *Signs, 9,* 434–453.

Gettys, Linda D., & Cann, Arnie. (1981). Children's perceptions of occupational sex stereotypes. *Sex Roles, 7,* 301–308.

Giarrusso, Roseann, Johnson, Paula, Goodchilds, Jacqueline, & Zellman, Gail. (1979, April). *Adolescents' cues and signals: Sex and assault.* Paper read at the meeting of the Western Psychological Association, San Diego, CA.

Gibbs, Robin. (1986). Social factors in exaggerated eating behavior among high school students. *International Journal of Eating Disorders, 5,* 1103–1107.

Giele, Janet. (1984).

Gigy, Lynn L. (1980). Self-concept of single women. *Psychology of Women Quarterly, 5,* 321–340.

Gilbert, Lucia A. (1985). *Men in dual-career families: Current realities and future prospects.* Hillsdale, NJ: Erlbaum.

Gilbert, Lucia A., Deutsch, Connie J., & Strahan, Robert F. (1978). Feminine and masculine dimensions of the typical, desirable, and ideal woman and man. *Sex Roles, 4,* 767–778.

Gilbert, Lucia A., Gallessich, June M., & Evans, Sherri L. (1983). Sex of faculty role model and student's self-perceptions of competency. *Sex Roles, 9,* 597–607.

Gilbert, Sandra M. (1984, December 30). Feisty femme, 40, seeks nurturant paragon. *New York Times Book Review,* p. 11.

Gilligan, Carol. (1977). In a different voice: Women's conception of the self and of morality. *Harvard Educational Review, 47,* 481–517.

Gilligan, Carol. (1979). Woman's place in man's life cycle. *Harvard Educational Review, 49,* 431–446.

Gilligan, Carol. (1982). *In a different voice: Psychological theory and women's development.* Cambridge, MA: Harvard University Press.

Gillis, John S., & Avis, Walter E. (1980). The male-taller norm in mate selection. *Personality and Social Psychology Bulletin, 6,* 396–401.

Gilman, Charlotte P. (1973). *The yellow wallpaper.* Old Westbury, NY: Feminist Press. (Original work published in 1891.)

Girls are different, look at the law. (1977, September 12). *Providence Evening Bulletin.*

Girls lose their lead. (1981, November). *Science 81,* pp. 6f.

Gitelson, Idy B., Petersen, Anne C., & Tobin-Richards, Maryse H. (1982). Adolescents' expectations of success, self-evaluations, and attributions about performance on spatial and verbal tasks. *Sex Roles, 8,* 411–419.

Glaser, Robert L., & Thorpe, Joseph S. (1986). Unethical intimacy: A survey of sexual contact and advances between psychology educators and female graduate students. *American Psychologist, 41,* 43–51.

Glass, Shirley P., & Wright, Thomas L. (1985). Sex differences in type of extramarital involvement and marital dissatisfaction. *Sex Roles, 12,* 1101–1120.

Glenwick, David S., Johansson, Sandra L., & Bondy, Jeffrey. (1978). A comparison of the self-images of female and male assistant professors. *Sex Roles, 4,* 513–524.

Godwin, Gail. (1977). A sorrowful woman. In N. Dean & M. Stark (Eds.), *In the looking glass* (pp. 167–173). New York: Putnam.

Godwin, Gail. (1978). *Violet Clay.* New York: Knopf.

Godwin, Gail. (1983). *A mother and two daughters.* New York: Avon.

Goffman, Erving. (1979). *Gender advertisements.* New York: Harper & Row.

Gold, Dolores, & Berger, Charlene. (1978). Problem-solving performance of young boys and girls as a function of task appropriateness and sex identity. *Sex Roles, 4,* 183–193.

Goldman, Joyce. (1972, August). The women of Bangladesh. *Ms,* pp. 84–89.

Goldman, Juliette D. G., & Goldman, Ronald J. (1983). Children's perceptions of parents and their roles: A cross-national study in Australia, England, North America, and Sweden. *Sex Roles, 9,* 791–812.

Gollin, Albert E. (1980). Comment on Johnson's "On the prevalence of rape in the United States." *Signs, 6,* 346–349.

Golub, Sharon. (1976). The effect of premenstrual anxiety and depression on cognitive function. *Journal of Personality and Social Psychology, 34,* 99–104.

Golub, Sharon. (1983). Menarche: The beginning of menstrual life. In S. Golub (Ed.), *Lifting the curse of menstruation* (pp. 17–36). New York: Haworth.

Golub, Sharon, & Harrington, Denise M. (1981). Premenstrual and menstrual mood changes in adolescent women. *Journal of Personality and Social Psychology, 41,* 961–965.

Gomberg, Edith S. (1979). Problems with alcohol and other drugs. In E. S. Gomberg & V. Franks (Eds.), *Gender and disordered behavior* (pp. 204–240). New York: Brunner/Mazel.

Gomes, Beverly, & Abramowitz, Stephen I. (1976). Sex-related patient and therapist effects on clinical judgment. *Sex Roles, 2,* 1–13.

Good, Paul R., & Smith, Barry D. (1980). Menstrual distress and sex-role attributes. *Psychology of Women Quarterly, 4,* 482–491.

Good, Thomas L., Sikes, J. Neville, & Brophy, Jere E. (1973). Effects of teacher sex and student sex on classroom interaction. *Journal of Educational Psychology, 65,* 74–87.

Goodman, Madeline J., Griffin, P. Bion, Estioko-Griffin, Agnes A., & Grove, John S. (1985). The compatibility of hunting and mothering among the Agta hunter-gatherers of the Philippines. *Sex Roles, 12,* 1199–1209.

Goolkasian, Paula. (1985). Phase and sex effects in pain perception: A critical review. *Psychology of Women Quarterly, 9,* 15–28.

Gordon, Barbara. (1979). *I'm dancing as fast as I can.* New York: Harper & Row.

Gordon, Jon W., & Ruddle, Frank H. (1981). Mammalian gonadal determination and gametogenesis. *Science, 211,* 1265–1271.

Gordon, Linda, & Erlien, Marla. (1981, November 28). The politics of Puritanism. *The Nation,* pp. 578–579.

Gornick, Vivian. (1982, April). Watch out: Your brain may be used against you. *Ms,* pp. 14–20.

Gough, Harrison G. (1952). Identifying psychological femininity. *Educational and Psychological Measurements, 12,* 427–439.

Gould, Lisa L. (1979, August/September). Adverse effects of obstetrical drugs. *Newsletter,* Association for Women in Psychology.

Gould, Stephen J. (1978, November 2). Women's brains. *New Scientist,* pp. 364–366.

Gove, Walter. (1979). Sex, marital status, and psychiatric treatment: A research note. *Social Forces, 58,* 89–93.

Gove, Walter R., & Tudor, Jeannette F. (1973). Adult sex roles and mental illness. *American Journal of Sociology, 78,* 812–835.

Grauerholz, Elizabeth, & Serpe, Richard T. (1985). Initiation and response: The dynamics of sexual interaction. *Sex Roles, 12,* 1041–1059.

Gray, Janet D. (1983). The married professional woman: An examination of her role conflicts and coping strategies. *Psychology of Women Quarterly, 7,* 235–243.

Gray, Mary W. (1985, September–October). The halls of ivy and the halls of justice: Resisting sex discrimination against faculty women. *Academe,* pp. 33–41.

Gray-Little, Bernadette, & Burks, Nancy. (1983). Power and satisfaction in marriage: A review and critique. *Psychological Bulletin, 93,* 513–538.

Green, Brent, Parham, Iris A., Kleff, Ramsey, & Pilisuk, Marc. (1980). Old age: Introduction. *Journal of Social Issues, 36*(2), 1–7.

Green, Rayna. (1977). Magnolias grow in dirt. *Southern Exposure, 4*(4), 29–33.

Green, Rayna. (1980). Native American women. *Signs, 6,* 248–267.

Green, Richard. (1978). Sexual identity of 37 children raised by homosexual or trans-sexual parents. *American Journal of Psychiatry, 135,* 692–697.

Green, Richard, Neuberg, Donna S., & Finch, Stephen J. (1983). Sex-typed motor behaviors of "feminine" boys, conventionally masculine boys, and conventionally feminine girls. *Sex Roles, 9,* 571–579.

Greenfield, Patricia M. (1981). Child care in cross-cultural perspectives: Implications for the future organization of child care in the United States. *Psychology of Women Quarterly, 6,* 41–54.

Greenhaus, Philip S. (1983, January 23). Letter to the editor. *New York Times Magazine,* p. 74.

Greenhouse, Linda. (1981, March 22). Equal pay debate now shifts to a far wider concept. *New York Times.*

Greenhouse, Steven. (1984, October 31). Former steel workers' income falls by half. *New York Times,* p. A17.

Greeno, Catherine G., & Maccoby, Eleanor E. (1986). How different is the "Different Voice"? *Signs, 11,* 310–316.

Greenwood, Sadja. (1985, May). Hot flashes: How to cope when the heat is on. *Ms,* pp. 79, 82, 151–152.

Greer, Germaine. (1970). *The female eunuch.* New York: McGraw-Hill.

Greer, William R. (1986, February 22). The changing women's marriage market. *New York Times.*

Gregory, Chester. (1974). *Women in defense work during World War II.* Hicksville, NY: Exposition Press.

Gregory, Mary K. (1977). Sex bias in school referrals. *Journal of School Psychology, 15,* 5–8.

Griffin, Susan. (1971, September). Rape: The all-American crime. *Ramparts,* pp. 26–35.

Griffin, Susan. (1981). *Pornography and silence.* New York: Harper & Row.

Griffitt, William, & Kaiser, Donn L. (1978). Affect, sex guilt, gender, and the rewarding-punishing effects of erotic stimuli. *Journal of Personality and Social Psychology, 36,* 850–858.

Gross, Alan E., Green, Susan K., Storck, Jerome T., & Vanyur, John M. (1980). Disclosure of sexual orientation and impressions of male and female homosexuals. *Personality and Social Psychology Bulletin, 6,* 307–314.

Gross, Jane. (1984, August 12). Women athletes topple sports myths. *New York Times,* p. E22.

Gross, Jane. (1985, January 6). Against the odds: A woman's ascent on Wall Street. *New York Times Magazine,* pp. 16–27, 55, 60, 68.

Gross, Jane. (1986, February 16). In federal war on drug trafficking, women are playing a greater role. *New York Times,* p. 52.

Groth, A. Nicholas. (1979). *Men who rape: The psychology of the offender.* New York: Plenum.

Group consciousness. (1982, Spring/Summer). *ISR Newsletter,* pp. 4–5. (Institute for Social Research, University of Michigan, Ann Arbor.)

Guffy, Ossie, & Ledner, Caryl. (1971). *Ossie: The autobiography of a black woman.* New York: Norton.

Gupta, Nina, Jenkins, G. Douglas Jr., & Beehr, Terry A. (1983). Employee gender, gender similarity, and supervisor-subordinate cross-evaluations. *Psychology of Women Quarterly, 8,* 174–184.

Gurin, Patricia. (1981). Labor market experiences and expectancies. *Sex Roles, 7,* 1079–1091.

Gutierres, Sara E., Patton, Deanna S., Raymond, Jonathan S., & Rhoads, Deborah L. (1984). Women and drugs: The heroin abuser and the prescription drug abuser. *Psychology of Women Quarterly, 8,* 354–369.

Guttentag, Marsha, & Bray, Helen. (1976). *Undoing sex stereotypes.* New York: McGraw-Hill.

Haas, Adelaide. (1979). Male and female spoken language differences: Stereotypes and evidence. *Psychological Bulletin, 86,* 616–626.

Hahn, Jon. (1977, November 2). Sex is fun; So is more, report says. *Providence Evening Bulletin,* p. D-4.

Hailey, Elizabeth F. (1979). *A woman of independent means.* New York: Avon.

Hall, Evelyn G., & Lee, Amelia M. (1984). Sex differences in motor performance of young children: Fact or fiction? *Sex Roles, 10,* 217–230.

Hall, Judith A. (1978). Gender effects in decoding nonverbal cues. *Psychological Bulletin, 85,* 845–857.

Hall, Mary H. (1969, July). A conversation with Masters and Johnson. *Psychology Today*, pp. 50–58.

Hall, Roberta M., & Sandler, Bernice R. (1982). The classroom climate: A chilly one for women? *Project on the Status and Education of Women*. (Association of American Colleges, Washington, DC)

Hall, Roberta M., & Sandler, Bernice R. (1984). Out of the classroom: A chilly campus climate for women? *Project on the Status and Education of Women*. (Association of American Colleges, Washington, DC)

Hammer, Signe. (1976). *Daughters and mothers: Mothers and daughters*. New York: New American Library.

Hammond, Judith A., & Mahoney, Constance W. (1983). Reward-cost balancing among coal miners. *Sex Roles, 9*, 17–29.

Hansen, Ranald D., & O'Leary, Virginia E. (1984). Sex determined attributions. In V. E. O'Leary, R. K. Unger, & B. S. Wallston, (Eds.), *Women, gender and social psychology* (pp. 67–99). Hillsdale, NJ: Erlbaum.

Harding, M. Esther. (1972). *Woman's mysteries: Ancient and modern*. New York: Putnam.

Hare-Mustin, Rachel T., Bennett, Sheila K., & Broderick, Patricia C. (1983). Attitude toward motherhood: Gender, generational, and religious comparisons. *Sex Roles, 9*, 643–661.

Hariton, E. Barbara. (1973). The sexual fantasies of women. In Psychology Today (Eds.), *The female experience* (pp. 33–38). Del Mar, CA: Communication/Research/Machines.

Harlow, Harry, & Harlow, Margaret K. (1966). Learning to love. *American Scientist, 54*(3), 244–272.

Harper, Lawrence V., & Sanders, Karen M. (1975). Preschool children's use of space: Sex differences in outdoor play. *Developmental Psychology, 11*, 119.

Harris, Janet. (1976). *The prime of Ms. America*. New York: New American Library.

Harris, Marvin. (1977, November 13). Why do men dominate women? *New York Times Magazine*.

Harris, Victor A., & Katkin, Edward S. (1975). Primary and secondary emotional behavior: Analysis of the role of autonomic feedback on affect, arousal, and attribution. *Psychological Bulletin, 82*, 904–916.

Harris, William H., & Levey, Judith S. (Eds.). (1975). *The new Columbia encyclopedia*. New York: Lippincott.

Harrison, Albert A. (1977). Let's make a deal: An analysis of revelations and stipulations in lonely hearts advertisements. *Journal of Personality and Social Psychology, 35*, 257–264.

Hartmann, Heidi I. (1981). The family as the locus of gender, class, and political struggle: The example of housework. *Signs, 6*, 366–394.

Hartup, Willard W., Moore, Shirley G., & Sager, Glen. (1963). Avoidance of inappropriate sex-typing by young children. *Journal of Consulting Psychology, 27*, 467–473.

Has French film star Brigitte Bardot become a recluse? (1983, April 17). *Boston Globe Magazine*.

Haseltine, Florence P., & Ohno, Susumo. (1981). Mechanisms of gonadal differentiation. *Science, 211*, 1272–1277.

Hasenfeld, Robin. (1982). *Empathy and justification: Two contextual cues related to gender differences in aggressive behavior*. Unpublished paper, Department of Psychology, University of Rhode Island, Kingston.

Haskell, Molly. (1974). *From reverence to rape: The treatment of women in the movies*. New York: Penguin.

Haugh, Susan S., Hoffman, Charles D., & Cowan, Gloria. (1980). The eye of the very young beholder: Sextyping of infants by young children. *Child Development, 51*, 598–600.

Hawthorne, Nathaniel. (1948). *The scarlet letter*. New York: Dodd, Mead. (Original work published in 1850.)

Hawthorne, Nathaniel. (1973). The birthmark. In M. Murray (Ed.), *A house of good proportion: Images of women in literature* (pp. 351–366). New York: Simon & Schuster. (Original work published in 1843.)

Hayden, Dolores. (1984, January). Making housing work for people. *Ms*, pp. 69–71.

Hayfield, Nancy. (1980). *Cleaning house*. New York: Farrar, Straus & Giroux.

Hayler, Barbara. (1979). Abortion. *Signs, 5*, 307–323.

Hays, Hoffman R. (1964). *The dangerous sex: The myth of feminine evil*. New York: Putnam.

Health-tex advertisement. (1982, March 14). *New York Times Magazine*.

Heilbrun, Carolyn G. (1973). *Toward a recognition of androgyny*. New York: Harper & Row.

Heilman, Joan R. (1980, September 7). Breaking the caesarean cycle. *New York Times Magazine*, pp. 84, 86, 88, 90–93.

Heilman, Madeline E., & Kram, Kathy E. (1984). Male and female assumptions about colleagues' views of their competence. *Psychology of Women Quarterly, 7*, 329–337.

Heiman, Julia R. (1975, April). Women's sexual arousal: The physiology of erotica. *Psychology Today*, pp. 91–94.

Heller, Kirby A., & Parsons, Jacqueline E. (1981). Sex differences in teachers' evaluative feedback and students' expectancies for success in mathematics. *Child Development, 52*, 1015–1019.

Helsing, Knud J., Szklo, Moyses, & Comstock, George W. (1981). Factors associated with mortality after widowhood. *American Journal of Public Health, 71*, 802–809.

Helson, Ravenna. (1986, March). *Advancing the social clock*. Paper presented at the meeting of the Association for Women in Psychology, Oakland, CA.

Helson, Ravenna, Mitchell, Valory, & Moane, Geraldine. (1984). Personality and patterns of adherence and nonadherence to the social clock. *Journal of Personality and Social Psychology, 46*, 1079–1096.

Hemmer, Joan D., & Kleiber, Douglas A. (1981). Tomboys and sissies: Androgynous children? *Sex Roles, 7*, 1205–1211.

Henahan, Donal. (1983, January 23). Women are breaking the symphonic barriers. *New York Times*, pp. 1, 19.

Hendrick, Susan, Hendrick, Clyde, Slapion-Foote, Michelle J., & Foote, Franklin H. (1985). Gender differences in sexual attitudes. *Journal of Personality and Social Psychology, 48*, 1630–1642.

Hendrix, Llewellyn, & Johnson, G. David. (1985). Instrumental and expressive socialization: A false dichotomy. *Sex Roles, 13,* 581–595.

Henig, Robin M. (1982, March 7). Dispelling menstrual myths. *New York Times Magazine,* pp. 64–65, 68, 70–71, 74–75, 78–79.

Henley, Nancy M. (1977). *Body politics: Power, sex and non-verbal communication.* Englewood Cliffs, NJ: Prentice-Hall.

Henley, Nancy M. (1985). Psychology and gender. *Signs, 11,* 101–119.

Henley, Nancy M., & Freeman, Jo. (1976). The sexual politics of interpersonal behavior. In S. Cox (Ed.), *Female psychology: The emerging self* (pp. 171–179). Chicago: Science Research Associates.

Her uncle and father were horrified but she just kept on dancing. (1979, April 2). *Providence Evening Bulletin.*

Herman, Jeanne B., & Gyllstrom, Karen K. (1977). Working men and women: Inter- and intra-role conflict. *Psychology of Women Quarterly, 1,* 319–333.

Herman, Judith, & Hirschman, Lisa. (1977). Father-daughter incest. *Signs, 2,* 735–756.

Herman, Judith, & Hirschman, Lisa. (1981). Families at risk for father-daughter incest. *American Journal of Psychiatry, 138,* 967–970.

Herzog, A. Regula, Bachman, Jerald G., & Johnston, Lloyd D. (1983). Paid work, child care, and housework: A national survey of high school seniors' preferences for sharing responsibilities between husband and wife. *Sex Roles, 9,* 109–135.

Heshusius, Lous. (1980). Female self-injury and suicide attempts: Culturally reinforced techniques in human relations. *Sex Roles, 6,* 843–857.

Hess, Beth B. (1985, June). Prime time. *Women's Review of Books,* pp. 6–7.

Hess, Robert D., & Miura, Irene T. (1985). Gender differences in enrollment in computer camps and classes. *Sex Roles, 13,* 193–203.

Hier, Daniel B. (1979). Genetic explanation for no sex difference in spatial ability among Eskimos. *Perceptual and Motor Skills, 48,* 593–594.

High court rejects definition of porn as violation of civil rights. (1986, February 25). *Providence Evening Bulletin,* p. A-4.

Hiltzik, Michael A. (1979, October 1). Prostitution not a victimless crime in West End. *Providence Evening Bulletin.*

Hines, Melissa. (1982). Prenatal gonadal hormones and sex differences in human behavior. *Psychological Bulletin, 92,* 56–80.

Hite, Shere. (1976). *The Hite report.* New York: Dell.

Hjelle, Larry A., & Butterfield, Rhonda. (1974). Self-actualization and women's attitudes toward their roles in contemporary society. *The Journal of Psychology, 87,* 225–230.

Hoffman, Joan C. (1982). Biorhythms in human reproduction: The not-so-steady states. *Signs, 7,* 829–844.

Hoffman, Lois W. (1977). Changes in family roles, socialization, and sex differences. *American Psychologist, 32,* 644–657.

Holden, Constance. (1984). Will home computers transform schools? *Science, 225,* 296.

Hollander, Edwin P. (1985). Leadership and power. In G. Lindzey & E. Aronson (Eds.), *Handbook of social psychology* (Vol. 2, 3rd ed.) (pp. 485–537). New York: Random House.

Hollender, John, & Shafer, Leslie. (1981). Male acceptance of female career roles. *Sex Roles, 7,* 1199–1203.

Holmstrom, Lynda L., & Burgess, Ann W. (1978). *The victim of rape.* New York: Wiley.

Holroyd, Jean C., & Brodsky, Annette M. (1977). Psychologists' attitudes and practices regarding erotic and non-erotic physical contact with patients. *American Psychologist, 32,* 843–849.

Holy or wholly wedlock: Maimonides 1174 A.D. (1972, November). *Intellectual Digest,* p. 53.

Holy Bible (Revised Standard Version). (1952). New York: Nelson & Sons.

Homiller, Jonica D. (1977). *Women and alcohol: A guide for state and local decision makers.* Washington, DC: The Council of State Authorities, Alcohol and Drug Problems Association of North America.

Homosexuality held a bar to the custody of children. (1985, June 20). *Providence Journal-Bulletin.*

Honey, Maureen. (1983). The working-class woman and recruitment propaganda during World War II: Class differences in the portrayal of war work. *Signs, 8,* 672–687.

Hooker, Evelyn. (1972). Homosexuality. In *National Institute of Mental Health Task Force on Homosexuality: Final report and background papers* (pp. 11–21). Rockville, MD: National Institute of Mental Health.

Hopkins, J. Roy. (1977). Sexual behavior in adolescence. *Journal of Social Issues, 33*(2), 67–85.

Hopkins, Joyce, Marcus, Marsha, & Campbell, Susan B. (1984). Postpartum depression: A critical review. *Psychological Bulletin, 95,* 498–515.

Horgan, Dianne. (1983). The pregnant woman's place and where to find it. *Sex Roles, 9,* 333–339.

Horn, Jack C. (1979, October). Fathers share the blame for Down's syndrome. *Psychology Today,* pp. 115–116.

Horn, Patrice. (1974, August). Newsline: Parents still prefer boys. *Psychology Today,* pp. 29–30.

Horney, Julie. (1979). Menstrual cycles and criminal responsibility. *Law and Human Behavior, 2,* 25–36.

Horney, Karen. (1967). Premenstrual tension. In H. Kelman (Ed.), *Feminine psychology* (pp. 99–106). New York: Norton. (Original work published in 1931.)

Horwitz, Allan V. (1982). Sex-role expectations, power, and psychological distress. *Sex Roles, 8,* 607–623.

Houseknecht, Sharon K. (1979). Timing of the decision to remain voluntarily childless: Evidence for continuous socialization. *Psychology of Women Quarterly, 4,* 81–96.

Houser, Betsy B., Berkman, Sherry L., & Beckman, Linda J. (1984). The relative rewards and costs of childlessness for older women. *Psychology of Women Quarterly, 8,* 395–398.

Houser, Betsy B., & Garvey, Chris. (1985). Factors that affect nontraditional enrollment among women. *Psychology of Women Quarterly, 9,* 105–117.

How firms use sex to win government contracts. (1980, June 26). *Providence Evening Bulletin.*

Howard, Elizabeth M. (1984, November). Miss Steak—And other beauties. *Ms,* p. 24.

Howard, Judith A. (1984). Societal influences on attribution: Blaming some victims more than others. *Journal of Personality and Social Psychology, 47,* 494–505.

Howard, Maureen. (1983, March). Forbidden fruits. *Vogue,* pp. 385–386, 428.

Howe, Florence. (1971, October 16). Sexual stereotypes start early. *Saturday Review,* pp. 76–77, 80–82, 92–93.

Hubbard, Ruth. (1982, October). The fetus as patient. *Ms,* pp. 28–32.

Hughey, Michael J., McElin, Thomas W., & Young, Todd. (1978). Maternal and fetal outcome of Lamaze-prepared patients. *Obstetrics and Gynecology, 51,* 643–647.

Hurst, Marsha, & Zambrana, Ruth E. (1980). The health careers of urban women: A study in East Harlem. *Signs, 5*(Suppl.), 112–126.

Hurwitz, Robin E., & White, Mary A. (1977). Effect of sex-linked vocational information on reported occupational choices of high school juniors. *Psychology of Women Quarterly, 2,* 149–156.

Hyde amendment has little effect. (1981, September 6). *New York Times.*

Hyde, Janet S. (1981). How large are cognitive gender differences? *American Psychologist, 36,* 892–901.

Hyde, Janet S. (1984). How large are gender differences in aggression? A developmental meta-analysis. *Developmental Psychology, 20,* 722–736.

Hyde, Janet S., Rosenberg, B. G., & Behrman, Joanne. (1977). "Tomboyism." *Psychology of Women Quarterly, 2,* 73–75.

IBM advertisement. (1985, January). *Psychology Today,* pp. 14–15.

Ickes, William, & Barnes, Richard D. (1977). The role of sex and self-monitoring in unstructured dyadic interactions. *Journal of Personality and Social Psychology, 35,* 315–330.

Ihinger-Tallman, Marilyn. (1982). Family interaction, gender, and status attainment value. *Sex Roles, 8,* 543–556.

Ilchman, Alice. (1986, January 7). Sex bias in the work place. *Providence Evening Bulletin,* p. A-11.

Imperato-McGinley, Julianne, Guerrero, Luis, Gautier, Teofilo, & Peterson, Ralph E. (1974). Steroid 5α-reductase deficiency in man: An inherited form of male pseudohermaphroditism. *Science, 186,* 1212–1215.

Improving longevity may have side effects. (1985, February 17). *New York Times.*

Instone, Debra, Major, Brenda, & Bunker, Barbara B. (1983). Gender, self-confidence, and social influence strategies: An organizational simulation. *Journal of Personality and Social Psychology, 44,* 322–333.

Ireson, Carol J. (1984). Adolescent pregnancy and sex-role. *Sex Roles, 11,* 189–201.

Israel, Allen C., Raskin, Pamela A., Libow, Judith A., & Pravder, Marsha D. (1978). Gender and sex-role appropriateness: Bias in the judgment of disturbed behavior. *Sex Roles, 4,* 399–413.

Jackman, Tom. (1983, January 9). Female professors gain little ground. *New York Times,* sec. 12, pp. 17–18.

Jackson, Linda A., & Cash, Thomas F. (1985). Components of gender stereotypes: Their implications for inferences on stereotypic and nonstereotypic dimensions. *Personality and Social Psychology Bulletin, 11,* 326–344.

Jacobs, Jerry A., & Powell, Brian. (1985). Occupational prestige: A sex-neutral concept? *Sex Roles, 12,* 1061–1071.

Jacobson, Marsha B. (1981). Effects of victim's and defendant's physical attractiveness on subjects' judgments in a rape case. *Sex Roles, 7,* 247–255.

Jacobson, Marsha B. (1983). Attitudes toward the Equal Rights Amendment as a function of knowing what it says. *Sex Roles, 9,* 891–896.

Jacobson, Marsha B., & Popovich, Paula M. (1983). Victim attractiveness and perceptions of responsibility in an ambiguous rape case. *Psychology of Women Quarterly, 8,* 100–104.

Jacoby, Susan. (1973, June 17). Feminism in the $12,000-a-year family: "What do I do for the next 20 years?" *New York Times Magazine.*

Janusonis, Michael. (1980, August 14). DePalma knows what audiences want to see. *Providence Evening Bulletin.*

Jaycox, Vicki. (1985). Letter to friends of Older Women's League. (1325 G Street, NW, Washington, DC 20005)

Jeffords, Charles R. (1984). The impact of sex-role and religious attitudes upon forced marital intercourse norms. *Sex Roles, 11,* 543–552.

Jennings, Kay D. (1977). People *versus* object orientation in preschool children: Do sex differences really occur? *Journal of Genetic Psychology, 131,* 65–73.

Johnson, Allan G. (1980). On the prevalence of rape in the United States. *Signs, 6,* 136–146.

Johnson, Dirk. (1986, June 15). Abused women get leverage in Connecticut. *New York Times,* p. E9.

Johnson, Maria M. (1985, November 8). Girls' aggression earns them recess separation. *Providence Journal-Bulletin.*

Johnson, Miriam M., Stockard, Jean, Rothbart, Mary K., & Friedman, Lisa. (1981). Sexual preference, feminism, and women's perceptions of their parents. *Sex Roles, 7,* 1–18.

Johnson, Paula. (1976). Women and power: Toward a theory of effectiveness. *Journal of Social Issues, 32,* 99–110.

Johnson, Sandy, Flinn, Jane M., & Tyer, Zita E. (1979). Effect of practice and training in spatial skills on embedded figures scores of male and females. *Perceptual and Motor Skills, 48* (part 1), 975–984.

Johnson, Sharon. (1984, May 22). Difference in life expectancy widens between the sexes. *New York Times,* p. C10.

Jones, Ann. (1980). *Women who kill.* New York: Fawcett Columbine.

Jones, Ernest. (1955). *The life and work of Sigmund Freud* (Vol. 2). New York: Basic Books.

Jones, Linda M., & McBride, Joanne L. (1980). Sex-role stereotyping in children as a function of maternal employment. *Journal of Social Psychology, 111*, 219−223.

Jong, Erica. (1973). *Fear of flying*. New York: Signet.

Jong, Erica. (1984). *Parachutes and kisses*. New York: Signet.

Josefowitz, Natasha. (1980). Management men and women: Closed vs. open doors. *Harvard Business Review, 58*(5), 56−58, 62.

Josefowitz, Natasha. (1984, May). Plums and prunes. *The Owl Observer*, p. 12.

Joseph, Gloria I. (1981a). Black mothers and daughters: Their roles and functions in American society. In G. I. Joseph & J. Lewis, *Common differences: Conflicts in black and white feminist perspectives* (pp. 75−126). Garden City, NY: Anchor.

Joseph, Gloria I. (1981b). Styling, profiling, and pretending: The games before the fall. In G. I. Joseph & J. Lewis, *Common differences: Conflicts in black and white feminist perspectives* (pp. 178−230). Garden City, NY: Anchor.

Joseph, Gloria I., & Lewis, Jill. (1981). *Common differences: Conflicts in black and white feminist perspectives*. Garden City, NY: Anchor.

Judge defends comments on abuse of children. (1982, March 6). *Providence Evening Bulletin*.

Judge says rape often provoked. (1977, September 9). *Providence Journal*.

Judge's recall sought. (1982, January 12). *Providence Evening Bulletin*.

Jung, Carl G. (1959). In V. deLaszlo (Ed.), *The basic writings of C. G. Jung*. New York: Random House.

Kagan, Jerome, & Klein, Robert E. (1973). Cross-cultural perspectives on early development. *American Psychologist, 28*, 947−961.

Kagan, Jerome, & Moss, Howard. (1962). *Birth to maturity*. New York: Wiley.

Kahn, Arnold. (1984). The power war: Male response to power loss under equality. *Psychology of Women Quarterly, 8*, 234−247.

Kahn, Ethel. (1984, March/April). The time has come for mid-life and older women. *Network News*, p. 2.

Kahne, Hilda. (1978). Economic research on women and families. *Signs, 3*, 652−665.

Kanarian, Mary A. (1980). *Attributions about rape*. Unpublished master's thesis, University of Rhode Island, Kingston.

Kanarian, Mary A., & Quina, Kathryn. (1984, April). *Sex-related differences in mathematics: Aptitude or attitude?* Paper read at the meeting of the Eastern Psychological Association, Baltimore, MD.

Kanowitz, Leo. (1969). *Women and the law*. Albuquerque: University of New Mexico Press.

Kanter, Rosabeth M. (1977). *Men and women of the corporation*. New York: Basic Books.

Kaplan, Jane R. (1980). Beauty and the feast. In J. R. Kaplan (Ed.), *A woman's conflict: The special relationship between women and food* (pp. 2−16). Englewood Cliffs, NJ: Prentice-Hall.

Kash, Sara D. (1984a, January). Birth-control survey. *Ms*, p. 17.

Kash, Sara D. (1984b, January). On the road to a second chance. *Ms*, p. 19.

Kassner, Marcia W. (1981). Will both spouses have careers?: Predictors of preferred traditional or egalitarian marriages among university students. *Journal of Vocational Behavior, 18*, 340−355.

Katzenstein, Mary F. (1984). Feminism and the meaning of the vote. *Signs, 10*, 4−26.

Kearney, Helen R. (1979). Feminist challenges to the social structure and sex roles. *Psychology of Women Quarterly, 4*, 16−31.

Keil, Sally V. W. (1982, April 18). Letter to the editor. *New York Times Magazine*, p. 130.

Keller, Evelyn F. (1983, September/October). Feminism as an analytic tool for the study of science. *Academe*, pp. 15−21.

Keller, James F., Elliott, Stephen S., & Gunberg, Edwin. (1982). Premarital sexual intercourse among single college students: A discriminant analysis. *Sex Roles, 8*, 21−32.

Keller, Marcia. (1984, October). Sexual love choices and regeneration. *Sojourner*, p. 15.

Kellerman, Jonathan, & Katz, Ernest R. (1978). Attitudes toward the division of child-rearing responsibility. *Sex Roles, 4*, 505−512.

Kelly, Rita Mae. (1983). Sex and becoming eminent as a political/organizational leader. *Sex Roles, 9*, 1073−1090.

Kenrick, Douglas T., Stringfield, David O., Wagenhals, Walter L., Dahl, Rebecca H., & Ransdell, Hilary J. (1980). Sex differences, androgyny, and approach responses to erotica: A new variation on the old volunteer problem. *Journal of Personality and Social Psychology, 38*, 517−524.

Kerber, Linda K. (1977, September 6). Point of View: "It must be womanly as well as manly to earn your own living." *Chronicle of Higher Education*, p. 48.

Kerber, Linda K. (1986). Some cautionary words for historians. *Signs, 11*, 304−310.

Kerr, Virginia. (1982, December). Supreme Court Justice O'Connor: The woman whose word is law. *Ms*, pp. 52, 80−84.

Kessler, Seymour, & Moos, Rudolf H. (1969). XYY chromosome: Premature conclusions. *Science, 165*, 442.

Kimball, Meredith M., & Gray, Vicky A. (1982). Feedback and performance expectancies in an academic setting. *Sex Roles, 8*, 999−1007.

Kimura, Doreen. (1985, November). Male brain, female brain: The hidden difference. *Psychology Today*, pp. 50−58.

King, H. Elizabeth, & Webb, Carol. (1981). Rape crisis centers: Progress and problems. *Journal of Social Issues, 37*(4), 93−104.

Kingston, Maxine H. (1977). *The woman warrior: Memoirs of a girlhood among ghosts*. New York: Vintage.

Kinsbourne, Marcel. (1982). Hemispheric specialization and the growth of human understanding. *American Psychologist, 37*, 411−420.

Kinsey, Alfred C., Pomeroy, Wardell B., Martin, Clyde E., &

Gebhard, Paul H. (1953). *Sexual behavior in the human female*. Philadelphia: Saunders.

Kinsman, Cheryl A., & Berk, Laura E. (1979). Joining the block and housekeeping areas. Changes in play and social behavior. *Young Children, 35*, 66–75.

Kirby, Darrell F., & Julian, Nancy B. (1981). Treatment of women in high school history textbooks. *Social Studies, 72*, 203–207.

Kitzinger, Sheila. (1979). *Women as mothers*. New York: Vintage.

Kiwanians vote to keep women out. (1986, June 25). *Providence Evening Bulletin*, p. A-4.

Kizer, Carolyn. (1973). From pro femina. In B. Segnitz & C. Rainey (Eds.), *Psyche: The feminine poetic consciousness* (pp. 131–135). New York: Dell.

Klein, Julia M. (1977, March). Is there a child in their future? *Radcliffe Quarterly*.

Kleinke, Chris L., Staneski, Richard A., & Mason, Jeanne K. (1982). Sex differences in coping with depression. *Sex Roles, 8*, 877–889.

Kleinman, Carol. (1983, July 26). Gender gap grows in educational executive posts. *Providence Evening Bulletin*.

Klemesrud, Judy. (1971, March 28). The disciples of Sappho, updated. *New York Times Magazine*.

Klemesrud, Judy. (1983, January 19). Mothers who shift back from jobs to homemaking. *New York Times*, pp. C1, C10.

Klemmack, Susan H., & Klemmack, David L. (1976). The social definition of rape. In M. J. Walker & S. L. Brodsky (Eds.), *Sexual assault* (pp. 135–148). Lexington, MA: Heath.

Knaub, Patricia K., Eversoll, Deanna R., & Voss, Jacqueline H. (1983). Is parenthood a desirable adult role? An assessment of attitudes held by contemporary women. *Sex Roles, 9*, 355–362.

Koblinsky, Sally A., & Sugawara, Alan I. (1984). Nonsexist curricula, sex of teacher, and children's sex-role learning. *Sex Roles, 10*, 357–367.

Koedt, Anne. (1973a). Lesbianism and feminism. In A. Koedt, E. Levine, & A. Rapone (Eds.), *Radical feminism* (pp. 246–258). New York: Quadrangle.

Koedt, Anne. (1973b). The myth of the vaginal orgasm. In A. Koedt, E. Levine, & A. Rapone (Eds.), *Radical feminism* (pp. 19–20). New York: Quadrangle.

Koeske, Randi K. (1983). Lifting the curse of menstruation: Toward a feminist perspective on the menstrual cycle. In S. Golub (Ed.), *Lifting the curse of menstruation* (pp. 1–16). New York: Haworth.

Koeske, Randi K., & Koeske, Gary F. (1975). An attributional approach to moods and the menstrual cycle. *Journal of Personality and Social Psychology, 31*, 473–478.

Kohlberg, Lawrence A. (1966). A cognitive-developmental analysis of children's sex-role concepts and attitudes. In E. E. Maccoby (Ed.), *The development of sex differences* (pp. 82–173). Stanford, CA: Stanford University Press.

Kolata, Gina B. (1979). Sex hormones and brain development. *Science, 205*, 985–987.

Kolata, Gina B. (1980a). Math and sex: Are girls born with less ability? *Science, 210*, 1234–1235.

Kolata, Gina B. (1980b). NIH panel urges fewer cesarian births. *Science, 210*, 176–177.

Kolata, Gina B. (1983). First trimester prenatal diagnosis. *Science, 221*, 1031–1032.

Kolata, Gina B. (1984a). Puberty mystery solved. *Science, 223*, 272.

Kolata, Gina B. (1984b). Studying learning in the womb. *Science, 225*, 302–303.

Komarovsky, Mirra. (1982). Female freshmen view their future: Career salience and its correlates. *Sex Roles, 8*, 299–314.

Korpivaara, Ari. (1982, February). Play groups for dads. *Ms*, pp. 52–54.

Koss, Mary P. (1981, September). *Hidden rape on a university campus*. Unpublished final report to the National Institute of Mental Health, Rockville, MD.

Koss, Mary P., Leonard, Kenneth E., Beezley, Dana A., & Oros, Cheryl J. (1985). Non-stranger sexual aggression: A discriminant analysis of the psychological characteristics of undetected offenders. *Sex Roles, 12*, 981–992.

Kotkin, Mark. (1983). Sex roles among married and unmarried couples. *Sex Roles, 9*, 975–985.

Kourilsky, Marilyn, & Campbell, Michael. (1984). Sex differences in a simulated classroom economy: Children's beliefs about entrepreneurship. *Sex Roles, 10*, 53–66.

Kozinn, Allan. (1985, March 24). An American woman conductor on the way up. *New York Times*, p. H23.

Kravetz, Diane, Marecek, Jeanne, & Finn, Stephen E. (1983). Factors influencing women's participation in consciousness-raising groups. *Psychology of Women Quarterly, 7*, 257–271.

Krieger, Susan. (1982). Lesbian identity and community: Recent social science literature. *Signs, 8*, 91–108.

Kropp, Jerri J., & Halverson, Charles F. (1983). Preschool children's preferences and recall for stereotyped versus nonstereotyped stories. *Sex Roles, 9*, 261–272.

Krulewitz, Judith E. (1978, August). *Sex differences in the perception of victims of sexual and nonsexual assault*. Paper presented at the meeting of the American Psychological Association, Toronto.

Krupa, Gregg. (1984, November 20). R.I. abortion law struck down. *Providence Evening Bulletin*.

Kuhn, Deanna, Nash, Sharon C., & Brucken, Laura. (1978). Sex role concepts of two- and three-year-olds. *Child Development, 49*, 445–451.

Kumagai, Gloria L. (1978). The Asian woman in America. *Explorations in Ethnic Studies, 1*, 27–39.

Kushner, Howard I. (1985). Women and suicide in historical perspective. *Signs, 10*, 537–552.

Kutner, Nancy G., & Levinson, Richard M. (1978). The toy salesperson: A voice for change in sex-role stereotypes? *Sex Roles, 4*, 1–8.

Kweskin, Sally L., & Cook, Alicia S. (1982). Heterosexual and homosexual mothers' self-described sex-role behavior and ideal sex-role behavior in children. *Sex Roles, 8*, 967–975.

LaBarbera, Joseph D. (1984). Seductive father-daughter relationships and sex roles in women. *Sex Roles, 11,* 941–951.

Ladner, Joyce A. (1971). *Tomorrow's tomorrow: The black woman.* Garden City, NY: Doubleday.

LaFrance, Marianne, & Carmen, Barbara. (1980). The non-verbal display of psychological androgyny. *Journal of Personality and Social Psychology, 38,* 36–49.

Lakoff, Robin. (1975). *Language and woman's place.* New York: Harper & Row.

Lamb, Patricia F. (1985, April). Heroine addicts. *Women's Review of Books,* pp. 16–17.

Lambert, Helen H. (1978). Biology and equality: A perspective on sex differences. *Signs, 4,* 97–117.

Lamphere, Louise. (1977). Anthropology. *Signs, 2,* 612–627.

Landau, Carol. (1986, May). *Critique of DSMIII-R.* Paper read at the meeting of the Rhode Island Association for Women in Psychology, Cranston, RI.

Landers, Ann. (1979, April 18). Dear Ann: Right off schedule. *Providence Journal-Bulletin.*

Landis, Bruce. (1983, September 20). Rapes increase in RI; Young girls at risk. *Providence Evening Bulletin.*

Landrine, Hope. (1983). *The politics of madness.* Unpublished doctoral dissertation, University of Rhode Island, Kingston.

Landrine, Hope. (1985). Race × class stereotypes of women. *Sex Roles, 13,* 65–75.

Lane advertisement. (1984, March). *Teen* magazine.

Laney, Billie J. (1970). A comparative study of expressive and comprehensive language development in male and female kindergarten children. Abstract in *Research in Education,* 1972, 7, 108. (Original is a dissertation, available from University Microfilms, Box 1764, Ann Arbor, MI 48106)

Langlois, Judith H., & Downs, A. Chris. (1980). Mothers, fathers, and peers as socialization agents of sex-typed play behaviors in young children. *Child Development, 51,* 1237–1247.

Lanier, Hope B., & Byrne, Joan. (1981). How high school students view women: The relationship between perceived attractiveness, occupation, and education. *Sex Roles, 7,* 145–148.

L'Armand, K., & Pepitone, Albert. (1982). Judgments of rape: A study of victim-rapist relationships and victim sexual history. *Personality and Social Psychology Bulletin, 8,* 134–139.

Lasker award stirs controversy. (1979). *Science, 203,* 341.

Latest rage in America: Traditional marriages. (1983, February 23). *Providence Evening Bulletin,* pp. A-1, A-10.

Latham, Caroline. (1985, February). How to live with a man. *Cosmopolitan,* pp. 98, 106–107, 112.

LaTorre, Ronald A., Yu, Lauren, Fortin, Louise, & Marrache, Myriam. (1983). Gender-role adoption and sex as academic and psychological risk factors. *Sex Roles, 9,* 1127–1136.

Laws, Judith L., & Schwartz, Pepper. (1977). *Sexual scripts: The social constructions of female sexuality.* New York: Dryden.

Laws, Sophie. (1983). The sexual politics of pre-menstrual tension. *Women's Studies International Forum, 6,* 19–31.

Lazarre, Jane. (1985, March 10). Writers as mothers. *New York Times Book Review,* p. 30.

Leahy, Robert L., & Shirk, Stephen R. (1984). The development of classificatory skills and sex-trait stereotypes in children. *Sex Roles, 10,* 281–292.

Lear, Martha W. (1972, January 30). Q. If you rape a woman and steal her TV, what can they get you for in New York? A. Stealing her TV. *New York Times Magazine.*

Leavitt, Judith W. (1980). Birthing and anesthesia: The debate over twilight sleep. *Signs, 6,* 147–164.

Lederer, Laura. (1980). Introduction. In L. Lederer (Ed.), *Take back the night* (pp. 15–20). New York: Morrow.

Lee, Harper. (1960). *To kill a mockingbird.* Philadelphia: J. B. Lippincott.

Lee, Patrick C., & Gropper, Nancy B. (1974). Sex-role culture and educational practice. *Harvard Educational Review, 44,* 369–407.

Leibowitz, Lila. (1970, February). Desmond Morris is wrong about breasts, buttocks and body hair. *Psychology Today,* pp. 16, 18, 22.

Leifer, Myra. (1980). Pregnancy. *Signs, 5,* 754–765.

Lemkau, Jeanne P. (1979a). Personality and background characteristics of women in male-dominated occupations: A review. *Psychology of Women Quarterly, 4,* 221–240.

Lemkau, Jeanne P. (1979b). Women and employment: Some emotional hazards. In C. L. Heckerman (Ed.), *The evolving female: Women in psychosocial context* (pp. 107–137). New York: Human Sciences.

Lemkau, Jeanne P. (1983). Women in male-dominated professions: Distinguishing personality and background characteristics. *Psychology of Women Quarterly, 8,* 144–165.

Lemkau, Jeanne P., & Landau, Carol. (1986). The "selfless syndrome": Assessment and treatment considerations. *Psychotherapy: Theory, Research, and Practice, 23,* 227–233.

Lenney, Ellen. (1977). Women's self-confidence in achievement settings. *Psychological Bulletin, 84,* 1–13.

Lenney, Ellen. (1981). What's fine for the gander isn't always good for the goose: Sex differences in self-confidence as a function of ability area and comparison with others. *Sex Roles, 7,* 905–924.

Lenney, Ellen, & Gold, Joel. (1982). Sex differences in self-confidence: The effects of task completion and of comparison to competent others. *Personality and Social Psychology Bulletin, 8,* 74–80.

Lerman, Hannah. (1976). What happens in feminist therapy? In S. Cox (Ed.), *Female psychology: The emerging self* (pp. 378–384). Chicago: Science Research Associates.

Lerman, Hannah. (1985). Some barriers to the development of a feminist theory of personality. In L. B. Rosewater & L. E. A. Walker (Eds.), *Handbook of feminist therapy: Women's issues in psychotherapy* (pp. 5–12). New York: Springer.

Lerner, Gerda. (1977). *The female experience: An American documentary.* Indianapolis: Bobbs-Merrill.

Lesbians: A consciousness raising kit. (1980). Cambridge, MA: Boston NOW.

Lessing, Doris. (1973). *The summer before the dark.* New York: Knopf.

Lessing, Doris. (1984). *The diaries of Jane Somers.* New York: Vintage.

Letters. (1982, December). *Ms,* p. 7.

Levenson, Robert W., & Gottman, John M. (1985). Physiological and affective predictors of change in relationship satisfaction. *Journal of Personality and Social Psychology, 49,* 85–94.

Lever, Janet. (1978). Sex differences in the complexity of children's play and games. *American Sociological Review, 43,* 471–482.

Levertov, Denise. (1973). From Stepping westward. In B. Segnitz & C. Rainey (Eds.), *Psyche: The feminine poetic consciousness* (pp. 100–102). New York: Dell.

Levin, Ira. (1972). *The Stepford wives.* New York: Random House.

Levine, Martin P., & Leonard, Robin. (1984). Discrimination against lesbians in the work force. *Signs, 9,* 700–710.

Levitin, Teresa E., & Chananie, J. D. (1972). Responses of female primary school teachers to sex-typed behaviors in male and female children. *Child Development, 43,* 1309–1316.

Leviton, Laura C., & Whitely, Susan E. (1981). Job seeking patterns of female and male Ph.D. recipients. *Psychology of Women Quarterly, 5,* 690–701.

Lewin, Tamar. (1984, July 22). Maternity leave: Is it leave, indeed? *New York Times,* pp. F1, F23.

Lewine, Richard R. J. (1981). Sex differences in schizophrenia: Timing or subtypes? *Psychological Bulletin, 90,* 432–444.

Lewis, Michael. (1975). Early sex differences in the human: Studies of socio-emotional development. *Archives of Sexual Behavior, 4,* 329–335.

Lewis, Robert A. (Ed.). (1981). *Men in difficult times.* Englewood Cliffs, NJ: Prentice-Hall.

Lewontin, R. C., Rose, Steven, & Kamin, Leon J. (1984). *Not in our genes: Biology, ideology, and human nature.* New York: Pantheon.

Lieberman, Morton A., & Bond, Gary R. (1976). The problem of being a woman: A survey of 17,000 women in consciousness-raising groups. *Journal of Applied Behavioral Science, 12,* 363–380.

Liebert, Robert M., McCall, Robert B., & Hanratty, Margaret A. (1971). Effects of sex-typed information on children's toy preferences. *Journal of Genetic Psychology, 119,* 133–136.

Life of fishing appeals to women. (1980, May 28). *Providence Evening Bulletin.*

Lifshin, Lyn. (1975). From The no more apologizing the no more little laughing blues. In *Upstate Madonna: Poems 1970–1974* (pp. 40–43). Trumansburg, NY: Crossing Press.

Lindsey, Karen. (1977, November). Sexual harassment on the job, and how to stop it. *Ms,* pp. 47–51, 74–78.

Lindsey, Robert. (1976, September 12). Women entering job market at an "extraordinary" pace. *New York Times.*

Lindsey, Robert. (1984, April 4). Sexual abuse of children draws experts' increasing concern nationwide. *New York Times,* p. A21.

Linn, Marcia C. (1985). Fostering equitable consequences from computer learning environments. *Sex Roles, 13,* 229–240.

Lippa, Richard, & Beauvais, Cheryl. (1983). Gender jeopardy: The effects of gender, assessed femininity and masculinity, and false success/failure feedback on performance in an experimental quiz game. *Journal of Personality and Social Psychology, 44,* 344–353.

Lipsitt, Lewis P. (1977). The study of sensory and learning processes of the newborn. *Clinics in Perinatology, 4,* 163–186.

Liss, Marsha B. (1981). Patterns of toy play: An analysis of sex differences. *Sex Roles, 7,* 1143–1150.

Living alone. (1984, August). *ISR Newsletter.* (Institute for Social Research, University of Michigan, Ann Arbor.)

Lobsenz, Norman M. (1974, January 20). Sex and the senior citizen. *New York Times Magazine.*

Lockheed, Marlaine E. (1985). Women, girls, and computers: A first look at the evidence. *Sex Roles, 13,* 115–122.

Loden, Marilyn. (1986, February 9). Disillusion at the corporate top: A machismo that drives women out. *New York Times,* p. F2.

Loewenstein, Sophie F. (1977, November). *Passion in women's lives.* Paper presented at Butler Hospital, Providence, RI.

Loewenstein, Sophie F. (1978). *Understanding lesbian women.* Unpublished paper, Simmons College, School of Social Work, Boston.

Loewenstein, Sophie F., Bloch, Natalie E., Campion, Jennifer, Epstein, Jane S., Gale, Peggy, & Salvatore, Maggie. (1981). A study of satisfactions and stresses of single women in midlife. *Sex Roles, 7,* 1127–1141.

Lombardo, William K., Cretser, Gary A., Lombardo, Barbara, & Mathis, Sharon L. (1983). For cryin' out loud—There is a sex difference. *Sex Roles, 9,* 987–995.

Longino, Helen E. (1980). Pornography, oppression, and freedom: A closer look. In L. Lederer (Ed.), *Take back the night* (pp. 40–54). New York: Morrow.

Looft, William R. (1971). Sex differences in the expression of vocational aspirations by elementary school children. *Developmental Psychology, 5,* 366.

Lorber, Judith. (1981). On *The Reproduction of Mothering:* A methodological debate. *Signs, 6,* 482–486.

Lott, Albert J., & Lott, Bernice E. (1963). *Negro and white youth.* New York: Holt, Rinehart & Winston.

Lott, Albert J., & Lott, Bernice E. (1968). A learning theory approach to interpersonal attitudes. In A. G. Greenwald, T. C. Brock, & T. M. Ostrom (Eds.), *Psychological foundations of attitudes* (pp. 67–88). New York: Academic Press.

Lott, Albert J., & Lott, Bernice E. (1972). The power of liking: Consequences of interpersonal attitudes derived from a liberalized view of secondary reinforcement. In L. Berkowitz (Ed.), *Advances in experimental social psychology* (pp. 109–148). New York: Academic Press.

Lott, Albert J., & Lott, Bernice E. (1974). The role of reward in the formation of positive interpersonal attitudes. In T. L. Huston (Ed.), *Foundations of interpersonal attraction* (pp. 171–192). New York: Academic Press.

Lott, Bernice. (1973). Who wants the children? Some relationships among attitudes toward children, parents, and the liberation of women. *American Psychologist, 28,* 573–582.

Lott, Bernice. (1978a). Toward the elimination of wife abuse: Social science in the service of social change. *Contemporary Psychology, 23,* 668–669.

Lott, Bernice. (1978b). Behavioral concordance with sex role ideology related to play areas, creativity, and parental sextyping of children. *Journal of Personality and Social Psychology, 36,* 1087–1100.

Lott, Bernice. (1979). Sex role ideology and children's drawings: Does the jack-o'-lantern smile or scare? *Sex Roles, 5,* 93–98.

Lott, Bernice. (1981). A feminist critique of androgyny: Toward the elimination of gender attributions for learned behavior. In C. Mayo & N. M. Henley (Eds.), *Gender and nonverbal behavior* (pp. 171–180). New York: Springer-Verlag.

Lott, Bernice. (1985a). The devaluation of women's competence. *Journal of Social Issues, 41*(4), 43–60.

Lott, Bernice. (1985b). The potential enrichment of social/ personality psychology through feminist research, and vice versa. *American Psychologist, 40,* 155–164.

Lott, Bernice. (in press). Sexist discrimination as distancing behavior: I. A laboratory demonstration. *Psychology of Women Quarterly.*

Lott, Bernice. (1986). *Sexist discrimination as distancing behavior: II. Prime time television.* Unpublished paper, University of Rhode Island, Kingston.

Lott, Bernice, Reilly, Mary Ellen, & Howard, Dale R. (1982). Sexual assault and harassment: A campus community case study. *Signs, 8,* 296–319.

Lott, Sara. (1979). *Mountains.* Unpublished poem.

Lott, Sara. (1985). *Shape I'm in.* Unpublished poem.

Lowe, Marian. (1978). Sociobiology and sex differences. *Signs, 4,* 119–125.

Lowe, Marian. (1983). The dialectic of biology and culture. In M. Lowe & R. Hubbard (Eds.), *Woman's nature: Rationalizations of inequality* (pp. 39–62). New York: Pergamon.

Lubinski, David, Tellegen, Auke, & Butcher, James N. (1981). The relationship between androgyny and subjective indicators of emotional well-being. *Journal of Personality and Social Psychology, 40,* 722–730.

Luginbuhl, James, & Mullin, Courtney. (1981). Rape and responsibility: How and how much is the victim blamed? *Sex Roles, 7,* 547–559.

Luker, Kristin. (1984). *Abortion and the politics of motherhood.* Berkeley: University of California Press.

Luria, Zella, & Meade, Robert G. (1984). Sexuality and the middle-aged woman. In G. Baruch & J. Brooks-Gunn (Eds.), *The middle-aged woman* (pp. 371–397). New York: Plenum.

Lynch, Jean M., & Reilly, Mary E. (1985–1986). Role rela-tionships: Lesbian perspectives. *Journal of Homosexuality, 12*(2), 53–69.

Lynn, Michael, & Shurgot, Barbara A. (1984). Responses to lonely hearts advertisements: Effects of reported physical attractiveness, physique, and coloration. *Personality and Social Psychology Bulletin, 10,* 349–357.

Lyons, Richard D. (1984, May 30). It's a boy? That's no surprise. *Providence Evening Bulletin.*

Maccoby, Eleanor E., & Jacklin, Carol N. (1974). *The psychology of sex differences.* Stanford, CA: Stanford University Press.

Maccoby, Eleanor E., & Jacklin, Carol N. (1980). Sex differences in aggression: A rejoinder and reprise. *Child Development, 51,* 964–980.

MacKinnon, Catharine A. (1979). *Sexual harassment of working women.* New Haven: Yale University Press.

MacKinnon, Catharine A. (1982). Feminism, Marxism, method, and the state: An agenda for theory. *Signs, 7,* 515–544.

MacKinnon, Catharine A. (1983). Feminism, Marxism, method, and the state: Toward feminist jurisprudence. *Signs, 8,* 635–658.

MacPherson, Kathleen I. (1984, March/April). Is osteoporosis inevitable? *Network News,* p. 8.

Maddi, Salvatore R. (1974, September). The victimization of Dora: Freud's most famous patient. *Psychology Today,* pp. 91–100.

Maeroff, Gene I. (1986). Making room at the top for women. *New York Times,* p. E9.

Major, Brenda, & Adams, Jeffrey B. (1984). Situational moderators of gender differences in reward allocations. *Sex Roles, 11,* 869–880.

Major, Brenda, Carnevale, Peter J. D., & Deaux, Kay. (1981). A different perspective on androgyny: Evaluations of masculine and feminine personality characteristics. *Journal of Personality and Social Psychology, 41,* 988–1001.

Major, Brenda, McFarlin, Dean B., & Gagnon, Diana. (1984). Overworked and underpaid: On the nature of gender differences in personal entitlement. *Journal of Personality and Social Psychology, 47,* 1399–1412.

Major, Jack. (1983, February 27). If it's new it's cool. *The Providence Sunday Journal.*

Malamuth, Neil M. (1981). Rape proclivity among males. *Journal of Social Issues, 37*(4), 138–157.

Malamuth, Neil M. (1983). Factors associated with rape as predictors of laboratory aggression against women. *Journal of Personality and Social Psychology, 45,* 432–442.

Malamuth, Neil M., Heim, Maggie, & Feshbach, Seymour. (1980). Sexual responsiveness of college students to rape depictions: Inhibitory and disinhibitory effects. *Journal of Personality and Social Psychology, 38,* 399–408.

Malamuth, Neil M., & Spinner, Barry. (1980). A longitudinal content analysis of sexual violence in the best-selling erotica magazines. *Journal of Sex Research, 16,* 226–237.

Malveaux, Julianne. (1985). Current economic trends and

black feminist consciousness. *Black Scholar, 16*(2), 26–31.

Mamay, Patricia D., & Simpson, Richard L. (1981). Three female roles in television commercials. *Sex Roles, 7,* 1223–1232.

Mandelbaum, Dorothy R. (1978). Women in medicine. *Signs, 4,* 136–145.

Manstead, A. S. R., Proffitt, C., & Smart, J. L. (1983). Predicting and understanding mothers' infant-feeding intentions and behaviors. *Journal of Personality and Social Psychology, 44,* 657–671.

Marden, Parker G., & Kolodner, Kenneth. (1979). *Alcohol abuse among women.* Washington, DC: U.S. Department of Health, Education and Welfare.

Marecek, Jeanne. (1977). *Power and women's psychological disorders: Preliminary observations.* Unpublished paper, Swarthmore College, Swarthmore, PA.

Marecek, Jeanne, & Kravetz, Diane. (1977). Women and mental health: A review of feminist change efforts. *Psychiatry, 40,* 323–329.

Margolin, Gayla, & Patterson, Gerald R. (1975). Differential consequences provided by mothers and fathers for their sons and daughters. *Developmental Psychology, 11,* 537–538.

Marini, Margaret M. (1978). Sex differences in the determination of adolescent aspirations: A review of research. *Sex Roles, 4,* 723–753.

Markson, Elizabeth W., & Hess, Beth B. (1980). Older women in the city. *Signs, 5*(Suppl.), 127–141.

Marriage vs. single life. (1982, Autumn). *ISR Newsletter* (Institute for Social Research, University of Michigan, Ann Arbor)

Marriages down in 1985; divorce up after a slide. (1986, March 27). *Providence Evening Bulletin,* p. A-5.

Marshall, Paule. (1975). Reena. In M. H. Washington (Ed.), *Black-eyed Susans* (pp. 114–138). Garden City, NY: Anchor.

Martin, Del. (1976). *Battered wives.* San Francisco, CA: Glide.

Marx, Jean L. (1979a). Dysmenorrhea: Basic research leads to a rational therapy. *Science, 205,* 175–176.

Marx, Jean L. (1979b). Hormones and their effects in the aging body. *Science, 206,* 805–806.

Mason, Karen O. (1980). Sex and status in science. (Review of *Fair Science,* by J. R. Cole.) *Science, 208,* 277–278.

Massachusetts Coalition of Battered Women Service Groups. (1981). *For shelter and beyond.* Boston: Author.

Masson, Jeffrey M. (1983). *The assault on truth.* New York: Farrar, Straus & Giroux.

Masters, John C., & Wilkinson, Alexander. (1976). Consensual and discriminative stereotypes of sex-type judgments by parents and children. *Child Development, 47,* 208–217.

Masters, William, & Johnson, Virginia. (1966). *Human sexual response.* Boston: Little, Brown.

Matthews, Karen A., & Carra, Joseph. (1982). Suppression of menstrual distress symptoms: A study of Type A behavior. *Personality and Social Psychology Bulletin, 8,* 146–151.

Matthews, Wendy S. (1981). Sex-role perception, portrayal, and preference in the fantasy play of young children. *Sex Roles, 7,* 979–987.

May, Clifford D. (1986, March 2). Behind a rise in sexual-abuse reports. *New York Times,* p. E8.

Maybelline advertisement. (1984, April). *Teen* magazine.

McBride, Angela B., & Black, Kathryn N. (1984). Differences that suggest female investment in, and male distance from, children. *Sex Roles, 10,* 231–246.

McClain, Edwin. (1978). Feminists and nonfeminists: Contrasting profiles in independence and affiliation. *Psychological Reports, 43,* 435–441.

McClintock, Martha. (1979). Considering "A biosocial perspective on parenting." *Signs, 4,* 703–710.

McClure, Gail T., & Piel, Ellen. (1978). College-bound girls and science careers: Perceptions of barriers and facilitating factors. *Journal of Vocational Behavior, 12,* 172–183.

McConahay, Shirley, & McConahay, John B. (1977). Sexual permissiveness, sex-role rigidity, and violence across cultures. *Journal of Social Issues, 33,* 134–143.

McCormack, Arlene. (1985). The sexual harassment of students by teachers: The case of students in science. *Sex Roles, 13,* 21–32.

McCormick, Naomi B. (1979). Come-ons and put-offs: Unmarried students' strategies for having and avoiding sexual intercourse. *Psychology of Women Quarterly, 4,* 194–211.

McCormick, Naomi B., Brannigan, Gary G., & LaPlante, Marcia N. (1984). Social desirability in the bedroom: Role of approval motivation in sexual relationships. *Sex Roles, 11,* 303–314.

McCoy, Elin. (1980, June 19). More mothers joining support groups. *New York Times.*

McGee, Mark G. (1979). Human spatial abilities: Psychometric studies and environmental, genetic, hormonal, and neurological influences. *Psychological Bulletin, 86,* 889–918.

McGhee, Paul E., & Frueh, Terry. (1980). Television viewing and the learning of sex-role stereotypes. *Sex Roles, 6,* 179–188.

McGraw-Hill Book Co. (1974). *Guidelines for equal treatment of the sexes in McGraw-Hill Book Company publications* (pamphlet). New York: Author.

McGuire, Linda S., Ryan, Kimberly O., & Omenn, Gilbert S. (1975). Congenital adrenal hyperplasia. II. Cognitive and behavioral studies. *Behavior Genetics, 5,* 175–188.

McLaughlin, Mary M. (1974). Survivors and surrogates: Children and parents from the ninth to the thirteenth centuries. In L. deMause (Ed.), *The history of childhood* (pp. 101–181). New York: Harper & Row.

McMahan, Ian D. (1982). Expectancy of success on sex-linked tasks. *Sex Roles, 8,* 949–958.

McMillan, Julie R., Clifton, A. Kay, McGrath, Diane, & Gale, Wanda S. (1977). Women's language: Uncertainty or interpersonal sensitivity and emotionality? *Sex Roles, 3,* 545–559.

McNulty, Faith. (1981). *The burning bed.* New York: Bantam.

Mead, Margaret. (1950). *Sex and temperament in three primitive societies*. New York: Mentor. (Original work published in 1935.)

Mead, Margaret. (1968). *Male and female*. New York: Dell. (Original work published in 1949.)

Meece, Judith L., Parsons, Jacquelynne E., Kaczala, Caroline M., Goff, Susan B., & Futterman, Robert. (1982). Sex differences in math achievement: Toward a model of academic choice. *Psychological Bulletin, 91*, 324–348.

Melson, Gail F. (1977). Sex differences in use of indoor space by preschool children. *Perceptual and Motor Skills, 44*, 207–213.

Menke, Edna M. (1983). Menstrual beliefs and experiences of mother-daughter dyads. In S. Golub (Ed.), *Menarche* (pp. 133–137). Boston: Lexington Books.

Men's life expectancy raised to 71.1 years. (1985, June 6). *Providence Evening Bulletin*.

Merritt, Shayne. (1982). Sex roles and political ambition. *Sex Roles, 8*, 1025–1036.

Merritt, Susan M. (1986, July 27). For women, a central role in computers. *New York Times*, p. E22.

Meyer, C. Buf, & Taylor, Shelley E. (1986). Adjustment to rape. *Journal of Personality and Social Psychology, 50*, 1226–1234.

Miller, Jean B. (1976). *Toward a new psychology of women*. Boston: Beacon.

Miller, Patricia Y., & Fowlkes, Martha R. (1980). Social and behavioral constructions of female sexuality. *Signs, 5*, 783–800.

Millett, Kate. (1971). Prostitution: A quartet for female voices. In V. Gornick & B. K. Moran (Eds.), *Women in sexist society* (pp. 21–69). New York: Basic Books.

Millett, Kate. (1978, November). Reply to "What do you think is erotic?" *Ms*, p. 80.

Milow, Vera J. (1983). Menstrual education: Past, present, and future. In S. Golub (Ed.), *Menarche* (pp. 127–132). Boston: Lexington Books.

Miner, Robert. (1980, June 15). Do fathers make good mothers? *Family Weekly*, pp. 4–6.

Misconceptions about women Ph.D.s challenged. (1982, Spring). *Project on the Status and Education of Women, 34*, pp. 6–7. (Association of American Colleges, Washington, DC)

Molestation story puts Fla. senator in spotlight. (1984, May 3). *Providence Evening Bulletin*.

Money, John. (1972, December). *Nativism versus culturalism in gender-identity differentiation*. Paper presented at the meeting of the American Association for the Advancement of Science, Washington, DC.

Montemayor, Raymond. (1974). Children's performance in a game and their attraction to it as a function of sex-typed labels. *Child Development, 45*, 152–156.

Moore, Helen A. (1985). Job satisfaction and women's spheres of work. *Sex Roles, 13*, 663–678.

More Americans going it alone. (1985, November 24). *New York Times*, p. E6.

More and more women forced into job market. (1985, October 29). *Providence Evening Bulletin*.

More fathers receiving paternity leave. (1984, July 26). *Providence Evening Bulletin*.

More people are living alone. (1985, November 20). *Providence Evening Bulletin*.

Morelock, Judy C. (1980). Sex differences in susceptibility to social influence. *Sex Roles, 6*, 537–548.

Morgan, Carolyn S. (1980). Female and male attitudes toward life: Implications for theories of mental health. *Sex Roles, 6*, 367–380.

Morgan, Kathryn P., & Ayim, Maryann. (1984). Comment on Bem's "Gender schema theory and its implications for child development: Raising gender-aschematic children in a gender-schematic society." *Signs, 10*, 188–196.

Morgan, Michael. (1982). Television and adolescents' sex role stereotypes: A longitudinal study. *Journal of Personality and Social Psychology, 43*, 947–955.

Morgan, Robin. (1970). *Sisterhood is powerful*. New York: Random House.

Morgan, Robin. (1978). *Going too far*. New York: Random House.

Morgan, Robin. (1982a). *The anatomy of freedom*. Garden City, NY: Anchor/Doubleday.

Morgan, Robin. (1982b, December). A quantum leap in feminist theory. *Ms*, pp. 101–106.

Morgan, Susanne. (1982, March). Sex after hysterectomy—What your doctor never told you. *Ms*, pp. 82–85.

Morokoff, Patricia J. (1985). Effects of sex guilt, repression, sexual "arousability," and sexual experience on female sexual arousal during erotica and fantasy. *Journal of Personality and Social Psychology, 49*, 177–187.

Morrison, Toni. (1971, August 22). What the black woman thinks about women's lib. *New York Times Magazine*, pp. 14–15, 63–64, 66.

Moss, Howard A. (1967). Sex, age, and state as determinants of mother-infant interaction. *Merrill-Palmer Quarterly, 13*, 19–36.

Most depend on social security. (1986, March 20). *New York Times*, p. C8.

Most law students in survey support allowing abortion, split on school prayer. (1985, April 22). *Providence Evening Bulletin*.

Mulac, Anthony, Incontro, Carol R., & James, Margaret R. (1985). Comparison of the gender-linked language effect and sex role stereotypes. *Journal of Personality and Social Psychology, 49*, 1098–1109.

Munro, Alice. (1977). Red dress—1946. In N. Dean and M. Stark (Eds.), *In the looking glass* (pp. 199–211). New York: Putnam.

Murphy, Mary. (1986, March 29). Sexual harassment in Hollywood. *TV Guide*, pp. 2–6, 10–11.

Murray, Ann D. (1979). Infant crying as an elicitor of parental behavior: An examination of two models. *Psychological Bulletin, 86*, 191–215.

Murray, Michele (Ed.). (1973). *A house of good proportion: Images of women in literature* (2nd ed.). New York: Simon & Schuster.

Murray, Saundra R., & Mednick, Martha T. S. (1977). Black women's achievement orientation: Motivational and cognitive factors. *Psychology of Women Quarterly, 1*, 247–259.

Myers, Harriet H., & Siegel, Paul S. (1985). The motivation to breast feed: A fit to the opponent-process theory? *Journal of Personality and Social Psychology, 49*, 189–193.

Myers, Linda J. (1978). *Black women in double jeopardy.* Unpublished paper, Ohio State University, Columbus.

Nash, Sharon C. (1975). The relationship among sex-role stereotyping, sex-role preference and the sex difference in spatial visualization. *Sex Roles, 1*, 15–32.

Nassi, Alberta J., & Abramowitz, Stephen I. (1978). Raising consciousness about women's groups: Process and outcome research. *Psychology of Women Quarterly, 3*, 139–156.

Nation ignoring problem of teenage pregnancies, says House subcommittee. (1986, February 10). *Providence Evening Bulletin.*

National Advisory Council on Economic Opportunity. (1981, September). *The American promise: Equal justice and economic opportunity.* Final Report. Washington, DC: U.S. Government Printing Office.

National Commission on Working Women. (1978). *An overview of women in the work force.* Washington, DC: Center for Women and Work.

National Commission on Working Women. (1983). *Women's work: Undervalued, underpaid.* Washington, DC: Center for Women and Work.

Nation's birthrate up in '84. (1985, March 30). *Providence Evening Bulletin.*

Naylor, Gloria. (1985). *Linden Hills.* New York: Ticknor & Field.

Near, Holly. (1974). Get off me baby. *Alive Album.* Ukiah, CA. Redwood Records.

Neiswender-Reedy, M., Birren, James E., & Schaie, K. Warner. (1981). Age and sex differences in satisfying love relationships across the adult life span. *Human Development, 24*, 52–66.

Nelson, Gayle. (1975). The double standard in adolescent novels. *English Journal, 64*, 53–56.

Nettles, Elizabeth J., & Loevinger, Jane. (1983). Sex role expectations and ego level in relation to problem marriages. *Journal of Personality and Social Psychology, 45*, 676–687.

Nevid, Jeffrey S. (1984). Sex differences in factors of romantic attraction. *Sex Roles, 11*, 401–411.

New asteroid is found within our solar orbit. (1978, September 10). *Providence Evening Bulletin.*

New laws recognizing marital rape as a crime. (1984, December 29). *New York Times.*

New police policy to stem domestic violence triples arrests. (1984, July 19). *Providence Evening Bulletin*, p. A-4.

Newcomb, Michael D. (1986). Nuclear attitudes and reactions: Associations with depression, drug use, and equality of life. *Journal of Personality and Social Psychology, 50*, 906–920.

Newcomb, Michael D., & Bentler, P. M. (1983). Dimensions of subjective female orgasmic responsiveness. *Journal of Personality and Social Psychology, 44*, 862–873.

Newcombe, Nora, Bandura, Mary M., & Taylor, Dawn G.

(1983). Sex differences in spatial ability and spatial activities. *Sex Roles, 9*, 377–386.

Newman, Lucile F. (1969). Folklore of pregnancy: Wives' tales in Contra Costa County, California. *Western Folklore, 28*(2), 112–135.

Newman, Lucile F. (1972). Birth control: An anthropological view. *Addison-Wesley Modular Publications*, Module 27. Reading, MA: Addison-Wesley.

News. (1981, May). National NOW Times.

Newton, Niles. (1970, November). Childbirth and culture. *Psychology Today*, pp. 74–75.

Newton, Niles. (1973). Trebly sensuous woman. In Psychology Today (Eds.), *The female experience* (pp. 22–25). Del Mar, CA: Communications/Research/Machines.

Newton, Niles, & Modahl, Charlotte. (1978, March). Pregnancy: The closest human relationship. *Human Nature*, pp. 40–49.

Nickerson, Eileen T., & Pitochelli, Elaine T. (1978, March). *Learned helplessness and depression in married women: Marriage as a depressing life style for women.* Paper presented at the meeting of the Eastern Psychological Association, Washington, DC.

Nicola-McLaughlin, Andrée. (1985). White power, black despair: Vanessa Williams in Babylon. *Black Scholar, 16*(2), 32–39.

Nies, Judith. (1977). Sarah Moore Grimké. In *Seven women: Portraits from the American radical tradition* (pp. 1–31). New York: Penguin.

9 to 5 in the news. (1985, May/June). *9 to 5 Newsletter*, p. 4. (Available from 1224 Huron Road, Cleveland, OH 44115)

99 ways to attract the right man. *TV Guide.* (1985, May 7).

No more Miss America! (1970). In R. Morgan (Ed.), *Sisterhood is powerful* (pp. 521–524). New York: Vintage.

Noble, Kenneth B. (1985, December 12). Low-paying jobs foreseen for most working women. *New York Times*, p. A20.

Nochlin, Linda. (1979, October 28). Women painters and Germaine Greer. (Review of *The Obstacle Race* by G. Greer.) *New York Times Book Review*, pp. 3, 46.

Norman, Colin. (1984). No panacea for the firewood crisis. *Science, 226*, 676.

Norman, Ralph D. (1974). Sex differences in preferences for sex of children: A replication after 20 years. *Journal of Psychology, 88*, 229–239.

Norwood, Christopher. (1985, May). In the name of science. *Ms*, pp. 36, 40.

Not victimless; The prostitutes are the victims. (1980, June 26). *Providence Evening Bulletin.*

NOW. (1983). *The myth of equality.* (Available from NOW Legal Defense and Education Fund, 132 W. 43rd St., New York, NY 10036)

Number of women in state legislatures. (1985, January/February). *Women's Political Times*, p. 7.

Nuns' group opposes anti-abortion effort. (1982, May 29). *Providence Evening Bulletin.*

Nyquist, Linda, Slivken, Karla, Spence, Janet T., & Helmreich, Robert L. (1985). Household responsibilities in middle-class couples: The contribution of demographic and personality variables. *Sex Roles, 12*, 15−34.

Oakley, Ann. (1979). A case of maternity: Paradigms of women as maternity cases. *Signs, 4*, 607−631.

Oates, Joyce C. (1981, March 29). Why is your writing so violent? *New York Times Book Review*, pp. 15, 35.

Oates, Joyce C. (1985). *Solstice*. New York: Dutton.

Oates, Joyce C. (1986). *Marya: A life*. New York: Dutton.

Oates, Mary J., & Williamson, Susan. (1978). Women's colleges and women achievers. *Signs, 3*, 795−806.

Oberstone, Andrea K., & Sukoneck, Harriet. (1976). Psychological adjustment and life style of single lesbians and single heterosexual women. *Psychology of Women Quarterly, 1*, 172−188.

O'Brien, Patricia. (1973). *The woman alone*. New York: New York Times Book Co.

Odent, Michel. (1984). *Birth reborn*. New York: Pantheon.

Offermann, Lynn R., & Schrier, Pamela E. (1985). Social influence strategies: The impact of sex, role, and attitudes toward power. *Personality and Social Psychology Bulletin, 11*, 286−300.

Offir, Carole W. (1975, January). Don't take it lying down. *Psychology Today*, p. 73.

O'Halloren, Bill. (1977, July 24). Nobody (in TV) loves you when you're old and gray. *New York Times*.

O'Keefe, Eileen S. C., & Hyde, Janet S. (1983). The development of occupational sex-role stereotypes: The effects of gender stability and age. *Sex Roles, 9*, 481−492.

O'Kelly, Charlotte G. (1974). Sexism in children's television. *Journalism Quarterly, 51*, 722−724.

Olds, Sharon. (1980). From The language of the brag. In *Satan says* (pp. 44−45). Pittsburgh, PA: Pittsburgh University Press.

Olejnik, Anthony B. (1980). Socialization of achievement: Effects of children's sex and age on achievement evaluations by adults. *Personality and Social Psychology Bulletin, 6*, 68−73.

Olejnik, Anthony B., Tompkins, Brigitte, & Heinbuck, Claudia. (1982). Sex differences, sex-role orientation, and reward allocations. *Sex roles, 8*, 711−719.

Olsen, Tillie. (1976). I stand here ironing. In *Tell me a riddle* (pp. 9−21). New York: Dell.

Olson, Sheryl L. (1984). The effects of sex-role taking on children's responses to aggressive conflict situations. *Sex Roles, 10*, 817−823.

Orbach, Susie. (1986). *Hunger strike: An anorectic's struggle as a metaphor for life*. New York: Norton.

O'Reilly, Jane. (1982). *The girl I left behind*. New York: Bantam.

Ortner, Sherry B. (1974). Is female to male as nature is to culture? In M. Z. Rosaldo & L. Lamphere (Eds.), *Woman, culture and society* (pp. 67−87). Stanford, CA: Stanford University Press.

Ortner, Sherry B., & Whitehead, Harriet (Eds.). (1981). *Sexual meanings: The cultural construction of gender and sexuality*. Cambridge, MA: Cambridge University Press.

Ostriker, Alicia. (1986, March 9). American poetry, now shaped by women. *New York Times Book Review*, pp. 1, 28, 30.

Packwood, Bob. (1984, April 21). Civil Rights Act: A recommitment. *Providence Journal-Bulletin*, p. A16.

PACs give women crucial assistance during campaigns. (1984, July 13). *Providence Evening Bulletin*, p. A14.

Padesky, Christine A., & Hammen, Constance L. (1981). Sex differences in depressive symptom expression and help-seeking among college students. *Sex Roles, 7*, 309−320.

Paige, Karen E. (1973). Women learning to sing the menstrual blues. In Psychology Today (Eds.), *The female experience* (pp. 17−21). Del Mar, CA: Communications/Research/Machines.

Pallak, Suzanne R., & Davies, Jacqueline M. (1982). Finding fault versus attributing responsibility: Using facts differently. *Personality and Social Psychology Bulletin, 8*, 454−459.

Palmer, Phyllis. (1983). "The racial feminization of poverty": Women of color as portents of the future for all women. *Women's Studies Quarterly, 11*(3), 4−6.

Paludi, Michele A., & Strayer, Lisa A. (1985). What's in an author's name? Differential evaluations of performance as a function of author's name. *Sex Roles, 12*, 353−361.

Papalia, Diane E., & Tennent, Susan S. (1975). Vocational aspirations in preschoolers: A manifestation of early sex role stereotyping. *Sex Roles, 1*, 197−199.

Paper urges therapists to remember wife. (1982, Summer). *Bradley Scope*, p. 7. (Emma Bradley Hospital, East Providence, RI)

Paradise, Louis V., & Wall, Shavaun M. (1986). Children's perceptions of male and female principals and teachers. *Sex Roles, 14*, 1−7.

Parlee, Mary B. (1973). The premenstrual syndrome. *Psychological Bulletin, 80*, 454−465.

Parlee, Mary B. (1982). Changes in moods and activation levels during the menstrual cycle in experimentally naive subjects. *Psychology of Women Quarterly, 7*, 119−131.

Parlee, Mary B. (1983). Menstrual rhythms in sensory processes: A review of fluctuations in vision, olfaction, audition, taste, and touch. *Psychological Bulletin, 93*, 539−548.

Parsons, Jacquelynne E., Ruble, Diane N., Hodges, Karen L., & Small, Ava W. (1976). Cognitive-developmental factors in emerging sex differences in achievement-related expectancies. *Journal of Social Issues, 32*, 47−61.

Patinkin, Mark. (1983, March 25). Hormone disharmony makes us do what we do. *Providence Evening Bulletin*, p. A-3.

Patrick, G. T. W. (1979). The psychology of women. In J. H. Williams (Ed.), *Psychology of women: Selected readings* (pp. 3−11). New York: Norton. (Original work published in 1895.)

Paul, Lois. (1974). The mastery of work and the mystery of sex in a Guatemalan village. In M. Z. Rosaldo & L. Lamphere (Eds.), *Woman, culture and society* (pp. 281−299). Stanford, CA: Stanford University Press.

Pear, Robert. (1985, August 29). Poverty data and families. *New York Times*, p. A17.

Pearce, Diana M. (1985). Toil and trouble: Women workers and unemployment compensation. *Signs, 10,* 439–459.

Pearson, Jessica. (1980). Women who farm: A preliminary portrait. *Sex Roles, 6,* 561–574.

Pedersen, Frank A., & Bell, Richard Q. (1970). Sex differences in preschool children without histories of complications of pregnancy and delivery. *Developmental Psychology, 3,* 10–15.

Peplau, Letitia A. (1976). Impact of fear of success and sex-role attitudes on women's competitive achievement. *Journal of Personality and Social Psychology, 34,* 561–568.

Peplau, Letitia A. (1979). Power in dating relationships. In J. Freeman (Ed.), *Women: A feminist perspective* (2nd ed.) (pp. 106–121). Palo Alto, CA: Mayfield.

Peplau, Letitia A. (1981, March). What homosexuals want. *Psychology Today,* 28–34, 37–38.

Peplau, Letitia A. (1982). Research on homosexual couples: An overview. *Journal of Homosexuality, 8*(2), 3–8.

Peplau, Letitia A., Rubin, Zick, & Hill, Charles T. (1977). Sexual intimacy in dating relationships. *Journal of Social Issues, 33,* 86–109.

Perry, David G., & Bussey, Kay. (1979). The social learning theory of sex differences: Imitation is alive and well. *Journal of Personality and Social Psychology, 37,* 1699–1712.

Persell, Caroline H. (1983). Gender, rewards and research in education. *Psychology of Women Quarterly, 8,* 33–47.

Person, Ethel S. (1980). Sexuality as the mainstay of identity: Psychoanalytic perspectives. *Signs, 5,* 605–630.

Personal Products Corp. (1957). *Growing up and liking it* (pamphlet). Milltown, NJ: Author.

Perun, Pamela J. (1981). Comment on Rossi's "Life-span theories and women's lives." *Signs, 7,* 243–248.

Petersen, Anne. (1983). Menarche: Meaning of measures and measuring meaning. In S. Golub (Ed.), *Menarche* (pp. 63–76). Boston: Lexington Books.

Peterson, Jonathan. (1983, February 8). Social security: A bias against working wives? *Providence Evening Bulletin.*

Peterson, Rolf A. (1983). Attitudes toward the childless spouse. *Sex Roles, 9,* 321–331.

Philips, Roger D., & Gilroy, Faith D. (1985). Sex-role stereotypes and clinical judgments of mental health: The Brovermans' findings reexamined. *Sex Roles, 12,* 179–193.

Philipson, Ilene. (1984). The repression of history and gender: A critical perspective on the feminist sexuality debate. *Signs, 10,* 113–118.

Phillips, Gerald M. (1983). *Loving and living.* Englewood Cliffs, NJ: Prentice-Hall.

Phillips, Sheridan, King, Suzanne, & DuBois, Louise. (1978). Spontaneous activities of female versus male newborns. *Child Development, 49,* 590–597.

Phillis, Diane E., & Stein, Peter J. (1983). Sink or swing? The lifestyles of single adults. In E. R. Allgeier & N. B. McCormick (Eds.), *Changing boundaries: Gender roles and sexual behavior* (pp. 202–225). Palo Alto, CA: Mayfield.

Phipps-Yonas, Susan. (1980). Teenage pregnancy and motherhood: A review of the literature. *American Journal of Orthopsychiatry, 50,* 403–431.

Piercy, Marge. (1975). *Small changes.* New York: Fawcett.

Piercy, Marge. (1976a). *Woman on the edge of time.* New York: Fawcett.

Piercy, Marge. (1976b). Rape poem. In *Living in the open* (pp. 88–89). New York: Knopf.

Piercy, Marge. (1979). *Vida.* New York: Summit.

Piercy, Marge. (1983). *Braided lives.* New York: Fawcett.

Piercy, Marge. (1984a). *Fly away home.* New York: Summit.

Piercy, Marge. (1984b). The inquisition. In *The moon is always female.* New York: Knopf.

Piercy, Marge. (1984c). Under red Aries. In *The moon is always female.* New York: Knopf.

Piercy, Marge. (1984d). The ordinary gauntlet. In *The moon is always female.* New York: Knopf.

Piercy, Marge. (1984e). Right to life. In *The moon is always female.* New York: Knopf.

Pines, Ayala, & Kafry, Ditsa. (1981). Tedium in the life and work of professional women as compared with men. *Sex Roles, 7,* 963–977.

Pitchford, Kenneth. (1978, October). The manly art of child care. *Ms,* pp. 96–99.

Pizzey, Erin. (1974). *Scream quietly or the neighbours will hear.* Harmondsworth, England: Penguin.

Plath, Sylvia. (1972). *The bell jar.* New York: Bantam.

Plumb, Pat, & Cowan, Gloria. (1984). A developmental study of destereotyping and androgynous activity preferences of tomboys, nontomboys, and males. *Sex Roles, 10,* 703–712.

Pogrebin, Letty C. (1972, September). Down with sexist upbringing. *Ms,* pp. 18, 32.

Pogrebin, Letty C. (1982a, February). Big changes in parenting. *Ms,* pp. 41–46.

Pogrebin, Letty C. (1982b, June). Anti-Semitism in the women's movement. *Ms,* pp. 66–67.

Pogrebin, Letty C. (1983, September 15). Hers. *New York Times,* p. C2.

Polivy, Janet, & Herman, C. Peter. (1985). Dieting and binging: A causal analysis. *American Psychologist, 40,* 193–201.

Poll says women are more tolerant of pre-marital sex. (1983, December 14). *Providence Evening Bulletin.*

Poll: Women belong in the workplace. (1986, June 17). *Providence Evening Bulletin,* pp. A1–A2.

Poll: Women more sensitive to "life-threatening" issues. (1983, October 3). *Providence Evening Bulletin.*

Pollis, Nicholas P., & Doyle, Donald C. (1972). Sex role, status, and perceived competence among first graders. *Perceptual and Motor Skills, 34,* 235–238.

Pollitt, Katha. (1985, December 12). Hers. *New York Times,* p. C2.

Pope, Kenneth S., Levenson, Hanna, & Schover, Leslie R. (1979). Sexual intimacy in psychological training: Results and implications of a national survey. *American Psychologist, 34,* 682–689.

Porter, Sylvia. (1985, August 23). What's a housewife worth? More than numbers show. *Providence Evening Bulletin.*

Posner, Judith. (1979). It's all in your head: Feminist and

medical models of menopause (strange bedfellows). *Sex Roles, 5,* 179–190.

Poverty hits minority women hardest. (1982, July). *Woman Power,* pp. 1–2. (National Association of Social Workers Committee on Women's Issues)

Powers, Marla N. (1980). Menstruation and reproduction: An Oglala case. *Signs, 6,* 54–65.

Prather, Jane, & Fidell, Linda S. (1975, January). Sex differences in the content and style of medical advertisements. *Social Science and Medicine, 9,* 23–26.

Pregnancy discrimination. (1985, Spring). *Civil Liberties,* p. 8.

Premenstrual syndrome keeps doctors guessing. (1986, January 6). *New York Times,* p. B5.

Presser, Harriet B. (1980). Sally's corner: Coping with unmarried motherhood. *Journal of Social Issues, 36*(1), 107–129.

Presser, Harriet B., & Cain, Virginia S. (1983). Shift work among dual-earner couples with children. *Science, 219,* 876–878.

Probber, Joan, & Ehrman, Lee. (1978). Pertinent genetics for understanding gender. In E. Tobach & B. Rosoff (Eds.), *Genes and gender: I* (pp. 13–30). New York: Gordian Press.

Pyke, S. W., & Kahill, S. P. (1983). Sex differences in characteristics presumed relevant to professional productivity. *Psychology of Women Quarterly, 8,* 189–192.

Quadagno, David M., Briscoe, Robert, & Quadagno, Jill S. (1977). Effect of perinatal gonadal hormones on selected nonsexual behavior patterns: A critical assessment of the nonhuman and human literature. *Psychological Bulletin, 84,* 62–80.

Queen, Stuart A., & Adams, John B. (1952). *The family in various cultures.* Philadelphia: Lippincott.

Quina, Kathryn, & Lott, Bernice. (1986, March). *Post-abortion personal issues and changes in life direction.* Paper presented at the meeting of the Association for Women in Psychology, Oakland, CA.

Rachlin, Susan K., & Vogt, Glenda L. (1974). Sex roles as presented to children by coloring books. *Journal of Popular Culture, 8,* 549–556.

Radicalesbians. (1976). The woman identified woman. In S. Cox (Ed.), *Female psychology: The emerging self* (pp. 304–308). Chicago: Science Research Associates.

Radloff, Lenore. (1975). Sex differences in depression: The effects of occupation and marital status. *Sex Roles, 1,* 249–265.

Radloff, Lenore S. (1980). Depression and the empty nest. *Sex Roles, 6,* 775–781.

Rador, Carol G., Masnick, Barbara R., & Hauser, Barbara B. (1977, November). Issues in feminist therapy: The work of a women's study group. *Social Work,* 507–509.

Radway, Janice A. (1984). *Reading the romance: Women, patriarchy, and popular literature.* Chapel Hill: University of North Carolina Press.

Ragan, Janet M. (1982). Gender displays in portrait photographs. *Sex Roles, 8,* 33–44.

Ramey, Estelle R. (1976). Sex hormones and executive ability. In S. Cox (Ed.), *Female psychology: The emerging self* (pp. 20–30). Chicago: Science Research Associates.

Rape case decision infuriates Hawaiians. (1978, March 6). *Providence Evening Bulletin.*

Rapin, Lynn S., & Cooper, Merri-Ann. (1980). Images of men and women: A comparison of feminists and non-feminists. *Psychology of Women Quarterly, 5,* 186–194.

Raskin, A. H. (1977, June 5). Women are still absent from labor's top ranks. *New York Times.*

Rawlings, Edna I., & Carter, Dianne K. (Eds.). (1977). *Psychotherapy for women: Treatment toward equality.* Springfield, IL: Charles C Thomas.

Recovery of women workers from recession lags greatly. (1984, March 23). *Providence Evening Bulletin,* p. A-15.

Re-entry women: Special programs for special populations. (1981a, April). *Project on the Status and Education of Women.* (Association of American Colleges, Washington, DC)

Re-entry women: Relevant statistics. (1981b, April). *Project on the Status and Education of Women.* (Association of American Colleges, Washington, DC)

Reid, Pamela T. (1978a, March). *Separate not equal: A behavioral analysis of black and white television characters.* Paper presented at the meeting of the Eastern Psychological Association, Washington, DC.

Reid, Pamela T. (1978b, August). *Black matriarchy: Young and old.* Paper presented at the meeting of the American Psychological Association, Toronto.

Reid, Pamela T. (1984). Feminism versus minority group identity: Not for black women only. *Sex Roles, 10,* 247–255.

Reilly, Mary Ellen. (1976). The family. *Population Profiles,* Unit No. 17. Washington, CT: The Center for Information on America.

Reilly, Mary Ellen, Lott, Bernice, & Gallogly, Sheila M. (in press). Sexual harassment of university students. *Sex Roles.*

Reinhold, Robert. (1985, December 15). Cherokees install first woman as chief of major American Indian tribe. *New York Times.*

Reinisch, June M. (1981). Prenatal exposure to synthetic progestins increases potential for aggression in humans. *Science, 211,* 1171–1173.

Reinisch, June M., & Karow, William G. (1977). Prenatal exposure to synthetic progestins and estrogens: Effect on human development. *Archives of Sexual Behavior, 6,* 257–288.

Reis, Harry T., Senchak, Marilyn, & Solomon, Beth. (1985). Sex differences in the intimacy of social interaction: Further examination of potential explanations. *Journal of Personality and Social Psychology, 48,* 1204–1217.

Reis, Harry T., & Wright, Stephanie. (1982). Knowledge of sex-role stereotypes in children aged 3 to 5. *Sex Roles, 8,* 1049–1056.

Reiter, Ed. (1981, July 26). Another breakthrough for women's rights. *New York Times.*

Rekers, George A. (1975). Stimulus control over sex-typed play in cross-gender identified boys. *Journal of Experimental Child Psychology, 20,* 136–148.

Rendely, Judith G., Holmstrom, Robert M., & Karp, Stephen A. (1984). The relationship of sex-role identity, life style, and mental health in suburban American homemakers: 1. Sex role, employment and adjustment. *Sex Roles, 11*, 839–848.

Renne, Karen S., & Allen, Paul C. (1976). Gender and the ritual of the door. *Sex Roles, 2*, 167–174.

Repetti, Rena L. (1984). Determinants of children's sex stereotyping: Parental sex-role traits and television viewing. *Personality and Social Psychology Bulletin, 10*, 457–468.

Report shows declining health among children; Reagan blamed. (1986, February 26). *Providence Evening Bulletin.*

Research dispels incestuous family myth. (1984, March). *NASW News*, pp. 3–4.

Resolution for the decriminalization and destigmatization of prostitution. (1984, August). Adopted by Division 35, American Psychological Association, at conference in Toronto.

Reuben, David. (1969). *Everything you always wanted to know about sex but were afraid to ask.* New York: McKay.

Reward for top work? Look for woman boss. (1986, June/July). *University of Utah Review.*

Rheingold, Harriet L., & Cook, Kaye V. (1975). The contents of boys' and girls' rooms as an index of parents' behavior. *Child Development, 46*, 459–463.

Ribble, Margaret A. (1944). Infantile experience in relation to personality development. In J. McV. Hunt (Ed.), *Personality and the behavior disorders* (Vol. 2) (pp. 621–651). New York: Ronald.

Rice, Berkeley. (1980, December). Enlightened talk, chauvinist action. *Psychology Today*, pp. 24–25.

Rich, Adrienne. (1977). *Of woman born.* New York: Bantam.

Rich, Adrienne. (1980). Compulsory heterosexuality and lesbian existence. *Signs, 5*, 631–660.

Richardson, Deborah C., Bernstein, Sandy, & Taylor, Stuart P. (1979). The effect of situational contingencies on female retaliative behavior. *Journal of Personality and Social Psychology, 37*, 2044–2048.

Richardson, Deborah C., & Campbell, Jennifer L. (1980). Alcohol and wife abuse: The effect of alcohol on attributions of blame for wife abuse. *Personality and Social Psychology Bulletin, 6*, 51–56.

Richardson, Deborah C., & Campbell, Jennifer L. (1982). Alcohol and rape: The effect of alcohol on attributions of blame for rape. *Personality and Social Psychology Bulletin, 8*, 468–476.

Richardson, Deborah C., Vinsel, Anne, & Taylor, Stuart P. (1980). Female aggression as a function of attitudes toward women. *Sex Roles, 6*, 265–271.

Richardson, John G., & Mahoney, E. R. (1981). The perceived social status of husbands and wives in dual-work families as a function of achieved and derived occupational status. *Sex Roles, 7*, 1189–1198.

Richie, Beth. (1985). Battered black women: A challenge for the black community. *Black Scholar, 16*(2), 40–44.

Ride claims she educated media. (1985, July 23). *Providence Evening Bulletin.*

Rierdan, Jill, Koff, Elissa, & Silverstone, Esther. (1978, March). *Human figure drawings of premenarcheal and postmenarcheal girls.* Paper read at the meeting of the Eastern Psychological Association, Washington, DC.

Riger, Stephanie, & Gordon, Margaret T. (1981). The fear of rape: A study in social control. *Journal of Social Issues, 37*(4), 71–92.

Riley, Pamela J. (1981). The influence of gender on occupational aspirations of kindergarten children. *Journal of Vocational Behavior, 19*, 244–250.

Rivers, Caryl. (1975, November 2). Can a woman be liberated and married? *New York Times Magazine.*

Roberts, Katherine, & Slade, Margot. (1984, April 29). Women's work in Nassau County. *New York Times.*

Roberts, Steven V. (1977, October 30). The old-age lobby has a loud voice in Washington. *New York Times*, p. E4.

Robertson, Nan. (1985, March 18). Theater festival for older women at the Public. *New York Times.*

Rodgers, Joann E. (1985, May). The best health kick of all. *Ms*, pp. 57–60, 140–141.

Rodin, Judith. (1976). Menstruation, reattribution, and competence. *Journal of Personality and Social Psychology, 33*, 345–353.

Rodin, Judith, Silberstein, Lisa, & Striegel-Moore, Ruth H. (1985). Women and weight: A normative discontent. In T. B. Sonderegger (Ed.), *Nebraska symposium on motivation 1984: Psychology and gender* (Vol. 32) (pp. 267–307). Lincoln: University of Nebraska Press.

Rogers, Lesley, & Walsh, Joan. (1982). Shortcomings of the psychomedical research of John Money and co-workers into sex differences in behavior: Social and political implications. *Sex Roles, 8*, 269–281.

Rollins, Judy, & White, Priscilla N. (1982). The relationship between mothers' and daughters' sex-role attitudes and self-concepts in three types of family environment. *Sex Roles, 8*, 1141–1155.

Romer, Nancy, & Cherry, Debra. (1980). Ethnic and social class differences in children's sex-role concepts. *Sex Roles, 6*, 245–263.

Rommel, Elizabeth. (1984, January). Grade school blues. *Ms*, pp. 32–35.

Rook, Karen S. (1984). The negative side of social interaction: Impact on psychological well-being. *Journal of Personality and Social Psychology, 46*, 1097–1108.

Rooney, James F., Volpe, Joan N., & Suziedelis, Antanas. (1984). Changes in femininity, masculinity, and self-regard among women alcoholics in residential treatment. *Sex Roles, 11*, 257–267.

Rosaldo, Michelle Z. (1974). Woman, culture and society: A theoretical overview. In M. Z. Rosaldo & L. Lamphere (Eds.), *Woman, culture and society* (pp. 17–42). Stanford, CA: Stanford University Press.

Rosaldo, Michelle Z. (1980). The use and abuse of anthropology: Reflections on feminism and cross-cultural understanding. *Signs, 5*, 389–417.

Rose, Hilary. (1983). Hand, brain, and heart: A feminist epistemology for the natural sciences. *Signs, 9*, 73–90.

Rosen, Marjorie. (1973). *Popcorn Venus: Women, movies and the American dream*. New York: Avon.

Rosenbaum, David E. (1980, July 27). Working women still seek man-sized wages. *New York Times*, sec. 4, p. E3.

Rosenberg, Florence R., & Simmons, Roberta G. (1975). Sex differences in the self-concept in adolescence. *Sex Roles, 1*, 147–159.

Rosenberg, Karen. (1984, April 14). Peaceniks and soldier girls. *The Nation*, pp. 453–457.

Rosenkrantz, Paul, Vogel, Susan, Bee, Helen, Broverman, Inge, & Broverman, Donald M. (1968). Sex-role stereotypes and self-concepts in college students. *Journal of Consulting and Clinical Psychology, 32*, 287–295.

Rosenthal, Naomi B. (1984). Consciousness raising: From revolution to re-evaluation. *Psychology of Women Quarterly, 8*, 309–326.

Rosenthal, Robert, Archer, Dane, DiMatteo, M. Robin, Koivumaki, Judith H., & Rogers, Peter L. (1974, September). Body talk and tone of voice: The language without words. *Psychology Today*, pp. 64–68.

Ross, Ellen. (1980). "The love crisis": Couples' advice books of the late 1970s. *Signs, 6*, 109–122.

Ross, Joanna, & Kahan, James P. (1983). Children by choice or by chance: The perceived effects of parity. *Sex Roles, 9*, 69–77.

Ross, Loretta J. (1981, July/August). Black women ponder: Why feminism? *New Directions for Women*, pp. 5, 16.

Rossi, Alice S. (1980). Life-span theories and women's lives. *Signs, 6*, 4–32.

Rossi, Joseph S. (1983). Ratios exaggerate gender differences in mathematical ability. *American Psychologist, 38*, 348.

Rossner, Judith. (1976). *Looking for Mr. Goodbar*. New York: Pocket Books.

Rossner, Judith. (1983). *August*. New York: Houghton Mifflin.

Rotary ordered to revive chapter with women in it. (1986, March 18). *Providence Evening Bulletin*, p. A-1.

Roth, Philip. (1969). *Portnoy's complaint*. New York: Random House.

Rothman, Barbara K. (1986). *The tentative pregnancy: Prenatal diagnosis and the future of motherhood*. New York: Viking.

Routh, Donald K., Schroeder, Carolyn S., & O'Tuama, Lorcan A. (1974). Development of activity level in children. *Developmental Psychology, 10*, 163–168.

Rowe, Mary P. (1973, December). *The progress of women in educational institutions: The Saturn's rings phenomenon*. Unpublished paper, Massachusetts Institute of Technology, Cambridge.

Roy, Maria (Ed.). (1977). *Battered women: A psychosociological study of domestic violence*. New York: Van Nostrand Reinhold.

Rubenstein, Carin. (1980, July). Menstruation: The shame of it all. *Psychology Today*, p. 38.

Rubin, Jeffrey Z., Provenzano, Frank J., & Luria, Zella. (1974). The eye of the beholder: Parents' views on sex of newborns. *American Journal of Orthopsychiatry, 44*, 512–519.

Rubin, Lillian B. (1976). *Worlds of pain: Life in the working class family*. New York: Basic Books.

Rubin, Lillian. (1981). *Women of a certain age*. New York: Harper & Row.

Rubin, Robert T., Reinisch, June M., & Haskett, Roger F. (1981). Postnatal gonadal steroid effects on human behavior. *Science, 211*, 1318–1324.

Rubin, Zick. (1970). Measurement of romantic love. *Journal of Personality and Social Psychology, 16*, 265–273.

Rubin, Zick, Peplau, Letitia A., & Hill, Charles T. (1981). Loving and leaving: Sex differences in romantic attachments. *Sex Roles, 7*, 821–835.

Ruble, Diane N. (1977). Premenstrual symptoms: A reinterpretation. *Science, 197*, 291–292.

Ruble, Diane N., Balaban, Terry, & Cooper, Joel. (1981). Gender constancy and the effects of sex-typed televised toy commercials. *Child Development, 52*, 667–673.

Ruble, Diane N., Boggiano, Ann K., & Brooks-Gunn, Jeanne. (1982). Men's and women's evaluations of menstrual-related excuses. *Sex Roles, 8*, 625–638.

Ruddick, Sara. (1983). Thinking about mothering—and putting maternal thinking to use. *Women's Studies Quarterly, 11*(4), 4–7.

Ruggiero, Josephine A., & Weston, Louise C. (1985). Work options for women in women's magazines: The medium *and* the message. *Sex Roles, 12*, 535–547.

Rush, Florence. (1971). The sexual abuse of children: A feminist point of view. *Radical Therapist, 2*(4).

Rushton, J. Philippe. (1976). Socialization and the altruistic behavior of children. *Psychological Bulletin, 83*, 898–913.

Russell, Diana E. H. (1982). *Rape in marriage*. New York: Macmillan.

Russell, Diana E. H., & Howell, Nancy. (1983). The prevalence of rape in the United States revisited. *Signs, 8*, 688–695.

Russell, John. (1983, July 24). It's not "women's art," it's good art. *New York Times*, sec. 2, pp. 1, 25.

Rutter, Michael. (1972). *Maternal deprivation: Reassessed*. Middlesex, England: Penguin.

Ryan, Kenneth J. (1982, November). Hospital or home births. *Harvard Medical School Health Letter*, pp. 3–4.

Ryff, Carol D., & Migdal, Susan. (1984). Intimacy and generativity: Self-perceived transitions. *Signs, 9*, 470–481.

Sacks, Karen. (1970). Social bases for sexual equality: A comparative review. In R. Morgan (Ed.), *Sisterhood is powerful* (pp. 455–469). New York: Vintage.

Sacks, Karen. (1979). *Sisters and wives*. Westport, CT: Greenwood.

Sadker, Myra, & Sadker, David. (1985, March). Sexism in the schoolroom of the '80s. *Psychology Today*, pp. 54–57.

Safer birth control pill on sale beginning Dec. 1. (1984, November 9). *Providence Evening Bulletin*.

Sanday, Peggy R. (1981). The socio-cultural context of rape: A cross-cultural study. *Journal of Social Issues, 37*(4), 5–27.

Sandidge, Susanne, & Friedland, Seymour J. (1975). Sex-role-taking and aggressive behavior in children. *Journal of Genetic Psychology, 126,* 227–231.

Sandoval, Chela. (1984). Comment on Krieger's "Lesbian identity and community: Recent social science literature." *Signs, 9,* 725–729.

Sanger, Margaret. (1920). *Woman and the new race.* New York: Truth.

Sattem, Linda, Savells, Jerry, & Murray, Ellen. (1984). Sex-role stereotypes and commitment of rape. *Sex Roles, 11,* 849–860.

Savin-Williams, Ritch C., & Demo, David H. (1983). Situational and transituational determinants of adolescent self-feelings. *Journal of Personality and Social Psychology, 44,* 824–833.

Sayre, Anne. (1975). *Rosalind Franklin and DNA.* New York: Norton.

Scanlan, Christopher. (1978, May 15). "Mother's little helpers" exact heavy wages. *Providence Evening Bulletin.*

Scarf, Maggie. (1980, July). The promiscuous woman. *Psychology Today,* pp. 78–87.

Schachter, Stanley, & Singer, Jerome E. (1962). Cognitive, social and physiological determinants of emotional state. *Psychological Review, 69,* 379–399.

Schaefer, Roy. (1984). The pursuit of failure and the idealization of unhappiness. *American Psychologist, 39,* 398–405.

Schafer, Alice T., & Gray, Mary W. (1981). Sex and mathematics. *Science, 211,* 231.

Scheinmann, Vivian J. (1981, August). Jewish feminists demand equal treatment. *New Directions for Women,* pp. 5, 16.

Schlesier-Stropp, Barbara. (1984). Bulimia: A review of the literature. *Psychological Bulletin, 95,* 247–257.

Schmidt, Gunter, Sigusch, Volkmar, & Schafer, Siegrid. (1977). Responses to reading erotic stories: Male-female differences. In D. Byrne and L. A. Byrne (Eds.), *Exploring human sexuality* (pp. 173–184). New York. Crowell.

Schmidt, Peggy. (1985, March 24). For the women, still a long way to go. *New York Times,* sec. 12, pp. 14–15.

Schneider, Claudine. (1985, November 21). Realities about comparable worth. *Providence Evening Bulletin.*

Schneider, Susan W. (1984). *Jewish and female.* New York: Simon & Schuster.

Schreiner, Tim. (1984, May 29). A revolution that has just begun. *USA Today,* p. 40.

Schullo, Stephen A., & Alperson, Burton L. (1984). Interpersonal phenomenology as a function of sexual orientation, sex, sentiment, and trait categories in long-term dyadic relationships. *Journal of Personality and Social Psychology, 47,* 983–1007.

Schwadel, Francine. (1985, March 14). Women move up in the military, but many jobs remain off limits. *Wall Street Journal,* p. 33.

Schwartz, Lori A., & Markham, William T. (1985). Sex stereotyping in children's toy advertisements. *Sex Roles, 12,* 157–170.

Sciolino, Elaine. (1985, September 11). Equality remains an elusive goal for U.N. women. *New York Times,* pp. C1, C4.

Scully, Diana, & Marolla, Joseph. (1981, December). *Convicted rapists' attitudes toward women and rape.* Paper presented at the meeting of the First International Interdisciplinary Congress on Women, Haifa, Israel.

Sears' acquittal ends more than just a case. (1986, February 10). *Providence Evening Bulletin,* pp. A1, A2.

Sears, Pauline S. & Barbee, A. H. (1977). Career and life satisfaction among Termann's's gifted women. In J. C. Stanley, W. D. George, & C. H. Solano (Eds.), *The gifted and the creative: A fifty-year perspective.* Baltimore: Johns Hopkins University Press.

Seashore, Marjorie J., Leifer, Aimee D., Barnett, Clifford R., & Leiderman, P. H. (1973). The effects of denial of early mother-infant interaction on maternal self-confidence. *Journal of Personality and Social Psychology, 26,* 369–378.

Seavey, Carol A., Katz, Phyllis A., & Zalk, Sue R. (1975). Baby X: The effect of gender labels on adult responses to infants. *Sex Roles, 1,* 103–109.

SEC enforcer quits after wife-beating story. (1985, February 27). *Providence Evening Bulletin.*

Seegmiller, Bonni R. (1980a). Sex-typed behavior in preschoolers: Sex, age, and social class effects. *Journal of Psychology, 104,* 31–33.

Seegmiller, Bonni R. (1980b). Sex-role differentiation in preschoolers: Effects of maternal employment. *Journal of Psychology, 104,* 185–189.

Seidler, Susan. (1984, March/April). ERT: Drug company sales vs. women's health. *Network News,* p. 7.

Selkin, James. (1975, January). Rape. *Psychology Today,* pp. 71–76.

Selkow, Paula. (1984). Effects of maternal employment on kindergarten and first-grade children's vocational aspirations. *Sex Roles, 11,* 677–690.

Selnow, Gary W. (1985). Sex differences in uses and perceptions of profanity. *Sex Roles, 12,* 303–312.

Senneker, Phyllis, & Hendrick, Clyde. (1983). Androgyny and helping behavior. *Journal of Personality and Social Psychology, 45,* 916–925.

Serbin, Lisa A., & Connor, Jane M. (1979). Sex-typing of children's play preferences and patterns of cognitive performance. *Journal of Genetic Psychology, 134,* 315–316.

Serbin, Lisa A., Connor, Jane M., Burchardt, Carol J., & Citron, Cheryl C. (1979). Effects of peer presence on sex-typing of children's play behavior. *Journal of Experimental Child Psychology, 27,* 303–309.

Serbin, Lisa A., Connor, Jane M., & Citron, Cheryl C. (1978). Environmental control of independent and dependent behaviors in preschool girls and boys: A model for early independence training. *Sex Roles, 4,* 867–875.

Serbin, Lisa A., Connor, Jane M., & Citron, Cheryl C. (1981). Sex-differentiated free play behavior: Effects of teacher modeling, location, and gender. *Developmental Psychology, 17,* 640–646.

Serbin, Lisa A., Connor, Jane M., & Iler, Iris. (1979). Sex-stereotyped and non-stereotyped introduction of new toys in the preschool classroom: An observational study of teacher behavior and its effects. *Psychology of Women Quarterly, 4,* 261–265.

Serbin, Lisa A., O'Leary, K. Daniel, Kent, Ronald N., & Tonick, Illene J. (1973). A comparison of teacher response to the preacademic and problem behavior of boys and girls. *Child Development, 44,* 796–804.

Serrin, William. (1984, November 25). Experts say job bias against women persists. *New York Times.*

Serrin, William. (1985, January 31). Women are turning to collective action as a key to power and protection. *New York Times,* p. A14.

Sex habits of single women detailed in national survey. (1986, June 2). *Providence Evening Bulletin,* p. A-4.

Sexual assault reports in R.I. increased 14.8% in last year. (1986, February 26). *Providence Evening Bulletin,* p. A-2.

Sexual harassment: A hidden issue. (1978, June). *Project on the status and education of women.* Washington, DC: Association of American Colleges.

Sexual harassment stirs high court's wrath. (1986, June 24). *Providence Evening Bulletin.*

Shakin, Madeline, Shakin, Debra, & Sternglanz, Sarah H. (1985). Infant clothing: Sex labeling for strangers. *Sex Roles, 12,* 955–964.

Shange, Ntozake. (1978). From With no immediate cause. In *Nappy edges* (pp. 114–117). New York: St. Martin's Press.

Sharff, Jagna W. (1983). Sex and temperament revisited. In M. Fooden, S. Gordon, & B. Hughley (Eds.), *Genes and gender IV. The second X and women's health* (pp. 49–62). Staten Island, NY: Gordian Press.

Sheehan, Susan. (1975). *A welfare mother.* New York: New American Library.

Sheehy, Gail. (1974). *Hustling.* New York: Dell.

Shehan, Constance L. (1984). Wives' work and psychological well-being: An extension of Gove's social role theory of depression. *Sex Roles, 11,* 881–899.

Shenon, Philip. (1986, May 18). A second opinion on pornography's impact. *New York Times.*

Shepard, Winifred. (1980). Mothers and fathers, sons and daughters: Perceptions of young adults. *Sex Roles, 6,* 421–433.

Sherfey, Mary Jane. (1970). A theory on female sexuality. In R. Morgan (Ed.), *Sisterhood is powerful* (pp. 220–230). New York: Random House.

Sherman, Julia A. (1967). Problem of sex differences in space perception and aspects of intellectual functioning. *Psychological Review, 74,* 290–299.

Sherman, Julia A. (1971). *On the psychology of women: A survey of empirical studies.* Springfield, IL: Charles C Thomas.

Sherman, Julia A. (1980). Mathematics, spatial visualization, and related factors: Changes in girls and boys, grades 8–11. *Journal of Educational Psychology, 72,* 476–482.

Sherman, Julia A. (1982, January). Premenstrual syndrome. *Division 35 Newsletter,* pp. 10–11. (American Psychological Association, Washington, DC)

Sherman, Julia A. (1983). Factors predicting girls' and boys' enrollments in college preparatory mathematics. *Psychology of Women Quarterly, 7,* 272–281.

Sherman, Julia A., & Fennema, Elizabeth. (1978). Distribution of spatial visualization and mathematical problem solving scores: A test of Stafford's X-linked hypotheses. *Psychology of Women Quarterly, 3,* 157–167.

Sherman, Julia A., Koufacos, Corinne, & Kenworthy, Joy Anne. (1978). Therapists: Their attitudes and information about women. *Psychology of Women Quarterly, 2,* 299–313.

Sherman, Susan R., & Rosenblatt, Aaron. (1984). Women physicians as teachers, administrators, and researchers in medical and surgical specialties: Kanter versus "Avis" as competing hypotheses. *Sex Roles, 11,* 203–209.

She's single—and prefers it. (1984, July 13). *Providence Evening Bulletin.*

She's the chief. (1985, January 27). *New York Times,* p. E6.

Shields, Stephanie A. (1975a). Functionalism, Darwinism, and the psychology of women: A study in social myth. *American Psychologist, 30,* 739–754.

Shields, Stephanie A. (1975b). Ms. Pilgrim's progress: The contributions of Leta Stetter Hollingworth to the psychology of women. *American Psychologist, 30,* 852–857.

Shields, Stephanie A., & Cooper, Pamela E. (1983). Stereotypes of traditional and nontraditional child-bearing roles. *Sex Roles, 9,* 363–376.

Shipp, E. R. (1985, July 5). More married women choosing sterilization. *New York Times,* pp. A1, B5.

Shotland, R. Lance, & Straw, Margaret K. (1976). Bystander response to an assault: When a man attacks a woman. *Journal of Personality and Social Psychology, 34,* 990–999.

Shreve, Anita. (1982, November 21). Careers and the lure of motherhood. *New York Times Magazine,* pp. 38–43, 46–52, 56.

Shusterman, Lisa R. (1976). The psychosocial factors of the abortion experience: A critical review. *Psychology of Women Quarterly, 1,* 79–106.

Sidovowicz, Laura S., & Lunney, G. S. (1980). Baby X revisited. *Sex Roles, 6,* 67–73.

Silvern, Louise E., & Ryan, Victor L. (1983). A reexamination of masculine and feminine sex-role ideals and conflicts among ideals for the man, woman, and person. *Sex Roles, 9,* 1223–1248.

Simon, William, & Gagnon, John. (1977). Psychosexual development. In D. Byrne & L. A. Byrne (Eds.), *Exploring human sexuality* (pp. 117–129). New York: Crowell.

Simpson, Gwyned. (1984). The daughters of Charlotte Ray: The career development process during the exploratory and establishment stages of black women attorneys. *Sex Roles, 11,* 113–139.

Sinclair, Molly. (1984, May 22). Steinem turns 50. *Providence Evening Bulletin,* p. A-6.

Singer, Dorothy G., & Singer, Jerome L. (1973). *Some characteristics of make-believe play in nursery school children:*

An observational study. Unpublished paper. (Available from authors, Dept. of Psychology, Yale University, New Haven, CT)

Singer, Jerome L., & Singer, Dorothy G. (1973, July). Experimental studies of imaginative and sociodramatic play. *Division 8 Newsletter*. (American Psychological Association, Washington, DC)

Singer, Jerome L., & Singer, Dorothy G. (1980). Television viewing, family style and aggressive behavior in preschool children. In M. R. Green (Ed.), *Violence and the family* (pp. 37–65). Boulder, CO: Westview.

Singer, Judith E., Westphal, Milton, & Niswander, Kenneth R. (1972). Sex differences in the incidence of neonatal abnormalities and abnormal performance in early childhood. In J. Bardwick (Ed.), *Readings on the psychology of women* (pp. 13–17). New York: Harper & Row.

Single parents head one-fourth of households with children. (1985, May 15). *Providence Journal-Bulletin*.

Singular, Stephen. (1978, April 30). Moving on: Reaping the rewards of the women's movement. *New York Times Magazine*, pp. 18–20ff.

Sinnott, Jan D. (1984). Older men, older women: Are their perceived roles similar? *Sex Roles, 10*, 847–856.

Skolnik, Ricki. (1983, March). A safe method lovers can share. *Whole Life Times*, pp. 24–25.

Skrypnek, Berna, & Snyder, Mark. (1982). On the self-perpetuating nature of stereotypes about men and women. *Journal of Experimental Social Psychology, 18*, 277–291.

Skultans, Vieda. (1979). The symbolic significance of menstruation and the menopause. In J. H. Williams (Ed.), *Psychology of women: Selected readings* (pp. 115–128). New York: Norton.

Slaughter, Carolyn. (1985). *A perfect woman*. New York: Ticknor & Fields.

Smedley, Agnes. (1973). *Daughter of earth*. Old Westbury, NY: Feminist Press. (Original work published in 1929.)

Smith, Barbara. (1985). Some home truths on the contemporary black feminist movement. *Black Scholar, 16*(2), 4–13.

Smith, Caroline, & Lloyd, Barbara. (1978). Maternal behavior and perceived sex of infant: Revisited. *Child Development, 49*, 1263–1265.

Smith, Elsie J. (1982). The black female adolescent: A review of the educational, career and psychological literature. *Psychology of Women Quarterly, 6*, 261–288.

Smith, Joan. (1984). The paradox of women's poverty: Wage-earning women and economic transformation. *Signs, 10*, 291–310.

Smith, M. Dwayne, & Self, George D. (1981). Feminists and traditionalists: An attitudinal comparison. *Sex Roles, 7*, 183–188.

Smith, Mary Lee. (1980). Sex bias in counseling and psychotherapy. *Psychological Bulletin, 87*, 392–407.

Smith, Patricia A., & Midlarsky, Elizabeth. (1985). Empirically derived conceptions of femaleness and maleness: A current view. *Sex Roles, 12*, 313–328.

Snitow, Ann B. (1980). The front line: Notes on sex in novels by women. *Signs, 5*, 702–718.

Snodgrass, Sara E. (1985). Women's intuition: The effect of subordinate role on interpersonal sensitivity. *Journal of Personality and Social Psychology, 49*, 146–155.

Snyder, Mark, Tanke, Elizabeth D., & Berscheid, Ellen. (1977). Social perception and interpersonal behavior: On the self-fulfilling nature of social stereotypes. *Journal of Personality and Social Psychology, 35*, 656–666.

Sobel, Suzanne B. (1982). Difficulties experienced by women in prison. *Psychology of Women Quarterly, 7*, 107–118.

Society's losers. (1981, Autumn). *ISR Newsletter*, pp. 4–5. (Institute for Social Research, University of Michigan, Ann Arbor.)

Sohn, David. (1982). Sex differences in achievement self-attributions: An effect-size analysis. *Sex Roles, 8*, 345–357.

Sommer, Barbara. (1983). How does menstruation affect cognitive competence and psychophysiological response? In S. Golub (Ed.), *Lifting the curse of menstruation* (pp. 53–90). New York: Haworth.

Sommers, Tish, & Shields, Laurie. (1978, Winter). Displaced homemakers. *Civil Rights Digest*, pp. 33–39.

Sontag, Susan. (1979). The double standard of aging. In J. H. Williams (Ed.), *Psychology of women: Selected readings* (pp. 462–478). New York: Norton.

Spacks, Patricia M. (1975). *The female imagination*. New York: Knopf.

Spacks, Patricia M. (1981). *The adolescent idea*. New York: Basic Books.

Speakers: Some are hot, some are not. (1982, December 17). *Providence Evening Bulletin*.

Specter, Joan. (1986, February 16). Philadelphia leads the way in parental leave. *New York Times*, p. E16.

Spence, Janet T. (1983). Comment on Lubinski, Tellegen, and Butcher's "Masculinity, femininity, and androgyny viewed and assessed as distinct concepts." *Journal of Personality and Social Psychology, 44*, 440–446.

Spence, Janet T. (1985). Gender identity and its implications for the concepts of masculinity and femininity. In T. B. Sonderegger (Ed.), *Nebraska symposium on motivation 1984: Psychology and gender* (Vol. 32) (pp. 59–96). Lincoln, NE: University of Nebraska Press.

Spence, Janet T., & Helmreich, Robert L. (1980). Masculine instrumentality and feminine expressiveness: Their relationships with sex role attitudes and behavior. *Psychology of Women Quarterly, 5*, 147–163.

Spence, Janet T., Helmreich, Robert L., & Stapp, Joy. (1974). The personality attributes questionnaire: A measure of sex role stereotypes and masculinity-femininity. *Journal Supplement Abstract Service Document*, Ms. No. 617.

Sperry, Roger. (1982). Some effects of disconnecting the cerebral hemispheres. *Science, 217*, 1223–1226.

Squire, Susan. (1983, October). Is the binge-purge cycle catching? *Ms*, pp. 41–46.

Stack, Carol B. (1974). *All our kin: Strategies for survival in a black community*. New York: Harper & Row.

Stack, Carol B. (1986). The culture of gender: Women and men of color. *Signs, 11*, 321–324.

Stake, Jayne E. (1983a). Ability level, evaluative feedback, and sex differences in performance expectancy.

Psychology of Women Quarterly, 8, 48–58.

Stake, Jayne E. (1983b). Factors in reward distribution: Allocator motive, gender, and Protestant ethic endorsement. *Journal of Personality and Social Psychology, 44,* 410–418.

Stake, Jayne E. (1985). Exploring the basis of sex differences in third-party allocations. *Journal of Personality and Social Psychology, 48,* 1621–1629.

Stallard, Karin, Ehrenreich, Barbara, & Sklar, Holly. (1983). *Poverty in the American dream: Women and children first.* Boston: South End Press.

Staples, Robert. (1977). Male-female sexual variations: Functions of biology or culture? In D. Byrne & L. A. Byrne (Eds.), *Exploring human sexuality* (pp. 185–193). New York: Crowell.

Stark, Elizabeth. (1986, April). Stand up to your man. *Psychology Today,* p. 68.

Starr, Barbara S. (1979). Sex differences among personality correlates of mathematical ability in high school seniors. *Psychology of Women Quarterly, 4,* 212–220.

State Dept. policies on women scored. (1984, April 19). *Providence Evening Bulletin.*

State of Rhode Island, 1979. Criminal offenses, Title II, Chapter 11–37. *An Act Relating to Rape and Seduction.*

Stearns, Beth C., Penner, Louis A., & Kimmel, Ellen. (1980). Sexism among psychotherapists: A case not yet proven. *Journal of Consulting and Clinical Psychology, 48,* 548–550.

Steel, Lauri, Abeles, Ronald P., & Card, Josefina J. (1982). Sex differences in the patterning of adult roles as a determinant of sex differences in occupational achievement. *Sex Roles, 8,* 1009–1024.

Steele, Daniel G., & Walker, C. Eugene. (1976). Female responsiveness to erotic films from a feminine perspective. *Journal of Nervous and Mental Disease, 162,* 266–273.

Stein, Aletha H., Pohly, Sheila R., & Mueller, Edward. (1971). The influence of masculine, feminine, and neutral tasks on children's achievement behavior, expectancies of success and attainment values. *Child Development, 42,* 195–207.

Stein, Peter J. (1976). *Single.* Englewood Cliffs, NJ: Prentice-Hall.

Steinem, Gloria. (1978a, February). A flash of power. *Ms,* pp. 87–88.

Steinem, Gloria. (1978b, October). If men could menstruate. *Ms,* p. 110.

Steinem, Gloria. (1978c, November). Erotica and pornography: A clear and present difference. *Ms,* pp. 53–54, 75, 76.

Steinmann, Marion. (1975, November 23). Now, the nurse-midwife. *New York Times Magazine,* pp. 34–45.

Steinmetz, Suzanne K. (1977–78). The battered husband syndrome. *Victimology, 1,* 499–509.

Stephen, Beverly. (1984, November). Rites of independence. *Ms,* p. 55.

Stericker, Anne, & LeVesconte, Shirley. (1982). Effect of brief training on sex-related differences in visual-spatial skill. *Journal of Personality and Social Psychology, 43,* 1018–1029.

Sterilization leads birth control survey. (1984, December 6). *Providence Evening Bulletin.*

Sternglanz, Sarah H., & Serbin, Lisa A. (1974). Sex role stereotyping in children's television programs. *Developmental Psychology, 10,* 710–715.

Steward, Margaret S., Steward, David S., & Dary, Judith A. (1983). Women who choose a man's career: Women in ministry. *Psychology of Women Quarterly, 8,* 166–173.

Stewart, Abigail J. (1980). Personality and situation in the prediction of women's life patterns. *Psychology of Women Quarterly, 5,* 195–206.

Stewart, Abigail J., & Salt, Patricia. (1981). Life stress, lifestyles, depression, and illness in adult women. *Journal of Personality and Social Psychology, 40,* 1063–1069.

Stipek, Deborah J. (1984). Sex differences in children's attributions for success and failure on math and spelling tests. *Sex Roles, 11,* 969–981.

Stitt, Christopher, Schmidt, Stuart, Price, Karl, & Kipnis, David. (1983). Sex of leader, leader behavior, and subordinate satisfaction. *Sex Roles, 9,* 31–42.

St. John-Parsons, Donald. (1978). Continuous dual-career families: A case study. *Psychology of Women Quarterly, 3,* 30–42.

St. Peter, Shirley. (1979). Jack went up the hill . . . but where was Jill? *Psychology of Women Quarterly, 4,* 256–260.

Stockard, Jean, & Dougherty, Maureen. (1983). Variations in subjective culture: A comparison of females and males in three settings. *Sex Roles, 9,* 953–974.

Stockburger, David W., & Davis, James O. (1978). Selling the female image as mental patient. *Sex Roles, 4,* 131–134.

Stokes, Henry S. (1982, October 17). Life and limbs are growing longer in Japan. *New York Times,* sec. 4.

Stone, Merlin. (1979). *Ancient mirrors of womanhood* (Vol. 1). New York: New Sibylline Books.

Stone, Morris. (1978, June 11). A backlash in the work place. *New York Times.*

Storms, Michael D., & Nisbett, Richard E. (1970). Insomnia and the attribution process. *Journal of Personality and Social Psychology, 16,* 319–328.

Straus, Murray A. (1978a). Wife beating: How common and why? *Victimology, 2,* 443–459.

Straus, Murray A. (1978b, December). *Stress and assault in a national sample of American families.* Paper read at Colloquium on Stress and Crime, National Institute of Law Enforcement and Criminal Justice, MITRE Corporation, Washington, DC.

Straus, Murray A., Gelles, Richard J., & Steinmetz, Suzanne K. (1981). *Behind closed doors.* Garden City, NY: Anchor/Doubleday.

Streissguth, Ann P., Landesman-Dwyer, Sharon, Martin, Joan C., & Smith, David W. (1980). Teratogenic effects of alcohol in humans and laboratory animals. *Science, 209,* 353–361.

Streshinsky, Shirley. (1975, September). The not so weaker sex. *McCall's,* p. 33.

Stricker, George. (1977). Implications of research for psychotherapeutic treatment of women. *American Psychologist, 32,* 14–22.

Strikers demand equal pay for women. (1981, July 6). *Providence Evening Bulletin*, pp. A-1, A-6.

Stringer-Moore, D., Pepitone-Arreola-Rockwell, F., & Rozée-Koker, P. (1984). Beliefs about and experiences with battering: Women and men in two populations. *Sex Roles, 11*, 269–276.

Stroebe, Margaret S., & Stroebe, Wolfgang. (1983). Who suffers more? Sex differences in health risks of the widowed. *Psychological Bulletin, 93*, 279–301.

Strong, Ellen. (1970). The hooker. In R. Morgan (Ed.), *Sisterhood is powerful* (pp. 289–297). New York: Vintage.

Strube, Michael J. (1981). Meta-analysis and cross-cultural comparison: Sex differences in child competitiveness. *Journal of Cross-Cultural Psychology, 12*, 3–20.

Study shows inequality in male-female financial aid. (1984, January 24). *Good 5¢ Cigar*. (University of Rhode Island, Kingston)

Studying love: Older set is enjoying new spirit of courtship. (1985, June 7). *Providence Evening Bulletin*.

Success, health linked in study. (1984, May 10). *Providence Evening Bulletin*.

Sun, Marjorie. (1984). Panel says Depo-Provera not proved safe. *Science, 226*, 950–951.

Superstition crumbles underground. (1981, December 14). *Providence Evening Bulletin*.

Supreme Court rules out use of sex-based tables. (1983, September–October). *Academe*, p. 7.

Swandby, Janet R. (1979). *Daily and retrospective mood and physical symptom self-reports and their relationship to the menstrual cycle*. Unpublished master's thesis, University of Wisconsin, Milwaukee.

Swertlow, Frank. (1982, June 12). TV update: Hollywood. *TV Guide*, p. A-1.

Taking a break to give birth: More firms will hold that job. (1981, January 28). *Providence Evening Bulletin*.

Tangri, Sandra S., Burt, Martha R., & Johnson, Leanor B. (1982). Sexual harassment at work: Three exploratory models. *Journal of Social Issues, 38*(4), 33–54.

Tanner, Nancy, & Zihlman, Adrienne. (1976). Women in evolution. Part I: Innovation and selection in human origins. *Signs, 1*, 585–608.

Tanzer, Deborah. (1973). Natural childbirth: Pain or peak experience? In Psychology Today (Eds.), *The female experience* (pp. 4–32). Del Mar, CA: Communications/Research/Machines.

Task Force on Issues in Research. (1977). Psychology of women. *Division 35 Newsletter, 4*(4). (American Psychological Association, Washington, DC)

Tavris, Carol. (1982, December). What's your P.Q.? *Ms*, pp. 49–50, 95.

Taylor, Marylee C., & Hall, Judith A. (1982). Psychological androgyny: Theories, methods, and conclusions. *Psychological Bulletin, 92*, 347–366.

Taylor, Shelley E., & Falcone, Hsiao-Ti. (1982). Cognitive bases of stereotyping: The relationship between categorization and prejudice. *Personality and Social Psychology Bulletin, 8*, 426–432.

Taylor, Shelley E., & Langer, Ellen J. (1977). Pregnancy: A social stigma? *Sex Roles, 3*, 27–35.

Taylor, Stuart. (1986, June 15). Abortion is affirmed, but in a lower voice. *New York Times*, p. E1.

Teenaged boys and girls suffer different—but equally serious—psychological problems. (1977, Summer). *ISR Newsletter*. (Institute for Social Research, University of Michigan, Ann Arbor)

Teltsch, Kathleen. (1985, September 19). Today's engineer is often a woman. *New York Times*, p. C1.

Terborg, James R. (1985). Working women and stress. In T. A. Beehr & R. S. Bhagat (Eds.), *Human stress and cognition in organizations* (pp. 245–286). New York: Wiley.

Teri, Linda. (1982). Effects of sex and sex-role style on clinical judgment. *Sex Roles, 8*, 639–649.

Tests change abortion attitudes. (1984, March 15). *Providence Evening Bulletin*.

The annual report on the economic status of the profession 1983–84. (1984, July/August). *Academe*, pp. 1–64.

The employment situation in the United States. (1981, October 11). *New York Times*, sec. 12.

The favored infants. (1976, June). *Human Behavior*, pp. 49–50.

The future of the family. (1981, Winter). *ISR Newsletter*. (Institute for Social Research, University of Michigan, Ann Arbor)

The paradox of well-being. (1981, Spring). *ISR Newsletter*. (Institute for Social Research, University of Michigan, Ann Arbor)

The pill—back in style. (1982, November). *The Harvard Medical School Health Letter*, pp. 2, 5.

The problem of rape on campus. (1978, Fall). *Project on the Status and Education of Women*. (Association of American Colleges, Washington, DC)

The war against pornography. (1985, March 18). *Newsweek*, pp. 58–67.

Therapists lose sex insurance. (1985, February 25). *Providence Evening Bulletin*.

There she goes, Miss America. (1984, August 4–11). *The Nation*.

They're not the marrying kind. (1986, May 8). *Providence Evening Bulletin*, p. A-1.

33 million in U.S. below poverty level; social cutbacks cited. (1985, December 2). *Providence Evening Bulletin*, p. A-5.

Thomas, Constance. (1985). The age of androgyny: The new views of psychotherapists. *Sex Roles, 13*, 381–392.

Thompson, John R. (1978, August). *One male psychotherapist's pilgrimage into his sexism*. Paper read at the meeting of the American Psychological Association, Toronto.

Thompson, Martha E. (1981a). Comment on Rich's "Compulsory heterosexuality and lesbian existence." *Signs, 6*, 790–794.

Thompson, Martha E. (1981b). Sex differences: Differential access to power or sex-role socialization? *Sex Roles, 7*, 413–424.

Thompson, Spencer K. (1975). Gender labels and early sex role development. *Child Development, 46*, 339–347.

Thompson, Spencer K., & Bentler, P. M. (1973). A developmental study of gender constancy and parent preference. *Archives of Sexual Behavior, 2*, 379–385.

Tidball, M. Elizabeth. (1980). Women's colleges and women achievers revisited. *Signs, 5,* 504–517.

Tieger, Todd. (1980). On the biological basis of sex differences in aggression. *Child Development, 51,* 943–963.

Tiffany, Sharon W. (1982). *Women, work and motherhood.* Englewood Cliffs, NJ: Prentice-Hall.

Tilby, Penelope J., & Kalin, Rudolf. (1980). Effects of sex-role deviant lifestyles in otherwise normal persons on the perception of maladjustment. *Sex Roles, 6,* 581–592.

Tinsley, Emiley G., Sullivan-Guest, Sandra, & McGuire, John. (1984). Feminine sex role and depression in middle-aged women. *Sex Roles, 11,* 25–32.

Tomasson, Robert E. (1985, March 27). State legislatures have more women. *New York Times,* p. C14.

Toth, Emily. (1984, February). Who'll take romance? *The Women's Review of Books,* pp. 12–13.

Touchton, Judy. (1983, May). Looking for leadership. *Comment,* p. 5.

Toufexis, Anastasia. (1982, July 12). What killed equal rights? *Time,* pp. 32–33.

Towson, Shelagh M. J., & Zanna, Mark P. (1982). Toward a situational analysis of gender differences in aggression. *Sex Roles, 8,* 903–914.

Trausch, Susan. (1986, April 20). Terrorism shakes the American psyche. *Boston Globe,* pp. 75–76.

Travis, Cheryl B. (1982). Sex comparisons on causal attributions: Another look at the null hypothesis. *Sex Roles, 8,* 375–380.

Treadway, C. Richard, Kane, Francis J. Jr., Jarrahi-Zadeh, Ali, & Lipton, Morris A. (1975). A psychoendocrine study of pregnancy and puerperium. In R. K. Unger & F. L. Denmark (Eds.), *Woman: Dependent or independent variable?* (pp. 591–604). New York: Psychological Dimensions.

Tremaine, Leslie S., Schau, Candace G., & Busch, Judith W. (1982). Children's occupational sex-typing. *Sex Roles, 8,* 691–710.

Trott, William C. (1981, March 20). Country gals have grown. *Providence Evening Bulletin,* p. B-6.

Trotter, Robert. (1982, March). Sex and the psychiatrist. *Science 82,* pp. 78–79.

Tuchman, Gaye. (1979). Women's depiction by the mass media. *Signs, 4,* 528–542.

Turkington, Carol. (1984, January). Ideology affects approach taken to alleviate PMS. *APA Monitor,* pp. 28–29.

20-year comparison, family roles. (1979, Winter). *ISR Newsletter.* (Institute for Social Research, University of Michigan, Ann Arbor.)

Two women survive in a macho world. (1978, September 20). *Providence Evening Bulletin.*

Ullian, Dora. (1984). "Why girls are good": A constructivist view. *Sex Roles, 11,* 241–256.

Unemployment: Higher for women across the board. (1981, Summer). *Project on the Status and Education of Women, 31.* (Association of American Colleges, Washington, DC)

Ungar, Sheldon B. (1982). The sex-typing of adult and child behavior in toy sales. *Sex Roles, 8,* 251–260.

Unger, Rhoda K. (1981). Sex as a social reality: Field and laboratory research. *Psychology of Women Quarterly, 5,* 645–653.

U.S. Bureau of the Census. (1976, April). *A statistical portrait of women in the U.S.* Current Population Reports, Series P-23, No. 58. Washington, DC: U.S. Government Printing Office.

U.S. Bureau of the Census. (1983, August). *American women: Three decades of change.* Special Demographic Analysis, No. 8. Washington, DC: U.S. Government Printing Office.

U.S. Bureau of the Census. (1985a). *Marital status and living arrangements: March 1984.* Current Population Reports, Series P-20, No. 399. Washington, DC: U.S. Government Printing Office.

U.S. Bureau of the Census. (1985b). *Statistical abstract of the United States.* Washington, DC: U.S. Government Printing Office.

U.S. Department of Labor. (1980, August). *Brief highlights of major federal laws on sex discrimination in employment.* Washington, DC: U.S. Government Printing Office.

U.S. Federal Bureau of Investigation. (1982). *Uniform crime reports.* Washington, DC: U.S. Government Printing Office.

U.S. study finds one in five births out of wedlock. (1985, September 29). *New York Times,* p. 65.

U.S. teenagers have more babies, abortions than counterparts abroad. (1985, March 13). *Providence Evening Bulletin.*

Unwanted births decline. (1985, May 14). *Providence Evening Bulletin.*

Unwed mothers. (1985, September 27). *Providence Evening Bulletin,* p. A1.

Vance, Brenda K., & Green, Vicki. (1984). Lesbian identities: An examination of sex behavior and sex role attribution as related to age of initial same-sex sexual encounter. *Psychology of Women Quarterly, 8,* 293–307.

Vance, Carole S. (Ed.). (1984). *Pleasure and danger: Exploring female sexuality.* Boston: Routledge & Kegan Paul.

Vance, Carole S., & Snitow, Ann B. (1984). Toward a conversation about sex in feminism: A modest proposal. *Signs, 10,* 126–135.

Vanek, Joann. (1974, November). Time spent in housework. *Scientific American,* pp. 116–120.

Van Gelder, Lindsy. (1979, February). When the Edith Bunkers unite!: National Congress of Neighborhood Women. *Ms,* pp. 53–56.

Van Hecke, Madelaine, Tracy, Robert J., Cotler, Sheldon, & Ribordy, Sheila C. (1984). Approval versus achievement motives in seventh-grade girls. *Sex Roles, 11,* 33–41.

Varro, Barbara. (1980, May 27). Why more couples aren't having kids. *Providence Evening Bulletin,* p. B-4.

Vatican seeks out U.S. nuns. (1986, March 20). *Providence Evening Bulletin,* p. C-22.

Veevers, Jean E. (1982). Voluntary childlessness: A critical assessment of the research. In E. D. Macklin & R. H. Rubin (Eds.), *Contemporary families and alternative lifestyles* (pp. 75–96). Beverly Hills, CA: Sage.

Vetter, Betty M. (1978). New data show uneven progress

for women and minorities in science. *Science, 202,* 507–508.

Vetter, Betty M. (1981). Degree completion by women and minorities in sciences increases. *Science, 212,* 35.

Vetter, Betty M., & Babco, Eleanor L. (1984). Women and minorities continue to grow in workplace. *Science, 226,* 159.

Views on sex still liberal—Pollster. (1985, April 25). *Providence Evening Bulletin,* p. A-2.

Villemur, Nora K., & Hyde, Janet S. (1983). Effects of sex of defense attorney, sex of jurors, and age and attractiveness of the victim on mock juror decision making in a rape case. *Sex Roles, 9,* 879–889.

Voda, Ann M., & Eliasson, Mona. (1985). Menopause: The closure of menstrual life. In S. Golub (Ed.), *Lifting the curse of menstruation* (pp. 137–156). New York: Haworth.

Voydanoff, Patricia. (1980). Perceived job characteristics and job satisfaction among men and women. *Psychology of Women Quarterly, 5,* 177–185.

Vrazo, Fawn. (1984, August 14). Joys and sadnesses of older mothers. *Providence Evening Bulletin.*

Waber, Deborah P. (1977). Biological substrates of field dependence: Implication of the sex difference. *Psychological Bulletin, 84,* 1076–1087.

Wade, Nicholas. (1975). Discovery of pulsars: A graduate student's story. *Science, 189,* 358–364.

Wagner, Irene. (n.d.). *Formerly battered women: A follow-up study.* (Available from 4761 22nd Ave. NE #4, Seattle, WA 98105)

Walker, Alice. (1976). *Meridian.* New York: Washington Square Press.

Walker, Alice. (1982). *The color purple.* New York: Washington Square Press.

Walker, Lawrence. (1984). Sex differences in the development of moral reasoning: A critical review. *Child Development, 55,* 667–691.

Walker, Lenore E. (1978). Treatment alternatives for battered women. In J. R. Chapman & M. Gates (Eds.), *The victimization of women* (pp. 143–174). Beverly Hills, CA: Sage.

Walker, Lenore E. (1979). *The battered woman.* New York: Harper & Row.

Walkowitz, Judith R. (1980). The politics of prostitution. *Signs, 6,* 123–135.

Wallace, Amy. (1985, August 11). Schooldays, workdays. *New York Times.*

Wallace, Michele. (1979). *Black macho and the myth of the superwoman.* New York: Dial.

Wallston, Barbara S. (1981). What are the questions in psychology of women? A feminist approach to research. *Psychology of Women Quarterly, 5,* 597–617.

Wallston, Barbara S. (in press). Social psychology of women and gender. *Journal of Applied Social Psychology.*

Walsh, John. (1983). Survey shows freshmen shift on careers, values. *Science, 219,* 822.

Walsh, John. (1984). Total doctorates edge up in science, engineering. *Science, 226,* 815.

Walsh, Mary R. (1985). The psychology of women course: A continuing catalyst for change. *Teaching of Psychology,* 12, 198–203.

Walshok, Mary L. (1981). *Blue-collar women: Pioneers on the male frontier.* New York: Doubleday/Anchor.

Warr, Peter, & Parry, Glenys. (1982). Paid employment and women's psychological well-being. *Psychological Bulletin, 91,* 498–516.

Warwick schoolgirls suing *Penthouse,* claim 'Amazon' comment a libelous slur. (1986, August 27). *Providence Evening Bulletin.*

Wash. court approves plan to end sex bias in state worker pay. (1986, April 12). *Providence Evening Bulletin,* p. A-3.

Washington, Mary H. (Ed.). (1975). *Black-eyed Susans.* Garden City, NY: Anchor.

Wasserman, Gail A., & Lewis, Michael. (1985). Infant sex differences: Ecological effects. *Sex Roles, 12,* 665–675.

Webb, Thomas E., & Van Devere, Chris A. (1985). Sex differences in the expression of depression: A developmental interaction effect. *Sex Roles, 12,* 91–95.

Weber, Ellen. (1977, April). Sexual abuse begins at home. *Ms,* pp. 64–67.

Weeks, M. O'Neal, & Gage, Bruce A. (1984). A comparison of the marriage-role expectations of college women enrolled in a functional marriage course in 1961, 1972, and 1978. *Sex Roles, 11,* 377–388.

Weideger, Paula. (1976). *Menstruation and menopause.* New York: Knopf.

Weingarten, Kathy, & Daniels, Pamela. (1981). *Sooner or later: The timing of parenthood in adult lives.* New York: Norton.

Weis, Lois. (1985, November–December). Progress but no parity: Women in higher education. *Academe,* pp. 29–33.

Weisheit, Ralph A. (1984). Women and crime: Issues and perspectives. *Sex Roles, 11,* 567–581.

Weisstein, Naomi. (1982, November). Tired of arguing about biological inferiority? *Ms,* pp. 41–46, 85.

Weitz, Rose. (1982). Feminist consciousness raising, self-concept, and depression. *Sex Roles, 8,* 231–241.

Weitzman, Lenore J. (1985). *The divorce revolution.* New York: Free Press.

Weitzman, Lenore J., Eifler, Deborah, Hokada, Elizabeth, & Ross, Catherine. (1972). Sex-role socialization in picture books for pre-school children. *American Journal of Sociology, 77,* 1125–1150.

Welch, Susan, & Booth, Alan. (1977). Employment and health among married women with children. *Sex Roles, 3,* 385–397.

Wenner, Kate. (1977, May 8). How they keep them down on the farm. *New York Times Magazine,* pp. 74, 80–83.

Werner, Dennis. (1984). Child care and influence among the Mekranoti of Central Brazil. *Sex Roles, 10,* 395–404.

Werner, Paul D., & LaRussa, Georgina W. (1985). Persistence and change in sex-role stereotypes. *Sex Roles, 12,* 1089–1100.

West, Joanne. (1984, March/April). Hysterectomy and the mid-life and older woman. *Network News,* p. 4.

Westoff, Charles F., & Rindfuss, Ronald R. (1974). Sex preselection in the United States: Some implications.

Science, 184, 633–636.

West's women making waves in labor force. (1984, January 23). *Providence Evening Bulletin.*

Wetzsteon, Ross. (1977, November). Woody Allen: Schlemiel as sex maniac. *Ms,* pp. 14–15.

Wheeler, Ladd, & Nezlek, John. (1977). Sex differences in social participation. *Journal of Personality and Social Psychology, 35,* 742–754.

White, Gregory L. (1980). Inducing jealousy: A power perspective. *Personality and Social Psychology Bulletin, 6,* 222–227.

Whiting, Beatrice, & Edwards, Carolyn P. (1973). A cross-cultural analysis of sex differences in the behavior of children aged three through eleven. *Journal of Social Psychology, 91,* 171–181.

Whiting, John W. M. (1941). *Becoming a Kwoma.* New Haven: Yale University Press.

Whitley, Bernard E. Jr. (1979). Sex roles and psychotherapy: A current appraisal. *Psychological Bulletin, 86,* 1309–1321.

Whitley, Bernard E. Jr. (1983). Sex role orientation and self-esteem: A critical meta-analytic review. *Journal of Personality and Social Psychology, 44,* 765–778.

Whitley, Bernard E. Jr. (1985). Sex-role orientation and psychological well-being: Two meta-analyses. *Sex Roles, 12,* 207–225.

Wiegers, Rebecca M., & Frieze, Irene H. (1977). Gender, female traditionality, achievement level, and cognitions of success and failure. *Psychology of Women Quarterly, 2,* 125–137.

Wielawski, Irene. (1985, June 27). Memorial told to curb caesareans. *Providence Evening Bulletin,* p. A-6.

Wiener, Jon. (1985, September 7). The Sears case: Women's history on trial. *The Nation,* pp. 174–176, 178–180.

Wiest, William M. (1977). Semantic differential profiles of orgasm and other experiences among men and women. *Sex Roles, 3,* 399–403.

Willett, Roslyn S. (1971). Working in "a man's world": The woman executive. In V. Gornick & B. K. Moran (Eds.), *Woman in sexist society* (pp. 367–383). New York: Basic Books.

Williams, Dorie G. (1985). Gender, masculinity-femininity, and emotional intimacy in same-sex friendship. *Sex Roles, 12,* 587–600.

Williams, Lenore R. (1983). Beliefs and attitudes of young girls regarding menstruation. In S. Golub (Ed.), *Menarche* (pp. 133–137). Boston: Lexington Books.

Williamson, Nancy E. (1976). Sex preferences, sex control, and the status of women. *Signs, 1,* 847–862.

Willis, Ellen. (1981, November 14). Betty Friedan's "Second Stage": A step backward. *The Nation,* pp. 494–496.

Wilmore, Jack H. (1977). The female athlete. *Journal of School Health, 47,* 227–233.

Wilson, Jean D., George, Frederick W., & Griffin, James E. (1981). The hormonal control of sexual development. *Science, 211,* 1278–1284.

Winakor, Bess. (1977, April 20). To get the gift that you want, it takes strategy. *Providence Evening Bulletin.*

Wise, Erica, & Rafferty, Janet. (1982). Sex bias and language. *Sex Roles, 8,* 1189–1196.

Wise, George W. (1978). The relationship of sex-role perception and levels of self-actualization in public school teachers. *Sex Roles, 4,* 605–617.

Wise, Paula S., & Joy, Stephany S. (1982). Working mothers, sex differences, and self-esteem in college students' self-descriptions. *Sex Roles, 8,* 785–790.

WITCH. New York Covens. (1970). In R. Morgan (Ed.), *Sisterhood is powerful* (pp. 539–540). New York: Vintage.

Withorn, Ann. (1986, June). New poor, old problems. *Women's Review of Books,* pp. 8–9.

Witkin, Herman A. (1979). Socialization, culture and ecology in the development of group and sex differences in cognitive style. *Human Development, 22,* 358.

Witkin, Herman A., Mednick, Sarnoff A., Schulsinger, Fini, Bakkestrom, Eskild, Christiansen, Karol O., Goodenough, Donald R., Hirschhorn, Kurt, Lundsteen, Claes, Owen, David R., Philip, John, Rubin, Donald B., & Stocking, Martha. (1976). Criminality in XYY and XXY men. *Science, 193,* 547–555.

Wittig, Michele A. (1976). Sex differences in intellectual functioning: How much of a difference do genes make? *Sex Roles, 2,* 63–74.

Wittig, Michele A. (1978). Letter to the editor. *Sex Roles, 4,* 331–332.

Wittig, Michele A. (1985). Sex-role norms and gender-related attainment values: Their role in attributions of success and failure. *Sex Roles, 12,* 1–13.

Wittig, Michele A., Marks, Gary S., & Jones, G. Alan. (1981). Luck versus effort attributions: Effect on reward allocations to self and other. *Personality and Social Psychology Bulletin, 7,* 71–78.

Wolfe, Linda. (1981, December 28–1982, January 4). The good news: The latest expert word on what it means to be single. *New York,* pp. 33–35.

Wolfe, Raymond, Lennox, Richard, & Hudiburg, Richard. (1983). Self-monitoring and sex as moderator variables in the statistical explanation of self-reported marijuana and alcohol use. *Journal of Personality and Social Psychology, 44,* 1069–1074.

Wolfson, Alice J. (1983, November/December). Access to abortion—The struggle continues. *Network News,* pp. 3–4.

Wolman, Carol, & Frank, Hal. (1975). The solo woman in a professional peer group. *American Journal of Orthopsychiatry, 45,* 164–171.

Wolowitz, Howard M. (1972). Hysterical character and feminine identity. In J. M. Bardwick (Ed.), *Readings on the psychology of women* (pp. 307–314). New York: Harper & Row.

Woman and psychotherapy. (1981). Washington, DC: Federation of Organizations for Professional Women.

Woman judge refuses to convict girl, 14. (1978, January 25). *Providence Evening Bulletin.*

Woman to head Columbia Law. (1986, January 5). *New York Times.*

Women at foot of pay ladder in federal jobs. (1984, December 6). *Providence Evening Bulletin,* p. A-8.

Women changing the Army's look. (1978, December 21). *Providence Evening Bulletin.*

Women face low pay after losing steel jobs. (1984, May 17). *New York Times.*

Women hitchhikers asking to be raped? (1977, July 21). *Providence Journal.*

Women in clerical jobs band together to learn 9-to-5 rights. (1985, February 20). *New York Times,* p. C9.

Women in college development earn 20 pct. less than men. (1982, July 7). *Chronicle of Higher Education.*

Women in poll tell of seducing men. (1980, July 30). *Providence Evening Bulletin.*

Women inmates win Ky. bias suit. (1982, July 27). *Providence Evening Bulletin.*

Women Marines a gang that can shoot straight. (1986, January 22). *Providence Evening Bulletin,* p. A-15.

Women, nonfliers, bring plane down. (1983, November 22). *New York Times.*

Women now hold most professional jobs. (1986, March 20). *Providence Evening Bulletin,* p. A-1.

Women on Words and Images. (1972). *Dick and Jane as victims: Sex stereotyping in children's readers.* Princeton, NJ: Author.

Women on Words and Images. (1975). *Channeling children.* Princeton, NJ: Author.

Women take the lead in enrollment. (1980, Spring). *Project on the Status and Education of Women, 26.* (Association of American Colleges, Washington, DC)

Women want more equality, more help around the house. (1986, June 10). *Providence Evening Bulletin,* p. A-1.

Women workers march on. (1978, August 17). *Providence Evening Bulletin.*

Women working less, filling dead-end jobs. (1984, July 18). *Providence Evening Bulletin.*

Women's health. Report of the Public Health Service Task Force on Women's Health Issues. (1985). *Public Health Reports, 100*(1), 73−106.

Women's hearts as healthy on job as home. (1980, January 25). *Providence Evening Bulletin.*

Women's pay still much below men's. (1982, February 6). *Providence Evening Bulletin.*

Women's well-being at midlife. (1982, Winter). *ISR Newsletter.* (Institute for Social Research, University of Michigan, Ann Arbor)

Wood, Elizabeth. (1980). Women in music. *Signs, 6,* 283−297.

Wood, P. S. (1980, May 18). Sex differences in sports. *New York Times Magazine,* pp. 30−33, 38, 96−104.

Wood, Wendy, Polek, Darlene, & Aiken, Cheryl. (1985). Sex differences in group task performance. *Journal of Personality and Social Psychology, 48,* 63−71.

Woodall, Martha. (1983, October 4). Late pregnancy risks exaggerated. *Providence Evening Bulletin,* p. B-12.

Wooden, Kenneth. (1976). *Weeping in the playtime of others.* New York: McGraw-Hill.

Woods, Nancy F., Dery, Gretchen K., & Most, Ada. (1983). Recollections of menarche, current menstrual attitudes, and perimenstrual symptoms. In S. Golub (Ed.), *Menarche* (pp. 87−97). Boston: Lexington Books.

Wooley, S. C., & Wooley, O. W. (1984, February). Feeling fat in a thin society. *Glamour,* pp. 198−252.

Worell, Judith, & Remer, Pamela. (1982, July). Sex fair guidelines for state association ethics committees. *Division 35 Newsletter,* pp. 9−10. (American Psychological Association, Washington, DC)

Working Women's Institute. (1980). *Sexual harassment on the job: Questions and answers.* (Available from 593 Park Ave., New York, NY 10021)

Working Women joins forces with national union. (1981, March 20). *Providence Evening Bulletin.*

Wrather, Joan. (1983). Programs provide a history lesson: Blacks and women in science. *Science, 220,* 186−187.

Wright, Chris T., Meadow, Arnold, Abramowitz, Stephen I., & Davidson, Christine V. (1980). Psychiatric diagnosis as a function of assessor profession and sex. *Psychology of Women Quarterly, 5,* 240−254.

Wright, Paul H. (1982). Men's friendships, women's friendships and the alleged inferiority of the latter. *Sex Roles, 8,* 1−20.

Wyer, Robert S. Jr., Bodenhausen, Galen V., & Gorman, Theresa F. (1985). Cognitive mediators of reactions to rape. *Journal of Personality and Social Psychology, 48,* 324−338.

Wylie, Philip. (1955). *A generation of vipers.* New York: Rinehart. (Original work published in 1942.)

Yalom, Marilyn, Estler, Suzanne, & Brewster, Wanda. (1982). Changes in female sexuality: A study of mother/daughter communication and generational differences. *Psychology of Women Quarterly, 7,* 141−154.

Yoder, Janice D. (1983). Another look at women in the United States Army: A comment on Woelfel's article. *Sex Roles, 9,* 285−288.

Yogev, Sara. (1982). Happiness in dual-career couples: Changing research, changing values. *Sex Roles, 8,* 593−605.

Yogev, Sara, & Vierra, Andrea. (1983). The state of motherhood among professional women. *Sex Roles, 9,* 391−396.

Yorburg, Betty, & Arafat, Ibtihaj. (1975). Current sex role conceptions and conflict. *Sex Roles, 1,* 135−146.

Zanna, Mark P., & Pack, Susan J. (1975). On the self-fulfilling nature of apparent sex differences in behavior. *Journal of Experimental Social Psychology, 11,* 583−591.

Zellman, Gail L., Goodchilds, Jacqueline D., Johnson, Paula B., & Giarusso, Roseann. (1981, August). *Teenagers' application of the label "rape" to nonconsensual sex between acquaintances.* Paper presented at the meeting of the American Psychological Association, Los Angeles, CA.

Zellman, Gail L., Johnson, Paula B., Giarusso, Roseann, & Goodchilds, Jacqueline D. (1979, September). *Adolescent expectations for dating relationships: Consensus between the sexes.* Paper read at the meeting of the American Psychological Association, New York.

Zimmerman, Bonnie. (1984). The politics of transliteration: Lesbian personal narratives. *Signs, 9,* 663−682.

Zimmerman, Ellen, & Parlee, Mary B. (1973). Behavioral changes associated with the menstrual cycle: An experimental investigation. *Journal of Applied Social Psychology, 3,* 335−344.

Zinn, Maxine B. (1982). Mexican-American women in the social sciences. *Signs, 8,* 259–272.

Zita, Jacquelyn N. (1981). Historical amnesia and the lesbian continuum. *Signs, 7,* 172–187.

Zucker, Kenneth J., & Cortes, Carol M. (1980). Sex stereotyping in adult-infant interaction: Some negative evidence. *American Journal of Orthopsychiatry, 50,* 160–164.

Zuckerman, Diana M., & Sayre, Donald H. (1982). Cultural sex-role expectations and children's sex-role concepts. *Sex Roles, 8,* 853–862.

Zuckerman, Miron. (1971). Physiological measures of sexual arousal in the human. *Psychological Bulletin, 75,* 297–329.

Names Index

Subject Index

CREDITS

This page constitutes an extension of the copyright page.

We have made every effort to trace the ownership of all copyrighted material and to secure permission from copyright holders. In the event of any question arising as to the use of any material, we will be pleased to make necessary corrections in future printings.

Pages 4, 103, 196: excerpts from *The Jewish Woman in America*, by Charlotte Baum, Paula Hyman, and Sonya Michel. Copyright © 1976 by Charlotte Baum, Paula Hyman, and Sonya Michel. Reprinted by permission of Doubleday & Company, Inc.

Pages 4, 5, 72: excerpts from *August* by Judith Rossner. Copyright © 1983 by Judith Rossner. Reprinted by permission of Houghton Mifflin Company.

Pages 13, 15–17, 98, 284: excerpts from *Myths of Gender: Biological Theories About Women* by Anne Fausto-Sterling. Copyright © 1985 by Basic Books, Inc., Publishers. Reprinted by permission of the publisher.

Page 53: table 4.1 from "Children's Perceptions of Occupational Sex Stereotypes," by L. D. Gettys and A. Cann. In *Sex Roles*, 1981, 7, 301–308. Copyright 1981 by Plenum Publishing Corporation. Reprinted by permission.

Pages 71, 134, 135, 139, 273: excerpts from *The Women's Room*, by Marilyn French. Copyright © 1977 by Marilyn French. Reprinted by permission of Summit Books, a division of Simon & Schuster, Inc.

Pages 76, 113, 114, 118, 136: excerpts from *Worlds of Pain: Life in the Working Class Family*, by Lillian Breslow Rubin. Copyright © 1976 by Lillian Breslow Rubin. Reprinted by permission of Basic Books, Inc., Publishers.

Page 86: excerpts from *The Subordinate Sex: A History of Attitudes toward Women*, by B. Bullough. Copyright © 1974 by Penguin Books. Reprinted by permission.

Page 91: Figure 6.1 copyright © 1976 by Paula Weideger. Reprinted from *Menstruation and Menopause: The Physiology and Psychology, the Myth and Reality*, by Paula Weideger, by permission of Alfred A. Knopf, Inc.

Page 102: excerpts from poem © Alta, by permission of the author.

Pages 133, 197: excerpts from *A Mother and Two Daughters*, by Gail Godwin. Copyright © 1982 by Gail Godwin. Reprinted by permission of Viking Penguin, Inc.

Page 147: excerpts from *Nappy Edges*, by Ntozake Shange. Copyright © 1972, 1974, 1975, 1976, 1977, 1978 by Ntozake Shange. Reprinted by permission of St. Martin's Press, Inc.

Page 163: lines excerpted from "Rape Poem." Copyright © 1974 by Marge Piercy. Reprinted from *Living in the Open*, by Marge Piercy, by permission of Alfred A. Knopf, Inc.

Pages 176, 185, 193: excerpts from *Small Changes*, by Marge Piercy. Copyright © 1972, 1973 by Marge Piercy. Reprinted by permission of Doubleday & Company, Inc.

Photo credits.

Page 4: "No Panacea for the Firewood Crisis," Norman, C., *Science*, Vol. 226, P. 676, photo by (Mark Edwards/Earthscan), 9 November 1984. Copyright 1984 by the AAAS.

Page 37: Carol A. Foote.

Page 83: Sylvia Plachy, Archive Pictures Inc.

Page 122: Record-A-Call.

Page 137: Carol A. Foote.

Page 162: AP/Wide World Photos.

Page 202: "Discrimination and Imitation of Facial Expressions by Neonates," T. M. Field, et al., *Science*, Vol. 218, Fig. 1, p. 180, 8 October 1982. Copyright 1982 by the AAS.

Page 218: UPI/Bettmann Newsphotos.

Page 223: American Home Products Corporation.

Page 291: Shoshana Rothaizer.

Page 292: Shoshana Rothaizer.

Page 299: Bernice Lott.

Page 308: AP/Wide World Photos.